lonely planet

Stuart Butler

Hiking
IN SPAIN

THE PYRENEES

1 PYRENEAN TRAVERSE

After a tough day's hiking on the Pyrenean Traverse (p73), savour some relaxation outside a *refugio* with new-found friends.

2 GRAND SESTRALES

Stifle the sickly sensation of vertigo and stomach-crawl to the lip of the Grand Sestrales on the Staggering Sestrales walk (p121) – you will be rewarded. Peer over the ledge to see vultures gliding gracefully on the thermals way, way below.

3 ALPINE LAKES

For a dip that even a polar bear would find bracing, dive gleefully into one of the numerous deep blue alpine lakes in the Pyrenees (especially on the Water World walk, p114).

4 SPRING & SUMMER DISPLAYS

The Pyrenees play host to some stunning seasonal colour displays (p69). In spring, the endless meadows are filled to bursting with a riotous floral show and, in summer, an extensive exhibit of butterflies float in the high-altitude skies.

5 MARMOT-SPOTTING

After days of hearing their warning whistles from afar, drop into a grassy valley to see the ever-wary marmots standing to attention watching you (p120).

6 ESTANY DE SANT MAURICI

Relish the natural assets of this glorious national park with a late-afternoon walk up to the Estany de Sant Maurici (p109) to watch the sunset colouring the mountains that rise above the lake.

SISTEMA CENTRAL

1 TOPPING LA MIRA

Make a crack-of-dawn clamber to the summit of La Mira on the Alta Ruta de Gredos hike (p44) to watch the sun rise over the cold teeth-like ridges of Los Galayos.

2 LAGUNA DE LOS CABALLEROS

Camp among the flowers on the edge of gorgeous Laguna de los Caballeros (p49). In the morning, trek to the summit of Covacha and count the frolicking ibex on the ridges below.

3 WINE & DINE IN MADRID

After a day's ridge-walking on the Valle de la Fuenfría walk (p56), return to the city with a hiker's hunger for a tapas-crawl around Madrid's superb bars and restaurants (p65).

BASQUE COUNTRY

1 PARQUE NATURAL DE URKIOLA

Take a moment's rest to ponder 'Will I, won't I' before you scramble those last hair-raising metres to reach the summit of Mt Anboto (p137). Manage it, and you'll delight in views of the whole world seemingly at your feet.

2 ATXULAR'S EYE

Be spoiled for choice choosing the perfect picnic spot on the Atxular's Eye walk (p133) – by a stream, in the mouth of a cave, or with a view over the Bilbao tower blocks…Decisions, decisions!

3 FRONTIER VIEWS

On the Frontier Views walk (p147), pick your way along a sheer ridge to reach the summit, where stunning views of the coastline of Spain and France are set before you.

CORDILLERA CANTÁBRICA

1 ÁLIVA

Amid a backdrop of huge snow-speckled peaks, take pleasure in the peace and tranquility of the Áliva pastures (p181) as you sit in silent contemplation of the world.

2 SAJA-BESAYA TRAVERSE

After a day on the 2000-year-old Roman roads of the Saja-Besaya Traverse (p163), feast on *pote* (a heavy stew) and *Queso de Cabrales* mountain cheese, and get bubbly on the local cider, *sidra*.

3 FUENTE DÉ CABLE CAR

The hair-raising Fuente Dé cable car ride (p181) kick-starts a fantastic walk through the best of the Picos on the Puertos de Áliva walk. Be prepared for mega-mountain views and idyllic meadows.

GALICIA

1 CELTIC INFLUENCES

Wonder whether you're still in Spain or have been magically transported to Scotland as men with bagpipes play in bars, the rain lashes down and the countryside glimmers green. Almost any walk in Galicia promises an experience unlike anywhere else on the Iberian Peninsula (p188).

2 BEACHCOMBING

Combing the coastline of the wildest and most magnificently bleak beaches in Spain, pluck goose barnacles and other shellfish straight out of rock pools on the Spindrift walk (p193). Then cook them up by firelight under the setting sun.

3 ANCARES RIDGE

On your way to a date with the clouds on the Ancares Ridge walk (p201), search for pine martens, wolves and capercaillies in the yew and birch woodlands of the Serra dos Ancares.

VALENCIA

1 PARQUE NATURAL DE LA TINENÇA DE BENIFASSÀ

Savour the lonely trails of the rugged sunburnt Parque Natural de la Tinença de Benifassá on a 100km dash through the dry gorges and narrow passes of the Els Ports Loop (p219).

2 RUTA LA MARINA ALTA

Ridge-walk among ruined Muslim castles and enjoy village hospitality on the Ruta la Marina Alta hike (p228), where another foreign walker is a rare sight.

3 MORELLA

Get your bearings at fairytale-like Morella – a fortified hilltop village, crowned with a castle – before starting the Ruta la Marina Alta hike (p228).

MALLORCA

1 TORRENT DE PAREIS

While the figures look okay – a six-kilometre, downhill-all-the-way walk – the Torrent de Pareis hike (p253), which winds down and down through a narrow gorge, is one tough little puppy.

2 BIRDWATCHING AT MONESTIR DE SA TRAPA

Keep your binoculars to hand on the Monestir de Sa Trapa hike (p241) that, as it climbs from sea level to peaceful highlands, passes through some of the best birding territory in Mallorca. Among the 80-odd species up for peeps are red kites, kestrels and peregrine falcons.

3 BARRANC DE BINIARAIX

Follow in the footsteps of pilgrims on the Barranc de Biniaraix & Embassament de Cúber hike (p246) as you ascend the Barranc de Biniaraix valley and trek through woodlands and plateaus, finishing at a pretty reservoir.

ANDALUCIA

1 SIERRA DE CAZORLA WILDLIFE

Hone your naturalist skills on the Sierra de Cazorla Loop (p264). As the trek rambles through the remote woodlands, hills and mountains of Andalucía, you have a superb opportunity to spot wild boar, mouflon, ibex and all manner of deer and birds. Just don't forget your field guide, David Attenborough!

2 MOUNTAINS & VILLAGES

After conquering the peninsula's highest mountain, Mulhacén (3479m), on the tough but truly fantastic Sierra Nevada Traverse (p278), descend into the snowy Alpujarras villages and ramble from hamlet to hamlet on two Alpujarras walks (p269).

3 BEACH BREAKS

Swap your hiking boots and sunglasses for flippers and snorkel to explore the underwater ridges and crags at any of the divine beaches you pass on the delightful Cabo de Gata Coast walk (p284).

CAMINO DE SANTIAGO

1 GLORIOUS CHURCHES

Be dazzled by the wealth of the holdings in churches and monasteries all along the Camino, such as Santa María de la Regla cathedral (p332). Even the churches of the tiniest villages are filled with the sort of treasures that are only found in museums. Your discoveries will highlight just how wealthy the church became from the donations of passing medieval pilgrims.

2 FEAST OF SANTIAGO PARTIES

If you arrive at the end of the Camino de Santiago on 25 July, you will find a city packed to the gills with people arriving for the Feast of Santiago (p309). Throw down your backpack, give thanks with the masses at the cathedral, then rush out to join the party!

3 FELLOW PILGRIMS

Nothing attracts interesting characters like a pilgrimage (p308), and the Camino is no exception. For everyone, the unforgettable highlight of the   is the encounters with people from all backgrounds and countries (and sometimes possibly from other planets!). Companions and conversation can be counted on at the route's many *albergues* (pilgrims' hostels).

HIKING IN SPAIN

Alone on a wind-blasted, snow-battered pinnacle of rock surveying an expanse of rolling peaks and troughs, it can be hard to believe that this is Spain – the land of more than 50 million visitors a year, the land of flamboyant and chaotic cities, the land of swarming sun, surf and sex *costas* (coasts). But the truth is that the jagged mountain on which you now stand, the rural valley you tramped up to get here and the silent-at-noon village you passed through are as much the real Spain as any beach-holiday excess. In fact, some might say that as Europe's second most mountainous nation, if you want to learn about the 'real' Spain then the place to do it is on the mountain trails.

And what trails they are. From the endless snowy majesty of the Pyrenees to gentle coastal rambles, Spain is a hiker's dream.

In this book we describe everything from hard multiday scrambles to day-long circuits catering to various levels of hiker, as well as easy, hands-in-the-pocket family excursions.

We take you on hikes starting near the gates of Madrid and Barcelona and send you up high in the Picos, Pyrenees and Sierra Nevada. We also lead you to more off-beat locales such as the water-logged fields of Galicia, the semi-barren wilderness of Valencia, the wildflower meadows of Andalucía, the coastal views of Mallorca, the forgotten mountains of the Basque Country, and finally on a rendezvous with God on the Camino de Santiago – Europe's most famous walk.

Lace up your boots. The mountains of Spain await.

Contents

THE MAPS

Table of Hikes

SISTEMA CENTRAL	DURATION	DIFFICULTY	TRANSPORT
ALTA RUTA DE GREDOS	5 DAYS	MODERATE–DEMANDING	BUS
LAKES & PEAKS	2 DAYS	MODERATE	BUS, TAXI
THE WAY OF THE EMPEROR	7–9 HOURS	MODERATE	BUS, TAXI
SIERRA DE CANDELARIO	2 DAYS	MODERATE	BUS
VALLE DE LA FUENFRÍA	5½–6 HOURS	MODERATE	TRAIN, BUS
CUERDA LARGA	3 DAYS	MODERATE–DEMANDING	TRAIN

THE PYRENEES	DURATION	DIFFICULTY	TRANSPORT
THE PYRENEAN TRAVERSE	17 DAYS	MODERATE–DEMANDING	BUS
BASSES DE LES SALAMANDRES	4¾–5¼ HOURS	MODERATE	BUS
ESTANYS DE SISCARÓ	4–4½ HOURS	MODERATE	BUS
PIC DE L'ESTANYÓ	6½–7½ HOURS	DEMANDING	BUS
ESTANY LLONG	5½–6 HOURS	EASY–MODERATE	BUS, TAXI
REFUGI DE COLOMINA	2 DAYS	MODERATE–DEMANDING	BUS, TAXI
PORT DE RATERA D'ESPOT	4½–5 HOURS	MODERATE	BUS, TAXI
WATER WORLD	6 HOURS	MODERATE	TAXI, CAR
FRONTIER RIDGE	3½ HOURS	EASY–MODERATE	BUS
LAGO DE CREGÜEÑA	5–5½ HOURS	MODERATE	BUS
BUTTERFLY VALLEY	3½–4 HOURS	MODERATE	CAR
PUERTO DE BARROSA	5½ HOURS	MODERATE	CAR
STAGGERING SESTRALES	3 HOURS	EASY	CAR

BASQUE COUNTRY & NAVARRAN PYRENEES	DURATION	DIFFICULTY	TRANSPORT
ATXULAR'S EYE	5 HOURS	EASY–MODERATE	BUS, TAXI, CAR
URKIOLA: ANBOTO RIDGE	5–5½HOURS	DEMANDING	BUS, TAXI
THE WONDERS OF ARALAR	4½–5 HOURS	EASY	BUS, TAXI
SAN SEBASTIÁN TO PASAI DONIBANE	2½–3 HOURS	EASY	BUS, TAXI
INTO THE WITCHES' LAIR	4 HOURS	EASY–MODERATE	BUS, TAXI, CAR
FRONTIER VIEWS	4½ HOURS	EASY–MODERATE	CAR
VULTURES & VERTIGO	5½ HOURS	MODERATE	CAR
PILGRIMS TO POTTOKS	5½ HOURS	MODERATE	BUS, TAXI, CAR

CORDILLERA CANTÁBRICA	DURATION	DIFFICULTY	TRANSPORT
SAJA-BESAYA TRAVERSE	2 DAYS	MODERATE	BUS, TRAIN
VIEWS OF THE ORDIALES	6–6½ HOURS	EASY	BUS, CAR
VEGA D'ARIO	6–7 HOURS	MODERATE	BUS, CAR
LAKE WALK	2½ HOURS	EASY	BUS, CAR
BULNES LA VILLA	4–5 HOURS	MODERATE	BUS, CAR
LA GARGANTA DEL CARES	6 HOURS	EASY	BUS, CAR
MACIZO DE ANDARA	3½–4 HOURS	MODERATE	CAR, TAXI
RUTA DE TRESVISO	5½–6 HOURS	MODERATE–DEMANDING	BUS, CAR
PUERTOS DE ÁLIVA	4 HOURS	EASY	BUS, CAR

GALICIA	DURATION	DIFFICULTY	TRANSPORT
MONTE PINDO	5–6 HOURS	MODERATE–DEMANDING	BUS
SPINDRIFT	2 DAYS	EASY–MODERATE	BUS
ILLA DO FARO	2–2½ HOURS	EASY–MODERATE	BOAT
ILLA MONTE AGUDO	2–2½ HOURS	EASY	BOAT
ANCARES RIDGE	5½–7 HOURS	MODERATE–DEMANDING	TAXI
PIORNEDO LOOP	4½–5½ HOURS	MODERATE	TAXI
DEVESA DA ROGUEIRA LOOP	6–7 HOURS	MODERATE–DEMANDING	TAXI
RÍO LOR MEANDER	2 DAYS	EASY–MODERATE	BUS, TAXI
VALENCIA	DURATION	DIFFICULTY	TRANSPORT
ELS PORTS LOOP	6 DAYS	MODERATE	BUS
RUTA LA MARINA ALTA	4 DAYS	MODERATE	BUS, TAXI
SIERRA DE BERNIA LOOP	5 HOURS	EASY–MODERATE	CAR
MALLORCA	DURATION	DIFFICULTY	TRANSPORT
MONESTIR DE SA TRAPA	4–4½ HOURS	EASY–MODERATE	BUS, TAXI
SÓLLER TO DEIÀ	3–4 HOURS	EASY	BUS
BARRANC DE BINIARAIX & EMBASSAMENT DE CÚBER	3½–4 HOURS	EASY–MODERATE	BUS
VALLDEMOSSA LOOP	5¼–5¾ HOURS	MODERATE	BUS
SÓLLER TO SA CALOBRA	6¼–7¼ HOURS	MODERATE	BUS, BOAT
TORRENT DE PAREIS	4–4½ HOURS	MODERATE–DEMANDING	BUS, BOAT
ANDALUCÍA	DURATION	DIFFICULTY	TRANSPORT
SIERRA DE CAZORLA LOOP	6½ HOURS	EASY–MODERATE	BUS
RÍO BOROSA	6–7 HOURS	MODERATE	BUS
ALPUJARRAS WALK I: THE LOW ROUTE	2 DAYS	MODERATE	BUS
ALPUJARRAS WALK II: THE HIGH ROUTE	2 DAYS	MODERATE	BUS
SIERRA NEVADA TRAVERSE	3 DAYS	MODERATE–DEMANDING	BUS
CABO DE GATA COAST	3 DAYS	EASY–MODERATE	BUS, TAXI
GRAZALEMA LOOP	6 HOURS	EASY–MODERATE	BUS
BENAMAHOMA TO ZAHARA DE LA SIERRA	5 HOURS	EASY	BUS
ALÁJAR FIGURE OF EIGHT	6 HOURS	EASY–MODERATE	BUS
CAMINO DE SANTIAGO	DURATION	DIFFICULTY	TRANSPORT
CAMINO DE SANTIAGO	30 DAYS	MODERATE–DEMANDING	BUS, TRAIN

The Author

STUART BUTLER

English-born Stuart Butler grew up walking around his native South Devon coastline and up on Dartmoor before moving onto bigger, though not necessarily better, mountains with walking holidays in the Indian and Nepalese Himalaya, Pakistan's Karakoram, Morocco's Atlas, Ethiopia's Simiens, the Scottish highlands, Norway, Kenya and all over France and Spain.

He now lives close to the Pyrenean foothills on the beautiful Basque beaches of the French/Spanish border. He has worked on a number of Spanish titles for Lonely Planet and stories from his travels can be seen on www.oceansurfpublications.co.uk.

MY FAVOURITE HIKES

Wow, what a question! Obviously I would have to choose one in my own area, the gorgeous green Basque country. Here I'd pick the Frontier Views (p147) or Urkiola (p137) walks both for their stupendous views. But then again maybe if I was feeling cold and blue I'd pick one in the southern sun. I'd never say no to the Sierra Nevada (p278) or, for something different, I'd go for the Cabo de Gata Coast walk (p284) – where I could combine both beach and boots. But good as these areas are, in the end it would have to be the Pyrenees (p73) – either going the whole slog on the traverse or, if I had to pick just one single day walk then definitely the Staggering Sestrales walk (p121).

CONTRIBUTING AUTHORS

Several authors contributed to the research and writing of sections of this book. See p385 for details.

Route Descriptions

This book contains route descriptions ranging from day trips to multiday megawalks, plus suggestions for other walks, side trips and alternative routes. Each walk description has a brief introduction outlining the natural and cultural features you may encounter, plus information to help you plan your walk – transport options, level of difficulty, time frame and any permits required.

Day walks are often circular and are located in areas of uncommon beauty. Multiday walks include information on campsites, mountain huts, hostels or other accommodation, and places where you can obtain water and supplies.

TIMES & DISTANCES

These are provided only as a guide. Times are based on actual walking time and do not include stops for snacks, taking photographs, rests or side trips. Be sure to factor these in when planning your walk. Distances are provided but should be read in conjunction with altitudes. Significant elevation changes can make a greater difference to your walking time than lateral distance.

In most cases, the daily stages are flexible and can be varied. It is important to recognise that short stages are sometimes recommended in order to acclimatise in mountain areas or because there are interesting features to explore en route.

LEVEL OF DIFFICULTY

Grading systems are always arbitrary. However, having an indication of the grade may help you choose between walks. Our authors use the following grading guidelines:

Easy – a walk on flat terrain or with minor elevation changes usually over short distances on well-travelled routes with no navigational difficulties.

Moderate – a walk with challenging terrain, often involving longer distances and steep climbs.

Demanding – a walk with long daily distances and difficult terrain with significant elevation changes; may involve challenging route-finding and high-altitude or glacier travel.

TRUE LEFT & TRUE RIGHT

The terms 'true left' and 'true right', used to describe the bank of a stream or river, sometimes throw readers. The 'true left bank' simply means the left bank as you look downstream.

MAPS

All maps in this book are indicative, and should be used as a guide in planning only (see p346). The most suitable commercial maps are recommended for each walk in the walk descriptions.

Planning

In every way Spain knows how to look after its guests. Its hotels are slick and good value, its cuisine delicious enough to make a tortoise race for a restaurant, its transport and communications systems fast and efficient, and its range of attractions and activities inexhaustible. In return for this welcome, Spain's guests come in ever increasing numbers – 50 million more than a year at the last count, more than anywhere else in the world. All this means that travelling and hiking around Spain is extraordinarily easy to plan and organise; but don't worry, that doesn't mean the high passes aren't among Europe's most thrilling challenges. The vast majority of hikers to Spain organise everything themselves, but should you want a helping hand there are plenty of excellent walking tour companies out there who can organise as much, or as little, as you want. If you choose to strike out alone then this book provides details on months and months worth of hikes: some easy coastal strolls, some multiday high-altitude challenges and one that promises you a place in

LOOKING FOR SOMETHING DIFFERENT?

Hiking through Spain needn't all be about snowy crags and challenging ascents. We've selected a few 'off the beaten mountain' hikes that'll show you a different side of Spanish hiking. See the Table of Hikes (p16) for more information.

BESIDE THE SEASIDE

For something at lower altitudes try these salty air walks along some of Spain's most beautiful, and little visited, beachscapes – but don't forget to pack a bucket and spade!

- Illa do Faro (p198) or Illa Monte Agudo (p199)
- Cabo de Gata Coast (p284)
- San Sebastián to Pasai Donibane (p143)

TREAD A LITTLE HISTORY

Join scenic wonders with cultural marvels on these walks through history.

- Camino de Santiago (p307)
- Pilgrims to Pottoks (p152)
- Alpujarras Walk II: The High Route (p275)
- Into the Witches' Lair (p145)
- Saja-Besaya Traverse (p163)

WILDLIFE

From the world's rarest big cat to meadows of butterflies, elusive bears and craggy colonies of vultures, Spain is one of the top wildlife-watching destinations in Europe. Keep your binoculars to hand on these wildlife-filled rambles.

- Monestir de Sa Trapa (p241)
- Sierra de Cazorla Loop (p264)
- The Pyrenean Traverse (p73)
- Alta Ruta de Gredos (p44)
- Butterfly Valley (p118)

heaven! Many people combine their hiking holiday with some general sightseeing or relaxing beach time and if you're one of these, then get your hands on Lonely Planet's *Spain*, which gives far greater detail than this book can on sightseeing, sleeping and eating throughout this wonderful nation.

WHEN TO WALK

The climate in Spain is as varied as each of the country's regions, and this climate affects where you walk and when; however, Spain's climatic variety means it's always perfect hiking weather somewhere. For example, were you to walk through a southern summer you'd quickly feel like a chicken on a spit-roast, but in the Basque Country, for example, with its much milder (and wetter!) summers, you'd be positively skipping across those mountain meadows.

The Camino de Santiago, at its best from June to October, can be walked at any time, though you may want to avoid the hottest and most popular months of July and August. Galician coastal routes are also accessible throughout the year, though heavy winter rains from the end of November until well into March can dampen enthusiasm.

The mild-season window for some of the high-level walks is open only briefly. In Andalucía's Sierra Nevada, the Picos de Europa in the Cordillera Cantábrica and on the higher walks in the Pyrenees, snow can block passes until the second half of June, and begins to fall again in early September.

Pyrenean *refugios* (mountain huts or refuges) are mostly open from mid-June to mid-September, though a minority of more accessible ones stay open year-round. Given their proximity to Madrid, parts of the Gredos and Guadarrama *sierras* (mountain ranges) can become quite crowded, especially at weekends. They're best walked in early or late summer when the climate is relatively benign and the trails emptier. And as for any of the coastal walks; well, we probably don't need to tell you that summers where it's at.

See Climate (p340) for more information.

Most residents of Spain and a fair percentage of those in western Europe holiday on the Iberian Peninsula from mid-July until the end of August, stretching facilities to the limit. At these times, as well as during *Semana Santa* (Easter Week), it's essential to reserve accommodation in *refugios* in advance.

DON'T HIT THE TRACK WITHOUT...

Organising a hiking holiday to Spain is as easy as adding two plus two and there is almost nothing that you can get at home that you can't get just as easily in Spain. Having said that there are a few things that are as essential as this book!

- Obtaining valid travel insurance that covers you for trekking (p344)
- Your passport and/or ID card (p350)
- Driving licence, car documents and car insurance (p356)
- Arranging car hire before you arrive – it's cheaper (p356)
- Binoculars for vulture spotting
- Rain jacket for Pyrenean thunderstorms (p360)
- Pleading with the god of blisters to spare you the pain

Overall, June and September are the best months for walking. Days are still relatively long; temperatures are milder; camping grounds, *refugios* and hotels are less overwhelmed; and the trails are less crowded.

COSTS & MONEY

Spain is, as locals will quickly tell you, not as cheap as it once was. What you spend on accommodation (probably your single greatest expense) will depend on various factors, such as location (Madrid is pricier than a *refugio* in the Sierra Nevada), season (December near a ski resort is expensive, but the same place in August can be half the price), the degree of comfort you require and a little dumb luck. At the budget end you'll pay €10 to €15 for a space in a *refugio* or €12 to €27 for a bed in a youth hostel (depending on the hostel, season and your age). A pitch on a campsite usually works out only a little cheaper than a space in a *refugio*.

The cheapest bearable *pensión* (small private hotel) or *hostal* (budget hotel) is unlikely to cost less than €25 (single) or €35 (double) a night – more in the cities and resorts. Depending on where you are, you can stumble across good single or double rooms with attached bathroom from as little as €30 or €45 (€60 or €80 in the more popular locations).

Eating out is still more variable. A *menú del día* (daily set menu) can cost as little as €8 to €12. Bank on spending at least €20 on a full dinner (including house wine). Note that many of the busier *refugios* along the more popular trails will provide meals as well, and a bed and full board (breakfast and dinner) can be had for around €30.,

---

GUIDED & GROUP WALKS

Most Spaniards tend to walk independently in small groups of friends or in larger packs from outdoor clubs. Organised tours do exist, such as the guided day walks led by national park staff. In popular tourist areas, such as Mallorca, outings are organised by private companies; however, unless your Spanish is good you'll miss out on a lot. There are no English-language walking tour operators based in Spain that operate nationwide, but there are plenty specialising in their region. See the relevant chapters for more information.

Most of the big British-based walking tour operators include Spain within their international programmes. Favourite destinations include the Picos de Europa, Andalucía, Mallorca, the Islas Canarias and the Aragonese Pyrenees. The operators include:

Alto Aragon (in the UK ☎ /fax 0208 3981321, in Spain 0974 371281; www.altoaragon.co.uk; 31 Heathside, Esher, Surrey, KT10 9TD, UK), a small company warmly recommended by more than one reader, has a base in both the UK and Spain. It organises walking holidays in the Pyrenees plus horse riding and cross-country skiing breaks.

ATG Oxford (☎ 01865 315678; www.atg-oxford.co.uk; 274 Banbury Rd, Oxford OX2 6PJ, UK)

Explore Worldwide (☎ 0845 0131537; www.explore.co.uk; Nelson House, 55 Victoria Rd, Farnborough, Hampshire, GU14 7PA, UK)

Exodus (☎ 020 8675 5550, www.exodus.co.uk; Grange Mills, Weir Rd, London SW12 0NE, UK)

Headwater (☎ 01606 720033; www.headwater.com; The Old School House, Chester Rd, Northwich, Cheshire CW8 1 LE, UK)

Ramblers Holidays (☎ 01707 331133; www.ramblersholidays.co.uk; Lemsford Mill, Lemsford Village, Welwyn Garden City, AL8 7TR, UK). The big daddy of them all, Ramblers is an offshoot of the Ramblers Association and has been in business for more than 50 years.

Sherpa Expeditions (☎ 020 85772717; www.sherpaexpeditions.com; 131A Heston Rd, Hounslow TW5 0RF, UK)

Public transport is reasonably priced, although high-speed trains can be expensive, and hiring a car (often the only feasible way of getting to some trailheads) is reasonable in comaprision to other parts of western Europe. Picking up a hire car from a big resort is almost always cheaper than hiring one from a small town (see Transport, p351, for more detail).

Hikers sticking to multiday treks and taking the full board option in *refugios* can get by easily enough on around €40 per day. Those using a town as a base for day walks and staying in youth hostels, eating snacks at lunchtime and travelling slowly could scrape by on €40 to €50 a day. A more comfortable midrange budget, including a set menu for lunch, a few tapas for an evening meal, a couple of sights and travel will be anything from €100 to €150 a day. From there, the sky's the limit. It is possible to spend hundreds on five-star lodgings and even in the occasional gourmet paradise.

BACKGROUND READING

For walking guidebooks and natural history titles specific to a region, see Books in the Information sections of regional chapters.

To set your own walking endeavours in perspective, pack *As I Walked Out One Midsummer Morning*, by Laurie Lee, an evocative account of Laurie's adventures walking from Vigo, in Galicia, to Málaga, down south on the Costa del Sol, during turbulent times just prior to the Spanish Civil War.

For an even more impressive – and contemporary – walking endeavour, read *Clear Waters Rising*, an un-put-downable account by Nick Crane of his epic trek from Finisterre, Galicia's most westerly tip, to Istanbul. The first third of the book describes his progress through Galicia, segments of the Camino Francés, the Picos de Europa and the Pyrenees.

Backpacks, Boots and Baguettes, by Simon Calder and Mick Webb recalls the pair's amusing adventures traversing the length of the Pyrenees. The action takes place on the French side, but the feeling is the same.

The Camino de Santiago, in particular, has captured the imagination of writers in English, and spawned a shelf or two of writing. *Spanish Steps* sees author Tim Moore and his donkey, Shinto, undertaking the walk from France to Santiago de Compostela, offering no shortage of laughs along the way. A more serious and superbly written account of the Camino can be found in Cees Nooteboom's *Roads to Santiago*.

There are literally hundreds of titles focusing on general Spanish culture and history. The current pick of the crop is *Ghosts of Spain*, by

THE COLOURFUL COUNT

The most eccentric of early walking pioneers was the half-French, half-Irish Count Henry Patrick Marie Russell-Killough, who bagged 16 first ascents of Pyrenean peaks. Among his many idiosyncrasies, he rented a sizeable hunk of the Vignemale massif in the Aragonese Pyrenees for the princely sum of one French franc a year and proceeded to haul himself to its summit 33 times, the last ascent in his 70th year.

When rather more spry, the count marked one successful climb by having an impromptu grave dug on the summit in which he asked his guides to bury him up to the neck. He excavated a number of caves in the mountain's lower slopes and lived in one for long periods between mountain walks. He was famous, too, for hosting dinner parties on the fringes of a glacier. Elegant Persian carpets were spread out and laden with fine food and wine carried up from the valley by a retinue of servants.

HISTORY OF WALKING

Until relatively recently, walking in Spain was primarily a utilitarian activity – to get from A to B. The Pyrenees, for example, today regarded as a magnificent resource for walkers, were for centuries the preserve of shepherds and hunters; they were seen as an obstacle – a natural frontier separating Spain from the rest of Europe – and not a source of enjoyment. The few passes leading into France were trodden mainly by merchants and smugglers, people walking to reach a goal, not walking for its own sake.

The Camino de Santiago (Way of St James) pilgrim route was always the exception. Walking the Way was considered to confer just as much merit as arriving at the goal. Every year, between 500,000 and two million pilgrims would make the journey on foot from all corners of Europe to Santiago de Compostela in Galicia. Its cathedral, believers say, houses the tomb of Santiago (St James) the apostle, and a pilgrimage to Santiago ranked in its time with one to Rome or Jerusalem. Nowadays, it's not only the faithful who make the journey. Many undertake the route for its own sake, staying at the ancient *hospitales* (wayside guesthouses) which mark the Way – or more accurately Ways (see Camino de Santiago chapter, p303).

Walking simply for pleasure was traditionally the preserve of the leisured and wealthy. However, many first-recorded ascents of the highest peaks were by surveyors or natural scientists, for whom the walk was merely the means to a greater end. It was, for example, the French botanist and geologist Louis-François Ramond de Carbonnières who, at the end of the 18th century, made the first known attempt to conquer the Glaciar de Maladeta in the Aragonese Pyrenees. A Russian officer, Platon de Tchihatcheff, was the first to scale the nearby Pico de Aneto in 1842. Similarly, it was as late as 1904 that the Spanish aristocrat El Marqués de Villaviciosa, Don Pedro Pidal, became the first to conquer El Naranjo de Bulnes in the Picos de Europa – guided by local shepherd Gregorio Pérez, who must have wondered what all the fuss was about.

Charles Packe was both a gentleman and a scholar. A member of the English landed gentry, his meticulously researched *Guide to the Pyrenees*, first published in 1862, was the seminal text for many years.

Nowadays, most major towns have an association of walking and climbing enthusiasts. The first walking group to be established in Spain was the Centre Excursionista de Catalunya (CEC), founded in Barcelona in 1876 and still going strong.

Giles Tremlett, which looks at contemporary Spain, a country in overdrive to catch up with the rest of the West but with its heart still planted in its tumultuous past.

Also highly recommended is *Between Hopes and Memories: A Spanish Journey* by Michael Jacobs, an amusing and personal reflection on contemporary Spain. Jacobs sets out from Madrid and crisscrosses the country, dipping into its historical, literary and cultural dimensions.

INTERNET RESOURCES

LonelyPlanet.com (www.lonelyplanet.com) can get you started with information on Spain, links and a forum of travellers trading information on the Thorn Tree.

Federación Española de Deportes de Montaña y Escalada (in Spanish; www.fedme.es) is the national walking organisation website with literally everything you need to know about hiking in Spain.

Turespaña (www.spain.info) is the Spanish tourist office's site, which offers lots of general information and useful links.

Walking World (www.walkingworld.com/home/index.asp?id=27) includes information on hiking throughout Spain, but with an emphasis on the south. You can even download route maps and descriptions (for a fee).

Renfe (Red Nacional de los Ferrocarriles Españoles; www.renfe.es) is the place for timetables and tickets for Spain's national rail network.

Environment

THE LAND

The Iberian Peninsula (Spain and Portugal), having previously floated around off the western end of Europe for millions of years, joined hands with the continent about 70 million years ago. Its collision with the European and African landmasses caused the peninsula's main mountain chains to rise up, most obviously the Pyrenees. The resulting rugged topography not only separated Spain from the rest of Europe for long periods, but also encouraged the rise of separate small states in the medieval period.

The Meseta

At the heart of Spain, and occupying 40% of the country, is the *meseta*, a sparsely populated (apart from a few cities, such as Madrid) tableland that's much given to grain growing. Contrary to what Professor Henry Higgins taught Eliza Dolittle, the *meseta* is not where most of Spain's rain falls. In fact, it has a continental climate: scorching in summer, cold in winter, and dry year-round. Nor is it really a plain: much of it is rolling hills, and it is split in two by the Cordillera Central mountain chain. Three of Spain's five major rivers – the Duero, Tajo and Guadiana – flow west across the *meseta* into Portugal and, ultimately, into the Atlantic Ocean. Like other Spanish rivers, these three are dammed here and there to provide much of the country's water and electricity.

The Mountains

The Sierra de Gredos, to the west of Madrid, and the Sierra de Guadarrama, to its north, both rise above 2400m. Cleaving through the *meseta*, they form part of the Sistema Central mountain range, which runs from the northeast of Madrid to the Portuguese border.

Mountain chains enclose the *meseta* on all sides except the west, where the terrain slopes more gently towards and then across Portugal.

At the northern limit of the *meseta*, Cordillera Cantábrica runs from near the Atlantic Ocean almost to the Basque Country, isolating central Spain from the Bay of Biscay (Mar Cantábrico). It rises above 2500m in the spectacular Picos de Europa, one of Spain's most popular walking areas. In the northwest, the more modest Montes de León and their offshoots cut off Galicia from the *meseta*.

The Sistema Ibérico runs from La Rioja in the northwest to southern Aragón, varying from plateaus and high moorland to deep gorges and eroded rock formations as in the Serranía de Cuenca. The southern boundary of the *meseta* is marked by the wooded Sierra Morena, which runs across northern Andalucía.

Spain's highest mountains lie at or near its edges. The Pyrenees mark 400km of border with France, from the Mediterranean to the Bay of Biscay, with stubby fingers reaching southwards into Navarra, Catalonia and Aragón and foothills extending west into the Basque Country. Aragón and Catalonia boast numerous 3000m peaks, the highest being Aragón's Pico de Aneto (3404m).

Across southern and eastern Andalucía stretches the Cordillera Bética, a rumpled mass of ranges that includes mainland Spain's highest peak, Mulhacén (3479m), in the Sierra Nevada, and an unusual spur radiating north, the Sierra de Cazorla. This same system continues east into Murcia

The highest peak in Spain isn't on the mainland at all, but is actually Teide (3718m), 1400km south-west of the mainland on the Canary Island of Tenerife.

and southern Valencia, dips under the Mediterranean, then re-emerges as the Balearic islands of Ibiza and Mallorca. On Mallorca it rises to more than 1400m in the Serra de Tramuntana.

SIGNS OF A GLACIAL PAST

Several of Spain's finest walks, especially in the Pyrenees, are through landscapes substantially shaped by glaciers. As a glacier flows downhill its weight of ice and snow creates a distinctive collection of landforms, many of which are preserved once the ice has vanished or retreated (as it is doing in Spain's few remaining high-mountain glaciers).

The most obvious is the U-shaped valley (1), gouged out by the glacier as it moves downhill, often with one or more bowl-shaped cirques or corries (2) at its head. Cirques are found along high mountain ridges or at mountain passes or cols (3). Where an alpine glacier – which flows off the upper slopes and ridges of a mountain range – has joined a deeper, more substantial valley glacier, a dramatic hanging valley (4) is often the result. Hanging valleys and cirques commonly shelter hidden alpine lakes or tarns (5). The thin ridge, which separates adjacent glacial valleys, is known as an arête (6).

As a glacier grinds its way forward, it usually leaves long lateral moraine (7) ridges along its course – mounds of debris either deposited along the flanks of the glacier or left by sub-ice streams within its heart. At the end – or snout – of a glacier is the terminal moraine (8), the point where the giant conveyor belt of ice drops its load of rocks and grit. Both high up in the hanging valleys and in the surrounding valleys and plains, moraine lakes (9) may form behind a dam of glacial rubble.

The plains that surround a glaciated range may feature a confusing variety of moraine ridges, mounds and outwash fans – material left by rivers flowing from the glaciers. Perched here and there may be an erratic (10), a rock carried far from its origin by the moving ice and left stranded when the ice melted (for example, a granite boulder dumped in a limestone landscape).

View of area before glacier's retreat

The Lowlands

Around and between all the mountains are five main lower-lying areas.

The basin of Río Ebro, Spain's most voluminous river, stretches from the central north to the Mediterranean coast, yielding a variety of crops, though parts of central Aragón are near-desert.

The lower Ebro flows through fertile Catalonia, composed mainly of ranges of low hills (but rising up to the mighty Pyrenees in the north). Further south, the coastal areas of Valencia and Murcia are dry plains transformed by irrigation into green market gardens and orchards.

The basin of Spain's fifth major river, Río Guadalquivir, stretches across central Andalucía.

The Coasts

Spanish Lynx

Spain's coast is as varied as its interior. The Mediterranean coast alternates between rocky coves and inlets, and flatter, straighter stretches with some long beaches and heavy tourism development – as on the Costa del Sol.

The Atlantic coast has cooler seas and whiter, sandier beaches. The Costa de la Luz, from the Strait of Gibraltar to the Portuguese border, is blessed with long sandy beaches. In the northwest, Galicia is deeply indented by long estuaries called *rías,* with plenty of sandy beaches. Along the Bay of Biscay, the Cordillera Cantábrica almost comes down to the coast, and the beaches are mostly coves and small bays, though still sandy.

WILDLIFE

Any of the walking areas we describe are a treasure-trove for botanists and birdwatchers (see p32, for some useful field guides). Spring, even in those regions that are brown and arid for most of the year, is spectacular

If you can find a copy, Spain (Wildlife Travelling Companion), by John Measures, is an excellent guide to the wildlife and wild places of the country.

LAST OF THE LYNX

The Iberian lynx (also known as the pardel lynx), Europe's only big-cat species, is without doubt the most majestic large creature in Spain. This beautiful cat once inhabited large areas of the peninsula, but in a tale we all know only too well, humans have done their utmost to wipe the cat out. Today only three populations remain: one in the Parque Nacional de Doñana another in the Sierra Morena, and a small group of 15 or so discovered in Castilla-La Mancha in 2007. Numbers are so critically low that there is now a real possibility that the Iberian lynx will become the first big cat to become extinct since the sabretooth tiger.

In 2000 it was estimated that 400 lynx remained throughout Spain and Portugal, but by 2005 that number had dropped to a mere 100 individuals. This dramatic reduction began with a crash in the rabbit population, the cats' main prey, thanks to disease. The situation was further worsened by habitat destruction through a change in farming techniques and road and housing developments. In fact, between 1960 and 1990 the lynx suffered an 80% reduction in its range.

However, there is a glimmer of hope. Against all odds the Sierra Morena population currently seems to be growing slightly and it's now thought these hills are home to around 150 cats. Most encouragingly, the first captive-breeding projects have started to bear fruit, with 14 baby lynx born in the last few years. Further captive-breeding centres are being constructed or have recently opened in different parts of Spain and Portugal, and the first cubs born from these are hoped to be released into the wild in 2010.

For more on the fate of the lynx, see the excellent website, www.iberianature.com/material/iberianlynx.htm.

THE END OF THE PYRENEAN GOATS

The Pyrenean goat *(bucardo)* has been hunted and harried into extinction. Once flourishing throughout the Pyrenees and Cordillera Cantábrica, its long history is confirmed in Palaeolithic cave paintings. Its last retreat was the Parque Nacional de Ordesa y Monte Perdido, where a tiny herd endured. But on 6 January 2001, a tree fell on the last surviving *bucardo*. Attempts at cloning failed and the world is now another species the poorer.

with wildflowers. Spain is on one of the main corridors for birds migrating between Europe and Africa, so if you manage to time your visit to coincide with the twice-yearly fly-past, you'll spot plenty of birds of passage as well as several endemic species you'll never see elsewhere.

Walkers stand a very good chance of seeing chamois and ibex. However, many of the larger mammals, as elsewhere in Europe's wilder regions have been shot, poisoned and starved to near-extinction. There are, nevertheless, wild boar and a very few brown bears clinging on precariously in the north. You might even be lucky enough to hear the distant howl of one of the estimated 2000 surviving wolves.

Animals
MAMMALS

Spain's wild terrain has allowed the survival of several species that have died out in many other countries – though the numbers of some are now perilously low. Many of Spain's wild mammals are nocturnal and you need to be both dedicated and lucky to track them down.

In 1900 Spain had about 2000 **brown bears** *(oso pardo)*. Today, it's estimated that only 60 to 80 survive in the Picos de Europa and further west in the Cordillera Cantábrica, and a handful, if that, remain in the Pyrenees. Though hunting or killing bears has been banned for over 30 years, numbers have failed to increase since the mid-1980s despite conservation programmes. Bear experts complain that local administrations give low priority to bear conservation – a contentious issue that arouses fierce opposition from many shepherds and landowners. The Pyrenean population is effectively extinct (although the French are attempting to boost numbers by importing bears from Slovenia) while the Cantabrian bears are seriously threatened. Hunting, poisoning (accidental and deliberate) and loss of habitat are the main reasons for the, perhaps terminal, decline in Spain of these shy creatures.

Wild Spain, by Frederic V Grunfeld (1999), is a useful practical guide to Spain's wilderness and wildlife areas, with illustrations of both animals and plants. It's getting a little dated but still does the job.

Equally threatened, primarily by hunting, **wolves** *(lobos)* are, by contrast, on the increase. From a population of about 500 in 1970, there are now over 1000 wolves in Spain. Their heartland is the mountains of Galicia and northwestern Castilla y León, but in recent years small groups have travelled huge distances to settle within 100km of Madrid. There are also a few further south, in Andalucía's Sierra Morena. Though heavily protected, they're still regarded as an enemy by many country people, and in some parts of the country wolf-hunting licences are still issued. Farmers complain that they have to wait far too long for compensation when wolves kill livestock.

Things look altogether better for the **Spanish ibex** *(cabra montés)*. The males of this stocky, high-mountain goat species sport distinctive, long horns. The ibex spends summer hopping agilely around high crags and descends to pastures in winter. Almost hunted to extinction by 1900, the ibex was protected by royal decree a few years later (though

Red Deer

MARMOTS

The reintroduction of the marmot *(marmota)* is an example of positive human intervention. Having become extinct in the Pyrenees, marmots were successfully brought from the Alps iin the 1950s, where they now thrive.

The first re-colonisers were let loose on the French side of the Pyrenees. But, not respecting man-made frontiers, they soon established themselves on Spanish slopes around boulder fields and rocky areas, where they live in family groups. Hibernators, their body temperature can drop to 10°C and their heartbeat to as low as five pulses per minute. Adults can weigh up to 8kg – a hearty dinner for the golden eagle, their public enemy number one.

Look out for – or rather listen out for – their distinctive whistle, since the lookout they always post will most likely spot you first.

the species still subject to controlled hunting today). There may now be around 38,000 in the country, the main populations being in Andalucía, which has around 30,000 individuals, and the Sierra de Gredos (see the boxed text The Gredos Ibex, p43), which are considered a separate sub-species and number around 8000. Sadly, its Pyrenean cousin (see the boxed text The End of the Pyrenean Goats, p30) is no more.

Unique to the Iberian Peninsula and smaller than the lynx of northern Europe, the **Iberian** or **pardel lynx** *(lince ibérico)* is the world's most endangered feline. Its numbers have been reduced to probably about 400 in Spain and under 50 in Portugal because of hunting and a decline in the number of rabbits, its staple food. Now stringently protected, it lives in wild southern and western woodlands, primarily in Andalucía. (See Last of the Lynx, p29, for more information).

You'll probably see traces of devastation from the indiscriminate snuffling of **wild boar** *(jabalí)*, though you'll be lucky to spot one since they're mainly nocturnal. They're not at all uncommon, and favour thick woods and marshes – especially those within striking distance of farmers' root crops.

Red *(ciervo)*, roe *(corzo)* and fallow *(gamo)* **deer** graze in forests and all types of woodland.

BACK FROM THE BRINK?

The *quebrantahuesos* (lammergeier or bearded vulture), with its majestic 2m-plus wingspan, is still a threatened species but is recovering slowly in the Pyrenees, where about 80 pairs now breed (the largest population in Europe). It has also been sighted in the Picos de Europa mountains after a 50-year absence, and an attempt is being made to reintroduce it to Andalucía's Parque Natural de Cazorla. The name *quebrantahuesos,* meaning 'bone breaker', describes the bird's habit of dropping animal bones onto rocks from great heights, so that they smash open, allowing the bird to get at the marrow.

Another emblematic and extremely rare bird is the *águila imperial ibérica* (Spanish imperial eagle). Long thought to be a subspecies of the imperial eagle, it's now widely regarded as a separate species and is unique to Spain. With the help of an active government protection plan, its numbers have increased from about 50 pairs in the 1960s to some 220 pairs today, in such places as Extremadura's Parque Nacional Monfragüe and Andalucía's Sierra Morena.

Spain's several hundred pairs of *buitre negro* (black vulture), Europe's biggest bird of prey, probably make up the world's largest population of these birds. Its strongholds include Monfragüe and the Sierra Pelada in western Andalucía.

Chamois *(rebeco)*, by contrast, live up high near the tree line of the Pyrenees and Cordillera Cantábrica, descending to pastures in winter. Since they live in such wide-open country, you stand a very good chance of spotting a family browsing. They resemble a smaller, shorter-horned version of the ibex but are actually a member of the antelope family.

With only a little more luck, you may spot a **red squirrel** *(ardilla)*, bounding through the mountain forests or scattering its discarded nut shells on you from above.

BIRDS

Around 25 species of birds of prey, some of them summer visitors from Africa, breed in Spain. You'll often see them circling or hovering above the mountains or *meseta*. The mountains of the Basque Country are a real hot spot for birds of prey.

The **golden eagle** *(águila real)*, with its square tail and splayed, upwardly turned wingtips, can soar for hours. The **griffon vulture** *(buitre leonado)* roosts on crags and cliff edges, and is the only member of the vulture family that's relatively light in colour. Other significant features are its dark tail and wing tips. The **Egyptian vulture** *(alimoche)*, unlike the golden eagle and griffon vulture, which live year-round in Spain, is a smaller, summer visitor. Black and white with a wedge-shaped tail and bare yellowish skin on its head and throat, it's relatively easy to identify.

Smaller birds of prey include the **kestrel** *(cernícalo)* and **buzzard** *(ratonero* – literally 'mouse catcher'), both of which are fairly common, the **sparrowhawk** *(gavilán)*, various **harriers** *(aguiluchos)*, and the acrobatic **red kite** *(milano real)* and **black kite** *(milano negro)*. You'll find many of them around deciduous or lowland woods and forests. Black kites are also fairly common over open ground near marshes and scavenging around rubbish dumps.

Spain is a haven for numerous water birds, thanks to some large wetland areas. Most famous and important of these is the Guadalquivir delta in Andalucía, where hundreds of thousands of birds winter, and many more call by during spring and autumn migrations. Other important coastal wetlands include La Albufera in Valencia and the Ebro delta in Catalonia.

Inland, thousands of **ducks** *(pato)* spend the winter in Castilla-La Mancha and at Laguna de Gallocanta, in Aragón. The later is Spain's natural lake (though it can virtually dry up in summer) and supports a sizeable **crane** *(grulla)* population. Laguna de Fuente in Andalucía is Europe's main breeding site for the **greater flamingo** *(flamenco)*, with as many as 16,000 pairs rearing chicks in spring and summer. You can see this beautiful pink bird in many other saline wetlands along the Mediterranean and southern Atlantic coasts.

There are two other large, uncommon birds, both famous for their elaborate male courtship displays. The **great bustard** *(avutarda)* lives mainly on the *meseta*, with small pockets in the Basque Pyrenees and Andalucía. An estimated 14,000 survive, severely under pressure from the modernisation of agriculture and illicit hunting. A mature male of what has been called the 'European ostrich' – and what is indisputably Europe's largest bird – can be over one metre tall and weigh imore than 18kg. The male in flight has been compared to a goose with eagle's wings. The **capercaillie** *(urogallo)* is a giant, black grouse. This shy bird, of which Spain still shelters around

Practical birdwatching guides include John R Butler's *Birdwatching on Spain's Southern Coast*, Ernest Garcia and Andrew Paterson's *Where to Watch Birds in Southern and Western Spain*, and Ernest Garcia and Michael Rebane's *Where to Watch Birds in Northern and Eastern Spain*.

Try birdwatching field guides such as *Collins Field Guide: Birds of Britain and Europe*, by Roger Tory Peterson, Guy Mountfort and PAD Hollom, or the slimmer *Collins Bird Guide: The Most Complete Guide to the Birds of Britain and Europe*, by Lars Svensson et al.

Hoopoe

PINE PROCESSIONARY CATERPILLAR

Even the birds turn up their beaks at the pine processionary moth, whose hairy caterpillars devour pine needles, threatening whole forests. Between October and March you can see their large silvery nests on the sunnier side of trees.

Come spring, they're on the march in single file, as fat as your little finger and 5cm long. Along the branch, down the trunk, into the roots: they bury themselves underground and enter the chrysalis stage. In July, the cycle begins again as the female moths fight their way loose and lay their eggs in another tree victim. Bristling with irritating hairs, the caterpillars can provoke a nasty allergic reaction if you touch them. Applying vinegar is said to provide relief.

1500, lives in northern mountain woodlands, mainly in the Cordillera Cantábrica and Catalan Pyrenees. The male doesn't just dance; he moonwalks, break dances, salsas and shimmies along while singing to his heart's content.

If you travel in central western Spain, you're certain to see storks. The **white stork** *(cigüeña blanca)* – in fact, black and white, with a red bill and legs – winters in Africa and, like so many tourists, chooses the best time of year to visit. It nests from spring to autumn on chimneys, towers, electricity pylons – anything nice and high – even right in the middle of towns. The **black stork** *(cigüeña negra)*, much rarer, also migratory and all black, has been reduced to around 200 pairs in Spain because of pollution of its watering and feeding places. Furtive – with good reason – its stronghold is the western part of the southern *meseta*, where it tends to build its nest on cliff edges.

Among the most colourful of Spain's birds are the **golden oriole** *(oropéndola)*, which spends the summers in orchards and deciduous woodlands (the male has an unmistakable bright yellow body); the orange, black and white **hoopoe** *(abubilla)*, with its distinctive crest and long bill, which is common in open woodlands, on farmland and golf courses; and the flamboyant gold, brown and turquoise **bee-eater** *(abejaruco)*, which nests in sandy banks in summer. All are more common in the south. Various **woodpeckers** *(pitos* or *picos)* and **owls** *(búhos)* inhabit mountain woodlands.

The English-language **Iberianature** (www .iberianature.com) is a terrific source of up-to-date information on Spanish fauna and flora.

Plants

In mainland Spain and the Balearic Islands around 8000 of Europe's 9000 plant species grow. Of these, 2000 are unique to the Iberian Peninsula (plus, in some instances, North Africa). There's such diversity and abundance because the last Ice Age did not blanket the entire peninsula, so plants that were frozen to death and extinction further north managed to survive in Spain.

HIGH- & MEDIUM-ALTITUDE PLANTS

Spain's many mountain areas claim much of the variety. The Pyrenees have about 150 unique species and even the much smaller Sierra Nevada in Andalucía has around 60. When the snows melt, the zones above the tree line bloom with small rock-clinging, ground-hugging plants.

Among the prettiest and most common of mountain plants is the gentian. The **trumpet gentian** is a deeper blue than the smaller, star-shaped **spring gentian**. Look out too for the great **yellow gentian**, its flowers arranged in bunches along the tall, single stem.

In spring, you'll come across whole fields of **poet's narcissus** (also called pheasant's eye narcissus). Like the gentians, its flowers are

The best guide to Spain's flowers and shrubs is *Flowers of South-West Europe,* by Oleg Polunin and BE Smythies. In the south, Betty Molesworth Allen's *Wildflowers of Southern Spain* is very helpful.

disproportionately large compared to the foliage in order to entice pollinating insects, which are much rarer at higher altitudes.

While many **orchids** flourish in damper, shadier woodlands, the alpine meadows of the Picos de Europa are a particularly rich area for these exotic flowers, boasting as many as 40 different species.

The **white crocus** (which can just as often be mauve) is one of the first flowers to push through the matted grass, still damp from snowmelt. In the brief high-mountain summer and well into autumn, the leafless crocus offers patches of pink or white colour. **Rhododendron** and **azalea** are colourful, low-level shrubs that grow to knee height.

MOUNTAIN FORESTS

On the cooler mountains of northern Spain, three kinds of conifer are dominant. Branches of the **silver fir** *(abeto blanco)*, so named because of the silvery colour of the underside of its needles, poke out almost at right angles. Often mixing it with beeches, or in stands of its own, its needles are set along side branches in two or three dense bunches. The long, tight cylindrical cones with a blunt top are a good identifier. With its flaking red bark the **Scots pine** *(pino albar)* – more accurately called the *pi roig*, or red pine, in Catalan – has needles in pairs and an egg-shaped cone that tapers to a point. Toughest of all, more of a loner and surviving as high as 2300m, the **mountain** or **black pine** *(pino negro)* is recognisable by its grey-black bark. Sparse on the windward side and more abundant to the lee, it's usually quite stunted in height because of the difficult conditions it endures. In more favourable conditions, however, it can grow taller than 30m.

LOWLAND FORESTS

Mixed evergreen and deciduous forests sprinkle the lowlands and *meseta*. Many contain two useful evergreen oaks. With a particularly hard wood at its core, the thick, lightweight bark of the **cork oak** *(alcornoque)* is stripped every nine years for cork. The **holm** or **ilex oak** *(encina)* is harvested for making charcoal. It also grows acorns, which are gobbled up by pigs whose fate is to become *jamon ibérico*, a particularly fine ham that's gobbled up in turn by humans. Although of the oak family, its shiny, evergreen leaves often have small, holly-like spines.

Where the tree cover is scattered, the mix of woodland and pasture is known as *dehesa*. Occurring mostly in the southwestern *meseta* and parts of Galicia and Andalucía, *dehesas* are bright with wildflowers in early summer.

The solitary **umbrella pine** *(pino piñonero)* has a large spreading top and edible nuts, prized in cooking; it grows near the coast.

Pyrenean oak and some of Europe's finest and most extensive forests of **beech** *(haya)* cover the lower slopes of the damp mountains in northern Spain.

SCRUB & STEPPE

Where there's no woodland or agriculture, the vegetation is often scrub, called *matorral* or *montebajo*, or steppe.

Scrub is quick to colonise where trees fail to take, have been logged long ago or have been wiped out by more recent forest fire. Herbs such as **lavender** *(lavanda)*, **rosemary** *(romero)*, **sage** (salvia) and **thyme** *(tomillo)* scent the air. In the south of the country and on Mallorca, shrubs of the prickly **rockrose** family abound. In the north and inland from the

Mediterranean, **gorse** *(aliaga)*, low **juniper** bushes *(enebro)*, varieties of **heather** *(brezo)* and the **strawberry tree** *(madroño)* predominate. If the soil is acid there may also be **broom** *(retama)*. **Asphodels**, **orchids**, **gladioli**, and **irises** may flower beneath these shrubs, which themselves can be quite colourful in spring.

Steppe is the result of overgrazing and can also occur naturally where the climate is hot and very dry. Much of the Ebro valley and Castilla-La Mancha are steppe, as is the almost desert-like Cabo de Gata in Andalucía. Steppe blossom with colour after rain.

NATIONAL PARKS & RESERVES

Spain's most ecologically important and spectacular walking areas – about 40,000 sq km if you include national hunting reserves – are almost all under some kind of official protection, with varying degrees of conservation and access. A *parque natural* (nature park), the most frequent category of protected area, may include villages, hotels and camping grounds; in others, access may be limited to a few walking trails, while a few reserves allow no public access. Controlled hunting is often still permitted – indeed in some parks, such as the Parque Natural de Cazorla, a combination of restocking and vigilance has actually led to an increase in the variety and quantity of larger species of wildlife.

National Parks

Spain currently has 14 *parques nacionales*, eight on the mainland and six offshore. Collectively they occupy over 3000 sq km, representing around 0.6% of the total landmass. Embracing some of Spain's most spectacular areas for walking, they enjoy the greatest degree of environmental protection – no mining, logging or other exploitation of natural resources, no hunting and a very strict control over construction.

The 1916 Ley General de Parques Nacionales (General Law for National Parks) stimulated a modest beginning. First to be designated was the small Parque Nacional de la Montaña de Covadonga, nowadays incorporated into the much larger Parque Nacional de los Picos de Europa (see p167), then the kernel, 20 sq km, of the Valle de Ordesa was approved for national park status. It too has been expanded over the years, these days forming part of the Parque Nacional de Ordesa y Monte Perdido, which embraces more than 150 sq km of rugged terrain.

Nearly 40 years passed before another outstanding natural area was accorded similar status. In 1954, the spectacularly barren volcanic area around Monte Teide, at 3718m Spain's highest peak, was established on Tenerife in the Canary Islands. A year later the Parc Nacional d'Aigüestortes i Estany de Sant Maurici was created in the Catalan Pyrenees.

In 1975 the Ley de Espacios Naturales (Natural Areas Law) tightened the rules and regulations for national parks; they now conform to internationally agreed norms for areas meriting such a title. Three years later came the long-overdue upgrading of Doñana, one of Europe's most important wetlands and a breeding and migratory haven for birds.

Spain's largest national park, Sierra Nevada, has received maximum protection since 2000. Newest of all is Extremadura's Parque Nacional Monfragüe; classified in 2007, the park is a hilly haven for a variety of raptors including the world's largest breeding population of Eurasian black vultures.

For official information on national parks, visit the website of Spain's **environment ministry** (www.marm.es; click on 'Red de Parques Nacionales'). It's in Spanish, French and English, and full of pretty graphs and pictures.

Other Protected Areas

These are administered by Spain's 17 regional governments. There are literally hundreds of such areas, falling into at least 16 classifications with a bewildering variety of terminology: *reservas naturales*, *parques ecológicos*, *áreas naturales*, *zonas protegidas*, just plain *parques* – and possibly every other permutation of these names. They range in size from 100-sq-m rocks off the Balearic Islands to the mountainous 2140-sq-km Parque Natural de Cazorla (see p262).

In 2008 Spain was awarded 527 blue flags for beach cleanliness – 49 less than in 2007, but still the most in the world. For more information, see www.blueflag.org.

ENVIRONMENTAL ISSUES

Humans have been shaping Spain's environment ever since hunter-gatherers scattered their first seeds and assumed a more sedentary life as cultivators of the land. Large-scale environmental changes are far from a late-20th-century phenomenon. It was the Romans who first began to hack away at the country's woodlands, which had until then, covered as much as half of the *meseta*.

Over the ensuing 2000 years, further deforestation along with overcultivation of the land and overgrazing (notably by flocks of several thousand sheep) has brought about substantial topsoil erosion.

By European standards, the country is sparsely populated and most of its people live in towns and cities, reducing their impact on the countryside. There's still lots of wilderness and plenty of unpolluted wild land to roam. However, Spain has particular environmental problems – some imposed by nature and others the result of human negligence.

RESPONSIBLE WALKING

Most of this is commonsense for most walkers but, without wanting to harp on like your parents did when you were a four-year-old playing with your food, it doesn't hurt to remind ourselves of the golden rules of walking does it?

RUBBISH

o If you've carried it in, you can carry it back out – everything, including empty packaging, citrus peel and cigarette butts, can be stowed in a dedicated rubbish bag. Make an effort to pick up rubbish left by others.

o Sanitary napkins, tampons and condoms don't burn or decompose readily, so carry them out, whatever the inconvenience.

o Burying rubbish disturbs soil and ground cover and encourages erosion and weed growth. Buried rubbish takes years to decompose and will probably be dug up by wild animals who may be injured or poisoned by it.

o Before you go on your hike remove all surplus food packaging and put small-portion packages in a single container to minimise waste.

HUMAN WASTE DISPOSAL

o If a toilet is provided at a campsite, please use it.

o Where there isn't one, bury your waste. Dig a small hole 15cm deep and at least 30m from any stream, 50m from paths and 200m from any buildings. Take a lightweight trowel or a large tent peg for the purpose. Cover the waste with a good layer of soil. Toilet paper should be burnt, although this is not recommended in a forest, above the tree line or in dry grassland; otherwise, carry it out – burying is a last resort. Ideally, use biodegradable paper.

o Contamination of water sources by human faeces can lead to the transmission of giardia, a human bacterial parasite.

Spain shares with its souther Mediterranean neighbours the problem of unpredictable and often deficient rainfall. Drought is perhaps its most serious environmental problem and strikes the country increasingly frequently. During the latest drought, in 2008 (the worst in a generation), the situation became so critical in Catalonia that the Catalan government proposed diverting water from the River Segre in order to supply water to Barcelona after water levels in reservoirs fell to just 19%. The central government in Madrid blocked this plan and the situation was eased after a wet summer.

It's not just a lack of rainfall that is leading to drought in Spain but the way in which the water is used. Intensive agriculture and the spread of towns and cities (including tourist resorts) have lowered water tables in some areas. For example growing vegetables under huge areas of plastic in the southeast – especially around Almería province – using intense fertiliser and pesticide use, and water pumped up from deep underground, is drying up some of the underground aquifers.

After agriculture it's the tourist industry that consumes the most water and, ironically, it's the south (the region that can least afford to waste water) that seems to be the most blasé about water use. Thirsty golf courses are a particular problem in this area as the average 18-hole course consumes as much water as a town of 20,000 people. Despite this, golf courses continue to breed like thirsty camels along the southern coast.

Spain has invested massively in reservoirs. These number around 1300 and cover a higher proportion of the country than any other nation

Sunseed Desert Technology, based in Almería, works to find sustainable solutions to living in a dry, semidesert environment. It accepts volunteers in a number of fields. See the website www.sunseed.org.uk for more information.

CAMPING

- In remote areas, use a recognised site rather than creating a new one. Keep at least 30m from watercourses and paths. Move on after a night or two.
- Pitch your tent away from hollows where water is likely to accumulate so that it won't be necessary to dig damaging trenches if it rains heavily.
- Leave your site as you found it – with no trace of your use.

WASHING

- Don't use detergents or toothpaste in or near streams or lakes; even if they are biodegradable they can harm fish and wildlife.
- To wash yourself, use biodegradable soap and a water container at least 50m from the watercourse. Disperse the waste water widely so it filters through the soil before returning to the stream.
- Wash cooking utensils 50m from watercourses using a scourer or gritty sand instead of detergent.

FIRES

- Use a safe existing fireplace rather than making a new one. Don't surround it with rocks – they're just another visual scar – but rather clear away all flammable material for at least 2m. Keep the fire small (under 1 sq m) and use a minimum of dead, fallen wood.
- Be absolutely certain the fire is extinguished. Spread the embers and drown them with water. Turn the embers over to check the fire is extinguished thoroughly. Scatter the charcoal and cover the fire site with soil and leaves.

ACCESS

- Many of the hikes in this book pass through private property – although it may not be obvious at the time – along recognised routes where access is freely permitted. If there seems to be some doubt about this, ask someone nearby if it's OK to hike through.

on Earth), but with scientists predicting that Spain will be among the countries worst affected by climate change these alone are unlikely to be enough to cope with future strain.

The soil of much of Spain is unyielding and impoverished. As everywhere, farmers supplement its deficiencies by adding fertilisers and increase its yield by using pesticides. This may be fine for the farmer, but problems are created downstream as the chemicals leech out. In La Albufera, a freshwater lake south of Valencia, fish and eels die every so often due to contamination upstream. The slow accumulation of toxic chemicals is not the only problem; in 1998 the fragile wetlands of the Parque Nacional de Doñana in Andalucía were assailed by an industrial spill of acids and heavy metals. Fortunately the authorities managed to prevent the worst of the spill seeping into the heart of the park.

It's not just potential environmental catastrophe threatening to wipe much of the wildlife of Spain off the map, but also hunting. Deeply ingrained in rural local culture, it raises heckles whenever it comes up for debate in Spain. The words *coto privado de caza* (private hunting area) daubed on rocks are a familiar sight and over 1.25 million shooting licences are issued annually. Birds are shot out of the sky, limed (caught in sticky bird-lime smeared on tree branches), netted and trapped, and older hunters especially resent limits on catches set for hunting and fishing seasons. Even though many species are now protected, poaching or winking at the law is commonplace and strict enforcement in Spain's vast countryside is impossible.

Despite all the human odds stacked against them, in some areas species such as wild boar and red deer have recovered to the point where they are now legally culled. The Spanish ibex, a kind of mountain goat, was almost extinct by 1900 but protection since then has raised its numbers to around 38,000.

The private car remains one of Spain's principal polluters. There are ecological movements in major cities, but the car rules. Politicians bend to the voting power of the car lobby, and the arteries of most large towns are clogged with traffic.

However, in popular walking areas there are signs of change. For example, in summer, the peak visiting season, you can now only enter the Parque Nacional de Ordesa y Monte Perdido on foot or by bus.

More generally, controls and legislation are beginning to bite as environmental awareness increases. The PSOE (Partido Socialista Obrero Español or Spanish Workers Party) government, in power from 1982 to 1996, made environmental pollution a crime and spurred on a range of actions by regional governments, which now have responsibility for most environmental matters. In 1981 Spain had just 35 environmentally protected areas, covering 2200 sq km. Today there are more than 400, embracing more than 25,000 sq km.

Sistema Central

HIGHLIGHTS

- Looking over the Circo de Gredos, the savage cliffs of Los Tres Hermanitos and Almanzor from the El Morezón ridge, on the **Alta Ruta de Gredos** walk (p44)
- Stumbling across the ridge of Covacha to pick a blissful spot to camp on the **Lakes & Peaks** walk (p49)
- Wandering through Hoyo Moros, a beautiful glacial corrie below Calvitero, on the **Sierra de Candelario** walk (p53)
- Exploring the eroded rock formations, fallen boulders, tall spires and narrow gullies of La Pedriza on the **Cuerda Larga** walk (p57)

Area: 94,224 sq km	Average summer high: 31°C	Population: 2.5 million

There's more to central Spain than Don Quixote, windmills and vast wheat fields. A spine of 2200m-plus mountains called Sistema Central rises rather unexpectedly from the *meseta* (high tableland) of Castilla y León and Castilla-La Mancha, providing an oasis of delightful alpine wilderness among the sometimes bleak expanse of Spain's heartland. A short drive from Madrid the well-watered valleys and rugged peaks are extremely popular with *madrileños* (people living in Madrid), but these attractions are little known by foreign tourists.

Sierra de Gredos forms the western and most dramatic section of Sistema Central and is the target for mountaineers and climbers as well as walkers in search of dramatic ridge traverses. Sierra de Guadarrama, while less grand than its western neighbour, is a very popular weekend getaway and winter ski destination. Its La Pedriza and the GR10 offer some rewarding challenges for walkers.

This chapter describes many of the most spectacular walks in Sistema Central. Some walks include popular tourist routes, but rest assured there's fantastic scope for getting well off the beaten track.

SISTEMA CENTRAL

SISTEMA CENTRAL

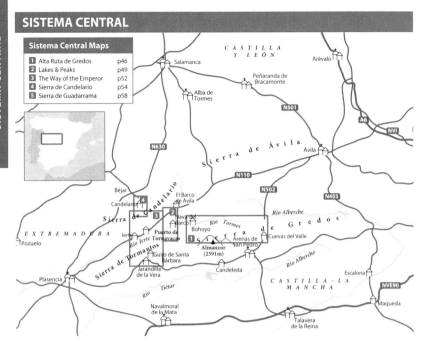

Sistema Central Maps

1	Alta Ruta de Gredos	p46
2	Lakes & Peaks	p49
3	The Way of the Emperor	p52
4	Sierra de Candelario	p54
5	Sierra de Guadarrama	p58

HISTORY

Evidence of Neolithic and Celtic peoples has been found on the southern slopes of the range. Generally speaking, the history of the Sistema Central reflects events unfolding in the *meseta* and rest of Spain, with the region resisting and succumbing to numerous invasions over the centuries, and repeatedly changing hands. The mountain terrain made an ideal base for guerrilla activity against the forces of Napoleon and Franco.

In 1978 Spain became a constitutional monarchy and a process of decentralisation began. Now the Sistema Central is governed by four regions: Castilla-La Mancha, Castilla y León (which has authority over most of the Sierra de Gredos), Extremadura and the Comunidad de Madrid (which governs the Sierra de Guadarrama). Recently these new authorities began promoting rural tourism in an effort to bring money and employment into the mountains.

ENVIRONMENT

Formed more than 300 million years ago in the late Palaeozoic period, then resculpted 275 million years later, the Sistema Central is divided by the Río Alberche into the western Sierra de Gredos and eastern Sierra de Guadarrama. The geology of the range (predominantly granite plus some gneiss and the odd seam of quartz) means springs well up close to the summits. These water sources as well as snowmelt from the highest peaks keep the valleys well watered year-round.

Massive glaciers carved many of the valleys in the range during the last Ice Age 10,000 years ago (glaciation is obvious in the central Gredos, far less so in the Guadarrama). The landscape then remained unchanged until the Middle Ages when humans began to make a significant impact on the environment. Until then the Sistema Central had a thick cover of deciduous trees such as holm, Pyrenean and cork oaks, with indigenous Scots pine appearing on the higher slopes. Only remnants of these forests survive today, mostly in river valleys and inaccessible areas. In places, ancient forests have been replaced with black or Corsican pine plantations, but a wide range of animals and plants is still found.

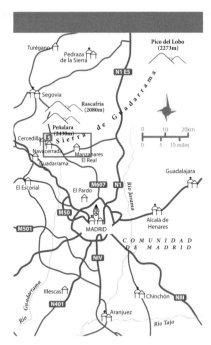

CLIMATE

The Sistema Central has a climate of extremes: fiercely hot summers and bitterly cold winters with icy northerly winds. However, unlike the surrounding *meseta* (that often receives less than 400mm of rain each year) the mountains are well watered, with between 1000mm and 1500mm of precipitation annually, a good third of it falling as snow in winter and the rest as heavy showers in autumn and spring.

Winter walkers should be prepared for blizzard conditions, while in autumn and spring the weather can change quickly, with low cloud bringing plummeting temperatures, fierce winds and almost horizontal freezing rain. These occasional storms can occur until mid-June when the last of the snow should have melted from the highest peaks and gullies. Indeed, many locals believe that the weather only becomes predictable after 1 June, which should bring three months of cloudless skies.

The Sierra de Guadarrama is usually snow-free earlier than the Gredos, its higher and grander neighbour, whose high passes

and north-facing gullies can be affected by snow until July.

PLANNING
Maps

The IGN Mapas Provinciales 1:200,000 *Ávila, Cáceres* and *Madrid* cover the Sistema Central, but for general planning check out Michelin's 1:400,000 map No 444 *Central Spain.*

BUYING MAPS

Some maps may be available in access or gateway towns, but Madrid is the place for map shopping.

La Tienda Verde (☎ 91 533 07 91; www .tiendaverde.es; Calle Maudes 38; metro Cuatro Caminos) is probably the best-stocked walking and mountaineering map shop in Madrid. The staff are knowledgeable and the company publishes an expanding range of own-brand walking maps and guides.

Librería Desnivel (☎ 902 24 88 48; www.libreriadesnivel.com; Plaza Matute 6; metro Antón Martín) is also excellent (and possibly better for books).

Books

It's pretty dated but *Mountains of Central Spain,* by Jacqueline Oglesby, is probably the only other English language book covering the Sistema Central.

Information Sources

For information about walking in the Sistema Central contact the national or local mountaineering federations. Organisations in Madrid include:

Federación Madrileña de Montañismo (☎ 91 527 38 01; www.fmm.es; Av Salas de los Infantes 1-5) It includes the Escuela Madrileña de Alta Montaña.
Grupo de Montaña del CSIC (☎ 91 547 77 06, fax 91 541 81 95; www.gmcsic.csic .es; Calle Hileras 4-5)
Montañeros Madrileños CAM (☎ 91 518 70 72; www.montmadrid.org; Barco 30)
RSEA Peñalara (☎ 91 522 87 43; www .penalara.org; Calle Aduana 17)

The websites of these organisations contain much useful information about weather, *refugios* (mountain huts or refuges) and events; many offices are open weekday evenings.

Guided Walks

Several groups run trips in Sistema Central:

Espacioaccion (☎ 91 326 72 92; www.espacioaccion.com; Calle Marcelino Álvarez 6, Madrid) The speciality here is climbing (including ice) and mountaineering. The company has an indoor climbing wall in Madrid.

Tierra de Fuego (☎ 91 521 52 40; www.tierrafuego.es; Trav. Conde Duque 3, Madrid) This company has a solid reputation.

Turismo Activo (☎/fax 920 34 83 85; www.turactiv.com; La Fragua, Barajas, Navarredonda de Gredos, Ávila) This operator runs all kinds of adventure and nature activities in the Gredos, from cross-country skiing to mushroom gathering.

GATEWAY
Where else but Madrid? (p65)

SIERRA DE GREDOS

This majestic and dramatic range consists of three overlapping ridges beginning in Extremadura and stretching northeast towards the Sierra de Guadarrama in the Comunidad de Madrid. The central section of the Gredos, stretching for 55km from Puerto del Pico (1391m) in the east to Puerto de Tornavacas (1274m) in the west, is the highest and most rugged of the lot. At its heart lies the Reserva Nacional del Macizo Central de Gredos, a 230-sq-km hunting reserve.

The two sides of the range differ greatly. On the northern side are stunning glacial valleys with clear turquoise lakes and rich *cervunales* (summer pastures) that lead through rolling *paramera* (moorland) down to the Río Tormes valley (running east to west) at 1500m to 1000m above sea level.

To the south, the terrain drops rapidly past the formidable barrier of dark, jagged pinnacles and fantastic granite cliffs to the villages of the Río Tiétar valley, some 500m above sea level.

ICE CLIMBING IN THE GREDOS

While the Gredos is primarily a summer walking destination, Refugio Elola is open on weekends throughout winter to cater for hardy walkers, mountaineers, adventurous skiers and ice climbers. The north-facing cliffs of Circo de Gredos are particularly suited to ice climbing and provide some excellent, challenging routes, most up frozen waterfalls. January to March is the best time for winter sports.

Several climbing and mountaineering companies operate from the *refugio* and some, including **Espacioaccion** (☎ 91 326 72 92; www.espacioaccion.com) run ice-climbing classes for beginners. Alternatively, approach the mountaineering organisations in Madrid: see Information Sources (p41) for details.

Bus services operate along both sides of the range and there's plenty of accommodation in the villages plus a network of *refugios* in the mountains. Great campsites abound.

While the Gredos might be dismissed as minor league by aficionados of the Pyrenees and Picos de Europa, the area has undeniable attraction – principally the accessibility of a beautiful and rugged alpine landscape and the variety of challenges presented by this small and relatively underpopulated area. Long ridge walks, peak bagging, leisurely strolls and serious mountaineering can all be undertaken here, just a short journey from Madrid. The popular areas receive hundreds of visitors, but a short walk up to a high ridge will leave the crowds behind and one thing you can be certain of, no matter how busy it gets, you'll be the only foreigner on the trails.

HISTORY
The southern slopes of the Sierra de Gredos have been settled since the Iron Age. While Roman settlement in the area was limited, the road over Puerto del Pico testifies to their presence. It wasn't until after the Reconquista that permanent colonisation of the northern slopes began and the native oak forests were cleared. Vegetables, cereals,

olives and vines on the southern slopes and rearing sheep on the northern side was a pattern of land use that continued until relatively recently.

The high mountains were exclusively the domain of shepherds and hunters until 1834 when the first recorded exploration of the mountains took place. However, it was not until 1899 that Almanzor was climbed.

More general interest in the Gredos began with Alfonso XIII, who liked to hunt in the region. He worked to protect dwindling stocks of Gredos ibex (see the boxed text The Gredos Ibex, below) and in 1926 actively encouraged the building of Spain's first *parador* (luxury state hotel) in Navarredonda. Though mountaineering *refugios* had been established in the area 10 years before sadly, many are now in ruins.

In the 1970s the region was 'discovered' by tourists and today tourism is highly concentrated around the Plataforma trailhead and Laguna Grande; this has had a negative impact on these environments.

ENVIRONMENT

From late spring the slopes of the Gredos are ablaze with flowers including region-specific crocuses such as St Bernard's and martagon lilies, and scented thickets of rock roses. Two regional endemics are Reseda gredensis, which has slender, white flower spikes, and the pale yellow-flowered snapdragon.

The granite uplands support a wide variety of heather and shrubs including two species of broom: one with white, pea-like flowers and the other with more characteristic yellow flowers (the latter forms dense waist-high cover and is the bane of walkers).

Several species of eagle are found in the Gredos: Spanish imperial (with a white crown and mantle); Bonelli's (quite rare); golden; booted; and short-toed. Griffons and black vultures soar above the peaks, while the mountains are one of the few havens for azure-winged magpies. Rock buntings (with striped heads) are seen at higher altitudes and occasionally red-legged partridges appear.

The Reserva Nacional del Macizo Central de Gredos helps protect a subspecies of Spanish ibex (see the boxed text The Gredos Ibex, below), as well as civets, wild boars, fallow and red deer.

The venomous viper is found locally. Other reptiles include the Iberian rock lizard, the striking turquoise-and-black mottled verdinegro lizard (found above 2000m) and the occellated or jewelled lizard (up to 80cm long, with beautiful blue spots on a green-and-brown back).

THE GREDOS IBEX

You are almost guaranteed to see the Gredos ibex while walking in the Sierra de Gredos. Large numbers of animals graze the remote high pastures at dawn and dusk. Males and females live in separate herds, except during the rut between November and January. Herds of females and young can number up to 30; male mixed-age groups are smaller, while old males are solitary and can often be seen perched on seemingly inaccessible peaks, silhouetted against the sky.

An endemic subspecies of the Spanish ibex, the Gredos ibex is a small, agile mountain goat with large eyes, a medium-brown coat, black markings and lighter areas on the neck and thighs. You'll often hear the animals' warning signal (a short, piercing whistle) before you see them.

At the beginning of the 20th century the Gredos ibex was hunted almost to extinction. The species was saved by King Alfonso XIII, who liked hunting the beautiful animals so much that in 1905 he declared the heart of the Gredos a *coto real* (royal hunting reserve, now known as Reserva Nacional del Macizo Central de Gredos) to protect the last stock. For the ibex it was a perverse kind of salvation, but since then the population has increased from a low point of fewer than 10 to around 8000.

No longer constantly threatened by people, the ibex are tame to the point of being cheeky. In fact, there are now so many of these animals that disease and overgrazing have become problems. Hunting – still practised in the area – helps a little with population management.

PLANNING
When to Walk
Facilities and bus schedules are geared towards July and August visitors, when the shore of Laguna Grande becomes a sea of campers and intense heat plagues ascent from the south. Snow permitting, the best time to walk is late June or September, when the crowds aren't around (Elola and Reguero Llano *refugios* are open daily from the beginning of June to the end of September). Avoid the busy summer weekends.

What to Bring
Bring all equipment and supplies from Madrid and wear a strong pair of boots. Few people bother to pitch a tent in summer – a three-season sleeping bag and mat will usually suffice, but do check the weather forecast!

Maps & Books
For planning, Adrados Ediciones' 1:135,000 *Parque Regional de la Sierra de Gredos* map is best – the 1:25,000 enlargement of the central Gredos is also very useful. The IGN 1:25,000 series is geographically accurate, but shows few paths. Numerous tourist maps cover the Gredos, but no single sheet displays all the paths, dirt roads and *refugios*.

Spanish-speaking readers have a wealth of detailed route guides to choose from (although many concentrate on day walks), including the excellent *Senderos de Montaña por el Sistema Central*, published by Anaya Touring Club, and *Vuelta a Gredos*, published by Ediciones Desnivel.

Information Sources
In Madrid the Castilla y León **tourist office** (Oficina de Promoción Turística de Castilla y León; ☎ 91 578 03 24; www .turismocastillayleon.com; Calle Alcalá 79; metro Retiro) is good for background information, not walking queries.

Tourist offices are found throughout the Gredos and mentioned under the relevant town headings in the Towns & Facilities section at the end of this chapter. In addition to national and local mountaineering organisations try contacting **Grupo Gredos de Montaña** (☎ /fax 920 37 26 45; www .grupogredos.com; Calle Triste Condesa 5,

Arenas de San Pedro) a small, but information-packed office, or **Oficina de Turismo del Valle del Jerte** (☎ 927 47 25 58; www .turismovalledeljerte.com; Cabezuela del Valle), where there is more than your average amount of walking information, including route guides for the western Gredos and Valle del Jerte.

Hundreds of *casas rurales* (rural houses or farmsteads) in the Gredos are available for rent, for more information contact **Casas de Gredos** (in Ávila ☎ 920 20 62 18, countrywide 902 42 41 41; www .casasgredos.com).

ACCESS TOWNS
El Barco de Ávila (p64) and Arenas de San Pedro (p62) are the best bases.

ALTA RUTA DE GREDOS

Duration 5 days
Distance 57km
Difficulty moderate–demanding
Start Cuevas del Valle (p64)
Finish Bohoyo (p63)
Transport bus
Summary A challenging traverse of the central Sierra de Gredos, with a side trip that includes the Cinco Lagunas and an ascent of Almanzor.

This undulating ridge-walk traverses the best of the central Gredos without relying on popular paths, conventional routes or complicated transport connections. It offers an opportunity to ascend Almanzor (2591m; the highest peak in the range) as part of a side trip that adds a day to the walk. The route is possible in three long, hard days, but allow for at least two nights at Refugio José Antonio Elola (Refugio Elola) if you want to explore the Circo de Gredos area at the heart of the range. Climbers have no problem finding challenging routes here, or at Los Galayos northeast of La Mira.

Refugios are scattered across the Gredos. Some are simple shepherds' huts; others offer a restaurant service. However, carrying camping equipment gives you more flexibility and there are some great campsites – when climbing Almanzor we found a group camped on ledges just 2m below the summit!

Simple exits to the south and north of the range are possible at regular intervals along the ridge and daily buses connect Madrid with villages on both sides. Adventurous souls prepared to do some scrambling can extend the route along the length of the main ridge past Covacha to Puerto de Tornavacas, although it doesn't stop there. A couple of difficult routes lead to Sierra de Candelario, enabling determined walkers to link all three Gredos walks described in this chapter.

PLANNING
Maps
It's possible to use IGN's 1:50,000 *Macizo Central de Gredos* map for the entire walk (there's a 1:25,000 section of the Circo de Gredos). However, for more topographical detail (but without many paths marked) use IGN's 1:25,000 map Nos 578-II *Mombeltrán*, 578-I *El Arenal*, 577-IV *El Raso*, 577-II *Laguna Grande* and 577-I *Bohoyo*.

Editorial Alpina's 1:40,000 *Sierra de Gredos* map shows more footpaths, but is a little inaccurate in positioning them.

GETTING TO/FROM THE WALK
If you're not going to make it to Cuevas del Valle the night before starting the walk don't fret. The Muñoz Travel bus from Arenas arrives at the trailhead before 8am and can drop you at Puerto del Pico 15 minutes later (removing the 1½ hour walk up the valley).

You could also catch a later bus to Cuevas del Valle from Arenas and cut the first day quite short (there are plenty of places to camp en route).

Another option is to catch the evening Muñoz Travel bus from Ávila to El Barco de Ávila and disembark at **Hostal Venta Rasquilla** (☎ 920 20 75 71; junction of the N502 & C500; s/d €25/40) 6km north of Puerto del Pico. Walk to Puerto del Pico to pick up the walk the next morning.

THE WALK
Day 1: Cuevas del Valle to Los Cervunales
5½–6½ hours, 12.5km
The day starts with a 547m climb (1½ hours or take the bus) north along the Roman road that leads from Cuevas del Valle to

the pass of **Puerto del Pico**. Although the Roman road starts lower down in the village, it is best to pick it up by walking along the main road uphill until you join it on your right-hand side.

From the pass, head west past the war memorial to a cairn-marked, well-worn path that climbs away across the southern slopes of **La Casa** (1847m), then settles into a 45-minute traverse southwest to the spur of Risco del Cuervo. Ignore paths heading south and head west through a jumble of rounded boulders and then towards a group of tall pines and the *fuente* (spring; also fountain or water source). The area is a fine, shaded **campsite**.

From here, following the cairns southwest for over an hour, passing over one spur and then south down a second spur to the end of a dirt road where a simple **hut** (with fireplace) and an animal enclosure are to be found (in bad weather, this is a good overnight option). Turn right (north) beside the hut and head up a well-made ancient trail that loops west past a *fuente* before climbing north, reaching **Puerto del Arenal** (1818m) in 1¼ hours.

Turn left at the pass (unless the rocky, rugged peak of La Fría (1983m) appeals to the scrambler in you) and work your way west around a small boulder-strewn peak (1891m) to a saddle where the path splits. Avoid the faint track that keeps close to the ridge and traverse northwest through the broom to Fuente del Cervunal and a beautiful area of high pasture (marked as **Los Cervunales**) that attracts ibex and wild boar at dawn and dusk. It's a great **campsite** and a private (locked) hut overlooks this beautiful spot.

Day 2: Los Cervunales to La Mira
4½–5 hours, 11km
Head southwest across the meadow for ten minutes to a pronounced gully, the source of Garganta de Cabrilla. Turn left (south) up to Puerto de la Cabrilla by following the gully. This is the beginning of 1½ hours without an obvious path, during which there's much broom to bash through. From the top, turn right (west) and walk for about an hour following the cairns along the ridge, passing into **Reserva Nacional del Macizo Central de Gredos**. Bear right to the large white quartz cairn and start

ALTA RUTA DE GREDOS

up and cut around the peak of Mojo de las Tres Cruces and southwest up to the top of **Mediodía** (2219m).

Head west from the peak to a granite post then southwest down to **Puerto del Peón** (2028m), where a well-marked trailheads southwest along the high ridge of the central Gredos. After an hour or so the track begins a gruelling, rocky climb to a stony and desolate area of flatter land northeast of La Mira before heading southwest to the ruins of **Refugio de los Pelaos**. Twenty metres from the ruin, there is a *fuente*. The ruins provide a sheltered campsite, while La Mira (2343m) itself is 15 minutes due south across the well-watered meadows (a popular ibex grazing area). On the summit is the ruined tower of a former optical telegraph station.

The best way to get to Refugio Victory (open all year) is to come back down (if you went to the top of La Mira) to the ruins of **Refugio de los Pelaos** and walk southwest across the meadow and climb down (274m – about one hour) steeply over the rocks to the *refugio*. The *refugio* is a simple affair with a large communal area downstairs and sleeping space for six people upstairs. The hut is popular with climbers drawn to the granite cliffs and vicious, teeth-like ridges of Los Galayos (there's some good climbing information at www.summitpost.com).

Day 3: La Mira to Refugio Elola
4½–6 hours, 12.5km

Head west from the ruined Refugio de los Pelaos and pick up a well-worn path that turns southwest along a ridge of small, rocky summits. After crossing a very rocky section below **Los Campanarios** (2162m), about 1¼ hours from La Mira, the trail splits. To the northwest a wide valley leads to the meadows surrounding **Refugio de Reguero Llano** (Refugio Llano; ☎ 689 41 26 39; accommodation per person €10; year-round but phone ahead) above Plataforma road head (about an hour away). Food is available if ordered in advance.

However, don't fork right: our route turns left onto a path heading southwest to **Puerto de Candeleda** (a popular route onto the ridge) where a faint trail cuts west through a meadow and up to the ruins of **Refugio del Rey** (the thick walls provide some shelter). There's a good *fuente* northwest of the *refugio*.

From the ruins an alternative route heads north skirting Morezón, but head west, picking up the trail leading across the northern flank of **Navasomera** (2299m) to an isolated meadow. Continue west up one of a host of paths climbing onto the rocky ridge of **Morezón** (2389m) that forms part of the Circo de Gredos, the horseshoe of cliffs encircling Laguna Grande. Possibly

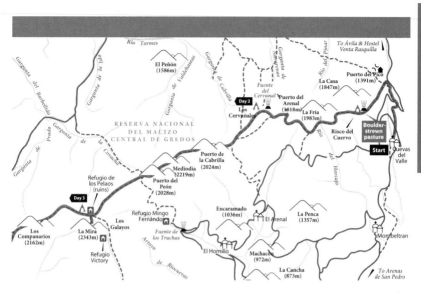

the easiest way is to climb through the grassy patch and near the top turn left to the peak. The views across to Almanzor (2591m) are fantastic.

There is considerable confusion as to the precise names and locations of many of the peaks found on this section of ridge, but we have followed the height and position of Morezón as marked on the IGN 1:25,000 series (and marked by a cross on the ground). Numerous mountaineering possibilities lead across the jagged peaks of Los Tres Hermanitos and you could descend steeply to Laguna Grande in several places.

From the peak, come back on yourself and head north to the flat, barren 2366m peak at the northern end of the ridge and then head northeast (directly towards Refugio Llano). One option is to descend gently off the summit through a narrow, shallow channel for about eight minutes to a small col that offers a steep route down (northwest) to the Laguna Grande. As this short cut is difficult with a heavy pack we suggest descending a little further onto a major ridge and trail which is also beautiful. Turn left and continue along the ridge for five minutes before bearing left and heading gently down to the Trocha Real (King's Way), a path linking Refugio Llano and **Refugio Elola** (☎ 920 20 75 76, 91 347 62 53 in Madrid;

www.galeon.com/refugioelola; accommodation per person €9; breakfast €4.20, dinner €13; Jun-Oct & weekends in May). Turn left and you'll reach the *refugio* 50 minutes later, after walking around Laguna Grande. There is a permanently open winter annexe, **restaurant** (three-course evening meal €9.95) and shop selling emergency rations such as beer and chocolate. Some English is spoken.

SIDE TRIP: ALMANZOR & THE CINCO LAGUNAS
6½–8 hours, 10km, 841m ascent/descent

This excellent side trip joins two attractions with one simple traverse, saving time and unnecessary climbing.

From Refugio Elola follow the cairned path that climbs behind the *refugio* and then heads southwest up the valley. After 25 minutes you will pass the end of a bold spur leading down from Ameal de Pablo (2509m). A couple of minutes from the *refugio* you pass the turn off to **Portilla del Venteadero** (see Day 4). Continue west across a dry river bed and then turn southwest. After a 20-minute climb bear right as the trail leads west up a narrow, steep, boulder-filled gully. After 45 minutes you'll reach a small col (2550m) just southwest of Almanzor. However, be warned that the last section involves climbing a passage of gully that's very worn by the feet of thousands of tourists. Many of the rocks are loose and there's a landslide waiting to happen.

From the col scramble/climb/traverse right (north) for about 20m. To your right (east) should be two corridors up the western face of the peak. Take the one on the left to arrive at **Almanzor** (2591m) after a 10-minute climb. Technically it's a simple ascent, but it's a little taxing and the summit is exposed. However, the views across the whole of the Gredos make it well worth the effort.

After descending from the summit don't return to the narrow gully, but turn right (north), passing through a small col onto the eastern side of the ridge. From here a steady 40-minute traverse to Portilla del Venteadero (Cerro del Venteadero; 2484m) is possible (although it seems out of the question when viewed from the *refugio*!). The summit of **La Galana** (2572m), due north of here, is not for non-climbers – a crevasse must be crossed and a narrow clifftop traverse is required.

From south of La Galana an obvious path leads northwest to a small pass overlooking Laguna de Güetre, which is reached via a scree slope. Turn left (west) to pick your way down a boulder field to the **Cinco Lagunas**.

You have two ways to complete the loop. Either follow the cairn-lined path on the eastern side of the largest lake east up a 300m scree slope to a 2378m pass (sometimes marked as Portilla del Rey). Otherwise take the path that leads from the northernmost lake to **Portilla del Rey** (2378m) before leading east into the Gargantón valley, across Risco Negro and back to Refugio Elola (about 2½ hours). Numerous other exits/entrances to/from the Cinco Lagunas are possible.

Day 4: Refugio Elola to Refugio El Lanchón
5½–6½ hours, 9km

Head west up behind the *refugio* on the trail to Almanzor (signed), but after a couple of minutes bear off right onto a cairn-lined path that climbs west along the northern side of a spur emanating from Ameal de Pablo. After about an hour you'll reach a rocky pass around the southern side of the crooked-looking summit. Continue west

across a small meadow and up a rocky slope to **Portilla del Venteadero** (Cerro del Venteadero; 2484m).

From the pass follow the rough path northwest, dipping down beneath the cliffs encircling the Cinco Lagunas and on past Portilla de las Cinco Lagunas (2358m) to flatter ground and a *fuente*. About 200m further north a wall running east-west marks the boundary of the Reserva Nacional del Macizo Central de Gredos and the beginning of the watershed that forms the Garganta de Bohoyo.

From here you could pick up the trail for the alternative finish. However, the main route heads northwest down to Bohoyo along the simple trail beside Garganta de Bohoyo. Break the journey at **Refugio El Lanchón** after about 1½ hours of beautiful valley walking (stick to the true right bank after about an hour when the valley becomes more vegetated). This overnight stop means you don't have to rush to catch a bus from Bohoyo and gives you time to appreciate the valley with its stark but beautiful landscape of streams, slabs of pink, weathered granite and bright green grass.

Refugio El Lanchón is very simple, much more a shepherds' hut than walkers' *refugio*. You could get about four people on the rickety sleeping platform and a couple on the floor.

ALTERNATIVE FINISH: NAVAMEDIANA
4–5 hours, 13km

A shorter alternative finish continues north across the western flanks of **Meapoco** (2396m) and **Plaza de Toros** (2311m) to the Garganta de Navamediana, which can be followed down a narrow, intimate valley to **Navamediana** in about 3½ hours (from Plaza de Toros). From this traditional Gredos village (which doesn't have so much as a public phone) it's less than 2km to a bus stop on the C500 (which is served by the same buses as Bohoyo).

Day 5: Refugio El Lanchón to Bohoyo
3–3½ hours, 12km

Downstream from the *refugio* the valley becomes increasingly vegetated and the trail becomes more obvious, cutting down through a meadow and arriving at **Fuente**

de la Redonda and a very simple hut. After a further 20 minutes the trail forks. Go right here then, a few minutes later, join a 4WD track that leads down the valley and into a wide, flat area of agricultural land.

Roughly 30 minutes after joining the 4WD track turn left beside a ruined farmhouse as the track climbs northeast through oak woodland. This trail soon leads across a cattle grid. Head north down the dirt road and as soon as you see the sealed road head towards it. Turn left then cross the now-wide Garganta de Bohoyo to **Restaurante El Vergel la Fuente de Gredos**, an ideal place to soak sore feet in the beautiful river, sink a few drinks and arrange a taxi.

The centre of Bohoyo is about 800m west and the bus stop is on the C500 a further 2.2km away.

LAKES & PEAKS

Duration 2 days
Distance 26km
Difficulty moderate
Start/Finish Nava del Barco
Nearest Town El Barco de Ávila (p64)
Transport bus, taxi
Summary A thrilling exploration of a glacial valley, a beautiful camping spot and some tricky ridge-walking around Covacha make this a memorable hike.

This walk is centred around an ascent of Covacha (2395m; highest peak in the western Gredos) after a beautiful walk up the glacial Valle de Garganta de Galin Gómez.

This would be an ideal continuation of the Alta Ruta de Gredos traverse (see Alta Ruta de Gredos Extension, p62, under More Walks) and there are loads of options for extensions and alternative routes from this popular peak.

Refer to the Editorial Alpina's 1:50,000 Valle del Jerte map, which has dozens of options.

PLANNING
What to Bring
You'll need to bring a full complement of camping gear along with you.

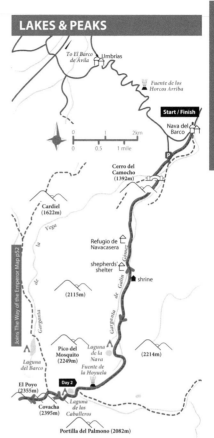

Maps
For accurate topographical detail (but without many paths marked) use IGN's 1:25,000 map No 576-III *Cabezuela del Valle* and 576-IV *Laguna del Barco*.

GETTING TO/FROM THE WALK
The easiest way to reach the trailhead is to take a taxi from El Barco de Ávila (Call Morena Lopez ☎ 920 34 03 48).

THE WALK
Day 1: Nava del Barco to Laguna de los Caballeros
4½–5 hours, 11km, 980m ascent
As far as the Laguna de La Nava this walk is well sign posted as the PR39. Walk down Nava del Barco's Calle del Puente to a

small square where you join a track going up past the Casa Rurales La Gargantera (these will be on your left) to a junction with a car park opposite where you turn left. Follow this track, which turns into a dirt road, and at the next fork turn right (southwest) as indicated by the PR39 sign and continue to the **Puente de La Yunta** (a bridge). Continue along this track ignoring any turn-offs until you pass through some green gates and into a pasture. For the next 15 minutes follow the faint track south up to a well-built shepherds' shelter, **Refugio de Navacasera**. Cairned trails lead to a second hut in about 30 minutes (both are open for use) and then, shortly afterwards, across the rocky riverbed to a small **shrine**.

The trail now changes into a beautiful, well-constructed path that zigzags up the now rugged, rocky valley, around a series of waterfalls. At the meadow, where the cairns momentarily disappear, bear left and within a few minutes you'll pick up the cairns again which will now lead you back to the final waterfall and on up to the **Laguna de la Nava**, about an hour from the shrine. Surrounded by towering peaks and scree slopes, the turquoise lake is a classic glacial creation and the dam wall makes a beautiful flat campsite.

From the eastern end of the dam head southeast, passing to the right of a ruin and, bearing slightly right, climb up over a rock area and onto a grassy patch where you bear left towards a stream. At the stream bear right and walk roughly southwest beside the humble beginnings of **Garganta de Galin Gómez**, cross the stream as it bears slightly right and make your way towards the head of the valley where you climb to the crest of a ridge on the stream's true right bank.

As you reach the top head roughly west and bear right, you may pick up the cairns among the broom, until **Laguna de los Caballeros** becomes visible up ahead to your left as the ground falls away. From here bushwhack west to a gully (and Fuente de la Hoyuela) before cutting down to the valley floor. It's not an easy (or quick) descent so pick the route that's most comfortable for you. The lake area is one of the most secluded and tranquil **campsites** in the Gredos.

Day 2: Laguna de los Caballeros to Nava del Barco via Covacha
5½–6 hours, 15km, 375 ascent

You shouldn't attempt to continue onto the summit of Covacha on wet or overcast days as the rocks can be very slippery and it's easy to lose your way.

Assuming it's fine then the path to **Covacha** (2395m) zigzags up to a col from the southern side of the lake. From the col turn right (west) following the cairns and a red arrow up and over a series of rocky slabs then bear slightly right and up into a narrow pass, before turning left (southwest) on the final push to the summit.

From the summit enjoy the spectacular views of the surrounding valleys and peaks and then continue the scramble west, following cairns over the rocky, often-exposed peaks and ridges of **El Poyo** (2355m).

From El Poyo simply turn tail and retrace your steps back to where you camped on the banks of the Laguna de los Caballeros and then onward back to Nava del Barco.

THE WAY OF THE EMPEROR

Duration 7–9 hours
Distance 28km
Difficulty moderate
Start Jarandilla de la Vera (p65)
Finish Tornavacas
Nearest Town El Barco de Ávila (p64)
Transport bus, taxi
Summary A gentle hike through gorgeous Gredos countryside retracing the steps of the men with blue blood.

A long, but relatively easy romp along the wonderful Ruta de Carlos V, or Camino Real (royal route), which passes through Reserva Natural de Garganta de los Infiernos, one of the last places in central Spain where you have a chance to see the rare black stork and other protected species.

PLANNING
Maps
Editorial Alpina's 1:50,000 *Valle del Jerte* map is very useful for trails and options, but is rather inaccurate: the path shown snaking up the true right bank of the

Garganta de Galin Gómez is a non-starter; Refugio Palomo near Puerto de Tornavacas has long-since closed; and the paths around Capilla-Refugio de las Nieves are marked incorrectly.

For accurate topographical detail (but without many paths marked) use IGN's 1:25,000 map Nos 576-I *Tornavacas* and 576-II *Solana de Ávila.*

GETTING TO/FROM THE WALK

See p65 for information on getting to and from Jarandilla de la Vera.

THE WALK

From Jarandilla de la Vera take the road out of town in a northerly direction towards the tiny village of Guijo de Santa Barbara then, two minutes after turning right off the C501 onto a concrete track, fork left onto Ruta de Carlos V. Follow the red-and-white markers (these mark the whole route, but are most easily seen when walking from Tornavacas to Jarandilla) to Puente de Palo, a footbridge. Cross the Garganta de Jaranda, head west to the dirt road, turn left then quickly cut back right to start a 10-minute climb northwest along a well-used dirt road to a tarmac road. Walk left for 60m, then turn right (west) onto a narrow trail leading up to a wide

CARLOS' WAY

The Way of the Emperor follows the route taken by the Holy Roman Emperor Carlos V in October 1556.

Son of the seemingly unlikely pairing of Juana the Crazy and Felipe the Handsome, Carlos inherited huge swathes of Spain, France, Germany and Italy at the tender age of 16. He later became the Holy Roman Emperor, but after 40 years of rule he abdicated and retired to Yuste monastery. He described his mountain crossing from Tornavacas to Jarandilla as the 'last pass of his life', but suffered little hardship – he was carried the whole way in a sedan chair. Something you'll be unlikely to convince local people to do for you now.

track. Turn right; then after about 10m bear left (northwest) onto a narrow trail that zigzags up the slope before bearing northwest across more open ground to **Fuente de los Pilones** and two large oak trees (a possible campsite). Continue northwest for 15 minutes, passing a large boulder before forking right (west) to a rocky promontory. A couple of minutes later, just past a collection of farm buildings, fork right (north) and head up through

TORNAVACAS TO CALVITERO LINK

An interesting and challenging route joins Tornavacas with the Sierra de Candelario walk. The 12.5km route takes 5½ hours, involves 1124m of descent and isn't recommended for those with heavy packs or a fear of heights, as some climbing and considerable exposure are involved. The best maps to use are IGN 1:25,000 map Nos 576-1 *Tornavacas* and 576-II *Solana de Ávila*.

From Tornavacas head north out of Plaza de la Iglesia, bear right across the stream and up Calle Real de Arriba. Fork right upon reaching a *fuente* and follow the red-and-white markers of the GR10 Puerto de Tornavacas for about 1¼ hours. Turn left, cross the N110 and head northwest up the dirt road opposite, climbing for about 25 minutes until the dirt road meets a stone wall and cuts back west. Bear right and climb northwest through the broom beside the wall. After an hour you'll reach a faint trail below the summit ridge of **Risco la Campana** (2093m); the trail leads around the peak to **Portilla de Galindo** (1983m).

From the pass you have two options. The main route heads west through the broom and along a rocky, tricky ridge to Cumbre de Talamanca (2394m), but after Portilla de Talamanca the route (marked with cairns) is very exposed – some sections are a nerve-wracking scramble/climb. The other route is slightly longer, although the terrain is easier. It cuts across Hoyo Malillo (an area of high pasture with an excellent campsite) then heads upstream along the Arroyo Malillo, around a waterfall – some straightforward but exposed climbing is required – and into an area of seasonal lakes and high pasture. To the west of this stunning glacial bowl a steep scree slope leads to Tranco del Diablo, 40 minutes northeast of Calvitero. To pick up Day 2 of the Sierra de Candelario walk, see Side Trip: Ascent of Calvitero (p55).

SISTEMA CENTRAL

THE WAY OF THE EMPEROR

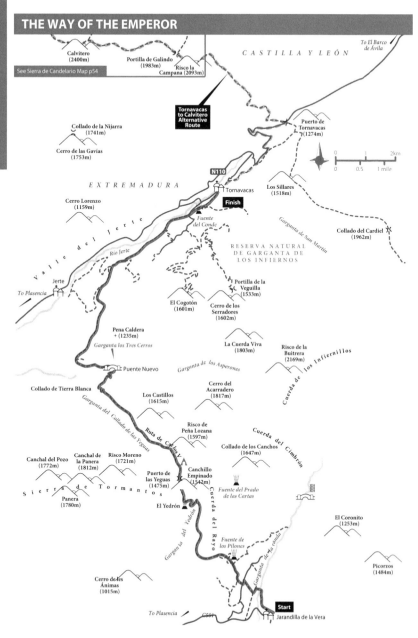

Calvitero (2400m)

Portilla de Galindo (1983m)

Risco la Campana (2093m)

CASTILLA Y LEÓN

To El Barco de Ávila

See Sierra de Candelario Map p54

Tornavacas to Calvitero Alternative Route

Collado de la Nijarra (1741m)

Cerro de las Gavias (1753m)

Puerto de Tornavacas (1274m)

0   1   2km
0   0.5   1 mile

N110

EXTREMADURA

Tornavacas

Finish

Los Sillares (1518m)

Cerro Lorenzo (1159m)

Fuente del Conde

Garganta de San Martín

Collado del Cardiel (1962m)

Río Jerte

RESERVA NATURAL DE GARGANTA DE LOS INFIERNOS

Valle del Jerte

Jerte

To Plasencia

Portilla de la Veguilla (1533m)

El Cogotón (1601m)

Cerro de los Serradores (1602m)

Pena Caldera + (1235m)

Garganta los Tres Cerros

La Cuerda Viva (1803m)

Risco de la Buitrera (2169m)

Cuerda de los Infiernillos

Puente Nuevo

Garganta de los Asperones

Collado de Tierra Blanca

Garganta del Collado de las Yeguas

Los Castillos (1615m)

Cerro del Acarradero (1817m)

Ruta de Carlos V

Risco de Peña Lozana (1597m)

Cuerda del Cimbrón

Canchal del Pozo (1772m)

Canchal de la Panera (1812m)

Risco Moreno (1721m)

Collado de los Canchos (1647m)

Puerto de las Yeguas (1475m)

Canchillo Empinado (1542m)

Fuente del Prado de las Cartas

Sierra de Tormantos

Panera (1780m)

El Yedrón

Cuerda del Rayo

Garganta del Yedrón

El Coronito (1253m)

Fuente de los Pilones

Garganta de Majedanda

Cerro de los Ánimas (1015m)

Picorzos (1484m)

To Plasencia

C501

Start

Jarandilla de la Vera

the broom into the **Valle de Garganta de Yedrón**. You'll reach the stream in roughly 35 minutes.

Cross the stream and follow the trail as it zigzags northwest up past a *fuente* onto the ridge of **Canchillo Empinado**

(1542m). Traverse north to **Puerto de la Yeguas** (1475m)then drop down and cross Garganta del Collado de las Yeguas heading northwest through a meadow at the beginning of a beautiful, 1¼-hour walk down the stunning, steep-sided valley towards Garganta los Tres Cerros.

Upon reaching a ridge marking the point two valleys meet high above Garganta los Tres Cerros, there's a tight zigzagging trail down to a junction of walking trails. Turn right and then right again at the next junction to head northeast up the valley to **Puente Nuevo** (a wonderful stone bridge), which you reach in 20 minutes. Cross and follow the trail west up to a 4WD track. Turn left, pootle along for about 10 minutes (avoiding switchbacks left) to a T-junction, then turn right before quickly cutting back left (north) down a narrow gully.

You'll soon join a 4WD track and the route northeast becomes fairly straight and simple. About 15 minutes after crossing a five-way junction (at which you should go straight ahead) turn left down a narrow track to another 4WD track that's soon joined by the GR10. You'll reach a tarmac road 50 minutes later. Turn left, left again across Río Jerte and then right onto a concrete road. Upon reaching a dead end turn left into **Tornavacas**.

SIERRA DE CANDELARIO

Duration 2 days
Distance 23.5km
Difficulty moderate
Start/Finish Candelario (p63)
Transport bus
Summary A leisurely two-day walk up a beautiful valley to one of the most stunning corries in the Gredos, with loads of scope for further exploration.

The Sierra de Candelario is divided from the western end of the Sierra de Gredos by the Valle de Aravalle, through which the N110 linking Plasencia and El Barco de Ávila passes. It's a small range and does not provide the scale and variety of landscapes found elsewhere in the Gredos. However, Hoya Moros – the tranquil, boulder-strewn corrie ringed by the stunning cliffs of Los

Hermanitos and Calvitero (2400m; the highest peak in the range) at the head of the Cuerpo de Hombre valley – is simply stunning and there are enough challenges in the area to occupy a number of days.

In theory this lengthy but enjoyable walk could be done in one very long day, but the climb from the picturesque (and touristy) village of Candelario is taxing. Camping in Hoya Moros is highly recommended and there are plenty of possible distractions and side trips. These include a loop around Los Hermanitos from Hoya Moros, a trip down to Lagunas El Trampal, an ascent of Canchal Negro (2364m) or an exploration of the ridges to the southeast and southwest into the Valle del Jerte (see the boxed text Tornavacas to Calvitero Link, p51).

Aside from rock cains there is no way-marking on this route.

PLANNING
Maps
Editorial Alpina's 1:50,000 *Valle del Jerte* map covers the walk, but is plagued by inaccuracies (Calvitero is incorrectly identified as El Torreón). IGN 1:25,000 maps Nos 553-III *Béjar* and 576-1 *Tornavacas* accurately cover the walk.

GETTING TO/FROM THE WALK
See Candelario (p63) for more information.

THE WALK
Day 1: Candelario to Refugio Cueva de Hoya Moros
5–5½ hours, 11.5km, 959m ascent
From the centre of Candelario walk up Calle Mayor, turn right (west) at El Canton (a building), to a small road where you take the upper left fork (more or less straight on) until the main road and turn left (signed towards 'Sierra'). Bear right towards **Hotel Cinco Castaños** and continue down the Camino del Calvario track. After about 10 minutes fork right past a building with a yellow-white marker on the wall and enter the woods past a red La Jarilla sign and continue steadily southwest to a sealed road east of Embalse de Fuente Santa (not visible). Turn left then, 10 minutes later, fork left (south) down a forestry road signed *La Dehesa* through green metal gates. Bear right over the bridge and again

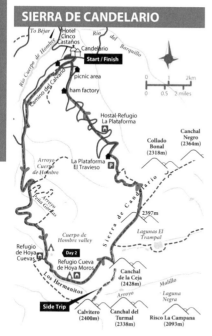

bear right through a second set of gates past the yellow-white marker to your right and into open oak woodland. Upon reaching a T-junction around 30 minutes later turn right (west) then bear right (south) at the next junction. After crossing the **Arroyo Peña Gordas** climb steadily through two obvious hairpin bends, ignoring a path off to the right at the first bend, before reaching a third (left) bend. As you reach the apex of the bend take a well-worn path immediately off to your right and marked by cairns that climbs southeast along a ridge parallel to the stunning, glacial **Cuerpo de Hombre** valley.

After 30 minutes, with Los Hermanitos in full view and a small meadow with stream on the left, the track bears right (south) through broom and across rock slabs to a set of falls. Small cairns mark the way along many paths, the lower path is possibly the easiest and quickest. At the waterfalls head upstream into a wide meadow. To the southwest, on a hill, lies the **Refugio de Hoya Cuevas**.

Head southeast across the meadow, picking out a suitable route for the steep, rocky climb to a second narrow meadow (by following the river course across the meadow you reach another small set of waterfalls; you can climb up on the right side of the falls and, when almost at the top of the falls, cut left across them and around the rocks into the meadow). Walk south beside the meandering river along a faint path marked with cairns. Cross over the river and head along its true left bank. Follow a faint path towards the huge rock slabs. Bear right around them, cross the river again and head northeast over and through the short section of moraine to some stepping stones which take you back over the river and into some pasture with the stunning glacial corrie of Hoya Moros. Make your way southeast through the soft pasture to a large cairn-topped boulder. One hundred metres east is **Refugio Cueva de Hoya Moros**. Walled rocks offer some shelter and this is a good place to camp. It does not offer shelter in the rain without a tent.

Day 2: Refugio Cueva de Hoya Moros to Candelario
4–4½ hours, 12km

From the *refugio* head northeast across the meadow, bear left to a grassy strip that leads northeast up between difficult rocky slopes and patches of broom. Climb steeply for 30 minutes where you begin to see the valley open out. On reaching the broom turn east, following the cairns up to flatter barren landscape to a path below a jumble of large, rounded rocks. Southeast of here is the level summit of **Canchal de la Ceja** (2428m). Head off along the right (south) trail here for the Ascent of Calvitero side trip (p55).

The main route turns left here. Follow the trail northeast, bearing up left past a large cairn and a metal sign, along the Cuerda del Calvitero passing along the east of a **peak** (2397m). As you begin to come around the side of the peak bear slightly left diagonally across the flat terrain following the cairns and trail in a more northerly direction. Ignore any cairns running off to the right or left of the main trail. As the valley down on your left starts to come into view as well as the road and **La Plataforma El Travieso** descend to the left and pick your route down through broom to the trailhead. Turn right along the road and, just before the bend, turn left to take a shortcut to the **Hostal-Refugio La Plata-forma** (☎/fax 923 40 18 00; Jul-early Sep). The hostel has a restaurant, good views and a gentle breeze.

From the hostel walk along the road signed to Candelario and then take the path off to the right which passes underneath the electricity pylons. This path crosses the road three times before arriving at the **Redondo de Iglesias**, (a ham factory). Turn right and head down the road to a right bend, where a track leads left into pine woodland. Follow it, turning immediately right (north) to a dirt road. Turn left northwest to a **picnic area** where you turn right and then left at the fork down past a viewpoint and three stone crosses.

Continue east for 50m before looping around a jumble of rocks and cutting down north to a road. Then turn left quickly, bear right down through more woods (this steep slope can be slippery after rain so you may wish to just stick to the road right to Candelario). Emerging from the woods 200 metres east of the **Hotel Cinco Castaños** turn right onto the road and head into Candelario.

SIDE TRIP: ASCENT OF CALVITERO
1½ hours, 4km

From the jumble of boulders and the main trail northwest of Canchal de la Ceja a cairn-marked trailheads south before turning southwest and crossing a saddle to **Calvitero** (2400m). You reach Calvitero after negotiating the Devil's Step – a steep channel in the rock (a fixed steel rope helps you do the simple climb).

The views are stunning, especially of Los Hermanitos, but on a good day the whole Sierra de Gredos is visible, as are the plains out to Salamanca.

Retrace your steps to rejoin the main route.

SIERRA DE GUADARRAMA

Slightly overshadowed by the Sierra de Gredos – its grander neighbour on the Sistema Central – the Sierra de Guadarrama

offers some great, easily accessible walking. The ski resorts and large number of day-trippers from Madrid may have taken their toll on some regions, but the high ridges and remote peaks are remarkably undisturbed. Certain areas demand attention despite being tourist targets – we highly recommend climbing Peñalara and the Siete Picos and exploring La Pedriza – while the GR10 and Cuerda Larga long-distance paths cross the bulk of the mountain chain.

Only 50km north of Madrid at the closest point, these mountains are well within day-trip range of the capital and efficient train and bus services bring the urban hordes into the mountains each weekend.

HISTORY
The history of the Guadarrama is similar to that of the Gredos. Additionally, the range has frequently played a role in defending Madrid (the mountains have long been known as Mons Carpetani, or protector of Madrid). During the Spanish Civil War Republicans defending Madrid (including the International Brigades) fought along the ridges around the watershed of the range – you can still come across evidence of trenches and other fortifications.

In 1923 a narrow-gauge railway from Cercedilla to the 1870m-high pass of Puerto de Cotos was opened. The subsequent influx of *madrileños* may have upset the Los Doce Amigos mountaineering society, which had established *refugios* in the range 10 years earlier, but a tourist industry was born. Increased car ownership and society's greater affluence in the 1970s led to the development of the limited, north-facing ski fields of the central Guadarrama, while a large number of second homes and chalet housing developments sprouted below the southern slopes.

ENVIRONMENT
The natural history of the Sierra de Guadarrama resembles that of the Gredos too (see Environment, p40). It also shares some of the differences between southern and northern slopes (see History, p40), although here the variation is often not as pronounced and there is certainly less glaciation.

The area of La Pedriza is an exception to the general terrain of the Sistema Central.

Here, numerous faults and extensive erosion of the softer, warmer-coloured rock have produced a strange landscape of towering rounded pinnacles, narrow passes, smooth domes and balancing rock sculptures.

The northern side of the range is almost completely covered by Scots pine. Spanish bluebells and toad flax, with its large, snapdragon-like flowers, thrive in the forests.

White storks, considered a good omen, are seasonal visitors to many villages in the mountains and foothills. Colonies of seven or eight nests can be seen at Manzanares El Real. You'll be very lucky to see Spanish ibex, wildcats or wild boars, but be wary of the hairy brown-and-black caterpillars of the pine processionary moth (see the boxed text The Pine Processionary Caterpillar, p33) and their large nests, like dense spiderwebs, in pine trees.

PLANNING
When to Walk
The area is busy all year and is often swamped at weekends between June and September. Some *refugios*, hostels, restaurants and tourist-oriented shops open only during the ski season, high summer or on weekends. Unlike areas of the Gredos, the snow cover has largely disappeared by mid-May, although freezing temperatures and driving rain and sleet can occur until June. Visit in May, June or September if you can.

Maps & Books
La Tienda Verde's 1:50,000 *Sierra de Guadarrama* map covers the whole of the range and can be used for most walks in the area. Editorial Alpina's 1:25,000 *La Pedriza* map covers the eastern half of the Cuerda Larga walk, while the 1:25,000 *Guadarrama* map covers the western half, and the whole of the Valle de la Fuenfría walk.

Domingo Pliego's *100 Excursiones Por La Sierra de Madrid* is a comprehensive Spanish-language guide to the area. The author has written dozens of guides to the Sistema Central.

Information Sources
Some information about the Sierra de Guadarrama is available at the Comunidad de Madrid's main **tourist office** (☎ 91 429 49 51; www.turismoco madrid.es; Calle Duque de Medinaceli 2, Madrid), but don't get your hopes up. A better bet are the many mountaineering federations in Madrid (see Information Sources, p41).

For details of more walks around Cercedilla, visit the **Centro de Educación Ambiental** (☎ 91 852 22 13; 10am-6pm), 2km north of Cercedilla, and pick up its pamphlet, *Sendas del Valle de la Fuenfría*. Its equivalent in Cotos, the **Centro de Interpretación del Parque Natural de Peñalara** (☎ 91 852 08 57) covers the trails and wildlife within this nature park.

ACCESS TOWN
Cercedilla (p64) is the take-off spot.

VALLE DE LA FUENFRÍA

Duration 5½–6 hours
Distance 21.5km
Difficulty moderate
Start/Finish Cercedilla (p64)
Transport train, bus
Summary A steepish climb to the rim of the valley followed by easy ridge-walking and a mostly gentle, though at times rocky, descent.

Thanks to good early-morning and evening rail and bus connections to Cercedilla, this loop around Valle de la Fuenfría is achievable as a day trip from Madrid. The trail is well marked and, although the valley is popular with *madrileños* throughout the year (ski-mountaineering takes over from walking once winter arrives), the route mostly avoids crowds.

The section from Pradera to Majalasna onwards is also the latter part of Day 3 of the Cuerda Larga walk (see p57), so walkers planning to tackle that could cut this walk short at Puerto de Fuenfría and take the Roman road back down to Cercedilla. Alternatively, from this pass the GR10.1 to Cotos could be picked up, combining the two routes described here into a four-day walk. Another possible extension would be along the GR10 southwest to El Escorial (see Western Guadarrama, p62, under More Walks).

GETTING TO/FROM THE WALK

For information on how to get to and from the start and finish of this walk see Cercedilla in the Towns & Facilities section (p64).

THE WALK

Turn left out of Cercedilla's train station and go straight after 100m, where the road goes left under the railway. Follow large circular blue markers up a winding, groomed footpath and climb a short flight of steps to turn right onto Camino de los Campamentos. This well-used dirt road climbs steadily for the next 25 minutes to an iron gate across the track. Following red dots, cut up left (west) across a large clearing, past a *fuente* and onto a trail that leads northwest through the woods to meet a forestry track after 45 minutes.

Cross the track and, now guided by smaller red dots, head northwest up the mountain to a ridge, the GR10 with its red-and-white flashes and a sturdy dry-stone wall marks the boundary between Castilla y León and the Comunidad de Madrid.

Turn right and follow the GR10 northwards, past a lesser peak (with a ruin at its base) and on to the summit of **Cerro Peña Águila** (2009m), identifiable by its large, conical cone and reached after around two hours of walking. There are spectacular views northwards over the *meseta* of Castilla y León while those northeast to **Siete Picos** (2138m) and, beyond, Peñalara (2430m) are equally majestic.

Follow the wall to **Collado de Marichiva** (1753m) to meet again the self same dirt road that you crossed about 1¼ hours earlier. Turn left at this col and walk past a *fuente* to reach Puerto de Fuenfría (1796m) after about 30 minutes. There's another *fuente* just north of the pass.

Head south of the pass then left after 250m to leave the GR10 and take a path that climbs southeast to a **viewpoint** overlooking the whole of Valle de la Fuenfría. At a T-junction with a broader trail, turn left and climb eastwards to **Collado Ventoso**, a grassy saddle with a *fuente* to the southwest. Pick up a trail (signed 'Senda de los Alevines' and indicated by yellow spots) that drops initially southwest, then south, across some fairly demanding boulder fields to **Pradera de Majalasna**.

Head south across this meadow, pass a *fuente*, then follow the trail markers down a wide, at times deeply sunken track to meet a dirt road beside a couple of giant boulders. Turn left (south) and walk as far as a hairpin bend and the two Los Miradores **viewpoints**. Bear left off the road and head to the southernmost viewpoint before swinging right (west) to undertake a 30-minute descent to a wide, open saddle. Here the route cuts back northwest (an alternative to the east leads down to the outskirts of Cercedilla). After a long, straight, mainly gentle descent, it crosses a footbridge after 30 minutes and cuts up to a sealed road. Turn left then, some 10 minutes later, take the path, signalled by blue dots, opposite the **Centro de Educación Ambiental**. Heading initially northwards, it soon loops south to become a wide, delightful track that gently descends through pine forest to reach the station after around 50 minutes – a glorious way to end the day.

CUERDA LARGA

Duration 3 days

Distance 54km

Difficulty moderate–demanding

Start Cotos (p64)

Finish Cercedilla (p64)

Transport train

Summary An enjoyable introduction to the Sierra de Guadarrama's peaceful valleys, high ridges and summits.

The walk begins in Parque Natural de Peñalara, continues along a short section of the Cuerda Larga long-distance path, and descends into La Pedriza, the most dramatic part of Parque Regional de la Cuenca Alta del Manzanares. Day 2 takes you along the tranquil upper valley of Río Manzanares

TAKING ON WATER

Be very careful where you refill your water bottles. Those upland streams look limpid and crystal clear but you're rarely higher than the highest cow. If there are flies buzzing around your head, there are probably cattle close too.

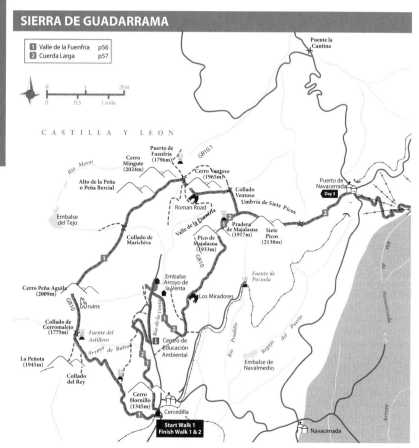

SIERRA DE GUADARRAMA

to Puerto de Navacerrada, saving the spiky Siete Picos (Seven Peaks) and their spectacular vistas for the shorter Day 3 with its gentle descent to Cercedilla.

It offers a taste of the great walking available once you leave the crowds behind. There are a number of possible extensions, side trips and deviations. The complete Cuerda Larga, a classic 18km walk, stretches across a section of high ridge running northeast from Puerto de Navacerrada to Puerto de la Morcuera and would be a worthy extension to this route.

Highly recommended as a warm up for this walk is an ascent of Peñalara (2429m; see Peñalara Ascent, p62) from Cotos, possibly including a loop through the Lagunas de Peñalara. It's also easy to spend at least two days in La Pedriza, scrambling around the eroded peaks.

GETTING TO/FROM THE WALK

From Cercedilla, mountain trains head up to Cotos (40 minutes, four daily) via Puerto de Navacerrada (25 minutes). The standard fare is €5. Twice as many services run on Saturday and Sunday.

A taxi from Cercedilla to Cotos costs about €30.

THE WALK
Day 1: Cotos to Manzanares El Real
6½–7½ hours, 21km

From Venta Marcelino in Cotos (1870m), walk southeast down a wide sealed road

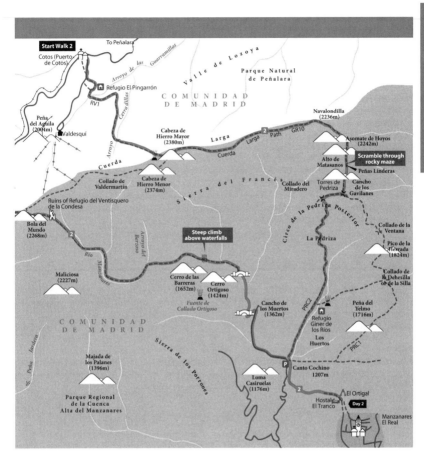

towards the Valdesquí ski area. After 10 minutes turn left onto a track that leads southeast to **Refugio El Pingarrón**.

From the *refugio* a path (marked RV1) descends south across Arroyo de las Guarramillas then loops around a spur through pine woodland down to a junction. Fork right off the RV1 and traverse south above Arroyo Cerradillas, towards which the trail now bends. Cross the stream to follow a meandering trail (indicated by faded yellow-and-white blazes) in a south-southeasterly direction across two more streams. At a third stream, leave the wood and head up the stream's true left (west) bank along a cairn-lined path all the way to the ridge of a spur, reached about an hour after turning into the valley. There's a *fuente* 50m southwest.

Proceed southeast, climbing to meet the Cuerda Larga (and GR10) at a saddle between **Cabeza de Hierro Menor** (2379m) and **Cabeza de Hierro Mayor** (2380m). Turn left and follow the red-and-white markers to the higher peak. The views are magic. Much of the Cuerda Larga can be seen and the cliffs of Circo de la Pedriza Posterior look as dramatic as anything in the Sistema Central.

Markers now lead you east along the undulating ridge for just over an hour to **Navalondilla** (2236m). Thin grass alternates with mostly brief boulder fields. You'll find the cairns a more reliable indicator than the less evident GR10 markers (diligently painted for walkers travelling east to west so keep looking over your shoulder!).

SISTEMA CENTRAL

LA PEDRIZA CIRCUIT

At the end of Day 1 of the Cuerda Larga Walk (p57) the route drops through Circo de la Pedriza Posterior, a near-perfect horseshoe of tall, rounded cliffs surrounding a rocky labyrinth. An adventure playground for climbers, scramblers and walkers.

With yellow-and-white trail markers the PRC1 makes a complete circuit of La Pedriza and requires you to occasionally crawl under huge balancing boulders, scramble up tall boulder stacks or squeeze through high, narrow passes. It's great fun, but can take 10 to 12 hours (with 1000m of ascent and descent). There are no *fuentes* close to the ridges, so carry plenty of water. It's a good idea to spend two days in the park or shorten the circuit by cutting down west to **Refugio Giner de los Ríos**, where the GR10 crosses the route at the Collada de la Dehesilla (also called Collado de la Silla). There are also dozens of alternative routes and the ascent of Peña del Yelmo (1716m) to consider. This ascent requires a couple of basic climbing moves and is best approached from the northeast.

La Tienda Verde's 1:15,000 *La Pedriza del Manzanares* map is essential. The circuit begins at Canto Cochino, around 2.5km from Hostal El Tranco and the El Ortigal camping ground, and about 4.5km from the centre of Manzanares El Real.

Cross the bridge and head northwest up the slope, following the trail markers to a junction. Turn right and follow the PRC1 (often marked as the PR1) across Cancho de los Muertos. The fun is just beginning.

Now for the day's one tricky piece of navigation; at Navalondilla, leave the Cuerda Larga and GR10, which bear away left (northeast). Instead, bear right (southeast) to another, rocky peak, **Asomate de Hoyos** (2242m), and pick up a cairn-lined path that leads south into the broom. Frequently branching in its early stages, it becomes a more evident trail as you descend. Scramble through a rocky maze on the west side of **Peñas Linderas** then work your way around the eastern flank of **Alto de Matasanos** (2106m) to reach **Cancho de los Gavilanes**, an evident col just north of the stunning eroded cliffs that form the boundary of **La Pedriza**. From this saddle, a level path heads southwest to **Collado del Miradero** (also called Collado de Prao Poyos; 1878m), a wider col, where there's a meeting of trails. The PRC1 forms a circuit around La Pedriza (see the boxed text La Pedriza Circuit, above – an excellent day out from the described route); instead, head south on the PRC2, which takes you through the heart of the park. After descending for a good 1½ hours, there's a sign for the well-equipped **Refugio Giner de los Ríos** (☎ 91 522 87 43, 659 021754; www.refugioginer .com; bed incl breakfast €10, half-board €21; Fri & Sat year-round, weekdays on reservation), a couple of minutes above the trail. To reach it, cross a footbridge and climb a low spur, passing a *fuente*. Otherwise, continue down the valley until the car park at Canto Cochino.

In **Canto Cochino**, which you reach 30 minutes beyond the *refugio*, there are two bar-restaurants. **Largo Ganta Zona de Acampada** (a camping ground with some facilities, but no drinking water) is 1.5km west, past the medical centre.

A beautiful 40-minute walk southeast beside the Río Manzanares brings you to a clutch of **restaurants** (like those at Canto Cochino, out of high season many open at weekends only) and a car park on the outskirts of **Manzanares El Real**. Close by is the smart campsite, **El Ortigal** (☎ 91 853 01 20; site per person/tent €6 each), while a little further downstream is the simple **Hostal El Tranco** (☎ 91 853 00 63; Calle del Tranco 4; s/d with shared bathrooms, price on application), which also runs a restaurant (the hostel is closed in Sep). The centre of Manzanares El Real is a 25-minute walk away.

Day 2: Manzanares El Real to Puerto de Navacerrada

5–6 hours, 18km

For almost all of its length, this route follows the upper reaches of Río Manzanares, followed by a climb to the Bola del Mundo, from where it's a simple descent to Puerto de Navacerrada.

Retrace your steps to Canto Cochino and walk upstream along the true left bank of Río Manzanares. Pine needles obscure what little path there is; just stick close to the river. After around 15 minutes, cross the river by some giant, smooth boulders and climb up to a road running parallel (it's possible to continue to the second of two footbridges but you'll find it tough going in places).

Turn right and follow the steadily climbing road for some 40 minutes to a road bridge across the Río Manzanares. Use the steps on the left just before the bridge to climb to a path that quickly leads past a reliable *fuente* to a simple footbridge. Cross; then zigzag up a clear, cairned path that heads west up through a gorge then stays fairly close to the river (the Alpina tracing is incorrect here), except for a steep climb around a series of waterfalls. The path is overgrown in places; in others there are several variants. Upon reaching a dirt road, walk left for 100m to a bridge. From here, a path on the true left bank follows the river northwest through the gentle, tranquil, grassy valley of the upper **Manzanares**. After about 30 minutes, curl west to follow a minor stream alongside a wide meadow, hopping freely from bank to bank, wherever the route's easier.

From the rubble of what was once **Refugio del Ventisquero de la Condesa**, it's a steep 200 vertical metres climb due west to **Bola del Mundo** (2268m), topped by what appear to be a pair of space rockets (possibly UFOs were active in the area when we passed!). From the summit, there are expansive views. The evening light beautifully illuminates the flat, arid plains of Castilla-La Mancha to the north and the outline of the Sierra de Gredos to the southwest. Madrid looks like a desert mirage. From here, a concrete road descends through ski infrastructure to **Puerto de Navacerrada** (p66).

Day 3: Puerto de Navacerrada to Cercedilla

3–4 hours, 15km

A word of warning: don't undertake this walk on a rainy day: the rock-face is hugely slippery and there's a danger of falling stones. With an early start from Madrid, this stage can also be undertaken as a wonderful, discrete day-walk. From

Puerto de Navacerrada's station, follow the sign, 'Sendero Arias', and turn left at a T-junction to reach the pass, just above and north of the village.

At the pass, head west from Bar-Restaurante Dos Castillas, straight up a short ski slope (signed 'Telégrafo') to meet a ridge. Turn left and follow a wide track just north of the ridge (a left fork offers a direct route across a series of rocky peaks) to a saddle with a giant boulder and a junction of trails. Head west along a wide track then, after 30m, fork left onto a cairn-marked trail that leads straight up the mountain to **Siete Picos**, the Seven Peaks. The first of these summits, distinguished by its triangulation point is, at 2138m, the highest. To reach the top requires a four-limbed scramble up a mass of eroded rock, best attacked from the northeast. If the climb seems daunting, ascend the second peak, a mere 19 metres lower, for an equally extravagant panorama. The trail now runs along the chain's northern flank with broad vistas of the dune plains of Castilla y León.

At a small col before the westernmost peak of the main summit ridge, pick up a steep, evident path that descends southwest through a stretch of open pine woodland to **Pradera de Majalasna** (1917m), a broad meadow, to join the last section of the Valle de la Fuenfría walk (see p56) for the last two hours or so of walking.

MORE WALKS

SIERRA DE GREDOS

Gredos Crossing

One popular three to four-day north-south crossing of the Gredos leads from Navalperal de Tormes (catch the Gredos bus from Madrid's Estación Sur de Autobuses) up Garganta del Pinar or across the Cuerda de los Barquillos (a long ridge) to the Cinco Lagunas and on to Refugio Elola. You then have the option of descending southwest along Garganta Tejéa from Lagunilla del Corral (which is northwest of Almanzor) to El Raso or heading east to Morezón and then south through Puerto de Candeleda down to Candeleda itself. Buses to Madrid run daily along the C501 south of the range. You'll need the IGN 1:50,000 *Macizo Central de Gredos* map.

Eastern Gredos

By basing yourself at Cuevas del Valle (see p64) and using the weekday Muñoz Travel buses to/from Ávila, you can do day walks up La Fría (1983m; west of Puerto del Pico) and Torozo (2021m; east of the pass). Both walks could also be turned into circular routes. The former goes straight up to the peak before descending to Puerto del Arenal and traversing back to the pass (or dropping down to El Arenal, which is also served by occasional buses). The latter peak could form part of a loop through San Esteban del Valle. IGN 1:25,000 map Nos 578-II *Mombeltrán* and 578-I *El Arenal* cover these walks.

Alta Ruta de Gredos Extension

It's possible to extend the Alta Ruta de Gredos to Puerto de Tornavacas. However, there's no set path from Portilla del Venteadero to Covacha, and broom and rugged, rocky peaks can make life difficult. El Butraco (2177m) is the most difficult (and rocky) section, but some of the ridge leading to it can be bypassed with a 30-minute detour along Garganta de Bohoyo. Around Cancho (2271m) is also tricky and it's essential to leave the ridge at Portilla del Palomo, thus avoiding the jagged cliffs of Riscos Morenos above Laguna de los Caballeros.

Four days allows for a comfortable traverse between Refugio Elola (see Day 3 of the Alta Ruta de Gredos walk, p44) and Puerto de Tornavacas, camping at the top of Garganta de Bohoyo on the first night, near Alto de las Becedillas Los Peones on the second and Laguna de los Caballeros on the third.

A good planning map for exploring the Gredos is Adrados Ediciones 1:135,000 *Parque Regional de la Sierra de Gredos*. Numerous IGN 1:25,000 maps cover the route.

SIERRA DE GUADARRAMA

Northeast Guadarrama

A number of good routes tag onto the Cuerda Larga Walk (see p57). A two-day option starts at Garganta de los Montes (which has a train station and bus links to Madrid), from where a pleasant trail runs the 10km to Cancencia and up to Puerto de Cancencia. From here the GR10.1 takes a fairly steady route to Refugio Puerto de la Morcuera (☎ 91 580 42 16), which lies 1km north of Puerto de la Morcuera (1796m). From the pass, the Cuerda Larga Walk can be reached via Najarra (2106m). The best map to use is the La Tienda Verde 1:50,000 *Sierra de Guadarrama*.

Western Guadarrama

The route between Cercedilla and San Lorenzo de El Escorial (a town that has drawn royals and *madrileños* for centuries) follows the GR10 across the ridges on the border with Castilla y León and the Comunidad de Madrid. En route is Valle de los Caídos (The Valley of the Fallen), which contains Franco's remarkable, perversely self-indulgent tomb. This walk would take at least three days and a number of simple *refugios* and huts lie en route. La Tienda Verde's 1:50,000 *Sierra de Guadarrama* map covers the walk.

Peñalara Ascent

The simple ascent of Peñalara (2430m; the highest peak in the Guadarrama) is excellent preparation for the Cuerda Larga Walk (see p57); you can stay overnight at the hostel in Puerto de Cotos and be bright eyed and bushy tailed for the Cuerda Larga Walk in the morning. Taking around three hours, the route has 600m of ascent and descent. To avoid retracing your steps from the summit it is possible to return to Puerto de Cotos via Laguna de los Pájaros or via Laguna Grande de Peñalara. The best map is the La Tienda Verde 1:50,000 *Sierra de Guadarrama*, plus the leaflet from the information office in Puerto de Cotos: see Information Sources (p41).

TOWNS & FACILITIES

ARENAS DE SAN PEDRO

☎ 920 / pop 6900

Arenas is a beautiful little town with a rather tumultuous history, having been much besieged. The town's motto roughly translates as 'Always burning and always faithful'. Hopefully it won't be quite so fiery when you pass through.

Information

The tourist **information office** (☎ 37 23 68; www.aytoarenas.com/turismo; Plaza San Pedro) is in the centre of town.

The **Grupo Gredos de Montaña** (see Information Sources, p44) is based at the information office as well.

Supplies & Equipment

On and just off Calle Triste Condesa (the main street) are a selection of local food shops, small supermarkets and **Mercado de Abastos** (Calle Maria Sanabria).

Sleeping & Eating

In a pleasant location beside the Río del Arenal, 1.9km out of town, is **Camping Riocantos** (☎ 37 25 47; Jul-Sep).

Hostal El Castillo (☎ 37 00 91; Carretera de Candeleda 2; s/d €23/33), beside the 14th-century Castillo de Don Álvaro de Luna Triste, is very pleasant.

Hostería Los Galayos (☎ 37 13 79; www.losgallayos.com; Plaza de Condestable Dávalos; s/d €40/48), a short distance away, has smart rooms but isn't stunning value. However, the restaurant is pretty good.

Cheaper places to eat are found along Calle Triste Condesa.

Getting There & Away

At least two buses run daily from Arenas de San Pedro to Madrid (€10.60, 2½ hours), except on Sunday. Two daily buses do the trip to Ávila (€5.30, 1¼ hours) from Monday to Saturday.

BOHOYO

☎ 920 / pop 400

At the end of the walk, this town has a pleasant centre with several bars and restaurants clustered around the church. There are few formal accommodation options.

Casa Rural Eltinao (☎ 34 71 34; d €65) is a recommended *casa rural* (rural guesthouse).

For passing royalty, the **Hotel Real** (☎ 34 72 31; www.hotelrealdebohoyo.com; d from €150) should do very nicely, ma'am.

Getting There & Away

Bohoyo's bus stop is 2.2km from the village (down) on the C500.

The daily **Cevesa** (☎ 91 539 31 32) bus from El Barco de Avila to Madrid passes through Bohoyo three times a day from Monday to Saturday and twice a day on Sundays and public holidays.

CANDELARIO

☎ 923 / pop 1000

Rubbing against a steep mountain face, this charming enclave is a popular summer resort and hiking base.

Information

Candelario's helpful **tourist office** (10am-2.30pm, 5-8pm Mon-Fri, 10am-2.30pm Sun) is situated at the bottom of the village. Candelario has a couple of ATMs, shops specialising in local delicacies and a number of bars, restaurants and hostels (some only open between Jul & Sep or at weekends).

Sleeping & Eating

Although not great, some of the cheapest accommodation in town is to be found at the **Hostal El Pasaje** (☎ 41 32 10; Calle Eras; s/d €24/39) which is open year-round.

Hotel Cinco Castaños (☎ 41 32 04; Carretera de la Sierra; s €39-54, d €54-60) is the best place to stay in town. It's set amid the hills within walking distance of the village and has simple, but pleasant rooms.

At weekends and during the high season a good bet is **Hostal La Sierra** (☎ 41 33 15; Calle Mayor 69; s/d €45/55).

Numerous cheap eateries are found on Ave del Humilladero and around Plaza de Solano, while **Bodega la Regadera** (top of Calle de Pedro Muñoz Rico) is an excellent little bar specialising in beef snacks and cheap red wine.

Mesón la Romana (Nuñez Losada 4; meals €15-20), off the top of Calle Mayor, is probably Candelario's best – and most expensive – restaurant.

Getting There & Away

Between Madrid's **Estación Sur de Auto-buses** and Béjar, **Ávila–Piedrahita–Barco Automotives** (APBA; ☎ 91 530 30 92) and **Cevesa** (☎ 91 539 31 32) both offer very similar services (€11.30; three hours, three daily, two on Sun & public holidays).

Alternatively, go via Salamanca. There are more frequent services and trains also go here, up to 15 services to Bejar not all direct (www.i-bejar.com/transportes). **La Serrana** (☎ 22 01 87) has services between

Béjar and Candelario (4.5km, at least five daily) or you could take a taxi from the bus station.

CERCEDILLA
☎ 91 / pop 7000

With several striking early 20th-century chalets and villas, sprawling Cercedilla has the feel of a holiday village. Nowadays geared to summer-season visitors, corporate training centres and second homes for *madrileños*, it has enough grocery shops, restaurants and bars open year-round to be a pleasant overnight stop, even though the excellent transport links to Madrid makes this optional.

Sleeping & Eating
A good option is large, friendly **Hostal El Aribel** (☎ 852 15 11; Calle Emilio Serrano 71; s/d with bathroom €35/45, without bathroom €20/30), 30m north of the train station, which has a good-value bar and café.

Up in the heart of town, **La Maya** (☎ 852 22 52; hostallamaya@hotmail.com; Carrera del Señor 2; d with bathroom €45) has reasonable food.

Another year-round eating choice is nearby **La Muñoza** (Plaza Mayor; 11am-11pm daily), which offers everything from a simple tapa to a full meal. You'll enjoy altogether more subtle fare at **Casa Gomez** (opposite the station).

Getting There & Away
From Madrid's Atocha station *cercanía* and regional rail services go to Cercedilla (€4.05; 1¼ hours, 15 per day) via Chamartín.

Larrea (☎ 851 55 92; www.auto buseslarrea.com) bus 684 runs between Madrid's Montcloa bus station and Cercedilla (€3.70; 1½ hours, every 30 minutes).

For a **taxi** call ☎ 619 226272 or 619 806452.

It's a 10-minute walk from the station to the pueblo. To avoid slaughter on the road, take the quiet, traffic-free lane beside Hostal El Aribel.

COTOS (PUERTO DE COTOS)
pop 100

Sleeping options are few, spartan and rarely open. Think seriously of overnighting in Cercedilla, then taking the first train up the mountain to Cotos the next morning.

Sleeping & Eating
Just off the road to Valdesquí is **Refugio El Pingarrón** (☎ 650 925854; bed €5; Sat & Sun Sep-Jun) Perched high above Arroyo de las Guarramillas, it sleeps 25 and reservations are essential. Its small annexe (push the door hard) is always open and sleeps four. Ski lifts blight the view south; northeast the beautiful Valle de Lozoya is fair compensation. And yes, that's not a typo; it really is shut in July and August!

At the top of the pass is **Venta Marcelino** (menús €12-35, mains €7.50-16), a friendly bar-restaurant. There's also a small bar at the train station. Both often close after the last train to Cercedilla.

CUEVAS DEL VALLE
☎ 920 / pop 600

Starting early from Madrid, you could reach this pretty little village and start walk on the same day.

Sleeping & Eating
On the main road through the village, a down-to-earth local bar and hotel **Casa Chato** (☎ 38 30 48; s/d with breakfast €25/50) is well worth your time. It also has a good restaurant.

Of the many *casa rurals* one in the centre is **Casa Rural los Moranegos**, (☎ 651 552273; per person €12).

For something more up market **Rinconcito de Gredos** (☎ 38 32 88; www .rinconcitogredos.com; s/d €45/60) located on the main road to Puerto del Pico, will satisfy most with its stylish rooms, some of which have exposed stone walls.

There are a couple a grocery shops, but it's best to bring supplies with you.

Getting There & Away
Direct services from Madrid are run by **Doaldi** (☎ 914 68 42 36; €11.15; 8.30am & 1pm). Two extra services run on Friday evenings (5pm & 7pm).

EL BARCO DE ÁVILA
☎ 920 / pop 2600

This picturesque little town is something of a hub for transport around the north side of the Gredos and is a nice spot to rest up or prepare for a walk.

Information

Make general inquiries at the **tourist information office** (☎ 34 08 88; Calle Mayor 2; Wed-Mon Jul-Sep, Sat & Sun Oct-Jun).

Reflo Papelería (Calle Mayor 24) has a fair selection of 1:25,000 topographical maps, plus other tourist maps and walking guides.

Sleeping & Eating

The best-value place in town, **Hostal Rosi** (☎ 34 00 55; Campillo 22; s/d with bathroom €25/50) has plenty of space.

Hotel Bellavista (☎ 34 07 53; Carretera de Ávila 15; s/d €57/71) provides good post-walk luxury.

Hotel Manila (☎ 34 08 44; Km 337 on the N110; s €40-56, doubles €50-70, breakfast €8.50) on the way to Plasencia, is El Barco's most upmarket choice. Sharply reduced weekday rates are often available.

There are also loads of *casas rurales* in and around town.

Local food shops and delicatessens line Calle Mayor. The best supermarket is on Carretera de Ávila.

The bars and restaurants around Plaza de España are the town's best. **Restaurante El Casino** (☎ 34 10 86; meals €28-36) is a cut above the rest.

Getting There & Away

Buses run by **APBA** (☎ 91 530 30 92) and **Cevesa** (☎ 91 439 31 32; www.cevesa.es) have very similar departure times from Madrid's Estación Sur de Autobuses (€12.20; 2½ hours, 8.30am & 4pm). Two of Cevesa's services continue through Puerto de Tornavacas to Plasencia.

Between Monday and Saturday **Muñoz Travel** (☎ 25 20 20) has three buses from Ávila bus station to El Barco de Ávila via the villages of Valle de Tormes (€5.80, two hours).

JARANDILLA DE LA VERA
☎ 927 / pop 3100

This is a pleasant little town, well-used to (mainly Spanish) tourists and weekenders.

Northwest of town, **Camping Jaranda** (☎ 56 04 54; www.campingjaranda.es; Km 47 on the C501; tent/person/car €4.70 each,

four-to-six person bungalows €64-80) is a decent place with a bar, restaurant, shop and swimming pool.

In town there's **Hostal Marbella** (☎ 56 02 18; on the C501; s from €25, d €39). At **Hotel Don Juan de Autria** (☎ 56 02 06; hotel@hoteljaranda.com; Ave Soledad Vega Ortiz 101; d €60) rates include breakfast. **Hostería Gante** (☎ 56 12 00; Plaza Soledad Vega; s/d/t €50/60/70) has slightly better rooms, but top of the heap is **Parador de Jarandilla de la Vera** (☎ 56 01 17; jarandilla@parador.es; d €80-155), which once provided a home away from home for kings, queens and other blue-blooded types.

One bus a day links Jarandilla de la Vera with Plasencia.

MADRID
☎ 91 / pop 3.2 million

The major walking areas of Sistema Central are within easy reach of Spain's capital, which has some good outdoor shops and information sources. Packed with bars and restaurants, Madrid is a great place to spend a few days; few people have rest and recuperation on their minds at the weekend, when the city doesn't get to sleep much before dawn.

Madrid also has a host of good parks and open spaces, famous art galleries and numerous open-air swimming pools.

Information

For information head to the **tourist information office** (☎ 429 49 51; www.esmadrid .com; Plaza Mayor; metro Sol). Other branches are found at Chamartín and Atocha train stations, and Aeropuerto de Barajas.

Supplies & Equipment

Gonza Sport (☎ 506 46 03; Calle Ribera de Curtidores 10-15) is a recommended mountain sports shop.

Sleeping & Eating

Although Madrid has hundreds of *pensiones* (guesthouses), hostels and hotels, finding accommodation can still be a problem between July and September.

Camping Osuna (☎ 741 05 10; Avenida de Logroño; site for four with car €42.20), near the airport, is about 500m from metro Canillejas; walk north across Avenida de

América and then follow Avenida de Logroño.

Los Amigos Ópera Backpackers (☎ 547 17 07; www.losamigoshostel.com; Calle Campomanes 6; dm €17-19) bright dorm-style rooms and plenty of interesting company.

Cat's Hostel (☎ 369 28 07; www.catshostel.com; Calle de Cañizares 6; dm €19, d from €24) Now here is something special. The internal courtyard is Madrid's finest – lavish Andalucían tilework, a fountain, a spectacular glass ceiling, surrounded on four sides by an open balcony. There's also a softly lit and supercool basement bar, where occasional live flamenco cohabits with free internet connections.

Albergue Juvenil (☎ 593 96 88; www.ajmadrid.es; Calle de Mejía Lequerica 21; dm €18-24) If you're looking for dormitory-style accommodation, you'd need a good reason to stay anywhere other than here. Opened in 2007, the Albergue's rooms are spotless, no dorm room houses more than six beds (and each has its own bathroom), and facilities include a pool table, a gymnasium, wheelchair access, free internet, laundry and a TV/DVD room with a choice of movies.

Hotel Plaza Mayor (☎ 360 06 06; www.h-plazamayor.com; Calle de Atocha 2; s/d from €65/85) Sitting just across from Plaza Mayor, here you'll find stylish decor, charming original elements from the 150-year-old building and extremely helpful staff.

Madrid is absolutely packed with places to eat and drink and it's relatively easy to find a restaurant offering a three-course *menú del día* (fixed-price meal) for less than €12. There are also excellent tapas bars by the bucket load. Good places to look include those in the La Latina district.

Getting There & Away
Hundreds of international flights arrive daily at Madrid's **Aeropuerto de Barajas**, 13km northeast of the city and, as you might expect, there are bus and train connections to a huge number of destinations across Spain, including most of the Gateways mentioned in this book.

Madrid has two main train stations: **Atocha** (☎ 506 68 46), south of the city

centre, which serves areas south of Madrid; and **Chamartín** in the north, which handles destinations north of Madrid (and international departures). *Cercanía* (short-range suburban trains) and *trens regionales* (regional trains) services to the Sistema Central usually leave from Chamartín.

Madrid's main bus station is **Estación Sur de Autobuses** (☎ 468 42 00; metro Méndez Álvaro), although other buses leave from **Intercambiador de Ave de América** (metro Ave de América).

For information on travelling between Madrid and destinations inside and outside Spain see Getting Around (p356), and Getting There & Away (p351).

NAVA DEL BARCO
pop 100
There are a couple of *casas rurales* in Nava del Barco (for contact information see Information Sources, p44) and some inviting overnight campsites just southwest of the village, which has a couple of grocery shops and a few bars.

PUERTO DE NAVACERRADA
☎ 91 / pop 2700
This place is geared towards a short, money-spinning ski season and can feel like a ghost town for the rest of the year.

Residencia Tiempo Libre (☎ 852 39 84) may take you in but requires full board (€30 per person).

Hotel Pasadoiro (☎ 852 14 27; www.pasadoiro.com; s/d €60/80), 50m south of the pass, has a restaurant. You'll eat more economically in bustling **Bar Restaurante Dos Castillas** (Tue-Sun), just across the road.

For alternative accommodation take the last train down the hill (6pm Mon-Thu, 8pm Fri, 7pm Sat & Sun) and overnight in Cercedilla (p64).

TORNAVACAS
pop 1200
Surrounded by cherry orchards that typify the Valle del Jerte, this village at the end of the walk is very pleasant indeed.

Tornavacas has an ATM and other services including grocery stores, delicatessens and the Centro de Interpretación (see Information Sources, p56).

Sleeping & Eating

At the beautiful **Casa Rural Antigua Posada** (☎ 927 17 70 19/608 852131; www.antigua posada.com; Ave de la Constitución 37; r per person €26) prices include breakfast.

About 1.5km northeast of Tornavacas is **Hostal Puerto de Tornavacas** (☎ 608 852131; hostalpuertodetornavacas@hot mail.com; Km 357 on N110; s/d with bathroom €25/40), which has a reasonably good restaurant.

Getting There & Away

The Plasencia-Madrid service (via El Barco de Ávila) run by **Cevesa** (☎ 91 539 31 32) passes through Tornavacas (€11, two daily). You can also flag the bus down at Puerto de Tornavacas.

The Pyrenees

HIGHLIGHTS

- Looking over all Andorra from the spine of Cresta de l'Estanyó on the **Pic de l'Estanyó** walk (p107)
- Walking just about anywhere in **Parc Nacional d'Aigüestortes i Estany de Sant Maurici** (p109)
- Looking back and saying 'Oh yes, the Pyrenees – they were nothing', as you stagger to the end of **The Pyrenean Traverse** (p73)
- Trying to keep a steady head while peering into the abyss on the **Staggering Sestrales** walk (p121)

Number of bears: 17 to 24	Number of summits above 3000m: 129

Like a chain of castles protecting Spain from the advances of the rest of Europe the Pyrenees burst out of the waters of the Mediterranean, climb to the heavens and then sink, Atlantis like, into the deep cold of the Atlantic Ocean.

These mountains have an edge of both Spain and France to them, yet they have a character and flavour that makes them their own little world. In fact, so different can the life, climate and look of each valley be that you could say that each tiny section of these mountains is a world unto itself. And it's this wonderful variety and vitality that brings more hikers from across the world to these mountains than any other range in Spain. They really are one of the hiking highlights of Europe.

The core of this chapter is a 17-day traverse across the highest, wildest and most breathtaking section of these mountains.

But 17 days or so is more time than many walkers can spare. For those who prefer to radiate out from a base, linger in a particularly scenic area or simply just return to a fancy hotel at the end of the day there are 12 single day or overnight walks. These take in an exploration of the surreal principality of Andorra and hikes that skirt the frontier of the two nations that share these delightful peaks. Enjoy!

HISTORY

The distressing news for walkers is that the Pyrenees no longer exist. So that air ticket was a waste of money wasn't it? No, only joking, as your soon-to-be-panting lungs will ascertain they are still very much there. It's just that many Spanish use the metaphor of the Pyrenees' disappearance to describe Spain's coming in from the cold after centuries of relative isolation from the rest of Europe – a process that began soon after the death of General Franco in 1975 and culminated in Spain's entry into the EU in 1986.

Hydro schemes in the Pyrenees contributed to Spain's economic recovery from the ravages of the Spanish Civil War. In the 1950s and 1960s Spain invested significantly in developing small-scale hydroelectric plants, mainly to service the towns and villages of the Pyrenean valleys. Most of the reservoirs are natural, though dams at their heads have often augmented their depths.

Traditionally the mountains have maintained an agricultural economy based on sheep and cows. Summer pastures were used not only by local villagers but also by shepherds and cowherds who transmigrated from much further afield (see the boxed text La Trashumancia, p104). Many of the trails described in this chapter were created to provide access to these lush, upland grasses. And many of the tracks still indicated on maps were once shepherds' routes and are now overgrown and underused except by occasional trekkers hacking their own way with compass and map.

ENVIRONMENT

The natural history of the Pyrenees is long and turbulent. Some 350 million years ago they were already a formidable mountain chain of igneous rock formed by solidified magma from the earth's molten heart, their summits capable of dwarfing today's 3000m giants.

Over tens of millions of years of slow erosion the mountains were ground down to a vast plain which was then invaded by the sea. Grain by grain, shell by shell, sediments accumulated in layers on the ocean bed. (In places such as the Parque Nacional de Ordesa y Monte Perdido you can still see sandstone bands, sometimes straight as a layer cake, often in convoluted whorls.)

About 25 million years ago the Iberian tectonic plate slammed into the European one with a force sufficient to compress and fold upwards slabs as big as today's peaks, from which the seas streamed and departed.

From this moment on, erosion has been the principal force shaping the range we see today. During the successive ice ages of the last million years ice covered all but the highest peaks and has left a distinctive imprint on the landscape (see the boxed text Signs of a Glacial Past, p28).

Mountain or black pine, squat with grey-black bark and hardiest of the conifers, occupies the reaches just below the tree line. Fir and Scots pine thrives at lower altitudes. Deciduous trees include rowan, hazel – a rich source of nutritious nuts in autumn – silver birch, elm, mountain oak, elder and, particularly in Aragón, forests of beech trees. Down in the damp lower valleys, goat willow, common ash and aspen abound.

In all but alpine environments, low banks of azaleas brush against your knees. Around them grow juniper bushes with their characteristic greyish berries, broom with bright yellow flowers, bilberries and wild raspberries (ready to pick in late summer), heather, dog roses and, at lower altitudes, clumps and stands of boxwood.

In general, June is the best time for viewing wildflowers. Common at subalpine level are white and leafless crocuses, the *carlina*

CHARLEMAGNE & THE THISTLE

As Emperor Charlemagne's army was passing through the Pyrenees, on its way to do battle with the Arab occupiers of Spain, the plague struck. When the emperor prayed to God for help, says the legend, an angel appeared to him and instructed him to fire an arrow into the air and whichever plant it pierced on its descent would prove to be an effective remedy. The arrow fell upon a kind of ground-hugging thistle, still common in the Pyrenees and still used as a natural remedy. It's called *carlina*, in both Catalan and Spanish, after Carlomagno – Charlemagne.

THE PYRENEES

THERE ARE BEARS IN THERE – MAYBE!

No-one seems to know exactly how many bears there are now living in the Pyrenees, estimates seem to suggest it's no more than 24. What is certain though, is that the original population is effectively extinct. The last surviving female Pyrenean brown bear, named Canelle, died in 2004, leaving only two males from a population that not so long ago numbered over 200 individuals.

In an attempt to 'restock' the mountains, 'immigrant' brown bears from Slovenia have been introduced in the last decade, which have been successfully breeding. Coexistence between human and bear has always been troublesome in the pastoral communities of the Pyrenees, for whom the bear was considered an enemy, killing sheep and other livestock. In fact the damage caused by bears is small compared to losses to accidents or stray dogs. Today, any farmer who has animals killed by bears is generously compensated by the government in order to deter hunting. The bears in the Pyrenees are understandably timid, not dangerous to humans, and you are extremely unlikely to encounter one, although you may find traces of their presence in tracks and droppings.

thistle (see the boxed text Charlemagne & the Thistle, p69) and various varieties of gentian including great yellow and – found everywhere when in season – bright blue trumpet gentians. Most flourish in meadows along with the pink stars of moss campions, alpine pasques, wild daffodils in abundance and mountain iris.

For more on the Pyrenees' typical alpine, subalpine and mountain vegetation, see Environment (p27).

You stand a reasonable chance of seeing chamois (*rebeco* in Spanish, *sarrio* in Aragonese and *isard* in Catalan), albeit at a distance. Roe and red deer are less timid but less widely distributed. Only a few brown bears survive in the Pyrenees and a positive but also contentious programme is under way to reintroduce them. Why contentious? Because many farmers claim that the bears attack and kill their livestock and that their respective governments are very slow in compensating them. Many foreign visitors will be amazed at the depth of feeling in mountain areas against the bears – this is most commonly displayed in anti-bear graffiti on roadsides. Listen for the characteristic warning whistle of marmots, the shaggy clowns of the high boulder fields. Strangest of all is the shy,

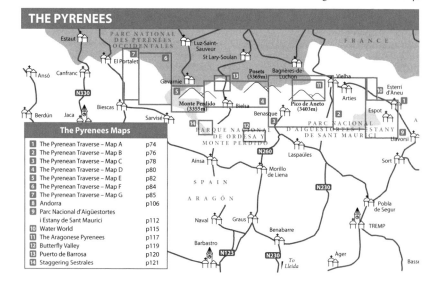

THE PYRENEES

rare desman, an aquatic, mole-like creature peculiar to the Pyrenees, whose closest relatives live in the Caucasus mountains of Georgia.

As your chances of spotting one of the 17 to 24 brown bears reputedly surviving in the Pyrenees are near nil, the only potentially harmful beastie on your path is the Pyrenean viper, a snake that, given a chance, will scuttle away before you're even aware of it.

Wheeling above the upland valleys and peaks are a variety of birds of prey, including golden, booted and Bonnelli's eagles. You'll probably spot griffon and Egyptian vultures. Rarer is the bearded vulture or, in Spanish *el quebrantahuesos* – the bone-smasher, from its habit of flying high and dropping bones onto the rocks so it can peck at the marrow.

CLIMATE

The weather can change in the twinkling of an eye. Summer mountain storms build up during the afternoon and break in the early evening. So aim for an early start each day – then you can dawdle or take evasive action, should the clouds build up. While such storms usually pass quickly, they can be intense: hailstones the size of marbles pelt down even in midsummer.

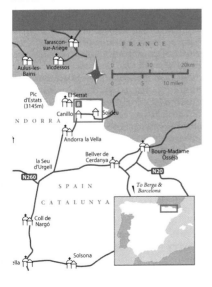

PLANNING

When to Walk

The walking season, unless you're an experienced mountain trekker comfortable with both snow and ice, is the window between mid-June and early September. Come any earlier and you'll be facing intimidating snow banks; come later and the weather is increasingly unreliable.

Maps

The Pyrenees are well endowed with maps for walkers.

BUYING MAPS

To be sure of getting the ones you need, buy all your maps in advance. Shops in popular tourist towns and villages such as Andorra la Vella, Espot, Benasque, Bielsa and Torla often sell the relevant map for their area but few, if any, alternatives.

SMALL-SCALE MAPS

Firestone produces a good overview map of the Pyrenees at 1:200,000, covering both the French and Spanish sides of the frontier. Editorial Everest does a worthy alternative, available in either book or folding format at 1:230,000.

LARGE-SCALE MAPS

The two most readily available maps are produced by Editorial Alpina (www.editorialalpina.com) and Rando Éditions (www.editions-suouest.com/nos-editions/rando-editions.html); they come in a variety of scales. For the lowdown on other worthwhile series and more detailed consideration of maps see the Planning sections of the regions and individual walks.

PLACE NAMES

We use the form the locals use, opting for the Catalan name in Andorra and the Catalan Pyrenees and the Spanish form elsewhere. You'll often find a variety of spellings from one map to another and even within the same text. One pass in the Catalan Pyrenees, for instance, is labelled variously as Port d'Onhla Crestada (Aragonese), Port de Collcrestada (Catalan) and Güellicrestada (Spanish). Further west in Aragón, a pass can be the Puerto Chisten, Puerto de Chistau or

Puerto de Gistaín, depending on which book or map you consult. This isn't necessarily cartographic carelessness; it reflects a shift in language or dialect from one valley to another – or the fact that, until quite recently, some place names had never been written down.

OTHER INFORMATION

If you're walking in late summer you may find that what we, or your map, present as a 'small tarn' is nothing more than cracked mud or a circle of more luxuriant grass. Such pools come and soon go after heavy rain or the early summer snow thaw.

By contrast, what may be a clearly identifiable track in late summer may be nothing more than a red line on the map after the snows have melted and the fresh spring grass begins to grow. Those same snows will also probably have demolished any small stone cairns last year's walkers may have laid.

When planning your walks, bear in mind that the times we quote cover only the actual walking time, not including stops for rest or food.

Books

Douglas Streatfield-James' *Trekking in the Pyrenees* is excellent, offering a wide range of walks, from half-dayers to demanding treks of a week or more.

Walks & Climbs in the Pyrenees, by Kev Reynolds, also well written, concentrates much more upon the French side than the Spanish.

Quite stimulating is *Pyrenees High Level Route*, an abridged and fairly pedestrian – forgive us but it's true! – translation of *La Haute Route des Pyrénées*, the classic French work by the granddad of all Pyrenees walkers, Georges Veron. However, he's not for beginners or even intermediate walkers. Master of navigation with an unparalleled knowledge of the mountains, he gives route descriptions that are often minimal and frequently just strikes out where no path exists.

Through the Spanish Pyrenees GR11: A Long Distance Footpath, by Paul Lucia, follows this long-distance Pyrenean trail.

For flowers, check out Lance Chilton's hard to find *Plant List for the Pyrenees*.

Bird-watchers will find *A Birdwatching Guide to the Pyrenees*, by Jacquie Crozier, an informative companion.

Information Sources

The two principal walking organisations in Catalunya are the **Federació d'Entitats Excursionistes de Catalunya** (☎ 93 412 07 77; www.feec.es) and one of its constituent groups, the **Centre Excursionista de Catalunya** (CEC; ☎ 93 315 23 11; www.cec.cat). Their equivalent in Aragón is the **Federación Aragonesa de Montañismo** (FAM; ☎ 976 22 79 71; www.fam.es).

GETTING AROUND

Public transport, rarely frequent and being chopped back year by year, runs rather more regularly in summer. Since most services are few and far between, check times with the local tourist office or look on www.alsa.es, which is the largest bus company and acts as an umbrella organisation for numerous smaller local companies.

For walks in Andorra the nearest town accessible by bus is Andorra la Vella (where there's also a good local bus service up the valley) from Barcelona, Madrid or Latour de Carol (France; also accessible by train).

For Parc Nacional d'Aigüestortes i Estany de Sant Maurici, go to La Guingeta from Lleida, Barcelona and Pobla de Segur.

For Vall d'Aran, buses go to Vielha (which also has a good local bus service) from Lleida and Barcelona.

For La Ribagorça and Posets massif buses reach Benasque from Lleida and Barcelona via Barbastro.

For Parque Nacional de Ordesa y Monte Perdido buses reach Torla from Jaca, Huesca and beyond via Sabiñánigo.

Buses from Sabiñánigo serve both Panticosa and Sallent de Gállego.

Where buses no longer ply, most villages have a taxi service, whether formally established or just someone who's prepared to do a run when asked. Inquire at the tourist office – in summer, there's a small office in most villages with tourism aspirations – or, for the real lowdown, in the local bar. A small investment can save you an hour or more of unexciting road walking.

A key train access point for the Catalan Pyrenees is Pobla de Segur, which is connected by train with Lleida (see p126).

GATEWAYS

Party in Barcelona (p124) and then head for the trails to recover. Lleida (p126) is another option.

THE PYRENEAN TRAVERSE

Duration 17 days

Distance 223km

Difficulty moderate–demanding

Start Espot (p126)

Finish Sallent de Gállego (p128)

Transport bus

Summary An exhilarating east-to-west trek through the most spectacular part of the Spanish Pyrenees, including a pair of national parks.

This challenging traverse starts on the eastern edge of the fantastic Parc Nacional d'Aigüestortes i Estany de Sant Maurici and ends in the village of Sallent de Gállego, deep in the Aragonese Pyrenees. Spectacular throughout, its major highlights are the two national parks that lie on the Spanish side of the border – the aforementioned Parc Nacional d'Aigüestortes i Estany de Sant Maurici and the Parque Nacional de Ordesa y Monte Perdido – plus Parque Posets-Maladeta, which is rugged and encompasses several of the Pyrenees' highest peaks.

We've set out a flexible itinerary to allow for varying amounts of time and fitness levels. Within most stages you'll find a campsite or unstaffed *refugio* (mountain hut or refuge) so you can knock off early or push on beyond the day's official end. The stages are, of course, an artificial division; on many days you can plan your own route, especially if you have the flexibility of a tent. We highlight some choice wild camping spots but practically any flat five square metres – provided you're not contravening *parque nacional* (national park) or *parque natural* (nature park) regulations – can be your bed for the night.

The two national parks areas within strolling distance of the shuttle-bus terminals can be thronged with walkers in high summer. Apart from these two tourist magnets, trails are lightly trodden and it can be quite an event to meet other trekkers. If you like to walk alone, you'll scarcely see another soul on the long and quite tough route between the Hospital de Vielha and Benasque.

This table lists the days of the traverse as we describe it (not including Alternative Days):

Day	From/To	Km
1	ESPOT REFUGI DE COLOMERS	18.5
2	REFUGI DE COLOMERS REFUGI VENTOSA I CALVELL	8
3	REFUGI VENTOSA I CALVELL REFUGI DE LA RESTANCA	6
4	REFUGI DE LA RESTANCA HOSPITAL DE VIELHA/REFUGI DE CONGALES	10
5	HOSPITAL DE VIELHA/REFUGI DE CONGALES MEADOWS BELOW COLLADO DEL TORO	8.5
6	MEADOWS BELOW COLLADO DEL TORO BENASQUE	20.5
7	BENASQUE REFUGIO ÁNGEL ORUS	10.5
8	REFUGIO ÁNGEL ORUS REFUGIO DE ESTÓS	14.5
9	REFUGIO DE ESTÓS REFUGIO DE VIADÓS	10
10	REFUGIO DE VIADÓS PARZÁN	20
11	PARZÁN VALLE DE PINETA	16
12	VALLE DE PINETA VALLE DE AÑISCLO	7.5
13	VALLE DE AÑISCLO TORLA	23
14	TORLA BUJARUELO	10
15	BUJARUELO BALNEARIO DE PANTICOSA	18
16	BALNEARIO DE PANTICOSA REFUGIO DE RESPOMUSO	12
17	REFUGIO DE RESPOMUSO SALLENT DE GÁLLEGO	10

PLANNING

Maps

Prames (www.prames.com) publishes a pack of 47 1:40,000 maps plus an accompanying booklet (in Spanish) that covers the whole of the GR11 trail from the Atlantic to the Mediterranean. It also produces excellent 1:25,000 maps for most of the Aragonese Pyrenees.

THE PYRENEAN TRAVERSE – MAP A

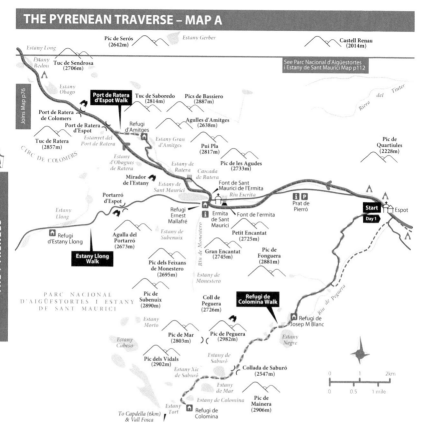

In a fruitful example of trans-frontier collaboration, Rando Éditions and the Institut Cartogràfic de Catalunya (ICC) have jointly published a series of seven 1:50,000 maps covering almost the entire Pyrenees. Contours are at 20m intervals and areas of steep terrain have clear elevation shading. However, not all paths, confidently indicated in red, exist on the ground.

You can cover all 17 days of the Pyrenean Traverse with only three sheets from this series, each of which contains considerable overlap:

Map Title	Map No	Days
PICA D'ESTATS ANETO	22	7–4
ANETO POSETS	23	4–10
GAVARNIE ORDESA	24	9–17

At €9.50, they're a bargain. But they're huge and will wrap you like an Egyptian mummy in high wind. Consider chopping them up into more manageable segments and maybe laminating them before setting out on the walk.

Editorial Alpina (www.editorialalpina .com) maps are the most readily available; come with scales of 1:25,000, 1:40,000 and an eccentric 1:30,000; and sell for €10.50. They're very reliable for topography as they have particularly clear elevation shading. However, the location of superimposed features such as the *refugios*, camping grounds and even some footpaths should sometimes be treated with scepticism. Be sure to buy the latest edition, which tends to be more accurate.

For the full traverse, you'll need:

Map Title	Days	From/To
SANT MAURICI	1	(LLERET TO REFUGI DE COLOMERS)
VALL DE BOÍ	2 & 3	(REFUGI DE COLOMERS TO REFUGI DE LA RESTANCA)
VAL D'ARAN	3 & 4	(REFUGI DE LA RESTANCA TO COLL DE MULLERES)
LA RIBAGORÇA	3 & 4	ALT 11 (REFUGI DE LA RESTANCA TO COLLADA DE BALLIBIERNA)
MALADETA ANETO	5	(LA BESURTA & BENASQUE)
POSETS	6–8	(BENASQUE TO REFUGIO DE VIADÓS)
BACHIMALA	10	(REFUGIO DE VIADÓS TO PARZÁN)
ORDESA MONTE	10–13	(PARZÁN TO BUJARUELO PERDIDO)
VIGNEMALE	15	(BUJARUELO TO PANTICOSA OR BALNEARIO DE PANTICOSA)
PANTICOSA	15 & 17	(BALNEARIO DE FORMIGAL PANTICOSA TO SALLENT DE GÁLLEGO)

THE WALK
Day 1: Espot to Refugi de Colomers
6½–7 hours, 18.5km

Day one and we're off with a bang, because this is truly a five-star day, passing Estany de Ratera, one of the national park's major jewels, crossing Port de Ratera de Colomers and finishing with a magnificent stepped, lake-stippled descent.

Exactly 2km along the pocked road from Espot turn right at a sign for Estany de Sant Maurici and Refugi Ernest Mallafré. Cross the Riu Escrita and follow its true left bank

through a mixture of broadleaf woodland, pine trees and meadow.

About halfway to the lake, after a pleasant hour's walking with few others for company, you meet the throng. Day visitors by the hundred stream in from the car park at **Prat de Pierró**, where an information cabin marks the entrance to the park and the limit for private vehicles. The riverside path from here to the lake is a conduit for around 95% of those park visitors who walk in. Many other visitors access Estany de Sant Maurici via 4WD taxis, which depart from Espot. One way €4.85 and return €9.70.

You can take water on board roughly 45 minutes beyond Prat de Pierró at the Font de l'Ermita, beside a small chapel, or a little further along from the Font de Sant Maurici (1910m), beside the northeast shore of the glimmering Estany de Sant Maurici **lake**. There is also a refugi Ernst Mallafre and a small information point beside the lake.

From the spring follow the lakeside track, signed 'La Cascada' (waterfall). Turn right (north) at a similar sign to refresh yourself in the rainbow spray of the **Cascada de Ratera**.

Continue uphill and the path bears away from the waterfall. Turn left at a sign, 'Estany de Ratera' and turn left again onto a 4WD track some five minutes later at a T-junction to rejoin the GR11 trail markers. Views south to the Pic dels Feixans de Monestero and the Gran and Petit Encantats – both official symbols of the park – are unsurpassed.

At a fork soon after the splendid tarn **Estany de Ratera** (2150m), about an hour from Estany de Sant Maurici, choose the left

THE PYRENEES

THE FAST LANE

Here are some possible short cuts and bypasses if your time in the mountains is limited. But don't bust a gut. Unless you're a human tornado, consider building in a rest day or two, for example, Benasque, at the end of Day 6. Another option, of course, is to do the traverse over a couple, or even three, holidays.

- Omit Days 2 and 3, walking directly from Refugi de Colomers to Refugi de la Restanca. Push on to the Hospital de Vielha (end Day 4) and save yet another day.

- Take the easy valley route between Benasque and Refugio de Estós (Alternative Day 7) and omit Days 6 and 7. Continue to Refugio de Viadós (end Day 9).

- Get an early start to Day 12, walk or take the shuttle bus from Pradera de Ordesa to Puente de los Navarros and continue to Bujaruelo (end Day 14).

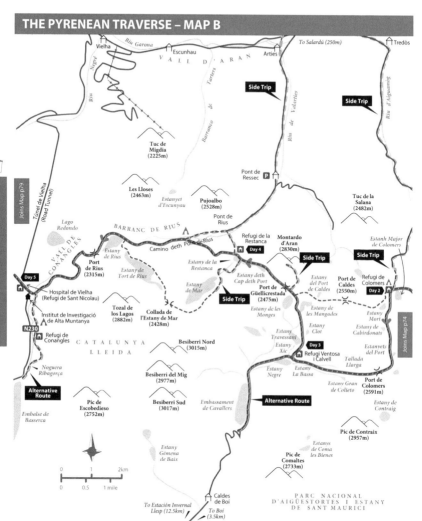

THE PYRENEAN TRAVERSE – MAP B

option then turn sharp right (northwest) to leave the 4WD track and take a well-trodden path. This soon crosses to the true left bank of the stream that you'll be following to its source at the lake just below Port de Ratera. About 15 minutes later ignore a side path for Refugi d'Amitges that turns away to the right. Keep looking for the poles that mark the trail from here until shortly before the col.

Once beyond **Estany d'Obagues de Ratera** (also known as Estany de la Munyidera) the path briefly crosses to the true right bank to avoid the worst of the first of a pair of boulder fields. It threads its way through the second, reducing, but not eliminating, the amount of scrambling required.

The grade stiffens briefly as you approach **Estanyet del Port de Ratera**, a tiny lake at the valley's head. Having curled around a bulge above its northeastern shore you reach **Port de Ratera d'Espot** (2580m), a mere 50m above the tarn and 2¼ to 2½ hours from Estany de Sant Maurici.

Stroll northwest along the flat, grassy saddle, passing **Port de Ratera de Colomers**, to begin the stepped descent. Take the left fork at a signed junction where the routes to the *refugios* of Colomers and Saboredo diverge. From here on there are infinite tempting campsites beside the lakes, big and small, which stipple the valley: the extensive **Estany Obago** (2242m), whose tip soon comes into view; **Estany Redon** (Round Pond); and **Estany Llarg**, also known as Estanh Long (Large and Long Pond). Full marks to the locals for accuracy, even if they fall short on originality. The route skirts to the southwest of each of the lakes, linked one to another by a stream, like beads on a necklace.

After the merest glimpse of Estanh Cloto and the low ranges behind the Vall d'Aran a wooden sign directs you left (west) over a small hill and down to **Estanh Major de Colomers**. Cross the dam. The old **refuge de Colomers**, now shut, is situated on the far side, two hours after crossing Port de Ratera d'Espot. Continue on past the old refuge for a further 300m to the new **Refugio de Colomers** (☎ 973 64 05 92; www.refugicolomers.com; dm €6.50, dinner €16.50), which is clearly visible on the other side of the lake. The *refugio* accommodates at least 66 people and has showers and toilets. The helpful warden, Josep Bacques, likes you to phone ahead to book for food but won't turn away a hungry or tired walker. Free camping is available to the right of the helipad or on any flat spot between the *refugio* and the stream (a popular spot with the local cows!).

SIDE TRIP: SALARDÚ
6–6½ hours, 24km
If you're camping or self-catering consider visiting Salardú, down the beautiful valley of the Riu d'Aiguamòg, or Arties from Refugi de la Restanca (see Side Trip: Arties, p83) stock up on food, as there are no shops until Benasque at the end of Day 12. This is also a convenient entry or exit point from the walk.

After half an hour of descent you can clip 3km or so from the walk by taking a 4WD shuttle taxi that runs between July and September. At the taxi's lower point you stand a reasonable chance of hitching

a lift to Salardú from one of the cars parked here at the limit for private traffic. A **taxi** (☎ 610 29 45 56) to Salardú from here will set you back a fat €40.

Here too are the hot springs, Banys de Tredòs. You can stay the night at **The Hotel Baños de Tredòs** (☎ 973 25 30 03; www .banhsdetredos.com; s/d €124.20/165.60) which may not be to your wallet's liking, but after a few days of minimal hygiene a half-hour hydromassage is a sensual delight.

Retrace your steps to return to the route.

Day 2: Refugi de Colomers to Refugi Ventosa I Calvell
3¾–4¼ hours, 8km
This is a relatively short day that diverges from the main GR11. After a steady ascent to the bowl of Circ de Colomers, a slippery, steep and potentially dangerous ascent to the Port de Colomers, it's downhill all the way past lakes and tarns to the dark Estany Negre and the night's *refugio*, perched above it.

It's a colour-coded start to the day. Continue on around the lake directly from the Refugio de Colomers, following the red and yellow blazes. Ascend southeastwards to cross the outlet of **Estany Mort** (literally, 'dead pool'), seething with frogs despite its name.

Where the red-and-yellow trail markers diverge stay on red, aiming for a multicoloured pole. Continue southwards up the true right bank of a stream that cascades from lake to lake. The path improves and cairns become more frequent as you pass to the east of **Estany de Cabirdonats**.

Tarns, some no bigger than puddles with attitude, others slowly evaporating under the summer sun, multiply as you push further into the grey moraine at the base of the awesome bowl of Circ de Colomers.

As you enter the Circ de Colomers, **Port de Colomers** (2591m), is an obvious notch to the west (right-hand side) while climbing the valley. No clear trail, markers or sign indicate where to begin the ascent. However, ensure that you do not continue to follow the red trail markers. The climb to the Port de Colomers is via a steep gully

THE PYRENEES

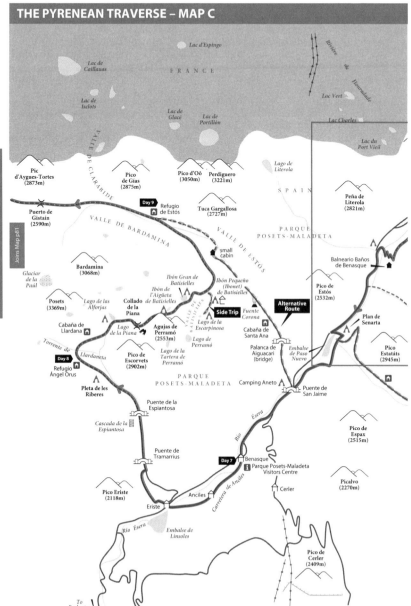

THE PYRENEAN TRAVERSE – MAP C

Lac d'Espingo

Lac de Caillauas

FRANCE

Rivière de Houradade

Lac de Isclots

Lac de Glacé

Lac de Portillón

Lac Vert

Lac Charles

Lac du Port Vieil

Pic d'Aygues-Tortes (2873m)

VALLE DE CLARABIDE

Pico de Gías (2875m)

Pico d'Oô (3050m)

Perdiguero (3221m)

Lago de Literola

SPAIN

Peña de Literola (2821m)

Puerto de Gistaín (2590m)

Day 9

Refugio de Estós

Tuca Gargallosa (2727m)

VALLE DE BARDAMINA

PARQUE POSETS-MALADETA

VALLE DE ESTÓS

small cabin

Balneario Baños de Benasque

Joins Map p81

Bardamina (3068m)

Ibón Gran de Batisielles

Ibón Pequeño (Ibonet) de Batisielles

Pico de Estós (2532m)

Glaciar de la Paúl

Ibón de l'Aigüeta de Batisielles

Side Trip

Fuente Corona

Alternative Route

Plan de Senarta

Posets (3369m)

Lago de las Alforjas

Collado de la Piana

VALLE DE BATISIELLES

Lago de la Escarpinosa

Cabaña de Llardana

Lago de la Piana

Agujas de Perramó (2553m)

Lago de Perramó

Cabaña de Santa Ana

Embalse de Paso Nuevo

Pico Estatáts (2945m)

Torrente de

Day 8

Llardaneta

Pico de Escorvets (2902m)

Lago de la Tartera de Perramó

Palanca de Aiguacari (bridge)

Refugio Ángel Orús

PARQUE POSETS-MALADETA

Camping Aneto

Puente de San Jaime

Pleta de les Ribéres

Puente de la Espiantosa

Ésera

Pico de Espax (2515m)

Cascada de la Espiantosa

Río

Puente de Tramarrius

Day 7

Benasque

Parque Posets-Maladeta Visitors Centre

Picalvo (2270m)

Carretera de Anciles

Cerler

Pico Eriste (2118m)

Anciles

Eriste

Río Ésera

Embalse de Linsoles

Pico de Cerler (2409m)

To Barbastro

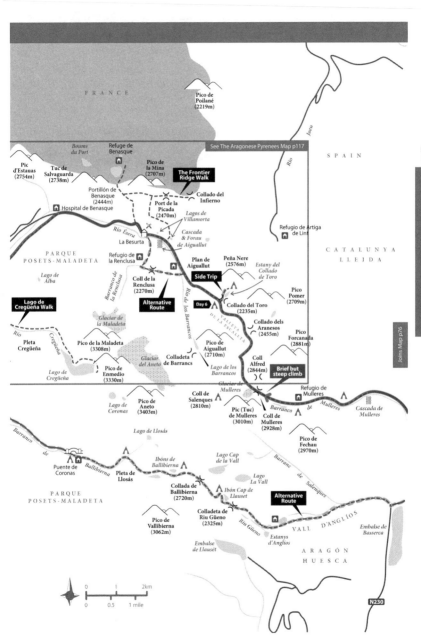

THE PYRENEES

THE PYRENEAN TRAVERSE – MAP D

full of loose scree and boulders. Extreme caution should be taken while ascending as it would appear recent movement has occurred. At the time of writing, there were cairns on both sides of the gully, but the safer side would appear to be the south (left hand) side.

From the pass you're rewarded for the hard slog of the last 100m of altitude change by heart-stopping views westwards to the severe Besiberri ridge on the horizon and a scattering of lakes in the valley at your feet.

After a little less than 15 minutes of steepish descent be sure to cross to and veer away from the true left bank of a small stream, following the main path and disregarding the cairns that entice you further down the valley. Dropping along a cairned trail, pass well above the marshy flats of **Tallada Llarga** to reach the first of the **Estanyets de Colieto**.

Now begins a joyous descent, hopping from lake to tarn, always with the snow-flecked Besiberri ridge as a backdrop. Three to 3½ hours into the day's walk, the trail meets the Carros de Foc route.

Turn right along this well signposted route to proceed towards Refugi Ventosa i Calvell. The trail follows the true right bank of the river passing the Estany Gran de Colieto. It enters a boulder field where scrambling is required and finishes with a short steep ascent to the refuge. At 2222m and overlooking Estany Negre, the **Refugi Ventosa i Calvell** (☎ 973 29 70 90; www .refugiventosa.com), is often full despite its capacity for 80, so it's particularly important to reserve. It is open from beginning June until end of September, and occassionally at other times; check the website.

ALTERNATIVE ROUTE: VIA CALDES DE BOÍ
4½–5 hours, 17km
You can end or join the Pyrenean Traverse quite easily by following this entry and exit route, popular with weekend walkers. A good path descends in 1½ hours from Refugi Ventosa i Calvell to the road head at the southern end of the **Embassament de Cavallers** (1725m), where you have a reasonable chance of hitching down. Around 4.5km of road walking brings you to **Caldes de Boí**, a spa with luxury hotels.

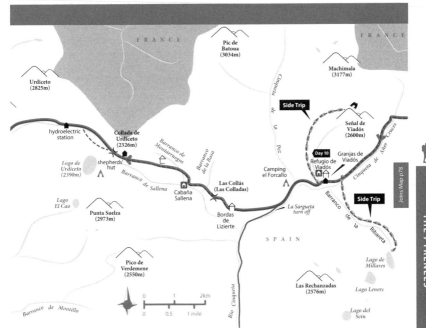

THE PYRENEES

For a wider choice of accommodation at more reasonable rates it's worth pushing on to Boí.

Day 3: Refugi Ventosa I Calvell to Refugi de la Restanca

2¾–3¼ hours, 6km

This is a brief stage, allowing time for one of two strongly recommended side trips: the ascent of Montardo d'Aran or a visit to the magnificent Estany de Mar.

Head north from the *refugio*, following cairns to pass by a chain of lakes. First comes tiny **Xic** and beside it, a sign 'Coret Oelhacrestada' (the Catalan form of Port de Güellicrestada), then **Travessani**, followed by **Clot**, **les Mangades** and **les Monges**.

Around half an hour into the day the path leaves the shore of Estany Travessani to climb above a large slab of granite on its south side. As you rejoin the lake look out for a far-from-evident but important junction that cries out for a sign. Here, the more lightly trodden path to the Port de Güellicrestada (Port d'Onhla Crestada in Aragonese) and Refugi de la Restanca – the option you take – continues due north,

splitting from the main and more evident trail, which bears northeast to Port de Caldes.

As you approach the lip of Estany de les Mangades after about an hour of walking aim for a multicoloured pole, cross the stream which drains from the lake, and head northwest towards **Port de Güellicrestada** (2475m). This must be one of the gentlest approaches to a pass in all of the Catalan Pyrenees.

SCARED? WE WERE PETRIFIED

Two chamois hunters, so the story goes, were rash enough to mock a group of pilgrims toiling by on their way to the tiny chapel below the lake of Sant Maurici. But God swiftly intervened on the side of His faithful. To this day, if you look back from the road leading to Estany de Ratera and apply an ample pinch of salt, you can see the hunters' forms, petrified for all eternity, nestling between the two Pics Encantats, the enchanted peaks.

THE PYRENEAN TRAVERSE – MAP E

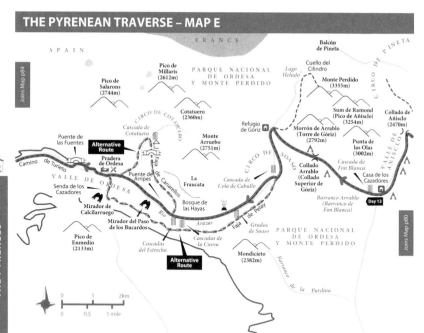

At the pass, 1½ to 1¾ hours from your starting point, you again pick up the red-and-white markers of the GR11. There's a sharp, 30-minute drop down a stony trail to **Estany deth Cap deth Port** that negotiates a massive, clearly signed and cairned boulder field along the way. Walk around the wall of the small dam that holds back this lake and follow the path beside the sluice as it drops very steeply to **Estany de la Restanca** (2010m). The smart **Refugi de la Restanca** (☎ 908 03 65 59) is at the near end of the dam. Allow 1¼ to 1½ hours from pass to lake. Run by Josep Mohedand, the 80-bed *refugio* does an excellent evening meal (four courses €16.50), and can provide snacks and drinks from the information bar upstairs.

SIDE TRIP: MONTARDO D'ARAN
2–2½ hours, 6.5km

The superb views from the summit of Montardo d'Aran repay in full the energy you'll burn in undertaking this popular detour. About 300m before reaching the Port de Güellicrestada break off to the right and head cross-country over the small plain

to join a clear path which rises northeast quite gently before zigzagging more severely northwards.

After mounting a rocky couloir the path reaches a relatively flat area leading to the base of a false summit (2781m). From here, cross a pronounced saddle and continue to the true **summit** (2830m), from where the panorama is superb.

SIDE TRIP: ESTANY DE MAR
2–2½ hours, 6km

From the *refugio*, head south along the east shore of Estany de la Restanca. A good path, with one tight spot of boulder clambering, scales the first bluff to a flat, grassy area flanking the outfall of the upper lake. It then zigzags up a second palisade to a chute from where you emerge, after no more than an hour, to a view over Estany de Mar (2230m).

The forbidding **Besiberri Nord peak** (3015m) to the south provides a suitable backdrop to the expanse of water that merits the name 'Mar' (sea). Having come this far, it's worth continuing at least a little further along the southeast bank of the lake on a vague, narrow trail marked by sporadic cairns.

If you can spare an entire day, consider taking in the lakes of Tort de Rius and Rius to do a popular loop walk that links with the GR11 to return to the *refugio*. To complete the full-day circuit of the three lakes continue along this trail as far as the Collada de l'Estany de Mar (2428m), then descend to approach the lakes of Estany de Tort de Rius and Estany de Rius from the southeast.

Return to the Restanca *refugio* from the latter by following in reverse the first section of Day 4 along Barranc de Rius.

SIDE TRIP: ARTIES
4½–5 hours, 18km

This is the second access route between the Pyrenean Traverse and Vall de Aran (the other drops from Refugi de Colomers to Salardú – see Side Trip: Salardú, p77). If you've been staying in *refugios* or camping wild for several days, you may welcome a break for rest and reprovisioning. Bear in mind that the next opportunity for stocking up is in Benasque, three days away.

From the Restanca lake it's about 45 minutes of pleasant descent through pine forest to the pretty Riu de Valarties valley. The path meets a river at a place still called Pont de Rius (Rius Bridge; 1700m), even though there hasn't been a bridge for decades. Between July and September a **4WD shuttle service** runs from here to Pont de Ressec, saving you, for the modest outlay of €4.40, around 3km of walking. From the car park at the limit for private vehicles you've a good chance of a lift along the sealed road that descends to Arties (1144m). Otherwise, you can slog it on foot (allow 1¼ hours at a brisk pace) or arrange a taxi.

Day 4: Refugi de la Restanca to Hospital De Vielha/ Refugi de Conangles
4–4½ hours, 10km

This is a day for striding out. From Refugi de la Restanca the altitude difference to the Port de Rius is 400m. Many walkers will start from Pont de Rius in the Riu de Valarties valley after visiting Arties and from here it's 650m. Either way, the ascent's fairly gradual along a clear, good-quality

---

TAKING A SHORT CUT

If you're intent upon progressing westwards from Refugi de Colomers, you can omit much of Days 2 and 3 and walk directly along the blazed GR11 to Refugi de la Restanca (see the end of Day 3). Quite a few GR11 walkers push themselves beyond Refugi de la Restanca as far as the Hospital de Vielha in one long stage, continuing along the Day 4 route and so saving themselves yet another day. You'll miss the awesome bowl of the Circ de Colomers and a spangle of lakes and tarns but, if time is at a premium…

---

trail that scarcely makes you pant, except for the steeper final push of 30 to 40 minutes to the shore of Estany de Rius.

If you've left the mountains to visit Arties and Naut Aran, rejoin the Pyrenean Traverse at Pont de Rius. Here, where the woodland trail that climbs to the Refugi de la Restanca takes off left, go straight ahead in defiance of a GR 'X' sign indicating no entry. (This unsigned route features incorrectly as the main GR11 tracing on the *Mapa de la Travessa dels Refugis del Parc Nacional d'Aigüestortes i Estany de Sant Maurici*, the national park map.) Cross the river to pick up a cairned – though, early in the season, very overgrown – path running above the true left bank. You're walking the **Camino deth Pont de Rius** (Camino del Pont de Rius) which, until the construction of the Túnel de Vielha, was a well-travelled access route to the upper Aran valley.

After about an hour and 250m of vertical ascent, you rejoin the GR11 about 2km west of Refugi de la Restanca. Just below the junction of the two trails is a glorious meadow, where marmots wolf-whistle you from the scree, ideal for a **campsite** if you've made an afternoon departure from Arties. A night here leaves you well poised to continue to Refugi de Mulleres (Molieres) on Day 5 and reach Benasque on the following day. For this reason, you might consider pushing on.

If beginning the day from Refugi de la Restanca, you have two choices. The easier and more travelled alternative is to stick to the GR11, which crosses the dam to curl

THE PYRENEES

THE PYRENEAN TRAVERSE – MAP F

Steep, slippery descent

Collado de Piedrafita (2782m)

Piedrafita (2916m)

new refugio

Lagos de Bramatuero

FRANCE

Cuello del Infierno

Upper Ibón Azul

Lower Ibón Azul

Embalse de Bachimaña

Picos del Infierno (3082m)

Cascada del Fraile

Dam wall

Pico de las Neveras (2902m)

Glacier des Oulettes

Ibón de Tebarray

Vignemale (3303m)

Glacier d'Ossoue

Mirador

Barranco de Batans (de los Batanes)

SPAIN

Balneario de Panticosa

Ibóns de Brazato

Day 16

Cuello de Brazato (2578m)

Pic de Pla d'Aube (2681m)

To Panticosa (1km)

Río Caldarés

Embalse de Brazato

Barranco Espelunz

Río Ara

Picos del Cardal (2543m)

Pico de Vilá (2583m)

Pico de Baldairan (2702m)

Arroyo Laulot

VALLE DE ORDISO

Río Ordiso

Alternative Route

Refugio de Ripera

Río Ripera

Pico de las Escuelas (2507m)

Pico de Mallaruego (2692m)

Ordiso (2319m)

Puente Oncins

Icona Refugio

Collado de Otal (1605m)

Day 15

Cabaña de Otal

Bujaruelo

Mesón San Nicolás de Bujaruelo

Ibón de Sabocos

CIRCO DE OTAL

VALLE DE OTAL

SIERRA DE TENDENERA

Collado de Tendenera (2325m)

VALLE DE BUJARUELO

Peña Sabocos (2755m)

Pico de Tendenera (2853m)

Peña de Otal o Arañonera (2709m)

Puente de los Abetos

Puente de Santa Elena (Puente Nuevo)

Puerto del

Barranco del

Puente de los Navarros

Río Ara

Mondiciero (2295m)

Barranco del Sorrosal

Puente de la Glera

Day 14 Torla

0   1   2km
0   0.5   1 mile

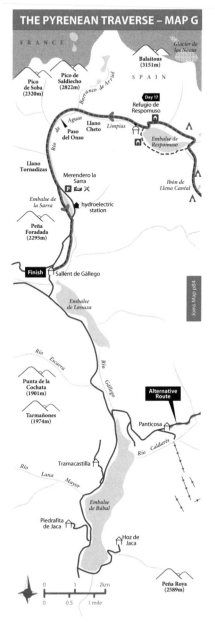

THE PYRENEAN TRAVERSE – MAP G

away northwestwards. Once over a hillock the path drops steeply leading from the dam into the main valley, and joins the Camino deth Pont de Rius. Cairns and signs are clearly visible along the whole route.

The even more scenic but considerably more arduous choice is to take in Estany de Mar and the equally large Estany de Tort de Rius (see the Side Trip: Estany de Mar, p82) and rejoin the main route at the eastern end of Estany de Rius. This will add about two hours' walking to what isn't a very tough day.

One to 1¼ hours after the junction of the GR11 and the path from the Riu de Valarties valley, you'll pass the remains of the dam construction buildings and a trash-strewn *fuente* beneath a small tower. Around five minutes later you draw level with the outlet of **Estany de Rius**.

From here it's well worth making a brief detour to visit the more appealing **Estany de Tort de Rius**, 10 minutes to the southeast. There's many a tarn and pool ahead but these are the last substantial lakes you'll see for the next several days of the traverse.

It takes about 40 minutes to circumnavigate all the arms and crannies of Estany de Rius to reach **Port de Rius** (2315m). From this pass you see for the first time the mountains of the Aragonese Pyrenees against the skyline, with Pico de Aneto, the highest summit of the whole chain, the northernmost pinnacle. Way below, traffic speeds along the road towards the tunnel to Vielha. The large building beside the highway is the University of Barcelona's high mountain research institute (Institut de Investigació de Alta Muntanya). Both appear deceptively near since the trail drops sharply in switchbacks then curls into the **Vall de Conangles**, away from your destination, reaching the valley bottom about an hour and a half from the col. From here you descend gently through pines, which yield to beech and birch.

The final 20 minutes of the day are an easy stroll down a wide cart track, from which you take a clear path left (watch out for this!) to drop into the valley. About 15 minutes further on, the wallker has a choice to make: proceed a further five minutes to the **Hospital de Vielha** or turn left, continuing on the GR11, for a further 15 minutes to the new **Refugi de Conangles** (both are clearly signed). Campers were also seen by the nearby river.

Hospital de Vielha (Espitau de Vielha in Aragonese) is also known as the **Refugi de Sant Nicolau** (☎ /fax 973 69 70 52; dm €11, half-board €27). Pension accommodation is also available at €35 for one person and €30 for groups of two to four. This includes breakfast and dinner. It is poised beside the southern entrance to the Túnel de Vielha. Modified over the centuries, its stone architecture is more distinctive than that of many alpine huts. Run by the *ajuntament* (local authority) of Vielha and with space for 50, it has a restaurant and genuine bar that gives it the atmosphere of a Spanish roadside inn.

Refugi de Conangles (☎ 619 847077/667 259651; www.refugiconangles.com) is a new establishment, keeping in character with other *refugios*. Friendly and extremely helpful, it is run by international alpiniste, Genis Roca, who can offer expert advice on local walks, including ascents of local peaks.

If you're tenting, you'll find decent campsites 45 minutes beyond the Hospital de Vielha on the route to the Coll de Mulleres (see Day 5) or at a popular picnic spot 20 minutes into Alternative Day 5.

Day 5: Hospital de Vielha to Meadows Below Collado del Toro

6–7½ hours, 8.5km

If you're in good shape it's possible to reach La Besurta and the shuttle-bus service to the Hospital de Benasque in one long day from the Hospital de Vielha. It's better, however, to either stretch Day 4 and stay overnight at Refugio de Mulleres or camp en route and take this tough walk at a less demanding pace. You'll find a pair of telescopic poles useful on both sides of the col. A further alternative, longer but less demanding, is to walk to Benasque via Collada di Ballibierna (see Alternative Days 5 & 6, p88).

This is the most challenging but also one of the most satisfying stages of the whole traverse. Up Barranco de Mulleres (Molières), over the col of the same name and down into Valleta de la Escaleta; it's easy enough to summarise but it's a tough one, with altitude changes totalling 2400m, of which 1300m is ascent. But the rewards match the considerable effort invested and, while it would be unwise to attempt the pass alone, this stage is nothing to shy away from. It's demanding because of the difficulty in following the trail during the last 45 minutes to Coll de Mulleres and because the last 10m to the col are steep enough to require a four-limbed clamber.

The route as far as the Estanyets de Mulleres tarns is uncomplicated and well marked. From the Hospital de Vielha (1630m) pick your way over the rubble around the mouth of the road tunnel to a clear cart track. Leave it after about 15 minutes to take a path that rises through beech wood beside the stream's true left bank. A further 15 minutes later pass the magnificent **Cascada de Mulleres** waterfall and, soon after a small, grassy flood plain that makes an ideal **campsite**.

EL TÚNEL DE VIELHA

It was 22 years after the first cut that the strategic road tunnel linking the Vall d'Aran with Spain was completed. Until it opened, the only communication between the valley and the outside world was northwards, to France, before the first snows of winter blocked the pass in September and until the spring snowmelt as late as June.

The Vall d'Aran had been politically affiliated to Spain since the 14th century. The purpose of the tunnel was to reinforce economic and cultural links with Spain and diminish the Gallic influence. Plagued by accidents and financial difficulties, the boring proceeded in fits and starts.

With the outbreak of the Spanish Civil War, work stopped completely. It resumed in 1941, with the forced labour of Republican prisoners. If you look around and above the tunnel entrance, you can still see traces of the bunkers that protected the project from the raids of their guerrilla comrades, fighting from their bases in the mountains.

Finally opened in 1948, at 5.3km it's the longest road tunnel in the Pyrenees.

EL HOSPITAL

You don't have to be sick to spend the night in a hospital. The history of these places, built at the base of important passes, goes back to medieval times and recalls the original meaning of the word: a place where hospitality is offered, a haven for rest and refuge. Often established and maintained by charitable foundations such as the Knights Templar, the Knights of St John of Jerusalem and the Orden (Order) de los Hospitalarios, they offered modest, safe lodging to foot travellers at a time when walking was more hazardous than it is today.

Some still serve as *refugios* for walkers. Two are possible overnight stops on the Pyrenean Traverse. The Hospital de Vielha was founded in 1192 at the base of an old *camino* that crosses the Coll de Toro into the Vall d'Aran. The Hospital de Benasque sits beside a *camino* leading to the Portillón de Benasque, once a popular smugglers' route into France.

About two hours out, clamber up the wall of a cirque, briefly using all four limbs. Around an hour later, a just-visible arrow on a granite boulder points towards **Refugio de Mulleres** (or Molières; 2360m), a bright-orange, 12-person, unstaffed *refugio*, only five minutes away above an icy lake. This is the first of four tarns that you'll pass as you work your way up Barranco de Mulleres, though some may be masked under snowpack. The patch of grass beside the *refugio* and the shores of the first two of the four tarns are all possible **campsites** – the last until you're well over the col.

From the *refugio* turn-off to Coll de Mulleres it's a two to 2½-hour ascent entirely over rock, varying from huge slabs to slippery scree, probably with some snow cover. Beyond the lakes, the track, now much less trodden, becomes more spindly and you're reliant upon cairns and the occasional ultra-discreet vermilion trail marker.

Coll de Mulleres (2928m), the highest pass on the Pyrenean traverse, isn't easy to distinguish against the skyline, even when it's almost on top of you. Just below the serrated rocks that mark the pass lock into the tracks of those who have gone before and head west across a narrow snowfield. The last 10m are a true climb and a real pig, especially if you're lugging a full pack.

The quite stupendous views of Pico de Aneto – the highest summit in the Pyrenees – and the Glaciar de la Maladeta to the west; the upper slopes of the Valleta de la Escaleta before you; and the peaks parting Aragón from Catalunya to your right more than justify every bead of sweat expended.

To avoid the **Glaciar de Mulleres** directly below you follow the ridge along its less steep, western side towards **Pic (Tuc) de Mulleres** (3010m), identified by the iron cross at its summit. Just west of the peak follow the intermittent line of cairns that drops northwards to join a feeder stream of the highest tarn of the Valleta de la Escaleta More simply, just dig in your heels and poles to yomp straight down the snow-covered glacier to the tarn, 35 to 45 minutes away. There's just enough flat space here for a **campsite**, but camping options increase in quantity and quality as you descend the valley.

Skirt around the tarn to its right. Once the glacier and snow give out you stride for a time over huge, smooth slabs of mottled granite, comfortable as the living room carpet after what you've recently experienced.

Shortly before drawing level with the evident **Collado dels Aranesos** (2455m), which leads back into Catalunya, pass a small tarn on its left (west) side then switch to the true right bank of the stream flowing from it. Beyond the tarn it's greenness once more, the gradient becomes less steep and there's even a hint of path again.

After passing over a rocky bluff above the west bank of a larger tarn you emerge into meadows just below the Collado del Toro, a clearly visible nick to the east (see Side Trip: Estany del Collado de Toro). Interlaced with streams, the meadows are a paradise for campers.

SIDE TRIP: ESTANY DEL COLLADO DE TORO
45 minutes–1 hour, 1km
Leave your backpack behind a boulder in the meadows below Collado del Toro and take an easy side trail to a minor pass, **Collado**

de Toro (2235m). Just beyond it is the pretty Estany del Collado de Toro, shaped like a figure of eight and hemmed in by Pomer to the east and Peña Nere on the north. If you want to walk further you can skirt the lake along its northwest shore, following cairns but no path, to a possible **campsite** overlooking the Vall d'Aran watershed.

ALTERNATIVE DAYS 5 & 6: VIA COLLADA DE BALLIBIERNA
10½–12 hours, 36km

This variant follows the GR11, which passes to the south of the Maladeta massif. With its familiar red-and-white blazes, it's a much longer, less demanding but still challenging route into Aragón. If you wish and if you get your timing right you can take a 4WD taxi from the *refugio* beyond Pleta de Llosás to Benasque or to Plan de Senarta and omit the final 10km of walking.

From the Hospital de Vielha follow the main N230 road south for 200m and turn left onto a path. After 20 minutes or so you pass beside a popular picnic spot that offers some tempting shaded **campsites** (bona fide trekkers, putting up their tent at dusk and moving on next day, are allowed to stay overnight here).

A few minutes later, fork right, go through a meadow and cross the Barranco de Besiberri, a tributary of the Noguera Ribagorçana. About an hour beyond the Hospital, cross to the true right bank of this more substantial river at a concrete footbridge and follow the main road for 200m.

At the far side of the road bridge where the Río Salenques flows into the Embalse de Basserca (Senet) dam turn right onto a trail that mounts the true right bank of the stream. You ascend fairly gently, walking a springy carpet of beech leaves, until, around 45 minutes beyond the bridge, you reach a flattish patch of terrain where Barranc de Salenques meets Vall d'Anglíos.

Continue west up the Vall d'Anglíos. The path, at first overgrown and difficult to distinguish early in the season, ascends very steeply with scarcely a zig or a zag through beech wood, which yields to silver birch, then fir and mountain ash. Wild strawberries and bilberries offer occasional and welcome refreshment. Once thickets of pine take over the gradient, though still

enough to make you puff, slackens a little, then levels out for the final kilometre to the first of the **Estanys d'Anglíos** lakes (2220m), reached after 3¼ to 3½ hours of walking.

Contour around the lake to the south, passing by a doll's house of a **refugio** which can just squeeze in four people (get there early if you want to bag a square metre or two). Just beyond, the GR11 splits. Take the westerly option to sneak between the second and third tarns, then head up a grassy bank to follow the small Riu Güeno upstream. You'll find this option frustratingly boulder-strewn but it's smooth as a helter-skelter compared with the alternative route.

Beyond the last of three small, inky tarns, reached some 35 to 45 minutes beyond the *refugio*, the route climbs steeply over boulders to the evident dip of **Colladeta de Riu Güeno** (2325m), after an altitude gain of 300m. The GR11 is well signed but you're just as well off picking your own way up and around the hefty granite slabs.

Drop steeply to curl around the western shore of the **Ibón Cap de Llauset** (*ibón* is Aragonese for lake). If you prefer to postpone the ascent to Collada de Ballibierna until the morrow (you're now about five hours into the walking day), the northwest corner of the lake makes a comfortable **campsite**.

To continue, follow the lake's outflow stream to rejoin the alternative GR11 route at a green sign. From this junction it's a further 300m of height gain over granite boulders to **Collada de Ballibierna** (or Vallibierna or Vallivierna or even Vallhiverna – all four variants are current!) at 2720m, with the possibility of snowfields on either side of the pass.

Drop westwards steeply from the pass. For the first 10 minutes you're better off picking your own route through the boulders rather than slithering down the skiddy, overtramped GR11 tracing. Once at the upper of the two **Ibóns de Ballibierna** you'll find that its grassy southeast shore makes a good **campsite**, after a total of 6½ to seven hours of walking.

To avoid unnecessary boulder hopping, keep high on the north side of the tight *barranco* connecting the two lakes, then wend your way around the north shore of the downstream one, reached one to 1¼ hours after leaving the col.

The descent beyond the lower lake is gentle, grassy and glorious. At valley level, the meadows of **Pleta de Llosás** (2200m) make a pleasant place to rest or **camp**. After entering sparse pine forest you reach, some 30 minutes beyond the meadows and eight to nine hours' walking from the Hospital de Vielha, **Puente de Coronas** (1950m) and an unstaffed **refugio** with room for 12 or so. The area around the hut has some inviting **campsites**.

From July to mid-September a **4WD taxi** descends from Puente de Coronas to Plan de Senarta at 1pm, 4pm and 6pm, allowing you to clip a good 10km off this stage (the 1pm and 6pm services continue as far as Benasque). Otherwise, it's an easy and uneventful stroll down a forested track that follows the northern flank of Barranco de Ballibierna.

Some 35 to 45 minutes beyond the first *refugio* is another. Domed, smaller and less inviting, it's fine if you fancy postponing the final haul into Benasque.

About an hour later, limbo dance under a barrier that prevents vehicle access from below and turn left (west) at a T-junction to follow a sign 'Benasque, Estós, GR11'.

Follow the east shore of the **Embalse de Paso Nuevo** reservoir. Some 15 to 20 minutes from the junction you can avoid a long hairpin in the 4WD track by taking an easily overlooked path to the right. After 50m bear left to descend through a thicket of boxwood, then turn right as you rejoin the track.

Half an hour later the route bears right to pass under the **Puente San Jaime** and the highway and almost goes through **Camping Aneto** (☎/fax 974 55 11 41; www.campinganeto.com; camping per person/tent €5.60 each). Set in large, attractive riverside grounds, it sells a good range of walking maps and guidebooks in Spanish and has a washing machine.

From the bridge it's a 3.8km walk south to Benasque (1140m).

Day 6: Meadows Below Collado del Toro to Benasque
5–6 hours, 20.5km

In a little under an hour of easy walking (look for the caves in the hillside, rated highly by speleologists), you emerge into the wide **Plan de Aiguallut**. Here, cows browse,

picnickers paddle and all is satisfyingly green and fertile.

A green metal *refugio* – even the huts are green around here – offering spartan space for eight, perches above the downstream end of the meadow. Just below it is Cascada de Aiguallut, down which the river hurtles before disappearing into Forau de Aiguallut.

At **La Besurta**, about 30 minutes walk from Plan de Aiguallut (or 1½ hours via Refugio de la Renclusa – see Alternative Route, p90), there's a small stall serving cold beer and soft drinks, snacks and *bocadillos* (€4-5) – a small gastronomic delight after a few days on the trail.

Shuttle buses (one way/return €2.40/4.20) travel the 6km from La Besurta to the Vano de Benasque (the car park past the Hospital de Benasque). They run at 5am and 5.30am and then from 8am they run every 35 minutes in each direction. Tickets are bought on the bus. Buses departing from La Besurta (six daily: 6am, 10am, 1.30pm, 5pm, 7pm and 9pm) continue to Benasque, stopping by request at Puente de San Jaime (for Camping Aneto – see the end of Alternative Days 5 & 6, previous column). At other times you shouldn't have too much trouble finding a lift down to town from the car park beside the lower bus terminal near the Hospital de Benasque. To check the times of buses, visit the **tourist office** (9.30am-1.30pm & 4.30pm-8.30pm in high season) or see the timetables at the bus stop or around the town.

While most walkers prefer to catch the bus to Benasque, it's possible to walk from

FORAU DE AIGUALLUT

The Forau (meaning cave or pothole in Aragonese) de Aiguallut is a cauldron into which swirl all the waters flowing from surrounding mountains – from Glaciar de Mulleres to the Maladeta massif. Once underground the run-off forms a subterranean river on a bed of limestone. It loses some 600m in height over only 4km before re-emerging at Artiga de Lin in Vall d'Aran. From here the river joins the Riu Garona, called La Garonne, once it crosses the French border, and flows into the Atlantic Ocean near Bordeaux.

La Besurta, for the most part off-road, via the old **Hospital de Benasque** (☎ 974 55 20 12/608 536053; www.llanosdelhospital .com; s/d €79/142) – see the boxed text El Hospital, p87. Around 500m east of the lower terminus of the shuttle bus running down from La Besurta, it offers hotel accommodation at a variety of rates but is no longer a refuge. An evening *menú* is available.

ALTERNATIVE ROUTE: VIA REFUGIO DE LA RENCLUSA
1½–1¾ hours, 3km

Refugio de la Renclusa (☎ 974 34 46 46), with capacity for 93, is staffed all year. Newly expanded in 2006, it offers excellent modern accommodation; the spacious rooms each containing about six beds have their own bathrooms. It's a very friendly place, offering meals, drinks and snacks all day. It's a very popular base camp for climbers and those planning an ascent of Pico de Aneto. Fork out €35.50 and you'll get dinner, bed and breakfast. There is a self-catering area if you wish to prepare your own food and just pay for a bed. A further €12.20 will buy you a picnic lunch for the next day. As it's also near vehicle access (whole coach loads of walkers are decanted daily from a 45-minute walk away at La Besurta), advance booking is highly recommended, especially at weekends

PARQUE POSETS-MALADETA

The park was declared a protected area in 1994. It covers 332 sq km and encompasses the two highest massifs in the Pyrenees and 13 of the range's major glaciers. Nearly all the park lies above 1800m, including the Pico de Aneto (3404m), the highest mountain in the Pyrenees.

It owes its shape, like so many other areas of the chain, to the ice ages, which created the characteristic U-shaped valleys, giant cirques at their head, hanging valleys high on their flanks and scooped depressions, today filled by more than 100 *ibóns*, or mountain tarns.

Following the region's upgrade to park status vehicle access is now restricted.

and in July/August. Just near the *refugio* is another impressive *forau* beside a small chapel.

From Plan de Aiguallut take a faint trail leading initially westwards from near the green metal shelter. The first part of the ascent to Coll de la Renclusa (2270m) is steep. Navigation isn't always easy as far as the pass but the trail is well cairned in its latter stages. To the *refugio* from Plan de Aiguallut takes about an hour, and La Besurta lies 30 to 40 minutes beyond, down the eastern flank of Barranco de la Renclusa.

Refugio de la Renclusa can be visited from La Besurta as an undemanding, well marked, 3km return trip. From La Besurta, head back towards Plan de Aiguallut and fork right (south) after about 10 minutes.

Day 7: Benasque to Refugio Ángel Orus
4–4½ hours, 10.5km

From Benasque cross the ring road beside Barrabes Ski Montaña and take the Carretera de Anciles. This quiet, leafy lane brings you to **Anciles** (1100m) after 1.5km. Even though you've scarcely had time to warm up, it's worth taking an early break to wander its lanes, bordered by 17th-and 18th-century *señorial* (stately) houses, roofed in the local slate. On the west side of this charming hamlet follow the dusty track, a continuation of the main street, that leaves the village, passing by a couple of flowing *fuentes*. Pick up yellow-and-white trail markers and take a right turn, signed 'Eriste', to follow a shady lane through hayfields as far as a bridge over the Río Ésera, opposite a power plant.

You should be in **Eriste** (1118m) within an hour. Go through the central square, to the left of the church and up to the top of the village. The trail that you follow into the ravine is signed 'Puente de Tramarrius, Refugio Ángel Orus'.

Eriste shows its most photogenic side as you climb above it – rooflines, hayfields and the head of the Linsoles reservoir with its canoes and sailing boats divert attention from the valley's industrial scars. Just under an hour later cross the old **Puente de Tramarrius** (1245m) to mount the east (true left) bank of the river and meet a

4WD track. Continue upstream along this wider trail.

Count on a bit more than another hour, or a total of two hours from Eriste, passing by an abandoned pyrite mine to reach the **Cascada de la Espiantosa** (1505m), an impressive waterfall. The area around the falls makes an excellent lunch stop. Cross the nearby Puente de la Espiantosa – a mundane concrete bridge that can't compare with the magnificent arch of the Puente de Tramarrius earlier. A sign above the car park gives an accurate duration of 1½ hours to the Ángel Orus *refugio*.

After 20 to 25 minutes the path levels out briefly before resuming its upward progression, moving away from but always heading back to the Aigüeta de Eriste, the splendid stream that cuts through the valley. You're following yellow-and-white blazes and also red plastic markers hanging from the trees – trail markers for winter walkers and skiers.

From **Pleta de les Riberes** (1815m), a small grassy area, the path zigzags steeply northwest up to **Refugio Ángel Orus** (2150m; ☎ 974 34 40 44; dm €15.50). You normally need to reserve ahead (essential at weekends), despite its capacity for 100, as it's the most popular base camp for an assault on Posets mountain. It's also the only choice other than the stark Cabaña de Llardana (see Day 8, next column) for noncampers walking this side of the massif.

ALTERNATIVE DAY 7: BENASQUE TO REFUGIO DE ESTÓS
3½–4 hours, 12km

If you take this easy walk – the main GR tracing – up Valle de Estós to the *refugio* of the same name, you can save a day by omitting Days 7 and 8. However, if you do, you'll be depriving yourself of some spectacular mountain walking in the shadow of Posets.

The valley route is a well-trodden one, a 4WD track for the most part and popular with day-trippers from Benasque. You can either savour a short stage and stay overnight at Refugio de Estós or continue to Refugio de Viadós (see Day 9, p93) – thus saving yourself yet another day. It makes for a long haul but many walkers undertake it.

Leave Benasque by the sealed road that heads north to La Besurta (if you'd prefer

to avoid this stretch of road take the La Besurta bus as far as Puente de San Jaime.

Valle de Estós takes off northwest from the Río Ésera. At **Puente de San Jaime**, 3.8km north of town, turn right then left to go under the road bridge, beside Camping Aneto and over an older arched bridge. After passing a small dam cross the **Palanca de Aiguacari** (*palanca* in Aragonese means bridge) onto the true right bank. Shortly beyond a pair of green metal gates, **Cabaña de Santa Ana**, once a chapel, can accommodate 12 for a spartan overnight stay. Soon the steepness abates and the valley broadens into fine meadow interspersed with hazel, ash and beech trees.

Forty-five minutes or so from Puente de San Jaime pause to refill your water bottles – and if the season's right, munch a few wild strawberries – at **Fuente Corona**. At a junction 10 minutes later take a right fork signed 'Refugio de Estós'. After a further hour the 4WD track dwindles to a broad footpath, sunken from the tramping of so many boots, just beyond a small, locked cabin, the upstream limit for motor vehicles.

Forty-five minutes later, after a final 10 to 15 minutes of steep climb, you reach **Refugio de Estós** with its welcome terrace and icy-cold drinks. For more about the *refugio*, see the end of Day 8.

Day 8: Refugio Ángel Orus to Refugio de Estós
6–7 hours, 14.5km

This makes for a long day. However, if the mood takes you there are several spectacular places en route where you can break off to camp.

From the *refugio* pick up the red-and-white flashes of the GR11.2 variant and head northwest (the northeasterly tracing on the Alpina map is no longer practicable), continuing beyond a sign, 'Posets, Llardaneta'.

After 35 to 45 minutes turn right where the trail splits, to follow a sign 'Collado de la Piana,' and cross the Torrente de Llardaneta. You have to rely on the low cairns but navigation is no problem as far as the **Cabaña de Llardana**, which is visible from the junction. This spartan hut can accommodate four people plus baggage and has abundant

CAMPING WILD IN ARAGÓN ALTERNATIVE ROUTE: CALDES DE BOÍ

As everywhere in the Pyrenees, camping is normally forbidden in national parks and designated conservation areas such as Parque Posets-Maladeta.

Outside these areas, regulation 79/1990 of 8 May 1990 decrees that above 1500m you can camp anywhere that's more than two hours' walk from a vehicle access point. Below 1500m you have the right to pitch your tent anywhere more than 5km from a designated camping ground and 1km from an urban centre. It's forbidden to camp within 100m of a river or road. If anyone should challenge you, just quote *'decreto 79/1990 del ocho de mayo'* back at them!

water from nearby seeps. There's also just enough space to pitch a tent.

Keeping the height, bear northeast over turfed-in boulders, forging your own way as the GR signing on this stretch is absurdly stingy. About half an hour beyond the cabin you need to drop steeply to intersect with a path coming up from the main valley. From here on the trail marking improves.

You reach the double **Lago de las Alforjas** (2400m) one to 1¼ hours past the cabin. It's one of a dozen or more lakes tucked around the eastern and southern slopes of the just-visible Posets and Bardamina crests. There are two to three good **campsites** around its western shores.

Allow one to 1¼ hours to reach the obvious Collado de la Piana, which is just north of Pico de Escorvets (2902m). Leaving the lake, head briefly – and implausibly – south along (oh joy!) a near-level gully before ascending northeast. Pick your way above the north bank of the often frozen tarn of La Piana (the southern route indicated on both Prames and Alpina maps is emphatically blocked by landslide) to reach **Collado de la Piana** (2660m). Here there are magnificent panoramas west to the Posets crest (second-highest in the Pyrenees at 3369m), and east to Maladeta and the Ixeia pinnacles.

At the saddle you meet the first of the rare wooden poles that mark the next stretch of this GR11 variant. They're so infrequent as to be all but useless – and totally so if there's the least wisp of mist. (A few years ago, when we asked one of the wardens at the Refugio de Estós if there were plans to improve the deficient signing, he just shrugged and pointed out that the cows would uproot most of the poles anyway!).

Drop eastwards and pass to the left (north) of a pair of tarns, both visible from the col, and two of a spattering of pools on this side of the massif. A steep, rocky descent of about 1½ hours brings you to the **Ibón de l'Aigüeta de Batisielles** and its satellite pools, each of whose banks offer attractive **camping**.

Cross to the true left bank of its outlet stream to drop steeply and curl around the south shore of the larger **Ibón Gran de Batisielles** (2260m), which also offers great camping. As you leave the lake be sure to stay well above and to the left of the steep valley that runs away southwards.

Now comes the payoff for all the scrambling since the Collado de la Piana as you lope down an easily identifiable path through sparse pine to emerge into the lush, though in places marshy, pine-ringed meadows that enfold the **Ibón Pequeño de Batisielles** (1950m), a reedy pond.

Here you can choose from various **campsites**, the best and driest being between the two forks of the Río de Batisielles. The only drawback to otherwise idyllic camping is that it's also a favourite grazing area of local cows and consequently the hunting ground of some particularly predatory horseflies. For the tentless there's a very basic, **green metal shelter**, sleeping three at a squeeze, on a knoll just southeast of the flats and another one beside the pool that can just accommodate four.

From the shelter beside the pool strike northeast along an evident, intermittently blazed trail. After an initial climb of about five minutes there's little net altitude gain as you stride through a mixture of pine forest and grassland. Enjoy the fine vistas across the Valle de Estós to the peaks of Pico de Gías, Pico d'Oô (no typing error here!) and the mighty Perdiguero. The Refugio de Estós, perched well above the riverside meadows, comes into sight long before you cross the Río de Estós by a stout wooden bridge for the final brief climb to its terrace.

Refugio de Estós (1890m; ☎/fax 974 34 45 15; dm beds €15.50) has beds for 99 walkers. Since it's a popular venue for groups, day visitors and overnighters from Benasque, reservations are essential. It serves drinks, snacks and meals, and has a hot shower and its own generator powered by a nearby torrent.

SIDE TRIP: LAGO DE LA ESCARPINOSA
1¾–2 hours, 4km
From the Ibón Pequeño de Batisielles head southwest through pine forest up an idyllic streamside path to the Lago de la Escarpinosa (2040m). Here, where the grass is limited but luxuriant, is another splendid spot for an overnight camp.

Day 9: Refugio de Estós to Refugio de Viadós
4–4½ hours, 10km
Two of the lime green national park signs greet you in quick succession as you leave the *refugio*. One posits two hours to the Puerto de Gistaín; the other, 1½ hours. Put your faith in the former, then add some.

The path descends gently on the north (true left) side of the river to meet the valley bottom after about 20 minutes' walking. The Clarabide stream descends southwards down a sheer valley to meet the main Río de Estós watercourse at about 2050m, 45 minutes to an hour above the *refugio*. It's a pretty spot to rest and replenish your water supplies – the last dependable water for quite some time.

Once you've crossed to the south side of the Río de Estós's first dribblings you face a rather monotonous westward haul over scree and rock up a long, dry tube of a valley. It's not too arduous, however, if you stick to the red-and-white trail markers of the GR11, which snakes smoothly between and around obstacles, avoiding most rock scrambling.

Aim for a notch on the south side of the bowl, then walk around the head of the valley to reach the true pass (2590m), known variously as the **Puerto de Gistaín**, Puerto Chistén and Puerto de Chistau, 2¼ to 2½ hours from the *refugio*.

There's really a double pass here, separated by a narrow moor. Before you move on take a last glance backwards at the Aneto massif, dominating the eastern horizon. Some 10 minutes from the second, minor col, cross to the true left bank of the gully which drops steeply away westwards. From here until the confluence of streams at Añes Cruces (2060m), it's a gentle, grassy descent, except for the last 10 minutes or so, which require all your attention as the path crosses steep scree.

At the confluence, reached about an hour beyond the pass, cross both tributaries, as well as an upstart little stream, to join the west (true right) bank of the river, from here on known as the Cinqueta de Añes Cruces. Conspicuous on the hillside are two **cabins**, one low and squat, the other newer. If the shepherds aren't in residence, the latter, especially, makes a good overnight flop.

The path is straightforward. As you gradually round the mountain, walking through wide, floral meadows, there are unsurpassed views of the entire west face of Posets. Allow 1¼ to 1½ hours from the confluence to **Granjas de Viadós** (Biadós), a hamlet of a dozen or so scattered farmhouses.

The privately owned **Refugio de Viadós** (1760m; ☎ 974 34 16 13; dm €10; Jul-Sep) is outstanding and extremely reasonable. With 65 bunks and a cosy bar and dining room, it's a friendly, popular family operation. The filling meals are a bargain at €13 for dinner and €5 for breakfast. Staff speak French, but minimal English.

The owner, Joaquin Cazcarra, also runs **Camping El Forcallo** (☎ 974 34 16 13; camping per person/tent €3.90 each; Jul-Aug), 1.3km down the hill. The fee includes a hot showers, excellent, flat pitches and clean facilities. There's no shop but it has a pleasant bar, where meals cost a very reasonable €13 for dinner and €5 for breakfast. The campsite and *refugio* are both accessible by car making them an ideal base for day walks or as a section end of the traverse.

SIDE TRIP: LAGO DE MILLARES
5–5½ hours, 10.5km
Time permitting, set aside a full day for the challenging yet satisfying return trip from Refugio de Viadós, up and out of the woodland around Barranco de Ribereta to the Lago de Millares (2400m), which

sparkles and spreads below the Pico de la Forqueta. The gradient is steep in places but you're on path the entire way.

SIDE TRIP: SEÑAL DE VIADÓS
3½–4 hours, 7km

Stunning 360-degree vistas make the 840m ascent from Viadós to Señal de Viadós (2600m) – a spectacular viewpoint – well worthwhile. Allow a generous half-day for this return trip, north-northeast of the *refugio*.

Day 10: Refugio de Viadós to Parzán
5½–6½ hours, 20km

After the challenge of the Posets rim, you deserve this easy, uncomplicated day of attractive walking, primarily through meadow and pine forest, which makes a gentle prelude to the altogether sterner stuff ahead. There's an ascent to 2300m but it's never too strenuous. Steel yourself, however, for the final unexciting 8.5km descent along a 4WD track from below Lago de Urdiceto to Valle de Bielsa. Few 4WDs venture this way so you're unlikely to get a lift.

From Refugio de Viadós the GR11 briefly takes to the trees but you're just as well off following the 4WD track downhill past Camping el Forcallo.

It's about 45 minutes from the *refugio* to the La Sargueta turn-off (1540m), 1km downstream from the camping ground. Take the track to the right, signed 'Urdiceto, Parzan'. After 30 minutes turn right at a cluster of farms, the **Bordas de Lizierte**, to

mount a steep path and briefly enter the welcome shade of a pine wood. You soon bear right to join a wider 4WD track and, within 20 to 30 minutes, reach the small pass and meadow of **Las Collás**, or Las Colladas (1846m).

The track dips briefly to Barranco de la Basa as **Cabaña Sallena**, the only structure on the opposite hillside, comes into view. The countryside is an appealing mix of piny ravines and turf. A view to the west of the bare **Punta Suelza** (2973m) provides a sample of the tougher terrain to come.

The 4WD track peters out at the *cabaña* (capable of sleeping up to six intimate friends) to become a clear footpath. About 30 minutes beyond the cabin there's a deep, inviting pool, ideal for a dunk on a hot day, where you cross to the stream's true right bank. No more than 10 minutes beyond is a tiny, tumbling stone **shelter** that could provide strictly emergency accommodation.

As you angle up the ridge separating the two *barrancos*, Montarruegos and Sallena, the path winds and undulates a little before slipping through **Collada de Urdiceto** (Ordiceto; 2326m), also known as Paso d'es Caballos, 3½ to four hours into the day. If you want to stay up high, try the wonderful **campsites** in the meadows before the pass.

At the pass there's a shepherds' hut that offers simple accommodation. Just beyond it the path meets a dirt access road that leads out left to Lago de Urdiceto (2390m), a stark, monochrome blot amid grimly

HYDROPOWER & HYDROTRASH

Purists deplore the tinkering with nature of the small-scale hydroelectric schemes that dam and distort high mountain tarns. But which is the least environmentally damaging and which takes most from the earth? A coal, oil or gas-fired generating station? A nuclear plant? Or whirring turbines, driven by a source of energy that drops from the sky and continues its downward journey unchanged?

There is something of a downside in the Pyrenees. Though many water pipes linking one lake with another are buried deep underground, there are some monumentally ugly wide-bore tubes that drop water from dam level to turbines further down in the valley. Around the dams you'll often see the abandoned debris of their construction: a twisted stretch of narrow-gauge railway line, the concrete pad of a demolished hut or the rusting pylons of long-abandoned cable lifts.

Then again, there's a special spin-off for walkers. Several Pyrenean mountain *refugios* started life as rest houses for workers on the dams and were given over to walking clubs and societies once construction was over.

rocky terrain – not really worth a detour. There are, however, a few turfy flat spots here for a **campsite** if you want to postpone the descent to Parzán.

Otherwise, turn right down the dirt road, then almost immediately left onto a path which cuts off a couple of long zigzags before rejoining the 4WD track 15 to 20 minutes later. After a further 15 minutes on the track turn left onto a path that runs beside a small dam and hydroelectric station and soon rejoins the 4WD track. From here on it's an uneventful descent, albeit with pleasant views, to the main highway, the Carretera de Francia, the trail emerging 1.5km north of the hamlet of Parzán.

Day 11: Parzán to Valle de Pineta
5½–6 hours, 16km

A fairly easy day following the GR11 tracing. After 8.5km of 4WD track up the attractive valley of the Rio Real it's a further climb through the jumble of rocks to springy turf and spectacular views of the Valle de Pineta and the impressive Cirque at its head. A gain of almost exactly 1000m in elevation to Collado de Pietramula is followed by a mostly undemanding walk down to the base of the Circo de Pineta.

Just north of Parzan turn left off the Carretera de Francia and follow the road to **Chisagües** 45 minutes after the junction. Continue past and round Chisagües along what becomes 4WD track, originally a path made to serve the long-abandoned silver and lead mines above Chisagües. It's a steady, uneventful rise up the valley with views improving at every bend.

About 6.5km beyond Chisagües at the acute hairpin bend that turns away up the mountain, leave the track down to the bridge crossing the Rio Real and work your way up the path going upwards and westwards through a jumble of rocks at the base of Pietramula, the slab of mountain to the left.

At the **Collado de Pietramula**, or Piedramula (2150m), about 30 minutes' uphill beyond the river crossing, you drink in the first dramatic views of the sheer western flank of the Valle de Pineta, the notch of the Collado de Añisclo, tomorrow's challenge, and the Glaciar de Monte Perdido.

A short, steep drop leads to the **Llanos de Estiva** plains, one vast potential

campsite, several football fields long, with a flowing water trough on its northern slope. At its limit, 20 to 30 minutes beyond the col, the grassy semblance of a path leads into a stony 4WD track. A couple of bends beyond a locked shepherds' hut on your right turn sharp right onto a pleasant, grassy path.

Shortly after the trail enters pinewood and begins to descend more steeply look out for an easily missed 90-degree turn southwest.

A couple more twists and the route descends emphatically and unambiguously southwestwards, down to the grassy **Llanos de la Larri** (1560m), 1½ to 1¾ hours beyond the col.

Cross over the rim of this wide hanging valley to drop through a wood of beech, holly and boxwood, each a delight after day upon day of conifers, to the small chapel of **Nuestra Señora de Pineta** (1250m) and its adjacent *fuente* about half an hour later.

Here, at the head of the valley, you've a binary choice of both accommodation and camping ground.

For a touch of four-star luxury at equivalent prices turn right for the **Parador de Bielsa** (☎ 974 50 10 11; r from €160). To fortify yourself for the morrow and the toughest ascent of the whole traverse, consider awarding yourself a gourmet dinner (€31 for their excellent set *menú*) at the restaurant, from where the views of the Circo de Pineta are stunning.

About 1.5km past the parador is the very pleasant **Refugio de Pineta** (☎ 974 50 12 03; www.fam.es; dm €14; open all year). While some places are kept aside for walk-in customers it's best to reserve in high season.

The **Camping Municipal** (per person with tent from €4) is nicely sited, however, the ratio of toilets and (cold!) showers to campers is woeful.

For comfort under canvas 6km further on from the camping municipal is **Camping Pineta** (☎ 974 50 10 89, fax 974 50 11 84; www.campingsonline .com/pineta; per person/tent €4.90 each; Mar–mid-Oct) which has great facilities including hot showers, large swimming pool, supermarket, bar and restaurant. At the reception it is also possible to purchase detailed maps of the region.

THE GR11 BACKTRACK

It's a principle of GR trails in Europe that they should be accessible to all. But from Collado de Añisclo the original GR11 route followed, and continues to follow, a potentially dangerous 500m traverse around the usually wet, often snowbound rock of Punta de las Olas.

In response to widespread criticism the GR11 committee approved an alternative, also marked with the red-and-white bars of the official GR trail.

Uniquely, the 'variant' now features in the official handbook as the recommended route, while the original life-threatener has been relegated to an option in italics.

Day 12: Valle de Pineta to Valle de Añisclo

4½–5¾ hours, 7.5km

Make no mistake, the major part of today is a tough, strenuous walk which will have you clambering up rocks and over fallen trees and negotiating minor landslides. Statistically speaking, the climb from the Pineta valley bottom to Collado de Añisclo represents a vertical ascent of just under 1200m in almost exactly 2km of walking and scrambling. Put another way, you're heaving your way up a gradient of just under 60%. The considerable compensation comes from the ever more spectacular views at your back of Valle and Circo de Pineta as you advance.

The GR11 crosses the true right bank of the river by way of the bridge beside the camping municipal. If you spent last night at the *refugio* or Camping de Pineta follow the path along the river westwards towards the bridge. After 10 to 15 minutes walking slip off your socks and shoes and cut across the river to pick up the track on the opposite side that heads back in the direction of the *refugio*.

The path meanders along the riverbed, crosses a water meadow, snakes along the base of the cliff then roughly 15 minutes beyond the *refugio* turning, begins to climb in earnest. A further 30 minutes later, cross a wide *barranco* and stream. Fill your bottles here as there's no more water until you're over the Añisclo pass. The obvious path mounts steeply through a tunnel of silver birch, boxwood, hazel and beech, their deep shade more than compensating for the absence of views.

At about 1900 metres the path intersects with the enviably flat Faja de Tormosa route to the right which contours around from Circo de Pineta to the west. Continue climbing on the path upwards, but keep your wits about you because as the dead trees testify, this slope is renowed for its springtime avalanches!

The steepest stuff is now behind you. Although there's plenty of scree ahead that will have you slithering, four-limbed manoeuvres are all but over, except for a short, mean traverse about 15 minutes before the saddle.

Walking times to **Collado de Añisclo** (2470m) vary enormously, from around three to five hours, but when finally you get to the top take a big gulp of fresh air and drink in the lovely views. If you're running short of energy, there's an unspolt spot with water and some level turf for a **campsite** no more than 50m vertical descent on the south side of the ridge.

At the pass it's time to make a decision between the high road: the original GR11 via the Puntas de las Olas traverse to Goriz or the more trodden low road down the Añisclo canyon. Unless you're an experienced mountaineer we strongly recommend that you avoid the former (see boxed text The GR11 Backtrack, previous column). Should you opt for it, take particular care when negotiating the tranche that requires cable support when there's snow around – which is most of the year. This variant takes between two and 2¼ hours as far as Collado Arrablo.

Even though you lose around 750m in altitude, we equally strongly recommend the GR11 variant via the alluring **Valle de Añisclo** both because its safer and for its own sake: it's a very pleasant and beautiful walk, taking only a couple more hours. Although note that if you're planning on continuing to Goriz this could make today's a whopping ten hours going this way!

To follow it, head briefly off to the right and westwards from the pass then the path begins to drop to the valley, but keeping fairly high up its eastern flank. A series of gentle drops, each ending in a waterfall and a pool deep enough to bathe in; green sward; alpine flowers; and a choice of campsites at each giant step make the upper valley one of the major highlights of the whole Pyrenees crossing. Just below the last of the inviting pools is a metal bridge across the river and the path that heads to Goriz where you will find plenty of spots to **camp**. You may however prefer to stay up high where there are fewer campers… Just over the bridge as the path starts to climb you will find a dry cosy hut – **Casa de los Cazadores** (Hunters House) a perfect option if you have no tent. It can accommodate five snuggled close. Just beyond here is a rocky overhang that also provides **shelter**.

ALTERNATIVE CAMPSITES
Should you have any stamina left when you reach Casa de los Cazadores, consider continuing for around a further 1¼ hours as far as the alpine meadows above the bare rock of Barranco de Fon Blanca. This may leave you drained but it will allow you to descend to Pradera de Ordesa comfortably the following day and maybe continue up Valle de Bujaruelo.

Day 13: Valle De Añisclo to Torla
7½–8½ hours, 23km
Steel yourself to rejoin the madding crowd. After an ascent to Collado Arrablo the route drops via the teeming Refugio de Góriz to the floor of Valle de Ordesa. As you draw closer to the shuttle-bus terminal at Pradera de Ordesa throngs of tourists seem to outnumber the trees. In fact, so popular is the end part of today's route that the way has even been paved, all be it with the natural stone of the park! If this doesn't sound like your idea of the wilderness, then you could take the route via Faja de Pelay (see p99).

Another option is to delay the inevitable, enjoy a short day and spend the night, probably in the company of a hundred others, in or around Refugio de Góriz. From here, the fit can undertake the demanding day trip to the summit of Monte Perdido (3355m; see Monte Perdido, p122).

Start out with some steep two-steps-up-one-back scree scrabbling just below the spectacular **Cascada de Fon Blanca** waterfall. Though it's abrupt and confronts you before you've time to catch your second wind, it's like a short stroll to the shops compared with yesterday's exertions as scree alternates with rocky outcrop, giving much more purchase.

As you continue to ascend the gaunt, narrow valley of the Barranco Arrablo (also known as the Barranco de Fon Blanca) the steepness eases markedly. After a little under 45 minutes cross to the true right bank of the shallow stream, dipping in your water bottles as you do; Ordesa is strictly limestone and surface water is at a premium away from the valley bottom.

Around 20 minutes later there's a brief, steep, hands-and-feet southwesterly traverse before the route resumes its westward progress below the valley's upper rim. Here, the path leaves behind the uniform grey rock of the canyon and emerges into a green alpine meadow – a perfect campsite shared only by marmots.

A short while later there is a final clamber then the descent to cross the stream (avoid taking the path straight ahead as you reach the stream) around which are several fine **campsites** and then a pleasant upland stride to the **Collado Arrablo** (2343m), also known as Collado Superior de Góriz, reached two to 2¼ hours into the day. From your right (east) the GR11 path from the Punta de las Olas traverse (see the boxed text The GR11 Backtrack, p96) trickles in, deceptively tame in its final stage.

From the saddle you have good views of the summits to the north: from right to left, Punta de las Olas (3002m), Sum de Ramond (also called Pico de Añisclo; 3254m), Morrón de Arrablo (or Torre de Góriz; 2792m) and, lording it over all, imperious Monte Perdido (3355m).

About 15 minutes beyond the pass there are several fine campsites where a large stream flows through a meadow. Once you reach **Refugio de Góriz** (2150m; ☎ /fax 974 34 12 01; www.goriz.es; dm €14, dinner €14.70), some 20 minutes later, you may well wonder why you've bothered. Multilingual signs inform you with commendable directness, 'those camping can't use any of the *refugio*'s services'. Such a proscription, however, doesn't apply to their drinks, snacks or, if you're lucky enough to be able to order one, meals.

The staff are pleasant enough, but the *refugio*, overstressed, overwhelmed and

CAMPING WILD IN THE PARQUE NACIONAL

Camping wild is not totally forbidden in the Parque Nacional de Ordesa y Monte Perdido. No-one will object to responsible *vivac* (bivouac) camping. This means you can pitch a small tent between dawn and dusk above certain altitudes, which vary from sector to sector:

Ordesa	2100m
Pineta	2500m
Añisclo & Escuaín	1800m

Within park boundaries there are a handful of *abrigos* (shelters). These, however, are intended for emergency use only.

understaffed, sits squarely astride several main routes: up to France via the Brecha de Rolando, through which French trekkers pour in their hundreds; to Pineta via the Cuello del Cilindro; down to the Ordesa canyon; back where you've come from – and, of course, the classic day trip up to Monte Perdido. In summer it's under enormous pressure to accommodate a huge number of walkers. It's wise to reserve both meals and sleeping space as much as two or three months in advance. The environs of the *refugio* are like an earthquake disaster zone from early afternoon onwards, with tents – which you can't erect until nightfall – and bodies everywhere.

It makes sense to stay overnight here if you're planning to use the *refugio* as a base for bagging Monte Perdido (see Monte Perdido, p122). Otherwise, do yourself, the wardens and the environment a favour and head down the valley to Pradera de Ordesa, still three to 3½ hours away.

About 40 minutes south of the hut, the path divides. The more evident – and somewhat more hazardous – route bears right just above the Circo de Soaso. The GR11, on this occasion prudence itself, describes a relatively gentle zigzagging course down the valley's southeastern flank. Some 20 minutes down the switchbacks the trail again divides. Take the right-hand path to reach the valley bottom, a little downstream from **Cascada de Cola de Caballo** (Horse's Tail Waterfall), a pleasant place for a rest break.

From here to Pradera de Ordesa you won't lack company for a moment. About 30 minutes below Cola de Caballo the canyon begins to lose some of its characteristic glacial shape and the woods become denser. Five minutes beyond the **Gradas de Soaso**, a series of natural steps down which the Río Arazas tumbles, there's a most welcome *fuente*. Another 30 minutes or so brings you to the turn-off for Faja de Canarellos and Circo de Cotatuero (see Alternative Route: Via Cascada de Cotatuero, p99).

At a sign for the Cascadas de la Cueva and del Estrecho waterfalls and La Pradera turn left and soon cross to the stream's south bank via **Puente de Arripes**. A few minutes later a short detour to the Mirador del Paso de los Bucardos lookout gives excellent views towards the cliffs of the Salarons and Cotatuero peaks.

Continue along the south-bank path and, at a junction with the Senda de los Cazadores trail (see Alternative Route: Via Faja de Pelay, p99), you cross back over the river to reach Pradera de Ordesa. The total time from Refugio de Góriz is around three hours.

If you've been on dehydrated goo for the past two days, **Bar-Restaurante La Pradera de Ordesa**, with its rich variety of tapas, *bocadillos*, icy-cold draught beer and a *menú* is a minor gastronomic paradise.

The car park (these days satisfyingly devoid of private cars) is the terminus for the Torla shuttle bus, the way most walkers enter and leave the park, and a way to save two hours. For service details see p128.

If you'd prefer to walk the 6.5km to Torla descend via an ancient track that links the village with the *bordas* (shepherds' huts) of Valle de Ordesa. It makes a pleasant, easy alternative to the shuttle bus.

Cross the small bridge a stone's throw from Pradera de Ordesa to meet the Camino de Turieto and follow downstream the true left bank of the Río Arazas. The *camino* drops gently through a wood of fir trees and open meadow. A pair of short detours to the right leads to small waterfalls.

At the park boundary, reached after about an hour, the *camino* forks south to Torla, already visible, and north (right) along the GR11 towards Valle de Bujaruelo. Take the Torla option, which soon becomes a sizeable dirt track. Roughly 30 minutes later, cross the river by Puente de la Glera and go up a cobbled lane that leads to Torla.

If you wanted to bypass Torla and extend Day 13 you could take the shuttle bus down as far as Puente de los Navarros to save a little boot leather and continue on. Another option is to begin Day 14 from Puente de los Navarros and continue to either Balneario de Panticosa (see Day 15, p100) or Panticosa (see Alternative Day 15, p101), but this makes for a very long day's walk.

ALTERNATIVE ROUTE: VIA FAJA DE PELAY
6½–7½ hours, 17.5km

'*Faja*', meaning belt or band, accurately describes this contour-hugging path, high above Valle de Ordesa. Beginning just south of Circo de Soaso, it continues as far as Mirador de Calcilarruego, where you launch yourself on the steep descent down the Senda de los Cazadores, the Hunters' Track.

Follow Day 13 as far as the point, well below Refugio de Góriz, where it bears away right and downhill to meet the valley bottom. Instead, continue straight with no loss of height to join the main Faja de Pelay path coming up from the meadows of Circo de Soaso.

After the hard, uphill work of the previous 1½ days, the Faja is an immensely enjoyable stroll, though the final descent down the ultra-steep Senda de los Cazadores may batter your kneecaps a little.

The path twists its way around one incised ravine after another, rarely rising above 1900m. The views are magnificent the whole way, except where obscured by trees. Keep your eyes focused on the middle ground as well as the canyon and mountain scenery. On this less-trodden trail you stand a good chance of spotting *sarrio*, as chamois are known in Aragonese.

From the point at which you leave the Day 13 route allow between 2¼ and 2½ hours to reach **Mirador de Calcilarruego**.

In the next 1¼ hours or so the path drops 600m vertically on the tight switchbacks of the Senda de los Cazadores, as mountain pine and fir trees gradually give way to silent, shaded beech wood. As you emerge from the wood turn left to reach the service area and shuttle-bus terminus of the Pradera de Ordesa, where you rejoin the main route within 10 minutes.

ALTERNATIVE ROUTE: VIA CASCADA DE COTATUERO
2½–3 hours, 6km

Head right at the turn-off to Faja de Canarellos and Circo de Cotatuero. The path briefly ascends to meet the Faja de Canarellos trail as it works northwest and the beeches become sparser, giving way to box, pine and fir.

The path hugs the 1700m contour around the flank of **Monte Arruebo** with the looming cliffs of **La Fraucata** above. Crossing the lips of numerous hanging valleys and narrowing on occasion to clear rock overhangs, it offers tremendous views of the opposite Faja de Pelay flank of the Ordesa canyon.

It will take you around 1½ hours from Bosque de las Hayas to reach the bridge and tiny shelter below **Cascada de Cotatuero**, which tumbles from Circo de Cotatuero. From here allow 40 minutes to rejoin the main north-bank path along Valle de Ordesa at a junction marked by a small shrine to the Virgen de Ordesa, and another 10 to reach Pradera de Ordesa, to rejoin the main route.

Day 14: Torla To Bujaruelo
3–3¾ hours, 10km

Given the twin attractions of Torla and the national park; where many walkers will want to linger; we've built in a very short day to allow flexibility to spend the morning having a look round Torla or take an early leisurely walk to Bujaruelo and spend the afternoon reading by the river.

Rather than slogging it up the highway, retrace your final steps at the end of Day 13 until, almost at the entry to the national park and with about half an hour's walking behind you, rejoin the GR11. Take the left fork, which soon brings you to the Puente de los Navarros.

At **Puente de los Navarros** (1045m), the bridge just to the west of the barrier marking the park entrance, the GR briefly takes the left fork up into the hills, rejoining the Ara valley at **Puente de Santa Elena**. However, unless you're particularly keen to slip in an extra gradient – and a brief, easily negotiated passage where you traverse while grabbing a chain – you'll save both time and energy by following the 4WD track that runs parallel to the Río Ara. It's a pleasant attractive walk northwards up Valle de Bujaruelo, sometimes the GR11 signs are hard to spot but if you follow the river you can't go wrong.

After 2.5km, where the track crosses the small Puente de Santa Elena (or Puente Nuevo), stay on the river's true left bank to take a charming footpath that leads through woodland to Bujaruelo.

Precisely 1.2km from Puente de Santa Elena, Puente de los Abetos leads to **Camping Valle de Bujaruelo** (☎ 974 48 63 48; www.campingvalledebujaruelo. com; camping per person/tent €4.50 each; Easter–mid-Oct). Alternatively, you can sleep in their **Refugio el Serbal** (d/t/q from €43/54/58). There's a bar, restaurant and a small shop (a good place to stock up if you've bypassed Torla).

A good option is to push on for a further 3km to Bujaruelo itself (1340m), a splendid spot where the valley broadens out. **Camping San Nicolás de Bujaruelo** (☎ 974 48 64 12; camping per person/tent €3.80/3.80; Easter-mid-Oct) is more spartan yet more walker-friendly. If there's no-one around, just pitch your tent and someone will turn up the next morning to collect the fee.

Beside the camping ground is **Mesón San Nicolás de Bujaruelo** (☎ 974 48 64 12; dm per person €12, dm half-board €29.95; d/quads per person half-board €38.65/32.65) on the site of what was once a hospital catering to pilgrims and travellers crossing into France by Puerto de Bujaruelo, also called Port de Gavarnie. Take time out before moving on to look at the ruins of the Romanesque chapel just behind the *mesón*. Though it's prudent to reserve ahead in July and August, the friendly manager will always squeeze you in (the Mesón record is 130 – in a place with a capacity of around 60 – one night when a Pyrenean storm raged and the adjacent camping ground was awash).

Also worthy of note if you've been high for several days and are beginning to smell the same way: the *mesón* and both the valley's camping grounds offer free hot showers.

Day 15: Bujaruelo to Balneario de Panticosa
6½–7½ hours, 18km

This route, following the GR11 tracing, is shorter, better marked and more popular than the Alternative Day 15 and arguably more varied. However, with a couple of substantial boulder fields to negotiate, it is, if anything, more difficult.

From Bujaruelo, the clearly marked GR11 route forms a sickle shape: straight up the Río Ara valley, then curving left to mount Barranco de Batans (de los Batanes). It then crosses the watershed at Cuello de Brazato and curls down to the spa resort of Balneario de Panticosa.

Cross Bujaruelo's fine single-arched stone bridge to follow the Río Ara's true left bank upstream – if, that is, you can resist taking a dip in the limpid blue pools.

At a T-junction, reached after about 20 minutes' walking, go right to take a 4WD track (left over the bridge is Alternative Day 15, p101) and follow it for 7.5km of gradual, effortless ascent of the Río Ara valley as far as the mouth of Barranco de Batáns at 2050m. The gorge narrows as you gain height. Just over the hour mark, there's a small cowherds' **refugio** (1640m) where the imposing Valle de Ordiso tumbles in from the west.

No more than 10 minutes later, cross a small col for the first breathtaking view of the imposing, unscaleable southwest face of Vignemale (3303m). From here on the landscape becomes altogether more rugged and alpine, but with an obvious path.

After a further hour, just beyond a second, spartan, cowherds' **refugio** and over a lateral moraine, the whole wide plain where Barranco Espelunz meets the main valley is a potential **campsite**.

Shortly after passing a solitary rain gauge about three hours from Bujaruelo, and with the cirque at the head of the valley already in view, stick to the river as the more distinct path heads away north to the frontier with France. Turn west just before a waterfall (it's the stream that you'll follow to its source going out with a splash as it tumbles into the beginnings of the Río Ara).

The trail climbs fairly gently, crossing the stream's true left bank after around 20 minutes. You're again among gritty granite boulders and slabs – hard nonporous rock where the water gurgles at surface level rather than percolating underground. The route soon shifts back to the right bank to avoid the worst of the chaos of boulder fields.

After passing the lowest of three small pools, it's boulder hopping for a good 20 minutes until you reach the top tarn. From here, the going underfoot, though scarcely smooth, eases as the path zigzags – sometimes in defiance of the GR's steeper, more punishing tracing – up to **Cuello de Brazato** (2578m), reached 1½ to 1¾ hours after leaving the Ara valley.

Immediately west of the pass keep well above the Ibóns de Brazato as you manoeuvre your way over more boulders and scree to cross a saddle and enjoy an easy yomp down to the head of **Embalse de Brazato**.

Balneario de Panticosa and its lake, though soon in sight, are still a good 1½ hours away. The trail from the dam head is even too easy, descending by long, shallow switchbacks that you'll be tempted to shortcut. There's no camping around the balneario so, about 30 minutes from Embalse de Brazato, where a giant wide-bore water pipe drops down the hillside from the north, you might want to detour a little off route to **camp** in a pleasant meadow with running water.

ALTERNATIVE DAY 15: BUJARUELO TO PANTICOSA VIA COLLADO DE TENDENERA

7½–8 hours, 23km

This alternative, but for a couple of tricky navigation points, is a day of clearly defined dirt paths with scarcely a stone to clamber over. You'll work hard as you ascend from Valle de Otal but, once over Collado de Tendenera, it's downhill all the way to Panticosa.

At the junction where Day 15 goes onto a 4WD track turn left to cross the river by Puente Oncins. Just over the bridge head west across a meadow for no more than 200m to pick up a vague trail marked by equally faint GR11 trail markers (the 'official' GR route now goes further north – see Day 15). As the trail enters evergreen wood and climbs southwestwards; navigation isn't easy. Once in open meadow again you'll probably lose the authentic

trail, overrun by new grass and competing cattle paths. However, if you keep on a southwest bearing and aim for **Collado de Otal** you shouldn't go wrong. If you do, extricate yourself by heading for the 4WD track (south), which describes a series of hairpin bends up the hillside.

Once over the col drop gently to the broad, grassy valley, through which the Río Otal snakes. Collado de Tendenera is obvious at the far, western end, flanked by its outriders, Pico de Tendenera (2853m) to the south and Pico de Mallaruego (2692m) to the north. From here it's easy, level striding on good-quality 4WD track to **Cabaña de Otal** – more cowshed than *refugio* but fine as an emergency shelter – reached after 1¼ to 1½ hours.

Continue due west and to the right of a small waterfall. Keep to the north (true left) bank of the stream that feeds it, passing a large metal rain gauge as you ascend to the head of the valley. Here the path veers north and climbs more steeply out of the bowl. About 50 minutes after the *cabaña*, beyond a metal sheepfold and before a multicoloured pole, follow the path, against all your instincts, as it turns back on itself and heads northeast, away from the col, for what seems an age.

Finally, after a good 25 minutes, the route turns sharply left beside a stream that crosses the main path. Overgrown and marked only by slowly decaying wooden pegs striped with the familiar red-and-white bars, it heads firmly northwest to become once more an evident path.

It's wild stuff up here. The rifts, whorls, bands and squashed contours of the rock become increasingly dramatic as you gain altitude in long arcs and there's not a sign of humanity except for the red-roofed *cabaña* below and the path at your feet. A little under an hour from the turn, at about 2200m, the trail passes over a small spring seeping from the rock just below the saddle. The grass here makes a cosy lunch spot or **campsite** if you've started the day south of Bujaruelo.

Collado de Tendenera (2325m) appears deceptively close but it takes another 20 minutes from the spring to reach the pass, where karst and sandstone meet. Take a last look east to where the border summit of Tallón (Taillon), at 3144m, guards Puerto de Bujaruelo, the nick you've had in view ever since the start of the day.

About 40 minutes below the col, pass a small *refugio* which sleeps four. There's water nearby and **camping** is possible if you beat down the long grass. Ten minutes later the path crosses to the true left bank of the stream it's been following, then veers away around a small bluff. Enjoy the unexpectedness of a magnificent view over the valley, through which the Río Ripera drains the cirque, and the giant wall of the Sierra de Tendenera. To the north juts the pronged peak of Balaitous (3151m) on the Franco-Spanish border.

After 15 minutes the path crosses the Río Ripera to meet a well-maintained 4WD track that mounts the valley. Some 20 minutes from the junction you pass a simple **refugio**, a possible overnight stop. From here on the challenges are over, the walking's simple and there remains only a considerable horizontal rather than vertical distance.

Some 10 minutes beyond the *refugio* the path crosses to the river's true right bank at a ford that may have you paddling when the river's in spate. A couple of minutes later it passes **Refugio de Ripera**, a spartan concrete block with capacity for six. From here on, the red-and-white flashes that, fresh or fading, have been around for most of the day, are supplemented by blue-and-white, then orange-and-white blazes as the path joins other trails coming up from Panticosa. Once it widens to become a track and makes a sharp left turn as the Arroyo Laulot stream comes in from the east it's an hour of fairly unexceptional walking to the *merendero* above Panticosa and a further 30 minutes into the village itself.

Once you hit the main road you have the option of hitching 5.5km up the road to Balneario de Panticosa (with a good *refugio*; for details, see the end of Day 15) so that you're poised for the next day's departure.

Day 16: Balneario de Panticosa to Refugio de Respomuso
6–6½ hours, 12km

The official GR11 handbook recommends a 21.5km marathon with more than 2500m of altitude change from Balneario de Panticosa to Sallent de Gállego, quoting an overly optimistic time of eight hours. We prefer to break the journey into one longish and one shorter day, staying overnight at the excellent Refugio de Respomuso with the possibility of camping nearby or breaking earlier to savour one of the fine **campsites** en route. Once you reach the *refugio* you could always race on downhill to Sallent de Gállego.

Leave Balneario de Panticosa by the path behind Casa de Piedra and head north up a well-established path, popular with day-walkers going to the Embalse de Bachimaña reservoirs. The progressively more splendid views back to the balneario and its lake compensates for the steepness of the ascent.

From the base of the **Cascada del Fraile** waterfall a series of steep zigzags leads to the head of the lower **Embalse de Bachimaña** (2180m), 1½ to 1¾ hours into the day. On the eastern shore of the reservoir are a pair of simple shelters and a potential **campsite**.

Towards the end of the reservoir's west shore, after passing a small island in the lake, there's a fork. Follow the GR11 as it ascends northwestwards and resist the temptation to stay on the evident, enticingly flat, track, which ends in nothingness at the lake's edge. On the opposite side of the lake you will see a soon to be completed new **refugio** which, once done and dusted, will offer an alternative finish to Day 15.

Ignoring the new *refugio* continue onwards and attack the steep 15 to 20-minute boulder clamber up to the lovely **Ibón Azul**. Unmarred by human construction and in a stunning setting below the Infierno and Piedrafita, which flank the obvious 'V' of Cuello del Infierno ahead, its lakeside meadows offer the best **campsite** east of the pass.

From the tarn allow an hour to reach **Cuello del Infierno** (Hell's Neck; 2721m), ascending through chaotic, fragmented rock where scarcely a blade of anything green grows. From the pass, nowhere near as hellish as its name implies, there are great views east over the lakes of Bachimaña and Bramatuero and over the often semi frozen Ibón de Tebarray, directly below you to the west.

Hell comes some 15 minutes later as you ease yourself over the rim of **Collado de Piedrafita** (2782m) to descend steeply on a slope of scree and shale where snow may persist until late summer. Negotiate this, curl around a shoulder, and heaven stretches before you: the bijou Ibón de Llena Cantal, a series of grassy, stepped meadows, and, glinting in the valley, Embalse de Respomuso.

Depending on conditions below the col (the tough stuff, brief in terms of distance, will take at least 15 minutes), it's around 45 minutes down to **Ibón de Llena Cantal** (2450m). On its east shore next to a striped pole is a **campsite** bordering on perfection.

Some 20 minutes of yomping descent over springy turf reaches a wide meadow and another five-star **campsite**. After a further 20 minutes there's scope for confusion as the GR11 splits both right and left around **Embalse de Respomuso** and a variant, marked in fading paint, goes straight ahead. For the Refugio de Respomuso the easiest way is to turn right on the level track to reach the *refugio* about 30 minutes later. The left-hand route takes you around the lake, much longer but maybe easier, this is also the route to take if you want to carry on to Sallent de Gallego avoiding a break at the *refugio*. On the other hand, if you want to **camp**, go straight ahead to the water meadows at the base of a small ridge running east-west as tents aren't allowed in the immediate environs of the *refugio*.

Refugio de Respomuso (2200m; ☎/fax 974 49 02 03; www.refugiosyalbergues .com; dm €15.50, dinner €14; May–mid-Dec), with draught beer, hot showers and Rioja and local Somontano wines, is a palace among mountain huts. The staff are friendliness itself and prices are *refugio* average. It's essential to reserve in July and August and advisable at other times since the place is often booked by groups.

Day 17: Refugio de Respomuso to Sallent de Gállego
3–3½ hours, 10km

The dam head, 15 minutes west of the *refugio*, is full of industrial detritus, abandoned after its construction. What's billed on the map as a *refugio* is now dilapidated and the chapel is locked – neither merit a detour. From a sign, 'La Sarra', head straight down the valley of the Río de Aguas Limpias on a good-quality path. It's a popular trail and, with under three hours to go on this, the very last leg

of the Pyrenean Traverse. You can have the satisfaction of acknowledging panting, overheated uphill toilers with a superior smile and a cheery, even-breathed greeting.

An hour from the dam the green bowl of **Llano Cheto** spreads out, watered by the twin cascades of the Río de Aguas Limpias and the Barranco de Arriel. At the narrows of **Paso del Onso**, around 1700m, the gorge bends south. The path tunnels through a fine wood of beech trees that offers the first real shade since above Balneario de Panticosa and harbours some attractive lunch spots.

Thirty to 40 minutes from Llano Cheto the track rounds a shoulder to reveal the wide meadows of **Llano Tornadizas** and the first distant glint of **Embalse de la Sarra**. Another 30 minutes brings you to the head of the dam, with a car park, picnic area and **Merendero la Sarra** (Jul-Sep), a bar-restaurant.

Take the reservoir's west bank, opposite the turbines of the hydroelectric station. At the dam head continue southwards along a sealed road then, about 10 minutes later, turn left and push your way down an overgrown path to the valley floor to meet a cart track that leads into **Sallent de Gállego** (1320m; see p128). Remove your boots and shed a tear of joy and sadness – it's time to head back to the traffic jams and chaos of the real world!

ANDORRA

Slip Andorra into the conversation and people will tell you, with horror or joy, that it's all skiing and shopping. They'll also probably add that it's a one-road, one-town ministate, its only highway, which links Spain and France, cutting a swathe through its only town, Andorra la Vella – which in turn is little more than a vast traffic jam bordered by cut-price temples to human greed.

They're right to a degree, but also very wrong. Free yourself from Andorra la Vella's tawdry embrace along good-quality secondary roads and you'll find villages as unspoilt as any in the Pyrenees. Despite the fact that Andorra, with a population of no more than 65,000 and an area of only 464 sq km, manages to absorb some eight million visitors a year, there are still areas where you can be completely alone. And Andorra's small, friendly tourist offices offer support that's second to none.

HISTORY

According to legend, Andorra was founded in around 784 AD by Emperor Charlemagne to thank the locals for guiding his troops through the mountains on their way to face the Arabs occupying the Spanish peninsula. Charlemagne's grandson granted the Valls d'Andorra (valleys of Andorra) to the count of Urgell from La Seu, further south in present-day Catalunya. He, in his turn, bequeathed the valleys to the local bishop of La Seu d'Urgell.

Following an obscure 13th-century dispute, a *modus vivendi* was established to share Andorra between the Catalan bishop and a feudal count over the French border. The contemporary consequence is that a very nominal suzerainty over Andorra – an independent state and member of the United Nations – is shared between France and Spain, whose governments only get upset if the smuggling, particularly of tobacco, gets out of hand.

Andorra is at the junction of two GR trails: the GR11, which links the Atlantic Ocean with the Mediterranean on the Spanish side of the Pyrenees, and the GR7, which runs from Lisbon all the way to the Black Sea.

ENVIRONMENT

Andorra's lines of communication are largely determined by its river valleys, which were created long before the cataclysms of successive ice ages. The principal river, the Riu Gran Valira, flows southwards into Spain. It's formed by the confluence of the Valira del Nord, which collects the headwaters of the catchment area around Soldeu; and the Valira d'Orient, fed by waters funnelled down the Arinsal and Ordino valleys.

PLANNING
Maps

Once in Andorra, pick up the excellent and highly detailed *Mutanyes D'Andorra* (1:10000) published by the Andorran government. Excellent for hiking and highly detailed, there are 14 of these, each covering a section of the principality. They are available in hiking shops and some supermarkets.

The 1:50,000 *Andorra & Cadi* map is produced by the French Rando Éditions with input from the Institut Cartogràfic de Catalunya. First issued in 2001, it's reliable and walker-friendly though some of the trails, indicated in firm red lines, are much less obvious on the ground. Unfortunately it's hard to come across in Andorra itself so snag a copy before you leave home.

Editorial Alpina covers the whole of the principality in one 1:40,000 map, *Andorra*, which gives a great overview, but be warned that not all paths are covered on this map, which can make things a little confusing!

Books

At tourist offices pick up the free booklet *Nature and Mountains* which contains

LA TRASHUMANCIA

Winter in the plains; summer in the mountains. As many a ruined *borda* or upland cabin eloquently tells, the annual migration of shepherds or cowherds and their animals is a dying – but far from dead – way of life.

It's estimated that around 150 families still depend upon the twice-yearly *anant de cabanera*, the migration to the mountains of some 100,000 sheep, the larger flocks with more than 4000 head. They follow centuries-old *camins ramaders*, tracks to the Pyrenees, nowadays sliced through by new roads, dams, housing estates and holiday developments.

In Aragón, too, there still exists a network of routes, known as *cabiñeras*. In spring and autumn, twice a year, the flocks are driven some 200km to and from the basin of the river Ebro, down in the plain, to the high alpine meadows of the Pyrenees.

A strange coincidence, the dates of departure – usually 24 June and 29 September – are, almost to the day, the opening and closing dates of mountain *refugios* for walkers. Is this merely obeying the weather or some deeper instinct?

various walks, mountain bike routes, climbing routes, plus nature and activity parks. The walk information would need to be supplemented with a detailed map.

Also at tourists offices the comprehensive *Mountain, Nature and Sports Guide* (€2), details everything from basic walking advice and trail safety to the animals, birds and flowers you might spot on the way. There are 25 walks detailed as well, but in scant detail.

Discovery Walking Guides *Walk Andorra!* by Charles Davis is easily available online before you leave and contains some thirty different walks.

Information Sources

For weather information see the national meteorology website www.meteo.ad.

GETTING AROUND

Ask at any tourist office for the free leaflet giving current timetables for the bus routes radiating from the capital, all run by **Cooperativa Interurbana** (☎ 806 555; www .interurbana.ad).

ACCESS TOWNS

See Canillo (p126), Andorra la Vella (p123) and Soldeu (p128).

BASSES DE LES SALAMANDRES

Duration 4¾–5¼ hours
Distance 12.5km
Difficulty moderate
Start/Finish Pont d'Incles
Nearest Town Soldeu (p128), Canillo (p126)
Transport bus
Summary A steep, semi-wooded climb from Vall d'Incles, a gentler ascent over open ground to four tarns, a lope down the Riu del Manegor valley and back along Vall d'Incles.

This walk gives you all the ingredients that make the Andorran experience: forest, mountain tarns, sheer rock formations, tumbling streams – and a gentle green valley to bring you home.

GETTING TO/FROM THE WALK

Walk out of Soldeu along the CG2 towards Canillo and Andorra la Vella. After 1km

you reach the bus stop (if you're coming from Canillo, hop off here) and tight bend at Pont d'Incles.

THE WALK

From the bus stop beside the CG2 at Pont d'Incles, 1km north of Soldeu, continue northwards along the narrow tarmac road that leads into Vall d'Incles to reach a sign, 'Roca de l'Home Dret', after 600m. Turn left to follow the yellow trail markers that lead you upwards beside a small stream and beyond a ruined *borda*.

After 20 to 25 minutes of fairly arduous uphill work through meadow and sparse forest the track veers southwest and levels out, offering fine views back to the head of Vall d'Incles, one of the prettiest valleys in all the Pyrenees. Follow the path as it curls around the flank of the mountain, maintaining a fairly steady height.

The path passes **Roca de l'Home Dret** (Straight or Upright Man), an isolated rock. After about 15 minutes' walking from the rock, the path drops down southeast briefly before continuing around the flank of the mountain in the welcome shade of a pine forest. Turn right to follow a sign, 'Estanys de Querol, de les Salamandres i dels Estanyons'. Continue uphill to another sign pointing to the right (northeast).

The trail crosses a broad meadow before the final shortish ascent to **Estany del Querol**, first of the pools, reached after 1½ to 1¾ hours of walking and an attractive spot for a breather.

Still heading northeast, pass another smaller pool that may be merely a peaty mire at the end of summer and push up to the twin **Basses de les Salamandres** (Salamander Pools), no more than 15 minutes beyond the first tarn.

Now comes the only piece of navigation that's in any way tricky: as the yellow blobs give out, head straight up a scarcely definable path to the top of the next ridge. Then, keeping a northeast bearing and dropping gently but not too significantly, work your way around the flank of the mountain until you intersect at right angles with a steep and more evident trail coming up from Vall d'Incles. There are several vague tracks to choose from, a few made by boots, most by the hooves of the wild horses that graze the

THE PYRENEES

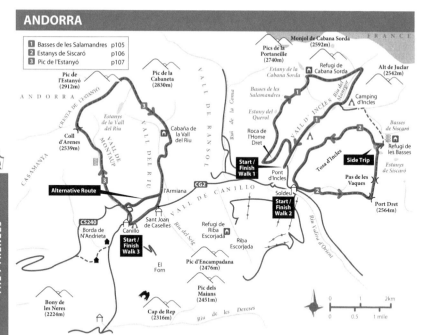

ANDORRA

1 Basses de les Salamandres p105
2 Estanys de Siscaró p106
3 Pic de l'Estanyó p107

lush summer grass. It really doesn't matter which one you select.

Once more guided by yellow circles, turn left (north) to follow a stream, soon crossing on stepping stones just downstream from a waterfall onto its true left bank to reach **Refugi de Cabana Sorda** (2295m), after a total walking time of 2¼ to 2½ hours. Just above the *refugio* is the pool of the same name, the biggest of the day, where you can replenish your water bottles, cool your feet and drink in the grandeur of the near sheer walls that enclose it.

From the *refugio*, strike east around the flank of Monjol de Cabana Sorda (2592m), now guided by red-and-yellow flashes. It's glorious walking of the kind you need towards day's end as the path descends gently through open meadow, then more abruptly to meet the narrow valley of the **Riu del Manegor**, some 45 minutes beyond the *refugio*.

Here the route describes a dog's leg, crossing to the true left bank of a gurgling beck. Once you reach Vall d'Incles, after some 20 minutes of easy descent, you can maintain a steady clip along the narrow,

lightly trafficked tarmac road. This follows the valley bottom, bringing you to the CG2 and your point of departure after 3km of easy walking. Alternatively, if you're staying in Soldeu, you can exit left along a signed cart track after 500m. This joins the last stage of the Estanys de Siscaró walk after 1km.

ESTANYS DE SISCARÓ

Duration 4–4½ hours
Distance 12km
Difficulty moderate
Start/Finish Soldeu (p128)
Transport bus
Summary A steep ascent to the col of Port Dret, brief level walking, then a short, precipitous drop to the Estanys de Siscaró, followed by woodland strolling around the flanks of the Tosa d'Incles.

We grade this walk moderate because of the steep ascent at the beginning of the day and the navigating required on the short stretch just before Port Dret.

You'll probably be walking alone for most of the day apart from the short section below the Estanys de Siscaró. These twin lakes are a popular spot for walkers who leave their vehicles beside Camping d'Incles at the end of the tarmac road.

THE WALK

At the head of the small lane beside Esports Calbó, an outdoor equipment shop on the main road near Soldeu's eastern limit, a sign reads 'Coma Bella, Clots de l'Os' and 'Port Dret'. Head straight up (not up the steps on the right) onto a path which flanks the top of Soldeu heading eastwards along the lane away from the village, following the clear yellow blazes. At a junction a little beyond a small farm, reached after about 10 minutes, keep left, following the main cart track. Beside a water tank opt for the narrow path that climbs beside the stream's true left bank, zigzagging its way up the mountainside in a generally easterly direction.

At a signpost, some 30 minutes from Soldeu, you have a choice: to go straight ahead, as the sign 'Estanys de Siscaró', beckons (rejoining the route at Pas de les Vaques) or, to turn right, following the sign 'Port Dret' for a more challenging variant.

Taking the Port Dret option, you enter a more open pine-stippled meadow about 10 minutes from the fork. Walk directly east up the lush turf above the tree line, still following reliable yellow blobs. When these peter out, keep heading consistently up the valley until you reach the pass at **Port Dret** (2564m), about 1½ hours from Soldeu. Once you've had your fill of the plunging vistas to the east, turn sharp left (north) along a clearly defined path to reach a second col, **Pas de les Vaques**, after 10 to 15 minutes of level walking. Identified by its giant cairn, it too offers a magnificent view of the twin lakes of the **Estanys de Siscaró**, like a pair of blue eyes gazing back at you.

It takes about 20 minutes of steep descent, guided by red-and-yellow markers, to reach the bank of the right-hand side of the eastern lake – an ideal spot for a breather or lunch break. The lakes take their name from the Catalan *siscall*, or glasswort, a rush-like plant that grows at their edges and in the flood plain below.

Leave the pool at its northern corner to drop steeply and beside the stream flowing from it towards the flood plain, **Basses de Siscaró**, and the tiny *refugio* of the same name in its northeast corner.

Around 10 minutes beyond the lake, and well before the valley bottom, strike left (northwest) to again pick up yellow trail markers. Less than 10 minutes later turn right as the path intersects with a more direct but less scenic variant dropping from the lakes. After intersecting with a path coming up from the *refugio* the trail enters woodland. Every now and again you'll catch glimpses of the Vall d'Incles below, but for the most part it's just you, the trees, and their welcome shade. Stick to the yellow trail markers – keep your gaze high since many of them are up on the trees – and you'll soon find yourself on an evident track. Threading its way through woodland, punctuated by clearings and streams, the track leads to a crossroads after about another hour of walking, where a sign points right to Incles and left to Soldeu. Turn left along the 4WD track to reach Soldeu around 30 minutes from the junction.

PIC DE L'ESTANYÓ

Duration 6½–7½ hours
Distance 15.5km
Difficulty demanding
Start/Finish Canillo (p126)
Transport bus
Summary An ascent to Coll d'Arenes, a scramble and clamber along Cresta de l'Estanyó to Pic de l'Estanyó, followed by a descent of Vall del Riu.

Make no mistake, this is a tough one that requires a good head for heights. The difficulty lies in the narrow (at times no more than 2m wide), jagged spine of the Cresta de l'Estanyó and in the length of the walk.

There's nothing we can do about the former but the route can be chopped quite neatly into less daunting sections. You can do the first and last sections of the walk, on either side of the crest, separately. Each is a pleasant up-and-down walk, of moderate difficulty, passing through meadows and beside *bordas*.

THE PYRENEES

The return trip to Coll d'Arenes takes four to 4½ hours, while an out-and-back walk to the lakes at the base of Pic de l'Estanyó takes six to 6¾ hours.

If you have wheels, you can drive up the CS240 for 4.6km and start the walk beside a sign for the Coll d'Arenes (see the walk description). There is nowhere to actually park here but continue along the road for another kilometre to a picnic area with limited parking. At the end of the walk head back to the highway from l'Armiana, thus saving yourself about 1¼ hours of walking.

PLANNING
Don't attempt the Cresta de l'Estanyó ridge on a wet day, when the slippery rock can be treacherous. If you're planning to do the ridge, keep your day pack light in case the wind throws you off balance. Check the weather forecast before setting out!

THE WALK
Walk up Carrer Major, 25m east of the tourist office in Canillo, pass beside Esglesia de Sant Cerni, the parish church, and continue up a track beside a stream. The route, which is a bit of a scramble, is clearly indicated with yellow circles. It crosses the CS240 and hugs the stream, which you'll be following almost to its source. After 30 to 35 minutes of steady ascent the route rejoins the road at a sign, 'Coll d'Arenes'.

The path zigzags up the east flank of Vall de Montaup to a stone building, where you turn left along a grassy cart track. Just beyond a second *borda* bear right along a blazed path. This rises gently to reach a series of waterfalls at a point where the valley closes in and becomes decidedly steeper.

About 45 minutes from the road you round a bend to enter a vast green amphitheatre. Just beyond a locked well a faint path climbs parallel to and well to the right (east) of the tumbling stream. Just beyond a steep 10-minute clamber to a false col there's a deep, shady overhang where the path crosses the stream. Refill your bottles here or at the pipe just above – there's no more water until you reach a tarn beyond Pic de l'Estanyó.

Keep to the left (west) side of the valley above this false col and don't worry if you deviate from the yellow blobs; it's easy cross-country work up and over a couple

of shale fields to **Coll d'Arenes**, two to 2¼ hours from Canillo.

From the pass a smudge of a path leads due north around a knoll, then veers right (northeast) towards the ridge. Don't worry if you lose the sparse, low cairns; keep a northerly bearing and you're bound to hit the ridge about 15 minutes from the pass. On the ridge, progress is *very* slow because of the jagged, friable rock but it's worth all the effort for the spectacular, changing views of the length and breadth of the principality and on into Spain and France. After a large cairn and a saddle that drops away to the east you can briefly pick up the pace by walking parallel to the cliff edge. But after a second small peak you're again gingerly picking your way along the knife-edge crest with the pools of the Estanys de la Vall del Riu now below to the southeast.

At the summit of **Pic de l'Estanyó** (allow up to 1½ hours from Coll d'Arenes) leave a slip of paper with your name in the sturdy metal box tucked into the rocks, as so many before you have done. To the southeast is the pine-clad valley through which you'll pass on the return to Canillo. Your immediate landmark, however, is a small tarn below and almost due east of the peak (at the end of a particularly dry summer this may be no more than a stain of darker grass). Follow the ridge until the first small breach (about 10 minutes from the peak), where you turn right to head down into the bowl in which the tarn nestles.

About five minutes beyond the tarn cross eastwards over a minor ridge to meet a pair of more substantial pools. On the far, southern shore of either, you'll pick up the yellow trail markers of the signed route connecting Canillo with L'Armiana, the largest of the pools that are known collectively as the Estanys de la Vall del Riu. From here on the route is again impeccably signed in yellow, in contrast with the inadequate marking as you descended from the ridge. High on the eastern flank of Vall del Riu the small Cabaña de la Vall del Riu is visible, still around 45 minutes away.

After the last of the day's boulder fields comes a brief squelch through the marshy headwaters of the river that tumbles down into the main valley. Follow the east side of the valley to pass by **Cabaña de la Vall del Riu** (2160m), an unstaffed *refugio*, something over 1½ hours from Pic d'Estanyó.

After a stretch of easy walking across a meadow turn *sharp* right at a sign, 'L'Aldosa Armiana, Canillo' (don't be seduced by the yellow dots bearing away right – they will lead you to the neighbouring Vall de Ransol). Some five minutes later pass to the right of an intact *borda*. The path descends fairly gradually and via a series of zigzags to cross the torrent by a wooden bridge.

The route curls gently westwards around the hill, leaving the stream to plunge away below. Savour the day's first extended stretch of near-level progress (that scramble along the ridge excepted!) until, about 20 minutes beyond the bridge, you meet a dirt road beside the abandoned houses of L'Armiana. If you've left your vehicle beside the CS240, continue along this road for 15 minutes to meet the highway, then turn right to recover it.

Otherwise, take the faint path that drops to the left and passes through the hamlet to make its way down to the CG2, debouching about 30 minutes later opposite the church of Sant Joan de Caselles, from where it's a 15 minute walk back to Canillo.

PARC NACIONAL D'AIGÜESTORTES I ESTANY DE SANT MAURICI

This national park is one of only two in the Spanish Pyrenees (the other being Parque Nacional de Ordesa y Monte Perdido). Despite its relatively small area (20km from east to west and a mere 9km from north to south), it sparkles with more than 50 lakes and tarns and includes some of the Pyrenees' most stunning scenery. The national park lies at the core of a wider wilderness area whose outer limit is known as the *zona periférica* and includes some magnificent high country to the north and south.

The park offers enough challenge and variety for a week or more of hiking along its numerous trails.

HISTORY
According to a well-attested story (see the boxed text, The General's Will, p110) it was by order of Generalissimo Franco himself that, in 1955, the area was declared a national park. It was expanded in 1996 to incorporate an additional 3890 hectares, so that its total area including the buffer zone is now 408 sq km.

ENVIRONMENT
The original granite and slate relief, now modified out of all recognition, was laid down some 200 million years ago during the Primary era. But, as elsewhere in the Pyrenees, it was the grinding, chewing, scraping action of glaciers during the successive ice ages of the Quaternary period that lent the landscape its present shape – its cirques and corries, scoured U-shaped glens and hanging valleys.

PLANNING
Maps & Books
The Rando Éditions/ICC 1:50,000 *Pica d'Estats Aneto* map gives complete and reliable coverage for the area.

Editorial Alpina 1:25000 *Parc Nacional d'Aigüestortes i Estany de Sant Maurici* is a two-maps-for-the-price-of-one deal. It's compact, and shows the all of the routes within the whole of the national park. It can be purchased for €10.

Also available from Editorial Alpina is the 1:25000 *Saint Maurici els entatats* map. This is actually just the Aigüestortes map from the double pack mentioned above, but if you buy it alone it comes with a very comprehensive guide to the park in English, containing everything from points of interest to walking itineraries.

The ICC map *Parc Nacional D'Aigüestortes i Estany de Sant Maurici* (1:25000) is an exceptionally detailed and easy-to-read map, available from tourist offices at €10. It's excellent for planning walks, but perhaps a little unwieldy for use out on the trail.

The Spanish government also publishes a 1:2500 scale map for €10, *Aigestortes i Estany De Sant Maurici*, available at park information offices.

Also available everywhere, in several different languages, is a leaflet *Aigestortes i Estany De Sant Maurici*, published by the

Spanish government, it gives an overview map of the park, and contains a wealth of information about the park, from its history to the flora and fauna within.

The book *Gina Alpina Aigüestortes Saint Maurici* (€20) contains a wealth of detailed information about the park for walkers, but is unfortunately only available in Spanish at the time of writing.

Visitors Guide to the National Park of Aigüestortes i Estany de Sant Maurici, sold at the national park information offices, gives impressively detailed information on the area's plants, animals and ecosystems – and also describes 25 walking trails within its boundaries.

Information Sources

Espot and Boí (see p125) both have park information offices. To reach the website of the park go to www.mma.es /parques/lared/aigues.

Refugios & Camping

There are six *refugios* in the park proper and another six within the *zona periferica*. The map Editorial Alpina 1:50000 *Parc Nacional d'Aigüestortes i Estany de Sant Maurici* has the names and phone numbers of each inside its cover, complete with web addresses where available. Most tend to be full by 3pm in July and August and we strongly recommend that you ring in advance to reserve. The overnight fee is €10 to €11 and meals are generally in the region of €11 to €12. Most keep a wing open for walkers and ski trekkers year-round but are only staffed between mid-June and mid-September.

Officially camping is not allowed in the park.

ACCESS TOWN

Espot (p126) is the best base for these walks.

ESTANY LLONG

Duration 5½–6 hours

Distance 17km

Difficulty easy–moderate

Start/Finish Estany de Sant Maurici

Nearest Town Espot (p126)

Transport taxi, bus

Summary A lake-to-lake traverse of the park along a classic route, with magnificent views from the intervening pass of Portarró d'Espot.

Crossing the park from east to west, this is a classic walk not only because of the spectacular scenery but also for its antiquity.

In medieval times the trail was a conduit for goods, people and animals travelling between the lands of the Count of Pallars in the east and those of the fiefdom of Erill to the west. In the first half of this century it became a fashionable leisure route as visitors, marvelling at the splendour of what the locals took for granted, rode on horseback between Espot and the small thermal spa of Caldes de Boí. Nowadays, it's closed to all motor traffic.

Most walkers do this route as a return trip in a day. It's also possible to stay

THE GENERAL'S WILL

In the early 1950s there was a flurry in the valleys when it was announced that no less a dignitary than General Franco himself would be paying a visit to inaugurate a couple of hydroelectric projects. For the first time in its long history, the track between the Estany de Sant Maurici and Aigüestortes was rolled and graded, while liberal quantities of whitewash were splashed around.

The cortège swept by. The general – a keen fly fisherman when cares of state allowed – was so impressed by the spectacle from the smart new road that he ordered the creation of Parc Nacional d'Aigüestortes i Estany de Sant Maurici, which was duly inaugurated in 1955.

Once the dust from the cavalcade had settled the road scarcely saw another vehicle. Eaten away by ice, sleet and rain, used again but briefly for equestrian outings, it was formally closed to all motorised traffic in 1995. Nowadays, there are still lingering traces of the general's route, but in a decade or two all evidence will be lost and nature will have reclaimed its own.

ESTANY DE SANT MAURICI

If you'd prefer to avoid the trip to and from Espot, it's possible to stay at the very friendly **Refugi de Ernest Mallafré** (1885m; ☎ 973 25 01 18) just above Estany de Sant Maurici, which accommodates up to 24 people. However, amazingly for so principal and long established a *refugio*, there's no shower, washbasin, or even the basic comfort of a squat toilet. If you can't bear to go *au naturale* however, there is an interesting earthworm powered public toilet 10 minutes walk away at the lake.

From Espot, you can undertake an agreeable walk (two hours, 8km) to Estany de Sant Maurici. However, many walkers prefer to save their energy for the even more spectacular scenery within the park and invest in a 4WD taxi ride (€4.85 one way, €9.70 return) as far as the lake (last descent 7pm). Taxis usually wait to leave until they're full. If you're short of time, and want to shortcut the walks, the taxis can take you pretty much to anywhere you might like to go in the park – see the taxi rank on the main street for itineraries. You can drive your own car as far as the barrier and parking area at Prat de Pierró (1640m), an hour's pleasant walk below the lake.

overnight at Refugi d'Estany Llong (advance reservations essential) or continue via Aigüestortes to Boí (see p125), about 9km further along the trail.

THE WALK

From the parking area at Prat De Pierro, take a right following the boardwalk signposted to Estany de Sant Maurici. Follow the well signposted path and a few minutes after passing the **Ermita de Sant Maurici**, turn left at the fork signposted Refugi de Ernest Mallafre.

From Refugi de Ernest Mallafré follow the sign to Monestro Sebenuix, ignoring the signs back to the lake. At the next fork turn right, signposted Subenuix and Potarro d'Espot, which takes you above and around the south side of Estany de Sant Maurici and through mixed wood of beech, birch and ash plus pine and fir. About 45 minutes out, the track passes a turn-off on the right to the Mirador de l'Estany lookout and then swings west, following and occasionally crossing the stream which tumbles down from the **Portarró d'Espot** pass (2425m).

It's worth pausing at the col to savour the views. To the west is **Estany Llong** (2000m), 3.5km and about one hour's steep descent away. The route here, as throughout the walk, is easy to distinguish.

At the western end of the lake is **Refugi d'Estany Llong** (2000m; ☎ 629 374652), the only *refugio* run by the national park authority. With capacity for only 36, reservations are essential. The *refugi* serves

meals, snacks and drinks, it also makes a pleasant rest stop before the return trip.

If you still have energy, consider continuing for a further 1½ to two hours as far as the particularly fine scenery at Aigüestortes.

At Aigüestortes, you can pick up a 4WD taxi which will take you as far as Boí, from where you can head out of the valley to Lleida by bus.

REFUGI DE COLOMINA

Duration 2 days

Distance 22km

Difficulty moderate–demanding

Start Estany de Sant Maurici

Finish Espot (p126)

Transport taxi, bus

Summary Easy walking to Estany de Monestero before the gradient increases, culminating in a steep final clamber to Coll de Peguera, then downhill all the way to Refugi de Colomina; return to the Riu Escrita valley via Collada de Saburó.

This walk is graded moderate to demanding due to the very steep ascent to Coll de Peguera.

A return trip of about 2½ hours as far as Estany de Monestero makes an easy, scenic option. Alternatively, you can stretch yourself a little more, add on another 1½ hours to the walk and continue to the cirque at the head of the Riu de Monestero valley before turning back.

PARC NACIONAL D'AIGÜESTORTES I ESTANY DE SANT MAURICI

See The Pyrenean Traverse – Map A p74

1 Estany Llong	p110
2 Refugi de Colomina	p111
3 Port de Ratera d'Espot	p113

THE WALK
Day 1: Estany de Sant Maurici to Refugi de Colomina
5½–6 hours, 10km

From the signposted fork on the track leading up to the lake, turn left (south) towards Refugii de Ernest Mallfré. Pass by the *refugio* to follow the Riu de Monestero. Half an hour out, a length of boardwalk takes you over a marshy section. Don't worry; the higher you climb, the less tamed the land. In fact, up top a few more clues and signs of humanity would be positively welcome. Beyond a boulder field about an hour from the lake you pass a tiny pool to reach **Estany de Monestero** (2170m) and, beyond it, a glorious, open alpine meadow.

Climbing gently along the true left bank of a stream which flows into Estany de Monestero, thread your way through another jumble of truly huge boulders (the massive square one marks an end to the scrambling), eventually crossing the stream to the true right bank.

Once you reach the cirque at the head of the valley the path climbs south-southeast. Stick to the east side of the bowl, resisting the temptation to head for the middle, which appears less arduous. Over the lip of a false col, reached after two to 2¼ hours, descend to a large, arid basin. Here begins the much steeper ascent to **Coll de Peguera** (2726m) between **Pic de Peguera** (2982m) and **Pic de Mar** (2803m) to its west.

THE WAR THAT WENT ON

It looks like the ruins of a fine baroque chapel, up there on the hillside above the Estany de Sant Maurici. In fact, until the 1960s it used to be a military barracks. Why, you may ask, in remote country not far from the frontier with a friendly neighbour and with no major population centre nearer than Lleida, several hours drive away, would anyone want to build barracks?

Their origins relate to the end of both the Spanish Civil War and WWII. In 1939, defeated Republicans and their families streamed across the passes into France. After 1945 Republicans returned and infiltrated the valleys along the frontier to mount a limited guerrilla struggle, which was savagely suppressed by the victorious Nationalist army. For a brief time, the *guerrilleros* (guerrillas) controlled Vall d'Aran and large areas of what is now the national park.

The barracks were constructed to drive out the Republican bands and cow the valleys' residents lest they be tempted to give support to the distant, lost Republican cause.

From the col, follow a sign to Refugi de Colomina and walk southwards to **Estany de Saburó**. Either take the path along the lake's western bank, which is steep yet stepped, or, for a less demanding alternative, pass close to the eastern shore of Estany Xic de Saburó.

Past the west shores of Estany de Mar and Estany de Colomina (2408m), is **Refugi de Colomina** (2395m; ☎ 973 25 20 00; mid-Jun–Oct) less than an hour's walking from Estany Xic de Saburó. This wooden *refugio* has 40 places and serves meals and drinks. If you prefer camping descend to Estany Tort, a short distance to the west, which has plenty of **campsites**.

Also near the electricity generating station, 1.8km below the village, is **Hostal Leo** (☎ 973 66 31 57), about which readers have reported very positively.

Day 2: Refugi de Colomina to Espot
5–5½ hours, 12km
You can retrace your steps over Coll de Peguera or vary the journey by crossing back into the main valley via Collada de Saburó.

The latter route is a variant of the GR11 and is well marked with red-and-white bars. Head east from the *refugio* and then swing northeast to follow the west bank of both Estany de Colomina and Estany de Mar. After ascending a steep gully pass a ruined building and descend to the dam head of **Estany de Saburó**; cross over. Curl around the lake and climb to **Collada de Saburó** (2670m) at the national park border.

Pass by three small lakes before dropping to **Estany Negre**. Once across the dam head, take a path that leads off north. From it a short detour leads left to **Refugi de Josep M Blanc** (2350m; ☎ 973 25 01 08), with capacity for 40 and normally full. Here you can get a drink or snack.

Continue until you reach another small lake and a forest *refugio* (not open to the public), from where the path descends in parallel with the Riu de Peguera to emerge on the sealed road on the outskirts of Espot.

PORT DE RATERA D'ESPOT

Duration 4½–5 hours
Distance 14.5km
Difficulty moderate
Start/Finish Estany de Sant Maurici
Nearest Town Espot (p126)
Transport taxi, bus
Summary Superb views as you leave the crowds behind, taking in Estany de Ratera, the lake and *refugio* of Estany Gran d'Amitges and Port de Ratera de Colomers; return via Mirador de l'Estany.

This circular route follows the early part of Day 1 of the Pyrenean Traverse, diverging to take in the three Estanys d'Amitges on the outbound leg and Mirador de l'Estany on the way back.

THE WALK
Follow Day 1 of the Pyrenean Traverse (p75) from Estany de Sant Maurici as far

as the instruction which reads 'at a fork soon after…**Estany de Ratera**…choose the left option'.

Here, if you fancy nothing more taxing than an easy 2½-hour stroll, keep left to pass by Mirador de l'Estany and return by the south bank of Estany de Sant Maurici. Otherwise, go right in the direction of the *refugio*. Now you'll be climbing more steeply, and the track nudges out of a pine forest to enter a rocky world with an occasional isolated copse of trees. Stay with the 4WD track to Estany Gran d'Amitges, the largest of a series of three tarns, behind which rise the spiky Agulles d'Amitges, the twin Pics de Bassiero and Tuc de Saboredo.

No more than 212m of vertical distance separate the shores of lakes Ratera and Amitges but the contrast between the former's pine-clad charm and the latter's harsh, denuded splendour is total.

The **Refugi d'Amitges** (2380m; ☎ 973 25 01 09; www.amitges.com; dm €15) beside **Estany Gran d'Amitges** (2362m), about 1½ hours from the start, is a popular overnight spot with spaces for 66. It does meals (€16.50), snacks and drinks and makes a congenial rest stop. A trail leads from it between the two upper lakes and across scree (here lies the only difficulty in what would otherwise be an easy walk). Continue up to **Port de Ratera d'Espot**, which you reach after a little less than another hour. At this point the trail rejoins Day 1 of the Pyrenean Traverse. It's well worth following it for another 10 minutes or so along the saddle as far as **Port de Ratera de Colomers**, from where there are great views of the necklace of lakes falling away to the southwest.

Returning to Port de Ratera d'Espot, take the Day 1 route in reverse around **Estanyet del Port de Ratera** and follow it until it rejoins the main track. You've now come full circle. One hundred metres beyond, where the paths meet, turn right to **Mirador de l'Estany** with its sweeping vistas of the mountains reflected in Estany de Sant Maurici. Continue along and you'll soon reach the trans-park route that links Estany Llong with Sant Maurici. Turn left along this path and return by the south bank of Estany de Sant Maurici to the point of departure.

WATER WORLD

Duration 6 hours
Distance 19km
Difficulty moderate
Start/Finish Parking Plan des Banhs
Nearest Town Salardu (p127)
Transport Taxi
Summary A magnificent loop past dozens of glowing alpine lakes with a scramble to a high and windy pass thrown in for good measure.

Put simply this is the Pyrenees at its best. This wonderful loop, which takes you over a rocky pass at the foot of Tuc del Grand Colomers, is a head-first plunge into a watery world of lakes, big and small and each more stunning than the last.

The whole circuit takes place just beyond the borders of the national park proper, but within the fringing, and still highly protected, buffer zone. It can be turned into a superb side trip between Day 1 and 2 of the Pyrenean Traverse or used as an extension of the Port de Ratera d'Espot walk (p113).

GETTING TO/FROM THE WALK
From Salardu drive down the narrow road to the Banhs de Tredos for 8km to the Parking Plan des Banhs where you have to leave your car and hop in one of the **taxis** (9am-6.30pm; €4 return; departures every few minutes in season), which drop you at the trailhead.

THE WALK
From the point at which the taxi drops you take the sign posted route left, and upwards through the forest towards the Refugi des Colomers. After seven or eight minutes the track emerges out onto a grassy plateau carpeted in riotous wild flowers in spring and early summer and also the first of the many lakes. It looks nice doesn't it? Trust us, this isn't anything! Follow the obvious path away from the lake and uphill where you'll start to get your first views of the dam wall of the **Estany Major de Colomers**, the path gets a little confusing at this point but as they all end up in the same place it doesn't make too much difference which

one you take, but make sure you end up on the left-hand (south) side of the dam wall where there's a small hut (rather than the right side where Refugi des Colomers gives those engaged in the Pyrenean Traverse a place to rest weary feet at the end of Day 1). At the foot of the dam wall the path veers off left (east) and is sign posted for Estany Obago. You're now following the red-and-white trail slashes of the GR11. The path climbs steeply up towards a gap between two small peaks from which you get a marvellous view of a picture-perfect lake surrounded by lush green grass just below (a thin path veers off the main route down to the lakeshore). Sticking with the main path you descend and then, a few minutes later, hit the aptly named **Estany Long**, which is a perfect picnic spot.

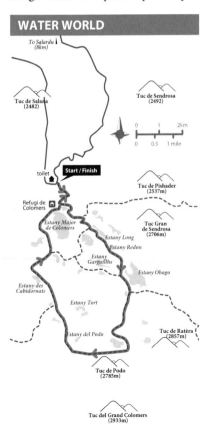

WATER WORLD

To Salardu (8km)

Tuc de Salana (2482)

Tuc de Sendrosa (2492)

0   1   2km
0   0.5   1 mile

toilet

Start / Finish

Refugi de Colomers

Estany Major de Colomers

Tuc de Pishader (2537m)

Tuc Gran de Sendrosa (2706m)

Estany Long

Estany Redon

Estany Gargullhs

Estany Obago

Estany des Cabidornats

Estany Tort

Estany del Podo

Tuc de Ratèra (2857m)

Tuc de Podo (2785m)

Tuc del Grand Colomers (2933m)

Continue along the right-hand bank of the lake to the head of the valley. Almost immediately after leaving Estang Long you arrive at the divine **Estany Redon** which again you pass by on the right bank, climb gently up a hill in a southeast direction toward **Estany Obago**.

As you approach the northern, furthest, end of Estany Obago the track forks with the GR11 branching off to the left and the route you want, which is marked with red paint splotches, veering off right and climbing to a low pass. Just beyond the pass you skip past a tiny baby-sized lake, cross a stream and continue upwards in a southerly direction. By now the flowery, green landscape of lower down has given way to one that is much more barren and boulder strewn. After fifteen minutes scrambling upwards you reach a deep blue L-shaped lake sitting at the base of tall mountain peak and flecked with snow year-round. Head around the left (east) side of the lake and continue to climb to a final rise and **Estany del Podu** pops into view. Rounding the easterly side of the lake and crossing the stream you then start to climb, and climb, and climb, all the while following the red paint markers. After a hard 30-minute climb in which both feet and hands are needed you make it to the col (2607m) at the base of **Tuc de Podu** (2785m) and are rewarded with enormous views of surrounding peaks including **Tuc del Grand Colomers** (2933m). From here on it's downhill all the way.

Clamber down off the other side of the col in a westerly direction, pass a little lake off to your left (south) and start to drop off the mountainside towards the ribbon of lakes in front of you. Be a bit careful around here as the red marker paint splotches have faded quite badly and are hard to see among the tumbling rocky landscape. It's actually easier to see those painted on the back of rocks intended for people going the other way around this loop. Look out also for the small rock cairns, but you're basically heading in a west southwest direction towards the small L-shaped lake. After an hour of steep, leg-jarring descent from the col things calm down a bit, grass and meadows start to replace rocks and boulders and the path becomes much more obvious again.

THE PYRENEES

You should now be walking in a north northwest direction. Fifteen minutes later and you come to the deep blue **Estany des Cabidornats**, easily one of the more sublime lakes, it sits in a big bowl surrounded by glowing grasslands. You pass by on the right hand side (east) of the lake and the trail is now very obvious. Continuing steeply downhill you meet up with the river that exits this lake and a series of beautiful waterfalls. At the base of these falls you must cross the river, using some stepping stones, so that the river is now on your right and you're on the western side of the river – attention: it's easy to go wrong here as another trail continues downwards on the wrong side of the river.

Finally, 35 minutes beyond Estany des Cabidornats, the Estany Major de Colomers that we passed at the start of the day comes back into view. The path now descends very steeply towards it – at one point it drops so much that a chain has been attached to the cliff wall to help ease you down (not as scary as it sounds!) a couple of metres. The path now works its way along the western edge of the lake and passes by the Refugi des Colomers where you rejoin the path back to the taxi drop off point.

THE ARAGONESE PYRENEES & PARQUE NACIONAL DE ORDESA Y MONTE PERDIDO

West of Catalunya lies Aragón, the land of the giants, within whose limits are Days 4 to 17 of the Pyrenean Traverse (see p73). Of the 12 tallest peaks in peninsular Spain, 10 rear up from Aragón. Three of these mountains – Pico de Aneto, Pico de Posets and Pico de Monte Perdido – are within easy reach of the Pyrenean Traverse (see p73) – though whether their summits are within easy reach of you is a challenge only you can answer.

If peak bagging and glacial heights leave you cold, there are also plenty of gentle valley walks to enjoy. This is tough country, however, with challenging passes between each valley and the probability of snow underfoot late into summer.

The rock subtly changes as you progress towards the setting sun. The upper Noguera Ribagorçana valley is a mix of shale and slate. Further west, the original granite bedrock is seen more frequently, especially around the Maladeta and Posets region. In some areas, such as Parque Nacional de Ordesa y Monte Perdido, bedrock is overlaid or cut through by limestone, with its characteristic underground rivers, potholes and caves.

But nothing is regular or ordered. The clash of the European and Iberian tectonic plates and later upheavals on a scale difficult to grasp have left the land folded, crumpled and profoundly askew.

To both east and west, Benasque is surrounded by Parque Posets-Maladeta. Established in 1994, the park contains 13 glaciers, the Pyrenees' highest peak (Pico de Aneto) – and about 2000 varieties of plants.

PLANNING
Maps
Rando Éditions 1:50,000 *Aneto-Posets* and *Gavarnie & Ordesa* maps are good bets as are the much more detailed Editorial Alpina's 1:25,000 *Maladeta-Aneto* and *Ordesa y Monte Perdido* maps. Harder to find is Prames' 1:40,000 *Ribagorza* map.

Books
Twelve signed walks around the Benasque region, ranging in length from 2km to 20km, are summarised in a free, bilingual leaflet, *Valle de Benasque: El Placer de Caminar (The Pleasure of Walking)*, available from the town's tourist office.

ACCESS TOWNS
For a pleasant and well-appointed base in the heart of the Aragonese Pyrenees, head for Benasque (see p124). The Parque Posets-Maladeta visitors centre is here. Parzán (p127) also makes an excellent base for walks around the Parque Nacional Ordesa y Monte Perdido.

FRONTIER RIDGE

Duration 3½ hours

Distance 9km

Difficulty easy–moderate

Start/Finish La Besurta

Nearest Town Benasque (p124)

Transport bus

Summary An ascent to Portillón de Benasque by a *camino*, easy traverse along the base of Pico de la Mina and a descent to La Besurta via the more westerly of the two Lagos de Villamorta.

You can make this stunning traipse along the Spanish–French frontier a modular day. To the basic walk of around 3½ hours you can graft on two side trips, described on p118.

GETTING TO/FROM THE WALK

For transport between Benasque and La Besurta, see Day 6 of the Pyrenean Traverse (p89).

THE WALK

From the bus stop 300m below La Besurta head northwards up the hill along a faint trail. After 15 minutes a better-defined track comes in from the left. This is the old and, in its time, much-travelled historical link between the Ésera valley and that of

Aran. These days, it's a *ruta hípica*, or pony trekking trail (signalled by red-tipped posts), that leads to Port de la Picada and on to Vall d'Aran or into France.

Continue up the trail in a series of fairly gentle zigzags for 40 to 50 minutes until you arrive at a junction, indicated by a pair of *ruta hípica* signs. Don't be seduced into following them and taking the path which heads northeast straight towards Port de la Picada. Instead, continue zigzagging towards **Portillón de Benasque** (2444m), now clearly in view and sitting snug between the twin masses of **Tuc de Salvaguarda** (2738m) and **Pico de la Mina** (2707m). After skirting a reedy tarn you should reach the pass about 1½ hours after setting out.

Surprisingly, there's little to see beyond the windy gap (for more spectacular views, see the two side trips on p118). You can, however, clearly identify the path threading eastwards from some ruined huts at the base of Portillón de Benasque. Marked '23' (it's part of a French trail that sneaks over the border), the path heads in a dead straight line over bare rock and scree to **Port de la Picada** (2470m), your next port of call, still some 45 minutes away, where you stand a very good chance of seeing eagles wheeling overhead.

If you're in the mood for a longer walk, 20 minutes down a trail from Port de la Picada brings you to Collado del Infierno.

THE ARAGONESE PYRENEES

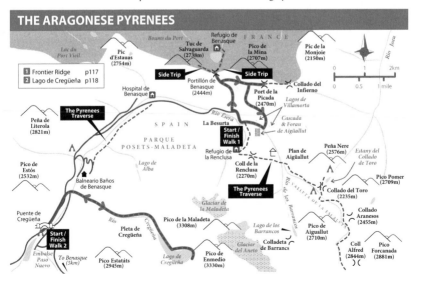

1 Frontier Ridge   p117
2 Lago de Cregüeña   p118

Turning back towards home from Port de la Picada, bear left (down and south), passing to the east of a small tarn. As you descend look out for the lower (nearer) of the two **Lagos de Villamorta**. Turn left (southeast) beside a medium-sized cairn onto a secondary trail. After passing a stony section flanked by stunted pine trees skirt the lower Villamorta pond on its south side. Beyond it the path is virtually invisible, but keep due south and within 10 minutes you should meet the stone 'stairs' on the main track linking the Plan d'Aiguallut and La Besurta, reached about 1¼ hours after leaving Port de la Picada.

SIDE TRIP: TUC DE SALVAGUARDA
1½ hours, 3km

For spectacular views in all directions, take the evident side trail from Portillón de Benasque to the summit of **Tuc de Salvaguarda** (2738m) to the west. It's much less daunting than the sight of spindly figures of other walkers against what appears to be a razor-edge ridge would have you believe.

SIDE TRIP: REFUGIO DE BENASQUE
1¼–1½ hours, 2.5km

Less strenuously, it's worth continuing beyond Portillón de Benasque, down into France, for a drink or a snack at the small, staffed **Refugio de Benasque** (2249m) run by the Club Alpin Français. It's in a glorious setting at the northeast tip of the first of three lakes called the Boums du Port. It is, however, substantially further than the 15 minutes claimed by a sign at the col.

LAGO DE CREGÜEÑA

Duration 5–5½ hours
Distance 11km
Difficulty moderate
Start/Finish Puente de Cregüeña
Nearest Town Benasque (p124)
Transport bus
Summary As the route ascends woodland briefly becomes plain before the steep climb resumes towards to the stark, rocky bowl in which the Lago de Cregüeña nestles.

An exhilarating ascent to the Pyrenees' third biggest lake, you'll cover steep, then flat,

then very steep and technical terrain;but the payoff is well worth the effort.

GETTING TO/FROM THE WALK

Take the shuttle bus that runs between Benasque and La Besurta (see Day 6 of the Pyrenean Traverse, p89) and ask to be dropped off at the Puente de Cregüeña bridge.

THE WALK

The path begins, wide and cairned, near Puente de Cregüeña, just off the main C139 highway between La Besurta and Benasque. It climbs, almost continuously and with little scope for error, all the way to Lago de Cregüeña. Following closely the course of the **Río Cregüeña**, it passes through shady woodland that opens out into a small plain, **Pleta de Cregüeña**, a brief, flattish respite before you attack the steeper and entirely rocky final 550m of altitude gain.

The western fingertip of the lake, which ranks as the third-largest (in terms of volume) in the Pyrenees, is only 3.5km from the Río Ésera as the eagle flies. All the same, the times we give are realistic as the ascent to the lake is steep (1200m over 11km). The setting, a savage cul-de-sac occasionally scaled by technical climbers aiming for the south face of Pico de la Maladeta, is ample compensation for the stiff climb. Return the way you came.

BUTTERFLY VALLEY

Duration 3½–4 hours
Distance 10km
Difficulty moderate
Start/Finish Parking Armeña, Barbaruens
Nearest Town Benasque (p124)
Transport car
Summary If you want to escape the crowds then this walk – through forests and meadows full of butterflies and onto a luminous green alpine lake – is hard to beat.

This dream-like walk to a beautiful secret lake is the stuff of postcards and of a thousand stories. Long after you've finished the walk and reluctantly farewelled the final butterfly, the images will stay with you.

GETTING TO/FROM THE WALK

There's no public transport whatsoever to the remote little village of Barbaruens. From Benasque drive southwest down the A139 to the village of Seira. Turn right onto the narrow country lane leading to Barbaruens and then, just as you enter the village swing hard left onto a dirt road (it's fine in a normal car) and drive for 3km to the fork in the road; take the left fork and carry on for a couple of hundred metres to the parking area.

THE WALK

From the parking area take the left (south) piste and follow it for around half an hour after which the piste turns into a narrow track through the pine trees. A hundred metres later you'll find yourself walking along the edge of a massive vertical cliff, that in wet and snowy conditions, when the path gets slippery, could send you very, very quickly down the mountain! It will be obvious that great care needs to be taken.

Twenty minutes later you move away from the vertigo cliffs and into a lightly forested glade with a gentle uphill ascent. There are several paths that all intermingle and twist and turn their way up the mountain but rock cairns should keep you on the right trail. The trail then moves back to the cliff edge and, if you weren't so busy watching your step, would provide marvellous views to the valley below.

This bit is especially dangerous in wet conditions as the rock here becomes lethally slippery in rain or snow. It can be quite changeable, so you should be prepared for bad weather regardless. The path alternates between steep ups and downs and passes over the debris of former landslides perilously close to the cliff edge. The final few hundred metres to the col are very steep and slippery – you will need poles for this part in bad weather.

The reward for this danger though is the grassy, flower filled **meadow** that greets you at the top of the col. The views of the surrounding mountains, including Cotiella (2912m), are astounding. This meadow is a truly blissful place with nothing but chirping birds and hundreds of colourful butterflies to disturb your contemplation of the mountains.

Follow the trail down into the bowl in the mountains where you'll catch your first glimpse of **Ibón d'Armeña**, a surreal green lake set among lush pastures and pine trees.

Pass along the southwest side of the lake (with the lake on your left) and enter a tranquil pine forest and areas of open meadow. Follow the trail in a northwest direction towards the **Refugio de Armeña** (four or five bunks, unstaffed) which you'll bump into in a gentle 20 minutes. The views through a gap in the mountains down to the fertile valleys far below from here are wonderful.

Take some time to enjoy the fruits of your toil and then return the way you came.

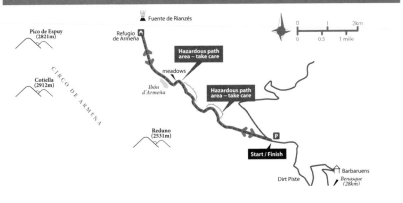

BUTTERFLY VALLEY

PUERTO DE BARROSA

Duration 5½ hours
Distance 19km
Difficulty moderate
Start/Finish Hospital de Parzán
Nearest Town Parzán (p127)
Transport car
Summary One of the finest day walks outside the national park, this route takes you up a river valley to the spectacular Circo de Barrosa and then up over a former smuggling track to a high ridge overlooking France.

If you're willing to navigate the demanding final section of this walk, you'll revel in the high-country companionship of marmots and chamois as well as soak in some spectacular views of France.

GETTING TO/FROM THE WALK

There's no public transport north of Parzán to the nearby trailhead at Hospital de Parzán, but hitching should be easy enough. In your own car head north of Parzán on the A138 and park in the small parking area by Hospital de Parzán.

THE WALK

This is a well waymarked and simple-to-follow walk, but its length, and a climb of 1154 metres makes it quite tough. Many people only go as far as the Refugio Barrosa, which would make the walk a family-friendly one of about three to four hours return.

From the car park follow the dirt piste uphill in a southerly direction. The path quickly starts zigzagging around and passes lots of remnants from the area's mining past. After 20 minutes of moderate upward climbing the valley suddenly opens out and you get your first view of the mountains up ahead. The walking gets easier as the path meanders through pine forest and along the banks of the **Río Barrosa** with lots of tempting toe-dipping spots. After an hour you enter the bottom of the **Circo de Barrosa** proper; a vast amphitheatre of barren snow-carpeted rocky peaks culminating

PUERTO DE BARROSA

in **La Munia** (3134m). Head across the grassy valley towards the unstaffed **Refugio Barrosa**. This is as far as many people come and after a riverside picnic they return by the way they came. But for us, our route goes upward to France.

The now lightly-trodden trail continues up in a northeast direction behind the *refugio*. It switchbacks sharply upward through tough grass pastures that are very popular with marmots (keep your eyes peeled early in the morning or late in the evening and you have a good chance of seeing some) and even chamois can sometimes be seen playing in the snowfields that lie year-round in the shady areas.

The further you go the wilder and more barren the landscape becomes, but the path always remains obvious. Finally, two hours after leaving the *refugio*, you reach the high, windy pass of the **Puerto de Barrosa** to be rewarded with amazing views over some of the bleakest, highest and coldest scenery in all the Pyrenees. Looking down into France you will see a series of icy blue lakes, the **Lacs de Barroude**, and beside them, the Refuge de Barroude, which you can walk to in a further half an hour if you wish. Otherwise return by the same route.

STAGGERING SESTRALES

Duration 3 hours

Distance 7km

Difficulty easy

Start/Finish Parking Plana Canal

Nearest Town Parzán (p127)

Transport car

Summary There are few more breathtaking views than the one from the sheer-sided Sestrales Alto. To the south are the plains of Spain, to the north Monte Perdido and below hundreds of metres of nothing!

Nothing can prepare you for the views that greet you at the end of this walk – find out if you suffer from vertigo by peering over the Sestrales ledge into the void below.

GETTING TO/FROM THE WALK

This is one walk that is very difficult, if not impossible, without your own wheels. From Parzán head south on the A138 turning

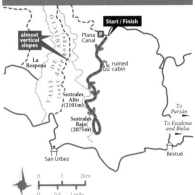

off at Escalona, continuing to Bestué and then it's 9km of dirt track to the parking at Plana Canal.

THE WALK

This is a very simple walk – you can already see your goal, the table shaped ridge to the south, from the car park. For the first half there is no real set trail so you have to beat your own path towards the summit, but don't worry this is very easy. Simply head past the gate at the entrance to the car park and walk over the brow of the grassy hill to the south. Almost straightaway you're rewarded with views of table-top mountains off to the east. From the top descend into the grassy valley towards a **ruined cabin** and join a light trail which takes you up and over another a light ridge on the other side of which is a much higher, and very steep, grassy hill.

When you reach the remnants of a fence running from east to west up the hill take a deep breath and follow the fence, and some rock cairns, up the hill. No, it's not fun, but it will be worth it! On the first col halfway up this hill you'll find a national park sign (which had fallen over at the time of research), a pile of rocks and a green sign post (although like the park sign this too had fallen off!). There's a wire fence here which you have to limbo dance your way under. From here the path is much more obvious as you simply follow the cairns all the way to the top.

For the final part of the walk you have some tantalising tasters of the views that await you at the top, but continue upward and the path suddenly flattens out and enters an enormous figure of eight-shaped grassy plateau covered in strange limestone formations that look for all the world like thousands of gravestones. Continue to the edge, and the highest, southwestern corner of the plateau and stand slack-jawed in awe of the view. The plateau simply stops and falls away almost vertically for a straight kilometre.

You're so high up above the **Valle de Añisclo** that eagles and vultures are likely to be soaring on the thermals below you. Southwards the plains of Spain seem to stretch forever while to the north the huge bulk of **Monte Perdido** (3355m) seems almost within touching distance and all around hundreds of giant peaks and canyons litter the horizon. It's truly one of the most breathtaking panoramas in all the Pyrenees.

To return, simply retrace your steps back to the car.

MORE WALKS

CATALUNYA
Pica d'Estats
Catalunya's highest mountain (3143m), straddling the Franco–Spanish frontier, has a special fascination for Catalan walkers.

From the pass at Port de Sotllo (2894m), there are two options. The shorter one requires 30 minutes of steep clambering up the ridge. The other, easier choice, despite the near-permanent snow on the northern slopes, descends to the little Estanyet de Barz in France. From here strike right (east) until you're between, though well below, the peaks of Estats and Montcalm (3077m). Make the final push up the gentler north slope via Coll de Riufred (2978m). Pack Alpina's 1:40,000 *Pica d'Estats* map.

ARAGÓN
Pico de Aneto
Aneto, at 3404m, is the highest summit in the Pyrenees, outstripped on the Spanish mainland only by Mulhacén in the Sierra Nevada. It's a challenge that draws many, both mountaineers and experienced

trekkers, and it's not to be underestimated. You'll need crampons and an ice axe – or walking poles at the very least – for the glacier. And don't attempt this strenuous day walk alone.

The classic route, with an altitude difference of 1265m, leads from Refugio de la Renclusa (see Alternative Route, p90). An early morning start is essential. You're well poised if you stay overnight at the *refugio* or else you can take the 4.30am bus from Benasque to La Besurta (see Getting There & Around for Benasque, p124). The additional distance from La Besurta to the *refugio* and back will add about an hour to the walking day.

Allow 4½ hours for the ascent from the *refugio*. Given the rough terrain, don't count on the descent being all that much shorter. Carry Alpina's 1:25,000 *Maladeta Aneto* map.

Pico de Posets
Views from Posets, at 3375m the second-highest peak in the Pyrenees, are – given its central position among the chain's loftiest peaks – even more staggering than those from Aneto. The ascent, or rather ascents, of Posets will tax you but it's neither as tough nor as dangerous as the haul up to Aneto.

Three popular routes thread from the three *refugios* that surround the massif in an equilateral triangle: Estós (see Alternative Day 7 of the Pyrenean Traverse, p91), Ángel Orus (see Day 7, p90) and Viadós (see Day 9, p93). Each, out and back, can be accomplished in a long day. Alpina's 1:25,000 *Posets Perdiguero* map covers all three approaches.

Monte Perdido
Monte Perdido (3355m) defers in height only to Pico de Aneto and Posets, and in popularity, only to Aneto. At any time of the year it's wise to come equipped with ice axe and crampons, or at least walking poles.

The well-cairned main route sets out from the Refugio de Góriz (see Day 13 of the Pyrenean Traverse, p97), the 7km return trip taking six to seven hours. A well-cairned path heads north as far as the tiny tarn of Lago Helado (Frozen Lake; around 3050m), reached some 2½ to three hours out. There you turn sharply right (southeast) for the final ascent up a steep couloir, then follow a rock-strewn snow ridge to the summit. Pack Alpina's 1:40,000 *Ordesa Monte Perdido* map.

TOWNS & FACILITIES

ANDORRA LA VELLA

☎ 376 / pop 22,800

Andorra la Vella, capital of the principality, has little to detain you unless you're keen to stock up on perfumes, handbags and cheap electronics. Most hikers will find Canillo (p126) or Soldeu (p128) better bases for the featured walks.

Information

The friendly municipal **tourist office** (☎ 827 117; Plaça de la Rotonda; 9.30am-1pm & 4-8pm Mon-Sat, 9.30am-1pm Sun Sep-Jun, 9.30am-9pm daily July-Aug) is well endowed with information about the city and the whole of Andorra.

Andorra has a mountaineering and walking group, **Club Pirinenc** (☎ 822 847; www.cpa.ad; Carrer Bonaventura; 5-8pm Mon-Fri).

For readers of Spanish, French or Catalan, **Libreria Jaume Caballé** (☎ /fax 829 454; Avinguda de Fiter í Rossell 31) has a splendid collection of antiquarian and new travel books and carries a comprehensive range of walking and travel maps.

Supplies & Equipment

There's no shortage of sports shops, mostly clustered around the bottom of Avinguda Meritxell. The largest of the three branches of **Viladomat** (☎ 800 805; Avinguda Meritxell 110), one of the best for walkers, also stocks walking maps. But it's not alone; browse around – if you can stand the intrusive traffic.

Sleeping & Eating

Should you find yourself stuck in town, **Pension la Rosa** (☎ 821 810; pensiolarosa @andorra.ad; Antic Carrer Major 18; s/d €18.22/29), just south of Ave Princep Benloch is a decent cheap place to see you through the night.

Papanico (Avinguda Príncep Benlloch 4) has tasty tapas from €2.10 and serves a range of sandwiches, *platos combinados* and mains. Grocery stores are bizarrely lacking in Andorra la Velle, so self-caterers will have to wander the aisles of the well-stocked **supermarket** on the 2nd floor of the Pyrénées department store (Avinguda Meritxell 21).

Getting There & Away

Unless you walk over the mountains the only way into or out of Andorra is by road – the mountain walk is preferable.

There are several buses a day between Andorra and Barcelona (€21; 3¼-4 hours).

ARTIES

☎ 973 / pop 100

Arties is a cluster of cheerful stone houses and makes a good base for the surrounding peaks and parks.

Information

There's a small **tourist office** (10am-1.30pm & 4.30-8pm daily Jul–mid-Sep) and an ATM in the village.

Sleeping & Eating

Camping Era Yerla d'Arties (☎ 64 16 02; camping per person/pitch/tent €5.15/13.35/5.15) Riverside and well maintained, this excellent site has a bar that serves a wide range of *bocadillos* (sandwiches).

Pensió Montarto (☎ 64 08 03; www .pensionmontarto.es; s/d/t €30/38/48), on the main road, is a good choice if you prefer a roof over your head.

There are plenty of cheap places to get stuffed with hearty mountain food.

BALNEARIO DE PANTICOSA

☎ 974 / pop 800

There's an excellent FAM-run *refugio*, **Casa de Piedra** (☎ 48 75 71; dm €14; dinner €11.60, breakfast €4.30), in town. Accommodation is in rooms for four to 14, with bathroom. Despite its capacity for more than 100, it's wise to reserve ahead in high summer. At such prices, it's the bargain of Balneario.

The only other place to stay is the luxurious **Hotel Continental** (☎ 48 71 37; r from €73) which, certainly makes a change from a night under canvas or in a *refugio*.

THE PYRENEES

BARCELONA
☎ 93 / pop 1.6 million

Set on a plain rising gently from the sea to a range of wooded hills, Barcelona is Spain's most cosmopolitan city and one of the Mediterranean's busiest ports. Restaurants, bars and clubs are always packed, as is the seaside in summer. You might get the impression it's dedicated exclusively to hedonism, but it's a hard-working, dynamic place hoping to place itself in the vanguard of 21st-century Europe with a heavy concentration of hi-tech and biomedical business.

Information
The **Oficina d'Informació de Turisme de Barcelona** (☎ 285 38 32; www.barcelona turisme.com; Plaça de Catalunya 17-S; 9am-9pm daily) gives city information and can book accommodation.

Supplies & Equipment
A first-class travel bookshop that also carries a wide range of maps is **Llibreria Altaïr** (☎ 342 71 71; www.altair.es; Gran Via de les Corts Catalanes 616).

Sleeping & Eating
Whatever the season, it's essential to book in advance. For online reservations consult www.barcelona-on-line.es.

Camping Masnou (☎ 555 15 03; Camí Fabra 33, El Masnou; two-person sites with car €30) Some 11km northeast of the city and only 200m from El Masnou train station (reached by *rodalies* trains from Catalunya station on Plaça de Catalunya), this camping ground offers some shade, is near the beach and is reasonable value.

Alberg Hostel Itaca (☎ 301 97 51; www.jo-oh.com/itaca; Carrer de Ripoll 21; dm €18, d €50-55) A bright option near La Catedral, Itaca has spacious dorms (sleeping six, eight or 12 people), with pleasant spring colours, and a couple of doubles with private bathroom. You can also make use of the kitchen.

Hostal Campi (☎ 301 35 45; hcampi @terra.es; Carrer Canuda 4; s/d from €31/54) is an excellent deal.

Hotel Jardi (☎ 301 59 00; www .hoteljardi-barcelona.com; Plaça de Sant Josep Oriol 1; s/d €79/106) overlooks a pretty square, but pick your room carefully – some are better value than others.

All three hostels are in the Barri Gòtic, the heart of the old town, which is rich in places to eat for all budgets.

Getting There & Away
Barcelona, one of Europe's most vibrant cities, has superb air connections to the rest of Europe and direct flights to/from North America. There are reasonable bus and train links to Andorra and the Catalan Pyrenees.

For airlines serving Barcelona's **El Prat airport** (☎ 902 40 47 04) see Air under Getting There & Away (p351). Many budget airlines serve **Girona-Costa Brava Airport**, 80km north of Barcelona and closer to the mountains. Both airports have plenty of car-rental outfits if you want to bypass the city and head straight for the hills.

Buses run to most large cities in Spain. A plethora of companies operates to different parts of the country, although many come under the umbrella of **ALSA** (☎ 902-42 22 42; www.alsa.es). The main intercity bus station is the **modern Estació del Nord** (☎ 902 30 32 22; Carrer d'Alí Bei 80).

Barcelona has good train connections to most major Spanish cities. Most services depart from **Estació Sants** (Plaça dels Països Catalans).

BENASQUE
☎ 974 / pop 2200

With its cobbled streets, 13th-century church and old greystone houses, roofed-in historic slates the shape of fish scales, Benasque's roots are deep. Nowadays, it's a small, bustling holiday centre where most of the new blends sensitively and harmoniously with the old.

If you fancy a day by the pool, the **Piscina Municipal** (€2.60; hours 11am-7pm) is over the bridge adjacent to Hotel Solana.

Information
The **tourist office** (☎ /fax 55 12 89; www .benasque.com; 9.30am-2pm & 4.30-8.30pm Tue-Sat & 9.30am-1pm & 4.30-8pm Sun & Mon) is on Calle Sebastián.

The small **Parque Posets-Maladeta visitors centre** (☎ 55 20 66; 10am-2pm & 4-8pm daily late Jun–mid-Sep, 10am-2pm &

3-6pm Sat & Sun mid-Sep–Easter, 10am-2pm & 4-8pm Sat & Sun Easter–late Jun), 1km from Benasque just off the road to Anciles (see Day 7, p90), has display panels and a good 15-minute video in Spanish about the park.

There are at least three ATMs in town.

Supplies & Equipment

There are a large number of shops across the town selling a variety of walking and outdoor clothing. On the main road, **Barrabés Esquí y Montaña** (☎ 55 16 81; www.barrabes.com; Carretera de Francia) sells a huge range of walking and outdoor equipment. It also stocks Benasque's best selection of maps and guidebooks.

Sleeping & Eating

For information on camping grounds near Benasque, see the end of Alternative Days 5 & 6 (p88).

Accommodation in Benasque itself is abundant, for any budget (there are at least 14 hotels, three camping grounds and five *casa rurales*) – though unless you've reserved you'll have difficulty finding a bed in this up-and-coming summer hiking and winter skiing resort.

Hostal Solana (☎ 55 10 19; Plaza Mayor 5; s/d from €28/38) is an economical place with clean, bright rooms.

Hotel Ciria (☎ 55 16 12, fax 55 16 86; www.hotelciria.com; Avenida de los Tilos; s/d with breakfast from €70/90) is a welcoming, family-run joint. The *menú* (€23) at its restaurant, El Fogaril, includes a range of local specialities.

For a meal there are many options along Avenida de los Tilos and its continuation, Calle Mayor. However, don't forget to explore the side streets as well!

Bar Plaza (Plaza Mayor; tapas from €0.90, *bocadillos* €2) is a friendly and popular place where you quickly start to feel like a local.

La Pizzeria (Calle Los Huertos; mains €9-12) has pizzas, pasta and salads to eat in or take away.

Restaurante Sayo (☎ 55 16 97; Calle Mayor 13) opens daily and serves filling *menú* from €12.

El Pesebre (Calle Mayor 45; menú €25) This is an intimate restaurant that serves an imaginative range of local dishes.

Getting There & Around

Regular buses run between Benasque and Barbastro (€7.25, two hours). There are two services daily except Sunday (one service). From Barbastro buses run to Barcelona, Lleida and Huesca. There are also six services a day from Barbastro to Monzón from where there are frequent trains for Zaragoza, Lleida and Barcelona.

From the end of June to mid-September a bus leaves Benasque for La Besurta (single/return €6.80/10.50) at 4.30am (a red-eye run for walkers wanting to attack Aneto – see Pico de Aneto, p122) plus 7.30am, 9am, 11am, 2.30pm and 6pm. The bus stop is outside Hotel Aneto on the main road. For details of the reverse run and of the shuttle service between Hospital de Benasque and La Besurta see the Day 6 description (p89).

BOÍ

☎ 973 / pop 1100

Boí is a quiet, relaxed, pretty, traditional village with a sense of community.

Information

If you're making Boí your base for any time visit **Casa del Parc** (☎ /fax 69 61 89; 9am-2pm & 3.30-5.45pm daily in Jul & Aug) is found through archways opposite the Parc Nacional d'Aigüestortes i Estany de Sant Maurici information office, where you will find more walk suggestions. This well-presented and informative office runs a 15-minute audiovisual introduction to the park, with an optional English version. They also sell walking maps and can provide you with a wide range of other information, including the low down on available *casas rurales*, as well as local bus times.

There's an ATM and a supermarket in town.

Sleeping & Eating

Hotel & Hostel Pey (☎ 69 60 36; r in hotel €65, r in hostel €50, both excluding tax) is in the heart of the village. Tasty meals are available for €13.50.

At the top of the village is **Pizzeria Casa Higinio** where pizzas start from €7 and pasta from €6. They also have a wide range of entrees and meat, as well as a daily *menú* for €14.

Getting There & Away

Taxis are available from Boí to take you further into the park (Cascada de Sant Esperit) for €9.70 return.

The bus (originating in Barcelona) which leaves Lleida at 9am for Vielha, passes by Pont de Suert at 11am. Here, between July and mid-September, it connects with a local bus which leaves at 11.15am for Caldes de Boí. In the opposite direction the bus departs from Caldes de Boí at 2pm, connecting with the return service for Lleida and Barcelona in Pont de Suert at 2.30pm.

CANILLO

☎ 376 / pop 3300

The Andorran village of Canillo tends to be much more subdued than Soldeu, 7km to its east. You'll find a helpful **tourist office** (☎ 753 600; www.vdc.ad) that's particularly helpful with assisting on hiking information. It runs daily guided walks throughout summer. You can relax after a day in the mountains at the sauna or swimming pool of the Palau de Gel, Canillo's local sports complex and ice rink.

Sleeping & Eating

Camping Casal (☎ 851 451; www .campingcasal.com; camping per person/ tent/car €3.50) is a basic campsite that's open year-round.

Camping Santa Creu (☎ 851 462; camping per person/tent/car €3.90 each) is the greenest campsite and, since it's the furthest from the highway, the quietest.

There are several other campsites in Canillo.

Pensio Comerç (☎ 851 020; s/d €15/29) This is a long-established hikers' favourite, to which regulars return year after year. Rooms are no-frills, but at this price who can complain?

Hotel Roc del Castell (☎ 851 825; hotelroccastell@andorra.ad; s/d €71/101) Sited on the main strip through town this large place offers the last tastes of luxury before the big adventure kicks off.

Cal Lulu (☎ 851 427; menú €14, mains €16-18, pizzas €7.50-10) Intimate, and as full of character as its punters this place serves great Catalan and French dishes which come in generous quantities.

The restaurant located at the Palau de Gel sports complex has an excellent value

weekday *menú* (€12.50) as well as decent pizzas. Its bar, with free Wi-Fi, is also a good spot for a snack.

Getting There & Away

Buses run roughly hourly from Andorra la Vella to Canillo before continuing on to Soldeu.

ESPOT

☎ 973 / pop 400

If you intend to make Espot the base for a walking holiday, call by **Casa del Parc** (☎ /fax 62 40 36; 9am-1pm & 3.30-6.45pm daily in summer, reduced hours in winter), the park information office, for more walk suggestions. This office runs a 15-minute audiovisual introduction to the park with an optional English version, and sells walking maps.

Sleeping & Eating

There's no shortage of camping grounds, each one beside the river.

Camping la Mola (☎ /fax 62 40 24; www.campinglamola.com; camping per person/tent €5.30/11.50; Jul-Sep), spacious and green, is the first you pass as you ascend from the Vall d'Aneu.

On the park (northwest) side of town is the small **Camping Solau** (☎ 62 40 68; www.camping-solau.com; camping per person/tent €4.75 each).

Casa Felip (☎ 62 40 93; d €50; Apr-Oct) is cosy and family-run.

Hotel Saurat (☎ 62 41 62; www .hotelsaurat.com; Plaça Sant Martí; s/d €70/100) is a popular walkers' choice.

The best grub can be found at **Restaurante Juquim** (mains €9-15; closed Mon).

Getting There & Away

The limited bus service (coming from Vielha from mid-Jun to mid-Sep, but from Esterri d'Aneu at other times) for Barcelona and Lleida passes through Vall d'Aneu, 8km from Espot (you then get a taxi to Espot). It leaves Lleida every day except Sunday, stopping in Pobla de Segur, Llavorsí and La Guingeta.

LLEIDA

☎ 902 / pop 131,700

Lleida is a likeable place with a long and varied history.

Information

Turisme Lleida's **Centre d'Informació i Reserves** (☎ 902 25 00 50; Carrer Major 31 bis; 10am-2pm & 4-7pm Mon-Sat, 10am-1.30pm Sun) is the best place for city information.

Sleeping & Eating

Hostal Mundial (☎ 973 24 27 00; Plaça de Sant Joan 4; s/d €27/42), with an entrance on Carrer Major, is a friendly place with worthy rooms. Snails, in all their slimy variety, are the speciality of **El Celler del Roser** (Carrer dels cavallers 24; meals €30). Enjoy!

Getting There & Away

Daily bus services by Alsina Graells include up to 14 buses (three on Sun) to Barcelona (€17.50, 2¼ to 2¾ hours) and two to El Pont de Suert and Vielha (€11.60, 2¾ hours). One bus a day (except Sun) heads to La Pobla de Segur and on to Sort, Llavorsí and Esterri d'Àneu (€18.35, three hours).

Lleida is on the Barcelona–Zaragoza–Madrid train line. Up to 34 trains run to Barcelona daily (3½ hours).

PANTICOSA

☎ 974 / pop 800

Retaining some old mountain charm Panticosa is a popular winter ski resort.

Information

The **tourist office** (☎ 48 73 18; Calle San Miguel 39; 9am-2pm & 4-9pm daily) delivers an offhand, uninformed service. There's a good website in Spanish, www .valledetena.com, listing facilities in the Tena valley, which embraces both Panticosa and Balneario.

Sleeping & Eating

Hostal Residencia Navarro (☎ 48 71 81; www.valledetena.com/navarro; r per person with bathroom €29), opposite the church, offers the most reasonable food and accommodation.

Panticosa has a couple of bakeries and supermarkets.

PARZÁN

☎ 974 / pop 320

Situated by the Carretera de Francia at the entrance to Parzán is a café, supermarket

and a grocery – an essential call as you won't meet another shop until Torla at the end of Day 13. Opposite the supermarket is the **Hotel La Fuen** (☎ 50 10 47; www .lafuen.com; s/d with breakfast €42/55), a small welcoming hotel with a bar and **restaurant** (menú del diá €12).

In the heart of the village you will find a couple of *casas rurales*. **Luis Zueras/Casa Marion** (☎ 50 11 90; s/d €30/50) has two comfortable apartments which come with a washing machine to make your clothes smile (and perhaps other walkers you meet!). **Maria Jesus Fumanal** (☎ 50 11 24; 24 Casa Quilez; s/d €20/30) is another option.

SALARDÚ

☎ 976 / pop 200

The village of Salardú (1268m), 'capital' of the Naut Aran (Upper Aran) region, offers groceries, accommodation (but no camping ground) and transport to the wider world.

Information

The **tourist office** (☎ 699 96 90 44; 10am-1.30pm & 4.30-8pm daily Jul-Sep) occupies a kiosk just off the main road. The village has an ATM.

Sleeping & Eating

Auberja Era Garona (☎ 64 52 71, fax 973 64 41 36; eragarona@aran.org; dm under 25/other €15.05/19.25) is a Hostelling International-affiliated youth hostel with capacity for 190. Rooms are for four or six people and it's advisable to reserve ahead. Breakfast is included.

Alberg Era Garona (☎ 64 52 71; carretera de Vielha s/n; dm student & under 26yr/over 26yr €22.45/26.30) This large hostel has rooms with up to four beds, each with a bathroom.

Hotel deth Païs (☎ 64 58 36; Plaça dera Pica; s/d €74/90) is a pleasant slate-roofed hotel with straightforward rooms.

Salardú has a grocery shop and supermarket. For something more subtle than hostel fare, you can dine agreeably at **Eth Cabilac** (☎ 64 42 82; Carrer Major 12; menú €15, mains €9.50-12.50), whose adjacent bar does good tapas and snacks.

Getting There & Away

From mid-June to September a daily bus from Vielha to Barcelona calls by.

Alternatively, take a local bus to Vielha from where the choice is a little wider.

SALLENT DE GÁLLEGO
☎ 974 / pop 1400

The pot of gold at the end of the traverse's rainbow, Sallent de Gállego is a lovely stone village with a bubbling brook running through it.

Information

The small **tourist office** (☎ 48 80 12; 9am-2pm & 4-9pm daily) functions from July to mid-September. See also www.vallede tena.com.

Sleeping & Eating

There's a basic **zona de acampada** (camping per person/tent €3.50 each; Jun-Sep) run by the municipality, just northeast of the village.

There are a couple of *casa rurales*. One of the cheapest options (which can be booked through the tourist office) is **Casa Serena** (☎ 48 81 94; Calle Peligno Desprendimmento de Nieve; per person €16).

Hostal Centro (☎ 48 80 19; www .valledetena.com/centro; per person with bathroom €26) is a small, family-run place with a restaurant.

Hotel Balaitus (☎ 48 80 59; www .valledetena.com/balaitus; s/d from €29/58) is a charming place, crammed with antique furniture and family mementoes.

Getting There & Away

From Monday to Saturday **Alosa** (www .alosa.es) buses go to Jaca via Sabiñánigo (two daily). From Jaca there is onward transport available to Zaragoza and Pamplona. From Sabiñánigo buses travel to/from Huesca, where there are links to Lleida and Barcelona. For a **taxi** call ☎ 664 487477.

SOLDEU
☎ 376 / pop 1100

Soldeu has a small **tourist office** (☎ 852 492; 10am-1pm & 3-6pm daily Dec-Apr, Jul & Aug).

For a place to rest your head try **Camping Font de Ferrosins** (☎ 347 119; camping per person/tent/car €3.20; mid-Jun–Sep), 1km into Vall d'Incles. It has showers, but is otherwise basic.

Hotel Roc de Sant Miquel (☎ 851 079, fax 851 196; hotelroc@andorra.ad; s/d with bathroom €26/32; Jun-Nov) is run by a pleasant young Anglo-Andorran couple. Both are ski instructors and experienced walkers and lead guided nature walks and hikes. Room rates include breakfast.

The friendly and comfortable **Hotel Bruxelles** (☎ 851 010; hotelbruxelles @hotmail.com; r from €36) is open year-round, with a restaurant offering an excellent and good value *menú*, and huge burgers. They also have internet access and offer packed lunches for walkers if ordered the day before.

Slim Jim's (☎ 852 567) offers packed lunches for walkers (€5) that you can order in advance by phone for pickup the next day. You can also revive yourself with a megamug of tea or beer at the end of the day and hop on the internet.

Hourly buses run from Andorra la Vella to Soldeu via Canillo between 8am and 8pm.

TORLA
☎ 974 / pop 300

A fine, stone-built village and gateway to the Parque Nacional de Ordesa y Monte Perdido, Torla gets crowded in high summer. This said, it is well endowed with restaurants and places to stay and makes an attractive rest stop. There are a couple of supermarkets, a public telephone, tourist office, ATM machines and more.

Information

Tourist Office (☎ 48 63 78; Calle Fatas; 9am-2pm & 4-9pm) This is a very informative office that also has the bonus of offering 15 minutes free internet access.

The official, and useful, website (in Spanish) for Torla and the national park is www.ordesa.com.

Sleeping & Eating

Of the three campsites **Camping Rio Ara** (☎ 48 62 48; www.ordesa.net/camping-rioar; per person/tent €4.10 each) is the handiest for Torla. It's approximately 15 minutes' walk from centre, off the main road. It also has a café and supermarket.

Camping San Anton (☎ 48 60 63; www .ordesa.net/camping-sananton; person/tent €4.50 each) Nearer to the park, but further from town, it has a bar, restaurant and supermarket and the shuttle bus drops and picks up here.

If you want to stay in Torla there are plenty of reasonably-priced hotels and hostels.

Albergue L'Atalaya (☎ 48 60 22; Calle Francia; www.ordesa.net/refugio-atalaya; dm €13, half board €26) A friendly and comforting mountain refuge in the middle of town with a welcoming bar-restaurant open to all.

Refugio Lucien Bret (☎ 48 62 21; www .ordesa.net/refugio-lucienbriet; dm/d €10/40) This is a very modern and comfortable *refugio* with excellent facilities situated right next to the supermarket in the centre of town.

Hostal Alto Aragon (☎ 48 61 72; www .pirineosguiadeservicios.com/hotelballarin; s/d €35/43) is run by the same family who run the slightly more expensive **Hotel Ballarin** (☎ 48 61 55; s/d/t €42/50/60), well situated near the main square and tourist office and with a good restaurant.

There are plenty of small restaurants offering Aragonese specialities. Enticing, but maybe a bit touristy, is **El Rebeco** on the main square. **El Duende** (Calle Inglesias) is also recommended.

Getting There & Away

Buses run to Torla from Sabinanigo, Jaca, and Huesca where you can get onward transport to Zaragoza, Pamplona and Barcelona.

VIELHA

☎ 973 / pop 5600

Vielha is the main town in the Vall d'Aran, though you wouldn't describe it as attractive.

Information

The **tourist office** (☎ 64 01 10; www .torismearan.org; Carrer Sarriulèra 10; 9am-9pm daily) carries information about the whole valley.

Sleeping & Eating

About a third of the Val d'Aran's hotels are in the capital. For some of the cheaper places, head down Passeig dèra Llibertat,

north off Avenguda de Castièro. High season for most is Christmas to New Year, Easter and a handful of other peak holiday periods: high summer (Jul-Aug) and much of the ski season (Jan-Feb). At other times, prices can as much as halve.

Hostal El Ciervo (☎ 64 01 65; Plaça de Sant Orenç 3; s/d €38/58) Some of the better rooms in this perfectly adequate, 18-room, old-style hotel overlooking a central square have the singular benefit of power showers.

If you've got your own wheels then you'll find some nice options just a few kilometres out of Vielha in the surrounding villages. In **Casau** (about 3.5km out of Vielha on the N230 road), high up above Vielha, you'll find three options, among them **Casa Cuny** (☎ 964 01 39; Carrèr Major 15; d €45), a three-storey white-washed house with magnificent views over the city and valley below.

In **Betrén**, a pretty village tacked on to the east end of Vielha's sprawl, seek out **Hotel Ço de Pierra** (☎ 64 13 34; www .hotelpierra.com; Carrèr Major 26; s/d €47/62), a new house that respects the stone-and-slate pattern of traditional housing. The 10 rooms combine stone, timber and terracotta for warmth. What's fabulous is that you are in a timeless village about a 15-minute walk from the centre of Vielha.

Quality dining is quite hard to come by in Vielha, but you will find no shortage of places serving average meals – many will dish up the local speciality, *olla aranesa* (a hearty hotpot).

Getting There & Away

From mid-June to the end of September **Alsina Graells** runs buses daily from Barcelona to Vielha Pobla de Segur, Llavorsí and La Guingeta. During the same period one bus daily leaves Vielha for Barcelona.

A year-round bus route connects Barcelona with Vielha via Lleida and the Túnel de Vielha.

From late June to mid-September several buses a day connect Vielha with villages such as Salardú and Arties. Off the main valley road you're dependent on taxis.

Basque Country & Navarran Pyrenees

HIGHLIGHTS

- Playing King of the Castle at the summit of Mt Autza on the **Frontier Views** walk (p147)
- Poking your nose through **Atxular's Eye** (p133) and picnicking in gorgeous alpine meadows
- Peering into the nests of massive griffon vultures and paying your respects at a pagan shrine on the **Vultures & Vertigo** walk (p149)
- Clinging precariously to the summit of Anboto, the scariest mountain in the Basque Country, on the **Urkiola: Anboto Ridge** walk (p137)

Area: 22,670 sq km	Average summer high: 28°C	Population: 3.04 million

The Basque mountains link Cordillera Cantábrica and the Pyrenees in a series of dramatic east–west *sierras* reaching a maximum altitude of 1551m. Parting the area's plentiful waters into those destined to wind up in the Atlantic and those bound for the Mediterranean (via the Río Ebro), these feisty, magnetic limestone ranges shelter endless walking opportunities. Inevitably, legends, curious cultural practices, or enticing history enhance the outstanding trails.

Euskadi is a small region (7261 sq km) composed of three provinces – Bizkaia (Vizcaya), Gipuzkoa (Guipúzcoa) and Araba (Álava) – poor in agriculture but abundant in raw materials, such as wood, iron and water. Bizkaia and Gipuzkoa border the Atlantic while inland Álava is distinctly Mediterranean. Navarra, a separate autonomous community or region in the Spanish system, shares historical ties with Euskadi. The name Euskal Herria refers to the historical Basque Country where Euskara, the mysterious Basque language, was and is still spoken. The remaining three of Euskal Herria's seven provinces are in France. Euskara bears no relationship to known languages, leading linguists to believe it's a Stone Age survivor. Megalithic burial chambers (dolmens and menhirs) are frequently concentrated on mountain passes and high pastures oriented towards the sun.

Coast-dwelling Basques have long enjoyed prosperity through commerce, fishing and emigration. Noncoastal Basques lived in urban areas or are dispersed across the rugged countryside in largely self-sufficient farmsteads called *baserria* in Euskara and *caseríos* in Spanish (see the boxed text Basque & Navarran Farmsteads, p135). Shepherding, as practised for thousands of years, is in decline. Stone huts on the high summer pastures are still constants, but shepherds now usually leave their flocks in the mountains and make periodic visits rather than live with them.

ENVIRONMENT

Geologically speaking, the Basque mountains are young when compared with the Cordillera Cantábrica or the Pyrenees. They are composed of limestone and sandstone formed from accumulated ocean-floor sediments, and have been shaped by karstification. This term is used to describe how limestone – calcium carbonate – reacts over time to the eroding properties of water and air. Karstification is the most important erosive process at work producing the dramatic, jagged peaks, rifts, caves and ravines found throughout the region. The area's only granite range, Aiako Harria (Peñas de Aia), is near San Sebastián.

Exploitation of the iron-rich hills is an ancient practice: foundries have produced high-quality iron since the 9th century. By the 14th century many ironworks lined river banks, using water to power their hammers and bellows, and severely damaging the rivers' ecosystems in the process. Beech and oak woods also suffered. To produce 100kg of iron, smiths needed nine sacks of hardwood (oak and beech) charcoal produced by carefully burning huge quantities of wood. Limestone was also painstakingly reduced to lime (to fertilise fields) in enormous ovens built in the woods. Nineteenth-century industrialisation dramatically depleted the ancient forests, leaving many hillsides barren. Monterey pine was planted to reforest and is used in paper mills and furniture, providing supplementary income for farmers. Red spruce, Japanese larch (a deciduous conifer) and Lawson cypress are also commonly planted for commercial harvest. Native mixed forests of ash, hawthorn, birch, hazel and maple are more limited in extent. Grand, extensive beech forests still thrive, fortunately.

Apart from deer, foxes and several other small mammals, birds are the primary wildlife you'll encounter. Atlantic-facing oak groves shelter woodpeckers, coal tits, woodcocks and the tawny owl all thrive. Above 600m, hanging out with the beech, look for black woodpeckers, thrushes and the nuthatch. Griffon and Egyptian vultures and red-billed choughs reign in the limestone heights.

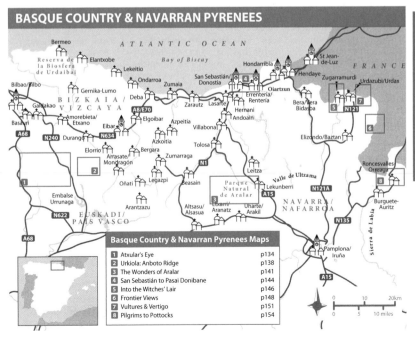

BASQUE COUNTRY & NAVARRAN PYRENEES

Basque Country & Navarran Pyrenees Maps	
1 Atxular's Eye	p134
2 Urkiola: Anboto Ridge	p138
3 The Wonders of Aralar	p141
4 San Sebastián to Pasai Donibane	p144
5 Into the Witches' Lair	p146
6 Frontier Views	p148
7 Vultures & Vertigo	p151
8 Pilgrims to Pottocks	p154

BASQUE COUNTRY & NAVARRAN PYRENEES

CLIMATE

Euskadi is one of Iberia's wettest regions. Winds and rain arrive from the northwest via the Atlantic Ocean year-round. Clouds dump rain primarily on the coast, with a pronounced rain-shadow beyond the highest hills further east and south around Vitoria (Gasteiz), and the southern half of Navarra. The maritime climate makes for mild winters and, for Spain, cool summers. Moving further inland and in mountain areas, expect greater extremes in temperature. Snow dusts the mountains in winter but rarely sticks, except in the Navarran Pyrenees east of Elizondo. May to October is the best period for walking.

PLANNING

Maps

Geo/Estel's 1:250,000 *Euskadi, Navarra, La Rioja* map covers the area described on a single, easy-to-read sheet.

Gobierno Vasco's (GV) 1:25,000 topographic maps are best for walking but can be hard to find. The IGN's 1:25,000 sheets are also reliable. In the series Cuadernos Pirenaicos, Sua Ediciones publishes 1:25,000 and 1:50,000 topographic maps and guides; these are good for planning, and highlight walks and climbs in specific areas. Nondik produces handy, water-resistant 1:40,000 topographic maps to the major Basque mountain areas. Finally, for routes in the Basque Pyrenees, close to the French border, then the French produced Cartes de Randonnées 1:50,000 maps to *Pays Basque Ouest* and *Pays Basque Est* are both excellent and easily available on both sides

of the border. Maps can be purchased in major cities and park information centres; don't rely on trailhead towns.

PLACE NAMES

Euskadi and Navarra have two official languages: Spanish and Euskara. Everybody understands Spanish. The percentage of Euskara-speakers varies regionally. All official signage in both regions, including that on the roads, is bilingual. Many maps may only use the Euskara version of place names. In the text, we either favour the most frequent usage or give both names to avoid confusion.

Books

With grave reservations we recommend Mark Kurlansky's engaging *Basque History of the World* as general background reading. Kurlansky's apologist take on ETA, the Basque terrorist group, is in our view morally reprehensible and one-sided journalism. If you can overlook this, then the book is well-written, entertaining and at times informative. For those interested in a far more serious, and less one-sided, look at the Basque Country then Paddy Woodworth's *The Basque Country: A Cultural History* is a much better bet, though it has to be said it's not as easy to read as Kurlansky's book.

In Spanish, the best general guide is Anaya Touring Club's *Pirineo Navarro y Montes Vascos*, which has natural and cultural history and route ideas. Iosu Etxaniz's *La Guía de Euskal Herria* is a cultural guide to Euskadi, Navarra and the

---

BEECH & OAK: SACRED TREES

Pago in Euskara and *haya* in Spanish, humidity-loving beech trees are regularly found above 600m on misty, water-soaked northern slopes. Constantly searching for light, the leaves and branches reach out and up producing a darkened forest and nearly plantless, though highly fertile, forest floor. In autumn, the tree's beech nuts provide a vital nutrient source for small mammals.

Communities commonly had a sacred oak (*haritz* in Euskara and *roble* in Spanish) where the traditional assemblies (*batzarrea*), uniting local representatives, were held and local laws (*fueros*) sworn. The Gernika oak tree, where Bizkaia's representatives would meet, is the most famous; at 300 years, it dried out in 1860. The present tree is its offshoot.

Beech and oak trees are pruned to prolong a tree's survival and productivity for hundreds of years. The main trunk is cut approximately 3m from its base to provoke a proliferation of shoots which grow horizontally and vertically. These are then cut for timber without harming the tree.

three French districts. Miguel Angulo is the resident walking and climbing expert. His numerous titles include *Montaña Vasca*, which has 400 itineraries. If you're a sea-lover, Tremoia Kolektiboa's *Rutas y Paseos por Parajes Naturales de Euskal Herria II: La Costa Vasca* describes great walks along Euskadi's 197km coastline.

Information Sources

Regional tourism offices (see Gateways, on this page) and park information centres have the most current information. In Euskadi tourism offices, ask for the free 1:200,000 *Euskadi* road map, and in Navarra, the 1:400,000 *Navarra: Mapa Guía*. A regional website is www.basquecountrytourism.net.

GATEWAYS

Bilbao (see p156) and San Sebastián (see p157), both in Euskadi, and Pamplona in Navarra are convenient major cities from which to enter the region. Thanks to cheap flights, with the likes of Ryan Air and easyJet, many people fly into the region via Biarritz just over the border in the French Basque country.

ATXULAR'S EYE

Duration	5 hours
Distance	10km
Difficulty	easy–moderate
Start/Finish	Pagomakurre
Nearest Town	Bilbao (p156)
Transport	bus, taxi, private car
Summary	The Itxina massif offers it all: forests, sacred caves, high pastures and limestone grandeur – all entered via the eye of Atxular.

The Parque Natural de Gorbeia, Euskadi's largest with 200 sq km, straddles the provinces of Bizkaia and Álava. While the highest peak in the area is emblematic Gorbeia (1482m), the huge rounded massif that sits at the centre of the park, this walk chooses instead to concentrate on the mesmerising Itxina massif, a craggy limestone labyrinth with vertical walls full of delightful surprises and some wonderful strolling through meadows, pastures,

grassy plateaus and beautiful beech forests. Some 500 caverns and 100 tortuous kilometres of galleries twist through the range's innards. Our walk takes you deep into Supelegor Cave, a name heavy with Basque folklore – it's considered one of the regular homes of Mari, the Basque goddess (see boxed text Mari, the Basque Goddess, p139). The largest cave in the range is actually Mairulegorreta (which at 12km long would constitute a decent hike of its own if this were a spelunking guide!), where Neanderthal remains have been discovered. For many though, the geological highlight is the famous Ojo de Atxular, a natural rock gateway through which you must pass to enter the magical world of Itxina.

The park is home to many bird and animal species, but it's the deer, reintroduced in 1958, that are the park's signature mammal. Come September, the ritual bellowing and brawling of the stags, as they stake claim on the harems, attracts numerous visitors.

The walk can be done from Bilbao using public transport, as a day-trip. The start and finish point consists of nothing but a car park and picnic/barbeque area, a couple of farmers' houses and an occasional summer shop.

PLANNING

When to Walk

Gorbeia receives winter storms, making May to October the best months for walking. The forest areas become very muddy after rain, which can really slow your walking times down. In foggy or rainy weather it would be very easy to get lost on this walk, so save it for sunny days only.

What to Bring

Carry plenty of water; there is no clean drinking water available en route.

Maps & Books

Sua Edizioak's 1:25,000 and 1:50,000 *Gorbeia* maps (they come in the same pack together with a Spanish language walking guide) offers the best detail.

Not one to slip in your pack (due to the weight), LP Peña Santiago's *Gorbeia: Montaña Vasca* gives sound advice on routes, with topographical maps.

ATXULAR'S EYE

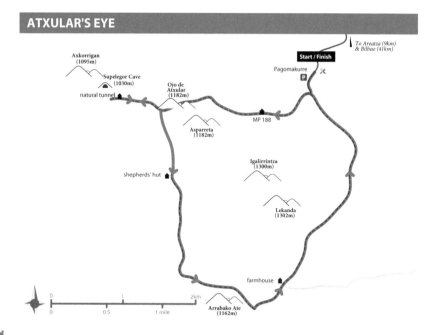

BASQUE COUNTRY & NAVARRAN PYRENEES

Information Sources

Providing basic information in English are two Parke Etxea interpretive centres. One is in Álava province in **Sarria** (☎ 945 43 07 09; 10am-2.30pm & 3.30-6pm Tue-Sun mid-Oct–June, 10am-7pm Tue-Sun June–mid-Oct), and the other in Bizkaia province in **Areatza** (☎ 94 673 92 79; 10am-2pm & 4-6pm daily).

Ask for the publication *Gorbeialdea* (in Spanish) in these centres and regional tourism offices. The centre in Sarria sells books and topographic maps. On the internet try www.gorbeialdea.com.

GETTING TO/FROM THE WALK

Bizkaia bus (☎ 902 22 22 65) runs regular buses from Bilbao to Areatza, the nearest village for the trailhead. From there you'll either have to take a taxi (€30) to the trailhead at Pagomakurre (and ask the driver to collect you at a given hour), or hitch (which should be easy enough on sunny summer days or at weekends). In your own car head to Areatza and, coming from the direction of Bilbao, turn right where you see the signs for the *parque natural* and follow the signs on

an increasingly narrow and bumpy road, 9km up the mountain to the Pagomakurre parking area.

THE WALK

From the car park at Pagomakurre (860m) follow the trail over the picnic-barbequre area in the direction indicated by the sign reading 'Atxular'. At the far end of the picnic area, where the trail diverges, follow the more obvious left-hand trail in a due west direction and enter a region of calm and beautiful beech forest where the trail is marked in red paint slashes. Numerous paths slide away from the main trail and although they all head in roughly the same direction it's best to stick to the waymarked trail. You'll know that you're still on the right path when, after 20 minutes, you come across a **MP 188 stone marker post**. Continue following the red paint marks up a gentle stone slope where the path starts to become obvious. Five minutes later you emerge out of the dense forest onto a grassy meadow, cross over a stile and continue straight ahead in a south-southeast direction, heading towards the rock-face.

A few minutes later you will need to cross over another stile and then continue on in the same direction. Above you, high in the rock-face, you will now be able to see the **Ojo de Atxular**, a huge window or gate-like natural stone arch (in reality it's all that remains of a large cave). Aim towards this, at first ascending gently over the pastureland before the trail starts zigzagging steeply up the cliff face to the *ojo* (eye). The heavy sweat you'll have built up on this part of the walk will be rewarded with ample views towards the coast and over the Durango massif.

Passing through the Ojo de Atxular and you enter Itxina proper – a strange world of forest, meadows and contorted limestone formations. The trail descends briefly from Atxular and rounds a hollow on the far side of which the trail forks. Take the right (and more westerly) fork which is indicated by the very faint word *supelegor* painted in red on a rock. Descend into the beech forest and follow the path, which now badly waymarked, remains obvious. After a few minutes green paint slashes and stone cairns start to sporadically appear to mark your route. When you see the very steep hollow veer, left (south) and work your way through the twisted limestone landscape. After five minutes the path again becomes a little more obvious and five minutes beyond that you reach a clearing full of incredible rock shapes that look as if they have been created by the mind of a twisted artist. The path forks here; look for the red 'S' painted on a rock following the path indicated in a westerly direction. There are plenty of stone cairns marking the way (although

they can be hard to see balanced on top of the piles of natural rocks!). When, after five minutes, you reach the hollow turn left and enter a large natural **tunnel** in the limestone cliff. Avoiding the cows that often shelter from the heat in here, you re-emerge into daylight on the far side of the tunnel and cross over another hollow in a westerly direction. When you come to yet another hollow the path forks. Ignore the turn off to the right and continue straight ahead before veering gently to the right; ahead of you is the massive entrance to the **Supelegor Cave**. You can venture quite far into the bowels of this gloomy cave.

When you've had your fill of life underground retrace your steps the way you came, back through the tunnel, past the rocky clearing and to the fork just this side of the Ojo de Atxular. Now turn right (south) at this fork and follow the faint red paint marks. The trail is now very obvious. After 20 minutes you reach a clearing which you cross and then, at the next clearing, bear left past some rocks and enter a large, gently sloping, and very beautiful, meadow. Following the obvious path through the meadow you'll see a partly hidden **shepherds' hut** off to your right. Keep following the clearly waymarked path across this meadow where you'll be rewarded with stupendous views to the coast and even the tower blocks of Bilbao to the north and, to the west, on across waves and waves of hills towards the mountains of Cantabria and the Spanish *Meseta*. It's truly one of the most magnificent views in the Basque Country. The trail climbs up and out of this meadow and you now have views

BASQUE & NAVARRAN FARMSTEADS

The large, three-storey stone houses often seen isolated in the countryside or high on a hill are *baserria* or farmhouses. They are fundamental to Basque life and a house's roots usually go back several centuries. All *baserria* have unchanging names, and families frequently go by their house's name rather than their own surname. Traditionally, the farmstead was passed on to the child (regardless of sex or birth order) deemed most apt to maintain its integrity.

The *baserri's* bottom level traditionally contains the stable for cows, henhouse and workshop. Winter hay and corn are stored on top, and domestic life occupies the 2nd floor, insulated between the other two floors. On average the farmstead occupies about 10 hectares – the majority replanted pine forest (for cash); then a smaller section dedicated to pasture (forage and hay for livestock); and the smallest part, crop land, to cultivate the household garden, corn and potatoes. Fruit (apple, pear, cherry) and nut (walnut and chestnut) trees once surrounded most farmhouses, but many have been replaced with pastures, fewer and less varied gardens, and pines.

BASQUE NATIONALISM

Basque nationalism is many-faceted, yet at its heart its motivation lies in the Basque peoples' compelling sense of identity and of cultural uniqueness, a passion that becomes evident to even the most casual traveller through the northern Basque provinces.

In 1959 a small group of Basques set up an organisation that became known as Euskadi Ta Askatasuna (ETA; Basque Homeland and Freedom). Its goal was to carve out an independent Basque state from the Basque territories of northern Spain and southern France. In 1968 the group carried out its first successful terrorist attack. Thus began a cycle of violence that became increasingly self-defeating as wide-ranging autonomy was granted in the early 1980s and 1990s. The antithesis of ETA was the emergence of a powerful, though peaceful, nationalism, especially among the young, that saw the Basque language as the most potent symbol of nationhood and independence. The central government has granted much autonomy to the Basque region, including its own police force and government; the region is currently run by the PNV, a moderate nationalist party.

In the last 40 years, however, ETA's grisly war has (according to Spanish government estimates) killed more than 800 people. Sporadic 'ceasefires' and peace initiatives have foundered on the unwillingness of both ETA and the central government to make major concessions. Relations reached a nadir in March 2004 when the government of José María Aznar made a desperate, and ultimately failed, election play by trying to blame ETA for the terrorist bombings in Madrid.

In March 2006 ETA declared a 'final' ceasefire. In response Prime Minister José Luis Rodríguez Zapatero stated that the Madrid government had 'the best opportunity for a peace process for more than 30 years'. Unfortunately, his optimism was misplaced and by December that year the process collapsed with a car bombing at Madrid's Barajas airport that led to the deaths of two people. Since then there has been a number of shootings and a series of recent car bomb attacks in Vitoria and other Basque towns. In January 2008 ETA stated again its call for independence and compared the Basque Country to Kosovo. In May 2008 a number of senior ETA members were arrested in the French city of Bordeaux.

No one would claim that all Basques are passionate nationalists, but with expanded autonomy on the cards for Catalonia, the realisation of the peaceful aspirations of a large majority of Basques seems more promising than ever. Complex and conflicting issues remain, however, not least the vexed question of the Madrid government's policy of imprisoning outside the Basque Country those whom many Basques see as political prisoners. The 2003 banning of Basque political party Batasuna for its alleged relationship to ETA and widely condemned support for terrorism has further aggravated the situation. Resolving this would be a major step forward.

going the other way over Gorbeia with its summit crowned with a radio mast (which from this distance looks like a miniature Eiffel Tower).

Continue following the red waymarking into a bowl where the red markings inexplicably become yellow, but the path remains obvious, though rockier, throughout. Fifteen minutes beyond the shepherds' hut and meadow, and the path sinks down into another bowl at the centre of which stands a pole with a red paint splash dabbed on it. Beyond this the path continues uphill through some forest in a south-southwest direction. A further 15 minutes on the path reaches the sheer walls that hem in the **Arrabako Ate** (1162m)

pass. Follow the path through the gap in the rock and descend on a rocky path and out of Itxina. Below you is a vast grassy plateau normally full of semi-wild horses and sheep and home to fantastic views over Gorbeia and onward towards the distant Pyrenees. Continue down into the meadow and stick to the trail which runs on the left side of a **stream** towards a small idyllic alpine **farmhouse**. Join the dirt road hemmed in by trees that leads away from the house and follow it for a couple of minutes to the end of the plateau where huge views into the valleys below await you. You will meet a motorable gravel road here which heads north-northeast down off the plateau. Now simply follow this road downhill for half an hour enjoying the views on the way back to Pagomakurre and your car.

URKIOLA: ANBOTO RIDGE

Duration 5–5½ hours
Distance 19.5km
Difficulty demanding
Start/Finish Puerto de Urkiola
Nearest Town Bilbao (p156)
Transport bus, taxi
Summary A gentle amble through shepherds' ancient pastures culminating in a thrilling and nerve-wracking scramble up a mythic karstic peak.

The 5958-hectare Parque Natural de Urkiola, established in 1989 in southeast Bizkaia, contains one of the Basque Country's most sacred peaks, Anboto, the mythical dwelling of La Dama (see the boxed text Mari, the Basque Goddess, p139). The tortured karstic landscapes of knife-edged white-grey ridges and dramatic, commanding peaks are definitely the stuff of myths. The limestone massifs of the Sierras de Aramoitz and Anboto part the Mediterranean and Atlantic waters, while the Arangio and Ezkubaratz ranges contain *urkia* (birch in Euskara), which give the park its name. Caves, fissures and curious formations such as the Jentilzubi (Bridge of the Gentiles), an impressive natural archway, and the Damaren Koba (Cave of the Lady), Urkiola's most famous cave, which opens onto Anboto's sheer vertical eastern face, add to the mystique.

The **Santuario de Urkiola**, an oddly situated, unfinished church dedicated to two San Antonios (San Antonio the Abbot, and San Antonio of Padua), dominates the trailhead. The mosaic behind the main altar and the stained-glass windows are particularly fine. San Antonio de Padua's feast day is celebrated on 13 June.

Evidence of human impact extending back thousands of years in the area of the park includes significant Neanderthal remains. Today shepherding and goat herding persist and the high green pastures are crowded with flocks. Forests cover 56%

of the park: 30% is reforested Monterey pine, Japanese larch and Lawson cypress, and 26% is native vegetation. Above 600m, on the steep limestone slopes, you'll see holm-oak and beech. In thick north-facing woodlands, beeches dominate. The griffon vulture, the park's largest bird, commonly soars in the skies.

The walk tackles the mythical summit of Anboto. It is rated demanding owing to the hair-raising final section to the top, which requires hands and feet (and guts!), but you can easily skip the final ascent, or adapt the walk to a moderate one of 14.5km (four to 4½ hours) by returning from Collado de Pagozelai and eliminating the Anboto section entirely. Two natural springs provide water en route.

PLANNING
When to Walk
The best months are May to October.

Maps & Books
Sua Edizioak's 1:25,000 and 1:50,000 *Durangaldea* maps (they come in the same pack together with a Spanish language walking guide) offer the best detail. The park's 1:20,000 *Parque Natural de Urkiola* map shows various itineraries but important routes are unmarked. Available from the park's information centre, *Urkiola: Guía del Parque Natural*, in Spanish, is a complete overview of the park's resources.

Information Sources
The **Toki Alai information centre** (☎ 94 681 41 55; 10am-2pm & 4-6pm daily), just west and up the hill from Puerto Urkiola, has a permanent park exhibit as well as English-language leaflets, maps and books.

GETTING TO/FROM THE WALK
Pesa run frequent buses between Bilbao and Durango and from there Alsa Buses head to Vitoria several times a day with all stopping at Puerto de Urkiola. A taxi from Durango will cost around €20.

Although Durango, a stinky (literally) industrial centre, is closer to the park, few people would choose to overnight there voluntarily. Bilbao (p156) makes a far better base.

THE WALK

From the church at **Puerto de Urkiola**, ascend to the car park's highest tier. Next to the entrance to this tier you will see a tarmac road continuing on straight up the hill to a barrier after which the road turns to dirt. Ignore this (we will return via this road) and instead take the track on your left heading southeast. After 50m use a stile to cross the fence (following red-and-white slashes) and go cross-country (east) straight up the wide grassy slope. Continue ascending towards a fire-break and cross it to a false summit. The impressive Aramoitz range (straight ahead) and Anboto (far right) come into view. Ascend, ignoring a trail to the right, and continue to the summit of **Urkiolagirre** (1009m), which is about 20 minutes from the car park. Here, as well as an orientation map, you'll have grand views of Anboto and the surrounding jagged limestone peaks. Continue east and descend 1km to a dirt road; the peaks loom ahead of you.

Turn left and in 150m, where the road curves sharp right, take the trail on the left, marked 'PRB202', indicating Larrano is 13 minutes away, and blazed yellow-and-white; you can see it ascending north along the limestone slope to grassy Larrano, the ridge's lowest point. Nearing the ridge-top, take a grassy path on the right to the ridge at the **Ermita de Santa Bárbara** (973m), surrounded by hawthorns and enjoying outstanding views. Return to the dirt road.

Ascend left (southeast) on the dirt road parallel to the mountains past a catchment reservoir, cabin (on the right) and quarry (on the left). Reaching a fork, veer left, gently ascending to **Collado de Pagozelai** (Beech Tree Pass). A wooden sign points left to the top of Anboto (35 minutes). If you'd rather not ascend, continue straight ahead (southeast) along a footpath down to a dirt road. Turn left and in 1km, through a dense beech wood, you'll reach Zabalandi pass (where descending Anboto summiteers rejoin the track).

To ascend Anboto from Collado de Pagozelai turn left and, 100m later, take a trail to the right through beeches. The blazed switchbacks begin. After 25 minutes the beeches disappear and beyond is a false

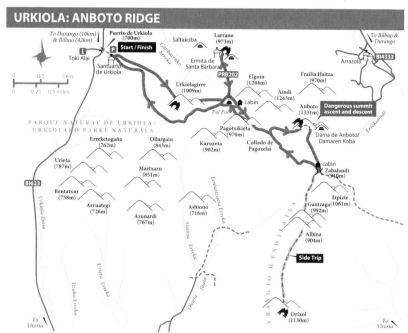

MARI, THE BASQUE GODDESS

Many Basque hilltops, crowned with crosses or chapels, were once the dominion of Basque divinities. Around the 11th century, Christianity began to make inroads into the Basque Country, primarily via the Puerto de Urkiola. Before (and well after) that time, belief in myriad deities was strong. Pre-eminent among them was Mari, or La Dama (the Lady), a beautiful feminine personification of the earth. Taking on diverse forms (tree-woman, horse on the wind, richly dressed or enveloped in flames), Mari dwelled inside the earth connected to the surface via caves or wells frequently filled with glittering gold. Mountain-top caves were her favourite dominions. Weather would improve or worsen whenever she was in residence: fog on Anboto, for example, was a sign of her presence.

Evoking great fear as well as honour and respect, Mari looked after villagers and despised lies, false accusations, vanity, failure to keep one's word and disrespect. Shepherds and other believers would often leave her offerings and explain natural disasters as evidence of her ire.

summit. The route now becomes more difficult and dangerous. Following the red-and-white paint slashes turn right and ascend, scrambling, to the visible summit of **Anboto** (1331m). Many people take one look at the sketchy, and sheer-sided, final ascent and, with slightly quivering legs, decide to go no further than the marker post on the false summit. If you do go the final few metres then just take it slow and steady, don't look down and keep close to the red-and-white paint slashes marking the safest route. From the summit you can either return the same way to Pagozelai or make an airy and daring descent along Anboto's southeastern face. To do this continue along the crest for a short way, then veer towards the right, initiating a steep descent on the limestone slope. The way is marked and the goal is clearly in sight: a dirt road next to a cabin in the grassy Zabalandi pass at the base of Izpizte (1061m), but be warned that the first part of this descent runs close to a terrifyingly sheer drop!

Reaching **Zabalandi** (910m), a sign indicates 'GR12 Orisol' to the south. The side trip described (see next column) leaves from here.

To return, take the dirt road descending westward, past a cabin with a roof of living grass. The road ascends and then levels out for 400m before veering right onto a marked, ascending footpath. In 10 minutes you'll reach Collado de Pagozelai. Return along the familiar road, and 200m before the cabin take a descending trail left through the grassy Campa de Azuntza. Take the footpath that borders, then enters,

the woods. From the iron-tasting **Pol Pol** spring, ascend to the dirt road. Turn left and descend 3.5km to the church and Puerto de Urkiola.

SIDE TRIP: ORIXOL PEAK
2½ hours, 8.3km

This splendid detour offers superb views and forest walking. From Zabalandi follow the 'Orisol' sign into a beech forest and go 500m to a fork. Head left, briefly ascending and then descending. In 400m the trail reaches a rocky section interspersed with young trees. In 175m, where the trees become more sparse, follow the blazes veering slightly left up the slope (requiring a bit of a scramble). Re-enter the forest for 300m and reach a pasture with a cabin. Take the road on the right past the cabin. Immediately take a footpath on the left for the final ascent (1.2km), initially through a beech wood. Ascend in zigzags. The trail is level for 800m, with Orixol's spur to the right. A few minutes later, after you pass a natural grassy balcony on the right, a group of rocks nearly blocks the path. At the rocks, without descending, turn right and ascend to the small, flat-topped summit of Orixol (1130m).

WARNING

Proceed with extreme caution on the last section to the summit of Anboto, which requires scrambling with hands and feet, as well as on the descent from Anboto. Neither should be contemplated in fog, rain or strong winds.

THE WONDERS OF ARALAR

Duration 4½–5hrs
Distance 14.3km
Difficulty easy
Start/Finish Casa Forestal de Aralar/Guardetxe
Nearest Town Lekunberri (p157)
Transport bus, taxi
Summary Taking in the Neolithic remains and unearthly karstic landscapes of the lonely Sierra de Aralar, this is an easy and varied plateau walk across one of Navarra's forgotten mountain scapes.

Largely lost among the glory of the nearby Pyrenees the Sierra de Aralar is a 208-sq-km slab of limestone rock, bleak undulating moorland, other worldly karstic rock formations and calming beech forests. Despite now being a natural park it remains little visited by foreign hikers all of which makes it a fantastic alternative to busier Pyrenean peaks.

The hills here have been inhabited for a very long time. Neolithic dolmens are widespread and testify to 5000 years of human habitation. Going even further back there are also cave systems in the lower reaches of the *sierra* that are said to have once been a home to fire-breathing dragons. Slightly more up to date is the Santuario de San Miguel de Aralar; an austere 9th-century chapel, which lies in the shadow of Mt Altxueta (1343m).

Our walk, an easy journey around the best of the *sierra*, takes in hawk-like views from the summit of Mt Irumugarrieta (1431m), endless rolling moorlands, beautiful beech forests and signs of our ancestors in the form of several Neolithic dolmens.

PLANNING
When to Walk
In the wet Basque lands the Sierra de Aralar stands out for its dampness. Seemingly days and days can pass with a permanent drizzly mist lying over the hills even when the coastal regions are bathing in sunshine. You should exercise extreme caution walking here during misty and cloudy days and not stray from the main path as it's very easy to become hopelessly lost among the karst landscape.

Maps & Books
Sua Edizioak's 1:25,000 and 1:50,000 *Aralar* maps cover the area of this walk in great detail. The two different scale maps are sold together in a pack complete with a Spanish language walking guide to the range.

GETTING TO/FROM THE WALK
To get to the departure point for the walk you'll either need your own wheels, a taxi or be prepared to walk (€25, 13km each way). Leave Lekunberri via the southern end of town and simply follow the signs for the Santuario de San Miguel de Aralar. This road takes you up into the natural park where, 13km from town, you reach the Casa Forestal de Aralar/Guardetxe, which is a large car park complete with a forest guards' house (being rebuilt at the time of research). Park here.

THE WALK
From the parking area walk back down the tarmac road in the direction you've just come from for 10 to 12 minutes. You will soon reach the **Albia dolmen**, the first of several prehistoric sites. Note that it's easy to miss this dolmen and that were it not for the small metal plaque revealing its identity most people would assume it was nothing more than a pile of rocks. Immediately after the dolmen you will see some roadside parking with a wide, gravelly track heading off into the trees on your left.

Follow this track and within a couple of minutes you will round a bend and see a **shepherds' hut** (which doesn't look anything like as quaint as you'd imagine a shepherds' hut to be). Continue to follow the track through silent and beautiful beech forest and after a further 10 minutes you'll pass another **shepherds' hut** where the gravel track becomes a grass one. Five minutes later and you come upon a clearing in the forest with a junction of paths. Take the path on your left, which heads gently uphill in a northerly direction and is indicated by red paint splotches and arrows. Continue following the obvious grassy trail (which now has plenty of red paint waymarkers) uphill through the forest. After 10 minutes

THE WONDERS OF ARALAR

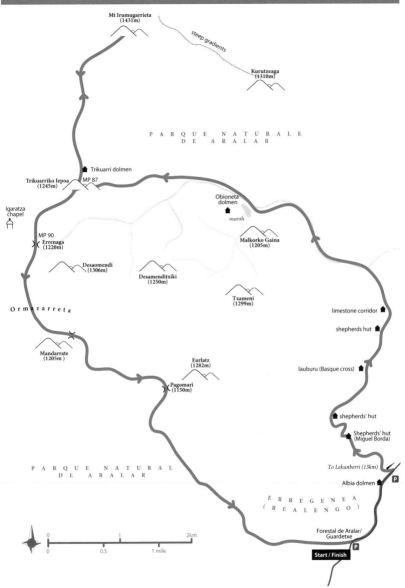

you will see a *lauburu* (Basque cross) under a cluster of fir trees.

From here the path becomes ever more ill-defined and faint but the red waymarkers will continue to guide you uphill in a roughly northerly direction. Pass over some open grassy patches and, 10 minutes from the cross, you will reach

THE OLDEST LANGUAGE

'The Basque language is a country,' said Victor Hugo, and language certainly encapsulates all things Basque. Known as *Euskara*, the Basque language is acknowledged as being one of Europe's oldest and most quixotic languages, with no known relationship to the Indo-European family of languages. Its earliest written elements were thought to be 13th-century manuscripts found at the Monasterio de Suso at San Millán de Cogolla in La Rioja province, but discoveries in 2006 at the archaeological site of Iruña-Veleia near Vitoria included inscriptions in Basque dating from the 3rd century AD.

Suppressed by Franco, Basque was subsequently recognised as one of Spain's official languages. Although Franco's repression meant that many older Basques are unable to speak their native tongue, it has now become the language of choice, and of identity, among a growing number of young Basques, fuelling a dynamic cultural renaissance and a non-violent political awareness. There are now Basque-language radio and TV stations and newspapers and you shouldn't be at all surprised to find yourself the only non-Basque speaker in a mountain bar. Being in a situation such as this is certain to make you want to learn a few words, but be warned. It's rumoured to be the hardest language in the world to learn!

a third **shepherds' hut** in the midst of a karst landscape and a grassy clearing. Just beyond the shepherds hut you squeeze through a short and narrow **limestone corridor** and emerge onto more open ground and out of the forest proper. You will now be following a very small stream in a northeasterly direction. The path becomes ever fainter and the red waymarkers a little less common but, keeping the stream on your right continue to march uphill for around 15 minutes. Eventually, as you reach its source, the stream will become little more than a few muddy pools. Continue right up to the head of the stream and the light valley it sits in and then, after the last of the red waymarkers has vanished, you will find yourself emerging onto the plateau itself at the end of the **Txameni ridge**. In the grass ahead of you is a very light 4WD track, turn left here and follow this for three or four minutes in a northerly direction until you hit the obvious gravelly road which you follow in a westerly direction (your left).

You're now on the GR12 and the walking, and route finding, becomes very simple. Follow the road which is indicated with red-and-white GR12 waymarkers every now and then. After 10 minutes you come to a fenced area containing a **marsh** full of bulrushes, frogs and alpine newts. You can cross a stile over the fence to take a closer look, but if it's summer watch where you step as the ground around

the marsh is literally crawling with tiny newborn frogs.

Back to the walking and the road undulates gently over a wild landscape of rolling moorlands and strange karstic rock formations. Semi-wild horses and sheep are common and constant companions to your walk. After 15 more minutes walking in a largely westerly direction you will pass the **Obioneta dolmen** a few metres off the road on your left. Another 15 minutes further on and you reach a marker stone with **MP 87** carved into it. From here take the lightly defined grassy trail on your right (north), which will lead you on a one-hour return trip to the summit of Mt Irumugarrieta (1431m). Within 30 seconds of leaving the MP 87 marker post you pass the **Trikuarri dolmen**. Continue to follow the grassy trail which is marked with red paint splotches every now and then. This leads you gently uphill and into a confused rocky landscape. Were it not for the red waymarkers it would be very easy to get lost here and in foggy weather you should not attempt to go to the summit. Ten minutes from the Trikuarri dolmen you will reach a large limestone rock painted in fading reds. Turn left here and continue to follow the red markers over ever more rocky terrain for a further five minutes until you reach another stone marker post this time with MP 83 carved onto it. Turn left (north-northwest) again here (do not descend into the bowl) and continue to follow the red markers up onto the main ridge. Ten minutes later you reach a fence, cross this and continue on up to the summit of **Mt Irumugar-rieta** (1431m) from where, on a clear day, you can glory in the views of the valley a vertical kilometre below you and beyond (outside of high summer) to distant snowy peaks. Descend the way you came.

Back on the main path continue to head in a west-southwest direction following the red-and-white GR12 marker posts for another few minutes until the road you're following meets another, even more distinct gravel and stone road next to a **MP 90** marker post. Turn left (south) here and follow the road to the **Errenaga pass** (1220m). There are some magnificent views down to the **Igaratza chapel** and refuge along this stretch of road (peer over the fence that follows the road on your right). From the pass the road drops slowly towards **Mandarrate**, a lovely grassy pass surrounded by bizarrely shaped rocks. From here all you need do is continue to follow the road in a southeasterly and downhill direction for a little under an hour. This will take you slowly off the plateau and back into the mottled beech forest before eventually arriving back where you started at the Casa Forestal de Aralar/Guardetxe parking.

SAN SEBASTIÁN TO PASAI DONIBANE

Duration 2½–3 hours
Distance 11.5km
Difficulty easy
Start San Sebastián (p157)
Finish Pasai Donibane (p145)
Transport taxi, bus
Summary Walk from the centre of one of Spain's coolest cities to wild sandstone cliffs covered in gulls and butterflies and finish in an enchanting Basque port.

This excellent coastal traverse, where the Atlantic laps against the Pyrenees, enjoys outstanding seascapes and Edam-cheese cliffs as well as wildlife, solitude and fresh sea air. It's an absolutely wonderful way to link together glitzy San Sebastián and its quaint neighbour, the port town

of Pasai Donibane. The walking is very easy and family friendly, but offers enough beauty and variety to appeal to hardened trekkers as well. A surprising array of coastal wildflowers thrive on the trail's borders, and intermittent woods contain examples of Mediterranean (holm oak, laurel, strawberry trees), Atlantic (chestnut, hawthorn, common oak), and exotic (eucalyptus, pine, mimosa) plant communities. From May to August nesting gulls fill the cliffs and cormorants can be seen diving for fish while the cliffs are positively aflutter with brightly painted butterflies and lizards.

PLANNING
When to Walk
The coast's temperate climate makes this walk feasible year-round. The driest months are July to September.

Maps
The IGN's 1:25,000 map No 64-II *Donostia-San Sebastián* covers the walk, though the waymarking is so good and trail so obvious that you won't really need anything other than the map provided here.

GETTING THERE & AWAY
For more information, see San Sebastian (p157).

THE WALK
Collect water before leaving San Sebastián.

Starting from the **town hall** overlooking San Sebastián's main beach, Playa de la Concha, take the maritime walkway right (north) towards the fishing wharf. Curve left past the aquarium to the Paseo Nuevo seaside walkway. Continue around Monte Urgull until you reach the art nouveau **Puente Zurriola** bridge (to shave off 1.5km, walk east from the town hall down Alameda del Boulevard to the bridge.) Turn left and cross the bridge, passing the Kursaal exhibition centre and the popular surfing beach, Playa de Zurriola (Gros), and continue towards Monte Ulía and the buildings ahead.

As you approach the end of **Playa de Zurriola** (Gros) the main road, Paseo de Zurriola, bends around to the right, away from the beach. Follow the road and, just before the petrol station, turn left (east) up Kalea Zemoría. You will see a set of

SAN SEBASTIÁN TO PASAI DONIBANE

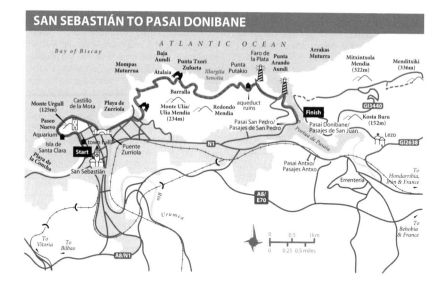

steps on your right and the first red-and-white waymarkers that indicate your route. Clamber up these steps to where the road eventually ends at the base of a hill and another, much steeper set of steps which merge into a paved trail curving left uphill to a paved road. Ignore stairs to the right near the top (which ascend to the Albergue Monte Ulía). Turn left (past a *mirador* – lookout) to a dirt trail marked with red-and-white slashes. Continue through a mixed wood, ignoring descending trails, for 10 minutes. When the trail re-enters the forest, look for gardens on the right and a hidden trail on the left (be warned that there is another left turn marked 'littoral' just before the one you want). Turn hard left and ascend through pines towards the coast. After 200m, the trail turns hard right and opens out onto a huge sea view at the top of sandy cliffs. Look down from here and you can make out the ruins of old buildings once said to have been used by smugglers.

Continue on the spectacular sandstone cliff-top trail, which soon descends southeast (right) into a pine forest filled with hydrangeas. Reaching a fork, make a hairpin left turn, descending out of the forest and onto a steeply descending cobbled lane towards the ocean. This was used by oxen in the 1890s to haul stone from the quarry below. For 20 minutes the

obvious trail zigzags down and around a huge, Swiss-cheese outcrop (gulls love the eroded holes) then undulates along the open hillside to a natural **lookout**. In the summer this area is awash in colourful butterflies (painted ladies are the most common). The extraordinary Faro de la Plata lighthouse, sandwiched between two tall sheaths of rock, comes into sight for the first time; 3.4km remain to the lighthouse.

The trail enters a beech, oak and chestnut forest and 10 minutes later reaches a cement road. Just a few metres before this the trail turns hard left and dives steeply through the forest for a few metres (in slippery conditions you might be better off just sliding down this bit on your bottom – or walking out onto the road, descending for 75m and, where it curves left, rejoining the trail on the right-hand side of the road) before bending right and meeting the cement road again. Cross over the road and, directly opposite, the trail heads off into the forest again. Ten minutes beyond the cement road and the small, rocky and delightful cove of **Illurgita Senotia** comes into view. Backed by greenery and, on a calm day, idyllic for snorkelling, this makes a good spot for a swim. To get down to the beach look for the tiny trail heading downhill on your left just after the bay first comes into view. Even in August you have a good chance of having this beach all to yourself. Ten minutes beyond the cove the trail ascends inland towards pastures, the brush thickens and the trail reaches a fork. The wider path continues straight on, inland, while the narrower trail turns sharp left. Take the left turning and at a T-junction a few metres later turn left again onto a wider sandstone, then cobbled path. In 15 minutes the lighthouse reappears, as well as a curious aqueduct in ruins. The trail winds around a gorge and aqueduct to the base of the romantic **Faro de la Plata**.

Turn right onto the road and continue for 500m. The whale-backed peak of Jaizkibel is to the east, and on the opposite side of the water, to you. Where the road curves right, turn left onto a wide sandstone path (still marked with red-and-white waymarkers) leading to a picnic area. Turn left at the picnic area and look for the marked, zigzagging footpath steeply descending to the lighthouse. Tankers, sailboats and even kayaks are often visible in the narrow channel leading to Pasaia, three burghs surrounding Gipuzkoa's largest port and dedicated to scrap transport and shipbuilding: Pasai San Pedro (Pasajes de San Pedro), Pasai Donibane (Pasajes de San Juan) and Pasai Antxo (Pasajes Antxo). Follow the footpath down to the maritime walkway and in 10 minutes reach San Pedro's port. Cross in the boat taxi (€0.60; every five minutes, all day) to picturesque **Pasai Donibane**, situated inside a cleft in the otherwise fortress like cliff walls. The protection these cliff walls afford make it harder to imagine a more perfect natural harbour and watching massive tankers motor out to sea through what appears to be no more than a narrow slit in the rock is a surreal experience indeed. Due to the limited building space the old town remains almost totally untouched by modern developments and, walking through the gloomy tunnels that line the old docks here brings forth strong sensations of having somehow slipped through a time portal and into a medieval fishing village. This feeling, and the town's general charm, is further enhanced by the need to catch a ferry over the narrow channel separating you from the town at the end of this walk.

Unfortunately, apart from some decent waterfront restaurants there are no real facilities for overnighting here so you will need to return to San Sebastián – easily done on one of the frequent buses which leave from just beyond the southern edge of the old town.

INTO THE WITCHES' LAIR

Duration 4 hours

Distance 9.5km

Difficulty easy–moderate

Start/Finish Zugarramurdi (p147)

Transport bus, taxi, car

Summary This fascinating walk takes in the dank cave homes of witches and the sort of views usually only possible when flying high above the clouds on a broomstick.

This fantastic walk, which crosses over the Spanish/French border, provides scenery in abundance, but maybe what really makes it stand out is the glimpse into the underworld of Basque life – literally and figuratively. Passing two sets of caves; one renowned for its natural artwork in the form of stalactites and stalagmites and the other renowned as a place where witches are said to have once mixed great cauldrons of evil. In addition to such a magical culture, this walk takes in one of the prettiest Basque villages and a couple of restaurants in which to break up the hike. The last section of this walk, from Sare to Zugarramurdi or vice-versa and back makes an ideal easy excursion for those with children.

PLANNING
When to Walk
The low altitude of this walk means it can be completed at any time of the year.

Maps & Books
Rando Éditions *Pays Basque Ouest* 1:50,000 is the most accurate map and has the route marked on it.

GETTING TO/FROM THE WALK
There are no buses to Zugarramurdi, but you can get a bus from Pamplona or San Sebastián to Elizondo several times a day for €4.60 from where you can take a taxi (about €25) 25km to Zugarramurdi. Another option is to actually start the walk from Sare,

WHALING

All along the Basque coastline eagle-eyed lookouts in watchtowers kept vigil for the unmistakable approach of the Biscayan whale. Seeing the spout, the lookout sounded the alarm shouting '¡Baliak! ¡Baliak!' (Whale! Whale!) and whalers quickly set out in their small boats. Once the oarsmen neared the huge mammal the harpooner, the elite among fishermen, summoned up his courage and launched his lance, hoping the tail wouldn't send them all into oblivion. Once on land the whale meat was divided (often the choicest piece, the tongue, went to the church as tribute) and the blubber was boiled down for oil. By 1059 fishermen from Bayonne (France) whaled commercially off the coast, and many coastal towns, including Bermeo, Lekeitio and Hondarribia, incorporated the whale into their town seal.

In the 16th century Basque whalers regularly practised their trade in Newfoundland. In 1978, a Basque galleon, the San Juan, sunk in 1565 with two whaleboats on board, was discovered in the waters of Red Bay, an important whaling station in Labrador, Canada. National Geographic covered the remarkable wreck and its discovery and subsequent investigation in its July 1985 issue (Vol 168, No 1).

on the French side of the border, which is connected to St Jean de Luz by bus several times a day. These buses pass right by the entrance to the caves thus allowing you to get straight off the bus and start walking.

THE WALK

From the entrance to the church in the centre of Zugarramurdi go uphill in a southerly direction following the sign to Etxalar and the yellow-and-white waymarkings. After 150m the road bends off to the left, but you veer off to the right (south) and continue on to the cemetrey on the outskirts of the village. Follow the road past the cemetrey and an apple orchard and descend slightly. Twenty metres past the cemetrey take the gravel track that veers off to the left (south) and, keeping the stream on your right-hand side, follow the track uphill. Five minutes beyond this you reach a ruined building where there is a fork. Ignore the fainter grass track and continue on the main track zigzagging uphill for 10 minutes to a small grassy ridge where there are pleasing views to the west over lush green valleys. Forty minutes into the walk you come to a narrow cement road halfway up the mountain. Turn left onto this road, following the direction of a wooden sign pointing to Ibaïneta. One hundred metres later you pass a house on your left called **Gaineko Borda** where the road ends and you follow a track veering off to the right (south) and enters a pine forest. Five minutes later at a fork in the track take the more obvious left-hand branch which continues uphill in

a southerly direction. An hour from the start you emerge out of the forest onto a grassy **col** (known as Ibaïneta Lepoa). As the numerous prehistoric dolmens indicate this col has been inhabited since time immemorial. Not surprising really as the views are lovely! As well as signs of your ancestors you'll find several signboards and information panels here pointing to every which way but the way we want (the sign pointing to Mt Atxuria has been pulled out of the ground and destroyed).

After a rest head west up the biggest of the two peaks; 10 minutes of strenuous leg action later you reach a false summit, carry on up beyond this in a westerly direction following the edge of the steep ridge and admiring the views down into France. After another few minutes you'll clamber

INTO THE WITCHES' LAIR

up onto the summit of **Mt Atxuria** which is either 759m according to most maps or 756m according to the marker post on the summit! Either way this short ridge summit sits smack bang on the border and offers marvellous views that on clear days take in half the French Basque coastline as well as a generous helping of hills and mountains to the east. Continue along the summit ridge in a westerly direction and, at the end of the summit start to descend in a northerly direction, blazing your own trail, along the ridge. You are now in France and on a clear day you should be able to see your goal, the car park at the Grottes de Sare. On a grey day you may just make out the sound of the odd passing motorbike far below. After around 30 minutes you'll reach a distinct path which zigzags down towards the car park passing by an area of forest. Forty-five minutes from the summit and after the faint path has become a very distinct path you'll reach a fork. Ignore the track heading off to your left which has a sign (with a green arrow and a pink flower painted on it) pointing down it. Instead follow the main path north northeast. Five minutes later you pass another flowery sign and a sign pointing downhill to the *grottes*. You now leave this main path and take a short cut down a smaller track in a northeast direction heading towards the obvious quarry and the car park. Note that this short cut path has been badly torn up by rainfall and requires a little caution. After five minutes you reach a fork where the torn up track continues straight ahead in a northerly direction. Instead turn right (east) and continue along a much smoother path; after 20 minutes this path almost doubles back on itself and descends through dense deciduous forest. An hour and a quarter after leaving the summit you finally reach the car park of the **Grottes de Sare** (☎ 05 59 54 21 88; adult/child €6.50/3.50; 10am-7pm Jul-Aug, much shorter hours throughout the winter).

From the cave entrance walk away from the car park and follow the sign for Zugarramurdi and the Restaurant-Venta Halty. The route is marked with blue triangles and a horse symbol and it's now almost impossible to get lost as there are markers every few metres. One hundred metres from the car park there is a paved track running along the southerly side of the road which you

can walk down in order to keep out of the road. After a few hundred metres the path rejoins the road, cross over the road and go around the corner to the left following the signs to the **Restaurant-Venta Halty**. As you approach the restaurant you'll see a little path on the right-hand side of the building marked with your friendly blue horse signs. Follow this as it vanishes into some pretty woodland. After 10 minutes you emerge out of the forest and onto a road from which you can enjoy views of the mountain you were earlier atop. Five minutes later you leave the road again and, instead, walk parallel but a little below the road, through some woodland and past the little **Grotte Lezea**. From here on our horsey arrows will all start pointing the other way – in other words back the way you've just come from, but nevertheless just keep following them towards Zugarramurdi. You drop to a stream, cross over a bridge and then climb steeply back up some steps in a southeast direction and onto a road. Turn right (southeast) and follow the road back to Zugarramurdi passing the **Cuevas de las Brujas** (Witches' Caves; ☎ 948 59 93 05; adult/child €3.50/2; 11am-dusk) on your right and, a moment or two later the bewitching **Museo de las Brujas** (☎ 948 59 90 04; adult/child €4/2; 11am-6pm Wed-Sun) on your left. The latter is a fascinating delve into the mysterious cauldron of witchcraft in the Pyrenees. Walk a couple of minutes back up the hill and, one hour after leaving the Grottes de Sare, you arrive back at Zugarramurdi's church. Zugarramurdi has plenty of *casas rurales* but no official hotel. There is also no public transport here.

FRONTIER VIEWS

Duration 4½ hours

Distance 10.5km

Difficulty easy–moderate

Start/Finish Puerto de Izpegi/Col d'Ispéguy

Nearest Town Elizondo (p157)

Transport car

Summary Tip-toe along a frontier ridge, saunter through beech forests and sweat your way up to some extraordinary views.

This memorable walk is one of the finest in the Basque Country – for minimal effort it rewards you with a view worthy of a hike twice as hard! It begins smack bang on the Spanish-French frontier (the road that leads to the starting point is spectacular enough to be a tourist attraction in its own right!) and then, criss-crossing between Spain and France, you skip along through gorgeous beech forests and up onto a grassy pass full of grazing *pottok* (miniature Basque ponies that are so small they make Shetland ponies look like shire horses), and lovely views over the surrounding mountains. The next stage of the walk is tougher. In a short distance you ascend over 500m, but the views, firstly along a knife-edged ridge and then from the summit of Mt Autza/ Mt Auza (1304m), are truly breathtaking. From the summit itself you have a 360-degree view that on clear days takes in the whole of the western Pyrenees as well as down to the French coast and the towns of Biarritz and St Jean de Luz. The first part of the walk, as far as the Elhorrieta pass is a superb family-friendly excursion of 1½ to two hours.

PLANNING
When to Walk
May to October are the prime months, although June-August can be a bit too hot for most people. Avoid misty, wet or snowy days when the path through the forest can become very boggy. Hunting season runs from October to November and walking the return leg from Elhorrieta back to the Puerto de Izpegi can become downright dangerous at this time!

Maps
Rando Éditions *Pays Basque Ouest* 1:50,000 is the most accurate map and has the route marked on it.

GETTING TO/FROM THE WALK
There is no transport whatsoever from Elizondo to the trailhead so you'll either need your own wheels or you'll have to hitch.

THE WALK
From the car park at the **Puerto de Izpegi** (672m) walk to the far southeast side and take the trail signed 'Banca'. This drops a few metres before levelling out and winding through lush ferns. The trail for this first

part is extremely obvious, well waymarked in green and white and in places the trail has even been nicely surfaced with gravel. After five minutes you'll pass by a gravestone oddly sited right on the edge of the trail.

After this the trail starts to climb fairly gently through some fantastic beech forest and opn areas of heathers. Ten minutes later the path forks; take the right -hand fork which doubles back on itself for a very short distance and then climbs quite steeply up the mountain in a zigzag fashion. After a further 45 minutes you emerge from the forest and onto the grassy knoll of the **Nekaitzeko Lépoa** (814m), a pass which is normally full of cute little *pottok* ponies awaiting a bit of fuss and attention. The signage here is a little confusing so simply ignore it and cross the pass in a southwest direction (keeping the **shepherds' hut** and a sheep pen on your right) aiming for the narrow surfaced road that is just visible from the Nekaitzeko Lépoa. On reaching this road, 10 minutes later, you'll be on the **Col d'Elhorrieta** (831m), which is marked with various signboards and an old and

FRONTIER VIEWS

faded B.F. 102 marker stone. This pass is notable for two reasons. First, it makes a great place for a picnic and secondly it marks the end of the easy part of the walk – if you're with children or less experienced walkers this might be the point at which you want to stop and, after a picnic and some time admiring the lovely views of the mountains around you, return to the Puerto de Izpegi via the Mt Olate route described further below.

If higher things await you then walk onto the road, past the BF 102 marker and the sign to Autza and, as you reach the bend in the road you'll see two grassy tracks leading off the road. The more obvious one goes downhill in a west-southwest direction. Ignore this one and instead take the much fainter and narrower trail that climbs steeply uphill into the forest in a more south-southwest direction. Start clambering upwards, pass through a gap in a fence, and continue ascending. You'll be running parallel, and in between, a barbed wire fence and a sheer ridge. After five minutes the path becomes clearer (although there are no waymarkers) and you now start to get the first of the evermore impressive views off the ridge. Fifteen minutes later you emerge from the forest and onto a small grassy pass with views over the French mountains that will blow your hiking boots off.

Mt Autza is clearly visible as the huge bulging peak immediately to the west (right), but instead of charging to the summit up the very steep slope next to you take the faint, and largely flat, trail marked by rock cairns that runs around the east side of the mountain until you reach another pass where the mountains on the Spanish side finally become visible for the first time. Turn west (right) here and start climbing to the summit following the cairns.

This final ascent follows a ridge with views across both sides of the border. Half an hour later and you finally reach the grassy summit of **Mt Autza** (1306m), which is marked with some crazy rock formations (not all of which are made by Mother Nature) and huge views over all the western Pyrenees and along the French coastline. On clear days you can easily spot the lighthouse down in Biarritz!

When you've finished soaring like a hawk on the summit return the same way you came back to the Nekaitzeko Lépoa pass from where, you can take a slightly shorter, but impressively scenic route over the humpback ridge of **Mt Olate** (935m) back to the car. To do this, look for the sign saying *Izpegi Olate* next to the sheep pen and follow it up the hill in a northeast direction. The trail is well waymarked in green and white and is obvious enough. Five minutes huffing and puffing will bring you to the top of the hill and a natural stone 'gateway'; pass through this and enter an area of beautiful beech forest. After a couple of minutes the path bears slightly right and weaves around a bit, but it remains well waymarked. Look out for the tree houses here from which hunters massacre the local birdlife each autumn. At other times of the year they give the rest of us an interesting tree's-eye view of the world. After 10 minutes you come out of the forest and onto an open hill carpeted in ferns. At the fork take the trail on the left which runs in a northwest direction and heads downwards rewarding you all the way with lovely views into the Spanish valleys. Shortly afterwards you will catch your first view of the main road snaking up from Elizondo to the Puerto de Izpegi and five minutes after that the pass itself and the car park come into view just below you. Follow the path back down to the car park.

VULTURES & VERTIGO

Duration 5½ hours

Distance 16km

Difficulty moderate

Start/Finish Col des Veaux

Nearest Towns Zugarramurdi (p147), Elizondo (p157), Bidarry (in France)

Transport car

Summary Veg out with the vultures on the vertiginous cliffs of the Peñas de Itsusi.

From valley low to mountain high this, at times, quite tough walk will have you soaring with masses of carrion-feeding griffon vultures and keeping an eagle-eyed lookout for other large birds of prey. In addition to being one of the finest places in the Pyrenees to see large raptors up close (vultures nest on the cliffs of the Peñas de Itsusi and are easily visible), this hike takes in a beautiful and remote Spanish valley complete with gushing river full of tempting places to have a paddle, an ancient pre-Christian shrine, and some glorious rolling mountain views.

Much of this walk is fairly easy, but there is one very steep, sweaty and rather hard to find section which leads from the valley floor up to the top of the Peñas de Itsusi.

Like many of the walks in the Basque Pyrenees this one sends you criss-crossing the Spanish/French frontier, but unlike any other walk in this book it's actually easier to access from the French side of the frontier.

PLANNING
When to Walk
May to October are the prime months, although June-August can be a bit too hot for most people. Avoid misty, wet or snowy days when route finding around the Peñas de Itsusi can be tough.

Maps
Rando Éditions *Pays Basque Ouest* 1:50,000 is the most accurate map and has the route marked on it.

GETTING TO/FROM THE WALK
There is no public transport whatsoever to the trailhead at the Col des Veaux, which exactly marks the Spanish/French border. Even with your own car getting there from the Spanish side can be a pain and most people drive there via France from the Pas de Roland and then take the tiny, winding road south through Laxia and onto the Venta Burkaitz, a shop that sits just off the Col des Veaux. If you're coming from Elizondo or Zugarramurdi drive along the N-121-B to Otsondo Gaina/Puerto de Otsondo where a small road forks off eastward to the Itzulegi parking. Just before this parking an even narrower and not always well-maintained farm track leads off to the left (northeast) and takes you, eventually, to the Col des Veaux.

Note also that the Col des Veaux is quite indistinct; the most obvious landmark there

is the Venta Burkaitz. Another option is to continue up from the Col des Veaux a couple of kilometres to the much more obvious Col de Méhatché. If you're reliant on public transport then the best bet is to head to France and hitch. On fine weekends this shouldn't be too hard.

THE WALK
From the parking at the **Col des Veaux** (567m) walk downhill along the road in a southerly direction. A hundred metres later you reach a junction of three roads; the one on the right heads slightly uphill and is marked with a blank white sign, another, the middle road, heads to the shop, Venta Burkaitz while the third one, which you want to take, is a concrete road that bends off left (east) and downhill and is marked with a sign for the Lezetako Borda. Follow this concrete road downhill through light woodland for half an hour until you reach the **Lezetako Borda**, a traditional Basque farmhouse that's been converted into a restaurant and serves excellent hearty mountain *menús* for €18–22. Follow the road, which now becomes a wide dirt piste behind the restaurant, pass over the cattle grid and start to walk gently uphill. For the next 40 minutes the path, which has no turn-offs or diversions, undulates through lovely woodland, past the odd farm and occasionally opens out to give views of the enviously green hills and mountain peaks surrounding you. Finally, you come to a crossroads, turn left here (east) and head gently uphill. You will now be running just above the Bastan river, though you'll still only be able to hear it rather than see it. Look out also for the gorgeous old chestnut trees that pop up along this section. As you walk along the path you gently descend past a small waterfall on your left-hand side and then, 10 minutes from the crossroads, you come to another fork. Ignore the narrower trail going uphill and stick with the wider, descending track. A moment or so later ignore the turning on your right leading to a stone farmhouse and continue straight ahead in an easterly direction. A few of minutes beyond you'll get your first views of the Peñas de Itsusi high up to your left and often clouded with soaring vultures. Looks high doesn't it? Yep, that's where you're off too! You then

reach another fork, take the downhill right hand path which continues down to the left bank of the chocolate brown **Bastan river**. A moment or so later you pass by a farmhouse with green shutters and reach a bridge over the river. Don't cross this bridge; instead leave the dirt road and veer off to the left along the little grassy path. The path is quite discreet and some might mistake it for an animal track. It starts just before the **bridge** and heads gently uphill in a northeast direction through the ferns. After about 20 minutes the path suddenly widens and comes to a fork with one branch heading downhill in a southeast direction and the other, right-hand branch, continuing uphill in a northeast direction. Take the right-hand branch and pass by the dry-stone wall, field and stable and continue into a patch of woodland until you reach a farm gate across the path. Go through this gate and continue another minute or so to the old stable on the right. As you reach the edge of this building, look for the very indiscreet, muddy track on the opposite side of the trail to the building. There's a small rock with a pink marker arrow on the ground next to this turn-off. Start to climb steeply up this track following the pink marker spots all the way. After a few minutes of hard climbing you get to a ruined farmhouse; walk

around the left-hand side of this (keeping the house on your right) and continue following the paint markers straight on up the now very steep narrow trail. This is the toughest part of the walk as, for the next 30 excruciating minutes, you are climbing towards the Peñas de Itsusi. Finally, high up the mountainside, you reach a crossroads where the insignificant path you've been following meets a much more trodden trail. You are now in France and this is part of the GR10; the trans-Pyrenean trail which runs east-west across the French Pyrenees and is marked with red-and-white paint slashes. As you haul yourself up onto this track turn right and head downhill for 15 minutes until you see a set of rough steps veering off uphill to your left for a few metres and into a cave (there is a rope handrail to help you pull yourself up here). This is **Harpeko Saindoa**, a part pagan, part Christian shrine full of torn up bits of clothing, plastic Virgins and other strange items. The origins of its mysterious lure on pilgrims of more than one persuasion is somewhat unclear but they have, nonetheless, been beating a fervent path up to the shrine for as long as anyone remembers, and their habit of leaving a personal offering to mollify the god or goddess of their choice endures to this day. The stalactite at the far end of the cave is said to cure skin complaints.

Exiting the cave, retrace your steps for 15 minutes back to where you joined the GR10 and then continue following it onwards and upwards along the northeast side of the steep valley. Although the path is always obvious, at times it can be quite hard going as you have to scramble over the debris of old landslides. Twenty minutes later, and right at the head of the valley, you come to a fork. The GR10 veers off right (north) and sails almost vertically up the cliff face. Breathe easy though because you're not going that way. Instead follow the pink paint splodges (that caused you so much pain earlier at the head of the valley), back into Spain and then south along the opposite wall of the valley with only a moderate rise in altitude. After a further 15 minutes you wind around the corner and climb onto a small grassy plain with memorable views over the Spanish mountains. Turn

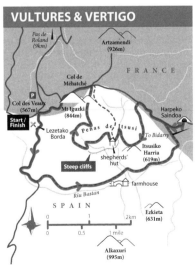

VULTURES & VERTIGO

right (west-northwest) here and continue to follow the pink waymarkers past the ruins of an old shepherds' cabin, and just beyond at the light fork, take the higher, right-hand path which leads you past two small **cols**.

The second col marks the start of the **Peñas de Itsusi**. Turn left (northwest) and follow both the pink paint splodges as well as some yellow arrows (pointing back the way you just came from) along the spectacular ridges and crags. Closeup vulture sightings are virtually guaranteed here and if you're lucky, in the spring and summer you might even be able to see vultures sitting on nests built into the cliffs below you. Keep heading northwest and downwards until you hit a stream. Walk 20 minutes upstream until you reach a pool and small waterfall (which makes a perfect picnic spot). Cross the stream here and you come to a clearing with a ruined shepherds' hut and another still habitable one. This clearing, sited on the edge of the cliff, gives easily the best view to the valley far, far below and is also popular with wildlife photographers after vulture shots. Turn inland here and continue to follow the waymarked path which meanders between a couple of hundred metres inland and the cliff edge before finally leaving the Peñas de Itsusi behind and heads north to the Col de Méhatché at the foot of **Mt Iguzki** (844m). When you reach the junction in the open countryside follow the pink waymarkers uphill and north, past a farmhouse, around the right hand side of Mt Iguzki and down onto the **Col de Méhatché**, which again marks the border of the two countries.

Turn left here onto the surfaced road and head downhill following the re-appearance GR10 paint slashes for 10 minutes until the road bends sharply off to the right. Following the GR10 markers leave the road here and follow the track straight ahead in a southwest direction. Turn right when you reach the fenced-in field and then left at the other end of the field join a farm track at a junction marked with a strange gravestone-like rock where you turn right. Thirty-five minutes beyond the Col de Méhatché you arrive back on the tarmac road and your car at the Col des Veaux.

PILGRIMS TO POTTOKS

Duration 5½ hours
Distance 17km
Difficulty moderate
Start/Finish Collada Lepoeder
Nearest Town Roncesvalles (p334)
Transport bus, taxi, car
Summary Looping through history, forests and mountain magnificence, this route flirts with the border, hangs out with Santiago-bound pilgrims and goes gooey over cute *pottok* ponies.

This is a fantastic walk taking you through the best of the Navarran Pyrenees, but there's more to this hike than just scenery. A sense of history abounds; the trailhead is located just a short way above the famous monastery of Roncesvalles – the first major port of call on Spanish soil for Santiago-bound pilgrims, and indeed a part of our route follows the Camino de Santiago as it rises up from France.

The Puerto de Ibañeta, just down the road from where we begin and end our walk (and if you want to add an extra hour and a half to the walk a good place for you to start and finish from), is immortalised in the 12th-century French epic poem *The Song of Roland* which recounts the slaughter of Charlemagne's rear guard. In more modern times, it was also from this pass that Napoleon launched his 1802 occupation of Spain and if that weren't enough history then a few dolmens help to stretch time right back to the Neolithic Age.

PLANNING
When to Walk
Mist and fog are possible at any time of year and can cause disorientation. You should not attempt to walk through the forest between the Col d'Orgambidé and the Cabane d'Urculu on such days and instead should take the alternative route described on p154, which follows the road through France. The most predictably dry and clear months are July to September. Hunting season runs from October through November. Hunters prize early October mornings and weekends.

Maps & Books

Rando Éditions *Pays Basque Est* 1:50,000 map covers this route although the detail isn't always quite what it could be. Make sure you buy the latest version of this map with the Crêtes d'Iparla on the cover as, on the older version the key has been thoughtfully placed right over the part you need! Buy all maps and books in either Pamplona or San Sebastián.

GETTING TO/FROM THE WALK

From Roncesvalles there is no public transport up to the border neither the Collada Lepoeder nor Puerto de Ibañeta, so you'll need to either have your own car, rent a taxi from Burguete (2.5km down the road from Roncesvalles), stick your thumb out and hitch (fairly easy to Puerto de Ibañeta, but much harder onwards to the Collada Lepoeder) or march along the Camino de Santiago pilgrimage route from Roncesvalles (add three hours if you do this). If you're driving actually finding the Collada Lepoeder can be a little confusing. From the Puerto de Ibañeta with its chapel and car park, follow the dirt road just at the entrance to the car park eastward and upward for 2.5km until you reach a distinct pass and a crossroads with driving tracks heading off in three different directions. This is the Collada Lepoeder, but there's no car park as such so just park on the grass verge.

THE WALK

Our walk begins on top of the world at the **Collada Lepoeder** with its stupendous views down to Roncesvalles – views that are normally being savoured by tired pilgrims who've just made it up from France and are getting their first long look at the way ahead. Take the wide left track heading north. This is both part of the GR11 and the Camino de Santiago and is superbly marked with blue and yellow signposts with a scallop shell on them (the symbol of the Camino), and the red-and-white slashes of the GR11. After five minutes veer off this main path and on to a small and faint path on the left, beside a group of trees. This takes you to the summit of **Mt Astobizkar** (1497m) where you can enjoy the views in relative peace. Walk along the gentle crest of the summit and

follow it back to the main GR11 path that you were on earlier.

A little over an hour from the start and you reach the **Col de Bentarte** (1344m) which sits smack on the French/Spanish border. We now say goodbye to the Camino and the main track which bears off into France and instead we veer right (east) following the red-and-white GR11 tracks along a grassy, and after the Camino, much quieter, trail. After a couple of hundred metres there's another fork, take the left-hand and more easterly fork, go through the gate and follow the trail along the side of a dry-stone wall and past various water troughs. You then reach the spectacular **Col d'Arnostéguy** which sits right on the frontier (a small tarmac road descends to St Jean Pied de Port in France from here), and has views down into the forested Spanish countryside (with normally quite a few *pottok* and other ponies around). Continue to follow the GR11 downwards in a southeast direction along the southern flank of Mt Urculu. The trail zigzags around, passes through areas of forests and at times drops fairly steeply. Fifteen minutes beyond the Col d'Arnostéguy you'll reach another slight col with some Neolithic **dolmens** off to the right and 15 minutes beyond these you'll pass by several **stone cabins**. Just past these, at a sign board, leave the GR11 behind (which continues southeast and downhill towards the Refugio Azpegi), and instead veer northeast and uphill along a motorable road. Keep following this road as it weaves uphill passing various livestock drinking troughs and a signpost to Azpegi. The road will eventually level out a little and winds over high moorland full of sheep, horses and cows.

Continue to stick to this track and 1½ hours after leaving the Col d'Arnostéguy you reach a crossroads where the cement road you've been following meets a tarmac road heading off to your right and left. This is the **Col d'Orgambidé**, which again identifies the border of Spain and France and is marked by a fake dolem just off to your left. You must now make a choice depending on the weather. If it's fine follow the instructions below. If it's rainy, misty or looks like it might change for the worse follow the description under Alternative Route (p154).

PILGRIMS TO POTTOKS

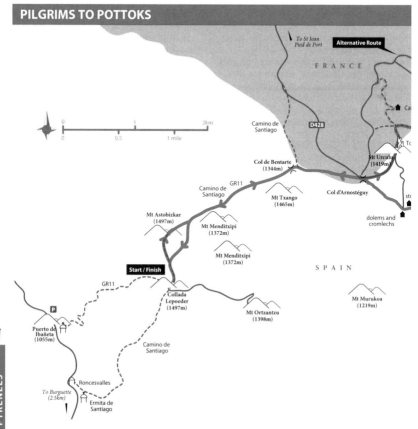

From the col retrace your steps 200m and then veer off west on the clear but unmarked path which disappears in and out of forests, grasslands and a strange karst landscape. Be very careful all along this section to avoid falling into one of the numerous sink holes! The path clambers along the side of a valley and becomes ever fainter but eventually you'll cross over into France between the BF 207 and BF 208 marker posts. Around an hour later you'll pass a large sink hole (doline) where you bear left uphill. From the summit you should be able to see a farmhouse, the **Cabane d'Urculu**. Walk on until you're directly above this house and then turn due south heading uphill to the summit of **Mt Urculu** (1419m). The summit is marked by the ruins of a stone tower, thought by 'experts' to date from anytime

between Roman times and the Middle Ages. After catching your breath, and the views, descend towards the Col d'Arnostéguy which we passed by earlier in a southerly direction before veering more to the west. For all of this descent you should be following the yellow paint splotches. Be warned this descent is very steep in places. From the Col d'Arnostéguy simply retrace your steps back along the GR11 in a westerly direction before re-joining the Camino at the Col de Bentarte and heading west-southwest back along the wide gravel track to your waiting car at the Collada Lepoeder.

ALTERNATIVE ROUTE
1½ hours, 5km

On days of bad visibility and weather you should not attempt the section between

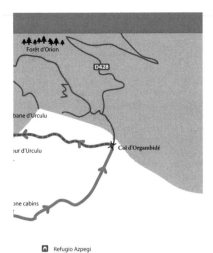

Refugio Azpegi

Mt Mendilatz
(1348m)

surfaced turn-offs to your left (and a couple of tracks) and a few farmhouses (there is a concentration of these by the second turn-off and one solitary one by the third turn-off). Eventually you'll find yourself outside the **Cabane d'Urculu**, a permanently inhabited farmhouse.

Continue past this house following the road, which now becomes a dirt track and after 10 minutes arrives at a half buried bunker on your left. From this bunker head due north towards the summit of **Mt Urculu** (1419m). It takes about 20 minutes of panting and puffing to crawl to the ruined tower on the summit where you rejoin the main route description. Taking this alternative route adds about half an hour to your walking time.

MORE WALKS

PARQUE NATURAL DE VALDEREJO
Desfiladero del Río Purón

The great attraction of Euskadi's most remote park, in Álava's extreme west (access via A2622), is the Río Purón's impressive gorge. Leaving from Lalastra, by the park's information centre, the short highlight walk passes through the abandoned village of Ribera and then enters the high, narrow gorge; at times the trail is excavated in the rock. The park centre has the free 1:16,000 *Valderejo Parque Natural* map, as well as information on other walks.

RESERVA DE LA BIOSFERA DE URDAIBAI
Elantxobe to Kanala

Northeast of Bilbao (via Gernika) is the 230-sq-km Urdaibai Reserve, taking in 12km of sandy shore along the Mundaka estuary and the surrounding hills. An attractive 13km moderate walk begins in Elantxobe, a fishing village that clings like a gecko to steep cliffs, and ascends to Cabo Ogoño, whose vertical walls drop 280m to the ocean. Continue to Akorda and then ascend to the grand *mirador* above the reserve, Ermita de San Pedro de Atxarre. Descend to Kanala on the estuary's shore. In summer, boats ferry across to Mundaka. Use the GV 1:25,000 maps, Nos 38-III and 38-IV.

the Col d'Orgambidé and the Cabane d'Urculu as the dangers of disappearing down a sink hole in the forest or getting hopelessly lost in the confusing landscape are much too high. Instead, take the longer, but safer route described here. Where the cement road meets the tarmac at the **Col d'Orgambidé** turn left (roughly north) and follow it for 500m over bleak moorland to a junction, a water trough and some signposts.

One sign points right (northeast) and downhill towards St Jean Pied de Port. Ignore this and instead turn left (which heads northwest and then almost immediately southwest before settling on a more westerly direction) to the Col d'Arnostéguy. Follow this tarmac road for a little over an hour passing three

PARQUE NATURAL AIAKO HARRIA

Visible from San Sebastián as a three-pronged crown, Aiako Harria (821m) is Euskadi's only granite massif. Take the GI363 Oiartzun-Irún road to the Alto de Elurtxe. From here a moderate 14km loop rounds the massif's perimetre via Arritxulegui and Castillo del Inglés. Alternatively, ascend the impressive crest, taking in Irumugarrieta, Txurrumurru and Erroilbide. Enjoy fantastic views of the city and ocean while walking in alpine forest. The IGN's 1:25,000 map No 65-I *Ventas de Irún* is helpful.

AROUND THE GR11
Selva de Irati

The 124 sq km of beech and white spruce northeast of Pamplona in the Irati Forest, one of Europe's largest forests, make for great walking. Take the NA178 via Ochagavía. The information centre is at the Casas de Irati, east of the Irabia reservoir. In an area famed for its abundant flora and fauna, there are eight easy, well-marked routes, all less than 6km in length. The highlight? Monte La Cuestión, northeast of the reservoir, shelters a section of forest untouched by human hands during the 20th century – difficulty of access prevented the lumber industry from removing wood. The recommended 1:40,000 *Irati, Valle de Salazar* map is available in many tourist offices, including Pamplona and Casas de Irati.

TOWNS & FACILITIES

BILBAO
☎ 944 / pop 353,400

Bilbao is a tough city that grew up surrounded by heavy industry and industrial wastelands, which for many years left it abused and bruised. However, a few wise investments have given it a shimmering titanium fish called the Museo Guggenheim and a horde of arty groupies around the world.

Today the city is a place of real character and hard-working, down to earth soul which, when combined with its plethora of cultural attractions make it a dynamic and exciting place to visit.

Information

The **tourist office** (☎ 79 57 60; www.bilbao.net/bilbaoturismo); **main office** (Plaza del Ensanche 11; 9am-2pm & 4-7.30pm Mon-Fri); **Teatro Arriaga (**Plaza Arriaga; 9.30am-2pm & 4-7.30pm daily Jun-Sep, 11am-2pm & 5-7.30pm Mon-Fri, 9.30am-2pm & 5-7.30pm Sat, 9.30am-2pm Sun Oct-May); and **Guggenheim** (Avenida Abandoibarra 2; 10am-7pm Mon-Sat, 10am-6pm Sun Jul-Sep, 11am-6pm Tue-Fri, 11am-7pm Sat, 11am-3pm Sun Oct-May) provide a wide-range of local and regional information.

The two best bookshops for maps and walking books (in English and French as well as Spanish) are **Tintas** (☎ 44 95 41; Calle del Generál Concha 10) and **Elkar Megadenda** (☎ 24 02 28; Calle de Iparragirre 26).

Sleeping & Eating

Camping Sopelana (☎ 946 76 21 20; sites for two people, small tent & car €25) is an xposed and crowded site within easy walking distance of Sopelana Beach. It's on the metro line, 15km from Bilbao.

Pensión Ladero (☎ 15 09 32; Calle Lotería 1; s/d €24/36) The no-fuss rooms here are as cheap as Bilbao gets and that mammoth climb up four storeys will be good training for your up-coming hiking adventures.

Hostal Begoña (☎ 23 01 34; www.hostalbegona.com; Calle de la Amistad 2; s/d from €53/64) has colourful rooms decorated with modern artworks, all with funky tiled bathrooms and wrought-iron beds.

Pensión Iturrienea Ostatua (☎ 16 15 00; www.iturrieneaostatua.com; Calle de Santa María 14; d/tw €70/96) Easily the most eccentric hotel in Bilbao, it's part farmyard, part old-fashioned toyshop and a work of art in its own right. Try to get a room on the 1st floor; they are so full of character there'll be barely enough room for your own!

Café-Bar Bilbao (Plaza Nueva 6; pintxos / Basque tapas €2-4) This place prides itself on very creative *pintxos,* so plunge straight in for a taste of *mousse de pata sobre crema de melocotón y almendras* (duck, cream, peach and almond mousse). Don't ask; just eat.

Abaroa (Paseo del Campo de Volantin 13; mains €7-12) This intimate place specialises in hearty countryside fare, but with a twist of today. The result is that black pudding and a bowl of beans have never been so well presented or tasted so good.

Rio-Oja (Calle de Perro 4; mains €8-10) specialises in light Basque seafood and heavy Riojan fare. To most foreigners the squid floating in pools of its own ink and sheep brains lying in its former owner's skull are the makings of a culinary adventure story that will be recounted for years. Don't worry: it really does taste much better than it sounds.

Getting There & Away
Bilbao's main bus station, **Termibus** (San Mamés), is the base for most bus companies. You can zoom from here to all big towns as well as most smaller centres throughout the Basque Country, Cantabria and beyond.

Renfe (☎ 902 24 02 02; www.renfe.es; Abando station, Plaza Circular 2) connects Bilbao to Madrid and Barcelona. **FEVE** (☎ 23 22 66; www.feve.es; Concordia station, Bailén 2) narrow-gauge rail trains serves the north coast west of Bilbao, and **Eusko Tren** (☎ 902 54 32 10; www .euskotren.es; Casco Viejo station, Plaza San Nicolás) goes to destinations within the Basque Country (San Sebastián, Durango and Hondarribia).

P&O ferries (☎ 902 02 04 61, 944 23 44 77; www.poportsmouth.com; Calle de Cosme Echevarrieta 1) leave three times a week for Portsmouth.

By car, take the N1 from Madrid to Burgos, the A1 to Vitoria and then the A68 to Bilbao.

ELIZONDO
☎ 948 / pop 1600
Elizondo is Valle de Baztan's capital and most important urban centre. The summer-only **tourist office** (☎ 58 12 79; Casa de Cultura, Plaza de los Fueros) provides information on local walks.

Antxitónea Hostal (☎ 58 18 07; www .antxitonea.com; Calle Braulío Iríarte 16; d from €72) has plain rooms with flower-ladened balconies. The attached restaurant has an excellent value €10 *menú del día*.

Several buses a day link Elizondo to Pamplona, which is 51km.

LEKUNBERRI
☎ 948 / pop 1100
There's not much to Basque-by-name, Basque-by-nature Lekunberri, the *sierra*'s main town, except a gaggle of solid Basque farmhouses in the old quarter and a growing estate of soulless modern housing beyond.

Information
The **tourist office** (☎ 50 72 04; oit .lekunberri@cfnavarra.es; Calle de Plazaola 21) is very helpful and can provide A4 sheets with simple valley-based local walks in English and harder and higher walks in Spanish.

Sleeping & Eating
Lekunberri has a number of hotels and restaurants. Hang with the ghosts of Sanfermines past at the beautiful **Hotel Ayestarán** (☎ 50 41 27; www.hotelayestaran .com; Calle de Aralar 27; s/d from €46/74) where Hemmingway stayed en route to the Pamplona party. The restaurant here is equally superb.

Getting There & Away
Most buses between Pamplona and San Sebastián stop here.

SAN SEBASTIÁN (DONOSTIA)
☎ 943 / pop 184,000
It's said that nothing is impossible. This is wrong. It's impossible to lay eyes on San Sebastián and not fall madly in love. This stunning city is everything that grimy Bilbao is not: cool, svelte and flirtatious by night, charming and well mannered by day. Best of all is the summer fun on the beach. For their setting, form and attitude the beaches of San Sebastián are the equal of any of the best city beaches in Europe.

Information
The city's friendly **tourist office** (☎ 943 48 11 66; www.sansebastianturismo.com; Blvd 8; 8.30am-8pm Mon-Sat, 10am-7pm Sun, Jun-Sep, 9am-2pm & 3.30-7pm Mon-Sat, 10am-2pm Sun Oct-May) offers comprehensive information on both the city and the Basque Country in general including some advice on local walks. There's also a smaller **tourist kiosk** (Paseo de la Concha;

10.30am-8.30pm Jul & Aug) at the city end of the Paseo de la Concha.

Elkar Megadenda (☎ 42 26 96; Calle de Fermín Calbetón 30) This excellent branch of the Elkar Megadenda Basque bookshop chain specalises in travel books and guides and has a dauntingly impressive range of hiking books and maps in a variety of languages – including virtually everything in print on hiking throughout Spain (in Spanish, French and English). If you need to pick up a map to an obscure Spanish mountain range then this is the place to do it. Almost opposite is its big brother which stocks a huge range of Basque language titles.

Sleeping & Eating

Camping Igueldo (☎ 21 45 02; www.camp ingigueldo.com; Paseo del Padra Orkolaga 69; sites for two people, car & tent or caravan from €25) This well-organised, tree-shaded camping ground is 5km west of the city and is served by bus 16 from Alameda del Boul-evard (€1.20, 30 minutes).

Albergue La Sirena Ondarreta (☎ 31 02 68; udala_youthhostel@donostia.org; Paseo de Igueldo 25; dm under/over 25yr from €17/18) San Sebastián's HI hostel is near Playa de Ondarreta and Monte Igueldo. It's immaculate and very secure. The midnight curfew extends to 4am on weekends, June to September.

Olga's Place (☎ 32 67 25; Calle de Zabaleta 49; dm €30) What you get here is the basics done exceedingly well; everything about this very popular hostel is immaculate and there's also a kitchen for guest use.

Pensión Amaiur Ostatua (☎ 42 96 54; www.pensionamaiur.com; Calle de 31 de Agosto 44; s/d without bathroom €55/60) Small rooms that have had a great deal of thought put into them – there's chintzy wallpaper in the hallways, brazen primary colours in the bedrooms and everywhere a

bizarre mix of African savannah and French street-scene paintings. There's a kitchen for guest use, and communal bathrooms only. In the high season you need to book months in advance.

Pensión Aida (☎ 32 78 00; www .pensionesconencanto.com; Calle de Iztueta 9; s/d €59/78) The owners of this excellent *pensión* read the rule book on what makes a good hotel. The rooms are bright and bold, full of exposed stone, and everything smells fresh and clean. For our money we'd say this one is hard to beat.

There are *pintxos* and then there are San Sebastián *pintxos*. Though every city in Spain likes to boast about the quality of its own *pintxos* or tapas, all will grudgingly agree that those of San Sebastián stand on a pedestal above all others. To prove it's not just a one-trick pony, San Sebastián has some superb restaurants and is home to more Michelin stars than even Paris. To find the best tastes head to the *Parte Vieja* (old quarter) where we could rave all day about the quality food to be found in the **Bar Goiz-Argi** (Calle de Fermín Calbetón 4), **Astelena** (Calle de Iñigo 1) and **La Cuchara de San Telmo** (Calle de 31 de Agosto 28).

Getting There & Away

From the **main bus station** (Plaza Pío XII) you'll find rides to every major and most minor towns in the Basque Country and Navarra as well as onward to most other large Spanish cities (sometimes with a change in Madrid). **Renfe** (☎ 42 64 30; Estación Norte, Avenida de Francia) has trains to Madrid and Barcelona among other places. If travelling east–west along the Basque coast it's better to take the **Eusko Tren** (Plaza Easo), which provides services to Bilbao, Durango and Hondarribia among other places.

Cordillera Cantábrica

- Following 2000-year-old Roman highways through the forests of the **Parque Natural de Saja-Besaya** (p162)
- Watching the indefatigable chamois as they leap around the steep and rocky mountain slopes of the **Parque Nacional de los Picos de Europa** (p167)
- Contemplating the awesome, sheer-walled spectacle of the **Garganta del Cares gorge** (p177)
- Relishing the peace and tranquillity of the high meadows found on many of the **Picos** walks (p167)
- Conquering your fear of heights and relishing the views on the **Ruta de Tresviso** walk (p180)

Area: 15, 925 sq km	Average summer high: 22°C

The Cordillera Cantábrica straddles the regions of Asturias, Cantabria and the Leonese part of Castilla y León. More than 250km long, it stretches from Serra dos Ancares in Galicia to Sierra de Peña Labra on the border between Cantabria and Castilla y León. Towering 2000m peaks rise from the Atlantic Ocean like huge sheer walls and form an imposing barrier that separates the sea from the great Castilian plains. Cut through by powerful river systems and low-lying, verdant valleys, these spectacular agricultural mountains are among Spain's finest.

It's not all about the peaks around here though; many walkers enjoy the lower mountains and rustic villages of the Parque Natural de Saja-Besaya, a region rarely strolled by foreigners. However, it's the Picos de Europa, composed of three magnificent limestone massifs – that are the highlight of walking areas in the Cordillera Cantábrica. They are simply magnificent. In fact many walkers rate them as the top hiking range in Spain.

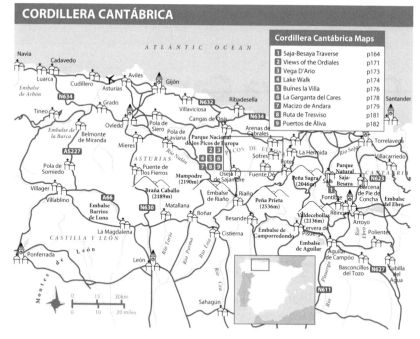

CORDILLERA CANTÁBRICA

Cordillera Cantábrica Maps

1	Saja-Besaya Traverse	p164
2	Views of the Ordiales	p171
3	Vega D'Ario	p173
4	Lake Walk	p174
5	Bulnes la Villa	p176
6	La Garganta del Cares	p178
7	Macizo de Andara	p179
8	Ruta de Tresvio	p181
9	Puertos de Áliva	p182

HISTORY

Palaeolithic cave art is found extensively in and around the Cordillera (see the boxed text Europe's First Artists, p161). Man's destructive hand appears in the Neolithic period (4000–2400 BC), with the spread of agriculture and livestock domestication provoking the first forest clearing. Around 2000 BC, immigrants from the north introduced metal technology and copper was actively mined. As the Roman Empire expanded, the Romans eagerly sought to control the Cordillera's wealth of iron, gold and copper and viciously subdued native tribes in campaigns from 29 to 13 BC. The area's 8th-century Arab presence is more legendary than factual, but nonetheless helped justify and initiate the Christian Reconquest of the peninsula. In 722 AD the Asturian King Pelayo won the first (legendary) battle against the Muslims at Covadonga (Cave of the Holy Mother) in the Picos de Europa. Over time, the cave and its magnificent waterfall evolved into a politico-religious symbol and an exceedingly popular pilgrimage site. Though the centuries-old cyclical practice of bringing the flocks from the low winter pastures of Castilla to the high summer pastures continues, *transhumance* (the oldest continuous economic activity of the Cordillera) is in decline.

Many of the indigenous forests of the lower slopes were felled to supply iron production, construction and fuel needs, opening up the land to new species of conifers and eucalyptues, the latter brought to the Cantabrian coast 160 years ago. The 20th century brought the most aggressive transformation of the landscape as technology made it easier to extract coal, ore and lumber, and to enter ecologically fragile areas – although, thankfully, conservation efforts now protect many areas.

ENVIRONMENT

Between 360 and 245 million years ago the rich coal deposits of the central Cordillera were formed from decaying ferns and moss pressed between layers of limestone and sand. Fossilised remnants of marine invertebrates – corals, crustaceans and molluscs – are also embedded in the rock. Forty million years ago, the African and

European tectonic plates collided. The Iberian subplate, sandwiched between the two, wrinkled and bulged, creating first the Pyrenees and then the Cordillera. Limestone (karst) landscapes are among the most significant geological features of the Cordillera and are characterised by dramatic, bare, open rocks, great high depressions and mountains riddled with underground waterways, interior vertical cavities and *simas* (caves; see the boxed text Caving in the Picos, p167). Glaciers dating from two million to 10,000 years ago created U-shaped valleys, polished walls, and dumped moraine.

The collision of Atlantic and Mediterranean climates, as well as dramatic variation in altitude, accounts for the Cordillera's wealth of flora and fauna. Up to 500m along the valley floors and riverways, forests include mountain ash, evergreen oak, common oak, beech, linden, chestnut, elm, alder, hazelnut, hawthorn, willow, maple and cherry trees. Shrubs include blackberry, sloe berry, wild roses and honeysuckle. In the wetter, northern valleys of Asturias, expect to see marsh orchids, globe flowers, ragged robins and marsh helleborines. In the more Mediterranean southern valleys, purple orchids and tassel hyacinths fill the meadows, and the forests include strawberry trees and cork oaks. From 500m to 1700m the plant life responds to the shorter summers and early frosts. Beech, birch, mountain ash, holly and holm-oaks dominate the forests. In the subalpine zone from 1700m to 2300m, you'll find beech and birch trees as well as juniper clinging to rock walls. The alpine area (2300m and above) supports small plants, including glacier fescue, columbine and toadflax.

In the forests, mammal species include brown bears, wild boar, mountain cats, wolves and red and roe deer. Along the river banks, otters and muskrats dwell with kingfishers and wagtails. In the skies goshawks, golden eagles, kestrels, common buzzards, griffon vultures and peregrine falcons dominate. Closer to the trees, listen for green and spotted woodpeckers as well as tawny, horned and barn owls. In rocky areas, tiny birds such as hedge and rock sparrows make their nests.

CLIMATE

Part of the Spanish region called 'España Verde' (Green Spain), the middle and lower elevations of the Cordillera have an Atlantic climate of temperate, wet weather. In winter and spring Atlantic cold fronts and air masses bring heavy rain and snow at high elevations. Winds tend to arrive from the northwest. The southern slopes and valleys have a drier, warmer climate, though anywhere in the Cordillera the weather can change rapidly. In general, snow leaves the lower slopes in April and May; at the highest elevations, snow may persist during June.

EUROPE'S FIRST ARTISTS

Imagine stepping back in time to Palaeolithic Europe (35,000–10,000 BC). Bone-chilling cold hits you (snow remains perpetually at 700m to 1000m) and the land is filled with almost mythical creatures – hairy mammoth and rhinoceros – and huge herds of bison, horses and deer: a hunter's paradise. You've arrived at a pivotal moment in human history. Along the Cantabrian coast, in the Pyrenees and southern France, the first and longest-lasting art form, cave painting, is being developed.

Using magnesium or carbon to create black lines and ochre or iron oxides to create brown, red, orange and yellow earth tones, artists filled walls and ceilings with animals, human figures, isolated hands and various symbols. Using the natural relief of the rock to convey a sense of volume, the movement and realism of the naturalistic animal figures richly contrasts with the distortion of faces and abstraction of symbols in these complex works.

West of Santander is Spain's most famous cave, Altamira. The site is virtually closed to visitors, but a complete recreation of the famous artwork, opened in 2001, provides an excellent sense of its grandeur. The many other caves open to visitors include Santimamiñe, 35 minutes from Bilbao towards the coast, El Castillo, one of four caves in Puente Viesgo 30km south of Santander, and El Buxu at the foot of the Picos de Europa just outside Cangas de Onís. Ask for the free brochure *Routes Through Prehistoric Asturian Art* in Asturian tourist offices.

OSO PARDO, THE BROWN BEAR

If you go down to the woods today you're sure to find – a bear! Well, OK the truth is you probably won't find a bear, but there are still some out there, just clinging on. Until two centuries ago, the brown bear (known in Spanish as *oso pardo*) inhabited nearly all of the Iberian Peninsula in large numbers, but uncontrolled hunting, habitat destruction and poisoning have caused the bears' progressive decline. Today, counting the 17-24 bears in the Pyrenees, the Cordillera Cantábrica has the greatest bear population. Their habitat covers 5000 sq km divided into two zones. The eastern zone has between 20 and 30 (2007 figures) bears; the western a slowly rising population of 100 to 110 (2007 figures). In fact, after some 34 cubs were born to the western population in 2009 the World Conservation Union has officially downgraded the western population status from critically endangered to endangered. For a long time it was thought that the two populations were actually separate and had no contact with one another, which could lead to problems with the gene pool, but in 2009 it was discovered that a female from the eastern population had given birth to two cubs fathered by a male from the western population.

Asturias, in the middle of the protected area, shelters 75% of the population and is the region most committed to the bears' regeneration. It has founded the Bear Foundation of Asturias (*Fundación Oso de Asturias*) in Casa del Oso in Proaza, and established areas of protection, policing hunters. The region also compensates landowners for damage to their land caused by the bears.

For more on these magnificent creatures see www.iberianature.com/spainblog/category/bears/.

PLANNING

Maps

IGN's 1:200,000 *Asturias, Cantabria* and *Cordillera Cantábrica* maps are widely available and useful for orientation.

Map details for the walks are in Maps under Planning for each walk.

PLACE NAMES

Bable, the local Asturian dialect, inconsistently appears on signs and maps, especially in the Parque Nacional Picos de Europa. It's easy to match Bable and Castilian names if they vary on maps and signs.

Books

Robin Walker's *Walking in the Cordillera Cantábrica* (available in Spanish as *Por la Cordillera Cantábrica*) is worthwhile. Widely available in English within Spain is Tino Pertierra and Eduardo Garcia's interesting cultural guide *Asturias: A Journey into Paradise*. In Spanish, the best general guide is Anaya's *Picos de Europa y Cordillera Cantábrica*, by Ramón Martín, with general background information and car and walking routes. For additional route ideas try the harder to find Juan Luis Somoano and Erik Pérez's *50 Excursiones Selectas de la Montaña Asturiana*.

GATEWAYS

If you want to bag a peak in the Picos (and elsewhere in the region) then get yourself to either Oviedo (p185) in Asturias or Santander (p187) in Cantabria. The city of León (see p332) also can be used as a southern access town.

PARQUE NATURAL DE SAJA-BESAYA

From Roman roads to shepherds' wild haunts and dense beech forests, the Parque Natural de Saja-Besaya, created in 1988, offers a combination of history and infrequently visited open spaces. Nestled between two of Cantabria's great north-south rivers, the Río Saja and the Río Besaya, the park is a 245-sq-km island in the middle of Spain's largest *reserva nacional de caza* (national hunting reserve), which occupies 30% of Cantabria.

The park's mountains are rounded, unlike the pinnacle-shaped Picos de Europa, and reach their highest at its southern limit: Iján (2084m) and El Cordel (2040m). The J-shaped park contains two *sierras* (the

CORDILLERA CANTÁBRICA

Sierra de Bárcena Mayor and the Sierra del Cordel) and numerous permanently green valleys formed by the Ríos Besaya and Saja and their tributaries: Argoza/Lodar, Queriendo, Bayones, Cambillas and Bijoz. Park flora and fauna is characteristic of the Cordillera: hill (Atlantic shrubs and oak) and mountain (beech, holly and birch) species (found between 500m and 1600m) dominate the area.

ACCESS TOWNS

Bárcena de Pie de Concha (p184) and Saja (p186) are the start and finish points respectively.

SAJA-BESAYA TRAVERSE

Duration 2 days
Distance 33.1km
Difficulty moderate
Start Bárcena de Pie de Concha (p184)
Finish Saja (p186)
Transport bus, train
Summary Walk from the Río Besaya to the Río Saja along Roman highways and ancient, stone-paved lanes; cross the Parque Natural de Saja-Besaya through lush forests and tiny villages.

This full traverse of the park follows part of the red-and-white waymarked GR71 (Cantabria's first Sendero de Gran Recorrido, or GR, long-distance trail). The GR71 begins its eight-day, 127.5km trajectory from Bárcena de Pie de Concha (where you begin) and leads to the foot of the Picos de Europa at Potes and west to Sotres. The section of the GR71 described frequently uses *empedrados*, stone-paved lanes that once neatly linked villages. Two recommended side trips head south from Bárcena Mayor village, where Day 1 ends and Day 2 begins, into the park's interior. Both are feasible on a third day. Note that though it takes two days to complete this route it's possible to polish it off in one long, and rushed, day.

PLANNING
When to Walk

July and August are the warmest and driest months, but May to June as well as

September are suitable. Avoid October to January, the hunting season.

Maps

The park itself has no topographic maps. IGN's 1:25,000 map Nos 83-I *Molledo*, 82-II *Los Tojos* and 83-IV *Espinilla* are best for the walk described.

Information Sources

For information on the area, use www.sajanansa.com. There is a small **tourist office** (9am-1pm & 3-6pm daily) in Bárcena de Pie de Concha. They have a fair amount of information on this, and other, walks. In Cabezón de Sal the **Centro de Interpretacion** has an exhibition on the park. See Barcena de Pie de Concha (p184) for more information.

THE WALK
Day 1: Bárcena de Pie de Concha to Bárcena Mayor

5½–6½ hours, 20.3km

Walk through Bárcena de Pie de Concha, following signs for '*Calzada Romana & Pujayo*', cross the Río Besaya from which the park takes its name, and the elongated one street neighbourhood of Pie de Concha. GR71 red-and-white slashes appear occasionally and 900m on the route passes a fountain then later a *rollo*, a pillar where punishments were meted out to anyone naughty (the locals are probably itching to use it on any annoying tourists passing by!). After 100m, a left hand detour leads to Cantabria's best preserved Roman *calzada* (highway). It runs for 5km from Pie de Concha to Somaconcha further south and retains original stone paving and diagonal drainage canals. Even old carriage-wheel marks are visible. Possibly of military origin, it was used until the 18th century to connect Castilla and Santander.

Back on the main route head out of the village along the main road veering right over the river and ascending 1.5km to **Pujayo** along the main road. At the church head straight and then veer right into the main plaza with a fountain and balconied houses. Every 10th August the village celebrates La Maya, San Lorenzo's feast day. Amid general festivities, the young men of the village cut down a beech limb, mount it in the village square, add grease to the trunk and then compete to scale it.

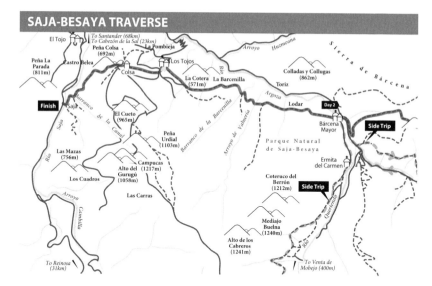

SAJA-BESAYA TRAVERSE

Take the left fork indicated by a marker on the lamppost in the plaza, continue down the street past a walled gate and 100m later veer right at the fork ascending a cement road (which quickly turns to dirt), go over a cattle grid, take a left fork and ascend for 5km up the **Barranco de Vaocerezo** to a ridge with spectacular views of the valleys and foothills of the Cordillera. Grazing cattle (most likely the area's local breed, *tudanca,* which are grey and black with widely separated horns) and horses roam semi-freely in these pastures.

You will see the path above zigzagging up in the same direction as the pylons. Reaching the crest with a water trough fed by a spring on your right, ascend 800m to a grassy path on the left that gradually circles around to the **Pico de Obios** (1222m), topped with a fire tower and antenna (alternatively you can continue straight on along the dirt path). Head west on the undulating dirt road along the summit, past the park sign, and continue for just over 4km crossing the Sierra de Bárcena to reach the foot of the conic **Pico la Guarda** (1085m).

The next portion can be confusing so follow the directions closely as the GR71 signs are not clearly visible. As the dirt road ascends towards the base of the summit and begins to curve right, leave it by taking a track on the left-hand (west) side; a small

marker lies on a stone in the road as you turn left towards a wooden post. In 400m, just before the track reaches a field, take a trailheading north (right) up a bank, past a broken post. Three red-and-white markers painted on the stones indicate that you're going in the right direction. Continue ascending briefly, then leave the trail to descend north–west along a path (badly waymarked and the path sometimes disappears) parallel to a low stone wall that you can just make out in the gorse. When the wall turns left, continue straight ahead descending cross-country through the gorse and heather, aiming all the time for the clearing (a round hill) in the oak grove below (towards the right, or north). Once at the clearing ignore the clear path that runs straight through the trees and instead descend left (west). When you reach the trees on your left (west) you will see a narrow gap and a stream (often dry in the summer), which has been made into a makeshift trail that is soon blazed (heading southwest, then west). To ensure that you're in the right place look out for the red-and-white marker post just ahead through the gap.

The path then makes its way down through an enchanting beech and oak forest and joins an ancient stone-paved road, which for lack of use and water erosion is

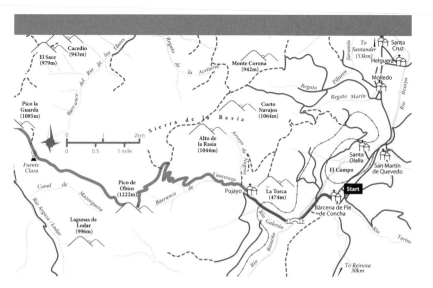

littered with loose stones and can be muddy and slippery. Continue 3.5km through the forest to the top of the village of **Bárcena Mayor** located on the river bank.

SIDE TRIP: VENTA DE MOBEJO
4½ hours, 14.5km
This unmarked forest walk runs partly along an ancient Roman highway, known as the Camino de Reinosa, that connected Castilla to Cantabria and along which, until the 19th century, Castilian wine and wheat were exchanged for Cantabrian carts, barrels and farm tools. Take water with you.

After leaving Bárcena via its only stone bridge, veer left onto a dirt road, passing an information panel which shows the Bárcena Mayor-Ozcaba route via Venta de Mobejo described here.

The trail, bordered on either side by high walls, passes a horse stable, huge chestnuts, oaks and a series of crosses (part of a Stations of the Cross). Ignore a left-hand trail at the first cross. After 20 minutes, the trail reaches a sharp, right-hand curve. Keep straight ahead along a dirt road which soon reaches the simple **Ermita del Carmen**.

From the chapel, take the old, southbound stone-paved trail (of Roman origin) that once linked Santander with Castilla. Keep going for 3.5km without detouring (passing through a replanted forest)

until the *empedrado* becomes a footpath and continues straight ahead. Reaching a shepherds' hut, turn right onto a path, nearly choked with blackberry brambles and ferns, that leads into a dense holly and beech forest before petering out.

Ascend west briefly through the forest cross-country, following a stone and wire wall that turns left to Casa de Avellanedo. From the cabin, take the footpath that undulates around the hillside first through ferns then gorse and heather to the beech forest visible on the next hill. Exit the forest to the fern-flanked hillside trail and then re-enter the beechwood along a cobbled section. Follow the path towards two shepherds' huts on the next hillside. Before reaching the huts, ignore a wide lane turning left in descent and continue straight along a footpath that in three minutes reaches **Venta de Mobejo**, a medieval wayside inn and stable, in ruins.

Here, either turn around and return to Bárcena Mayor or, if you're looking to stretch your legs further, continue 3km to the C625, before retracing your steps to Bárcena Mayor.

SIDE TRIP: FUENTE CLARA
2–2½ hours, 6.6km
This circuit walk goes along an open hillside and back along the river. Leave the

CULINARY MUSTS

With so many milk-producing animals running around the Picos de Europa's high pastures, the cheese-lover will not be disappointed. The most famous cheese, Queso de Cabrales, is produced on the Picos de Europa's north side. Part of the blue cheese family, Cabrales is a semihard, pasty cheese with distinctive bluish-green veins and a pungent smell and taste. The mould (genus Penicillium) is crucial to the three-to six-month maturation process. Made with cows', goats' and sheep's milk, the cheese is left in caves with 90% humidity and at a temperature of 8° to 12°C.

The area's rich, steaming stews will satisfy any hunger. *Pote* or *potaje*, named after the dish in which it is cooked, is a stew made with chick-peas or white beans, meat, chorizo (red sausage), potatoes and leafy green cabbage. *Fabada* is an Asturian variant of *pote* and contains a mixture of pork, beef and sausage – chorizo and morcilla (blood sausage) – to create a tangy delight for all the senses.

To wash it down, Asturian *sidra* (cider) is a refreshing accompaniment. Dating from at least the 12th century, this lightly alcoholic cider is made from pressed apples fermented in oak barrels. Drunk during fiestas as well as simply on afternoon breaks, *sidra* is widely popular not only for its smooth flavour but for the social atmosphere that accompanies its consumption.

village, head south along a sealed road. In 800m, after passing a corral on the right, look for the left-hand trail marker. Ascend left along makeshift stairs and enter a pine and chestnut forest soon dominated by pines. The sight and sound of the rapids and pools of the Río Argoza/Lodar are below. The footpath crosses a brook with a small waterfall and turns left, switchbacking uphill until it levels out and leaves the forest. The trail gently curves southeast around a hill. Using a stile to climb over a wire fence across the footpath, drop to cross a wooden footbridge over the **Fuente Clara** spring. Visible on the hillside are outcrops with ferns, heather and gorse bushes. Descend towards the Río Argoza below, on the way scaling another wire fence, and cross the river via a wooden bridge. Climb to the dirt road and go northwest for 3km through a rich forest back to Bárcena Mayor.

Day 2: Bárcena Mayor to Saja
3½–4 hours, 12.8km

The last day of the walk undulates through forest and the villages of Los Tojos and Colsa, (fountains can be found in both villages). Leave Bárcena Mayor via its stone bridge and turn right (an information panel incorrectly states 14km to Saja) entering a forest. Immediately fork left marked with red-and-white sign, ascending a stone-paved lane which crosses a brook, a wet zone, and two clearings along a footpath. The path then heads right down into what

looks like a stream bed, turns left and follows a barbed-wire fence (on the right). After five minutes, fork right at a junction onto a footpath past two large oaks on the left. A barbed-wire fence to your right will be a constant reference over the next 2km; take care as this path may be muddy and slippery. Continue until you pass a shepherd's hut in the field up to your left and then another modern shepherds' hut on your right. As you pass this descend right (northwest) and then left past a marker post, down to and across a stream and continue straight up, sporadic markers and piles of stones indicate the direction. You follow the fence for a short while longer and eventually ascend to the crest of a hill. At the top the path turns right and makes a zigzagging descent to the **Arroyo de Valneria** which you cross via a bridge (the route is marked by yellow signs on the trees indicating *Los Tojos*). From the bridge continue uphill on a wider trail and at the fork turn left, climbing steeply until the trail opens to a fire-break for an electricity transmission line. Turn left on reaching the fire-break and continue for 500m, quickly re-entering the forest, until the village of Los Tojos comes into sight. The dirt lane joins a gravel and earth road that continues for another 2.2km to **Los Tojos**. On reaching Los Tojos, the trailheads left onto the main road, as shown by a red-and-white marker on a lamppost, and through the village where you can refresh yourself or eat at one of the restaurants. Continue along on the main road roughly 1km to **Colsa** (no bars). Just at the entrance to the village turn left as indicated by a marker on a lamppost. At the last house, by the sign to *Saja-Ozcaba,* turn right downhill onto a dirt and gravel road. Reaching a monument on the left, leave the road where it curves right and head straight on the old pathway that reaches Saja in 2.5km. En route pass a beautiful wayside chapel and descend through a leafy forest (attention: the footpath may be muddy and slippery).

PARQUE NACIONAL DE LOS PICOS DE EUROPA

The Picos de Europa with their knife-edge, irregular limestone summits, are the highest, most rugged and awe-inspiring mountains of all the Cordillera. Despite lying only 15km from the Bay of Biscay, the peaks soar dramatically to 2600m. Extending into Asturias (277 sq km), Cantabria (131 sq km) and Castilla y León (94 sq km), the Picos de Europa are 40km long (west to east) and 20km wide. The chain is separated into three massifs by rivers and deep gorges.

The Macizo Occidental (Western Massif), delimited by the rivers Sella and Cares, is the largest and arguably the most beautiful of the massifs, with the greatest variety of

landscapes: forests, *majadas* (high pastures with shepherds' huts), gorges, lakes and imposing mountains. Its highest point is the Torre de Santa de Castilla at 2596m.

The Macizo Central (Central Massif), with more rock than flora, lies between the rivers Cares and Duje and includes the highest peak of the Picos, the Torre de Cerredo (2648m). Its rugged and abrupt relief, dotted with rocky bowls known as *jous* in the local tongue Bable (*hoyos* in Spanish), gives it a lunar look. The massif also harbours the Picos' signature peak El Naranjo de Bulnes, or Pico Urriellu (2519m), and Pico Tesorero (2570m), at the region's geographical centre. Finally, the Macizo Oriental (Eastern Massif), demarcated by the rivers Duje and Deva, is the gentlest and lowest massif, though still with wild summits reaching well over 2000m.

On 21 July 1918, at the instigation of Pedro Pidal, Marqués de Villaviciosa, King Alfonso XIII declared the Parque Nacional de la Montaña de Covadonga Spain's first national park. Initially, only the Macizo Occidental fell within the 169 sq km of protected area. During the 1980s and 1990s, campaigns were waged by both Spanish and non-Spanish activists to bring the other two massifs under national protection. Finally, on 30 May 1995 the park limits were extended to 646 sq km.

ENVIRONMENT

Karstification, the transformation of a limestone landscape by percolating groundwater, is the most outstanding active geological process in the Picos de Europa. Besides causing the area's many cracks and

---

CAVING IN THE PICOS

Walking along the upper reaches of the Picos, it's surprising to learn that underfoot the porous, limestone mountains are riddled with caves hollowed out by the effects of water erosion. Teams from (primarily) Spain, France and England have explored more than 3000 horizontal and vertical Picos cavities.

Caving began here in 1918 but did not take off until the 1960s, culminating in several major feats. In 1985, members of Oxford University's Cave Club descended 1135 spectacular metres into the Macizo Occidental's Sistema del Jito.

Also in the park is El Farfao, a natural spring that surges out of a fissure in the rock wall. It's believed to be a natural release point for water from the Sima del Trave, the deepest cave (1441m) yet to be explored in Spain and the fourth-deepest in the world. The national park information offices can provide further information on caving permits and speleological clubs.

caves, the process of water erosion acting upon lime also creates scree, *jous* and river gorges. Water filters through rocks and springs forth in unlikely spots. These mountains are havens for technical rock climbers as well as for cavers exploring the Cordillera's innards (see the boxed text Caving in the Picos, p167).

Owing to the lack of topsoil and the large amount of land cleared for pasture, woodlands cover less than 20% of the park. Protected from extremes of climate by deep gorges, Mediterranean species (strawberry, cork and holm oak) cohabit with alder, ash, willow, elm, oak and linden. Mixed deciduous forests of oak, hazel, holly, mountain ash and yew reign at altitudes up to 800m, with birch and beech beyond. Wildflowers are rich: you'll find wood anemone, purple saxifrage, Cantabrian thrift, great yellow gentian, pheasant's eye daffodil and flag iris.

The park's most representative mammal is the chamois, known locally as the *rebeco*. Some 6500 of them skip along on hooves well adapted to the steep, rocky slopes. Wild boar, foxes, wolves (in decline), deer, badgers, martens, hedgehogs, mountain cats and stoats also scrape out a living. Golden eagles, griffon and Egyptian vultures, peregrine falcons and common buzzards can be seen in the skies. Accompanying the walker at the highest altitudes, with their unmistakable caws, are red-billed choughs and yellow-billed alpine choughs. Also integral to the park are domestic animals including cows (brown alpina and casina breeds), goats, sheep and Asturian horses (called *asturcón*).

PLANNING
The following planning information applies to all the walks in this section.

When to Walk
July, August and September are all good walking months, though shepherds agree that September, still clear and warm, is the ideal time as the heat lessens and crowds disappear.

Maps
Many Picos de Europa maps are riddled with errors. Adrados's three maps – *El Cornión* and *Picos de Europa: Macizos Central y Oriental* at 1:25,000, and *Picos de Europa*

y Costa Oriental de Asturias at 1:80,000 – are outstanding. Editorial Alpina's *Parque Nacional de Picos de Europa* 1:40,000 map comes in two sheets (sold together) which sensibly divide the park into central and western zones and the eastern zone. It's the easiest map to come across. The park's 1:25,000 topographical map, divided into four sheets, contains the routes waymarked in 2002.

Books
Several books in English (original and translated) cover the Picos de Europa. A general book laden with photos is *Picos de Europa: Asturias, León, Cantabria*. For technical climbs, Robin Walker's *Walks and Climbs in the Picos de Europa* is your best bet.

With its topographical map, the park also sells a guide to 30 marked PRs and two GRs. On the park's flora, Modesto Luceño & Pablo Vargas's *Guía Botánica de los Picos de Europa* is best.

Information Sources
The national park maintains three main information centres open year-round: in **Cangas de Onís** (Asturias) at the **Casa Dago** (☎ 985 84 86 14; Avenida Covadonga 43; 8am-9pm summer, 9am-2pm & 4-6.30pm winter); in **Posada de Valdeón** (León, ☎ 987 74 05 49; Travesía de los Llanos; 8am-9pm summer, 9am-2pm & 4-6.30pm winter); and in **Camaleño** (Cantabria, ☎ 942 73 32 01; between Potes & Fuente Dé; 8am-9pm summer, 9am-2pm & 4-6.30pm winter). The **Centro de Visitantes Pedro Pidal** (10am-6pm daily Easter–mid-Dec), within the park near the Lagos de Covadonga, has an audiovisual show and dioramas giving an overview of the park's highlights, as well as selling books. Other, smaller, information centres operate in the months of July, August and September at Los Lagos, Poncebos and Fuente Dé, Panes and Valdeón. It's possible to join free guided tours of the park – enquire at the main visitor centres. Be warned that not all the staff at the various information centres are guides, or have even walked the mountains much, and if you need more accurate information on walks it is not always easy to find the right person to talk to. The information booths are lacking in

REFUGIOS IN THE PICOS DE EUROPA

Although none of the walks we describe here require sleeping overnight in the mountains there are a number of *refugios* should you wish to. All *refugios* serve meals, sell basic canned food and most are close to natural springs. Almost all have showers, bathrooms and phones. *Refugio* wardens provide helpful walking information. A standard nightly fee of €4.40/10 for members/nonmembers of federated mountain clubs is charged. Bring your mountain club card from your country of residence to receive the members' rate. Meals work on the same system: with breakfast and dinner for members clocking in at €4.50 and €11 respectively, while for non-members breakfast is €5.20 and dinner €14. Meals are not provided at the Refugio de la Terenosa. For more information on other Picos *refugios*, contact the **Federación de Montañismo del Principado de Asturias** (☎ 985 25 23 62; www.fempa.net; Avenida Julian Claveria, Oviedo), or a national park office. Reserve early, especially if planning an August trip, and always at Refugio Vega de Urriellu.

LOCATION	ALTITUDE	SPACES	TELEPHONE	SEASON
Vega de Ario	1630m	40	☎ 515 62 15 65	Open with warden May–Oct
La Terenosa	1300m	24		Closed at time of research
Vega de Urriellu	1953m	96	☎ 985 92 52 00	Open year-round
Jou de los Cabrones	2100m	20	☎ 515 62 15 55	Open with warden May–Oct; Open without warden rest of year
Cabaña Verónica	2325m	3	☎ 942 73 00 07	Open with warden year-round
Collado Jermoso	2064m	27	☎ 636 998 727	open with warden May–Oct; call rest of year
Vegarredonda	1460m	68	☎ 985 92 29 52	Open with warden Feb–Oct

good advice and offer very few maps and walk route descriptions. Therefore you rely on the marked PR and GRsigns although they can become less visible and hard to follow on certain routes.

A tonne of useful information can be found on www.liebanaypicosdeeuropa.com.

Emergency

The **Grupo de Rescate** (Mountain Rescue; ☎ 942 73 00 07; Cuartel de la Guardia Civil, Obispo 7) is in Potes – or call ☎ 112 for any emergency.

Permits & Regulations

There are no permits or fees. Camping in the park is permitted only around the *refugios* (which have a 10-tent maximum) and above 1600m wherever you can find relatively flat ground. Tents can only be erected an hour before sunset and must be taken down during the day.

ACCESS TOWNS

Santander (p187) and Oviedo (p185) are the nearest big cities with international connections while Cangas de Onís (p185), Arenas de Cabrales (p183), Sotres (p187), Potes (p186), Fuente Dé (p185) and Posada de Valdeón (p186) all make good bases for one or other of the following walks.

VIEWS OF THE ORDIALES

Duration 6–6½ hours
Distance 10.2km
Difficulty easy
Start/Finish Buferrera car park
Nearest Town Cangas de Onís (p185)
Transport bus/car
Summary Choose a clear day for this easy, scenic return trip that leads to a stunning lookout, Mirador de Ordiales.

A popular walk both for its superb views from a natural balcony with its dizzying kilometre deep drop to the valley of Angón, and for its historical significance. Taking you past the Lago de Enol and into wilder countryside, this enjoyable walk ascends easily up through charming *vegas* (fertile valleys) and grasslands to the Refugio de

Vegarredonda where the views begin to open out.

An interesting change of landscape comes with a short steep climb across the limestone hills, where you might spot many a chamois, to reach the *mirador* and final resting place of Pedro Pidal; pioneer conservationist whose dedication to the Picos helped lead it to becoming Spain's first national park. He was also the first person to reach the summit of El Naranjos (2519m) in 1904. Standing on the cliffs by his grave, marvelling at the views, you'll fully understand why he chose to be buried here. Should you wish to climb higher take the option at the end of the walk to the Pico Coltaba (2026m).

GETTING TO/FROM THE WALK

Access to the trailhead is limited due to parking and the narrow mountain road. There are four car parks situated before Covadonga (per day €2) and a bus then takes you to the Buferrera car park at the Lakes (€7; 9am-7.30pm, every 15 minutes).

THE WALK

Choose a clear day for this scenic walk through *vegas* (meadows) and grasslands and scree slopes to a spectacular viewpoint and the final resting place of Pedro Pidal. Sunshine and crisp light will open up the high contrasts here and the mountain sky is at its best and most immense when it's a dazzling azure.

From the Buferrera car park take the road back towards the **Lago de Enol** and fork right along its southern side, eventually taking a wide track on the left-hand side (west) of the lake signed the 'PR5' and marked with yellow-and-white markers. After 400m you pass the turn-off for the Refugio Cabaña de Pastores on your right (currently closed). Ignoring the *refugio* turn off, continue along the 4WD track through the **Vega de Enol**, where further walking tracks branch off on your left, and the **Vega la Cueva** on your right with its small huts (*majadas*) to reach, after 40 minutes, a fork in the road (this is the Pan de Carmen). Take the left fork which descends past a **car park**, where the track narrows, and continues briefly through a beech wood and the **Vega del Huerto** with its pool (dedicated to Robert Frasinelli, environmental champion

of the Picos). Take the well-marked path that in a few minutes crosses a small bridge over the **River Pomperi**. The paved path then turns right to ascend past a spring and water trough before turning southwest to the grasslands of the **Vega de Piedra** (named after the large rock to your right), and a few huts. You should now be able to see some small limestone cairns indicating your route. This well-marked path leaves the meadow and climbs southeast to Collado de la Prida and then, passing another large slab of rock, the route takes you into a meadow, where livestock often graze. As a well-used grazing ground it pays to make sure you cause as little disruption as possible to the bovine tenants – they're regarded as locals, whereas you'll just be visiting. You may lose the path here, but ahead you should be able to make out a path that continues to climb to the Canal de Canraso. Stick with this path and after the Canal de Canraso you cross the los Vahos stream with its Roman-style stone markers. A short, steep zigzag up then brings you to **Majada de la Rondiella** (1380m) a group of shepherd's huts. Continue onwards until you reach a marker in the middle of the field, head straight across past more huts into an area of rocky country. After 20 minutes climbing to the **Collado Gamanal** you'll get the first view of the Refugio de Vegarredonda where the scenery changes noticeably to areas of loose rocky scree. Ten minutes later, and two to 2½ hours from the start of the walk, you'll be cruising on past the **Refugio de Vegarredonda** (1410m). There is a spring to fill up your water bottles or you can break momentarily from your frontier minimalism and purchase drinks, sandwiches (from €6) and hot meals (from €8).

Behind the *refugio* and past a spring you'll see a marker post where the route turns left and then right (west) to climb through the rocks and zigzag up a wide gully (*cuenya cerrada*). The path is fairly obvious here and it climbs steeply through limestone hills and depressions to a pass where the views begin to open out, at this point you may spot frolicking chamois. From here the path is more gentle and curves around to the broad clearing of **Ordiales** where there is also the abandoned **Refugio Icona**. The path may now start

VIEWS OF THE ORDIALES

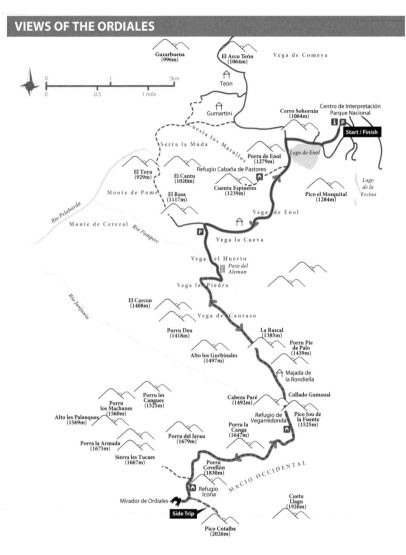

to disappear occasionally, but climb to the left of the *refugio* and head southwest passing by a cave and then zigzag up to the ***mirador*** (1691m), the natural balcony overlooking the valley of the Río Dobra and the grave of Pedro Pidal. It was his last wish to be buried here, but he had to wait eight years for his wish to be granted. Engraved in the rock it reads 'Lover of the Picos, I would love to live; die and

eternally rest here in Ordiales. In the enchanted kingdom of the chamois and the eagles…' The return journey is via the same path.

Should you wish to climb higher to the Pico Coltaba (2026m) return to the hut and take the path that winds sharply up behind it. You may lose the path in some parts, but follow the small piles of stones that serve as route markers.

VEGA D'ARIO

Duration 6–7 hours
Distance 12–14kms
Difficulty moderate
Start/Finish Buferrera car park
Nearest Town Cangas de Onís (p185)
Transport bus, car
Summary A rewarding climb through varied terrain and impressive limestone landscapes to the rocky col of El Jito and Refugio de Ario, returning via the pastures of the Majadas de La Güelga.

A classic Picos de Europa walk, the trail quickly leaves the lakes and climbs (630m) through pastures to remarkable limestone areas and summits with stunning views of the Macizo Central, returning partly via a different route. The Vega D'Ario sits in an undeniably beautiful position with its *refugio* situated at a passing point for people from various routes. Although a long, and at some points steep, climb it is worth the effort.

GETTING TO/FROM THE WALK

Access to the trailhead is limited due to parking and the narrow mountain road. There are four car parks situated before Covadonga (per day €2) and a bus then takes you to the Buferrera car park at the Lakes (€7; 9am-7.30pm, every 15 minutes).

THE WALK

From the Buferrera car park head towards the visitors centre and past the Buferrera mines to the car park and bar by the **Lago de la Ercina** (1160m) and follow the well-worn path along the lake's eastern shore. Roughly half-way along cut across left to the limestone crag and up an eastbound marked path that ascends above the lake. From the **El Brazu Cabin** at the base of the Pico Llúcia there are splendid lake views. The obvious earth and stone path runs uphill alongside a stream, the Riega El Brazu which heads off right, as you follow a tributary and then traverses through gorse, heather and blue thistles. Ignore a path heading left and traverse the **Cuenye Las Bobias** ridge from where you'll begin to see a forest of beech trees. The path descends and then levels out

at the Vega Las Bobias pasture noted for its **shepherds' huts** and grazing cattle. Pass the huts to your right and head straight through the middle of the pasture until you reach a flat-topped rock with a water trough, fed by a spring, built into its left-hand side (this is where you could start a return journey if you're tired). If you're made of stronger stuff continue straight ahead abandoning the grass and ascending through an area of stones and beech trees, following yellow painted markers. A few minutes later the path levels out and starts to descend across the Llaguiellu grassland where the path zigzags up ahead. Here the path splits, but as they all eventually go to the Llaguiellu it hardly matters which you take; although the upper right path is possibly the easiest to follow. Llaguiellu is a tiny wet *vega* to the right of the path, cross over the stream and start the steep climb. Here the effect of the runoff water over the whole mountainside gouges out gullies that expose the red earth which sometimes gets confused with the path. After 20 minutes you reach the top where the landscape turns to large expanses of limestone. Continue upwards across a succession of small depressions to reach the **Llanos Los Jitos** marked by a boundary post. Descend slightly before ascending a long valley where you can make out two cairns at the top, towards which you are heading. After a last steep climb up a series of zigzags you arrive at the **Collado El Jito** (1650m) where the path then levels out. One of the most impressive views of the Macizo Central – jagged peaks souring up into the sky – is on the eastern horizon. Closer, to the south, the rounded bulk of **Mt Jultayu** (1950m) appears (see p174 for more on climbing this). From the summit of El Jito, to the right of the trail, is one of three entrances to one of the deepest cave systems in the Picos (see boxed text Caving in the Picos, p167). A sign indicates that the Refugio de Marquis is not far; head past the marker post depicting the names of the surrounding peaks and take the path shown by the small piles of stones and yellow markers. Quarter of an hour later the path curves left to the **Refugio de Ario** (1630m:, ☎ 515 621 565 42 satellite phone so no code is required; dm €10, half-board €29.90; May-Oct). Note that toilets are not available to day-visitors as water is limited.

However, lunch or dinner (from €14) is available (and then presumably toilet use!) as are other refreshments or there is a spring in front of the *refugio*.

Return via the same route as far as the flat-topped rock with the spring that you passed earlier and turn right onto a path leading down towards the limestone rocks. The path bends around to the right across a limestone outcrop (there may be small mounds of stones indicating the path), emerging onto a small grassy opening with a short cliff on the right. Turn left (northeast) and downhill where you will see a pile of rocks indicating the path, and huts below you in the valley. The path disappears but just before reaching the huts and the valley bottom, turn left and you should begin to see a path curving back below the direction

you just came from. Always keep the valley bottom to your right. You come into a small grassy clearing and continue straight ahead to ascend a small section of limestone rocks. As you reach the top the valley veers around to your right, and down to your left an obvious path runs diagonally ahead climbing towards a larger crop of limestone. Make your way to this path through bracken and heath pasture and ascend towards the rocks; below to the right you can see the group of barns known as the **Majada de La Güelga**. Contour your way around the first set of rocks while maintaining your height and, ignoring the paths leading up from the right, go through the middle of another crop of rocks and head towards the ridge where you'll see the path from the right reaching a spur. Continue along the

VEGA D'ARIO

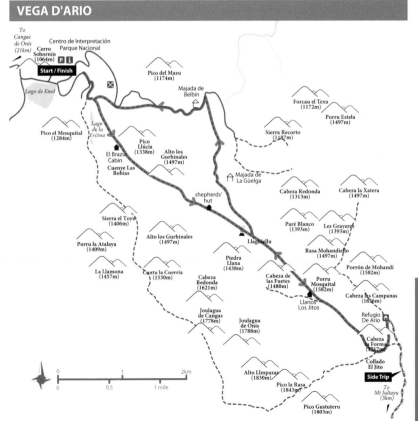

ridge until the **Majada de Belbin** becomes clearly visible in the depression to your left and a 4WD track running west, which is the continuation of your route. Cut down to the *majadas* and follow the track up. At the second right-hand bend after a grassy plateau there is a little path forking left from the track (more or less straight on) that undulates back towards the track and the ridge ahead. Make your way up to the ridge past the track that leads off to your right and the Lago de la Ercina comes into view. Head down the grassy slope back to the car park and bar for a well-earned beer!

SIDE TRIP: JULTAYU
2½ hours, 6km, 330m ascent
To feel on top of the world, try the ascent of Jultayu. From the *refugio*, cross the meadow southeast. At the end of the meadow, near a hut, the path veers right and winds through the rocks, following yellow trail markers. At the oxidised iron sign, turn right (south) towards the mountain. At the base of the peak, 25 minutes from the start, a yellow arrow points down and left (southeast). Ignore this and continue straight (south), ascending 370m to the summit following cairns along the mountain's north face. In less than an hour from the fork you'll reach the natural watchtower.

LAKE WALK

Duration 2½ hours
Distance 5km
Difficulty easy
Start/Finish Buferrera car park
Nearest Town Cangas de Onís (p185)
Transport bus, car
Summary A relaxed short walk perfect for families it takes in two pretty lakes, flower meadows, shepherds' huts and beech forests scattered among the surrounding peaks of the Picos.

This easy walk, with a short ascent of 110m, is just as enjoyable as other parts of the Picos. Begin the walk with a stop at the visitors centre with its displays of the park's different habitats and extensive information on the flora and fauna. The Mirador de Entrelagos (between the lakes)

provides views of both glacial lakes in all their splendour.

GETTING TO/FROM THE WALK
Access to the trailhead is limited due to parking and the narrow mountain road. There are four car parks situated before Covadonga (per day €2) and a bus then takes you to the Buferrera car park at the lakes (€7; 9am-7.30pm, every 15 minutes).

THE WALK
From the Buferrera car park follow the signs to the visitors centre, go through the arboretum, past some mines (with displays), up the steps to the bar/restaurant and across to the lake. Head along the right-hand side of **Lago de la Ercina** through the meadows which are full of wildflowers in the spring. The lake, which provides a home to various waterfowl, has a maximum depth of only 2m yet is 550m long and 350m wide.

Pass the water trough to your right and continue on the path towards the end of the lake. Follow the upward right-hand (south) trail just after the sign to El Bricial by the Pico el Mosquital. At the fork you can either take the gentle climb to the upper meadows or continue onwards to the brick wall at the end of the lake and then take the steeper climb up to the right through a limestone rock garden. Whichever route you choose, both paths take you onto the meadow of **Las Reblagas**; the second path coming out onto the left of the meadow. Bear right across Las Reblagas on a well-marked path around the hillside and continue onto the next meadow **Vega Bricial** to a path running between the *majadas* (brick huts now uninhabited). This

is **El Bricial**. Here you continue straight across to the base of some rocks where you will find a marked path – ignore the wider path running off to the right up the hillside. Yellow-and-white markings and stone cairns guide you through the rocks and up the gully which bears roughly right. This is a prime habitat for *té de roca* (sideritis hyssopifolia) plant, which is used to make a calming infusion. The path is well trodden and takes you through areas of bracken, grass and rock along the path of a small stream. The Vega de Enol will come into view with its pastures scattered with *majadas* set among ash trees and a 4WD track at the far side. Once inside the **Vega de Enol** turn right around the limestone rocks and running parallel to the 4WD track head towards the **Lago de Enol**. At the southern edge of the lake, ignore the sign indicating 'Buferrera' to the left and instead turn right onto a narrow path that runs along the lake shore. This takes you under a large overhanging rock where large stones have been laid in the lake waters to enable the path to continue. From here the path winds up around and away from the lake passing areas of short springy turf and various limestone outcrops to the plateau of La Piedra. Head away from the cluster of small barns and onto the paved trail which leads to the top of the **ridge** (La Picota) and a magnificent view from the **Mirador de Entrelagos**. Afterwards simply climb back down to the car park where you began.

BULNES LA VILLA

Duration 4–5 hours
Distance 11.5km
Difficulty moderate
Start/Finish Poncebos
Nearest Town Arenas de Cabrales (p183)
Transport bus/car
Summary A spectacularly steep and steady zigzag along a cliff ledge that winds up the river valley of the Arroyo del Tejo to Bulnes la Villa, which is followed by a descent back via Collado Pandebano to the start point on a funicular railway.

This route was once one of the only ways to reach the isolated village of Bulnes la Villa,

with a population of possibly 20. There's still no road access to the village and mains electricity has only been a part of life here since the 1980s. The funicular railway, which runs 2km up the mountainside and now offers considerably easier access, was opened on 17 September 2001.

Much of this walk consists of a tough climb up the mountain slope, but once up in the pretty village Bulnes La Villa, with its cafés and restaurants, you can choose between jumping straight onto the funicular or continuing on to Pandébano with its exceptional views of Naranjo peak.

GETTING TO/FROM THE WALK

Coming from Arenas take the AS264 to the car park at the base of the funicular. Buses from Arenas to Poncebos depart on the hour from 9am and on the half-hour going the other way until 7pm. For **taxis** call ☎ 985 84 64 87/985 84 67 98. The funicular runs every half-hour (single/return €14/18; 10am-8pm Easter & Jul-Sep, 10am-12.30pm & 2-6pm rest of the year).

THE WALK

From the Hospedaje la Garganta del Cares, just beyond the car park, take the tarmac road with the river to your left and follow it through the tunnel. Just past the tunnel as the road turns to limestone chippings you will see a sign to your left saying Camino de Bulnes. Follow this down to your left across the river. Once over the river the path begins to climb and about 10 minutes later you'll reach the **Puente Zardo** where you again cross the river. The path now starts to zigzag steeply uphill.

While climbing be sure to take a look back towards Poncebos you will see a spectacular path winding up to the small hamlet of Carmemeña. Continuing onwards you will soon pass a path leading off to the right and marked with a yellow sign – ignore this and carry on climbing upwards. Follow the obvious path until about an hour later it eventually levels out onto an open grassy patch with a **river**. The **El Castillo** district of Bulnes should come into view on the cliff above.

You now start to climb again until you come to a bridge, **Puente Colines**, but don't cross the bridge, instead continue straight on. Just under 10 minutes later you'll pass

BULNES LA VILLA

the entrance to the funicular on your left and then another five minutes later you'll cross a **bridge** into the village of **Bulnes la Villa**. Here you can decide between calling it a day and taking the funicular back down or, much more worthwhile, continuing onwards to the Mirador de Naranjo and Pandébano as described here. But first let's have some lunch. Bulnes La Villa has several cafés and restaurants including some situated on the peaceful riverbank.

After a rest, cross back over the bridge that led you into the village and by the large tree turn right and climb; as you reach a the large slab of rock turn left to the **Mirador de Naranjo** a minute or so away. Return to the main trail by the rock and start to ascend in a southeast direction along a rocky path that leads you through a woodland of walnut and hazelnut trees with the river off to your right providing a musical accompaniment as it tumbles downwards.

After around 10 to 15 minutes you'll see a red-and-white marker indicating the path, continue upwards and at a bend ignore the small path off to the right which takes you to a cascade and an alternative, but less scenic route up. The path begins to get steeper and may be wet and slippery. After 20 minutes you pass a small pool,

which makes a tempting bath and shady picnic spot. A short while further on the path forks, take the right fork following the markers. The left path leads you up to a pasture and a spectacular picnic spot with views back to Monte Castiello and Pico de Alba.

The lane then crosses the **Río Tejo** and as you come around a bend the view opens out ahead and you get your first beautiful view of Naranjo peak. After crossing the river again the path turns left and is indicated with a marker, (if you get as far as the hut then you've gone wrong!). The stone path ascends a short while further through the trees then turns into a dirt path. Keep right at a fork and continue through the ferns and a gate and eventually you will arrive in the **La Jelguerra** meadow with its huts. Just beyond these huts, is the highest point of the meadow, is the **Collado Pandébano**.

A blanket of lovely views is laid out below you. Sotres village is visible to the east, (you could continue onwards downhill through the meadows to the village if you feel like stretching your legs some more, and then even connect up to the Macizo de Andara walk, p178). Return via the same route to Bulnes La Villa and hop on the funicular back to where you left your car.

CORDILLERA CANTÁBRICA

LA GARGANTA DEL CARES

Duration 6 hours

Distance 20km

Difficulty easy

Start Poncebos

Finish Caín

Nearest Towns Poncebos (p186), Caín (p184) or Arenas de Cabrales (p183)

Transport bus, car

Summary An outstanding, but very popular, trail that is carved into the cliffs of the breathtaking Cares gorge.

Despite this the classic Picos walk being almost too popular it's earned this popularity for a very good reason and it's well worth braving the maddening crowds to get a piece of the action. The walk, though long, is easy and is undertaken by all ages and walking abilities. The trail, carved high up into the gorge walls, was constructed by the electricity company Viesgo in the 1940s in order to service the hydroelectric canal that runs between Caín and Camarmeña along the Río Cares. Those with vertigo may find it slightly difficult as it is a high trail, at some points 200m above the river, but the trail is wide and is walked by hundreds every year. There is however not much shade. Keep an eye on the heavens for griffen vultures soaring in the thermals high above.

This walk can be done in reverse just as easily.

GETTING TO/FROM THE WALK

Coming from Arenas take the AS-264 to the car park at the base of the funicular.

Buses from Arenas to Poncebos depart on the hour from 9am and on the half-hour going the other way until 7pm. For **taxis** call ☎ 985 84 64 87/985 84 67 98. The funicular runs every half-hour (single/return €14/18; 10am-8pm Easter & Jul-Sep, 10am-12.30pm & 2-6pm Oct-Jun).

THE WALK

From the Hospedaje la Garganta del Cares, just beyond the car park, take the road that has the Río Cares on your left and continue through the tunnel past the sign to Bulnes off to your left. The path turns to one of limestone chippings and you'll quickly come to a visitors information booth. To the right of the booth, indicated by a small sign next to a rock is the start of the trail. A steady ascent of 250m takes you above the river to some old barns. The going starts to get a little energetic at this point as you ascend for a while. Continue zigzagging upwards into ever more impressive scenery and views. You will be able to see the continuation of your route desperately hugging the cliff-face further on, and this is a good spot to fire off a few well-sited photos and to take in the vista. The trail descends a little, then levels out and passes under some wide overhangs and natural arches. After a little under 1½ hours you pass a stone-built hut by a sluice gate. The path stays level for about 4km eventually passing **Culiembro** roughly halfway along the route. A former settlement which was almost destroyed in the construction of the aqueduct, Culiembro is also the site of a complex cave system featuring many passages, cascades and underground waterfalls; at the time of writing, a team of cave-divers and surveyors was in the process

RÍO & GARGANTA DEL CARES

The Río Cares springs forth 16km south of Caín, near the Pico Gildar (2078m), and flows through the Valle de Valdeón, Posada de Valdeón, Cordiñanes and numerous low-lying winter pastures. It reaches Caín and the Garganta del Cares at its narrowest point (near the dam) and cuts through the gorge for 10km to Poncebos. Wider and calmer, it descends to Arenas de Cabrales village and continues for another 26km before joining the Río Deva in Panes.

A remarkable engineering feat, the 3m-wide path running the length of the gorge was gouged out of its sheer walls in 1946 to provide access to the Canal del Cares, made by the Viesgo electricity company in 1921. The canal runs from Caín at the top of the gorge to Camarmeña, from where it is funnelled in tubes to the Poncebos hydroelectric plant 230m below. Before the path was hewed into the walls of the gorge, the only way along it was via a trail much higher on the slopes of the Macizo Central – a daring undertaking reserved for the shepherds of Caín.

LA GARGANTA DEL CARES

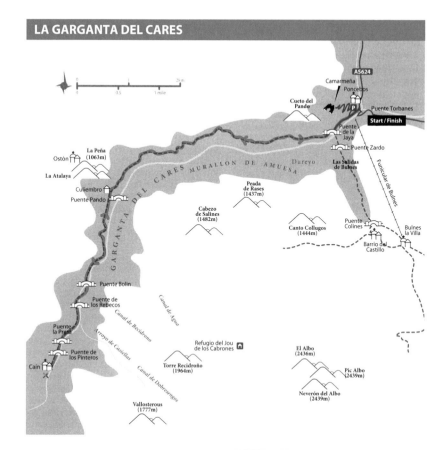

of exploring and mapping the system. The gorge from here narrows and goes through a series of arched windows, you will note you are walking just above the canal. A short while later you pass over the two bridges of **Puente Bolin** and **Puente de los Rebecos**. Passing over the last bridge you descend towards the river where a ributary called **Arroyo de Casiellas** joins the main river and makes an excellent picnic spot or good place for a dip. After a series of tunnels, where a torch might come in handy, the trail reaches and passes over a fish ladder and a weir which diverts water from the Río Cares Canal. A short while later, crossing over the last bridge, you come into the village of **Caín** (500m) with plenty of restaurants and bars and two small supermarkets. After a drink and a nap by the river take the same path back.

MACIZO DE ANDARA

Duration 3½–4 hours

Distance 16km

Difficulty moderate

Start/Finish car park, 3km from Sotres on road to Tresviso

Nearest Town Sotres (p187)

Transport car, taxi

Summary This undulating route, following an old mining trail, offers a wonderful variety of scenery and is a pleasant change from the crowded walks of Bulnes and Garganta.

The walk begins from a car park approximately 3km along the road to Tresviso from Sotres and can be done either way around but the route described here keeps you in the shade for the uphill section. The trail mostly follows a 4WD track, but offers all the ingredients the Picos are renowned for: vast views, traditional *majadas* (used for cheese-making), beech forests, a mildly challenging ascent followed by an easy romp back down. The Refugio Caseton de Andara makes a welcome refreshment stop.

GETTING TO/FROM THE WALK

There are no buses to Sotres from Arenas. If you're in your own car leave Sotres and take the road to Tresviso. After 3km you will come to a car park where the walk starts. If staying in Sotres you can walk the 3km along the road or you could probably hitch without much stress. Alternatively take a **taxi** starting in Arenas (☎ 985 84 64 87, 985 84 67 98).

THE WALK

Start from the PR28 sign 'Ruta de Andara' and descend almost immediately past the breeze-block huts on your right and shortly afterwards passing some yellow-and-white waymarkers on your left. As the road bends (16 minutes later), ignore a track on your left and carry on along the well-marked track until reaching a grassy opening, the **Vega del Tronco**, just after which a faintly painted 'A Beges' sign (40 minutes from the start) can be seen on the rocks. The path levels out, passes through some forest and slips around the side of the **Sierra de la Corta** where the views open out a little down the valley and across to Tresviso. Ignore any small paths running off and stay on the main track. At one bend there is the possibility of confusion as there's a well-worn path going off the track, but stay on the main track which bends around to the left and emerges out of the trees to where you will see a group of barns down to your left. Shepherds can sometimes been seen here making *queso picon*, a blue cheese. Pass a sign saying 'Monte de Llama' just before re-entering the forest and passing the Riega del Torno stream. Ignore the path running

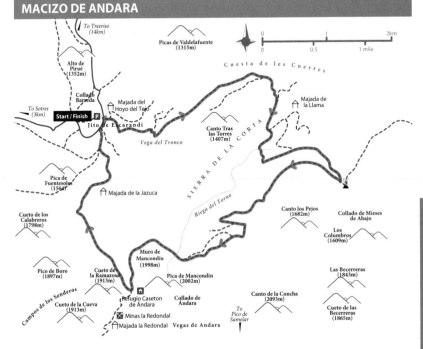

off to your right just before reaching a fork, where you should take the upper path heading straight on in a northeast direction past a water trough. When you reach a bend in the road with another water trough and **fountain** (fill your water bottles here), beside it the road forks again – take the right fork which bends back towards the way you just came and starts to ascend some 550m. The first part of the climb is within the shade of the beech trees of La Llama, but as you round a bend the trees vanish and are replaced with a rocky and open landscape with great views back down the valley. The track winds up towards **Muro de Macondiú** (1998m) reaching its east face and a wonderful viewing spot at a junction. Continue along the path straight on in a southeast direction, curving around Macondiú for a final 30-minute ascent to the fairly unpleasant **Refugio Caseton de Ándara** (1750m; ☎ 671 40 42 77; dm €8, half-board €25) which only comes into view as you are virtually on top of it. Just past the *refugio* is the entrance to the mine shafts which was used to extract zinc and lead in the 19th century. The small *refugio* is housed in the old headquarters of the mining company and cannot be described as an attractive place to spend the night. They do however sell refreshments.

From here the well-marked path continues past the mine entrance under the rails of the mine truck and descends over rocky limestone landscapes and pastures for about an hour back to the Jito de Escarandi (wide open space) and the parking.

RUTA DE TRESVISO

Duration 5½–6 hours

Distance 11.5km

Difficulty moderate–demanding

Start/Finish Urdón

Nearest Town Potes (p186)

Transport bus, car

Summary A challenging 800m ascent along an old mining trail with magnificent views all the way.

Until the late 20th century this dramatic and spectacular route was the only link to the remote village of Tresviso. Those

with vertigo might find it a bit unnerving, but fear not, the trail is wide and popular and your sense of achievement once at the top makes up for any amount of vertigo-inspired sickness! The path is obvious and easy to follow with no detours along the way as it snakes its way up from the Desfiladero de la Hermida gorge. If staying in Sotres you can make your way to Tresviso and take the trail going down, but take care if wet as it can be slippery.

GETTING TO/FROM THE WALK

Buses passing between Panes and Potes can drop you at the walk's trailhead in Urdón. Travelling by car from Panes take the N621 to Urdón where you will find some parking.

THE WALK

Start the walk from the dirt road that leads to the hydroelectric plant, cross the bridge over the Río Urdón, followed by a second bridge crossing over a tributary and finally cross a third bridge back over the Urdón. Pass through an area of trees to the first set of zigzags up the gully where you'll reach a gate beyond which the path starts to ascend much more steeply along the cliff edge. At one point the path forks, but with both routes taking you to the **Balcón de Pilates** (where an electricity pylon perches precariously on the cliff edge), it doesn't matter which you take.

There are some splendid views here looking back the way you've just come from and across the gorge to the peak of Cuetodave, Osina Pass and the water channel of the hydroelectricity plant. After drinking in the view carry on zigzagging up and up and up towards another set of electricity pylons (just over two hours from the start) flanked by meadows and limestone rock gardens.

You pass through the **Inverniales de Frías** meadows where the path narrows to become just a small track and pass a barn before the final bendy-wendy zigzag up to a *mirador* just before **Tresviso**. You enter the village next to a cemetrey and though you might by now feel like you belong in said cemetrey we'd recommend pushing on into the village centre to the bar. When you've got your breath back, retrace your steps.

RUTA DE TRESVISO

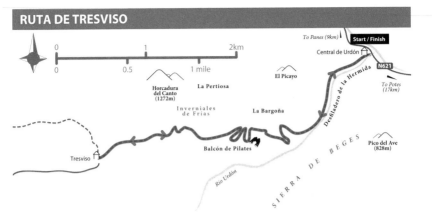

PUERTOS DE ÁLIVA

Duration 4 hours

Distance 14km

Difficulty easy

Start/Finish Fuente Dé (p185)

Transport bus, car

Summary This classic walk starts with a scary cable car ride and rewards you for your bravery with an enjoyable hike through flower-strewn meadows blessed with enormous views.

This route follows the well-marked PR24 along the pastures of the Áliva down to the village of Espinama. The Puertos de Áliva range separates the eastern and western massifs of the Picos and there are some great views from the start of the walk of the many surrounding peaks. The ascent back from Espinama is steady and short and offers a memorable view of the natural amphitheatre of Fuente Dé.

Note that in July or August you need to arrive at the cable car by 9am at the latest, otherwise the queues are so long you probably won't want to bother.

GETTING TO/FROM THE WALK

The cable car (single/return €8/14) runs from 9am to 8pm in the summer and 10am to 6pm in the winter. After purchasing a ticket your turn will be called by number. There is a small cafeteria and self service next to the cable car. At the top you emerge into the tourist centre with souvenir shop, café/restaurant and toilets. For information on getting to Fuente Dé see p185.

THE WALK

After wobbling in fear off the cable car at the upper station you might well want to take some time out to admire the views before taking the path climbing gently away from the cable car station. After 20 minutes you arrive at a junction just below the **Peña Olvidada**; take the right hand path indicated PR24 and descend on the 4WD track. Continue past the **Chalet Real** (a former royal family hunting lodge) and onto the **Refugio de Áliva** (☎ 942 73 09 99; s/d €47/75; Jun–mid-Oct). After enjoying a rest on the terrace continue onwards between the *refugio* buildings following the waymarkers which send you meandering off down a wide track. At the junction with the trail to **Sotres**, take the right path, then ignore the path to the left, and head more or less straight on in southerly direction through the lush meadows of **Puertos de Áliva**. At another junction (with the PR22 trail) continue straight on past two water troughs, a spring and a headstone to arrive at the **La Portillas de Boqueron gates** and a cattle grid. As you turn the corner the scenery changes and you reach the tree line. The track wanders past the **Inverniales de Igüedri** (barns) where the cattle spend much of the early winter. Here you have the impression that you are nearly down but it is at least 30

PUERTOS DE ÁLIVA

minutes more along the main track until you reach Espinama. As you reach the cattle grid and first houses of **Espinama** you emerge at a junction onto a main road marked with a water trough in front of you. Turn right past the **Posada/Bar Sobrevilla** on your right and another bar on your left, to emerge again at a junction onto the main road that leads up to Fuente Dé. The **Bar-Restaurant Vincente Campo** is opposite you on the other side of the road, cross the road here and take the small concrete road that leads down to the right, indicated by a waymarker on a pole.

Follow the signs to Hostal Puente Deva which you pass on your left and then bear left down towards the river which is also signed to the village of **Pido**. Cross the bridge and climb steeply through the trees and past a meadow. As you reach the end of the meadow and the first houses, bear right past a grain store on stilts (known as *hórreo*, it's raised off the ground on stone mushrooms in order to keep rats and mice out) then left to reach a junction where opposite you will see a GR202 sign and a path straight ahead. Ignore both the sign and the path and turn right along the tarmac road past the cheese shop and, at the fork, bear left taking the upper branch where some railings will be on your right. Continue straight ahead bearing slightly right until you come to a junction of small roads.

Diagonally opposite you should see a lamppost with a waymarker on it. Take the road going up to the left just in front of the lamppost and head out of the village ignoring a left turn. If in doubt, you should now be following the line of electric cables past a National Park sign, a water trough and the last of the village houses. Continue along this main track, which takes you past the **Peña Remoña goats' cheese factory** and crosses two bridges over two rivers, the Río Canalejas and the Río de Cantigan from where you'll start to get your first views of the large natural amphitheatre of Fuente Dé.

Just after passing the second bridge, and an opening into a field on your left, take the path (25-30m past the second bridge) that climbs up left from the main track in a northeast direction. Ignore any tracks running off to the right and left, and carry on straight up. At one stage the track forks; take the right fork and again ignore any tracks leaving it. You'll eventually pass an Invernes las Berrugas (barn) on your right just beyond which is another junction. Turn right and continue down through the trees to eventually emerge at the turning point above **Fuente Dé** with the cable car ahead.

MORE WALKS

PARQUE NATURAL DE SAJA-BESAYA
GR71 Continuation
From Saja, the GR71 continues in daily stages to Tudanca (17km), Pejanda (16km), Cahecho (20km), Potes (8km), Bejes (16.5km) and Sotres (16km). Accommodation is available at the end of each day. For transport and lodging information in Potes and Sotres, see Towns & Facilities (p187). The maps in Juan Miguel Gil and Fernando Obregón's *El Sendero de la Reserva de Saja* book are sufficient.

ELSEWHERE IN THE CORDILLERA PARQUE NATURAL DE SOMIEDO
The beautiful Parque Natural de Somiedo, one of the last strong-holds of the brown bear, has a number of excellent hikes. The park's office has more information.

Ruta del Camín Real
Two walks leave from Puerto de San Lorenzo along the Ruta del Camín Real.

Once a Roman highway linking Asturias with Astorga, this road was later used by the Muslims on their way to sack Oviedo. The first walk heads southeast to Puerto de la Mesa in 21.5km; the second goes northwest for 6km to Bustariega.

Ruta de la Pornacal
Starting in Villar de Viladas (west of Pola de Somiedo), the route ascends 6km to the *teito*-filled pastures of La Pornacal and Los Cuartos.

Ruta de las Brañas de Arbellales
This walk to Salienca (east of Pola de Somiedo) passes six *brañas* in an easy 6km.

Ruta de el Cornón
This is a day of climbing Somiedo's highest peak, El Cornón (2194m). From Santa María del Puerto, ascend west to the conical summit in 7km (3½ hours). Return the same way or via Collado los Moñones.

Senda Arcediano
In the 17th century this route, possibly a Roman highway, received its name when an archdeacon from Oseja de Sajambre poured money into its improvement. It connected Castilla with Asturias via the Puerto de Beza, avoiding the imposing Garganta de los Beyos gorge created by the Río Sella. We recommend starting in Soto (5km from Oseja) and continuing 15km north to Amieva. Feasible in five to 5½ hours, this moderate route is partially marked with red-and-white trail markers and has stunning views of the Macizo Occidental.

From Soto, ascend to the Portillera de Beza pass and then cross the Valle de Toneyo, La Majada de Saugu, a high summer pasture, and the Collado del Cueta pass to finish in Amieva village. The Adrados 1:25,000 *El Cornión* map and Marta Prieto's booklet *La Senda del Arcediano* cover the area.

TOWNS & FACILITIES

ARENAS DE CABRALES
☎ 985 / pop 800
Arenas de Cabrales lies at the confluence of Ríos Cares and Casaño, 30km east of Cangas

de Onís. The busy main road is lined with hotels, restaurants and bars, and just off it lies a little tangle of quiet squares and back lanes. Buses stop next to the **tourist office** (☎ 84 64 84; 10am-2pm & 4-8pm Tue-Sun Easter & Jul-Sep), which is a kiosk in the middle of town at the junction of the Poncebos road.

On the second-last or last Sunday in August, the **Certamen del Queso** (Cheese Festival) is held in this home of fine smelly cheese. Thousands come to enjoy the exhibitions, processions, cheese-making demonstrations and tastings.

Sleeping & Eating

Arenas has a camping ground and about 10 other accommodation options, as well as holiday apartments.

Camping Naranjo de Bulnes (☎ 84 65 78; sites per two people, car & tent €24.50) This large and efficiently-run camping ground sits within a chestnut grove, 1.5km east of the town centre on the Panes road.

Hostal Naturaleza (☎ 84 64 87; d €36) About 800m from the centre of Arenas along the road to Poncebos is this quiet little house with a series of smallish but well-scrubbed rooms. The owner, Fina, also has a couple of houses for rent in Arenas.

Hotel Rural El Torrejón (☎ 84 64 11; www.eltorrejon.com, in Spanish; r €55, with breakfast) A bright-red country house welcomes the weary traveller with tastefully decorated rooms in a rural style with lots of fragrant wood. The setting is idyllic, beside Río Casaño, and a couple of minutes' walk from the village centre.

Restaurante Cares (meals €25-30; daily Jun-Sep, Tue-Sun Oct-May) On the western approach into town, this is one of the best restaurants for miles around. Dig into a hearty *cachopo* (breaded veal stuffed with ham, cheese and vegetables) and finish with *delicias de limón* (between lemon mousse and yogurt).

Getting There & Away

To reach Arenas, you can either connect from Oviedo via Cangas de Onís or from Santander via Panes. ALSA buses connect Cangas and Arenas. By car from Cangas, continue east on the AS114.

BÁRCENA DE PIE DE CONCHA
☎ 942 / pop 800

This small village has a **tourist office** (9am-1pm & 3-6pm), with some information on walks in the area, a bar-shop, market, pharmacy, bank and public phone. Sleeping and dining options are limited: **Casa Ferrero** (☎ 84 13 03; s/d with bathroom €18/36), can sometimes prepare meals on request.

Getting There & Away

Fifty-three kilometres south of Santander, Bárcena is easy to access with buses from Santander as well as trains. By car from Santander, head southwest on the N611 towards Torrelavega and then south towards Reinosa.

BÁRCENA MAYOR
☎ 942 / pop 600

An EU grant for economically depressed areas gave this picturesque village a massive face-lift that's left it looking very happy with itself. There are a few shops offering local produce as well as a small **tourist office** (9am-2pm, but don't actually rely on it). Accommodation is limited. Near the church try **Posada Reserva Verde** (☎ 74 10 13/652 960213; www.reservaverde.com; s/d/tr with bathrooms and breakfast €50/65/95), which is a small and stylish place run by two very friendly local ladies. They also offer an excellent evening meal with wine included for €15. There's also a campsite (no showers) to the south of village but at the time of writing it was closed and there was no indication as to whether it would reopen.

No buses travel to Bárcena Mayor so you will need your own car or to walk in.

CAÍN
☎ 987 / pop 400

Caín is surrounded by jagged peaks, mostly over 2000m or more, and its residents honour Gregorio Pérez (1853–1913), a village shepherd who made the first recorded ascent of Naranjo de Bulnes with Pedro Pidal in 1904. From a village where in summer they used to vend linden blossoms, Caín has grown with tourism and has a supermarket, public phones in bars, and a tourist kiosk. The fountain is near the church.

You can camp in the fields along the river for €2. The fields' owners will collect the money. For somewhere indoors, **Casa Cuevas** (☎ 74 27 20; d €40) has basic rooms. There are at least two fancier places to stay, plus a couple of bars and restaurants. You'll find further lodgings in the string of villages south of Caín, including Cordiñanes and the rather drab Posada de Valdeón.

No buses travel to Caín.

CANGAS DE ONÍS
☎ 985 / pop 6700

Good King Pelayo, after his victory at Covadonga, moved about 12km down the hill to settle the base of his nascent Asturian kingdom at Cangas in AD 722. Cangas' big moment in history lasted 70 years or so, until the capital was moved elsewhere. Its second boom time arrived in the late 20th century with the invasion of Picos de Europa tourists. In August especially, the largely modern and rather drab town is full to bursting with trekkers, campers and holiday-makers, many desperately searching for a room – a common story throughout eastern Asturias in high summer.

Information
The **tourist office** (☎ 84 80 05; www.cangasdeonis.com; Jardines del Ayuntamiento 2; 10am-9pm daily Jul & Aug, 10am-2pm & 4-7pm Mon-Sat, 10am-2pm Sun Sep-Jun) is just off the main street, Avenida de Covadonga. **Casa Dago** (☎ 84 86 14; Avenida de Covadonga 43; 9am-2.30pm, sometimes open in afternoon) provides national park information. Cangas has a fair smattering of banks with ATMs.

Sleeping & Eating
Cangas has loads of hotels and a few *pensiones,* and there are plenty more of both, plus numerous *casas rurales,* in nearby villages. Along the road towards Arenas de Cabrales, Soto de Cangas, Mestas de Con and Benia de Onís all have several options. Most places in town can also inform you of rental apartments.

Hostal de Casa Fermín (☎ 84 84 91; 676 015377; Paseo de Contranquil 3; d €50) Located 500m past the Capilla de Santa Cruz, in a vaguely bucolic setting, this brick structure has bright, simple rooms and a popular summer *sidrería.*

Hotel Santa Cruz (☎ 84 94 17; www .hotelsantacruz.net; Avenida Constantino González 11; s/d €67/90) Between the Capilla de Santa Cruz and a big riverside playground, this modern hotel goes for the rustic look. You can increase the comfort factor by opting for a double with its own jacuzzi (€120).

Mesón Puente Romano (menú del día €12) The terrace is just below the bridge, or you could opt for the lugubrious cellarlike dining room. The set lunch is *fabada* (a hefty Asturian bean stew) followed by *arroz con leche* (rice pudding). The management warns that both dishes are 'abundant'.

Getting There & Away
You will find the bus stop and local ALSA bus company office opposite the Jardines del Ayuntamiento on Avenida de Covadonga. From July to early September, buses run between Cangas and Lago de la Ercina.

FUENTE DÉ
☎ 942 / pop 200

Sitting literally at the feet of the Picos de Europa at the end of a box canyon and offering a beautiful natural amphitheatre, this small village has grown up around the cable car. There are no services other than hotels and restaurants and while it cannot be called attractive it's a convenient stop for accessing the walks. **Camping El Redondo** (☎ 73 66 99; camping per person/car €5/7.10) has a supermarket, bar and washing machines. **Hotel Rebeco** (☎ 73 66 01/02; s/ d with bathrooms inc breakfast €57/65) is a handsome stone lodge that represents good value. It has an excellent restaurant; try the fresh fish meals from €10.

Buses trundle several times a day along the scenic road between Potes and Fuent Dé.

OVIEDO
☎ 985 / pop 220,700

Oviedo is a charming, slightly inland city with a refined feel throughout its central core.

Information
The **tourist office** (☎ 21 33 85; www .infoasturias.com; Calle de Cimadevilla 4; 10am-8pm mid-Jun-mid-Sep, 10am-7pm

rest of year) provides useful information for walkers. Ask for the free 1:75,000 *Picos de Europa* map and the detailed brochure *Mountain Routes*, which gives excellent ideas for walking in the area.

Sleeping & Eating

In the historical quarter, you'll find decent rooms at **Hostal Los Arcos** (☎ 21 47 73; Magdalena 3; s/d €35/50). A quick stroll from the train station is **Hostal Belmonte** (☎ 24 10 20; calogon@teleline.es; Calle de Uría 31; s/d €39/49), a charming 3rd-floor (there's a lift) lodging offering cosy rooms with timber floors and an at-home feel. Cheaper rooms with shared bathroom are also available. Oviedo's *sidrería* rules include getting good grub at reasonable prices. Most of those on Calle de la Gascona serve *raciones* from €8 to €18. Two or three constitute a full meal. One highly recommended place is **Tierra Astur** (Calle de la Gascona 1; meals €20-25), a particularly atmospheric *sidrería/restaurant*, famed for its grilled meats and prize-winning cider.

Getting There & Away

Buses run by **ALSA** (☎ 902 42 22 42) connect Madrid and Oviedo (from €29.90; 5½ hours, 10 daily) as do Renfe trains. By car, take the A6 tollway from Madrid to Benavente (northwest) and then the N630 to León. Continue on the A66 to Oviedo.

Between Santander and Oviedo there are several buses a day (from €12.60).

PONCEBOS

☎ 985 / pop 100

There's no real village here, just a smattering of buildings but it offers easy access to the cable car and is a convenient base for the walks starting from the northern end of the El Garganta del Cares gorge. **Hospedaje la Garganta de Cares** (☎ 84 64 63; s/d €38/62 with breakfast) is a comfortable hotel with free parking, restaurant (meals from €8) and bar. Classier digs can be found at the **Mirador de Cabrales** (☎ 84 66 73; s/d €75/79).

Buses run up to five times a day between Arenas de Cabrales and Poncebos.

POSADA DE VALDEÓN

Of all the Picos access towns, Posada is closest to León, south of the park. It has

a pharmacy, supermarket, and bars and restaurants. There are two camping grounds nearby, in Santa Marina and Soto de Cangas, as well as a handful of cheap lodgings.

Buses run by ALSA connect León and Posada from where you can reach Caín.

POTES

☎ 942 / pop 1500

With its well-preserved medieval quarter, Potes is an ideal base for the southern Macizo Oriental and Macizo Central.

Information

The **tourist office** (☎ 73 07 87; Plaza de la Serna; 10am-2pm & 4-7pm Mon & Thu-Sat, 10am-2pm Sun) shares a building with the bus station on the west side of town.

Sleeping & Eating

With 13 hotels and *pensiones*, there is no shortage of accommodation here. They are by and large simple, straightforward places, all clustered fairly close to one another.

Casa Cayo (☎ 73 01 50; www.casacayo .com; Calle Cántabra 6; s/d €30/50) This is the pick of the bunch in Potes, with helpful service and attractive, comfy, wood-beamed rooms. You can eat well in the excellent restaurant for about €20.

Getting There & Away

Buses run between Potes and Santander three times daily on weekdays and twice daily at weekends. The journey takes a little over two hours.

SAJA

☎ 942 / pop 300

Limited accommodation is available at **Casa de Labranza Seijos** (☎ 74 12 23; d with shared bathroom €30), which has clean ample rooms. Dining is limited to a restaurant 300m out of village on the main road.

Getting There & Away

Public transport options are limited; there's one bus a week (Mon) to Torrelavega via Cabezón at 8.45am and from there onward transport is easy, with connections to Bárcena de Pie if you left your car there at the start of a walk. Other options including hitching or take a **taxi** (☎ 70 05 18; €40) between the two villages. Some of the local people may offer to take you for less. By car take N625 to Cabezón, then N634 to Torrelavega and finally A67 to Santander.

SANTANDER
☎ 942 / pop 182,300

This large seaport city offers all services and last-minute supplies.

Information

The **city tourist office** (☎ 20 30 00; Jardines de Pereda; 9am-9pm mid-Jun–mid-Sep) provides good local information. Note: hours may vary widely. The **regional tourist office** (☎ 31 07 08; www.turismocantabria .com; Calle de Hernán Cortés 4; 9am-9pm daily Jul–mid-Sep, 9am-1pm & 4-7pm daily rest of year) gives accommodation and transport information as well as free brochures on walking in Cantabria and the Picos de Europa.

Librería Estudio (Avenida Calvo Sotelo 21) stocks English titles as well as walking guides and maps.

Sleeping & Eating

Hospedaje Botín (☎ 21 00 94; www .hospedajebotin.com; Calle de Isabel II 1; s/d €38/55) The homey Botín has some spacious rooms with showers and *galerías* (glassed-in balconies). In the historical quarter, **Pensión La Corza** (☎ 21 29 50; Hernán Cortés 25, 3rd floor; d with/without bathroom €55/42) has good rooms.

For something different to eat check out **A,11** (Calle del Arrabal 11; tapas and *raciones* €1.30-12) with its gourmet sophistication and big-city-style bright lights.

Getting There & Away

Buses connect Madrid and Santander (from €26.50, five hours, six daily) as do Renfe trains. By car from Madrid, take the A1 to Burgos and then the N623 north. Brittany Ferries link Santander with the UK (see p356).

SOTRES
☎ 985 / pop 100

Sotres is a high-altitude village, located 16km from Arenas. You can sleep and eat well at **Casa Cipriano** (☎ 94 50 24; www.casacipriano.com; s/d €30/50), a favourite haunt of mountain aficionados. Aside from the simple but cheerful rooms, the staff offer a professional mountain-and-caving guide service and simple restaurant.

Hotel Peña Castil (☎ 94 50 80; www .hotel.penacastil.com; s/d €40/60) offers 10 impeccable if smallish rooms in a renovated stone house. The rooms have graciously tiled floors, some wood panelling and fine showers, and some have perky balconies.

Getting There & Away

No buses ascend to Sotres from Arenas. Take a taxi from the stand next to the tourist office, or hitch. By car, take the scenic winding AS264 up through the Garganta del Duje.

Galicia

HIGHLIGHTS

- Marvelling at the treacherous beauty of the **Costa da Morte** (p191) with the ocean licking at your feet
- Reaching the top of Monte Pindo on the **Monte Pindo** walk (p192) and seeing the 'end of the earth' amidst the massive blue expanse of the Atlantic
- Sharing the solitary, green ridges of the eastern serras with agile deer on the **Serra dos Ancares** walk (p210)
- Following a sinuous canyon through timeless villages and ancient chestnut groves on the **Río Lor Meander** walk (p206)

Area: 29,574 sq km	Average summer high: 24°C	Population: 2.77 million

Quietly nestled in Iberia's northwest corner, Galicia has a great wealth of natural riches for the walker eager to experiment in this largely rural corner of Spain. Plunging sea cliffs and expansive dunes, deep forests and water-fed mountain slopes, are enhanced by fascinating cultural history: prehistoric sites; medieval monasteries, churches and bridges; and surprising vestiges of arcane ways of living – thatch-roofed houses, unique stone granaries and yoked oxen driving wooden ploughs.

The walks detailed here explore parts of Galicia's 1200km of coastline along the isolated Costa da Morte (Death Coast) and the Illas Cíes (Cies Islands), which form part of Spain's newest national park. In the Serras dos Ancares and Courel mountain ranges of Galicia's magical, rural interior are rounded crests, river systems and enclosed lush valleys.

Despite these attractions, don't expect excellent walking infrastructure (good trail markers, English-language guides and easy public transport). Galicians are not avid recreational walkers and no private or public agency regularly maintains trails. Hopefully, this situation will change.

HISTORY

Megalithic peoples (around 3500 BC) intentionally changed the landscape leaving behind dolmens (burial chambers built with huge stones) and later petroglyphs. Around 600 BC Iron Age peoples (some of them Celts) intensively settled the area, filling Galicia with some 3500 castros – permanent, fortified, circular settlements. There are excellent examples of dolmens on the coast and castros all over Galicia. Romans arrived in 137 BC and eventually conquered the area in search of mineral wealth. Iberia's oldest (and still functioning!) Roman lighthouse, La Torre de Hércules, protects La Coruña (A Coruña). Roman walls still

encircle Lugo. Both of these monuments are Unesco World Heritage sites.

The 9th-century discovery of James the Apostle's tomb in Santiago de Compostela (see History in the Camino de Santiago chapter, p304), forever put Galicia on the map and the region achieved its maximum glory by the 13th century. The mid-19th-century Rexurdimento, Galicia's political and cultural renaissance spawned a nationalism which embraced a largely imagined (and romanticised) Celtic past.

Galicia's economic mainstays have been animal husbandry, agriculture and fishing. When these proved to be inadequate, many Galicians fled to richer areas (such as the Americas and other parts of Europe).

GALICIA

Emigrants' money, tourism, agricultural efficiency and, somewhat surprisingly, a hugely successful fashion industry all worked to invigorate the weak economy between the 1970s and 1990s. Despite generalised prosperity, young people still seek employment in the urban areas, the fishing industry is currently in grave crisis and an ageing population is left to tend the fields.

ENVIRONMENT

Split into four provinces (La Coruña, Lugo, Pontevedra and Ourense), Galicia's 29,482 sq km form a complex topography from the coast to the inland mountains. Mainly composed of igneous (granites) and metamorphic rocks (schists and gneiss), Galicia is, geologically speaking, the Iberian Peninsula's oldest area.

Tectonic movements were largely responsible for leaving behind a coast of high (500m to 1100m), steep coastal ranges divided dramatically by magnificent, silty *rías*, or tidal estuaries, created by the perpetual battle between ocean waves and river water. Into the Atlantic pour some 38 rivers and the coast is adorned with more than 50 islands. The interior region undulates well below the level of the coastal ranges before reaching 2000m in the

---

WARNING

Eight types of snake inhabit the region. Two are venomous though their bites are rarely fatal. They are small (maximum 50cm to 60cm) and inhabit forest, field and brush habitats. Keys to their identification are their vertical pupils and triangular heads. For a discussion of treatment for snake bites, see Bites & Stings (p369).

---

rounded eastern serras (Ancares, Courel and Eixe).

Galicia was once densely covered with humidity-loving carballo, or common oak, but only 10% of the original oak groves remain. The rest have been largely converted into agricultural land or replanted with fast-growing pines and eucalyptuses. Galicia's best autochthonous, mixed Atlantic forests are found in the Serra dos Ancares. Walkers inevitably encounter scrub characteristic of Galician monte (low-hill country) – heather, genista, broom and gorse. Individual walks may feature unique and rare species of flowers; these are covered in the relevant parts of this chapter. Common all over the region are deer, wild boar, hares, foxes, weasels and occasionally otters, pine martens and there are even a few wolves out there.

CLIMATE

In general, the Atlantic gives Galicia a temperate, wet climate, although its hilly topography makes for numerous microclimates. Precipitation tends to be heaviest on the northern coast and western mountains (up to 3000mm of rainfall annually) and lowest in the southeastern serra (600mm annual rainfall). See each walk for local information.

PLANNING
When to Walk

All walks are feasible from May to October; mid-June to mid-September is best. Outside of these months, rain is common and snow occasionally hits the mountains.

When planning your walks, bear in mind that the times quoted are actual walking times.

CRACKIN' GOOD SHELLFISH

Galician shellfish and seafood is plentiful, fresh and may well be the best you have ever tasted. The region's signature dish is *pulpo a la gallega*, tender pieces of octopus sprinkled with olive oil and paprika (*pulpo á feira* has chunks of potato added). Mollusc mavens will enjoy the variety of *ameixas* (clams) and *mexillons* (mussels). Special shellfish of the region include *vieiras* and *zamburiñas* (types of scallop), *berberechos* (cockles), *navajas* (razor clams) and the tiny, much-prized goose barnacles known as *percebes*, which bear a curious resemblance to fingernails. Other delicacies include various crabs, from little *necoras* to the great big *buey del mar* – the 'ox of the sea'. Also keep an eye open for the *bogavante* or *lubrigante*, a large, lobster-like creature with two enormous claws.

Maps

For orientation, the following 1:250,000 maps are recommended: Ediciones Sálvora's *Mapa de Galicia* and the Xunta de Galicia's *Mapa Autonómico*. They are widely available in Galician bookshops. The regional tourist office in Santiago de Compostela has the free 1:400,000 *Galicia, North of Portugal* map, which is excellent.

Maps for individual walks are detailed under Planning for each walk.

PLACE NAMES

Road signs are in Galician. City dwellers are primarily Spanish speakers but Galician is the mother tongue of the rural population (who, if they don't also speak Spanish, at least understand it). In general, maps use Galician place names rather than Castilian. The only exceptions to this rule are some of the older IGN and SGE maps. Differences are minimal enough to be easily recognised in either language.

Books

Galicia, published by Guía Azul (Serie Verde), is a good, general guide (in Spanish) which focuses on the area's natural resources. Walking guides are almost exclusively written in the Galician language.

Purchase maps and books at either **Follas Novas** (Montero Ríos 37) or **Abraxas** (Montero Ríos 50) in Santiago de Compostela. Maps and books for individual walks can be bought in the Access Towns or Nearest Towns for the walk unless otherwise stated.

Information Sources

In Santiago de Compostela, the regional **tourist office** (☎ 981 58 40 81; Rúa do Vilar 30-32; 10am-8pm Mon-Fri, 11am-2pm & 5-7pm Sat, 11am-2pm Sun) provides regional (and local) transport and accommodation information for Galicia and the Camino de Santiago. Ask for the useful brochures: *Galicia: Nature's Garden* and *Galicia: Pathways*. The latter, although great in concept (it briefly describes walking routes with simple maps and points of interest), is inadequate; most routes are neither maintained nor consistently waymarked.

Useful websites on Galicia are: www.turgalicia.es and www.galinor.es.

GATEWAY

See Santiago de Compostela (p213).

COSTA DA MORTE

The Galician coast is broken into three sections: Rías Altas, Costa da Morte and Rías Baixas – the upper and lower *rías* with the Death Coast in between.

Seeing a winter storm batter the Atlantic coast, the meaning of Costa da Morte is immediately clear. Countless ships lost off this rugged coast are mute testimony to its treachery (see the boxed text The English Cemetery, p197). The area extends from the cliffs of Malpica, in the northwest around Cabo Fisterra (Finisterre), to the dazzling white dunes of Carnota. Three *rías* (Corme, Laxe and Corcubión) interrupt the coastline, which reaches out to the sea in a series of juts and capes; lighthouses crown seven of these. The *rías* are less windswept, with waveless beaches, dense woods and villages.

Several rare and endangered plants are found almost exclusively on the Galician coast: herba de namorar, the 'falling in love plant', a type of thrift, used to enchant the desired partner; camariña, which gives Camariñas its name, a small bush that produces a tiny, white fruit; and angélica, a 1m-high plant with bright green leaves and umbrella-shaped yellow flowers, unique to this part of the world.

Seabirds thrive on the Galician coast, attracting bird-watchers from around the world. Of particular note are shags (a species of cormorant) that nest in furnas, or cliff-side caves; the penguin-like guillemot; and the yellow-legged gull. While walking it's common to see dolphins and porpoises playing just offshore.

Wind and clouds from the southwest generally indicate the imminent arrival of rain.

PLANNING

Costa da Morte: Guía Turística-Cultural, by Xan Fernández Carrera, provides excellent and extensive historical and cultural information, and has an English translation at the back.

An lutsta website on the Costa da Morte is www.finisterrae.org.

GALICIA

MONTE PINDO

Duration 5–6 hours
Distance 16km
Difficulty moderate–demanding
Start/Finish O Pindo (p212)
Transport bus
Summary Salty breezes, pine forests, odd granite formations, 360-degree summit views – this loop features a stunning array of natural sculpture on one of Galicia's most celebrated coastal mountains.

Rising abruptly out of the Atlantic, rose-gold granitic Monte Pindo is Galicia's Mt Olympus. From its summit, A Moa (627m), there are unbeatable views from Fisterra (north) to Carnota (south). Local legends are extensive: Celts committed mass suicide here rather than submit to Roman colonisation; fertility rites were celebrated on pagan altars on the summit; ancient treasure is hidden in secret caves. The wondrous moraine and erosion-produced granite formations are a highlight. Semi-wild horses are often spotted on the walk's upper reaches.

Sporadic yellow-and-white slashes mark the 3.5km trail up to A Moa. The easiest way to descend from the summit is to take the same trail back down. A much longer and more demanding alternative descent heads down Pindo's backside through the Río Xallas canyon and allows you to make a loop through this impressive countryside. This section is marked with occasional yellow-and-white slashes, cairns and wooden signage and a compass is recommended. Harnessed since the early 20th century, the river was dammed in 1988 and lost its ecological viability. Spectacular nonetheless, the final 100m waterfall is Europe's longest freshwater-to-ocean drop, forming a 20m-deep pool below. Each year, on major holidays and on Sundays from 21 June to 21 September, the dam is opened from noon until 2pm and the Xallas once again roars majestically.

You'll find water at the trailhead and in Fieiro, 6.5km into the walk.

Maps

The IGN's 1:25,000 map Nos 93-I *Brens* and 93-III *O Pindo* cover the route.

GETTING TO/FROM THE WALK

See O Pindo p212 for transport information.

THE WALK

A metal 'Monte Pindo' sign located adjacent to O Pindo's church marks the trailhead. Head southeast past the playground (with fountain) into the forest, crossing a small stream bed to a narrow path. The dirt and rock trail ascends for 20 minutes through dense foliage, first along a low stone wall and then zigzagging uphill. Where the trail begins to level and veers notably left, look for the Olimpo Celta – soon, with some

WARNING

Marine fog makes it easy to get lost on this mountain. When the dam is opened occasionally for rain overflow in December and January (and as previously described), keep in mind that there are no warning sirens.

MONTE PINDO

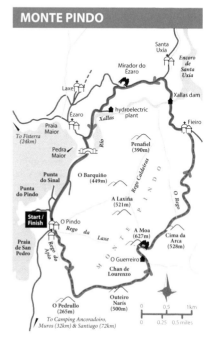

imagination, heads, angels and animals are visible in the granite. During the next 20 minutes the forest thins, the coastal views preview the glory ahead and then the trail steepens, through charred pines, to a T-junction. Looking southwest (right), **O Pedrullo**, a small peak, is recognisable by the cascade of small rocks at its base. A 10th-century watchtower built here protected the inhabitants from Viking raids. Peasant uprisings in 1467 provoked its destruction.

Turn left through the open granite landscape. About 250m after the T-junction don't miss a poorly-marked left fork. Continue steadily uphill for 15 minutes through a narrowing canyon. A stone barrier between two huge boulders hems in semi-wild horses. Cross the barrier and continue ascending for another 20 minutes to the surprising alpine plateau, **Chan do Lourenzo** (Lorenzo's Floor). Horses often graze here amidst the heather and broom. Looking left, A Moa's light, rounded summit appears. Carnota's 6km of white beach lie to the south. A wolfram (aka tungsten) mine, exploited by locals desperate for pesetas during WWI and WWII, lies behind the shepherds' hut. The mineral was used to strengthen weaponry and coveted by the Germans who controlled the local mines.

Go northwest towards A Moa, keeping left to avoid the boggy centre, and in 100m look for 6m-high **O Guerreiro** (the Warrior) sitting with his back to you. Follow the trail on this sentinel's right. About 300m beyond O Guerreiro, the trail ascends through woodland and heads left on a poorly-marked fork. Continue up for another 10 minutes to a plateau at A Moa's base.

Circle around to A Moa's northeast face following a high granite wall. In a grassy saddle where Xallas canyon (with water pipes visibly shooting down the hillside) comes into view to the north, turn left (west) and continue ascending for 100m along a narrow footpath through boulders to the summit. Punctured with erosion pools, enjoy excellent 360-degree views. From right to left is Cabo Fisterra, Illas Lobeiras (last breeding ground of monk seals, exterminated in the 19th century), O Pindo, Quilmas and Carnota. To avoid navigational difficulties, descend the same way you came up.

If you want to make the long loop, descend from A Moa's top to the saddle where the Xallas canyon is visible. Turn left (north), descending towards the canyon. After 100m the trail veers right (east) into a pine forest. Keep heading east towards the windmills visible on the far hills. Reaching a plateau, aim east towards large granite boulders and follow the cairns over large granite slabs. At the base of the boulders, turn left along a descending trail towards a low granite range directly ahead. After reaching an information panel at the range's base, the trail veers left and returns to pine and oak woods. Ferns can overgrow the trail here. In five minutes of descent, the trail opens up to an obvious wider trail that keeps descending for 20 minutes in a northerly direction (except one hairpin turn) until it empties onto a dirt track. Turn left and in 10 minutes this road brings you to **Fieiro**.

Turn left onto the sealed road and in 1km the trail crosses the Xallas dam. To reach Ézaro continue 4.5km along the sealed road. Initially the road veers left and then makes a steep descent past the **Mirador do Ézaro**. One kilometre further fork left onto a cement road descending towards the hydroelectric plant and then continue to Ézaro village. It's possible to detour to the waterfall's base by turning left onto the hydroelectric plant's service road. The hydroelectric plant has a small Centro de Interpretación open mornings and afternoons.

Once at the highway, turn left over the bridge and continue to O Pindo to finish the loop or turn right to enter Ézaro.

SPINDRIFT

Duration 2 days
Distance 39km
Difficulty easy–moderate
Start Laxe (p212)
Finish Camariñas (p211)
Transport bus, taxi
Summary With the ocean never out of sight, this walk provides an excellent introduction to the often desolate and always hauntingly beautiful Costa da Morte.

If the sea is your passion, then this is your walk. From start to finish, the ocean

GALICIA

acts as a constant right-hand companion, its breaking waves a lyrical commentary on your progress. Linking the Costa da Morte's two northernmost *rías*, the walk provides peace and isolation; only fishing villages, and the time-worn patterns of their daily routines, interrupt the otherwise desolate but tranquil coast. The walk ends in Camariñas, famous for its lace (see the boxed text Galician Lace-Making, below).

PLANNING
What to Bring
Make sure to get sufficient water for the short first day in Laxe. On Day 2, water is available in several spots and the trail is sporadically marked with yellow-and-white slashes.

Maps
The IGN's 1:50,000 map Nos 43-IV *Laxe* and 67-II *Muxía* cover the route.

GETTING TO/FROM THE WALK
To return to Laxe from Camariñas, take a taxi (☎ 981 73 61 69) from the stand next to Bar Praia on the main street (€25) or a bus with transfers. With Aucasa/Autos Carballo buses take the 6.30am Camariñas-Santiago bus and then transfer at Ponte do Porto (10 minutes from Camariñas) for Laxe (originating in Muxia). Alternatively, take the Camariñas-Carballo line (€5; five daily Mon-Fri, three Sat, two Sun) and transfer in Carballo for either Laxe or Santiago.

THE WALK
Day 1: Laxe to Camelle
3–3½ hours, 12km
Leave the main Praza Ramón Juega along the quaint Rúa Río. Ascend 600m along the cement road (ignore the yellow-white slashes leading right on a wide trail) to the chapel, Santa Cruz da Rosa. Local women keep the candles burning for their men at sea.

From the chapel, take a wide southbound dirt lane. Just past a small house, the trail, flanked by stone walls separating fallow fields, narrows and heads towards the long stretch of gorgeous, rolling coastline ahead. In 200m, where several trails join, turn right and cross the fields to an obvious track marked with yellow-and-white slashes. Turn left and follow the wide trail down to **Praia de Soesto**, a surfers' favourite hangout. Pick your way across the small river and dunes and walk down the crescent beach. At the far end take a small footpath bordering the coast – spindrift may brush your skin – and continue for 15 minutes.

Reaching a small stone beach the path becomes a dirt lane. At the next sandy beach the lane becomes a wide dirt road. Twenty minutes later, when the road curves left and separates from the sea, continue along the road and turn right onto the first wide dirt lane you reach. Follow the lane to a grassy parking area. Take the left-hand trail and continue 400m until the trail opens on the right and gently slopes down to the flat rocks and **Praia de Traba**, a great stretch (2.5km) of white sand. Cross the beach.

GALICIAN LACE-MAKING
Observing women (*palilleiras*) swiftly manipulate tens of bobbins (*palillos* or *bolillos*) to slowly produce intricate patterns of delicate lace, known as *encaixe*, is a most impressive sight. Sitting at the doors of their homes, or grouped together, *palilleiras* practise an art whose origin is unclear. Some say a Flemish soldier of Carlos I, based on the coast, first imported the lace; others, that it came via the Camino de Santiago (Way of St James). The most romantic version suggests that a strange, foreign woman, saved from a shipwreck by helpful locals, gave them the gift of lace in thanks.

The oblong, pillowed work-board is stuffed with tightly packed hay inside a soft sack. Two wooden sticks project from the top, providing support. Around the board the women wrap drawn pattern and position countless coloured pins at crucial intersections. Between the pins they skilfully braid linen threads, each attached to walnut *palillos*. Camariñas is the most famous centre of lace-making in the Costa da Morte. Several shops specialise in lace-making and there's a **Museo do Encaixe** (Lace Museum; ☎ 981 73 63 40; Praza Insuela; admission €2; 11am-2pm & 5-8pm Tue-Sat, 11am-2pm & 4-7pm Sun) by the town hall.

GALICIA

MAN, EL ALEMÁN DE CAMELLE

As you approach Camelle, eye-catching, coloured circles on the village breakwater seem oddly out of place. Signs for 'Museo' along the maritime walkway lead past salty types chewing the fat over fishing nets to the unexpected museum of Man (Manfred), a German who came to Camelle in the 1960s and set himself up on the breakwater, where he stayed until his death in late 2002. Man built a highly creative open-air museum using the flotsam brought by the waves – tree roots, nets, floats, shoes, whale vertebrae, scraps, plastics, etc. Pinnacle-shaped sculptures made from stones fixed with cement, and several paths covered with local plants completed this fantastical wonder. Man, a true modern-day hermit, explained his vision simply – life is a circle.

During the November 2002 Prestige oil spill Man's museum was extensively polluted (and it's said that the broken heart from which Man suffered after the spill may very well have contributed to his death shortly afterwards). Man's final public request was for his museum to be left untouched as a reminder of the devastating effects of the spill. Still a tourist attraction, the sea is slowly taking the museum back again and it now shows a marked decline from when Man was alive.

Early in this stretch, a river drains into the sea. Fording it barefoot may be necessary. Halfway down the beach, an optional detour (left) ascends the dunes to Lagoa de Traba, a protected freshwater lagoon. Marsh birds such as coots and grebes thrive. At the beach's far end, a boardwalk will take you back into the village of **Mórdomo** which has a small bar.

At the beach's end, 4km remain to Camelle. Continue on a right-hand dirt lane that promptly forks right onto a narrow access trail (a wider stone trail here rejoins the narrow path). For 30 minutes the trail rolls (sometimes disappearing) through granite boulder fields to a wide dirt lane. With Camelle in sight, the trail veers left, comes to a fork (go right), narrows through dense brush and reopens at a stone beach. Take the sealed road for 500m. Follow the curve around the bay of Camelle to get to its port and commercial centre.

Day 2: Camelle to Camariñas
7–8½ hours, 27km

Leave Camelle's port via Rúa do Porto. Climb for 200m and make a hairpin right turn onto a sealed road leading to desolate **Arou** (1.8km). Follow the maritime walkway around Arou's beach

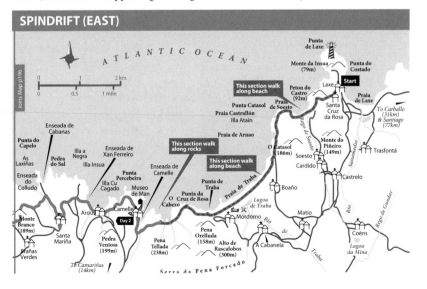

SPINDRIFT (EAST)

to the boardwalk. Continue to the sealed road and turn right following the coast for 700m. Turn left onto the ascending cement road. Fifty metres later, turn right onto a rocky road that steeply ascends for 1km to a sealed road. Turn right and go 1.2km to the crossroads of **Santa Mariña**, which fills the steep valley stretching below. Turn right and descend in hairpins through the houses of this lonesome enclave. Descend towards the port and, about 300m above it, turn left down a dirt road that, after a slight dip and ignoring a dirt track on the left, launches into the longest (1.4km) and hardest ascent of the day – straight on. On reaching the summit, head right to the wide road.

In 10 minutes the road skirts Monte Branco (White Mountain), named for its sandy composition. For the next 45 minutes the walking is easy along the wide track that takes you above the dunes and Praia do Trece, and makes a long, gentle descent to the ocean and the **Cemiterio dos Ingleses** (see the boxed text The English Cemetery, p197).

Continue along the road at sea level for an hour (3.8km). Soon views of the windmills, lighthouse of Cabo Vilán and the islets off the cape dominate the horizon. Upon reaching a sign (left) that describes how wolves (lobos) were once trapped, continue another five minutes to where the road begins to ascend and curve left. Either take the road, or, continue straight along a footpath that shortcuts up the steep hillside and returns to the road. Sheep and goats often graze in this area and there's a natural spring. Once at the top of the hill, follow the road towards the lighthouse and continue 1.7km to the first windmill on your right. Just after the windmill, take a small footpath to the right that makes a beeline for the lighthouse (1km) and avoids the enormous Stolt sole fish farm, or keep to the main road to avoid the prickly scrub. The majestic **lighthouse** sits 135m above the sea, is 25m high and was the first in Spain (1896) to function with electricity. Ships can see it from 60km away.

From the lighthouse follow the sealed road. Where it curves sharp left (100m below the dirt road), search on the right for an obvious southbound trail. Follow the coastline for 35 minutes aiming for the hill topped by a chapel. Nearing the hill, the

trail veers left and, before reaching a soccer field and granary, turns right. From the hill's base make a five-minute ascent up the well-defined trail to the **Capela da Virxe do Monte**. Excellent views southwest to the Ría de Camariñas, the village of Muxía and Cabo Touriñán are worth the climb.

Descend the same way to the base. Before the soccer field, turn right onto a descending sea-access road. After 200m make a hairpin turn left towards the beach. Notice stacks of drying seaweed used to fertilise fields. Skirt the beach and then ascend along stone walls following the beach contour. Continue along the obvious dirt track for 15 minutes, ignoring any smaller footpaths, until you reach a T-junction. You will pass forest as well as cultivated fields of potatoes, beans and cabbage. Turn left and walk for five minutes until the dirt track converts to cement running between houses. Pass between two houses and veer right. In 200m pass the 17th-century ruins of Carlos III's Castelo del Soberano. The castle's stones were used to construct the port and the cannons became mooring posts. Turn left to reach Camariñas.

SPINDRIFT (WEST)

THE ENGLISH CEMETERY

On 10 November 1890 the British training vessel Serpent ran aground off the coast between Cabo Vilán and Praia do Trece. The attempts of nearby villagers to help were futile. Of the 173 hands on-board all but three were lost. The humble cemetery at the foot of the rocks shelters their remains. In thanks for the heroics of the local people and the burial of the sailors, the British Admiralty gave a rifle to the priest of nearby Xaviña, a gold watch to the mayor and a barometer to the town hall (embedded in the wall of a house in Camariñas). In addition, whenever a British military ship passed the area it was to sound cannon in honour of the lost sailors. Within the cemetery walls is a stone cross dedicated to the thousands of nameless *náufragos* (shipwrecked) off the Death Coast.

ILLAS CÍES

In 2007 the Cíes, a 9km breakwater protecting Vigo from the Atlantic's fury, topped the *Guardian's* 'Best Beaches in the World' list with their crystalline waters and white-sand beaches. The 434-hectare archipelago consists of five tiny islets and three islands: Monte Agudo, the largest and most rugged; O Faro, linked to Monte Agudo by a white sandy crescent (Praia das Rodas) which forms a lagoon (O Lago); and San Martiño, separated from the other two and only accessible by private boat.

The Cíes were first protected in 1980. In July 2002 they, together with the Ons and Sálvora archipelagos and Illa Cortegada, were declared Galicia's first and Spain's 13th national park, Parque Nacional Marítimo Terrestre de las Islas Atlánticas de Galicia. The park covers 1665 terrestrial and 1135 maritime hectares.

Since pre-Roman times humans have inhabited the islands. During the 14th century each island had a monastery, but pirate raids precluded the establishment of a stable population up until the 19th century; the last inhabitants left in the 1970s.

Owing to the islands' low altitude (maximum 197m) and proximity to the mountainous mainland, rainfall is very low – with a marked summer drought – giving the islands a mixed Mediterranean-Atlantic climate. The granite massifs, shaped by wind and water into steep 100m cliffs on their eastern faces, and gentler, forested and dotted with dunes and beaches on their western sides, harbour excellent examples of rare Galician flora (375 species), as well as a unique species of thrift (Armeria pungens), rare specimens – for example, Corema album and Mediterranean species such as rockrose, cork-oak and wild asparagus.

Key populations of marine birds find sanctuary here. The largest colony in the world (22,000 breeding pairs) of the yellow-legged gull is found on the Cíes, and 1000 breeding pairs of shags thrive here. From the two bird observatories that the walks visit you can view the cliff-side nests of both species. Nesting occurs from January to August; chicks are born in June and July. And, unlike the overfished coastal waters nearby, the protected seabeds teem with life.

PLANNING

There is a limit of 2200 visitors per day, and the islands' only lodging facility, the camping ground, has an 800-person nightly limit (see Illas Cíes, p212). Especially in August, the islands are overwhelmed by visitors; a reduction of permitted maximums is imperative to protect the islands' delicate ecosystems. All the islands' services (ferry, bars and restaurants, camping, Red Cross, ranger service and information) are open at Easter and from 15 June to 15 September. Both walks are easily combined as a single day trip (don't forget your swimsuit!), but to stay longer, plan ahead. The islands have no potable water source. Either bring your own or pay a high price on the islands. Visitors are responsible for taking all of their rubbish back to the mainland for disposal.

Maps & Books

The IGN's 1:10,000 *Parque Natural Islas Cíes* map covers the walks. The islands' information centres have free self-guided walks with simple maps.

The islands' information centre lends (but does not sell) guides to visitors. In English, find the *Visitor's Guide to Galicia's Atlantic Islands Land-Maritime National Park*. The guide is for sale at bookstores in Vigo.

GALICIA

Information Sources
Staffed by park rangers, the **information centre** (10am-2pm & 4.30-7.30pm daily), located in a small cabin 100m from the ferry dock, offers free brochures in English covering the four marked routes, the cultural history and the flora and fauna as well as guided visits in Spanish. Fifteen minutes by foot from the dock, on O Faro island, the 17th-century remains of the **San Estevo monastery** (Punto de Información) houses an exhibit on the islands' flora and fauna and an audiovisual programme, but was closed for renovation at the time of writing. The mainland **park office** (☎ 986 246 517; CETMAR Building, Calle Eduardo Cabello s/n) is in Bouzas (Vigo).

Permits & Regulations
Permits are not necessary to visit but a return ferry ticket is required if making a day trip, and reservations with a camping voucher at the camping ground if staying longer. The authorisation of the National Park Authority is necessary to sail, anchor or scuba dive.

The following are prohibited:

- camping beyond established facilities
- disturbing flora and fauna (at sea or on land)
- entering designated Marine Birds Sanctuary areas
- fires (except Campingaz stoves in the campground)
- making excessive noise
- bringing animals onto the islands
- swimming in the lake

ACCESS TOWN
See Vigo (p214).

ILLA DO FARO

Duration 2–2½ hours
Distance 7.7km
Difficulty easy–moderate
Start/Finish Muelle das Rodas
Nearest Town Vigo (p214)
Transport boat
Summary A gentle ascent to a bird observatory and Monte Faro lighthouse offering outstanding views.

If birds and beacons are your thing, this pleasant, relaxing walk delivers handsomely.

GETTING TO/FROM THE WALK
Naviera Mar de Ons (☎ 986 22 52 72; www.mardeons.com) ferries operate from Vigo (€35 return, 45 minutes, four daily from mid-Jun–mid-Sep) to the Muelle das Rodas jetty on Illa de Monte Agudo. Buy tickets online and avoid summer lines at the ferry's ticket offices. Ferries also leave from Baiona (€35 return, one hour, four daily from late Jun–mid-Sep) and Cangas (€28 return, 45 minutes, twice daily from late Jun-early Sep). With good weather more ferries are added. Children up to 12 years ride free.

THE WALK
From the boat jetty, fronted by **Bar-Restaurante Playa de Rodas** (sandwiches from €2.50, meals €10), walk left down the obvious trail 100m to the information centre.

From the information hut turn left (south) along the obvious trail which circles **O Lago**, via a sea wall (built in the 1960s) joining the two islands. Sea life in the pool, clearly visible from the wall, abounds. Ascend past the camping ground to the **Punto de Informacion** (under restoration at the time of writing), a two-storey stone building on the right. Another 250m further on, you'll reach a crossroads. Wooden signs clearly indicate where the different trails lead. Turn right (following the Faro de Cíes/Pedra de Campá sign) up a clear path that zigzags for around 20 minutes, forking right once, before opening up to a lookout and the hollowed-out 'bell-tower rock' **Pedra da Campá**. A further 100m ahead is the bird observatory, a small blind with space for four to observe birds and an information panel in English.

Return the same way to the fork. Veer right and continue on the wide trail for 30 minutes up to the lighthouse crowning **Monte Faro** (172m). Enjoy outstanding views of Illa San Martiño and the mainland. Descend five minutes the same way until reaching a trail on the right marked 'Faro da Porta'. Descend right, at first steeply, along the dirt trail to a T-junction. Turning right leads to the **Faro da Porta**

ILLAS CÍES

1 Illa do Faro   p198
2 Illa Monte Agudo   p199

200-year-old cemetrey, at Praia das Rodas' extreme southern end, and return to the ferry dock via the beach.

ILLA MONTE AGUDO

Duration 2–2½ hours
Distance 7.3km
Difficulty easy
Start/Finish Muelle das Rodas
Nearest Town Vigo (p214)
Transport boat
Summary Outstanding lookouts, crashing waves, cliffs and a chance to end at the island's best beach.

This enjoyable amble around dunes, through forest trails, up to dramatic coastal lookouts and down to serene beaches is sure to reveal a host of delights.

GETTING TO/FROM THE WALK

For details of ferry access to the Muelle das Rodas jetty, where the walk starts and ends, see Getting to/from the Walk (p198).

THE WALK

From the jetty, turn left and walk 100m to the information hut. Turn right (north) along the pine-lined cement path. A wooden sign indicates 'Faro do Peito, 2.1km'. The protected **Dunas de Figueiras-Mixueiro**, where many endangered plants survive, are to the right. About 300m from the start ignore the 'Area de Figueiras' sign (it's the islands' nudist beach). The trail becomes enveloped by eucalyptus trees and progressively ascends, offering fantastic views of the Ría de Vigo. Growing amidst the eucalyptus are a few native oak, holly, strawberry and willow trees. Continue ascending to a crossroads clearly marked with wooden signs giving distances and directions.

To reach the **Alto do Príncipe** (122m), a magnificent lookout, turn left (west) onto an ascending trail which quickly turns south. Sloe berries, torvisco (Mediterranean mezereon) and rockrose flank the trail. Fifteen minutes from the crossroads the trail briefly dips before turning right to an open area and ascending to the lookout. Enjoy the excellent views of Monte Faro

lighthouse in 580m. Instead, turn left and wind down towards Carracido beach and the port. Sailboats dock here frequently. In six minutes pass **Fonte de Carracido** (of dubious drinkability) and a beach to reach the crossroads. Just down the hill (and clearly marked) is the pleasant, sandy beach **Praia da Nosa Señora**, popular with summer boaters.

Take the trail straight towards the Caseta de Información. After 200m turn right on an unmarked descending cement road. Upon reaching another fork, either turn left along the trail, first past **Casa de Comidas Serafín** (meals from €3), with very pleasant open-air seating and a Playa Rodas beach access, and then back to the start via the camping ground, or alternatively you could head right to descend to the islands' and its lighthouse as well as the granite rocks, cliffs and erosion pools. Return to the crossroads.

Turn left (north) towards 'Faro do Peito'. After 400m a wide trail briefly heads left to a lookout before rejoining the main trail. Surrounded by open grassland, continue 10 minutes to a clearly marked fork. Here, the route makes a short loop. Ascend left towards the bird observatory and stay on the main trail for five minutes. Reaching a T-junction, head left and continue briefly to a granite outcrop and, visible below on a small trail, the bird observatory (Monte Agudo is to the left). Return to the fork and descend left briefly to another fork (marked with a wooden post). Head downhill 160m to the old lighthouse and a large sea cave, **Furna de Monte Agudo**, via the access port ramp. Return to the fork and turn left continuing straight on for 10 minutes to complete the small loop.

Return to the crossroads for the last time. Take the trail to the left marked 'Campo de Traballo'. Descend for six minutes along the cement track through forest. Ten metres after the cement track ends and before reaching a log cabin, take a right-hand path towards the ocean and the rocky area **O Bufardo**. Keep straight (south) on the narrow (and sometimes rough) forest trail just above the white beach for six minutes to **Praia de Figueiras** (the nudist beach). Either descend and cross the beach or continue along the obvious forest path. Both trails rejoin at the beach's southern end and, 10 minutes further reach, the information hut.

SERRA DOS ANCARES

The Ancares range (composed of granite, slate and sandstone) runs for 30km and covers an area of 127 sq km, reaching its maximum heights at Pico Cuíña (1987m) in León and O Mostallar (1935m) in Galicia. In the Ancares, the westward-flowing rivers include the Ser, Rao and Navia while the Cua, Ancares and Burbia head east. Due to its isolation, ruggedness of life and political marginalisation the Ancares were slow to modernise, maintaining their customs and ancient dwellings, the *pallozas*, (see the boxed text Galician Vernacular Architecture, p203). In the 1990s the area began to receive EU development grants and the government's tourism branch realised that 'the past' sells. Money has primarily been funnelled into rural guesthouses rather than conservation of the enormous natural assets. Ancares is a *reserva nacional de caza* (national hunting reserve), though area supporters optimistically label it a *parque natural* on signs and stickers.

Not overwhelmed by eucalyptuses and pines, the Ancares woodlands are distinctly Atlantic (oak, birch, laurel, hazel, yew and holly). Chestnut, oak and walnut groves are also an intrinsic part of the landscape. Retaining its leaves and fruit in winter, holly plays a crucial role, providing 50% of the herbivores' nourishment and shelter; it's 5°C warmer under its canopy. Due to human exploitation of the environment (cutting trees for timber and pastures), scrub (including tasty blueberries) covers much of the range. The great yellow gentian is a beautiful companion on the range's heights.

The Ancares woodlands contain rare and endangered mammals such as pine martens, wolves and the *urogallo*, or *capercaillie*, known locally as the *pita do monte* (mountain chicken). Its spectacular nuptial song once filled the woods in spring. The *urogallo* has been protected from hunting since 1971, but only 10 pairs are believed to survive. Expect to see roe deer, diminutive creatures which skip across scree.

PLANNING

Ancares winters are long, cold and wet (1500mm to 2000mm of rainfall). Autumn colours are particularly appealing for walking. A compass is recommended for navigation here.

Maps & Books

Everest's 1:80,000 *Os Ancares: Mapa de Carretera* is ideal for orientation. For both walks described the IGN's 1:50,000 *Sierra de Ancares* topographic map is best. Cumio's 1:50,000 topographic map and guidebook *Ancares: La gran sierra Galaico-Leonesa* are also good and informative.

Information Sources

Area information is best acquired through the town halls in Pedrafita do Cebreiro or Becerreá. Camping in the wild is frowned upon; ask for permission in the San Román de Cervantes (known as Cervantes) town hall. Get petrol at access towns as none is available within the Ancares.

ACCESS TOWNS

See Pedrafita Do Cebreiro (p213), Becerreá (p210), Piornedo (p213).

ANCARES RIDGE

Duration 5½–7 hours

Distance 19km

Difficulty moderate–demanding

Start Refuxio dos Ancares (see below)

Finish Piornedo (p213)

Transport taxi

Summary Walking among the clouds, this south–north traverse climbs five high peaks before descending to the hamlet of Piornedo with its pre-Roman style dwellings.

Beginning from Refuxio dos Ancares, just outside Degrada, and ending in Piornedo, this outstanding ridge walk can also be done in reverse; although the Mostallar ascent is taxing. Carry plenty of water as there are no fountains, other than a natural spring, en route and supply from there cannot be guaranteed at all times of the year.

Adjacent to the Ancares Ridge walk trailhead, **Refuxio dos Ancares** (☎ 982 18 11 13; dm €10; s/d with bathroom €25/35) is 1.5km from Degrada, which is little more than a crossroads with several houses. Food is available (menú €10). In Mosteiro 5km south of Cervantes (on the Becerreá-Degrada road) find **Camping Os Ancares** (☎ 982 36 45 56; camping per adult/child/tent/car €3.50/3.30/3.70/3.30).

GETTING TO/FROM THE WALK

Degrada lies roughly 40km from either Becerreá (9km towards Navia de Suarna then towards Cervantes) or Pedrafita (towards Doiras); both approaches follow seemingly endless winding roads. Hire a taxi (around €50) from Becerreá or Pedrafita if travelling on public transport.

THE WALK

From Refuxio dos Ancares (1350m), take the sealed road that heads southeast among broom, ferns and heather for 30 minutes (1.3km) until the sealed road converts to dirt track. Over the next easy 5km the trail passes a fountain trough, the Campa de Ortigoso and a holly and oak forest. The track peters out at **Campa de Tres Obispos** (1579m) at the base of Pico Tres Obispos. There are spectacular panoramic views of the serra's highest peaks from here. You may, on occasion, encounter a fellow hiker who also shares a passion for artistic endeavour, quietly sketching or painting the inspiring country before them. From left to right (northeast to southwest) are Cuíña, O Mostallar, Lagos or Lanzas, Corno Maldito, das Charcas, Penedois, Tres Obispos and, on the far right, the hooked Pena Rubia.

Take the southbound footpath that ascends towards Pico Tres Obispos. For 25 minutes climb steeply through heather and then grass along the ridge towards the peak. You may need to stop to draw breath once or twice on the way up, but it's a pretty spectacular place to do it. Keep along the peak's right slope to a meadow at the base of the summit. Search for a trail on the left that climbs to the rocky summit of **Pico Tres Obispos** (1795m). Views of the serra and a good part of León and Lugo provinces are yours from this legendary gathering spot of the bishops of Astorga, Lugo and Oviedo – the shared corner of their dioceses.

Descend briefly southeast. Take the ridge trail northeast, crossing the irregular peaks of **Os Penedois** (1754m). The trail will disappear underneath the stones. Instead of ascending the next peak, Pico das Charcas (1793m), take a trail from its base and follow its left-hand slope to the base of the conical **Corno Maldito** (Damned Horn).

Circle around the base of Corno Maldito's right slope through open pasture, then turn left (northeast) ascending to the ridge. Once on the ridge, if you want to go to Corno Maldito's summit turn left and in five minutes reach the summit cairn (1849m). Return to the ridge. Follow the left slope of the next hill and descend to the wide saddle, **Golada de Boca do Campo**. A small cirque lies off to the right. You are now halfway through the walk.

GALICIA

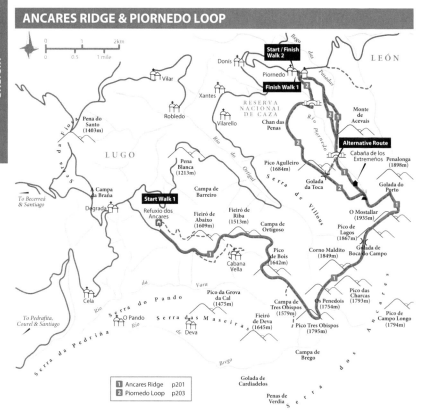

ANCARES RIDGE & PIORNEDO LOOP

1 Ancares Ridge p201	
2 Piornedo Loop p203	

Ascend the ridge heading north for 25 minutes to **Pico de Lagos** (Pico de Lanzas; 1867m). From the summit, also cairned, O Mostallar comes into spectacular view to the northeast. Descend towards it along the ridge. Look for a level trail through scree along Mostallar's west face. Once through the scree the trail remains level and converts to grass before turning sharply and steeply right.

This is the only tricky part and you may need to use your hands to help guide your progress for a short distance. Aim for the ridge 30m away. Once on the ridge turn left, quickly reaching the flat-topped and grassy summit of **O Mostallar** (1935m). Continue to the cairn and then head left (north) in descent along a wire fence (a footpath runs parallel to it). Follow this

all the way down to the saddle, **Golada do Porto**.

Turn left (west) and descend across the basin (an example of a glacial hanging valley – see the boxed text Signs of A Glacial Past, p28) for 30 minutes to a shepherds' hut, **Cabaña de los Extremeños**. En route, pass a natural spring, cross a stream (the origin of Río Piornedo) and, if it's late August or September, ripe blueberries. From the dilapidated cabin take a road descending to the left for 30 minutes to another open valley.

Cross the river again via an old wooden bridge. Continue straight ahead, first ascending and then continuously descending (for 3km) to Piornedo along the wide lane. Enter the village past its chapel.

PIORNEDO LOOP

Duration 4½–5½ hours
Distance 13km
Difficulty moderate
Start/Finish Piornedo (p213)
Transport taxi, bus
Summary A varied walk through lush forest, mountain pastures and high valleys to the origin of the sparkling Río Piornedo.

The walk starts and ends in Piornedo. Drinking water is available only at Piornedo's public fountain. Ask Manolo in the Hotel Piornedo if the last section around Chan das Penas has been recently cleared otherwise turn down the Golada da Toca-bridge trail as navigation can be a real challenge when the post-Golada da Toca section is overgrown with brush.

GETTING TO/FROM THE WALK

See Piornedo (P213) for transport information.

THE WALK

Ascend through Piornedo and then past the chapel on a dirt road. Pass through the livestock gate and continue ascending for 25 minutes (1.2km). Two hundred metres after the area where the road briefly descends and before it veers left beginning a steep ascent, look for a 3m-high boulder to the right of the road. Head south crossing a narrow stream to pickup a footpath that veers left (south) along the southwestern slope of the open hillside sprinkled with holly, birch and rowan. Looking right, the valley below is clearly visible, as are the ridge, forest and zigzagging trail that the walk reaches later. After five minutes the footpath enters a dense forest and gently ascends for 20 minutes along an intermittently rocky trail.

As the ascent ends, continue south, keeping left through the high broom and pastures. The trail reaches the second, lower valley described in the Ancares Ridge walk. Cross the wooden bridge and ascend the wide trail for 35 minutes to the shepherds' cabin, **Cabaña de los Extremeños**. Head eastward, towards the **Golada do Porto saddle** (left of O Mostallar) aiming for the centre of the great basin. Look for the multi-coloured snow-marker. Once you spot it, turn right to face southwest, and look for the only visible path up to the ridge (some sections are open dirt). Aim for this path and ascend steeply for

GALICIAN VERNACULAR ARCHITECTURE

Inhabited until the 1980s, *pallozas* are dwellings that were first developed during pre-Roman times and well adapted to the Ancares. Upon an oval floor, 1m-high stone walls rise to meet the conical roof of rye-thatch that prevented the accumulation of snow and water. People shared the inside – separated into various rooms with the hearth at the centre – with their animals, taking advantage of their heat. Constructed with a southern exposure and on a slant to improve drainage, they had small windows but no chimneys; smoke filtered up through the thatch.

Near to the dwellings are *hórreos*, free-standing granaries elevated on columns or solid blocks and used to store the harvest free from humidity. Between the column and the granary's base a projecting horizontal rock prevents hungry rodents from gaining access. Asturian *hórreos* are square with wooden walls and a four-sided tile, slate or even thatch roof. The Galician ones are quite diverse but are usually rectangular and made of stone, with a pitched tile roof often decorated with a cross.

Constructed on riverbanks, *molinos* milled corn and wheat using water power. River water was diverted through a canal then released, dropping onto a turbine that moved a huge stone wheel which ground the grain. Mills either had one owner, who kept a percentage of the flour milled, or several who took turns milling. In the 19th century more than 8200 *molinos* functioned in Galicia.

Albares or *cortines*, appearing on mountain hillsides near villages, are circular or oval stone walls up to 1.5m high with horizontally projecting stones rimming their tops. These prevented sweet-toothed bears robbing honey from the beehives kept inside them. Examples are found in both the Ancares and Courel.

GALICIA

15 minutes, out of the basin to the ridge, which has outstanding views.

Turn north (right) along the crest of the ridge (if you went left, you would reach Pico de Lagos) and head towards the next peak. After 20 minutes (1km) the trail descends to a narrow saddle, Golada da Toca. Continue ascending the ridge to the summit of **Pico Agulleiro** (1684m).

On a poorly-marked westbound trail, begin the gentle descent on a high open plain for 300m. Turn right (northeast) and descend 200m, going cross-country, towards the forest. Reaching the magical birch forest, look for the clear left-hand (north-northwest) descending trail. It stays close to the edge of the forest.

Descend for 20 minutes until the trail reaches another, wider trail. Turn left onto the new trail, which immediately leaves the forest. Turn right, keeping a couple of boulders on your left. A thick tunnel of broom leads to a deep trail that becomes enveloped in holly forest before reaching an open plain surrounded by huge boulders, **Chan das Penas**. The trail peters out here.

Turn right (north-northeast) for 100m along the grass and when the trail re-appears continue straight ahead (north) ignoring another trail leading left. The trail makes a serpentine 30-minute descent, primarily in the forest, passing two large, dry oaks on the right, before reaching the valley floor. Cross the stone bridge, spanning the **Río Piornedo**, and take the dirt road straight ahead which ascends directly to the village (near the chapel) in 20 minutes.

SERRA DO COUREL

Lying on a northeast-southwest axis, the Serra do Courel or Caurel (210 sq km) is divided and demarcated by three mighty rivers – the Lor (west), Quiroga and Sor (east). Its steep, forested hillsides and rounded, open peaks reach a maximum height at Pico Formigueiros (1643m). The iron-rich limestone and slate mountains were the focus of Roman mining operations and evidence of these activities is found throughout the area. The Courel's main attractions are its rustic mountain villages and extraordinary flora.

The soils, orientation, slopes, minimal pollution and the convergence of Atlantic and Mediterranean climate systems have produced more than 1000 floral species that flourish between 400m and 1600m. Remarkably, 40% of Galicia's flora is represented in the Courel, which constitutes only 1% of the total territory. Special forests called *devesas* – humid, north-facing mixed woodlands of carballo (common oak), Pyrenean oak, maples, hazel, beech (Spain's westernmost examples), holly, birch, rowan and yew trees – thrive here. Mediterranean species include holm and cork-oaks and strawberry trees as well as the aromatic rockrose and lavender bushes. Wildflowers

---

CHESTNUTS, SOUTOS & SEQUEIROS

Huge *soutos* (chestnut groves) grow thickly around Courel villages. The chestnuts' enormous trunks, often twisted and gnarled, support odd-looking small limbs intentionally cultivated this way for two reasons: to provide lumber without killing the whole tree, and to produce more chestnuts. The carbohydrate-rich fruit, wrapped in prickly husks, was long fundamental to the local diet (before the potato's arrival). Come autumn, the Courel turns rich tones of yellow, and the husks (known locally as *ourizos*, or literally 'hedgehogs') turn brown and fall to the ground. Continuing an ancient cycle, the Courel's signature tree is ready for harvest. Soon the air fills with the delicious scent of roasting chestnuts.

Today a *magosto* (chestnut roast) is still celebrated each November in alternating years in Seoane and Folgoso. Roasted, stewed, stuffed in birds, boiled and mashed, or simply raw – chestnuts are integral in regional dishes. For year-round use, chestnuts were dried during a laborious 20-day process in *sequeiros*, stone and slate-roofed drying cabins frequently grouped together. As the old ways die out, some of these buildings as well as the *cabañas* used to store hay – both of which are commonly seen on walks – are being converted into weekend homes.

are particularly rich and include purple orchid, columbine, butterwort, toadflax and purple flag iris.

Bats inhabit the area's limestone caves, and it's possible to encounter rare mountain cats and martens, and to see the endangered golden eagle (only five reproductive pairs remain) in the sky.

GETTING AROUND

Public transport consists only of expensive taxis and inconveniently infrequent summertime **Empresa Courel** (☎ 982 42 82 11) buses connecting Quiroga, on the Courel's southern extreme, with Folgoso do Courel (see p211) and Seoane do Courel.

ACCESS TOWNS

See Pedrafita do Cebreiro (p213), Seoane do Courel (p214), Folgoso do Courel (p211), Quiroga (p213).

DEVESA DA ROGUEIRA LOOP

Duration 6–7 hours

Distance 20km

Difficulty moderate–demanding

Start/Finish Moreda (p212)

Nearest Town Seoane do Courel (p214)

Transport taxi

Summary An ascent through magical forest with more than 1000 species to the Serra do Courel's crest, Galicia's only glacial lagoon and a unique natural spring.

Initially enveloped in the enchanting *devesa*, this trail reaches the open ridge for superb views of the Courel. The return leg leads down to the rustic village of Moreda. Most of the Courel was once covered by *devesas* but these were nearly logged to death at the turn of the 20th century. Information panels in Spanish accompany the trail for 20 minutes and explain how many of forest's trees were traditionally used. The trail is intermittently marked as the PR50.

The walk ascends 870m through the forest. In spring both the Fonte do Cervo and the glacial Lagoa A Lucenza will be full (but don't expect a dazzling, icy cirque at any time of the year), while the changing leaves make autumn an attractive time. To shorten the walk by 5km simply descend back through the forest where indicated in the text. Water is available at several natural springs en route.

PLANNING
Maps
The IGN's 1:25,000 map No 157-I *Seoane do Courel* covers the route.

GETTING TO/FROM THE WALK
See Moreda (p212) for transport information and options.

THE WALK
From Moreda's **interpretive centre**, head southeast into a chestnut grove. Five minutes later cross a stream adjacent to a *sequeiro* (and, further along, some *cabañas*). For 25 minutes the walk ascends along a trail (ignore field-access trails) and enjoy views of the *devesa* and ridge to be climbed. Where the trail crosses a stream, make a hairpin left turn, and five minutes later reach a fork.

Take the right fork and begin a series of switchbacks through forest for 20 minutes. The trail levels and passes a stretch where the stream descends in cascades. Immediately after fording the stream, the trail steepens again and the hardest section begins – 30 minutes uphill through woodland. On reaching a fork go right. Continue ascending to a T-junction and turn right (turning left will take you to Moreda). A few minutes later there's another T-junction – with the upper loop trail. Turn left and in five minutes reach the **Fonte do Cervo**. From the high rock-face two springs flow – one red (rich in iron), the other clear (calcareous). They taste and smell differently and are said to be medicinal.

Left (east) of the Fonte de Cervo, the trail continues for 30 minutes through forest and then dense, prickly brush to the ridge. This trail is not regularly maintained and will probably be closed. Consequently, we recommend the following:

To reach the ridge, Lagoa A Lucenza and the **Mirador de Piolín**, backtrack from the Fonte de Cervo to the first junction and continue straight maintaining the same altitude level for 15 minutes until the trail breaks open at an old slate quarry and a wide dirt track.

DEVESA DA ROGUEIRA LOOP

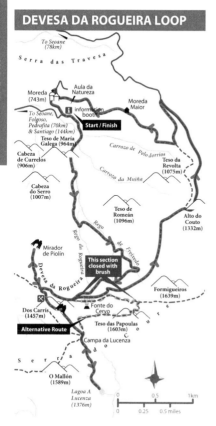

of turning left along the trail you came up on the ascent (returning this way saves 5km), continue straight on. After 100m ignore a footpath that goes left. During the next hour the obvious trail fords two streams, passes through an area rich in yews (and wild blueberries in mid-summer), and twists through the forest in gradual descent. It continues by breaking through the forest to an area with hazels, scrub oaks, rowan and birch, and reaches a sealed road hemmed in by pines, near the top of **Alto do Couto**. Where the forest opens, it's easy to spot the descent route: look north for the *cabañas* and Moreda below.

Turn left down the road; after 100m there's a fountain and water tank. Continue for 1.4km (25 minutes), ignoring dirt roads. Branch left off the sealed road onto a dirt trail that zigzags downhill and in 15 minutes reaches the first cabin. Turn right and descend (ignore two dirt trails left) to pastures and continue straight. *Cabañas* are visible at the foot of a section of scree. Continue through a wet zone and trees and take a descending fork left. The cobbled path widens as it descends steeply in 10 minutes to Moreda Maior, some cabins surrounded by walnuts. Continue for 15 minutes on the clear trail; a chestnut grove indicates Moreda is close. Reaching a fork, head left and, once past some small gardens, enter Moreda via the cement road. At the guesthouse, 100m further on, turn left and in 300m reach the interpretive centre, or turn right down to Moreda's plaza and fountain.

RÍO LOR MEANDER

Duration 2 days

Distance 22km

Difficulty easy–moderate

Start Seoane do Courel (p214),

Finish Froxán (p211)

Transport bus, taxi

Summary An outstanding village-to-village walk through the steep-sided canyon of the sinuous Río Lor, passing inhabited villages, *soutos* and a pre-Roman fort.

To visit the **Mirador de Piolín** and get great views over the *devesa*, turn right in descent along the 4WD track and continue for 10 minutes until the trail peters out at a right-hand lookout point. Return the same way to the quarry.

To visit the lagoon, continue uphill from the quarry along an obvious 4WD track for 20 minutes to the ridge and a crossroads in a wide saddle called **Campa da Lucenza**. Continue straight ahead at the crossroads and veer left onto an unmarked grassy area. A path soon appears and descends to the base of a hill. From here go right on a footpath to reach the shore of **Lagoa A Lucenza** (1376m). Retrace your steps to Campa da Lucenza, descend back to the slate quarry and return to the junction.

Take the left fork and descend the trail to the next junction (three minutes). Instead

This route invites you to see the Courel through the eyes of the river. Primarily undulating along the canyon of the Lor's true left bank, it uses ancient pathways traversed for millennia by villagers travelling to the foundry, to the *albares* to get honey (see the boxed text Galician Vernacular Architecture, p203), to the *sequeiros* to tend chestnuts (see the boxed text Chestnuts, Soutos & Sequeiros, p204), or just to get from place to place. Marked with 'Ruta do Lor' wooden signs, yellow-and-white slashes and yellow arrows (the latter two both haphazardly), the recently rehabilitated trail is the work of local people wishing to recuperate a not-so-distant yet abandoned past. Day 2 ends in Froxán. From here are outlined two additional day hikes which would make a good third day and allow you to spend two nights in this village. If you are short on time, we recommend Day 2 as the highlight. Parts of the walk may be overgrown, especially during Day 1. Long trousers are advised. Water is readily available at village fountains.

PLANNING
Maps
The IGN's 1:25,000 map Nos 157-I *Seoane do Courel*, 156-II *Folgoso do Courel* and 156-IV *Salcedo* cover the route.

GETTING TO/FROM THE WALK
See Seoane do Courel (p214) and Froxán (p211).

THE WALK
Day 1: Seoane do Courel to Folgoso do Courel
3½–4 hours, 12km

Left of Bar Gloria in Seoane look for yellow-and-white slashes and take a descending paved road past houses towards the canyon and river. Descend 200m to the village's last house, and take a paved right-hand fork (ignoring a gated trail on the right) and steeply descend towards the river. On the left, just before the trail passes under a house, is a 19th-century water-powered foundry. Turn left over the bridge and continue to a wooden 'Ruta do Lor' sign 100m ahead. Distances are clearly marked.

Take the ascending trail curving right to a chestnut grove. After passing a house on the right and between two impressive vertical boulders, the trail continues for 4km along

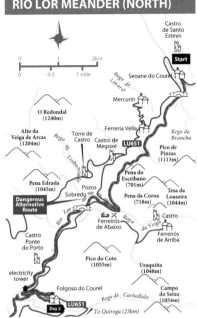

RÍO LOR MEANDER (NORTH)

roughly the same contour while rounding the great flanks of the hill on the left. The trail never reaches the river, although it is audible much of the way. About 20 minutes into the walk take a left fork and 10 minutes later, at a T-junction, go left again and pass some *sequeiros*. Take a fork to the right after a further 100m or so. Just before entering the village there are fantastic views down the canyon. The trail curves left past several houses, becomes a paved road and descends to **Ferreirós de Abaixo**, on the river, and **bar-restaurant O Pontón** (meals €13) serving outstanding meals. Don't miss this place! The owner, Manolo Álvarez, is an resourceful local artist who transforms chestnut trunks into magnificent pieces of furniture.

Head to the road (the guard-rail shows Ruta do Lor distances). From here there are two options which rejoin further downstream. The first option is the marked trail. Turn left and ascend along the road 100m. After several large chestnut trees marked with yellow arrows, veer right down a footpath. For 15 minutes the trail gradually descends through chestnuts, a burned area and then back through forest. The trail reaches a fork. The trail coming from the right is the alternative and in 50m leads to a wooden bridge.

The second option adds 600m and takes you closer to the river and beautiful natural pools ideal for a dip. Caveat: there is a 100m hair-raising section near the union with the other trail that requires caution. Turn right in descent along the road for 600m to a left hand sign marked *pozos* (pools). Descend the obvious zigzagging trail following yellow arrows to a wooden bridge. Cross and continue for three minutes in descent to the Pozo de Mulas – a cluster of massive boulders, dripping with vines, guarding a deep inviting pool. Continue downstream and where the pool ends take a left-hand ascending trail to a natural lookout over the canyon. Keep following the yellow arrows back down to the river. The trail follows the steep left bank and makes a brief ascent requiring hands and feet and continues for 100m along a narrow path with a vertical drop to the river. Soon thereafter the trail reaches a wooden bridge and one minute later joins the main trail as described in the first option.

At the junction of the two trails, continue downstream (left if coming off the main trail). During the next 2km (25 minutes) the trail rolls through the forest past a waterfall (on the left), then branches left (ascending away from the Lor past a *sequeiro*) and finally reaches a wider trail, initially slate. Fork right and head downhill through the forest. Ascend along an open hillside with the main road above you, and in 10 minutes pass a crumbling *albar* on the left. Fifteen minutes later, when an electricity tower is visible to the southwest on a hilltop, veer right, downhill, at an unmarked fork (the left fork leads to an impassable, abandoned dump). You can spot the outlines of *albares* on the other side of the canyon. Look ahead to the next bend and aim for the trail visible on a contour below yours. You may need to go cross-country in places. At the bend continue on roughly the same contour for five minutes, ascending only gradually to meet the trail, marked with yellow arrows, at a slate outcrop. Briefly ascend, with the arrows, to a curve in a wide slate road. Turn left (uphill) to reach Folgoso; to the

right (downhill) the road continues to Valdomir (see Day 2).

Ascend 1.5km along a zigzagging dirt road. Folgoso is visible most of the time. Continue to the top along the road, to the tower, and turn right onto the main road to reach Folgoso in 400m.

Day 2: Folgoso do Courel to Froxán
3–3½ hours, 10km
Return to the Folgoso–Valdomir juncture along the slate road from the previous day. Continue downhill to a wooden bridge and cross, then veer left. In five minutes cross another wooden bridge, **Ponte de Sudrios**, spanning the Lor near the Río Loúzara affluent. Over the bridge turn left and continue for 20 minutes, passing **O Touzón** (its small chapel, dedicated to San Roque, is worth a peek) and the houses of **A Pendella** before reaching the main road and a bridge at Valdomir. Cross the bridge to the Mesón Catuxo, which is a great spot for a drink or meal (from €12).

From the parking lot, take the trail past the chapel (well worth a glance) and ascend to the Ruta do Lor sign. Turn left, reaching an old aqueduct in 150m, and then take a fork to the right uphill along a narrow, steep trail which opens to a *souto*. Look for arrows and ascend straight to a zigzagging trail up to **A Campa**. Arrows accurately lead left, right, left and right through the maze of houses. From A Campa's last house, Vilamor's church, high on the opposite side of the canyon, dominates. The good trail undulates for 2km: go left at four forks. Where the trail ascends steeply to a wide slate road, go right downhill (the fifth fork) and pass below Vidallón. Visible in the distance are the houses of Vilar, nestled in chestnut trees at approximately the same elevation as you. Mediterranean species suddenly appear on this section: rockrose, cork-oaks and strawberry trees. In 10 minutes reach a 'Ruta Castro do Vilar' sign and a *cabaña*. Leave the road and take a narrow but obvious descending trail towards Vilar. The trail is magnificent through here as it winds around cliffs. In another easy 20 minutes you'll reach **Vilar**.

At the concrete plaza turn left to the fountain or continue straight through a

RÍO LOR MEANDER (SOUTH)

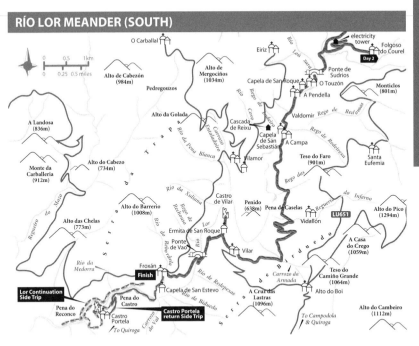

GALICIA

tunnel (formed by a balconied house) to a fork. Immediately to the right is a small **museum** (admission €1) run by a fascinating local man who has salvaged everything from harnesses and saddles to pots and spinning tools from Vilar and neighbouring villages. The route to Froxán (signposted) veers left through the village past the hamlet, *souto* and gardens. Veer right, past the **San Roque chapel**, to the ruined 2nd-century **Castro de Vilar** upon a rocky spur above the Lor. In spite of the overgrowth, it's possible to discern defensive walls and the ruins of circular dwellings.

Returning to the chapel, continue back towards Vilar for 50m and take the footpath that descends right (west) through chestnuts and then open hillside for 20 minutes to the **Río Lor**. Cross the wooden bridge, **Ponte de Vao** (the last PR51 sign), and ascend left along a wider path. Where it levels out, look for cork-oaks. At the next fork veer left, entering **Froxán**, a hamlet of medieval appearance, and continue to its plaza. The village fountain (Fonte de Milagro) is up to the right.

SIDE TRIP: FROXÁN TO CASTRO PORTELA RETURN

1½ hours, 5km

From Froxán's upper plaza, head straight down between the houses. After the last house turn left and immediately go right on a cobbled lane that descends in 10 minutes to a sealed road on the banks of the Lor.

Cross the **Río Lor** on the road (there's a great swimming hole on the right) and continue for 1km along the road. Turn right onto a descending lane that appears when the road makes its first left turn, initiating the 2.5km loop of Castro Portela. Continue straight, ignoring a descending trail right, for 15 minutes on a hillside trail among chestnuts above the Lor.

After the trail eventually descends and curves left, passing a restored *sequeiro*, it curves right to a fork. Veer right through pastures and huts and after 300m turn left in ascent to **Castro Portela**. Wend your way up through the village, past a fountain and then onto the sealed road. Turn left, return to the bridge along the road and continue to Froxán.

GALICIA

SIDE TRIP: LOR CONTINUATION
1½ hours, 5km

Exploring the Lor's true right bank below Castro Portela, this walk offers the longest continuous section along the river.

From Froxán's fountain 'Fonte de Milagro' turn left along the sealed road and in 400m you will reach a hairpin curve with cork-oaks and a crumbling albar. Turn right down a dirt trail that once linked the villages and descend towards the river. The path parallels the river, offering spectacular views for 2km until it reaches some cabins in a field surrounded by chestnuts. Return the same way.

MORE WALKS

PARQUE NATURAL FRAGA DO EUME

Under the lush shelter of Galicia's last great Atlantic woodland, this circuit walk descends along the Río Eume's canyon, continuing along its river bank to reach the Caaveiro monastery. This easy to moderate 12km walk is accessed via Pontedeume, starts at the Camping Fraga do Eume and is intermittently marked as the GR50. Use the IGN's 1:25,000 map Nos 22-III *Pontedeume* and 22-I *Fene*.

SANTIAGO DE COMPOSTELA
Monte Pedroso

A must if staying in Santiago, this easy 10km-return walk leaves from the Praza do Obradoiro and ascends Monte Pedroso (Rocky Hill) to the north. Panoramic views of Santiago and the surrounding countryside are exceptionally fine. From the *parador*, descend the ramp to the Carmen de Abaixo church. Turn right immediately after the bridge. Veer left up the first road until it converts to dirt, winding to the top.

Sobrado dos Monxes

North of Melide, but reached from Arzúa, is one of the best conserved (and still functioning) monasteries of Galicia, Sobrado dos Monxes. Around the monastery is a 12km loop. Leaving from the Barrio de Alvariza the trail covers the monastery's lands, a lagoon, oak woods and various hamlets. IGN map Nos 71-III *Sobrado* and 71-IV *As Cruces* cover the walk.

SERRA DOS ANCARES
Picos Cuíña & Penalonga

East of Piornedo, accessible by car and just within León's borders, is the Porto dos Ancares. From here a trail (at first poorly marked) heads south (constantly veering right) and ascends two large hills before reaching the summit of Pico Cuíña (1998m), the highest peak in the Ancares. From its base, a trail leads right to the summit of Penalonga (1898m). This hard return trip takes seven hours. Use the IGN's 1:50,000 *Sierra de Ancares* map.

Campa de Brego Loop & Pico Pena Rubia

This 15.5km easy to moderate walk starts at Refuxio dos Ancares (Degrada) and descends to tranquil valleys within the most well-preserved and beautiful forest in the range. The loop initially uses the same trail as the Ancares Ridge walk, then diverts at Campa de Tres Obispos descending to the Golada de Vara and back via Cabaña Vella. A 4.5km detour ascends to Pena Rubia (1822m) from the *golada*, adding challenge and views to the walk. Use IGN's 1:50,000 *Sierra de Ancares* map.

SERRA DO COUREL
Courel Ridge

Ten kilometres from Seoane, along the highway from the camping ground (heading towards Visuña) at the Alto do Couto, a dirt road turns off right. Over the course of 10km, the track snakes along the crest of the serra, passing Formigueiros, Mallón, Pía Paxaro, Cobaluda and ending at the Alto do Boi (10km from Folgoso). Use IGN's 1:25,000 map Nos 157-I *Seoane do Courel* and 156-IV *Salcedo*. This 20km-return trip is feasible in a day.

TOWNS & FACILITIES

BECERREÁ
☎ 982 / pop 3300

Nicknamed the 'Gateway to the Ancares', Becerreá offers all general services. The town hall (☎ 36 00 04; 9am-2pm Mon-Fri) will help you find your bearings.

To overnight here, convenient **Hostal Herbón** (☎ 608 588768; s/d €25/45) is across from the bus stop.

ALSA (☎ 902 42 22 42; www.alsa.es) runs daily buses to Becerreá from Santiago de Compostela and Madrid.

Taxi drivers congregate at Calle Carlos III, **Bar Centro** (☎ 36 00 16) or you can contact the local driver on ☎ 689 563393. Tariffs from Becerreá are: to Camping Os Ancares €15, to Degrada €35, and to Piornedo €50.

By car from Santiago, take the N634 (towards Oviedo) to Guitiriz and then head for Becerreá on the A6 (towards Madrid) via Lugo.

CAMARIÑAS
☎ 981 / pop 6300

This fishing town has a full range of services.

Sleeping & Eating

For an impersonal, functional atmosphere, try **Hotel Parranda** (☎ 70 54 68; Calle Casadillo 1; d with bathroom €40).

Your best bet is the charming **Hotel Rústico Puerta Arnela** (☎ 70 54 77; www .puertoarnela.es; Plaza del Carmen 20; d with breakfast and bathroom/terrace €50/60) has clean, new rooms, and tasty local food meals.

You'll eat well, inexpensively and abundantly at both **Restaurante Villa de Oro** (Areal 7; menú €8) and **Restaurante O Meu Lar** (Pinzón 26; menú €8). The caldeirada (seafood stew) is especially good at the latter.

Getting There & Away

Autos Carballo/Aucasa (☎ 58 88 11) buses run daily (except Sundays) between Camariñas and Santiago.

By car from Camariñas, take the AC432 to Vimianzo. Continue to Baio to pick up the C545 (via Santa Comba) to head southeast to Santiago.

CAMELLE
☎ 981 / pop 900

In Camelle, **A Molinera** (☎ 71 03 28; Calle Principal 79; 2-4 persons €40) has four immaculate self-catering apartments with bathroom and kitchen. **A Chalana** (meals €10), several doors away, serves excellent coastal fare. **Bar Rotterdam** (Calle del Muelle 20; mains from €9) has delicious seafood. Try the caldeirada or paella. There is a supermarket and other basic services. To get a taxi, call ☎ 73 01 18.

FOLGOSO DO COUREL
☎ 982 / pop 1300

Folgoso is the Courel's largest community and serves as the administrative centre. The only information centre within the Courel is Folgoso's **town hall** (☎ 43 30 01; www.caurel.fegamp.es; 9am-3pm & 5-8pm Mon-Fri), which provides the basics in Spanish. There are ATMs, a pharmacy and the area's **health centre** (doctor's surgery; mornings only).

Sleeping & Eating

O Mirador (☎ 43 30 64; d with bathroom €40), run by a warm French woman on the lower road towards Vilamor, has the best rooms in town and meals for around €11.

Also off the upper road, **Bar-Hospedaxe Novo** (☎ 43 30 07; d with/without bathroom €30/25) has comfortable rooms and simple fare. An Albergue (youth hostel) Municipal, located in the old town hall building, is advertised as an option for hikers but at the time of writing it was closed. For supplies there are markets in centre of the village.

Bus access is as for Seoane do Courel (see p214). By car, continue from Seoane for 12km on the LU651. Folgoso's taxi driver (also the town's baker at Casa de Puentes supermarket off the upper road), **Alejandro** (☎ 43 30 87), makes runs to Pedrafita (€28), Seoane (€12), Vilamor (€9) and Froxán (€12).

FROXÁN
☎ 982 / pop 100

With one foot in the past and one in the present, Froxán has experienced a small Renaissance in the last 10 years; many village homes have been restored and it is full of life in August with visitors and fiestas. There are no shops or services, but the beautifully restored **Casa da Aira** (☎ 19 96 73; www.casadaaira.com; d with bathroom €55) is a surprise for rooms and meals (breakfast €5, lunch & dinner €16).

No buses reach Froxán. From Quiroga it's possible to get a taxi through **Empresas Courel** (☎ 42 82 11). Within the Courel, **Carlos** (☎ 15 51 00) drives from Froxán to Seoane (€15), Pedrafita (€40) or Quiroga (€30). By car, continue on the LU651 for 6km from Folgoso.

ILLAS CÍES

Camping Illas Cíes (☎ 986 68 76 36; www.campingislascies.com; 9.30am-9.30pm; camping per day adult/child/tent €7.90/5.95/7.90) is the only lodging option. To camp, it is obligatory to have a *tarjeta de acampado* (camping voucher), purchased for €10 from the camp's office in the Estación Marítima in Vigo (see Vigo, p214) or through the campground's website. Alternatively, if arriving from Baiona or Cangas, reserve by phone or internet and then pay at the camp's reception upon arrival. When reservations are made, the date and time of departure must be fixed. The return can be modified once there, if necessary.

The camping ground has a self-service cafetería, restaurant and small supermarket. If self-catering, mainland prices are cheaper.

For access, see Getting to/from the Walk, p198.

LAXE

☎ 0981 / pop 3400

Laxe's tiny historical quarter still retains remnants of its nobler days, including the 14th-century Gothic church, which boasts excellent sculpted figures. There are several markets, ATMs and pharmacies along the main drag.

Sleeping & Eating

Past the church. **Hostal/Bar Bahía** (☎ 72 82 07; www.bahialaxe.com; Rúa Besugueira 24; d with bathroom €50) has attractive, clean rooms, some with terraces overlooking the port. Manolo, the owner, eagerly acts as Laxe's unofficial tourism wonk and can help with transport to trailheads in the off-season.

Hotel/Restaurante Playa de Laxe (☎ 73 90 00; www.playadelaxe.com; Avenida Cesáreo Pondal 27; d with bathroom €80). Meals are good but pricey.

Good seafood as well as grilled fish and beef, is prepared at the trendy **Mesón O Salvavidas** adjacent to the Hotel Playa de Laxe. On the main plaza **Café/Bar O Mirador** serves a wide variety of *raciones* and has great photos of historical Laxe. **Bar Bahía**, across the street from the local bakery on the main street, does great light fare – *calamares fritos* and *bocadillos*.

Getting There & Away

Autos Carballo/Aucasa (☎ 58 88 11) buses go from Santiago to Laxe four times daily Monday to Friday and one Saturday. Additional Autos Carballo buses link Santiago and Laxe via Carballo with transfers daily. There's one weekday return from Laxe to Santiago at 6.30am.

By car from Santiago, take the C545 northwest to Zas, then the AC430 north, and finally the AC422 west to Laxe.

MOREDA

☎ 982 / pop 300

Moreda is laid out on a steep hillside at the base of the Devesa da Rogueira. It has a fountain and a charming, rural guesthouse, **A Casiña da Rogueira** (☎ 15 56 23; d €27, five-person house with kitchen €87), near the walk's end.

At the trailhead, 300m down the road, is the **Aula de Natureza** (10am-2pm & 4-8pm daily), an interpretive centre that is staffed year-round and has a public toilet. Displays on flora, fauna and local life are worth a look. Also available are the free leaflets (in Spanish), *Mapa do Courel* and *O Courel Rutas de Senderismo*. The latter outlines four hard-to-follow walking trails.

Moreda is 7km from Seoane. Either take a taxi (see Seoane do Courel, p214) or drive. Travelling towards Folgoso, turn left towards Parada/Moreda.

O PINDO

☎ 981 / pop 800

Set on a hill and the curve of a tranquil, white-sand beach, O Pindo is an attractive fishing town. It has a supermarket, ATM and pharmacy.

A Revolta (☎ 76 48 64; s/d €25/40) has basic rooms and outstanding coastal fare (menú €9). For accommodation closest to the trailhead **Pensión Sol e Mar** (☎ 76 02 98; s/d with bathroom €30/45) has attractive, clean rooms.

Located on a gorgeous stretch of coast nestled in a seaside pine grove, you'll find **Camping Ancoradorio** (☎ 87 88 97; www .rc-ancoradoiro.com; per person/tent/car €5.90/5.90/3.75) 15km from the trailhead between Muros and O Pindo. It has a popular seafood restaurant serving mains for around €12, but no store. By bus, make for O Pindo and ask the driver to drop you at the camping ground or take a taxi from Muros.

From Santiago take a **Castromil** (☎ 55 57 60; www.monbus.es) Santiago–Muros–Finisterre bus direct to O Pindo.

By car, take the C543 to Noia and then the C550 (for Fisterra) to Muros and O Pindo.

PEDRAFITA DO CEBREIRO
☎ 982 / pop 1300
Straddling the most important pass connecting Galicia to Madrid via the NVI highway (the A6 *autovía* bypasses the town proper), Pedrafita is a gateway to either the Ancares (north) or the Courel (south). You'll find all general services here. A culinary must is the local cows'-milk cheese, Queixo do Cebreiro. With its original cream-cheese-like texture and flavour, it is divine alone or with local honey or cherries.

The **town hall** (☎ 36 71 03; 9am-2pm Mon-Fri) has basic information on the Ancares.

Hostal Restaurante Pazos (☎ 936 70 85; Avenida Castilla 1; d with bathroom €35) and **Casa Garcia** (☎ 36 70 21; Camiño da Feira 2; d with bathroom €40) both have simple rooms and serve meals (from €10). **Rustic Cebreiro**, 5km south on the Triacastela road, also has lodgings.

ALSA (☎ 902 42 22 42; www.alsa.es) runs buses to Pedrafita from Santiago de Compostela and Madrid (two daily).

Find taxis from Bar Galicia on the main street or call **Fermín** (☎ 609 67 43 03), who operates daily from June to August and at weekends the rest of the year. From Pedrafita to Degrada he charges €28 and to Seoane do Courel, €25.

By car from Santiago, take the N634 (towards Oviedo) to Guitiriz and then head for Pedrafita on the A6 via Lugo. From Madrid take the A6 (towards A Coruña).

PIORNEDO
☎ 982 / pop 100
Nicknamed the 'pre-Roman hamlet' for its fine grouping of *pallozas*; the **palloza museum** (admission €1) is a must. Of the four lodgings, the best are **Cantina O Mustallar** (☎ 915 17 17; d with/without bathroom from €40/18), which serves excellent home-cooked meals (menú €9); and the delightful mountain lodge **Hotel Piornedo** (☎ 15 13 51, 982 16 15 87; www.hotelpiornedo.com; d with bathroom from €40). Enjoy a read in the lounge with its magnificent panoramic window overlooking the valley. It also sells books and maps of the area and has good meals for €12.

Piornedo lies 10km beyond Degrada. To travel between Piornedo and Degrada (€25) or Becerreá (€60) by taxi contact **Pedrete** (☎ 982 15 13 59) in Piornedo. On weekends and afternoons, **Pepe** (☎ 36 45 46) in Cervantes also runs from Piornedo (€46) and Degrada (€32) to Becerreá.

QUIROGA
☎ 982 / pop 4000
If using public transport in Serra do Courel you will need to spend a night in Quiroga on the range's southern end. The **tourist office** (☎ 42 89 46; Rúa Xardins; open daily) supplies area information, and adjacent **Librería Celia** has books and maps. **Hostal Quiper** (☎ 42 84 51; Rúa Real 62; d with bathroom €36) doubles as the bus stop. For a bite to eat, try **Restaurante O Roxo Vivo** (Pereiro 8; menu €10). There's a **Monbus** (☎ 902 29 29 00; www.monbus .es) bus between Santiago and Quiroga via Monforte daily. **Taxis** (☎ 982 42 80 35) run from Bar Cine on Rúa Real to Froxán Folgoso (€25) and Seoane (€34).

SANTIAGO DE COMPOSTELA
☎ 981 / pop 94,400
Splendour in stone awaits you in this magnificent medieval city. Whether wandering the labyrinth of stone arcades amidst pilgrims arriving from the far reaches of the globe or enjoying the modern district's hip scene, Santiago provides an excellent gateway for walks in the rest of the region. Getting to the walks is possible by public transport as described, but if you want great flexibility to see the many

nooks and crannies off the beaten path, then definitely rent a car in Santiago. For historical background, see the introduction to the Camino de Santiago chapter (p304). The city **tourist office** (☎ 55 51 29; www .santiagoturismo.com; Rúa do Vilar 63; open 9am-9pm Jun-Sep, 9am-2pm & 4-7pm Oct-May) has city maps and local information.

Toribio (Hórreo 5) and **Piteira** (Huérfanas 38), both on Praza de Galicia, are good sports shops for last-minute equipment needs.

Sleeping & Eating

On the city's northeast side is **As Cancelas Camping** (☎ 58 02 66; Rúa 25 de Xullo 35; camping per person/tent/car €6/6.30/6.30).

Hotel Pico Sacro (☎ 58 44 66; Rúa San Francisco; s/d with bathroom €45/60) has a great location (150m from the Cathedral) and immaculate, quiet rooms.

An excellent small hotel with a beautiful garden in the historical quarter is **Costa Vella** (☎ 56 95 30; Porta da Pena 17; d from €70); ask for balconied rooms.

For style, try the five-star parador **Hostal dos Reis Católicos** (☎ 58 22 00; d €220).

Even if you're not buying, the Praza de Abastos morning public market is worth a visit; vendors at permanent stalls and local country folk ring the edges hawking everything from delicious local cheese, pigs' heads and live hens to enormous cabbages and fresh fruit.

For *pinchos* (as tapas are known in northern Spain) head to the bars on Rúa da Raíña, where they're free with your drink. Most establishments also serve *bocadillos* (sandwiches), *raciones* (main courses) and a *menú del día*, a three-course set meal which comes with a beverage included.

Restaurante 42 (Rúa do Franco 42; mains €8-14) does an excellent Galician meal.

For a filling, inexpensive meal head to the pilgrim's hotspot **Casa Manolo** (Praza de Cervantes; menú €8).

Getting There & Away

Santiago de Compostela is connected by **ALSA** (☎ 902 42 22 42; www.alsa.es) buses with Madrid (€59; nine hours; two daily) and, on the same line, Oviedo (€37; six hours; four daily), Santander (€43; nine hours; two daily), Bilbao (€50; 12 hours; three daily) and San Sebastián (€57; 13

hours; two daily). Santiago's **bus station** (☎ 981 54 24 16; www.tussa.org; San Caetano) is east of the centre.

Santiago's **train station** (☎ 902 240 202; www.renfe.es; Avenida de Lugo) is a 10-minute walk south from Praza de Galicia. Trains run to/from Madrid (€45; nine hours; twice daily). Regional trains run roughly every hour up and down the coast, linking Santiago with Vigo, Pontevedra, and A Coruña.

Santiago is on the A9 tollway off the A6 from Madrid. The N550 is parallel, slow and free. The N634 connects to Oviedo.

SEOANE DO COUREL
☎ 982 / pop 300
Seoane, 25km south of Pedrafita, has a bank (with ATM), post office and a pharmacy.

Sleeping & Eating
Located 1.5km from Seoane, towards Visuña, **Acampamento O Caurel** (☎ 43 31 01; camping per person/tent/car €4/4/4; two/four-person bungalows €42/67; Easter & Jul-15 Sep) has a cafetería, telephone and information sheets with details of nearby walks.

Casa Ferreiro (☎ 43 30 65; d with/without bathroom €35/29) has comfortable rooms and an attractive dining room (meals €10).

Try **Restaurante Anduriña** (meal €8) at the village centre for a meal with great views, or the small market for basic foodstuffs.

Empresa Courel (☎ 42 82 11) makes runs to Folgoso and Seoane from Quiroga only on the 10th and 27th of each month making this a highly impractical service.

Javier out of **Bar Hydra** (☎ 43 30 81) and Jesús from **Bar Gloria** (☎ 43 30 51) double as taxi drivers. They drive between Seoane and Pedrafita (€28), Moreda (€12), Folgoso (€28), Vilamor (€28) and Froxán (€30).

By car, head south from Pedrafita (towards Triacastela) on the LU651. Just before Hospital da Condesa, turn left to Seoane.

VIGO
☎ 986 / pop 296,000
The major gateway to the Cíes, Vigo, is Galicia's largest port city. The regional **tourist office** (☎ 43 05 77; Rúa Cánovas del Castillo 22; 9.30am-2pm & 4.30-6.30pm

Mon-Fri, 10am-1.30pm & 5-6.30pm Sat) is across the street from the Estación Marítima (ferry terminal), de la Ría de Vigo, on the Muelle de Transatlánticos. In the Estación Marítima there's a cafetería and ticket windows for the Naviera Mar de Ons ferry and the **Camping Illas Cíes** (reservations ☎ 986 43 83 58; www .campingislascies.com; open 8.30am-1.30pm & 2.30-7pm daily). For more information, see Illas Cíes (p212).

Sleeping & Eating

Hostal La Palma (☎ 43 06 78; Palma 7; s/d with bathroom €20/28; mid-Jun–Sep) has very good rooms, some with balcony, and does excellent seafood (menús €8-10).

The contemporary **Hotel Náutico** (☎ 12 24 49; www.hotelnautico.net; Rúa de Luís Taboada 28; s/d/tr incl breakfast €37/53/66) has a clean, crisp style and a pleasant nautical look. Enjoy free wi-fi and a heated towel rack in the bathroom.

One street up from the bustling port, the old fishing quarter bursts with tapas bars and restaurants. The public market is on Rúa Pescadería.

Getting There & Away

Vigo's airport is in the low-cost airline market and services national and international destinations.

From Santiago, **Castromil/Monbus** (☎ 981 58 90 90; www.monbus.es) buses connect to Vigo. Regular train services run to/from Santiago and Madrid.

By car, the A9 tollway runs to/from Santiago via Pontevedra.

Valencia

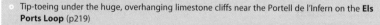

HIGHLIGHTS

- Tip-toeing under the huge, overhanging limestone cliffs near the Portell de l'Infern on the **Els Ports Loop** (p219)
- Oohhing and ahhing over the gorgeous views from the medieval city of **Morella** (p219)
- Eating great Valencian cuisine in the mountain restaurant of El Trestellador, overlooking the Valle de Guadalest, on the **Ruta La Marina Alta** walk (p228)
- Dipping your toes into the crystal clear waters of the Mediterranean after the spectacular ridge walk along the **Sierra de Bernia Traverse** (p232)

Area: 23,255 sq km	Average summer high: 32°C	Population: 4.4 million

Mention to someone that you're going off hiking in Valencia and you'll probably be rewarded with a quizzical stare. Valencia, they will tell you, just isn't walking country. Valencia, they will knowingly nod, is sun, sea and sangria country. Well move over sangria and make way for Valencia's rugged interior. A region of extreme beauty that's well covered by long- and short-distance footpaths all little travelled by hikers. In fact, of all the areas of Spain covered in this book Valencia – the land of Benidorm – is, ironically, the most adventurous area to explore.

On the northwestern fringes of the Comunidad Valenciana (region of Valencia), abutting both Aragón and Catalonia, the end of the Sistema Ibérico forms a complex of ravines and craggy summits known as Els Ports – 'the region of the mountain passes'. The fairy-tale-like walled city of Morella is the gateway to these seemingly endless *sierras*.

In the south, closer to Alicante, the rocky, arid mountains of La Marina tower above the Mediterranean, tempting walkers to explore thin gullies and narrow ridges.

With a variety of terrain and a long walking season, the region's mountains are a great alternative to the skyscrapers and sun lounges of the Costa Blanca.

HISTORY

Valencia's Iberian peoples were already trading with Greek and Phoenician merchants by 800BC, and the Mediterranean coast ensured prosperity for Valencian communities through Roman, Visigoth and Islamic occupations.

Islamic influence on the region was considerable between the conquest in AD 709 and 1238 when the Christian armies of Jaime I of Aragón captured the city of Valencia. By 1245 the Christian *Reconquista* (Reconquest) of the region was complete, but Valencia retained considerable political and legal independence. The marriage of Fernando II of Aragón and Isobel I of Castilla in 1469 unified Castilla and Valencia, with other counties of the Aragonese crown following suit in 1479.

Despite the *Reconquista* thousands of Muslims remained, not least in order to tend the irrigation systems that watered the inland terraces and coastal *huerta* (fertile plain). The final Muslim expulsion began in 1609 and was an economic disaster that the region didn't fully recover from until the 19th century. While tourism is now the region's biggest money-spinner, Valencia's fertile lands produce vast amounts of fruit (oranges in particular), vegetables and cereals, including rice.

The Comunidad Valenciana was established in 1982 and includes the provinces of Castellón, Valencia and Alicante.

ENVIRONMENT

Away from the resorts Valencia has a diverse coastline containing *salinas* (salt pans; at Santa Pola, close to Alicante, you'll see flamingos), freshwater lagoons teeming with bird life, towering cliffs and rugged outcrops as well as miles of beautiful beach.

Move west, inland from the coastal plain, and sierras, stepped with stone terraces where almond and fruit trees once thrived, roll to the horizon. Further west the *meseta* (high tableland of central Spain) begins, although down south on the border with Murcia are areas of semi-desert.

Valencia's mountains are contrasting. The relatively low, arid peaks in the south (such as the red-and-white limestone massifs of La Marina) are offshoots from the Sistema Bético that rises up in Andalucía. In the northwest El Maestrazgo is an extension of the Sistema Ibérico and the mountains are higher and wetter.

These different habitats support contrasting fauna and flora and 22 *parques naturales* (nature parks) have been established since 1982. Each is a necessary corrective since Valencia's wildlife has suffered significantly from agricultural and tourist development.

CLIMATE

Valencia has a mild Mediterranean climate. When it rains (around 400mm to 500mm per year) it does so in downpours, and mostly between September and December, with another burst from April to June.

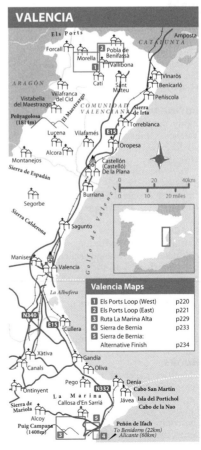

VALENCIA

Valencia Maps

1 Els Ports Loop (West)　　p220
2 Els Ports Loop (East)　　p221
3 Ruta La Marina Alta　　p229
4 Sierra de Bernia　　p233
5 Sierra de Bernia:
　 Alternative Finish　　p234

Average maximum temperatures are 13°C in winter and around 31°C in summer. Generally speaking, the mountains of the south are warmer than those in the north, which are intermittently snow-covered in winter.

PLANNING
When to Walk
Anytime that's not high summer is the basic rule. Actually, there's more variation than that; winters can be damp and cold at altitude and likewise high summer on the peaks isn't quite as hot as you might imagine – at least in comparison to the coast. Spring and autumn are without a doubt the prime periods though.

Maps
A trio of IGN 1:200,000 Mapa Provincial sheets cover Valencia's three provinces. The Alicante map covers La Marina while the Castellón map covers Els Ports. The best overall map of the region is Michelin's No 577 *Comunidad Valenciana & Murcia* (1:400,000).

BUYING MAPS
Easily the best map shop in the region is Valencia's **Librería Patagonia** (☎ 96 393 60 52; www.libreriapatagonia.com; Calle Hospital 1).

In Alicante **Librería International** (☎ 965 21 79 25; Rafael Altamira 6) carries an excellent range of 1:25,000 maps covering the La Marina region.

PLACE NAMES
Valenciano (regarded by linguists as a dialect of Catalan and as a language in its own right by many locals) is increasingly the only form used for signage and on maps, and this is practised in this chapter. Fortunately, Valenciano forms are often very similar to the Spanish version (for example, *font* instead of *fuente*, *serra* instead of *sierra*) so there's little scope for confusion.

Books
For titles covering the Alicante region, see p227. No walking books in English yet cover Els Ports. Readers of Spanish, however, will have a wide choice, including the comprehensive *Montañas Valencianas* series, by Rafael Cebrián.

WHAT'S COOKING IN VALENCIA?
Rice underwrites much Valencian cuisine – such as *paella* – first simmered here and exported to the world. For a more original experience, try alternatives such as *arroz a banda* (simmered in a fish stock), *arroz negro* (with squid, including its ink) or *arroz al horno* (baked in the oven). For *fideuá,* Valencian cooks simply substitute noodles for rice.

Other regional specialities include *horchata,* an opaque sugary drink made from pressed *chufas* (tiger nuts), into which you dip large finger-shaped buns called *fartons.* Finally, despite its name, *Agua de Valencia* couldn't be further from water. It mixes *cava* (sparkling Champagne-method wine), orange juice, gin and vodka.

Information Sources
The best place for walking information is the **Centro Excursionista de Valencia** (☎ 96 391 16 43; www.centroexcursionista.org; Plaza Tavernes de Valldigna 4; 5-9pm Mon-Thu, 5-8pm Fri), which has a library and café. The organisation runs excursions and expeditions and also publishes a list of Valencian footpaths plus other general walking literature.

Leaflets promoting rural tourism cover many popular walking areas (providing a good overview) and are available from most tourist offices. Information on rural tourism is also available on www.comunitat-valenciana.com and www.gva.es.

GATEWAY
Valencia is the main gateway to the region, see p236.

PARQUE NATURAL DE LA TINENÇA DE BENIFASSÀ

A spectacular wilderness of sunburnt and rugged terrain indicates that you have entered the newly created Parque Natural de La Tinença de Benifassà. For a hiker this new playground provides endless opportunities for striking off down a dusty trail with nobody but you for company.

ACCESS TOWN
See Morella (p236).

ELS PORTS LOOP

Duration 6 days

Distance 106.5km

Difficulty moderate

Start/Finish Morella (p236)

Transport bus

Summary From the medieval walled city of Morella, this flexible walk loops through a remote landscape along ancient tracks and walled lanes, crossing through spectacular gorges and over narrow passes.

This sparsely populated region has an excellent network of lightly trodden trails – in particular, the GR7 long-distance route, whose red-and-white trail markers guide you between Morella and Refugi de Font Ferrera. Most of the remainder of the walk follows various shorter trails, each numbered PRV (short for *senderos de pequeña recorrido valencianos*) and blazed with yellow-and-white markers.

The route takes you through lands from which humankind has all but withdrawn, giving up the struggle to tame the spectacular, rugged, unforgiving terrain. Most farmsteads are tumbling, their fields and orchards abandoned. Yet the dry-stone terracing and walls, kilometre after kilometre of them, remain as testimony to human endeavour.

It's a land of bare, rocky hilltops, steep ravines and dense woods, cut through by old drovers' ways and ancient paths, trodden for centuries and linking lonely villages, until the motor car came along.

Most of the walking falls within the Parque Natural de La Tinença de Benifassà, created in 2006 in recognition of the area's rich fauna and flora. Most communities en route offer accommodation and the walk can be lengthened or shortened to suit. In particular, Day 3 could be skipped or done only in part.

HISTORY
Thanks to its location on the route from the coast to Zaragoza, the town of Morella has long dominated the cultural and economic landscape of Els Ports. It's one of Spain's oldest towns in one of the country's earliest inhabited regions. Prehistoric cave paintings were discovered at Morella la Vella and evidence of Mediterranean man (from around 6000 BC) has been found in the Ríu de la Sénia gorge, where archaeologists believe the trail snaking up to Bellestar has been used since 3000BC.

After the *Reconquista*, Monasterio Santa María de Benifassà in La Tinença de Benifassà (a grouping of hamlets known as the 'Seven Settlements of Benifassà') exerted considerable power and influence over the region, but the contemporary picture is one of rural dereliction that has stimulated a huge EU/national programme of renovation and rejuvenation seeking to boost rural tourism. However, many houses in Els Ports are now second homes for city dwellers or occupied for only a few weeks each year.

ENVIRONMENT
It's the eastern fringes of the Sistema Ibérico that form the heavily eroded network of jagged limestone peaks and deep gorges in Els Ports. This decidedly un-Mediterranean landscape is a habitat more typical of Aragón, with woods of holm, gall, cork and kermes oak. Boxwood (the village of El Boixar bears its name), traditionally used by craftsmen to make ploughing equipment and tableware, is also widespread.

This wild, remote area has an abundance of unique plants and you're more likely to see wildcats or red squirrels here than anywhere

WATER
Many of the *fuentes* (fountains) indicated are seasonal, and often dry in summer. Play safe and check with your hosts at the beginning of each stage. Similarly, most rivers and streams – rarely difficult to leap over or ford – simply don't exist for several months. On the plus side, nearly every village you pass through has its constantly flowing *fuente*, usually in the Plaza Mayor (Plaça Major), the main square.

VALENCIA

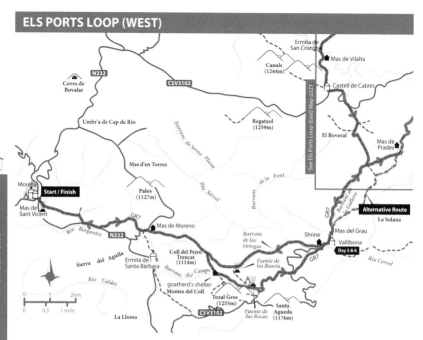

ELS PORTS LOOP (WEST)

else in the Valencia region. Wild boar, Spanish ibex and recently re-introduced roe deer often forage near mountain villages. Birds to look for include the golden eagle, griffon vulture, peregrine falcon, kestrels, robins, coal tits and nightingales.

PLANNING
When to Walk

Els Ports experiences more variable weather, harsher winters and more rain than elsewhere in the region. Compared with Valencia city, Morella is generally 5.5°C cooler and has 200mm more rainfall.

Walking is possible from spring to late autumn, although both ends of the season are susceptible to occasional snow and June to August is hot. Between November and April the rivers and streams in *barrancos* (gullies or ravines) flow. Late April to June and September to mid-October are the best times to walk.

Maps

Two excellent 1:30,000 maps, designed for walkers and available from the Morella tourist office among other outlets, cover the

whole of the route. Published by El Tossal Cartografies, *La Tinença de Benifassà* takes in everything except the first part of Day 1, which features on *Els Ports*, the adjacent map.

Information Sources

Morella's **tourist office** (☎ 964 17 30 32; www.morella.net; Plaza San Miguel 3) is a good general resource that carries some information about walking.

GETTING TO/FROM THE WALK

See Morella (p236) for getting there and away.

THE WALK
Day 1: Morella to Vallibona
4¼–4¾ hours, 17.5km

Go through Portal de Sant Mateu and head left down an intermittently stepped lane to a sealed road. Here, you can play safe and stay with the GR7 and its red-and-white markers. This, tediously, follows sealed roads for the next 3km. More interestingly (it will require a bit of navigational nous unless the route has been re-signed since we passed), turn

VALLIBONA & THE SIGNIFICANCE OF SEVEN

Every seven years, on Ascension Day, the people of Vallibona undertake a 30km pilgrimage to Peñarroya (Pena-Roja in Valenciano), over the border in Aragon. They're sustaining a tradition that goes back at least to the 14th century. Legend has it that the plague devastated the village, sparing only seven young men and a handful of old people. The seven youths set out in search of brides and, arriving in Peñarroya, were received by an old woman called Petronella (Petronila), who, conveniently, had taken in seven orphan girls. Paired off and married, the couples returned to Vallibona. Seven years later, the seven men, each now a proud father, fulfilled a vow and returned to give thanks to Peñarroya's Virgen de la Fuente for having restored life to their village, giving birth to a tradition that will next be marked in 2012.

left and head down to the N232. Go right, then after 25m, left down a dirt road. Cross a stream at **Mas de Sant Vicent** – a mill with a 600-year-old *fuente* (spring) – and head generally upwards and eastwards, aiming for a pair of electricity pylons at the crest of the hill. Descend on a clear 4WD track then, just beyond a couple of farm buildings, strike east on a footpath that's very faint in places. Plug on through three gates, walking just north of a pine plantation, and turn right at a junction beside a tall poplar tree to rejoin the N232 and GR7 about 30 minutes after having left them.

Walk eastwards to the N232's 'Km 59' marker. Fork left down a 4WD track beside a bridge over the Ríu Bergantes, then ford right across a stream 10 minutes later beneath a grove of poplars. Stay parallel with the stream for another 15 minutes before recrossing it to follow the track upstream past a beautiful seasonal waterfall and deep pool, then along a 4WD track to a sealed road.

Turn left, passing a deep well and pleasant rest spot in a poplar grove, then after 100m fork right (east) up a concrete farm track, climbing steadily, (look back for great views

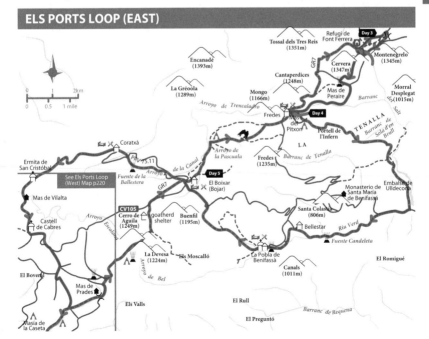

ELS PORTS LOOP (EAST)

of Morella) around **Mas de Moreno**, a working farm, and up to the southern fringe of holm-oak woodland. Continue roughly east along a wide, rocky, walled lane that leads through sparse woodland to a gate and up the northern side of a gully in a slightly surreal landscape of juniper trees that look like escapees from an ornamental garden.

Upon reaching a 4WD track turn right (east), then fork left, up to **Coll del Peiró Trencat** (1114m) and its small shrine. Here at a junction of trails, where two GR7 variants meet, there are splendid views eastwards and back to Morella.

Turn right (south) up a faint 4WD track and parallel dry-stone wall until a metal fence, where you turn sharp left to follow its line along a ridge. From the fence, the GR7 bears left off the ridge and southeast. After a 20-minute gentle descent through oak woodland, you reach a 4WD track and **Fuente de las Rocas** (a possible campsite). Head east a little way, then fork left (north) down a spur before turning right off this 4WD track. Follow the GR7 eastwards around a couple of gullies, with Vallibona soon in sight, through a group of houses and northeast to the CV111. Cross and pick up a well-worn path that zigzags down an oak-wooded gully back to the road. Turn right, cross the Riu Cervol and fork left up to **Vallibona** (665m), a typical mountain hamlet of precisely 42 residents.

Manel, a professional photographer (he took most of the photos on your reference map) and his partner Tere run Vallibona's only overnight option. Their Hostal-Restaurante **La Carbonera** (☎ 964 17 20 00; Plaza Sant Antoni; s/d €30/45 with breakfast; dinner €10; Tue-Sun), a hugely welcoming haven, does excellent value meals (replenish your energy with Tere's chickpea soup and juicy chops from lambs that latterly gambolled in the very fields you're walking).

Day 2: Vallibona to Refugi de Font Ferrera
6¾–7¼ hours, 23km

Turn right out of the hotel, then right again onto the higher of the two roads leading north into a gorge. Loop around and up the gorge's eastern side. The GR7 then takes the original, cobbled track to re-emerge on the road, just west of Mas del Grau.

(From here an alternative route, a clear dirt track, allows walkers to avoid wet feet between November and April, when the river is swollen. It leads northeast along a well-used dirt road to Mas de Prades in about two hours.)

Following the main route, leave the road, now dirt, to follow the GR7 upstream along Barranc de la Gallera following a faint 4WD track that crisscrosses the river into a beautiful narrow gorge. Some 20 minutes later the 4WD track disappears and so (except in winter) does the water.

A narrow trail now leads upstream, hopping from bank to bank. After around an hour within the gorge, it zigzags up the true left bank to avoid a set of waterfalls (and past the 4WD track descended on Day 5), then opens out to become a wide, easily strode forest track. Continue northeast for about 30 minutes to the head of the valley and bear right up to a dirt road (the alternative route to Vallibona) and **Mas de Prades**, perched on a saddle. To the east is Arroyo de Bel, a dramatic gorge.

Head north along the dirt road for 100m, then bear right onto a narrow path that zigzags up the pine-covered slope past another farmhouse to a 4WD track. Turn right, then right again at the next junction (a *fuente* is reached in 15 minutes by turning left) to climb roughly northeast for 10 minutes to another junction. Continue straight ahead, then after 80m peel off right with the GR7, heading northeast across a clearing, left of a low wall and out into a large bowl. Meadows and a muddy spring lie to the south (a beautiful **campsite** if you have enough water on board).

Continue northeast over the barren terrain and head straight over a 4WD track. Turn right onto a second one and follow it for around 30 minutes as it snakes between the summits of Cerro de Aguila (1249m) and La Devesa (1224m). It winds in a northerly direction, past a wonderful, igloo-shaped, dry-stone **goatherd shelter** (possible campsite) to the 'Km 25' marker on the CV105. Turn right and walk 200m down the road before bearing left up the slope and northeast along an ancient track that crosses a scrub-covered ridge to **El Boixar** (Bojar), reached in about 4¼ hours of walking. For accommodation and other services see the end of Day 4 (p224).

Walk to the eastern end of the village, then head south, across CV105 and down to the old village washhouse and a stream of *fuentes*. Go left, heading east down to a T-junction. Turn left here, then continue north along a 4WD track and across a stream. Trail markers now lead along the stream's bed but it's easier to turn right along a 4WD track that the GR7 soon joins. Continue northeast along the firm track for around 10 minutes until, just after crossing a small stream (and with an old farmhouse and some good **campsites** 150m north), the GR7 cuts up right and northeast beside **Barranc de la Pasquala** (Arroyo de la Pasquala). Cross the stream after about 15 minutes then bear right (northeast) up the slope along a thin footpath before traversing to an excellent **viewpoint** above the head of the valley.

Follow the trail easterly for a couple of minutes to a 4WD track at the edge of a stunning canyon. Turn right and then, after 50m, bear left onto a faint track leading to a shallow gully. Stay on the southern side of the valley as it widens until the GR7 bears left (north) following power lines to a dirt road. Turn right and head northeast to **Fredes**, reached 1½ to 1¾ hours after leaving El Boixar. For accommodation in Fredes, see the end of Day 3. For the nearby beautiful **Mas del Pitxon campsite**, see early on Day 4 (p224).

Walk for a further 1½ hours (6km) northeast along the GR7, which winds around the wooded gullies and cliff-tops of Roca Blanca, offering superb views of the canyon below, then cuts north to a dirt road. At a four-way junction, look for a GR7 signpost, half hidden behind a pine tree. After a while, the 4WD track peters out to become a trail (inside the small structure, astride the path, that resembles a dog kennel is a GR7 logbook, where you can leave your mark). The trail finally descends to **Refugi de Font Ferrera** (☎ 647 84 71 05, office 977 58 86 68; www.feec.cat; dm €11; dinner €13; daily mid-Jul–mid-Sep & most weekends year-round). The *refugi* (mountain hut or refuge), at 1220m and just over the border into Catalonia, has space for 40, hot showers and a small guest kitchen. Guti, the cheerful warden, himself a mountaineer and climber, cooks hearty meals (book in advance). The *refugi* may be

---

THE GR7 (VERY) LONG DISTANCE TRAIL

You're walking a mere fragment of a very long route. The GR7 runs for approximately 6000km (600 of them in the Valencia region), from the temple of Delphi in the Peloponnese in Greece, taking in eight countries on the way, entering Spain via Andorra, high in the Pyrenees, and eventually terminating at Tarifa, mainland Spain's southernmost point, within sight of north Africa. You will need to pack a couple of changes of clothes if attempting this whole route!

---

open more often than the official opening hours suggest, so do call to check.

Day 3: Refugi de Font Ferrera to Fredes
4½–6 hours, 12.5km

This day could be cut down to a simple two-hour loop to Montenegrelo or done as a long day walk from Fredes.

From the *refugi*, take the 4WD track and turn right (east) at a T-junction. Follow this wide dirt track for around 10 minutes, then bear right onto a narrow trail (still the GR7) at another T-junction. A 20-minute traverse brings you onto a small **saddle** where a path turns right (south) off the GR7 (look for a jagged blue arrow painted on the rock) and climbs to a wonderful cliff edge east of **Montenegrelo** (1345m). Turn right and follow the trail past a weather and fire watch station to the peak, reached after about an hour of walking, with the Embalse de Ulldecona (see Day 4) glinting to the south. As well as eagles and vultures swirling around the summit you may also see magnificent, solitary male ibex.

Head west from the peak along a 4WD track. Continue straight ahead (southwest) at a switchback, reached some 15 minutes from the peak, and stay with the ridge until you meet a crossroads of trails just beyond two large boulders. Turn right (west), descending to another junction in about eight minutes. Refugi de Font Ferrera is 10 minutes away (northwest), but cut back left (southwest) following the yellow-and-white trail markers up and over the ridge to a 4WD track. Turn right and head down

VALENCIA

southwest for 15 minutes before turning left and descending sharply to another 4WD track. Turn right, ignore a right turn a few minutes later and continue east to **Mas de Peraire**, an area of grassy terraces with a large natural water cistern.

The trail begins a steep 45-minute descent through imposing rock outcrops to the **Barranc del Salt**. Cross the stream and turn right, scrambling along the rocky trail through a dramatic gorge to a beautiful set of falls. The trail now climbs for 35 minutes to a 4WD track and a tricky junction (keep an eye on the trail markers). Take the second right switchback, then climb steeply west to another 4WD track. Turn right and right again onto a track leading west to Fredes 10 minutes later.

Fredes has one *casa rural*, **Casa Nuri** (☎ 977 72 91 02; per person €25; year-round). Ask for Nuri – she's used to short-stay walkers. In friendly **Bar-Restaurante La Taberna** (☎ 977 72 91 52; www .latabernadefredes.es; menú €14; 9am-11pm Tue-Sun) there's everything from a simple sandwich to a full scale meal. It also sells bread.

Day 4: Fredes to El Boixar
6½–7 hours, 22.5km
From Fredes as far as La Pobla de Benifassà, the trail is blazed intermittently but sufficiently with yellow-and-white markers.

Retrace your steps along the last 10 minutes of Day 3 and then continue east along the PRV75.1, which almost immediately bears left off the track onto a former mule trail. This heads southeast, up to and across a 4WD track, then down to **Mas del Pitxon**, a ruined farmhouse with a fantastic view that makes a fine campsite (take on water at Fredes' public *fuente*).

Follow the trail as it zigzags southeast and through the narrow **Portell de l'Infern** ('gate to hell'), then along a lengthy spur below overhanging cliffs (one with a *fuente*). The landscape here is just splendid and this short traverse is probably the most stunning section of the whole walk.

Constantly descending, the path soon enters shady pinewood, then heads generally southeast across more open ground before ducking down a narrow gully that quickly

opens out. Continue down to a cluster of holiday homes beside the reservoir **Embalse de Ulldecona**, reached about an hour from Portell de l'Infern. Here at the reservoir's extremity, if the water's low you can make out the old terracing and field boundaries.

Turn right and walk for 2.2km along the lakeside road as far as the CV105 and a dam. In an attractive site beside the dam, **Mesón-Hotel Molí l'Abad** (☎ 977 71 34 18; www.moliabad.com; s/d €35/60) has a large self-service **restaurant-bar** (Tue-Sun) and comfortable rooms.

From the restaurant head west along the CV105. After a couple of minutes, take a path on the left. Clearly defined, it runs between the road and a long finger of the reservoir as far as a forestry nursery. Turn left to cross the Ríu Verd, pass through metal gates, then loop right (west) around a stout farmhouse. Recross the river and then follow it upstream for around 15 minutes before crossing to the true right bank and continuing upstream to **Fuente Candeleta**. The track soon becomes a trail that winds westwards, ever higher up the valley, beneath sandstone cliffs. Then, one to 1¼ hours from the forest nursery, bear right (northwest), up the side of the gorge and along an ancient path that leads to **Bellestar** (715m), invitingly perched on its hillock. The only place for food and drink is **Mesón Bellestar** (☎ 977 72 91 00, 628 335434; Carrer Major 43).

Just west of the village, bear left down a concrete track. Beside a market garden, ignore the PV sign pointing west, instead, head southwest along a 4WD track, then

---

A HOUSE IN THE COUNTRY

Casas rurales, country accommodation at reasonable prices, are undoubtedly a way of regenerating dying villages. But the scheme, underwritten by generous local and European financing, can be abused. Once five years have elapsed after a grant has been spent upon improvements, owners are free to sell their property, as many do, thus making themselves a nice little profit and often becoming a part of the rural exodus the subsidies were designed to arrest.

right up a lane that leads to the CV107 and, after 1.5km, **La Pobla de Benifassà** (705m). In the village there are a couple of bar-restaurants and **Hotel la Tinença** (☎ 977 72 90 44; r per person €30, half-board €45), which does tapas and *bocadillos* and will sell basic provisions to hotel guests. Just outside the village, **Auberge la Font Lluny** (☎ 977 72 91 25; www.lafontlluny .com; s/d €25/44 with breakfast, half-board €34 per person) is a more hostel-like alternative.

From the western end of Carrer Major, walk northwest past Auberge la Font Lluny (with its *fuente*) along a dirt road. Fork left after 10 minutes, leaving the concrete track and keeping parallel to a stream that you soon cross. Turn right at a T-junction and climb northwest for around an hour to the cliff-top CV105. Take a last look back at La Pobla and Bellestar, now way below, and stride out for 1.5km along this flat, sealed road to reach **El Boixar**.

At **Casa-Refugi El Boixar** (☎ 977 72 90 71, 660 401822; www.elboixar.net; Carrer Major 28; per person €23, half-board €41) Ximo Alemany and his wife Marisa offer excellent accommodation and country cuisine to match. Ximo, a keen walker and mountain biker, is hugely knowledgeable about hiking in the area. The kitchen functions from Friday to Sunday, year-round (daily in Aug). On other days of the week, guests eat at the tiny bar (maximum capacity 15, squeezed tight) in the lower part of the village, which does simple food.

Day 5: El Boixar to Vallibona
6–7 hours, 15.5km

Turn right out of the *refugi*, then right (north) again at a sign for Coratxà that leads you down a concrete track, straight across the CV109 and into a gully. Cross the stream and continue northwestwards up the valley for 20 minutes before zigzagging up to meet the CV109 again.

In quick succession, turn left, then right after 20m, then right again after 50m and left after 40m (it's much clearer on the ground!) to follow a footpath that leads you north, then west as it broadens into a 4WD track. Bear right (northwest) at a cairn with marker and follow the footpath into a wood. Head northwest, down to a broad meadow, **Fuente de la Ballestera**

and, for the last time, the CV109. Walk left along it for 100m, then bear right onto a track that leads steeply upwards to **Coratxà**, with its *fuente*.

Hostelería Sant Jaume (☎ 977 72 91 90; www.corachar.com; Plaça Major; r €52, half-board €46 per person) has eight trim rooms and a great restaurant.

From Coratxà to Ermita de San Cristóbal, it's mostly easy walking. Head east from Plaça Major, then turn left beside the village rubbish containers. After two minutes, fork left at a pilgrim stone, signed 'Pena-Roja' (see the box, p221), onto a concrete 4WD track that leads through a shallow valley. After around 15 minutes, fork left (west), leaving the main track to climb northwestwards. Bear left just past a *fuente* and head southwest before cutting up and over the ridge. It's now a gentle descent to **Ermita de San Cristóbal** (1248m). The 270-degree views from this ruined chapel, perched on the edge of Sierra de los Aragoneses, are staggering.

Head back east to a signpost and large cairn, then descend southeast, following cairns and frustratingly sparse markers towards Mas de Vilalta, a sturdy farmhouse (behind it is Font Juana). Turn right (south) and work your way southwest around a saddle.

Cut down south below the saddle and then traverse, initially eastwards, beneath a row of cliffs on an ancient trail that zigzags down and across a 4WD track (a PR variant goes right and rejoins the main route before Castell de Cabres) to meet a stream. Once over, traverse west to a 4WD track and PR signpost around five minutes later.

Follow the PR (the trail markers are sketchy in places) roughly south, past a grave, down through a gully and across a wide stream bed to begin the 30-minute or so, snaking climb to a complex set of **terracing.** From the terracing continue south to a ridge, then curl around the west side of the 1189m peak overlooking **Castell de Cabres**. Here, **Bar-Restaurante La Espiga** (☎ 977 72 90 25) serves up decent fare and there's a spurting *fuente* in the main square.

On the CV105 at the village's eastern limit, avoid some dull roadwork by turning left onto a signed path. After around 10 minutes, turn sharp right (south) along a 4WD track to rejoin the road at a bridge. Head southeast down a wide dirt road, following it for about 20 minutes, up to a three-way junction by a water cistern. Turn left (south) and take a switchback right after a few minutes to keep with the track, which heads generally southeast.

At a fork, take the left option to stay with the 4WD track. Although longer, it descends more gently than the right arm, which takes you past a ruined farmhouse, followed by a extremely steep drop. Both options bring you to **Barranc de la Gallera** and the GR7. Turn right and follow the trail back to Vallibona, retracing the outward route on Day 2 (see p222).

Day 6: Vallibona to Morella
4–5 hours, 15.5km

From the village's western limit, add spice to the return leg to Morella by taking the signed 'Camí Vell GR7', the old route between Vallibona and Morella.

The trail traverses west, high above the Riu Cervol, passes a small **shrine**, then slopes down to the river. Cross below a fine, walled gully and head upstream before bearing left, up and into the mouth of Barranc de las Ortegas.

Continue southwest through the gorge, past **Fuente de los Baseta**. After about 30 minutes, cross to the true left bank of the *barranco* and continue southwest past a set of overhanging cliffs. At the end of the gorge, follow trail markers through oak woodland to a wide, walled lane. At a multiple junction, where a track leads right to a sturdy farmhouse, go straight (west), keeping with the line of the stone wall.

On meeting a 4WD track, turn right and follow it northwestwards all the way up to the signpost, shrine and heart-stopping panorama at **Coll del Peiró Trencat**, reached after 1¾ to two hours of walking. With Morella already in sight, simply retrace your steps to Morella, following Day 1's outward route (see p220).

LA MARINA

North of the high-rise blocks, sun-loungers and all-night discos of Benidorm are the beautifully rugged, arid mountains of La Marina. Made up of numerous east-west ridges, the range is divided into *baja* (lower) and *alta* (higher) regions and occupies a huge headland that juts out into the Mediterranean between Alicante and Valencia.

These mountains are not giants – the highest peak is Aitana at 1557m – but the area has a variety of interesting terrain and the village hospitality is first class. Dry, rocky *monte bajo* (scrub) terrain is common, but good trails and a network of forestry tracks crisscross the region allowing for dramatic ridge walks, traverses down precipitous gullies and peak-bagging. Despite the tourist hordes a stone's throw away, for nine months of the year it's perfectly possible to pick up your pack, disappear into the mountains and not speak to another person all day.

HISTORY
The greatest historical and cultural influence on La Marina, which has been occupied since about 5000BC, came from the period of Islamic occupation. Mozarabic trails (see the boxed text Mozarabic Trails, p231), irrigation systems and terraced hillsides remain as evidence of the collective industry of the times, while ruined hill forts are a sign of the struggle between Christians and Muslims. Also found in the mountains are watchtowers built to warn of piracy and Berber raiding parties – common in the 17th century when Valencia lacked stability and strong leadership.

Before the tourist boom Benidorm was a poor coastal village, and agricultural production dominated La Marina's economy. More recently agriculture on the more marginal lands has been abandoned and old terraces have fallen into disrepair following massive migration from inland villages to the coast.

ENVIRONMENT
Scarred by fissures and crags, the rocky, arid limestone slopes of La Marina provide habitats for lime-tolerant plants such as the spring-blooming yellow anthyllis, and early summer-blooming black, vanilla, mirror, frog and Bertoloni's bee orchids. Local specialities include the rusty foxglove, found on scree, and the tiny rush-leaved daffodil. The scent of sage, thyme, rue,

curry plant and cotton lavender fills the air during the intense heat of summer, when pink century and red valerian bloom.

Rabbits, hares and foxes are found in the mountains, but you'll be lucky if wildcats and wild boar cross your path. You may see the bold, brown-and-black hoopoe (said to bring bad luck if hunted), along with eagles, many species of harriers and warblers, colourful rollers and bee-eaters, and you'll often startle partridges in long grass.

Lataste's viper, which is yellow with a triangular head and a wavy line down the spine, is the only poisonous viper found here. The caterpillar of the pine processionary moth (see the boxed text The Pine Processionary Caterpillar, p33) also spins its silken nests up in the trees.

CLIMATE

The coastal regions enjoy a mild winter but, at that time, you should be prepared to walk in 7°C, regular frosts and occasional snowfalls on the higher peaks. Cold, wet winds sporadically blast the mountains from October until June.

PLANNING
When to Walk

Few people are crazy enough to walk from July to September, when temperatures can soar above 35°C, even at altitude. Much of the region's annual 490mm of rainfall descends during the *gota fría*, a stormy period in September and October, but mild winters mean that the walking season runs from October to June. March to May, when many wildflowers bloom, is ideal.

What to Bring

In late spring and autumn, it's a delight to sleep out under the stars, but don't skimp on walking boots suited to rocky terrain.

Maps

There are no regional maps specific to the La Marina area; it is covered by those mentioned in Maps under Information (p218). For large-scale maps see the Planning sections of individual walks.

Books

Four good books intended for the day-walker covering La Marina and the wider

Costa Blanca area are *Costa Blanca Walks* (volumes 1 & 2), by the late Bob Stansfield; *Costa Blanca Walks* by the very much alive Charles Davis; and *Landscapes of the Costa Blanca*, by Christine and John Oldfield.

Information Sources

The website of the active Costa Blanca Mountain Walkers and also www.costa blancawalking.info have helpful information and provide a useful entrée to the local expatriate hiking world. Also worth checking out is http://bobandjeanhall .blogspot.com, which describes a host of La Marina walks, supplemented by the couple's photos.

Guided Walks

The Costa Blanca Mountain Walkers (www .cbmwalkers.org) have been exploring La Marina for more than a couple of decades and walkers are welcome to join them on their regular outings. Details of their walks are usually published in the weekly Costa Blanca News.

Three outstanding enterprises with deep knowledge of the area are based in La Marina and offer walking holidays: **Terra Ferma** (☎ 96 589 03 92; www. terraferma.net), an eco-sensitive operation run by two young Spaniards who speak excellent English; **Mountain Walks** (☎ 96 551 10 44; www.mountainwalks.com, www.elsfrares.com), run by Brits Pat and Brian Fagg, who have been running self-guided or accompanied walking tours from their lovely rural hotel in Quatretondeta for nigh on 20 years; and in Castell de Castells, British residents Gary and Sarah Neal manage an equally

---

NÍSPERO

Níspero, or loquat trees, grow by the thousand under vast netting systems (for protection against spring storms) that cover the slopes around Callosa. The climate and soil around Callosa particularly suit *níspero* trees, which produce a yellow, tangy, apricot-like fruit. So famous are the *níspera* of Callosa that they have been awarded a *denominación de origen* label, something more usually associated with the better wines.

sensitive operation, **Mountain Walking** (☎ 96 551 82 54; www.mountainwalking -spain.com).

ACCESS TOWNS

See Alicante (p234), Benidorm (p235) and Callosa d'En Sarriá (Callosa; p235).

GETTING THERE & AWAY

Alicante's **El Altet** airport (☎ 902 40 47 04) is served by budget airlines, charters and scheduled flights from all over Europe.

RUTA LA MARINA ALTA

Duration 4 days

Distance 53km

Difficulty moderate

Start Confrides

Finish Bolulla

Nearest Towns Callosa (p235), Confrides (see next column)

Transport bus, taxi

Summary This S-shaped exploration of La Marina Alta includes the region's highest ridge, the intriguing ruins of Islamic castles and a number of ridge walks.

Forestry tracks and marked paths, intermittently blazed in yellow-and-white, lead across the Sierra de Aitana, through Valle de Guadalest, over the Serra de Serrella and around the Serra d'Aixorta. A highly recommended day walk (see Serra d'Aixorta, p230) joins the route at Castell de Castells.

You have a range of options here. It's possible to do the walk staying in village accommodation, but equally possible to break it up into more leisurely segments and sleep in the mountains. You can spin the walk out to around seven nights if you prefer to take your time. Alternatively, it's also quite possible to conflate Days 1 and 2, especially if you omit the Aitana detour. Accommodation is the key. If you're not camping, you'll need to conflate Days 1 and 2 (quite possible with a reasonably early start).

Determined walkers could link this walk with the Sierra de Bernia Traverse (see the boxed text Bolulla to Fonts de l'Algar Link, p232).

PLANNING
Maps

Marina Baixa, Serra d'Aitana, published by Editorial Piolet at a handy scale of 1:20,000 covers all except the second half of Day 4, for which you'll need a fragment of the IGN 1:25,000 map *No 822-III Parcent*.

GETTING TO/FROM THE WALK

From Callosa, one **ALSA** (☎ 96 680 39 55; www.alsa.es) bus runs daily to Confrides (45 minutes), leaving from opposite Hostal Avenida at 9.30am. A Callosa-based **taxi** (☎ 661 445777, 619 589306) to Confrides costs around €25.

At the end, a taxi from Bolulla to Callosa costs around €10 and, to Benidorm bus station €25. One alternative is to walk to Fonts de l'Algar at the end of the walk (see the boxed text Bolulla to Fonts de l'Algar Link, p232).

THE WALK
Day 1: Confrides to Fuente Forata
3–3½ hours, 11km

From the CV70 Benidorm-Alcoy road, walk up Calle San Antonio, Confrides' main street, and bear left, signed 'Font de l'Arbre'. Go straight to follow a sign, PRCV-22 Puerto de Tudons. Continue along this quiet tarmac road (we saw one vehicle in two hours) as it twists and turns, climbing steadily and eventually giving views of the antennae and radar domes atop Sierra de Aitana before it plunges to the few scattered buildings of Casas de Aitana with a **bar** (Tue-Sun year-round) that does snacks, simple meals and cold drinks. Below it, the shaded Font de l'Arbre with its flowing spring makes a possible **campsite.**

From the *fuente*, zigzag south up a wide forestry track, signed 'Cumbre d'Aitana', that runs beneath the northern escarpment of Sierra de Aitana, then follow it eastwards below the cliffs, passing *neveras* (see the boxed text Neveras: the Original Fridges, p230) on the left after approximately 30 and 50 minutes. About five minutes after the second *nevera*, ignore a sharp left turn and fork left a couple of minutes later onto a stony path that descends gently to **Fuente Forata**, a gorgeous campsite, where ice-cold water gushes from the mountain to flow through a series of man-made troughs.

There's a *nevera* nearby and you can clearly see a *forat* (hole through the rock) to the southeast. There are stunning views across Valle de Guadalest to the Serra de Serrella and north to the Sierra de Bernia.

Spending the night in Confrides makes it easy to walk the first two days in one.

Pensión el Pirineo (☎ 96 588 58 58; s/d €35/45; open year-round) does a cracking menú for €14. Also in the village, **Casa a Faragulla** (☎ 96 595 60 45, 654 665 054; Plaza del Nogal 8; per person €16) is a spacious *casa rural*.

Day 2: Fuente Forata to Benimantell

3½–4 hours including Aitana detour, 12km

You might want to pull on a pair of long trousers today since the path passes through several spots of prickly *montebajo* (undergrowth). Fill up your water bottles too; there's no source until Font del Molí.

From Fuente Forata, leave the main track and, from the spring's head, take a well-worn path, signed 'Sender Botánic del Passet de la Rebosa', that leads southeast below the *forat* and through a protected microreserve, where illustrated signs (unfortunately only in Valenciano) indicate mountain flora. After crossing a scree slope, clamber up a boulder-strewn gully, guided by yellow-and-white flashes. Bear left halfway up (just below a yew tree) and climb through **Puerto de Tudos** (or 'Fat Man's Agony'), the second of two very narrow gaps leading to the summit ridge of Sierra de Aitana.

Once through traverse left (east), above a large fissure down to a marked, chest-high rock-face and trail junction. From here, a strongly recommended 35- to 45-minute round trip detour leads towards the summit of **Aitana** (1557m), the highest peak in La Marina. Follow the yellow-and-white flashes and pegs up a rocky path. The summit itself is within the military radar station to the west, but before the boundary fence a lesser summit – a mere 8m lower – gives uninterrupted views of La Marina. Particularly impressive is Puig Campana (1408m) to the southeast, said by locals to resemble Mussolini's craggy Roman features, and the Isla de Benidorm (Benidorm Island) beyond it.

VALENCIA

RUTA LA MARINA ALTA

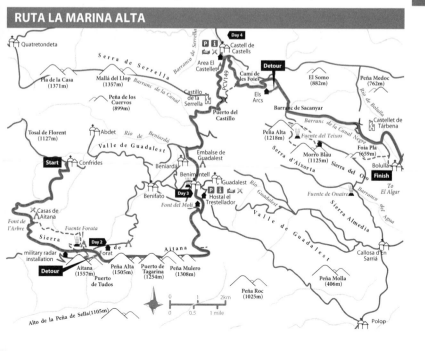

NEVERAS: THE ORIGINAL FRIDGES

Neveras are deep, cylindrical pits, usually constructed on the northern slopes of high mountains and once used to make ice from snow. Normally about 15m deep and 10m wide, the larger ones had supporting beams and wooden tiled roofs. Smaller neveras had domed, dry-stone roofs.

In winter, the pits were filled with snow which was compacted into ice, insulated with straw and left until the summer months when local men (nevaters) would come up from the villages at night to cut the ice into usable blocks, transporting it by mule down to the valleys before sunrise.

Neveras were mainly used during the 17th and 18th centuries, but older men in the village of Confrides maintain that the practice continued into the early part of the 20th century. Neveras fell into decay with the introduction of electric refrigeration, but good examples remain below the cliffs of Aitana.

Back at the junction, head south, then east, to pass below **Peña Alta** (1505m), the beginning of an enjoyable hour or so ridge walk east to Puerto de Tagarina, a pass crossed by the forestry road linking Benifato and Sella. Continue east, up and over **Peña Mulero** (1308m) on a 4WD track that makes for easy walking. The views of Alto de la Peña de Sella (1105m; a great place for a ridge walk) and El Realet, a jagged barrier between Sella and Puig Campana, are excellent.

Descend eastwards, again on stony path, to a small saddle (1043m) marked by a couple of cairns, reached 35 to 40 minutes after Puerto de Tagarina. Cut back left along a narrow rock gully. Cross a small scree field and turn left to walk above an almond grove. Less than 10 minutes later, go straight ahead where four tracks meet to descend through more almond groves, turning right onto a concrete track after 20 minutes. Keep descending and hairpin left to stay with the main track as far as **Font del Molí**, where you can replenish your water bottles. Turn left (north) along a tarmac road then fork right. Around 250m later a right turn leads to **Hostal El Trestellador** (☎ 96 588 52 21; www.hostaltrestellador .com; s/d €40/55; menú €15), which offers truly excellent Valencian cooking (restore your energy with a huge, steaming bowlful of rabbit stew).

Benimantell itself is 20 minutes north of Hostal El Trestellador and 20 minutes west of Guadalest. Both villages have bars, restaurants and grocery shops. **Guadalest** is something of a tourist trap but delightful once the last coach has pulled out. It has bus connections to Callosa (four daily),

the wonderful **Castillo de San José** and a good casa rural choice, **Cases Noves** (☎ 96 611 20 64, 676 010171; Calle Achova 2; s €40–50, d €70–80; menú €14).

Day 3: Benimantell to Castell de Castells

3½–4 hours, 12.5km

From Plaça Major in the centre of Benimantell head northwest around the church and downhill, filling your bottles at a fuente. At the far side of the school, turn right down a narrow tarred lane past the cemetery and zigzag roughly north towards Embalse de Guadalest. At the end of the sealed road, turn left onto a 4WD track. Around 10 minutes later, turn sharp left onto a narrower trail. This descends to the broad track that runs alongside lake **Embalse de Guadalest,** where there are one or two potential **campsites**. Turn right along the track, which becomes blacktop and ascends to join the road just north of Beniardá.

Go right, passing a fuente, to cross Río de Beniardá and turn right along a tarmac road (good quality except for one brief washed-away section) that curls around the edge of the lake to a gully, Barranco de les Coves. Here, at a T-junction 30 to 40 minutes beyond Beniardá, go straight (north) to join the PR-CV18 trail and begin the climb of around 75 minutes to **Puerto del Castillo**, a high pass. As you ascend, there's an increasingly splendid panorama of the whole of yesterday's route and the lake beneath you.

At the pass is a crossroads. To the right (east) a track leads onto Serra d'Aixorta; to the left are the ruins of **Castillo de la**

Serrella, one of the last Islamic strongholds in La Marina. About 40 minutes away, the ruins can easily be reached by heading west along the dirt road from the pass, then climbing up.

From the crossroads, descend straight ahead for a couple of minutes, then turn left (signed 'Area el Castellet') onto a dirt road that loops westwards. Turn right less than 10 minutes from the junction to descend the PCV-149, a stony footpath that follows an old Mozarabic trail (see the boxed text Mozarabic Trails, below), zigzagging down to **Area El Castellet** (four-bed cabins €28). It has a couple of *fuentes* and plenty of space for camping, which is free. Reserve cabins through **Silvoturismo** (☎ 902 10 708 4, 96 537 62 31; www.silvoturismo.com).

Fifteen minutes further on, **Castell de Castells** has two great overnight options.

Pensión Castells (☎ 96 551 82 54; www.mountainwalking-spain.com; Calle San Vicente 18; s/d €40/55; dinner €18; open year-round) is a wonderful walker – and cyclist – friendly option. English owners Sarah and Gary Neal know their mountains inside out, care for the landscape and will prepare you a packed lunch. See p227.

Hotel Rural Serrella (☎ 96 551 81 38; www.hotel-serrella.com; Calle Alcoy 2; s/d €40-60, half-board per person €50-60) is an equally cosy choice run by the village mayoress.

You'll find a cluster of bar-restaurants and a couple of grocery shops near the village church.

Day 4: Castell de Castells to Bolulla

5–6 hours including Els Arcs detour, 17.5km

Today, though longer than Day 3 is less demanding. It also offers considerably more shade, especially in the first few hours. Long trousers are an advantage since the undergrowth clutches in places.

Head east along the CV752, then, 50m beyond the turn-off to Area El Castellet, turn right to climb a dirt road that leads to Puerto del Castillo. At a hairpin bend after about 20 minutes bear left (south). From here, it's easy walking, following for the most part the contour line of the hill and you'll maintain a steady clip along an ancient track, the Camí de les Foies. A short ascent brings you to a signboard and junction with the PRCV151, reached about 50 minutes after the hairpin bend. Follow the sign for Plan d'Aialt and, after roughly seven minutes, turn right to leave the PR route and follow a good, sandy track. Soon after, do make the 30 minute round trip detour to Els Arcs, a dramatic pair of interlinked *forats*, through which you can see the twisting, upwards route that you've been following.

Back en route and less than five minutes beyond the detour, turn left at a blacktop road and, some eight minutes later at a bend with an open patch of ground, take the track that leads right, then quickly left (southeast; look for the pair of small cairns).

This soon becomes a narrow, evident footpath that threads its way up the

MOZARABIC TRAILS

During the early centuries of southern Spain's Islamic occupation a large percentage of the local population converted to Islam. Those who chose to remain Christian were not persecuted, but given full legal protection secured by the payment of tax. Christians mixed freely with Muslims and the two slowly became indistinguishable in appearance, causing the Christians of northern Spain to name them the mozárabes, the 'Arabised' or Arab-like. Elements of Arab culture (such as craft and building skills, which in turn filtered into the northern Christian kingdoms) were also adopted by the mozárabes, who even built churches in an Arabic style.

Ancient stepped tracks through the mountains of Valencia (and Andalucía) are also the work of the mozárabes. Typically, these cobbled trails zigzag across the steepest slopes and down into the deepest ravines, making navigable once treacherous routes. It's also likely that many of these trails were constructed by the Mudéjars, Muslim settlers who stayed after the Reconquista and converted to Christianity.

Many of these paths are still in quite good condition, testament to the merits of solid construction and skill of mozárabe and Muslim craftsmen.

southern flank of steep Barranc de Sacanyar. Stay with the path as it threads around a long abandoned dam at the head of the gully. This is quite a good spot to take a break if you wish to rest and re-fuel. At the watershed, cross a broad, stony plateau, guided by cairns, to descend the northern flank of spectacular **Barranc de la Canal Negre**. Both flanks of this valley were once elaborately terraced and cultivated. Those productive and fertile days are passed now and nowadays, terraces tumble, farms and barns are collapsed and roofless and prickly, alienating gorse colonises the land.

Eventually, you arrive at a saddle and dirt road. Due east, atop a precipitous but breathtaking peak, are the ruins of **Castellet de Tárbena** (called Penya del Castellet on the IGN 1:25,000 map). Just north of the **pass** is an area of pasture that makes an exceptional campsite (though finding water can be a bit of a hike). Even if you don't stop to set up camp here, do take the time to walk this way for a few minutes for the sake of the views east to the row of dramatic cliffs and ravines that line the upper reaches of Río de Bolulla.

Back at the pass turn right (south). The road soon becomes tarmac, crosses a bridge and leads you down to Bolulla in around one hour.

Can Capelletes (☎ 96 588 04 52; www .capelletes.com; Avenida Capelletes 2; s/d €50/70) is a large, welcoming villa, just south of the village, where you'll find all the comforts to reward your efforts.

BOLULLA TO FONTS DE L'ALGAR LINK

A simple 45-minute route leads 2.5km from Bolulla along sealed tracks through *níspero* orchards to the start of the Sierra de Bernia Traverse.

Cross into the large car park opposite the centre of Bolulla, turn right and pick up the road (marked as a pista on the recommended IGN 1:25,000 map *Nos 848-I Altea* and *822-III Parcent*) that leads happily southeast and then south, down through a couple of zigzags, to the restaurants of El Algar at Fonts de l'Algar.

SIERRA DE BERNIA LOOP

Duration 5 hours
Distance 13.25km
Difficulty easy–moderate
Start/Finish Fonts de l'Algar or Bernia
Nearest Town Callosa (p235)
Transport car, bus, taxi
Summary A circular route below the ridge that offers excellent mountain and coastal views. For experienced walkers, we describe an optional clamber and walk along the crest that requires nerve and agility.

This exhilarating walk around the jagged western ridge of Sierra de Bernia begins at Fonts de l'Algar, a popular tourist spot, 3km from Callosa. For a shorter option (2½ to 2¾ hours) that's a favourite with local walkers, start and finish in the hamlet of Bernia, omitting the ascent from Fonts de l'Algar, to walk an oval that retains the best of the views.

There's also the possibility of heading south off the ridge to L'Olla on the coast and picking up public transport from there.

PLANNING

It's a good idea to bring swimming togs for a refreshing post-walk dip in the waterfalls and gorges of **Fonts de l'Algar** (admission €2.50–4).

Maps

Marina Alta, Sierra de Bernia, published by Editorial Piolet at a scale of 1:20,000, covers the whole of the route

GETTING TO/FROM THE WALK

For Fonts de l'Algar, you'll need to take a taxi from Callosa (see p235). For a Bernia start, drive the spectacular CV749 from Benissa.

From L'Olla, the alternative finish, catch a No 10 bus via **Altea** (€1.25, five daily) or the **FGV trenet** (€2.25, hourly) back to Benidorm.

THE WALK

Head southeast up the road to the limit of Fonts de l'Algar. Turn left at a T-junction to begin the 1.1km climb southeast up

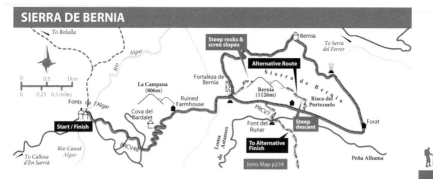

a sealed road through *níspero* groves. After around 20 minutes, fork left onto a track, following yellow-and-white trail markers of the PRCV48, which zigzags on a 45-minute climb up the lower slopes of La Campana (Penya Severino; 792m). Beyond **Cova del Bardalet** (a *cester* or livestock shelter), the trail turns east to a ruined farmhouse and threshing circle. Pick up the wide track heading east and then bear left onto a narrow track that leads up to **Fortaleza de Bernia** in about 20 minutes.

The fort was built for King Felipe II in 1562, but subsequently occupied by Muslims escaping persecution and expulsion. Felipe III had it dismantled in 1612 to deny the fugitives the use of it, but substantial sections remain.

Following the main route, head east along a generally well waymarked path. PR blazes (that occasionally and inexplicably follow the less easy of a pair of options) are supplemented by multicoloured smudges of spray paint, both useful and superfluous.

The views of Altea and the length of coastline are breathtaking. A mix of easy walking and more tortuous work over scree fields brings you, in a little over an hour beyond the fort, to a *forat*, a low, narrow 20m-long tunnel, leading through the *sierra*, that may have you on all fours. Once through, pick up the obvious trail that descends northwest down to a *fuente* and a well-defined 4WD track. Turn left for Bernia, reached about an hour from the *forat*.

A DEMANDING SCRAMBLE

For a challenging clamber and scramble along the crest, head northeast from the ruins, zigzagging up a scree slope. About 20m below the cliff wall a red arrow and various red dots (markers that illustrate the whole ridge walk) lead left (northwest). Traverse across the wide ledge and around the western buttress of Sierra de Bernia to an exposed ledge. From here, scramble and clamber east up onto the main ridge, from where it's a 30-minute scramble (exposed in places) to **Bernia peak** (1126m). It's a stunning viewpoint (Ibiza is visible on a clear day) and from here the trail leads across a lesser peak and up to the 1104m peak 20 minutes after the main summit.

Special care is needed for the next section as the trail drops steeply from the main ridge (stick to the northern side) to a col (999m), before which a few climbing moves are required to complete a traverse (a little exposed) across a rock-face and around a tree. After this crossing the trail cuts back to the southern side of the ridge and it's a simple walk up to the 1007m peak. On the southern side of the peak a trail leads to **Risco del Portezuelo** – an impressive col. Again, it's very steep, but like big steps and not too unnerving.

At the col, red dots lead northeast back onto the main ridge (the trail reportedly covers the whole range), but instead turn right (south) down a steep, but manageable scree slope to rejoin the main route.

At an information board, some 100m before the often closed **Restaurant Serra Bernia**, turn left, following the wide, rocky track through vineyards, almond and olive grovess and up to a saddle between the Bernia massif and Serra del Ferrer. Fortaleza de Bernia and the route back down to Fonts de l'Algar lies just south of here, about 45 minutes from Bernia.

ALTERNATIVE FINISH: L'OLLA
3 hours, 9km
Approximately 20 minutes beyond Fortaleza de Bernia, following the eastern traverse, the PRCV7 (also blazed in yellow-and-white) heads down past Font del Runar, along a tarmac road, southeast through a parking area and onto a narrow trail that descends to a dirt road in about an hour. Follow this road south, passing a few houses, to a T-junction. Turn left (northeast) following the tarmac southeast for 100m before turning left onto a rough track by an electricity substation just before a roundabout. Descend through the woods to another tarmac road, turn right and continue south to Altea la Vella. Turn left onto the CV755 and after 800m turn right onto a tarmac track that leads under the motorway (A7) and across a bridge. Turn left, then bear left, heading south to Olla-Altea FGV station (and the pleasant **Barbacoa Bar**). Alternatively, continue south across the N332 to a couple of restaurants on the **pebble beach** of Playa L'Olla.

TOWNS & FACILITIES

ALICANTE
☎ 96 / pop 332,000
Benidorm has more direct access to La Marina, but Alicante is a pleasant city and with so many cheap flights arriving here you may choose to spend the night.

Information
The main **tourist office** (☎ 520 00 00; Rambla de Méndez Núñez 23) offers a wealth of information for walkers while **K2 Esports** (☎ 520 65 62; Calle Belando 5) and **El Corte Inglés** (☎ 592 50 01; cnr Ave Maisonnave & Calle Churruca) are the best places for walking and camping equipment.

Sleeping & Eating
Pensión La Milagrosa (☎ 521 69 18; www .hostallamilagrosa.com; Calle de Villavieja 8; s/d €25/40, with bathroom €35/50) has simple rooms, a small guest kitchen, washing machine and roof terrace.

In El Barrio (the old town) **Hostal Les Monges Palace** (☎ 521 50 46; www .lesmonges.net; Calle San Agustín 4; s €30-36, d €45-52) is a wonderful, agreeably quirky choice.

Guest House Antonio (☎ 650 718353; www.guesthousealicante.com; Calle Segura 20; s/d €40/50) is a magnificent budget choice.

There are dozens of cheap restaurants in El Barrio.

Getting There & Away
Dozens of cheap flights arrive and depart from Alicante's **Aeropuerto El Altet** (☎ 902 40 47 04).

Bus C-6 (€1.25; every 40 minutes) runs the 12km from the airport to Plaza del Mar in Alicante via the bus station, from where there are **ALSA** (☎ 902 42 22 42; www.alsa .es) buses to Madrid (€27.35; 5¼ hours, at least 10 daily), Valencia (€21; 2½ hours; more than 10 daily) and Benidorm (€4; one hour; every 30 minutes).

SIERRA DE BERNIA: ALTERNATIVE FINISH

Joins Map p233

To Alternative Finish

El Paradiso

Barranc de las Peñas

Barronc del Riquel

Sierra Altea

Urlisa

To Callosa d'En Sarrià

Altea la Vella

A7

Ermita de Santa Barbara

Olla Altea Train Station

A7

Alternative Finish

L'Olla

Cap Negret Train Station

MEDITERRANEAN SEA

0   0.5   1km
0   0.25   0.5 miles

From **Estación de Madrid** (☎ 902 24 02 02; Avenida de Salamanca) trains leave for Madrid (€43; 3¾ hours; seven daily) and Valencia (€27.30; 1¾ hours; 10 daily).

TRAM (☎ 900 72 04 72; www.fgvalicante .com) runs a smart tram to Benidorm (€4.40; 70 minutes; every half hour) along a coastal route that's scenically stunning at times. Take it from the Mercado terminus beside the covered market.

BENIDORM
☎ 96 / pop 70,200

Tacky tourism at its most heinous? Perhaps, but a lot of people look down their noses at Benidorm without ever having been there. With reasonable bus links into La Marina, it's the most sensible place to stay before or after the walk. The old town is an enjoyable place to spend an evening and – who knows? – the place might even grow on you.

Information
The main **tourist information office** (☎ 585 13 11; www.Benidorm.org; Avenida Martínez Alejos 16) does not have much information for mountain walkers.

Supplies & Equipment
Beni-Algar Sports (Intersport; ☎ 585 77 20; Calle Mercado 3) carries a decent range of walking equipment. The town's well endowed with supermarkets.

Librería Francés (☎ 585 15 01; Avenida Ruzafa 4) has a limited selection of walking maps.

Sleeping & Eating
Log on to Benidorm Spotlight (www .Benidorm-spotlight.com) before you travel; it often lists significant discounts.

Camping Villasol (☎ 585 04 22; www .camping-villasol.com; Avenida Bernat de Sarrià 13; site per person/tent €7.20/7.70) is a great campsite.

Hotel Iris (☎ 586 52 51; www.iris-hotel .net; Calle Palma 47; s €19-30, d €25-45) is a friendly budget choice that has a cosy ground floor, guests-only bar.

Hotel Los Ángeles (☎ 680 74 33; Calle Los Ángeles 3; s/d €43/76) is another pleasant, informal, family-owned hotel. Prices drop significantly in the off-season.

Calle Santo Domingo and Plaza de la Constitución in the old town are the best areas for Spanish food and drink.

Standing room only, **La Cava Aragonesa** (☎ 96 680 12 06; Plaza de la Constitución; lunch menú €9.80-12.80, mains €12-18)) has a magnificent selection of tapas and juicy canapés. Next door is its sit-down restaurant, where you can select from 20 different wooden platters of mixed foods.

Topo Gigio (Edificio Marianne 9, Avenida del Mediterráneo) is an authentic Italian place that prepares superior pizzas and pastas (around €8) and also offers a selection of mains from across the Mediterranean (€10-19).

Getting There & Away
ALSA buses run to Madrid (€30-48; 5½-6½ hours; at least eight daily), Valencia (€14.75; 1¾ hours; at least seven daily), Alicante (€4; one hour; every 30 minutes) and Alicante's El Altet airport (€8; 45 minutes; hourly). All leave from the bus station (served by local bus 41 or 47) on Calle Francisco Llorca.

The tram to Alicante (€4.40; every half hour) leaves from the train station north of town.

CALLOSA (CALLOSA D'EN SARRIÀ)
☎ 96 / pop 8300

Once the most important town in La Marina, Callosa is a historic little place with just enough of interest for a pre-walk diversion.

Information
Callosa has a small **tourist office** (☎ 588 01 53; Calle San Antonio 2; 9.30am-2.30pm Mon-Fri).

Sleeping & Eating
The nearest campsite is **Camping Fonts d'Algar** (☎ 639 520365; www .campingfontsdalgar.co.uk; site per person/ tent €5.50 each), 3km east of town and handy for the Sierra de Bernia walk. It's well equipped, but stark, and some facilities close in the low season. A bunch of nearby bars and restaurants cater for the tourist crowds drawn to the gorges and waterfalls of Fonts de l'Algar.

Fonda Galiana (☎ 588 01 55; Calle Colón 15; s/d €20/40) has simple rooms, shared facilities and a restaurant specialising in local cuisine.

Hostal Avenida (☎ 588 02 89; Carretera Alicante 9; s €20, d with/without bathroom €40/30), opposite the bus stop, is a simple, friendly and functional place with a popular bar-restaurant.

El Repòs del Viatger (☎ 588 23 22; www.casaruralelreposdelviatger.com; Calle Mayor 3; s/d €40/60), on the main street, is a charmingly restored town house.

Mesón San José (Carretera de Bolulla) is good for regional cuisine.

Getting There & Away

Hourly **ALSA** (☎ 902 42 22 42; www .alsa.es) buses run between Callosa and Benidorm bus station.

Another option is a **taxi** (☎ 661 445777, 619 589306). The fare to Bolulla or Fonts de l'Algar is about €10, while Confrides costs around €25.

MORELLA
☎ 964 / pop 2900

Perched on a hilltop, crowned by a castle and surrounded by its wall, Morella is an impressive sight. The Els Ports Loop walk begins and ends here, where you can happily spend an hour or two exploring the town (the Gothic Basílica de Santa María la Mayor is stunning) and sampling rich mountain cuisine.

Morella is a wonderful place to stock your rucksack with locally cured cheeses, sausages and cold meats. Several mini-markets offer more mundane supplies.

Sleeping & Eating

Between dusk and dawn you can bivouac north of the castle beside the municipal swimming pool (which has hot showers).

Hostal La Muralla (☎ 16 02 43; www .hostalmuralla.com; s/d €27/46), just around the corner, is scrupulously clean and great value.

Hotel El Cid (☎ 16 01 25; www .hotelelcidmorella.com; s/d €33/52, half-board €57), just inside Portal de Sant Mateu, has trim rooms. The bar is a regular haunt of retired men playing cards and there's a reasonable **restaurant** (menú €12).

Built in the 16th century as the cardinal's palace, **Hotel Cardinal Ram** (☎ 17 30 85; www.cardenalram.com; Cuesta Suñer 1; s/d

€37.50/59) is a couple of notches up and runs a good restaurant.

Restaurante Casa Roque (☎ 16 03 36; Cuesta San Juan 1; mains €10-20) offers regional specialities such as *sopa morellana con buñuelos* (broth with dumplings) and *gallina trufada* (chicken with locally dug truffles). **Mesón del Pastor** (☎ 16 02 49; Cuesta Jováni 5-7; mains €8.50-13.50) also does hearty mountain fare.

Getting There & Away

Morella is best reached via Castellón, which has good train connections south and north (see Getting There & Away for Valencia, p236).

From Monday to Friday, **Autos Medi-terráneo** (☎ 22 00 54) runs two daily buses (€9, 2¼ hours) between Morella and Castellón's train station. There's one Saturday service.

Morella has one **taxi company** (☎ 659 487861).

VALENCIA
☎ 96 / 807,200

The prosperous capital of the region and Spain's third-largest city has great nightlife, fantastic historical buildings and a contemporary architectural masterpiece, the Ciudad de las Artes y de las Ciencias (City of Arts and Sciences). If you are around for the festival of Las Fallas in mid-March you'll experience one of Europe's wildest street parties.

Information

The **regional tourist office** (☎ 398 64 22; www.comunitatvalenciana.com; Calle Paz 48) has some good walking material, plus lots of background information about the region as a whole. **Turismo Valencia** (VLC; ☎ 315 39 31; www.turisvalencia.es), mainly concerned with Valencia city, has its main office on Plaza de la Reina.

Supplies & Equipment

Close to the regional tourist office, **Base Deportes Altarriba** (☎ 392 21 99; Calle Paz 11) is a good central choice for outdoor and camping gear. There's no shortage of supermarkets and specialist food outlets. Valencia's **Mercado Central** (Plaza Mercado; 8am-2.30pm Mon-Sat) – a swirl of smells, movement and colour with more than 900 stalls – is Europe's largest fresh produce market.

Sleeping

Valencia is particularly well endowed with well-priced, well-run private hostels such as **Hilux** (☎ 391 46 91; www.feetup hostels.com; Calle Cadirers 11), **Hôme Youth Hostel** (☎ 391 62 29; www.likeathome.net; Calle Lonja 4), **Red Nest Hostel** (☎ 342 71 68; www.nesthostelsvalencia.com) and its sibling, **Purple Nest Hostel** (☎ 353 25 61; Plaza Tetuan 5) and **Indigo Youth Hostel** (☎ 315 39 88; www.indigohostel.com; Calle Guillem de Castro 64).

Other excellent budget choices are **Pensión París** (☎ 352 67 66; www .pensionparis.com; Calle Salvá 12; basic s/d €22/32, d with bathroom €40) and **Hostal Antigua Morellana** (☎ 391 57 73; www .hostalam.com; Calle En Bou 2; s €45-55, d €55-65) with full en-suite facilities.

For something altogether fancier, try **Ad Hoc** (☎ 391 91 40; www.adhochoteles .com; Calle Boix 4; s €76-101, d €89-125) for friendly, sybaritic R&R.

Eating

In the heart of town, **Pepita Pulgarcita** (☎ 391 46 08; C de Caballeros 19) and **Bodeguilla del Gato** (☎ 391 82 35; C de Catalans 10) are a pair of great tapas places.

For great Mediterranean cuisine, head for **La Lola** (☎ 391 80 45; www .lalolarestaurante.com; Subida del Toledano 8) or, the best of Valencia's bunch of Italian restaurants, **La Pappardella** (☎ 391 89 15; C de Bordadores 5).

Getting There & Away

Air Valencia's **Aeropuerto de Manises** (☎ 159 85 00) is 10km west of the centre and serviced by Metro Lines 3 and 5. Regular flights connect Valencia with other major Spanish towns and European cities such as Paris, Milan, Geneva, Amsterdam and Brussels. easy Jet flies to London (Gatwick) and Bristol, and Ryanair to London (Stansted).

BUS

From Valencia's **bus station** (☎ 346 62 66), Avanzabus (☎ 902 02 00 52; www .avanzabus.com) operates hourly bus services to/from Madrid (€23.50, four hours). **ALSA** (☎ 902 42 22 42; www .alsa.es) has up to 20 daily buses to/from Barcelona (€25.50-30, four to 5½ hours) and over 10 to Alicante (€18.50, 2½ hours), most passing by Benidorm (€15.75, 1¾ hours).

TRAIN

From Valencia's Estación del Norte, up to 10 Alaris express trains travel daily to/from Madrid (€46, 3½ hours), at least 12 to Barcelona (€40, three to 3¾ hours) and 10 to Alicante (€28, 1¾ hours).

Trains run every half hour to Castellón (€4.20, one hour).

VALENCIA

Mallorca

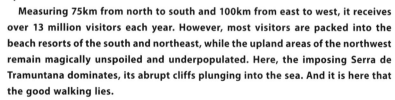

HIGHLIGHTS

- Feeling the salty wind in your hair and the warming sun on your back as you hike the cliffs above the sparkling Mediterranean on the **Sóller to Sa Calobra** walk (p250)
- Savouring the views of the Sóller valley, way below, from the Mirador d'en Quesada on the **Barranc de Biniaraix & Embassament de Cúber** walk (p246)
- Enjoying the superb seascapes from the Camino del Archiduque on the **Valldemossa Loop** (p248)
- Clambering down Mallorca's deepest gorge, the **Torrent de Pareis** (p253)

Area: 3700 sq km	Average summer high: 28°C	Population: 702,000

Mallorca is the largest of the Islas Baleares (Balearic Islands), an archipelago of four inhabited and several smaller islands that spangle the Mediterranean off Spain's eastern coast.

Measuring 75km from north to south and 100km from east to west, it receives over 13 million visitors each year. However, most visitors are packed into the beach resorts of the south and northeast, while the upland areas of the northwest remain magically unspoiled and underpopulated. Here, the imposing Serra de Tramuntana dominates, its abrupt cliffs plunging into the sea. And it is here that the good walking lies.

MALLORCA

HISTORY

Over the centuries, Mallorca was occupied by wave after wave of invaders; Phoenicians, Carthaginians, Romans, Visigoths and Arabs have all touched Mallorca and left their mark.

The Arabs built the first water channels for irrigation and introduced the *sínia* (water wheel) to raise water from wells and underground reservoirs. They also constructed the island's earliest *marjades* (banks of terracing), which increased cultivable space on the flanks of the steep valleys. Then, in 1229, the Catalan army of Jaume I, king of Catalunya and Aragón, put an end to more than three centuries of Islamic occupation.

After the 'discovery' of the Americas, Spain's attention was drawn increasingly to its transatlantic possessions, to the neglect of its offshore Mediterranean islands, which were repeatedly battered by raiding Barbary pirates and Turkish warships. In Pollença and Sóller commemorative events recalling this period are held every year.

Mass tourism, which began as a trickle in the 1950s and has gushed in greater volume with every subsequent year, has been the economic saviour of the islands but at considerable environmental cost.

Throughout recent Mallorcan history the Serra de Tramuntana was mainly the preserve of olive farmers, charcoal-burners and *neveras*, or snow-collectors (for more about *neveras*, see the boxed text Neveras: the Original Fridges, p230). Nowadays, the major part of the range, which is classified as Áreas Naturales de la Serra de Tramuntana, enjoys a degree of environmental protection.

There's no longstanding tradition of walking for pleasure among Mallorcans. Until relatively recently life was hard for most and leisure time limited. You walked for a purpose – to get where you needed to be – and not for the intrinsic pleasure of the journey. To this day, many walks follow ancient paths between villages and a lot of the walkers on the trails are still foreign visitors.

ENVIRONMENT

Mallorca is a continuation of the Andalucían mountains, also known as the Baetic Plate, on the Spanish mainland. Limestone,

uplifted from the sea floor by tectonic forces some 150 million years ago, constitutes the core of the Serra de Tramuntana. There, north-facing crags and cliffs are much steeper than those facing south, in many places making access to the coast impossible from the landward side.

Evergreen oak (*alzina*), its leaves waxy and shiny to reduce evaporation in the heat of summer, is common. Its subspecies, the holm-oak, once the charcoal-burners' favourite, thrives at lower altitudes. Seeds of the carob or locust bean, formerly fed to livestock, are now mainly used as a substitute for chocolate and as a guaranteed, flush-you-through laxative.

At higher levels pines predominate, surviving up to about 1000m. Most common

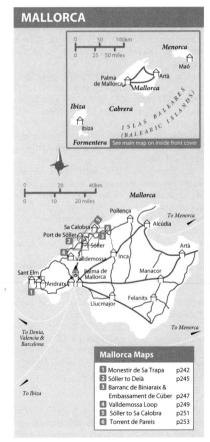

MALLORCA

Menorca
Maó
Palma de Mallorca · Artà
Mallorca
Ibiza · Cabrera
Ibiza
Formentera · See main map on inside front cover
ISLAS BALEARES (BALEARIC ISLANDS)

Mallorca
Pollença · To Menorca
Sa Calobra · Alcúdia
Port de Sóller
Sóller · Artà
Valldemossa · Inca
Sant Elm · Palma de Mallorca · Manacor
Andratx
Felanitx
Llucmajor
To Denia, Valencia & Barcelona
To Menorca
To Ibiza

Mallorca Maps	
1 Monestir de Sa Trapa	p242
2 Sóller to Deià	p245
3 Barranc de Biniaraix & Embassament de Cúber	p247
4 Valldemossa Loop	p249
5 Sóller to Sa Calobra	p251
6 Torrent de Pareis	p253

WHAT'S COOKING IN MALLORCA?

Fish and seafood are the lead items in many a Balearic kitchen. In the marshlands of S'Albufera, in eastern Mallorca, rice and eels are traditional mainstays. The former is used in many dishes, while the latter most usually pops up in the *espinagada*, an eel and spinach pie. Valldemossa is famous for its versions of *coca*, a pizza-like snack that you will find around the island. One of the local specialities is the potato version, *coca de patata*.

The interior of Mallorca is serious wine country, with two Denominación de Orígen (DO) areas, Binissalem and Pla i Llevant (roughly the southeast sector of the island).

is the Aleppo pine, which, despite its name, may have originated in the Balearic Islands and only later became established in the Levant.

The main cultivated trees are olive trees (some veterans are reputed to be more than 1000 years old), fig trees – pendulous and often supported by sturdy poles – and almond trees, whose blossoms tint the countryside pink in spring. Orange and lemon orchards proliferate, especially in the mild Sóller valley.

In springtime the hills blaze yellow with broom. Aromatic rosemary, with its characteristic blue flower, and wild rockroses stay in flower longer. *Asphodelus* colonise land low in nutrition and somewhere, sometime, you're bound to get your boots tangled in *carritx*, a type of grass with long, sharp-edged leaves.

Migratory birds use the islands as a staging post in spring and autumn. You're certain to spot raptors such as red kites, kestrels, black vultures, hawks and both Eleanor's and peregrine falcons.

Keen bird-watchers can contact fellow enthusiasts at the **Grupo de Ornitología Balear** (GOB; ☎ 971 49 60 60), also known as the Grup Balear d'Ornitologia i Defensa de la Naturalesa, in Palma.

CLIMATE

The major rains fall between late October and February. But even December, the dampest month, has an average of only eight days rain, a statistic that walkers from soggier climes regard with envy.

PLANNING

When to Walk

The best period for walking is from late February to May, when the countryside is green and blossoming and temperatures moderate, or September and early October, after the summer crowds have gone but before the rains arrive. This said, winter walking, when the average daily temperature rarely drops below 10°C, can be splendid and many enthusiasts actually prefer it. Nevertheless if you choose technical routes at this time the going can be tough.

Between late June and August, daily average temperatures are around 25°C and hiking the tops without even a bush for shade can be a sticky experience. But if summer – when there's no rain to speak of – is the only time you can get away, don't despair. Make an early enough start and you can be cooling off in the sea by the time the sun reaches its zenith.

When planning your walks, bear in mind that the times we quote are actual walking time, and do not include rest stops.

Maps

The most detailed options are Editorial Alpina Walking Maps' 1:25,000 *Mallorca Tramuntana*. These cover three different areas (north, central and south) and each pack contains both a map and a hiking guide (Spanish only) and feature all the main routes.

An overall map of the island for outdoor enthusiasts is Kompass' 1:75,000 *Mallorca*, with walking and mountain bike routes superimposed. For driving and general orientation, the free *Las Islas Baleares* map, available from any tourist office, is quite adequate.

Discovery Walking Guides (also known as Warm Island Walking Guides) publishes three reliable walking maps of the island, based on IGN 1:25,000 originals, together with a detailed route description in English. Their 1:40,000 *Mallorca Mountains Walking Guide* presents 19 enticing walks around Sóller and Port de Sóller. *Mallorca North & Mountains Tour & Trail Map* at the same scale covers almost all the Serra de Tramuntana. This map, like the Freytag & Berndt 1:50,000 *Mallorca Tramuntana* map, covers all the walks in this chapter except the Monestir de Sa Trapa walk.

Foment del Desenvolupament de Mallorca (Fodesma), a branch of the Consell Insular (the island's governing body), has produced several good walking brochures. In addition to a large-scale plan of the walk, each contains a wealth of background information. They are available in Spanish, English and French amongst others.

Books

Walking in Mallorca, by June Parker, describes more than 50 walks on the island. It's solid on background and extremely well researched and written; its only deficiency is the spindly monochrome maps.

Mallorca, by Valerie Crespi-Green, in the Sunflower series is, by comparison, thin beer. Even so, it describes several worthwhile hikes and the 1:40,000 colour maps are easy to follow.

Birdwatching in Mallorca, by Ken Stoba, is worth slipping into your pack. *Wild Flowers of Majorca, Minorca and Ibiza*, by Elspeth Beckett, the best guide for amateur botanists, is no longer easy to obtain.

Information Sources

You'll find gigabytes of information about the island at www.visitbalears.com and www.infomallorca.net.

Tourist offices carry a free pamphlet *20 Walking Excursions in Mallorca*. It gives pointers but needs to be supplemented with a good map.

GATEWAYS

All the walks in this chapter, except Monestir de Sa Trapa, are accessible by public transport from Sóller (p257) or Port de Sóller (p256), so it makes sense to base yourself in one or the other. Palma de Mallorca (p255) is the logical base for the Monestir de Sa Trapa walk – and you may find yourself spending a night there on your way to or from the other trails. Pretty Pollenca (p256) makes a pleasant base although it's further from most of the walks.

MONESTIR DE SA TRAPA

Duration 4–4½ hours

Distance 12km

Difficulty easy–moderate

Start Sant Elm

Finish S'Arracó

Nearest Town Palma de Mallorca (p255)

Transport bus, taxi

Summary A robust ascent from the coastal resort of Sant Elm to the ex-Trappist monastery of Sa Trapa is followed by a gentler inland return walk to the village of S'Arracó.

The coastal stretch of this walk, where more than 80 bird species have been recorded, is particularly rich for ornithologists; that's why local ecological group, the Grup Balear d'Ornitologia i Defensa de la Naturalesa, purchased the dilapidated monastery of Sa Trapa in 1980. It's gradually renovating the monastery, the intricate system of irrigation

MALLORCA'S BLOCKED PASSAGES

Not so long ago you could do a magnificent circuit around the lip of the bowl of mountains in which Sóller nestles – until a farmer up on the top erected a series of locked gates to bar the way. It is possible to cross his territory but only as part of an organised group with a guide who pays the proprietor. It's not what walking, wild, free and harming no-one, should be about.

Another favourite walk used to be the Puig Roig circuit, much of it following an old *corniche* path once used by smugglers. But here, too, property owners have blocked the route, allowing access on Sunday only. On another trail near the Monestir de Lluc the landowner exacts a €4 toll.

Unfortunately, there's little tradition of walking for walking's sake on the island. So there's no pressure group with the clout of, say, the admirable Ramblers Association in the UK which, at the click of a barred gate, can drum up a posse of walkers to challenge closed footpaths and militate for freedom of access.

MONESTIR DE SA TRAPA

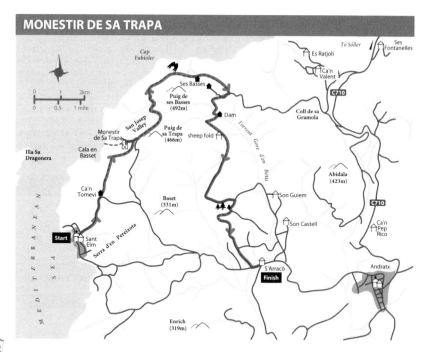

fed by a single stream, and the fine stone terracing.

The first part of the walk offers superb seascapes to compensate for the huffing and puffing. You stand a good chance of seeing red kites, kestrels, alpine swifts and maybe even a hawk or peregrine falcon. Once you reach the *mirador* (lookout point) at Cap Fabioler, it's flat or downhill all the way home, though the route is indistinct in a couple of places.

PLANNING
What to Bring
It's well worth slipping your binoculars into your day pack.

Maps
Editorial Alpina Walking Maps' 1:25,000 *Mallorca Tramuntana South* is the king of maps to this area. Another option is the SGE 1:50,000 map No 37–27 (697) *Andratx*, though not all of the route is indicated.

GETTING TO/FROM THE WALK
Bus No L102 between Palma and Andratx (pronounced an-dratch; €2.90, 1¼ hours)

leaves Palma every 45 minutes from Plaça d'Espanya, beside the train station.

Bus No L100 leaves Andratx for Sant Elm via S'Arracó (six daily). Convenient buses head back to Andratx from Sant Elm (two daily), calling by S'Arracó about 10 minutes after departing Andratx. The service may vary in winter. For the current schedule, ring **Autocares Andratx** (☎ 971 20 45 04).

Radio Taxi Andratx (☎ 971 13 63 98) will run you from Andratx to Sant Elm for about €10. At the end of the walk, ring them from S'Arracó and they'll be round in two shakes to pick you up (€7 to return to Andratx).

THE WALK
From Sant Elm's bus terminus in Plaça Mossen Sebastia Grau, head northeast up Avinguda de Sa Trapa. After 15 minutes, when you reach the farm of Ca'n Tomevi and a four-way junction with a signboard, go straight ahead along a narrow path and NOT right, as the sign indicates. Both ways lead to Sa Trapa. The one we recommend makes for a rather tougher ascent but offers

MONESTIR DE SA TRAPA

Expelled from France in 1791 in the wake of the French revolution and its anticlericalism, a small group of Trappist monks (hence the name, Sa Trapa) travelled to Tarragona, on the Catalan coast south of Barcelona. A few years later, when France invaded Spain, they had to flee again and found their way to Mallorca. At the desolate southwest tip of the island, they founded a monastery.

Never numbering more than 40, the monks returned to the mainland in 1820. But during their 10 short years of occupation they built a small monastery, channelled the intermittent stream which flows down the San Josep valley into a network of irrigation canals, established agriculture and constructed a corn mill, threshing house and banks of terraces with dry-stone walls – all of which remain to this day.

After many years of neglect, the property and its land were acquired by Grup Balear d'Ornitologia i Defensa de la Naturalesa, in whose trust the complex remains.

more shade and more spectacular views. (If you only fancy a short outing from Sant Elm, you can ascend to Sa Trapa by one of these alternatives and return by the other.)

As the intermittently cairned path comes out of the woods and onto a cliff, the steep stuff begins in earnest, as do the great views of the coast and the uninhabited island and nature reserve, Illa Sa Dragonera.

At the top of the last rocky crag, watch out for the red arrows directing you right and up a series of large, steep boulders. Miss these and you'll find yourself facing a sheer drop to the sea.

Once over the brow, you see the ruins of the **Monestir de Sa Trapa** below, less than 10 minutes' walk away. The once-rich setting which induced a group of Trappist monks to establish their self-contained community here (see the boxed text Monestir de Sa Trapa) is now bleak as a result of a devastating fire in 1994 which left most of the pines no more than twisted black fingers. Despite extensive replanting, and even though grasses and *montebajo* (scrub) are reasserting themselves, it will be a generation before the valley fully recovers. Below the monastery, the old cereal mill and the circular threshing area is a *mirador* with a simple plaque to one Joan Lliteras, who fell to his death when only 18.

Retrace your steps along the well-defined track and continue beyond the junction with the path from Sant Elm. At a steep hairpin, where a sign indicates S'Arracó and Sant Elm to the right, take instead the narrow path heading north, away from the bend. You're now at the heart of the area

devastated by the fire, much of it replanted with young pines encased in chicken wire to protect them from feral goats, their principal threat.

After a straightforward ascent to 400m, the route again levels out, letting you maintain a steady clip. At a giant cairn about 45 minutes from Sa Trapa, don't miss the brief (precisely 2½ minutes brief!) diversion left (west) to the **mirador** at Cap Fabioler. This, with its sweeping views of sea and coast, makes an agreeable rest stop.

Only a few metres beyond the cairn, you finally kiss goodbye to Illa Sa Dragonera, now in your wake, as the views open out to reveal the rocky coastline and the Serra de Tramuntana range, the southwestern extremity of which you're walking. Aim eastwards towards the first significant clump of live trees since you entered the area of the fire's devastation. Within this copse is **Ses Basses**, 25 to 30 minutes beyond the *mirador* and the first intact building since Sa Trapa. Written records reveal a building on this site as early as 1389.

For the Torrent alternative, take the narrow, sandy track to the right, which briefly doubles back before swinging southeast. The track ends beside a **small dam**. Take the path which veers away right over a small bluff, following an ancient wall. Stick with it as, by now well cairned, it runs west up the flank of a side valley to curl around its top. About 20 minutes beyond the dam, you reach a sheepfold, where the path all but disappears briefly under yet more burnt pines. However, if you keep the building on your right, you'll soon pick it up again.

MALLORCA

After dropping gently southwestwards for some 10 minutes, you enter the welcome semi-shade of a **pine grove** with a small, neglected almond orchard to your right. Just beyond, the path runs parallel with a terrace wall, still heading southwards, to become a wide, rocky track that steadily descends. Ruined farmsteads and abandoned cultivation give way to chic, renovated second homes as you approach your destination, S'Arracó.

SÓLLER TO DEIÀ

Duration 3–4 hours
Distance 10km
Difficulty easy
Start Sóller (p257)
Finish Deià (p245)
Transport bus
Summary A straightforward, well-signed walk beside olive groves and pasture, with a coastal path to Cala de Deià and an ascent by an ancient track to Deià.

The walk links two interesting communities on Mallorca's northwest coast. The optional cut-out to Deià at the end of the Camí de Castelló saves 3km and can make a good warm-up walk after a midday arrival in Sóller.

HISTORY

Until the Sóller–Deià road was thrust through in the 19th century, the Camí de Castelló was the main thoroughfare between the two villages. Superseded and thus neglected, it became the preserve of hunters, charcoal-burners and shepherds. Recently restored, it's now a well-signed and popular track for walkers.

The Camí de la Mar, less well defined nowadays, also has a long history. In late medieval times, for example, it was deliberately sabotaged in places to make access more difficult for Arab coastal raiders.

PLANNING
When to Walk

Reasonably shady, the route can be walked comfortably even at the height of summer, when you can also dunk yourself in one of the small coves or at the Cala de Deià.

What to Bring

Pack your bathers if you fancy cooling off in one of the coves.

Maps

The best map is Editorial Alpina Walking Maps' 1:25,000 *Mallorca Tramuntana Central*. An alternative is Discovery Walking Guides' 1:40,000 *Mallorca North & Mountains Tour & Trail Map*, and the Freytag & Berndt 1:50,000 *Mallorca Tramuntana* map also covers the route.

GETTING TO/FROM THE WALK

Buses run between Deià and Sóller, and Port de Sóller (30 minutes; three daily, Mon-Sat, one daily Sun).

THE WALK

From Sóller, head for the Repsol **petrol station** on the bypass road that goes to Port de Sóller. If you take Carrer de Bauçà from the main Plaça de sa Constitució and keep heading west as directly as the turnings allow, you won't miss it.

Cross the bypass to a sign, Camí del Rost, which also marks the beginning of the Camí de Castelló. After about 15 minutes, the sealed road narrows to a footpath that, once over a stream bed, becomes a fine stone stairway.

Just over the half-hour, the cobbles stop and you descend briefly among olive trees, ignoring both a potential fork and a manifest turn to the right. The way is now a wide cart track.

A little under an hour out, you arrive at a minor crossroads, signed for Deià. Soon, a couple of giant fig trees overhanging the path offer juicy refreshment as you skirt the estate of C'an Carabasseta.

At a junction beside a small 17th-century **chapel**, now sadly ruined, mount the less obvious cobbled path to the left of the chapel. It's indicated by the first of the GR signs that help what's already easy navigation until you reach the C710.

The path ascends to **Son Mico**, also known as Ca'n Prohom, a large farmhouse with roots at least as deep as the 15th century. There, you can fortify yourself with fresh orange juice and cakes. Queen Isabel II, who's reputed to have spent the night here when she visited Sóller in 1888, enjoyed, no doubt, more sumptuous fare.

Take the track on the left just after the houses. Some 200m beyond Son Mico, leave the track and turn sharp left just before an electricity pylon to mount a clearly signed cobbled track – stay on this small track ignoring any deviating trails.

Once the cliffs of the Cala de Deià come into view, there's a clearly signed potable spring, the **Font de ses Mentides**, in a gully just off route. Here you have a choice of routes. You can either take the little path on the right just after the fountain marked with stone cairns which will lead you downhill and to the left until you hit the C710 road. Cross the road and take the path directly onward to **Lluc Alcari**. This route avoids having to walk along the C710 road. Otherwise, continue in a straight line over the brow of an incline, to where you'll see Lluc Alcari, a cluster of coastal houses, ahead. About two hours into the walk, turn right at a T-junction to follow a sealed driveway and cobbled lane to meet the C710 main road. Here, you can either cut out to Deià by walking west for about 30 minutes or turn east to continue the walk via Lluc Alcari, as described here.

After a little less than 10 minutes of roadwork, go left at the Lluc Alcari turn-off (signed 'Hotel Costa d'Or') then right at a fork (the left option leads to the hotel). After a bend, look for some steps leading to

a narrow path on the right (signed 'playa'). Follow it for some 200m above an olive grove then bear left to thread your way downhill. When you intersect with **Camí de la Mar**, the coastal path, turn left to follow the coastline. Although debris from recent logging (the clear-up after a particularly destructive storm) makes the path indistinct in places, wayfinding is, in general, uncomplicated.

From a **mirador**, reached 20 minutes after having hit the coast, you can pick out the 17th-century **Torre de sa Pedrissa**, a defensive tower on the headland beyond Cala de Deià. The latter's pebble beach, reached after around three hours' walking, may well be crowded but the water is clean and inviting.

There's only one way out of the tight valley; head inland along a dirt track that soon becomes a narrow sealed road. After 10 minutes, cross the bed of the Torrent Major by a wooden bridge onto the true left (west) bank to ascend an excellent, recently restored cobbled path. You're now following the Camí des Ribassos, another ancient pathway linking Deià with its small sea outlet. Turn left where it joins a well-defined track. From the Cala to the village is about 40 minutes. **Deià** is an attractive cluster of some 75 houses on the lower slopes of the Puig des Teix. It can

SÓLLER TO DEIÀ

be massively crowded during the day as convoys of tourist coaches deposit their cargo. Then, like Sóller, it becomes itself again each evening as the buses pull out.

The village has a high proportion of expats, a longstanding tradition, going back to the days when it was a thriving artist colony with the late Robert Graves its most famous denizen.

BARRANC DE BINIARAIX & EMBASSAMENT DE CÚBER

Duration 3½–4 hours

Distance 11km

Difficulty easy–moderate

Start Sóller (p257)

Finish Embassament de Cúber

Transport bus

Summary An ascent of the tight Barranc de Biniaraix valley to the small upland plateau of l'Ofre, crossing a col to descend through woodland and on to the Embassament de Cúber reservoir.

This classic walk follows part of an old pilgrim route which ran between Sóller and the Monestir de Lluc. The earliest documented evidence of its use as a pilgrim route is a letter dated AD 1438 from the local bishop to his priest in Sóller, granting an indulgence of 40 days to those who helped to maintain the track.

ENVIRONMENT

Few evergreen oaks, the valley's original cladding, remain. They've been superseded by olive and orange groves, carob trees and, in the upper reaches, pine trees and juniper bushes. In the humid areas near the banks of the Torrent des Barranc is a rich variety of ferns, some of them endemic to Mallorca.

PLANNING
Maps

Once again Editorial Alpina Walking Maps' 1:25,000 *Mallorca Tramuntana South* is the map to get. Discovery Walking Guides' 1:40,000 *Mallorca North & Mountains Tour & Trail Map* and the Freytag & Berndt 1:50,000 *Mallorca Tramuntana* map also cover the route.

GETTING TO/FROM THE WALK

The later of the twice-daily buses linking Pollença and Port de Sóller via Sóller passes by Embassament de Cúber reservoir, at the end of the walk, between 5.05pm and 5.20pm (€1.10). Miss it and you've one helluva hike home. If you opt to do the route in reverse – an easier but less fulfilling option – take the morning bus which leaves Port de Sóller at 9am, calling by the Repsol petrol station on the Sóller bypass at 9.10am, and get off at the reservoir. Note that there is no bus service on Sundays.

THE WALK

From Plaça de sa Constitució in Sóller head northeast along Carrer de sa Lluna, which becomes Carrer de l'Alquería del Comte. Continue straight onto Carrer d'Ozones. After 15 minutes, cross a bridge onto the true right bank of the Torrent des Barranc – the stream that you'll be following to its source. At **Biniaraix**, an attractive little village that merits a brief stop, go up a flight of steps beside a telephone box and turn right up a cobbled street to emerge in Plaça de la Concepció, about 25 minutes from Sóller. Beyond it is a wash house and – mercifully upstream – a drinking-water fountain.

THRUSH NETTING

Mallorca is rich in bird life, but it could be a whole lot richer. In spite of the efforts of local environmental groups such as Grup Balear d'Ornitologia i Defensa de la Naturalesa, many islanders still think that if it's got wings, it's up there to be brought down and eaten.

One particularly cruel practice is thrush netting. In October and November flocks of *tords* (thrushes) migrating from Europe to warmer African climes briefly drop in on Mallorca to feed and fortify themselves for the next leg. Special nets, called *filats*, are slung between the olive trees. In them, the thrushes are trapped and struggle to exhaustion. 'It's better than being slowly poisoned by insecticides', aficionados will tell you, but that really doesn't wash if your other option as a thrush is to be up there flying, wild and free.

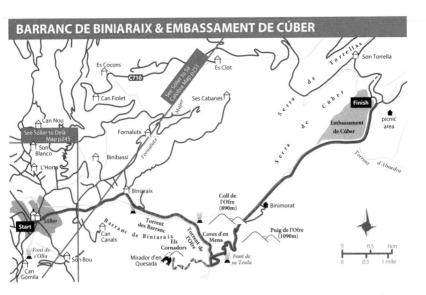

BARRANC DE BINIARAIX & EMBASSAMENT DE CÚBER

Take the track to the right, signposted 'A l'Ofre'. From here on, navigation is made simpler by fresh GR signs at strategic points, marking a completed section of the Ruta de Pedra en Sec long-distance trail (see the Sóller to Deià walk, p244). After five minutes, cross the stream bed and begin the long haul up well-maintained cobblestone steps.

The lower reaches of the stream will probably be dry, its waters siphoned off further upstream. Higher up, you walk beside waterfalls and enticing pools and over stepping stones. Throughout the valley, there are tight terraces of olive trees above neat dry-stone walls, superbly constructed and maintained.

Pass beneath the russet **Coves d'en Mena**, a huge scar on the precipitous cliff face that's clearly visible from Sóller, now in sight way below, together with the lighthouse and upper buildings of Port de Sóller.

As you pass through a green gate, ignore for once the sign saying 'l'Ofre, Propiedad Privada'. The area proclaims itself a private property at every turning, but you're grudgingly allowed through. Pay heed, however, to the bull sign, although we can't be sure whether the bull – if he exists – is there primarily to serve the cows or the farmer's interests in keeping pesky walkers out.

The track dwindles to a narrow pathway, still progressing southward. From it, the way to the splendid **Mirador d'en Quesada** (see the Side Trip p248) branches off.

To continue to Embassament de Cúber, go through a green gate to bypass the farm with its sign emphasising 'no entry'.

The path soon joins a wide forest track. Around 20 minutes beyond the Mirador d'en Quesada turn-off, avoid a bend or two in the track by turning left (northeast) up a rocky path that debouches at the **Coll de l'Ofre** (890m) some 15 minutes later.

From the pass, 2½ to 2¾ hours' walking from Sóller, there are fine views eastwards to the cone of **Puig de l'Ofre** (1090m), the reservoir below and, beyond it, Puig Mayor – at 1443m, the highest point on the island and crowned by telecommunication aerials. Shortly after the col, take another short cut on the left to rejoin the track at the lone building of **Binimorat**. Leave the less than welcoming l'Ofre land by the lower of two gates after about three hours' walking.

When you reach the reservoir minutes later, follow its east bank over the dam head until you hit the main road, which today's travellers use to get from Sóller to the Monestir de Lluc.

If you've time on your hands before the bus is due, drop down the road for less than five minutes to **Sa Font de Noguer**, a shaded picnic area with a delightfully cool spring. The bus will happily stop to pick you up here if you signal.

SIDE TRIP: MIRADOR D'EN QUESADA
1–1¼ hours, 3km
From the sign 'Mirador d'en Quesada', about two hours out of Sóller, head right just below a concrete cistern. As you climb, there's only one point where you might go astray; at a sharp bend where the track turns west, go with the turn and disregard the smaller path heading away from it. At a col about 35 minutes from the turnoff, take a signed path up to the right (northeast). After passing a stone *refugio* (mountain hut or refuge), this leads you to the *mirador*.

Once you've savoured the magnificent, expansive views of the entire Sóller basin and the coast beyond, retrace your steps.

VALLDEMOSSA LOOP

Duration 5¼–5¾ hours
Distance 15km
Difficulty moderate
Start/Finish Valldemossa
Nearest Towns Sóller (p257), Port de Sóller (p256)
Transport bus
Summary A steepish ascent leads to the plateau of Es Pouet, the Mirador de ses Puntes, the splendid Camino del Archiduque, a detour to the summit of Es Teix and home via the Vall de Cairats.

This is a pick-and-mix day; if you don't want to do the whole walk there are two points where you can take a significant short cut. You can also omit the ascent to the summit of Es Teix. Do any of these and the difficulty of the walk becomes easy–moderate; you'll still enjoy some splendid coastal views from the main section of the Camino del Archiduque.

Both landowner and villager have made their contribution to the landscape. Walkers have Archduke Ludwig Salvator of Habsburg, (see the boxed text El Archiduque, below), to thank for laying out the *camino* (way), a dramatic trail that follows the cliff-tops.

HISTORY
In the late 19th century, Archiduque Luis Salvator built a series of paths through his estate of Miramar. In the spirit of high Romanticism, these private bridleways allowed him to ride his lands – and to impress his constant stream of visitors with spectacular coastal views and seascapes. The finest of these are from what is known today as the Camino del Archiduque.

PLANNING
What to Bring
The broken rocks and stones used to repair and improve the *camino* are, paradoxically, potential ankle-twisters. While most of the walk is fine if you're wearing runners, this major stretch makes boots advisable.

Maps
Editorial Alpina Walking Maps' 1:25,000 *Mallorca Tramuntana Central* is the best map.

The runner-up position goes to Discovery Walking Guides' 1:40,000 *Mallorca North*

EL ARCHIDUQUE

Archduke Ludwig Salvator (Luis Salvator in Spanish) of Habsburg, Lorraine and Bourbon was much more than just another romantic, northern European aristocrat doing the Grand Tour. Captivated by the Islas Baleares, and Mallorca in particular, he bought the estate of Miramar in 1872 and made it his home for more than 40 years – notwithstanding spells at his castle outside Prague and other homes at Ramleh in Egypt and Zinis, near Trieste, plus visits to the imperial court in Vienna and long Mediterranean cruises in his prized yachts, Nixe 1 and Nixe 2.

Polymath and ecologically sensitive before the term had even been invented, he restored decaying farmhouses and dwellings, created a magnificent garden of indigenous plants and shrubs at Miramar, bought up trees that farmers were about to fell and entertained a constant procession of visitors – while still finding time to write more than 70 books and scientific treatises, of which the most famous *is Les Balears Descrites per la Paraula i el Gravat* (The Balearics in Words and Images).

VALLDEMOSSA LOOP

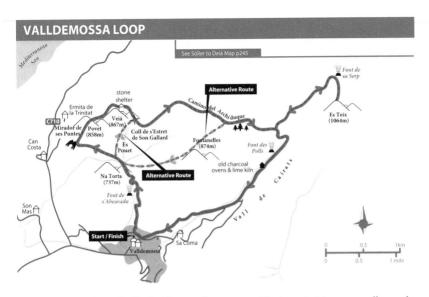

& *Mountains Tour & Trail Map,* and the Freytag & Berndt 1:50,000 *Mallorca Tramuntana* map covers the route, but don't attempt the path traced on this map linking Coll de s'Estret de Son Gallard and Deià; it's no longer walkable.

GETTING TO/FROM THE WALK
Bus No L210 runs between Valldemossa and Port de Sóller, passing by Sóller's Plaça de América (almost every hour).

THE WALK
From the bus stop in Valldemossa, walk towards Palma and take Carrer de la Venerable Sor Aina, the first road on your left. Turn right along Carrer de Joan Miró, the first intersection. Go straight ahead up a flight of steps beside a school then zigzag left-left-right at the rear of the school along Carrers Alzines, des Ametlers and de les Oliveres. At the end of this cul-de-sac, take the track heading northwest beside a sign which says, alarmingly, in English, 'Danger: Big Game'. The more trustworthy Spanish version merely warns that you're entering a hunting zone!

Take the path beside the sign. A couple of minutes later, where the broad track is blocked by a fence, turn left (north) up a rocky path, which was once an old charcoal-burners' track. Pass through gateposts, then

over a stile, to maintain a generally north-northwest bearing, ignoring any side trails, through, for the most part, shady oaks and under the shadow of Na Torta (737m).

A little under 45 minutes from Valldemossa, go through a gap in a dry-stone wall to emerge onto a small plateau. Disregarding tracks to right and left, continue straight ahead through spindly oak trees, passing beside a *sitja* (charcoal-burners' circle) to reach the well of **Es Pouet** (don't drink from its murky depths).

For a short cut, you can follow the dominant track to the right (bear initially north, then east) to bypass the *mirador*, save yourself around an hour of walking and rejoin the route at Coll de s'Estret de Son Gallard. Mind you, if you do, you'll miss out on a spectacular panorama.

For the Mirador de ses Puntes, take the minor path which heads initially straight ahead (north) then very soon turns west. Climbing at first, then gently descending through pine, oak and scrub, you skim the southwestern flanks of Povet and Veià to arrive, something over the hour from Valldemossa, at the **Mirador de ses Puntes.** From here, there are spectacular views of the village of Puigpunyent, squat on top of the first hill to the west, the Tramuntana chain trailing away westwards and, to the south, the suburbs of Palma.

Here, with an initial hairpin east, the **Camino del Archiduque** begins. After 15 minutes you pass alongside the knoll of **Veiá** (867m), clearly identifiable by its trig marker. Ten minutes later the trail arrives at a **crumbling stone shelter** from where you can see the next hour or so of the route snaking before you. As you leave the ruins, the path heads briefly towards the sea before resuming its easterly progression.

After around 1¾ hours of hiking you arrive at the **Coll de s'Estret de Son Gallard** with a welcome stone bench. To the right (south) is that short-cut path coming up from Es Pouet.

A 15-minute ascent from the col leads to the most spectacular portion of the causeway, with sheer drops to the seaward side.

After 2½ hours of walking in total, you skirt a copse of trees, isolated on the bleak plateau. This is about the only shaded picnic stop until you reach the Vall de Cairats towards the end of the walk. To its right, a narrow path heads back to Es Pouet and offers a slightly shorter return to Valldemossa.

Thirty minutes later, take the turn-off left (east) at a large cairn to bag the peak of **Es Teix** (1064m), marked by two iron crosses (allow 45 minutes to one hour for the round trip). Es Teix means the yew tree in Catalan – though most of the yews were felled long ago. Bountiful, Es Teix furnished local villages with water and ice for the hotter months. It was also a provider of firewood for the hearth, of charcoal and of stones that, once crushed, fed the kilns to produce lime.

For views toward Sóller and Ses Cornadors, be sure to climb Es Teix's left-hand (easterly) summit, not the one with multiple crosses – otherwise you'll see nothing new. Some 10 minutes from the cairn is a small plain with a spring, the **Font de sa Serp**, where for most of the year you can replenish your water bottles.

Return to the junction with the main path at the head of the Vall de Cairats. Some 4¼ hours into the day, you reach the end of the archduke's path as the track widens and steepens to plunge down past a *casa de sa neu* (ice pit).

Just below is a shelter, originally the bunkhouse for the *neveras*, or snow

collectors. With benches and a hearth, it's pleasantly cool and dark on a hot day. But resist the temptation to lunch here if you've held out this far because in under 10 minutes you reach the **Font des Polls** (Spring of the Poplar Trees) with water and shaded benches (don't confuse it with the stagnant cistern a couple of minutes below the *refugio*). As you continue to descend, you pass several charcoal-burning circles with their characteristic green moss or sward and a lime kiln, where rock from Es Teix used to be crushed and slow fired to make lime for whitewashing houses.

About 4¾ hours into the walk, cross a large stile beside a locked gate to leave the estate of the eponymous archduke. Continue along the track and, at a fork, bear right over a cattle grid. Once you hit a sealed road about 15 minutes from the stile, bear right, then first left to drop to the main road. Turn right for Plaça Campdevànol and the bus stop – an anticlimactic final 15 minutes of blacktop at the end of an exhilarating day.

SÓLLER TO SA CALOBRA

Duration 6¼–7¼ hours

Distance 18km

Difficulty moderate

Start Sóller

Finish Sa Calobra

Nearest Towns Sóller (p257), Port de Sóller (p256)

Transport bus, boat

Summary A steepish, optional climb leads to the Mirador de ses Barques, from where the route descends to the Vall de Bàlitx and rises to the Coll de Biniamar to follow the cliff-side *corniche* to Cala Tuent and pass over the col to Sa Calobra.

A warm-up stroll through the Sóller valley is followed by a fairly hard slog up to the Mirador de ses Barques (which you can omit – as many walkers do – by taking the morning bus to this point). Woods give way to cultivation as you descend to the pleasantly fertile Vall de Bàlitx. Just after the Coll de Biniamar, a detour to the abandoned farm of Sa Costera (which you could omit, and save 45 minutes, if pushed for time) makes for a pleasant lunch stop. The great views of the bay of Racó de sa Taleca continue as you walk the cliff path.

At Cala Tuent, you can take time out for a swim, and also, in summer, catch a boat back to Port de Sóller. If you're continuing to Sa Calobra – as you must between October and May – allow yourself plenty of leeway to catch the last boat back to Port de Sóller (as there is only one, or sometimes two boats a day). The short sea trip, with spectacular views of the cliffs you recently walked, isn't the least of the day's pleasures.

If you begin at the *mirador*, deduct around 45 minutes from the total walking time. If you finish at Cala Tuent, knock off about an hour.

PLANNING
Maps
The best map is Editorial Alpina Walking Maps' 1:25,000 *Mallorca Tramuntana Central*. You can also try Discovery Walking Guides' 1:40,000 *Mallorca North & Mountains Tour & Trail Map* and the Freytag & Berndt 1:50,000 *Mallorca Tramuntana* map which both cover the route.

GETTING TO/FROM THE WALK
To begin the walk at the Mirador de ses Barques, take the morning bus for Pollença, which leaves Port de Sóller at 9am, calling by the Repsol petrol station on the Sóller bypass at 9.10am.

You need to catch the last boat back from Sa Calobra to Port de Sóller. The boat leaves at 2pm or 4.45pm, (€13), from April to October or just once a per week between November and March (check availability); miss it and we don't have to tell you that you're in trouble. The service is run by **Barcos Azules** (☎ 971 63 01 70; www .barcosazules.com). From Monday to Friday only in September, the boat also puts in at Cala Tuent at around 4.50pm.

THE WALK
Leave Plaça de sa Constitució in Sóller by Carrer de Sa Lluna. Take the second left onto Carrer de la Victoria 11 Maig and bear right beside a small bridge to follow the sign for Fornalutx. After about 10 minutes, turn right just before the high wall of the

village football stadium. Take the left turn at a three-way fork onto Carrer ses Moncades to meet a sign directing you towards Tuent and Sa Calobra. The trail, zigzagging quite steeply, crosses the sealed C710 road and continues northwards to the **Mirador de ses Barques**, reached around 45 minutes after leaving Sóller.

Leave the *mirador* by the steps on the upper, northeast side of the car park at a sign for Bàlitx, Sa Costera and Tuent. The path passes over a hillock to join a track, which you take to the left. Soon after, this merges with a wide cart track that runs beside an extensive olive plantation. About 25 minutes from the *mirador*, at the entrance to the farm of Bàlitx de Dalt, veer right through a gateway to enter the richly cultivated Vall de Bàlitx. Savour the twisted, gnarled olive trees – some of them reputed to be over 1000 years old. Ahead, on the valley's wooded northern flank, you can make out the winding path that will lead you up to the Coll de Biniamar.

About 300m into the valley, leave the main track at a hairpin bend to go straight ahead and down some cobbled steps. Just off route is the **Font de Bàlitx**, a reliable source of water except towards the end of summer in particularly dry years. Rejoin the wide cart track just before the forlorn, abandoned **Bàlitx d'es Mig**. Continue to a sign 'Agroturismo, Bàlitx d'Avall'. Don't follow it; turn left to take the more direct pedestrian route to the farm, down several flights of stone steps. This finely engineered way descends to **Bàlitx d'Avall** (also known as Bàlitx d' Abaix) to complete approximately 1¼ hours of walking from the *mirador*. It's well worth pausing at this substantial farm to down a glass of fresh orange juice, squeezed from the fruit of the surrounding orchards.

The track crosses the Torrent d'es Llorés stream bed to begin climbing in earnest. Blue trail markers stay with you as you toil until, 35 to 40 minutes from the farm, you reach the **Coll de Biniamar**. Thick tree foliage at first obscures views in any direction, but within five minutes a red-blazed side trail, overgrown in places, meanders off left to lonely **Sa Costera**.

This former farm overlooks the bay of Racó de sa Taleca, tantalisingly inaccessible some hundreds of metres below. The grounds themselves make an excellent picnic stop, with year-round water available

from a spring in a cave on the terrace behind and to the right of the house.

Return to the main trail, which narrows soon after the wooded vegetation begins to dwindle and becomes an exposed but quite safe walk along the flank of the cliff. Though it appears to run parallel to the contour lines, there's a surprising amount of up and down work, yet nothing too taxing, and the views are positively inspirational. About 35 minutes from the col, pass a side trail that drops to an abandoned shoreline hydroelectric plant. Continue along this fine *corniche* route through successive stone gates, until it meets a wide track and a lone farm about 1¼ hours beyond Coll de Biniamar and three hours from the *mirador*. Turn left and, after only 20m on a newly graded track, don't miss the flight of steps leading downwards to the left. After a brief stretch on another new road, drop left again down a path signed 'Tuent es Vergaret', then turn left yet again at a gravel road to take a path, marked by two cairns, down through the wood.

The path ends beside a **bar-restaurant**, perched on a knoll overlooking Cala Tuent, reached after about 3¼ hours from the *mirador*. From here, it's easy to drop down to the beach of sand and pebbles for a swim or a laze. (Here, on weekdays in summer, you have the option of catching a boat back to Port de Sóller; see Getting to/from the Walk, p251).

To continue to Sa Calobra, take the sealed road which leads via a series of bends to **Ermita de San Lorenzo** (Sant Llorenç), a 13th-century chapel clearly visible at the breach in the saddle to the northeast. As you follow the winding road up to the pass, resist the temptation to short-cut the hairpins; the distance saved is outweighed by the energy you'll expend clambering over boulders and forging your way through the scrub. Instead, resign yourself to this stretch of very lightly trafficked road and enjoy the changing perspectives of Cala Tuent below you.

Once at the col, go through a gate just beyond the *ermita* and take an ancient paved track, now sadly overgrown, its steps and stones ill-maintained, yet still discernible. At its end, turn left at the first house you meet, then left again when you hit the sealed road for an easy 15-minute descent to the clamour of Sa Calobra, teeming with day-trippers. Reward yourself with a drink at one of the **café terraces** as you wait for the boat to arrive.

Allow a generous 90 minutes to reach Sa Calobra from Cala Tuent. This gives you enough leeway to catch the late afternoon boat back to Sóller.

TORRENT DE PAREIS

Duration 4–4½ hours
Distance 6km
Difficulty moderate–demanding
Start Escorca
Finish Sa Calobra
Nearest Towns Sóller (p257), Port de Sóller (p256)
Transport bus, boat
Summary A steep descent along a switchback trail leads to the even steeper gorge of the Torrent de Pareis, Sa Calobra and the sea.

It's downhill all the way and it's only a little more than 6km. But you'll expend as much energy as you would on a full-day hike when you negotiate the Torrent de Pareis, Mallorca's deepest canyon – mostly by walking but sometimes scrambling and bringing all four limbs into play.

ENVIRONMENT

The Torrent de Pareis, believe it or not – and it is difficult to credit for much of the year, when it's reduced to a few residual pools – is the island's principal watercourse. Over the millennia rainwater has gouged a narrow gorge, in places more than 200m deep, through the soft limestone. The side valley of Sa Fosca, leading to the Torrent des Gorg Blau, is a Mallorcan mecca for cavers.

PLANNING
When to Walk

This is the one walk on Mallorca that's better done in summer. In winter, you may have to wade through pools. In the hotter months, although the first part of the walk down from the plateau is unshaded, the sun only fleetingly penetrates to the depths of the ravine. Even so, it's best to set off early

in the morning in order to avoid the worst of the heat.

What to Bring

Consider packing a pair of runners – lighter than boots and providing a better grip when you're scrambling over boulders or stretched at full length. After rain (see the Warning) you may need to take a length of rope.

Maps

You guessed it; the Editorial Alpina Walking Maps' 1:25,000 *Mallorca Tramuntana Central* is the best map. Discovery Walking Guides' 1:40,000 *Mallorca North & Mountains Tour & Trail Map* and the Freytag & Berndt 1:50,000 *Mallorca Tramuntana* map both cover the route, but you don't really need them.

GETTING TO/FROM THE WALK

For Escorca, take the morning bus for Pollença, which leaves Port de Sóller at 9am, calling by the Repsol petrol station on the Sóller bypass at 9.10am. Ask the driver to drop you off – Escorca, at the milepost signed 'Km 25', is only a couple of houses and is easily overrun. To return, you need to catch the last boat back from Sa Calobra to Port de Sóller (for details see p256).

THE WALK

Walk down the steep path opposite Restaurante Escorca. You can take lightly the litany of warnings on the adjacent sign; the advice to pack a wetsuit seems particularly like overkill. Follow the level path that runs along the boundary of **Ses Tanques de Baix**, a series of sheepfolds.

TORRENT DE PAREIS

WARNING

After a rainstorm, or if a cloudburst is predicted, there's a real risk of flash floods. Ring the **Grup d'Excursió Mallorqui** (☎ 871 94 79 00) – see also Palma de Mallorca (p255) – to ask about conditions in the gorge. Even if the descent is practicable, the rocks can be treacherously slippery until they dry.

After a little more than five minutes, take a sharp left through a metal gate and continue straight to the lip of the gorge, from where a well-defined path, rocky in places, makes a zigzagging descent (look out for its beginning about 10m before a natural hole in the rock-face overlooking the valley).

After 25 minutes you reach a small, round terrace with close-cropped sward. This former charcoal-burners' site is an ideal spot to pause and savour the view, where the only other evidence of humanity is the distant farm of Son Colomí on the opposite flank.

Soon after, the trail improves as you negotiate a series of long switchbacks. A **lone fig tree** marks around 45 minutes of unremittingly downhill hiking from the lip. Twenty metres beyond it, a seasonal spring drips from the rocks and a narrow trail, briefly much steeper and more of a clamber, begins its descent through rock and long grass to the bed of the Torrent de Lluc. Angle up onto its true left bank to find a path. This, though heavily overgrown with sharp grasses, is less taxing than battling your way over the boulders in the riverbed.

After passing between two giant, perpendicular cliffs and feeling pretty small, return to the stream bed; 20 minutes beyond the fig tree you'll reach **S'Entreforc**, the confluence where the smaller Torrent des Gorg Blau (Blue Ravine) joins the main valley from the southwest. Here begins the true Torrent de Pareis ('Pareis' meaning 'pair' in the Mallorcan dialect of Catalan).

On a large rock are four very faded, painted arrows labelled: 'Lluch' (Lluc), pointing back upstream; 'Sa Fosca', left; 'Calobra', straight ahead; and Millor no anar (Better not go), pointing at the

sheer, unassailable cliff wall on your right. Ho, ho!

Though the Torrent des Gorg Blau is for experienced cavers only, it's well worth briefly detouring to explore the first few hundred metres, known as Sa Fosca (The Darkness), an apt name for this narrow canyon, where the sun rarely penetrates to the base of its near-vertical walls.

Continue along the main gorge by taking a path on the true right bank, signalled by a green arrow, in order to avoid a jumble of boulders. This threads back to the riverbed after little more than five minutes.

Now the fun really begins as you climb down the first of the three areas of giant boulders, easing yourself through a pair of narrow chimneys. Take care as the rock is slippery from the rubbing of so many boots and bums – and particularly treacherous after rain. Then comes a brief easy stretch where you can stride out along the unencumbered stream bed before the valley narrows drastically.

When you're about 1¼ hours from the confluence, look for a path on the true left bank that will take you above and around another boulder-strewn defile. Work your way around the right face of a huge monolith then left of another giant (aided by a rope anchored around the rock). Your reward is the **Font des Degotis**, a spring where water drips from the fronds on the rock wall. Here you can quench your thirst and even take a natural shower.

Two hours from the confluence you must again take evasive action, this time up the true right bank to bypass a pair of monoliths and what, in summer, may still be a couple of late-season pools.

Soon after, the gorge at last opens out. A final flat stretch takes you to the small **beach** of Sa Calobra's eastern cove where, if you can find a spare square metre, you can relax on the shingle and cool off in the sea. A pedestrian tunnel leads to the thronged port and the boat to **Port de Sóller**.

MORE WALKS

Some good walks radiate out from the hamlet of Lluc (also spelt Lluch), east of Sóller and at the eastern limit of the most exciting stretch of the Tramuntana. The village has at least three places to eat and you can stay in the austere 18th-century monastery, **Santuari de Lluc** (☎ 971 87 15 25, fax 971 51 70 96; s/d/tr/six-beds with bathroom €21/32.50/37/42).

Editorial Alpina Walking Maps' 1:25,000 *Mallorca Tramuntana North/Central/South* includes all routes, Discovery Walking Guides' 1:40,000 *Mallorca North & Mountains Tour & Trail Map* covers the first two walks. The Freytag & Berndt 1:50,000 *Mallorca Tramuntana* map includes all three.

Lluc to Embassament de Cúber

This 14km, 4¼- to 4¾-hour walk interlinks with the route between Sóller and the Embassament de Cúber described earlier in the chapter. It continues the old pilgrim route. Make an earlyish start so that you can pick up the return bus to Lluc that passes by the dam head at about 3.30pm.

Lluc to Torre de Lluc

You'll have to plan ahead for this one since access is only permitted on Sundays (see the boxed text, Mallorca's Blocked Passages, p241). The route (19km, 4½ to five hours one way) leads from the monastery to a magnificent coastal viewpoint beside an old watchtower. About 1¾ hours of walking brings you to the cave houses of Coscona, while a little over 15 minutes beyond are the ruins of an old customs house, unattractive in themselves but offering great views (you can always make this more easily accessible spot your goal for the day).

Lluc to Pollença

This route takes you from the Monestir de Lluc to the attractive inland town of Pollença, following the old *camino* – now little travelled and superseded by the modern highway. It's an undemanding 20km walk that will take you between 4½ to five hours – and luckily you don't have to be up with the dawn to arrive in time to catch the 4.35pm bus back from Pollença to Lluc.

The Dry-Stone Route (GR221)

A fantastic new long-distance trail covering 135km is partially ready and waiting for keen hikers. Much of the route takes advantage of the old cobbled paths linking the villages and estates on the Serra and passes through a memorable human landscape of olive groves built onto row after row of dry-stone wall terraces. The GR221 crosses the Serra de Tramuntana from the Port d'Andratx (in the south of the island) to Pollença (in the north) and some buildings have been restored as mountain hostels. Various alternative sections have been planned, which will go by way of Peguera, Es Capdellà, Castell d'Alaró, Bunyola and Cala Tuent. The work restoring the paths and the buildings is being carried out by the Department of the Environment of the *Consell Insular de Mallorca*. The currently open sections follow public paths and cross public land, but the fact that most of the Serra is private property will likely lead to delays in opening the entire route. In time, it will be an eight-stage walk with a mountain hostel (*refugis*) waiting for you at the end of each day.

TOWNS & FACILITIES

PALMA DE MALLORCA

☎ 971 / pop 396,600

The islands' only true city, this is an agreeable, albeit crowded, spot to pass through.

Information

The Consell de Mallorca's **tourist office** (☎ 17 39 90; Plaça de la Reina 2; 9am-8pm Mon-Fri, 10am-2pm Sat) covers the whole island.

La Casa del Mapa (☎ /fax 22 59 45; Carrer Sant Domingo 11) has a comprehensive selection of large-scale Mallorca maps. **Librería Fondevila** (☎ 72 56 16; Costa de la Pols 18) also carries a good stock of maps and guidebooks.

The **Grup d'Excursió Mallorqui** (GEM; ☎ 71 88 23; www.gemweb.org; Carrer Doctor Andreu Feliu 20; 7-9pm Mon-Fri) has friendly members and a pretty good library.

Supplies & Equipment

A good range of walking gear, and a smaller selection of walking books, are available at **Es Refugi** (Vía Sindicat 21) and **Foracorda** (Carrer Miquel Marquès 20).

MALLORCA

Sleeping & Eating

Hostal Pons (☎ 72 26 58; Carrer del Vi 8; s/d without bathroom €25/45) Seemingly untouched since the 1880s the downstairs rooms are cluttered with antiques and artwork.

Hostal Corona (☎ 73 19 35; www.hostal -corona.com; Carrer de Josep Villalonga 22; s €30, d €45-55) Simple rooms with timber furnishings and old tiled floors and a fantastic botanical bonanza garden make this a firm favourite.

A mess of eateries and bars caters to Palma's visitors in the maze of streets between Plaça de la Reina and the port. **Bar España** (☎ 72 42 34; Carrer de Ca'n Escurrac 12; mains €15-20), is enormously popular, offering excellent Basque *pintxos* (tapas) at reasonable prices. Veggies should head to **Sa Pastanaga** (☎ 72 41 94; Carrer de Sant Elies 6B; meals €12.20; Mon-Sat, lunch only) which does a fantastic set vegetarian lunch.

Getting There & Away

There's a daily stream of charter flights into Palma from Europe, especially from the UK and Germany, for details see Air (p351).

Iberia, Air Europa, Veuling and Spanair operate scheduled flights from major Spanish cities.

If coming from the mainland then it's far more romantic, though not a lot cheaper, to travel by boat. **Trasmediterranea** (☎ 902 45 46 45; www.trasmediterranea.com) runs daily sea transport between Palma and both Barcelona (3¾ to seven hours) and Valencia (4¼ to 7¼ hours). Duration and price (€47-90) to/from each depends upon the kind of vessel.

Palma's train station is on Plaça d'Espanya. The bus station is on Carrer Eusebi Estada, just northeast of the train station. Tourist offices and both stations carry a pamphlet listing bus times and routes throughout the island, and Palma–Sóller train times.

POLLENÇA
☎ 971 / pop 16,500

Pollença is the prettiest village in the north of the island and the natural finish to the long-distance GR221 trail, which runs from Port d'Andratx along the whole Tramuntana mountain range to Pollença.

Information

Tourist office (☎ 53 50 77; Carrer Sant Domingo, 17; 9am-2pm & 2.30-4pm Mon-Fri, 10am-1pm Sun Mar-Oct).

Sleeping & Eating

A 10-minute walk from the main square, near a stone bridge built by the Romans, is **Refugi del Pont Romà** (☎ 17 37 00; dm beds €11). A comfortable place, it provides meals as well.

Pensión Bellavista (☎ 86 46 00; www .pensionbellavista.com; Carrer Monges 14, Port de Pollença; s/d with bathroom €35/60) Located in a traditional house with a fresh, green garden in nearby Port de Pollença, this is a solid choice with a great atmosphere and friendly management.

Pollença and Port de Pollença are full of restaurants, for all budgets.

Getting There & Away

Buses leave every hour for Palma with **Autocares Transunion Mallorca** (☎ 43 04 01) and twice daily between Port de Sóller and Port de Pollença – a spectacular drive over the mountains.

PORT DE SÓLLER
☎ 971 / pop 11,000

Port de Sóller has a fairly wide choice of hotels. It's essential to reserve ahead in high summer.

Information

There's a small **tourist office** (☎ 63 30 42; Carrer Canonge Oliver 10; 9am-1pm & 2.30-5pm Mon-Fri, 10am-1pm Sat Mar-Oct).

Sleeping & Eating

A 45-minute walk from Port de Sóller, beside the lighthouse, is **Refugi Muleta** (☎ 17 37 00; dm beds €10). Open only to walkers and cyclists who all share one large dorm, it also provides meals and the warden is a qualified mountain guide and a mine of information about walking in the Tramuntana.

Hotel Brisas (☎ 63 13 52; www.hotel -brisas.com; Camí del Far 15; d with break-fast €60), on the lighthouse road, is small by Port de Sóller standards and family run.

The whole sweep of the bay is bordered by restaurants and cafés for every palate and pocket.

Getting There & Away

A rumbly tram (€4), with regular departures about every half-hour between 7am and 9pm, runs between Sóller and Port de Sóller. There's also an express bus that runs hourly between Palma and Port de Sóller via Sóller's Plaça de América. See also Getting There & Away for Sóller (below).

SÓLLER

☎ 971 / pop 1400

The ochre town of Sóller, set amid citrus groves and completely dominated by the solid walls of the Serra de Tramuntana is one of the more attractive villages on the island. This is especially so after the huge numbers of day visitors, who travel up here on the train from Palma and the rickety tram from Port de Sóller, retreat back home.

Information

The **tourist office** (☎ 63 80 08; www .sollernet.com; Plaça d'Espanya; 9.30am-2pm & 3-5pm Mon-Fri, 10am-1pm Sat & Sun, closed Sun Nov-Feb) is in an old train carriage beside the station.

Librería Calabruix (☎ 63 26 41; Carrer Sa Lluna) stocks a limited range of walking maps and guidebooks.

Forn de Campos (Calle Jeroni Estades 8) bakery has a couple of internet points.

Sleeping & Eating

The countryside around Sóller is jam packed with stylish boutique hotels many of which are featured on www.sollernet.com.

Hotel El Guía (☎ 63 02 27; www .sollernet.com/elguia; s/d with bathroom €51/80) is handily located beside the train station. It's a great place to meet fellow hikers. The bright rooms feature timber trims and good amenities including modern bathrooms.

It's advisable to book rooms ahead – except, paradoxically, between July and September, when most visitors to Mallorca are stretched out on the beaches.

THE SLOW CHUG NORTH TO SÓLLER

A delightful journey into the past is also a pleasing way to head north for Sóller. Since 1912, a **narrow-gauge train** (☎ 971 75 20 51, 902 36 47 11; http//:trendesoller .com; one way/return €10/17, child 3-6yr half price, under 3yr free) has trundled along this winding 27.3km route. The teetering timber-panelled train trundles out of Plaça de l'Estació seven times daily and takes 1¼ hours. You pass through ever-changing countryside that becomes dramatic in the north as it crosses the Serra de Alfàbia, offering fabulous views over Sóller and the sea on the final descent into town.

Cas Carreter (☎ 63 51 33; Carrer del Cetre 9; meals €25-30) occupies an old cart workshop, and produces excellent cooking using as many local ingredients as possible.

Getting There & Away

For information on trains between Palma and Sóller see the boxed text above.

An express bus runs hourly between Palma and Port de Sóller stopping in Sóller's Plaça de América and in Port de Sóller.

For a taxi, call **Radio Taxi Sóller** (☎ 63 84 84). Prices to/from Sóller include Port de Sóller €8, Deià €21, Embassament de Cúber €26, Valldemossa €31 and Sa Calobra €48.

VALLDEMOSSA

☎ 971 / pop 1900

Valldemossa is an attractive blend of tree-lined streets, old stone houses and impressive new villas. There is little in the way of accommodation aside from the superb **Es Petit Hotel** (☎ 61 24 79; s/d €113/125). For food you'll find a sprinkling of cheerful restaurants decorating the streets.

MALLORCA

Andalucía

- Poking your nose into the beautiful green valleys and endlessly varied karstic mountainscapes of the **Parque Natural de Cazorla** (p262) and **Sierra de Grazalema** (p288)
- Zigzagging along medieval stone paths between the blisteringly white villages of the **Alpujarras** (p267)
- Playing peek-a-boo with the clouds while scrambling through mainland Spain's highest range on the **Sierra Nevada Traverse** (p278)
- Dancing along dramatic desert cliffs above moonstone-blue Mediterranean waters on the **Cabo de Gato Coast** walk (p284)

Area: 87,000 sq km	Average summer high: 36°C	Population: 7.9 million

Andalucía is all the clichés of Spain rolled into one sensory overload. It's searing light, sultry flamenco nights and blood-soaked bull-fighting afternoons. It's Islamic art and holiday excess on the Costas. It's everything that you ever hoped Spain would be and much that you didn't expect. And of the unexpected, the most delightful surprise is the region's natural attractions – large tracts of beautiful, rugged mountain country, gorgeous green river valleys, abundant wildlife and long stretches of dramatic coast that are a far cry from torrid Torremolinos. Half of Andalucía is hills or mountains, including mainland Spain's highest peak, Mulhacén (3479m), and for now the trails and back paths of this steamy southern region remain blissfully uncluttered with other hikers.

Northerners might imagine Andalucía is too hot for much walking; in fact, for about half the year the climate is ideal. But in some areas trail-marking is still relatively sparse, so there is ample opportunity to use your navigational skills. Walking for pleasure took off much later in Andalucía than in northern Spain, and you'll rarely encounter anything like a crowd on any walk. Remember the walk times we give do not include stops, so allow extra time to look at maps, chew olives, peer through your binoculars at eagles and flamingos, snooze under oak trees and gaze at all those gorgeous Andalucían panoramas.

ANDALUCÍA

HISTORY

In AD 711 the Muslim general Tariq ibn Ziyad landed at Gibraltar with 10,000 men. Somewhere on the Río Guadalete in western Andalucía, his forces decimated the Visigoth army, and within a few years the Muslims had overrun most of the Iberian Peninsula.

The Andalucían cities Córdoba (756–1031), Seville (1040–1248), then Granada (1248–1492) took turns as the leading city of Muslim Spain or, as it was called, Al-Andalus (from which Andalucía is derived). At its peak in the 10th century Córdoba was the biggest, most cultured city in Western Europe. Andalucía's Islamic heritage is one of its most fascinating aspects. This is not only a matter of great buildings, such as Granada's Alhambra and Córdoba's Mezquita, but also of gardens, food, music and more. Many of the villages you walk through preserve their labyrinthine Muslim street layout, and the irrigation and terracing of much of the Andalucían countryside have similar roots.

Andalucía fell to the Christian *Reconquista* in stages between 1214 and 1492. The Muslims soon faced a variety of repressive measures, which sparked revolts in Andalucía in 1500 and 1568. They were finally expelled from Spain between 1609 and 1614.

Columbus' 'discovery' of the Americas in 1492 brought great wealth to the ports of Seville and, later, Cádiz, but the Andalucían countryside sank into a profound decline, with noble landowners turning formerly productive food-growing land over to sheep. By the late 19th century rural Andalucía – especially the west – was a hotbed of anarchist unrest, and during the Spanish Civil War Andalucía split along class lines, with savage atrocities committed by both sides. The hungry years after the war were particularly hungry here, and between 1950 and 1970 1.5 million Andalucíans left to find work in industrial northern Spain and other European countries.

Since the 1960s a coastal tourism boom, a series of community works schemes, better welfare provisions, massive EU subsidies for agriculture and tourism-driven construction have made a big difference. Andalucía today is increasingly prosperous, its major cities are bright, cosmopolitan places, its villages full of life and its people the most flamboyant in Spain.

ENVIRONMENT

In basic geographic terms, Andalucía consists of two east–west mountain chains separated by the valley of the Río Guadalquivir, plus a coastal plain. Of the two mountain chains, the low Sierra Morena rolls along Andalucía's northern borders, while the higher Cordillera Bética is a mass of rugged ranges that broadens out from the southwest to the east; it includes mainland Spain's highest peak, Mulhacén (3479m), in the Sierra Nevada southeast of Granada, and the collection of ranges that make up the Parque Natural de Cazorla in northeast Andalucía, where several peaks top 2000m. Much of the Cordillera Bética is limestone, the erosion of which over the millennia has produced some wonderful karstic rock formations.

With more than 80 protected areas, covering some 15,000 sq km (well over half of all the environmentally protected land in Spain), Andalucía has huge appeal for nature lovers. Its vast range of plants (around 5000 species, some 150 of them unique) is largely due to the fact that the last Ice Age was relatively temperate at this southerly latitude, allowing plants which were killed off further north to survive. The mountains harbour much of the variety.

Among animals, the ibex numbers perhaps 30,000 in Andalucía and you may see it on several walks. In the Parque Natural de Cazorla, chances are high of spotting fallow deer, and reasonable for red deer, wild boar and mouflon, a wild sheep.

Andalucía is a magnet for bird-lovers, with 13 resident raptor species and several summer visitors from Africa. The Sierra de Grazalema has a large population of griffon vultures. Andalucía is also a haven for water birds, mainly thanks to extensive wetlands along the Atlantic coast. The beautiful greater flamingo can be seen in large numbers in several places including on the Cabo de Gata Coast walk.

CLIMATE

Andalucía is the most southerly and, overall, warmest part of peninsula Spain. On the coast it's temperate in winter and

ANDALUCÍA

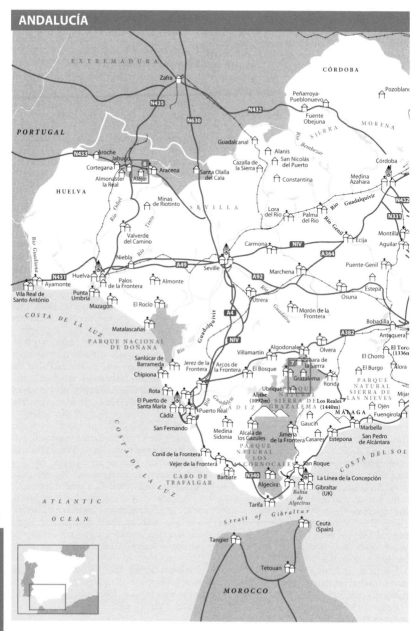

hot in summer. Inland, temperatures are more extreme and the climate can be cold and inclement from November to February but sizzling in July and August. Daytime temperatures in these hottest months reach 36°C in inland cities, and about 30°C on

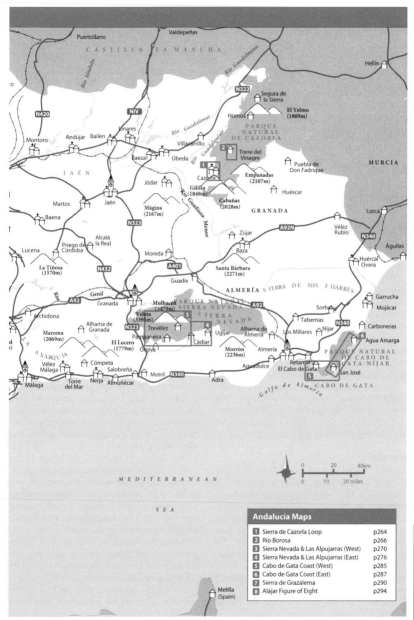

the coasts. From December to February it regularly gets down to near-freezing at night in Granada.

Average daily minimum temperatures in the high Sierra Nevada in winter can get as low as -9°C.

Most places get 400mm to 500mm of rain a year (a little less than London), the majority of it falls from October to March; there's little from June to September. Most mountain ranges get at least a dusting of snow most winters, and the upper Sierra Nevada is white for eight or nine months a year.

PLANNING
When to Walk
The best months are April to June, September and October – when the weather is warm, but not too warm, and the vegetation is at its most colourful (spring flowers, autumn leaves). The one major exception is the Sierra Nevada (best in July and August).

Maps
Michelin's 1:400,000 *Southern Spain* map, is good for overall planning. It's widely available in and outside Andalucía.

Published large-scale maps of Andalucía should be regarded as approximations to reality – useful, but never fully to be trusted. They're OK on contours, courses of rivers and other natural features, but when it comes to paths and tracks, they show a lot that don't exist, and ignore many that do exist. See the Planning sections of individual walks for specific recommendations.

Most recommended maps are fairly easily obtained in the walk areas, but it's always worth visiting map and bookshops in cities on the way, such as the Gateways and Access Towns in this chapter.

Books
Lonely Planet's *Andalucía* fills out the picture for those who want to experience everything this amazing region offers. It includes plenty of detail on all the walking areas featured in this book. *Walking in Andalucía*, by Guy Hunter-Watts, has detailed descriptions and maps of 36 good day walks. Among Spanish-language walking guides, we recommend the two-volume *Excursiones por el Sur de España*, by Juan Carlos García Gallego. Volume I includes Las Alpujarras and the Sierra Nevada; Volume II covers the Parque Natural de Cazorla.

For historical, cultural and social background, the erudite but irreverent *Andalucía*, by Michael Jacobs, is hard to

beat. It's hard to locate but naturalists will find *A Selection of Wildflowers of Southern Spain*, by Betty Molesworth Allen, and, the much easier to find, *Where to Watch Birds in Southern & Western Spain*, by Ernest Garcia, Andrew Paterson and Christopher Helm, very useful, but you will want a field guide with pictures to complement the latter. See Planning (p25) for further book recommendations.

GATEWAYS
Malaga (p300), Granada (p298) and Seville (p301) are the big smokes you should be aiming to arrive at. Malaga is best for the Sierra Nevada region and the Sierra de Grazalema, Granada for the Sierra Nevada and the Parque Natural de Cazorla, while Seville, the capital of Andalucía is the top choice for the Sierra de Grazalema and the Sierra de Aracena.

PARQUE NATURAL DE CAZORLA

The Parque Natural de las Sierras de Cazorla, Segura y Las Villas (to give it its full title), in Jaén province in northeast Andalucía, is, at 2143 sq km, the largest protected area in Spain. It's a crinkled, pinnacled region of several complicated *sierras* (mountain ranges) – not extraordinarily high, but memorably beautiful – divided by high plains and deep river valleys. Much of the park is thickly forested and wild animals are abundant and visible– a big attraction.

The park stretches 90km from north to south, with most of its ranges aligned roughly north–south. The Guadalquivir, Andalucía's longest river, rises in the south of the park, between the Sierra de Cazorla and Sierra del Pozo, and flows 60km north into the Embalse del Tranco de Beas reservoir, where it turns west towards the Atlantic.

It's in the south of the park – where millions of years of erosion of limestone and dolomitic rocks have created the most marvellous karstic mountainscapes – that we have chosen the day-walks in this section. They're separate walks, not one circuit, because in this southern area the only bus service and all the places to stay – including the camping grounds, which are the only places you are allowed to camp – are along the Guadalquivir valley. Thus anywhere more than half a day's walk from the Guadalquivir or from the park's fringe towns is out of reach for people without a vehicle. The ideal way to explore the park is with a vehicle to reach day walks in some of its more remote areas.

HISTORY

In the 18th century these sparsely populated *sierras* were turned over to the Spanish navy, which had many of the native oaks and black pines floated downriver to be made into ships at Cádiz or Cartagena. In 1960, 710 sq km in what's now the southern part of the park were declared a *coto nacional de caza* (national hunting reserve). This greatly increased the numbers of larger animals by subjecting hunting to strict controls, reintroducing species that had been hunted to extinction here such as the red deer and wild boar, and introducing new species.

The *parque natural* (nature park) was created in 1986 in response to a surge in tourism that was threatening the area's ecological balance. The park attempts to conserve the environment while promoting compatible economically beneficial activities, such as responsible forestry, agriculture and tourism.

ENVIRONMENT

The Parque Natural de Cazorla has Andalucía's biggest forests, with pine species predominant. The tall black pine, with its horizontally spreading branches typically clustered near the top, generally likes the higher terrain above 1300m. The other two main pine species, introduced here for timber, are the maritime pine, with its typically rounded top, growing at elevations up to about 1500m, and the Aleppo pine, with a bushy top and separated, often bare branches, predominant at warmer, drier levels up to 1100m.

PLANNING

When to Walk

The walking is best from April to June and in September and October. At these times temperatures are moderate and the number of other visitors (except in Semana Santa – Easter Week) should be well below the summer holiday peak.

Maps

The Editorial Alpina 1:40,000 *Sierra de Cazorla* map is the best for all three walks. You should be able to find it in Cazorla town if you haven't obtained it beforehand.

Information Sources

The park's main visitors centre is the **Centro de Visitantes Torre del Vinagre**

CAZORLA WILDLIFE

The big five animal species here are the ibex, mouflon, wild boar, red deer and the smaller fallow deer. All are subject to controlled hunting: indeed the fallow deer and the mouflon (a large, reddish-brown, wild sheep) were introduced here in the 1960s specifically for hunting.

The ibex lives mainly on rocky heights but we have also seen it on the Río Borosa walk. It numbers several thousand and increasing. The other four big animals prefer forests – as does the fairly common red squirrel.

The likelihood of seeing wildlife improves as you get further away from the beaten track. The chances are also higher early and late in the day – deer are most likely to emerge onto open grassy areas at these times. While walking it's very likely you'll come across areas of upturned earth where wild boars have rooted for food. If you're lucky enough to see some boar then don't worry as, unlike popular myth states, they aren't dangerous and are far more likely to just scamper off in the opposite direction as soon as they notice you.

Some 140 bird species nest in the park. Rocky crags are the haunt of golden and Bonelli's eagles, griffon and Egyptian vultures and peregrine falcons. Something of an emblem of the park, but one you'd be very lucky to see, is the lammergeier, Europe's largest bird of prey. In 1986 it disappeared from the park, its only Spanish habitat outside the Pyrenees, but an attempt is being made to reintroduce it.

(☎ 953 71 30 40; 10am-2pm & 4-7pm Apr-Jun, 10am-2pm & 5-8pm Jul-Aug, 10am-2pm & 4-6pm Nov-Mar), on the A319 16km northeast of Empalme del Valle and 33km northeast of Cazorla. The centre provides plenty of information on the park as well as various interactive displays and a small museum and botanic garden. Tourist information offices in Cazorla town can also be useful.

ACCESS TOWN

See Cazorla (p297).

SIERRA DE CAZORLA LOOP

Duration 6½ hours
Distance 17km
Difficulty easy–moderate
Start/Finish Cazorla (p297)
Transport bus
Summary A panoramic loop in the Sierra de Cazorla combining mountain and woodland scenery.

This walk takes you right round the hills that rise impressively to the south and east of Cazorla town. Take water for the walk.

GETTING TO/FROM THE WALK

For more on getting to and from the walk see Cazorla p297.

THE WALK

Leave Cazorla's handsome Plaza de Santa María by Camino de San Isicio, which runs behind the 400-year-old Fuente de las Cadenas. Continue straight ahead until you reach the fork where you'll see a sign pointing left to Castillo de Cinco Esquinas. Follow this and, roughly five minutes later, you'll reach the start of the track proper, which is now signed to Puerto del Guililo and heads off to the left. You simply follow these signs and the green and white waymarking, past views of the Castillo de Cinco Esquinas (Castle of Five Corners) for around 40 minutes until you lay eyes on the 17th-century Monasterio de Montesión in a beautiful fold of the hills just off to your right. The monastery was built in 1625 by Julian Ferrer and was once busy with monks and the routine of their ministrations. Today only one monk of a hermitic order remains.

From the leftward (southeast) bend where the monastery came into view, take a lesser track up to the east following the green and white waymarking. After a few minutes turn right along the second track crossing this. Immediately bend left and wind up through pines to emerge on a broad vehicle track after 15 minutes. Go left along this for nearly 10 minutes then, where you see the sign for Puerto del Guililo, turn sharp right as the sign indicates (almost doubling back on yourself). After about 15 minutes, turn left (south) onto a lesser path at a small cairn. This soon becomes an excellent, clear path, climbing gradually through the pine woods. After about 25 minutes you emerge from tree cover and start to enjoy ever better views of the crags above and the sea of olive trees rolling over the plains below (Jaén province produces 10% of the world's olive oil). A further 25 minutes upward brings you to the 1750m **Puerto del Gilillo** pass, where fine eastward views open out and give you the chance to relish in the beauty of the park's contours

SIERRA DE CAZORLA LOOP

all around you. There's a small stone shelter just below the pass.

To cap **Gilillo** (1848m), the highest peak in this area of the park (just over 1000m higher than Cazorla), head 15 minutes south from the pass. Back at the pass, take the northward path from the left-hand (west) side of the stone hut again following the green arrows. This wends through dry, scrubby vegetation along the **Loma de los Castellones** ridge, with alternating eastern and western panoramas. Griffon vultures like to cruise the air currents along here. The path is mostly clear but after 15 minutes, going down the far (north) side of the hump marked 1732m on the Editorial Alpina map, you need to fork left at a faint green arrow on a rock; you're soon continuing in the same direction as before. Ignore a right turn by three cairns around 15 minutes later, and after another 20 minutes cross a grassy basin to join a track coming from the right. A further 10 minutes along you reach the **Puerto del Tejo** pass (1556m), with a three-way path junction.

Go left and follow the path as it winds around **Cerro de la Laguna** and descends northward. Around an hour from Puerto del Tejo you reach the *cortijo* (farm) **Prado Redondo**, an enchanting spot. A few metres before the house turn left at the fork and head downhill, keeping the house on your right and following the waymarkers. The path can be a little hard to follow over this section but if you stick to the following directions then you should be fine. The path bends left (southwest) and descends into a gully, around seven minutes from Prado Redondo: follow it down the gully right. Soon after it curves westward out of the gully to pass above the Castillo Templario de la Iruela (the Knights Templar castle of La Iruela village) and arrives at the **Ermita de la Virgen de la Cabeza** (45 minutes from Prado Redondo), with views over Cazorla town below. From the chapel turn left and head downhill along the path running through forest to emerge on the paved La Iruela-El Chorro road opposite the **Mirador Merenderos de Cazorla**. A path down to the right of the *mirador* (lookout) heads down into Cazorla and you'll reach the town centre in 20 minutes.

RÍO BOROSA

Duration 6–7 hours
Distance 24km
Difficulty moderate
Start/Finish Centro de Visitantes Torre del Vinagre
Nearest Town Cazorla (p297)
Transport bus
Summary Exquisite valley and mountain scenery as you ascend a tributary of the Guadalquivir, via a narrow gorge and two tunnels, to two beautiful mountain lakes.

The Cazorla park's best-known walk follows the Río Borosa (also called Aguas Negras) upstream through scenery that progresses from the simply pretty to jaw-droppingly majestic.

PLANNING
Try to avoid the times when there will be large numbers of other people on the route: Easter, July, August and fine spring and autumn weekends.

The route is dotted with good trackside springs, the last of these at the Central Eléctrica. Carry a water bottle that you can fill there with enough water to take you to the top of the walk and back (about three hours). A torch (flashlight) is comforting, if not essential, in the tunnels.

GETTING TO/FROM THE WALK
The start and finish point is the Centro de Visitantes Torre del Vinagre (see Information Sources, p263). Using the Cazorla-Coto Ríos bus service, which stops at Torre del Vinagre, you can do the walk in a day trip from Cazorla.

Carcesa (☎ 953 72 11 42) runs buses from Cazorla's Plaza de la Constitución to Coto Ríos via Torre del Vinagre.

THE WALK
This walk starts off very easy and becomes gradually more difficult, but its there-and-back nature means that you can make an about-turn at any point along the route.

Opposite the Centro de Visitantes Torre del Vinagre, take a road east off the A319 signed 'Central Eléctrica'. This crosses the

RÍO BOROSA

The first section is along a dirt road which twice crosses the tumbling, trout-rich river as you move up the narrow, lush valley. After 40 minutes, where the road starts climbing to the left, take a path forking right. This leads through a beautiful, 20-minute section where the valley narrows to a gorge, the **Cerrada de Elías**, and the path briefly takes to a wooden walkway to save you from swimming.

You re-emerge on the dirt road and reach the Central Eléctrica, a small hydroelectric transformer station, 40 minutes later.

A path passes between the power station and river to a 'Nacimiento de Aguas Negras, Laguna de Valdeazores' sign directing you upwards. The karstic mountainscape begins to look like a Chinese landscape painting as the river beside you descends a series of high rock steps in waterfalls. Unfortunately the flow here is sometimes diminished because some of the waters have been diverted for the power station. Around 40 minutes from the power station, the path turns left to cross below a cliff, then within 10 minutes turns sharp right to enter a **tunnel** inside the cliff. Water for the power station passes through the tunnel too: your narrow path is separated from the watercourse by a fence. The tunnel is dimly lit by a few openings in the rock wall for most of its five-minute length.

Then there's five minutes in the open air before you enter a second tunnel, one minute long. From this you emerge just

Guadalquivir and, 1.5km from the A319, passes a *piscifactoría* (fish farm), with parking areas close by. The road then crosses the Río Borosa. Turn right at this point and follow the track along the north side of the river.

COTO

You see this word scrawled over every part of the Spanish countryside. On rocks, signs, walls, on the ground, by roadsides, in forests. With a variety of companion words – Coto Privado, Coto Nacional, Coto Deportivo de Caza, Coto Municipal San Isidro, Coto X4204, Coto Torrox – but most mysteriously on its own, over and over again: COTO, COTO, COTO.

Is it a football team? A political movement? The latest teen music sensation? No. Like so many things in the Spanish countryside, it's to do with *la caza* (hunting). One – perhaps the original – meaning of *coto* is cairn or boundary marker, but it has come to mean an area on which hunting rights are restricted to a certain person or group – be they private individuals (*coto privado*), a municipality (*coto municipal*), or even the nation (*coto nacional* or *reserva nacional de caza*). *Cotos privados* are often also signalled by small, rectangular signs divided diagonally into a black triangle and a white triangle. Publicly owned hunting rights are normally shared out, by methods including lottery, among individuals who apply for them for a season. So that there will still be animals and birds to be hunted the following year, there are complicated rules and regulations, even on *cotos privados*, about which animals can be shot, where and when.

As for plain old *coto* on its own, the only thing you can be sure of is that – even if you were inclined to – you can't shoot nothin' in there.

SLEEPING AROUND TORRE DEL VINAGRE

While Cazorla is an adequate base for this walk there's also a variety of places to stay on and near the A319 within a few kilometres of Torre del Vinagre. All the following can be reached by the Cazorla-Coto Ríos bus service (see Getting to/from the Walk).

Hotel de Montaña Los Parrles (☎ 953 12 61 70; s/d €35/44, half/full board €12.50/22.50 per day extra) Along the road to Hornos this cheerful place has idyllic views of the reservoir and a country-style dining room.

Hotel de Montaña La Hortizuela (☎ 953 71 30 13; www.lahortizuela.com, in Spanish; s/d €38/58), 2km north from Torre del Vinagre, then 1km up a side road, is a cosy small hotel in a tranquil setting, with a good restaurant offering a €12 *menú del día* (fixed-price meal). There are wild boar in the surrounding woods.

Further north is **Camping Chopera Coto Ríos** (☎ 953 71 30 05; camping for two people with tent and a car €15), with a rather cramped but shady site by the side road into Coto Ríos. From October to April it's worth ringing to confirm it's open.

below the dam holding back the **Laguna de Aguas Negras,** a picturesque little reservoir surrounded by hills and trees. You have ascended 550m from the Río Guadalquivir to reach this point. A few minutes up the valley to the southeast is the **Nacimiento de Aguas Negras,** where the Borosa wells out from under a rock. A 15-minute walk south from the reservoir brings you to a similar-sized natural lake, the **Laguna de Valdeazores** – altogether about 3½ hours walking from Torre del Vinagre.

Return the way you came, unless you happen to have vehicle support, in which case you could continue 4km southwest to be picked up at the Collado de la Fuente Bermejo.

SIERRA NEVADA & LAS ALPUJARRAS

A casual visitor to the Alhambra in Granada will see, except perhaps from July to October, an imposing line of snow-topped mountains to the southeast. This is the western end of the Sierra Nevada, which includes mainland Spain's highest peak, Mulhacén (3479m), and two others over 3000m.

On the south side of the Sierra Nevada lies one of the oddest, most picturesque crannies of Andalucía, the 70km-long jumble of valleys called Las Alpujarras,

or La Alpujarra. Here, deep ravines cut through arid hillsides, and oasis-like villages are surrounded by vegetable gardens and groves of olives, figs, almonds, chestnuts, holm-oaks and other useful trees.

The walks in this section – the two two-day Alpujarras walks and the three-day Sierra Nevada Traverse – can be linked together. A snag however is that their optimum seasons differ (see the Planning section of each walk): the second half of June and the first three weeks of September are the least uncomfortable crossover times. The Alpujarras walks are easily divisible or extendable.

The upper parts of the Sierra Nevada form the 862-sq-km Parque Nacional Sierra Nevada, Spain's biggest national park, created in 1998. Surrounding this on the lower slopes of the range, and including many Alpujarras villages, is the separate, 848-sq-km Parque Natural Sierra Nevada, less stringently protected.

HISTORY

In Muslim times Las Alpujarras grew prosperous supplying the textile workshops of Almería, Granada and Málaga with silk thread, spun from the unravelled cocoons of the silk moth. Together with irrigated agriculture, this activity probably supported a population of more than 150,000 before the fall of Granada in 1492.

Christian promises of tolerance for the conquered Muslims soon gave way to forced mass conversions and land expropriations, and in 1500 Muslims rebelled across

ANDALUCÍA

ALPUJARRAS VILLAGES

Travellers who have been to Morocco may notice a resemblance between villages in the Alpujarras and those in Morocco's Atlas mountains, from where the Alpujarran style was introduced in the Moorish era times by Berber settlers. The huddled white houses seem to clamber over each other in an effort not to slide down the hillsides. Streets too narrow for vehicles ramble between them, decked with flowery balconies.

Somewhere in most villages stands a solid 16th-century *mudéjar* church – one built by Muslims living under Christian rule in medieval Spain. Most houses have two storeys, with the lower floor used for storage and/or animals. *Tinaos* – flat terraces – stretch across streets, turning them into tunnels, and the characteristic *terraos* (flat roofs), with their protruding chimneypots, consist of a layer of *launa* (a type of clay) packed onto flat stones, which are themselves laid on wooden beams. Nowadays there's often a layer of plastic between the stones and the *launa* for extra waterproofing.

Andalucía. Afterwards, they were given the choice of exile or conversion to Christianity. Most converted – to become known as *moriscos* – but the change was barely skin-deep. A new revolt in Las Alpujarras in 1568 led to two years of vicious guerrilla war, and ended only after the rebel leader Aben Humeya was assassinated by his own cousin.

Almost the whole Alpujarras population was then deported to other parts of Spain, and some 270 villages and hamlets were repeopled with settlers from northern Spain. More than 100 others were abandoned. Over the following centuries the silk industry fell by the wayside and swathes of Alpujarras' woodlands were lost to mining and cereal growing.

PLANNING
Information Sources

In the Alpujarras village of Pampaneira, the **Punto de Información Parque Nacional de Sierra Nevada** (☎ 958 76 31 27; Plaza de la Libertad; 10am-2pm & 5-7pm Tue-Sat Easter–mid-Oct, 10am-2pm & 4-6pm Tue-Sat rest of year, 10am-3pm Sun & Mon year-round) has information on the Alpujarras and Sierra Nevada, including maps for sale, and can inform you on walks and *refugios* (mountain huts or refuges). Pampaneira is the starting point of the Alpujarras walks, and this is also the nearest information office to the start of the Sierra Nevada Traverse.

For additional day hikes, Charles Davis' *Walk! The Alpujarras* (Discovery Walking Guides) is a great resource, with full-colour maps.

GETTING THERE & AROUND

Alsina Graells/ALSA (in Granada ☎ 958 18 54 80, in Órgiva 958 78 50 02, in Málaga 952 34 17 38, in Almería 950 23 51 68) operates buses to the Alpujarras. From Granada, they run on two routes: one twice daily on the low road through Cádiar and Válor; the other three times daily to the higher villages and ending in Trevélez or Bérchules; see the boxed text, below, for details. Return buses start before 6am and in mid-afternoon. There is a Málaga–Órgiva bus and a bus from Almería runs to Cádiar.

A taxi between Trevélez and any of the Barranco de Poqueira villages will start around €40 but availability may be an issue in busy periods so it's worth trying to book ahead.

LAS ALPUJARRAS BUS SERVICE

Destination	Cost	Duration	Daily Freq.
Bérchules	€8.50	3 hours	2
Bubión	€6	2¼ hours	3
Cádiar	€7.50	3 hours	2
Capileira	€6	2½ hours	3
Lanjarón	€4	1 hour	6–9
Pampaneira	€5.50	2 hours	3
Pitres	€6	2¾ hours	3
Órgiva	€4.50	1¾ hours	6–9
Trevélez	€7	3¼ hours	3
Válor	€9	3¾ hours	2
Yegen	€8.50	3½ hours	2

ACCESS TOWNS

See Trevélez (p302), Capileira (p297), and Mairena (p300).

ALPUJARRAS WALK I: THE LOW ROUTE

Duration 2 days

Distance 26.5km

Difficulty moderate

Start Pampaneira (p300)

Finish Alquería de Morayma (p274)

Nearest Towns Trevélez (p302), Pampaneira (p300)

Transport bus

Summary Linking several of this unique region's picturesque Berber-style villages, this route starts at the edge of a dramatic gorge and works its way through pine forests into arid, eroded *ramblas*, ending along a lush river valley. An optional third day by bus and on foot can link you to the Alpujarras Walk II: The High Route.

The old paths connecting the villages of Las Alpujarras pass through constantly changing scenery. Though tourism here, especially in the western villages, is ever-increasing, the area remains a world apart, with a rare sense of timelessness. Reminders of the Moorish past are ubiquitous in the form of Berber-style architecture and the terracing and irrigation of the land.

Many villages along the route – including virtually all those we mention here – are hubs of good day-walk routes. With rarely more than two hours between villages, and plenty of food, water and lodgings along the way, there's infinite scope for subdividing and varying the stages of our route. With plenty of time, you could spend more than one night in some places and explore the surrounding areas on day walks. Most of our recommended places to stay can furnish local route information.

The walk begins in the Barranco de Poqueira, one of the deepest gorges in the southern flank of the Sierra Nevada. The Poqueira villages – Pampaneira, Bubión and Capileira – are three of the most picturesque (albeit most visited) in Las Alpujarras. If you have time, it's rewarding

to spend a day or two exploring the whole gorge, which reaches close up beneath the Sierra Nevada's highest peaks. You can obtain information on local walking routes from the information office in Pampaneira (see Information Sources, p268).

For several stretches our route follows the well-marked GR142 or GR7 long-distance footpaths. The GR142 runs 140km from Lanjarón in the western Alpujarras to Fiñana on the north side of the eastern Sierra Nevada; the far more scenic GR7 runs the length of Spain from Andorra in the north to Tarifa in the south, and is part of the European E4 route from Greece to Andalucía.

PLANNING

The best times are April to mid-June and mid-September to early November. The summer months can be stiflingly hot, especially in the low-lying easterly part of the route, and winter is often cold in the higher villages.

It's best to ring ahead for rooms in your preferred lodgings. The larger villages have banks with ATMs. All Alpujarras villages have fountains where you can drink and fill water bottles. If in any doubt about water quality, just ask a local '¿Es potable?' ('Is it safe to drink?').

Maps & Books

The IGN 1:50,000 *Sierra Nevada* map covers both the routes we feature here but is hard to obtain locally. Try for it at CNIG offices or specialist map shops such as Cartográfica del Sur in Granada (see p298). Editorial Alpina's 1:40,000 *Sierra Nevada, La Alpujarra* map and Editorial Penibética's 1:40,000 *Sierra Nevada* map are fairly good but cover only about half and three-quarters of our routes, respectively. The Alpina and Penibética maps come with booklets, available in English or Spanish, describing various walking routes in Las Alpujarras and the Sierra Nevada.

South From Granada, by Englishman Gerald Brenan, who settled in the Alpujarras village of Yegen, is a fascinating and amusing picture of an isolated corner of Spain in the 1920s.

Another Englishman, Chris Stewart, settled as a sheep farmer near Órgiva in

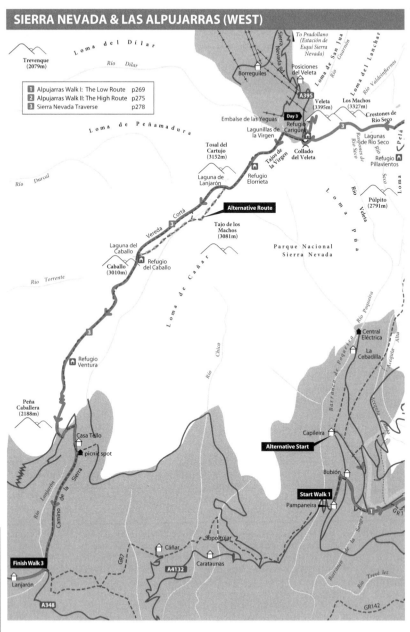

SIERRA NEVADA & LAS ALPUJARRAS (WEST)

the 1990s, and his *Driving over Lemons* tells entertainingly of modern life as a foreigner in Las Alpujarras.

GR142 Senda de la Alpujarra, by Mariano Cruz Fajardo and Ramón Fernández del Real, and *GR7 Senda Granadina*, by

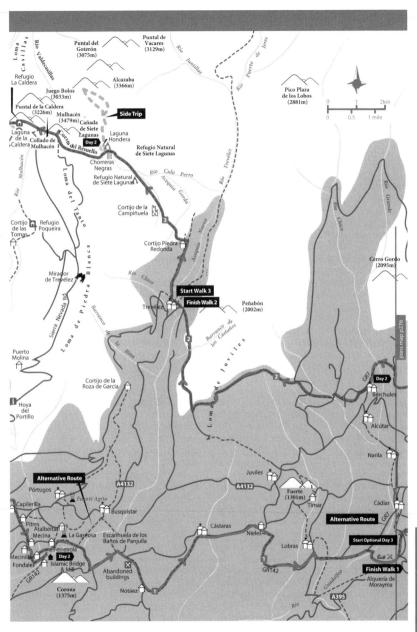

Mariano Cruz, Jesús Espinosa and Natalio Carmona, are fine Spanish-language trail guides, full of fascinating local

background. The Punto de Información in Pampaneira (see Information Sources, p268) sells the best selection of maps and books locally. You'll also find some in shops in Trevélez.

THE WALK
Day 1: Pampaneira to Ferreirola
4¼ hours, 9km

The actual walking time is relatively short, but the villages along the way invite exploration, and there's a lot of up-and-down between them.

From Pampaneira's central square (1055m) take the uphill street beside Taberna Narciso, marked with a 'Bubión 1.5km' sign. At the first junction, bear right, then at each division or meeting of streets, take the most upward option, eventually bearing left on level ground, away from the houses. A 'Camino a Bubíon' sign points up a switchback, and GR7 trail posts begin just below Calle Castillo and the top edge of the village. The path winds up among orchards, poplars and chestnuts to the bottom edge of **Bubión** (1300m). Work your way uphill to the main road and turn right; 70m downhill from the Teide restaurant, turn left where a GR7 signpost indicates 'Capilerilla 3.5km'. This street becomes a narrow dirt road, climbing through chestnuts and holm oaks and making several switchbacks. Eventually a narrower track heads straight off the road, marked by green-and-red marker posts; this makes a hard right, and a 'Sendero Monte Pecho' sign and a GR7 post indicate the trail leading up. From here, your path follows red-and-white paint markers up the fairly steep hillside to cross the ridge by an electricity pylon.

The path dips and crosses a broader track running north-south. Continue following red-and-white posts and paint markings. The path crosses the upper **Barranco de la Sangre** (Ravine of Blood; scene of a battle during the 1568–70 rebellion). At a crossroads among pines, follow the GR7 sign for Pitres and Capilerilla. This is where the Alternative Start (see p273) joins the route. A little further along, follow a red-and-white GR7 post at a downward right fork. Another 15 minutes winding down (only intermittently marked as the GR7), and you're on the edge of the hamlet of **Capilerilla**. Turn left into the hamlet, and after passing under a *tinao* (terrace over the street) look for a sign, 'Pitres 0.5km', on the right by a water tank. Follow the path

downwards and you emerge on the plaza of Pitres, the next hamlet, around 10 minutes later (two hours from Bubíon).

Pitres (1245m) is not quite so picturesque – but also not as visited – as the villages in the Barranco de Poqueira. Just east of town, down a signposted path off the A4132, the main road, **Refugio Los Albergues** (☎ 958 34 31 76; dm €8; 16 Feb-14 Dec) is a friendly little German-owned walkers' hostel in a beautiful setting. It has a kitchen and hot showers. On the western side of town, just above the A4132, **Camping El Balcón de Pitres** (☎ 958 76 61 11; www .balcondepitres.com; camping per person/ tent/car €5/5/4.50, three-person cabins & cottages from €60) also has an inexpensive restaurant.

The hamlets in the valley below are grouped with Pitres and Capilerilla in the municipality of La Taha, a name that recalls the emirate of Granada, when the Alpujarras was divided into 12 administrative units called *tahas*. Today these tranquil lower hamlets form a tiny world almost of their own, where the air seems thick with accumulated centuries. The tinkle of running water is ubiquitous, and ancient paths wend their way through lush woods and orchards.

Entering Pitres' plaza, take a right and follow the street down to the A4132. Cross over, following the street down beside Restaurante La Carretera. This becomes a partly cobbled road, then a *sendero local* (local trail), marked with green-and-white posts. It will have you at the top edge of **Mecina** in 15 minutes; from here, bear right to meet the main road and the village church. Two places to stay and eat here may prove useful if the lodgings in Ferreirola are full.

Just off the main road, **Hotel Albergue de Mecina** (☎ 958 76 62 54; Calle La Fuente; s/d with bathroom €52/65) is a tasteful, modern 21-room hotel with a good restaurant and a pool.

On the east edge of the village, **L'Atelier** (☎ 958 85 75 01; www.ivu.org/atelier; Calle Alberca; s/d €35/50) is a welcoming French-run vegetarian guesthouse, serving gourmet international meat-free meals. Rates include breakfast.

For **Mecinilla**, the next hamlet just a few minutes along, head down the road to the right of the Mecina church, marked with a green-and-white post and a 'Camino de Mecinilla' plaque. At **Bar Aljibe** (which serves good-value *raciones*), continue straight, heading downhill at each junction until a left turn off Calle Laurel turns into a dirt path. This descends, meeting a paved road, where you make a short jog to the right, picking up the path again just past a block of garages.

Entering **Fondales**, the lowest Taha village, bear left but ignore the 'Camino de Ferreirola' plaque and the green-and-white *sendero local* posts, and head downhill on the village street, making several turns. A 'Camino de Órgiva' plaque points the way to a GR142 post near a three-spout fountain. Head down to the Río Trevélez ravine at the bottom of this deep valley. The path reaches an old **Islamic-era bridge** over the gorge, with a ruined mill beside it. You have descended 420m in 45 minutes from Pitres to reach this marvellous spot.

At this point, you can return the way you came, then, back at the top of Fondales, follow the 'Camino de Ferreirola' signs at the top of Fondales.

Or you can take another route out of the ravine to meet the same trail further along – but the path is faint in some spots and heavily overgrown in others. Take the eastward path along the river's north bank, immediately crossing a small side-stream and forking left up its far bank along a very faint trail – just keep heading up, and be prepared for a bit of a scramble in spots. After 15 minutes you come out onto the green-and-white marked *sendero local*. Turn right, and in five minutes you enter Ferreirola, see p298 for more information on where to sleep.

ALTERNATIVE START: CAPILEIRA
45 minutes, 3.2km
Starting in Capileira (see p297) avoids the steep uphill in the first hour from Pampaneira through Bubión. Walk southeast up the Sierra Nevada road from Capileira for 2km, then branch right along a track signed 'Cortijo Prado Toro'. Some 600m south down this track, fork left at another 'Cortijo Prado Toro' sign. In another 600m you reach a crossroads among pines. Turn left here to join the main route, following the same GR7 sign to Pitres and Capilerilla.

Day 2: Ferreirola to Alquería De Morayma
7 hours, 17.5km
The later stretch of trail, especially past Notaez, is through dry, prickly brush – wear tall socks or trousers if you have them. From Ferreirola's central fountain, follow the street down past Villa Kiko. On the east edge of the village, follow the GR142 signpost to Busquístar. In a few minutes you reach **La Gaseosa**, a spring with tiles around its water spout. The water is mildly fizzy and good to drink. At a fork 10 minutes later, take the broader, right-hand option, marked with a red-and-white painted X, indicating that you are leaving the GR142. (The Alternative Route: Via Busquístar, p274, diverges here.) The path descends to a ruined mill beside a bridge over the Río Trevélez, then zigzags up the south side of this steep valley by an ancient, part-cobbled path, the **Escarihuela de los Baños de Panjuila**. The path becomes wider and less steep 20 minutes from the bridge, and winds around in a further 15 minutes to a small group of houses where a vehicle track joins it from the right. Go left (east) along the track and in 150m you emerge on a paved road. Go left along this for 15 minutes to a junction amid a scattering of buildings. The Alternative Route: Via Busquístar rejoins the main route here. (On the hillside nearby, abandoned buildings mark the former departure point of an aerial conveyor system carrying iron ore from the Conjuro mines, just northeast of here, to Rules, 20km west. The mines and conveyor functioned from 1955 to 1968.) At the road junction, take the right-hand option, signposted 'Cástaras', and after five minutes turn down a path to the right with a GR142 signpost to Notaez. The narrow path – very well marked with red-and-white marker posts and paint stripes – leads downhill through almond groves and shiny, silver-grey soil, for 40 minutes to the pretty, quiet village of **Notáez** – there are no services here, except a central fountain. A GR142 signpost to Cástaras indicates your onward direction.

From Notáez follow the GR142 steadily upward; the route is narrow and not very regularly marked. After about an hour, it meets a wide dirt track within sight of the village of **Cástaras**, set on a rock outcrop with greenery all around. Clamber down the rise, cross the road and continue on the trail, slightly to the left – a faint red-and-white paint marker is visible on the rocks after a few steps. From here, it's another 15 minutes or so to the centre of the village, where there is one bar. Along the left wall of the village church, take the street signposted 'Nieles, Jubiles'. The street soon turns right and becomes the road to **Nieles**, 40 minutes east. After the Nieles church, take the first path down to the right, with a GR142 signpost to Lobras. After 1¼ hours winding down into and up out of two valleys (the last 30 minutes on a dirt track), you emerge on a tarmac road just south of **Lobras village**. Go right (south), following a GR7 (not GR142) signpost to Cádiar. After about 220m, by an exercise park, a GR7 signpost ('Cadiar, 5km') points down a dirt road to the left. At the time of research, however, a new road was being laid, leaving no reliable landmarks for the trail start off the road to the right. If you can't find the trail start, work your way downhill, staying south of the power lines, and in about 10 minutes you will reach the trail at the bottom, where you cross two *ramblas* (seasonal watercourses) in immediate succession (between the two you cross the GR142, here following a separate, longer route to Cádiar). Cross the second *rambla* and follow red-and-white paint dashes ahead. After 100m the path turns uphill to the right. Fifteen minutes later it crests a ridge, crosses a vehicle track and starts descending towards the Río Guadalfeo valley. About 20 minutes from the ridge, on a rightward bend of the GR7, is a sign to **Alquería de Morayma** (☎ 958 34 32 21; www.alqueriamorayma.com; d & apt €61-91) down to the right off the GR7. A great place to stay, this old *cortijo* has been lovingly renovated in meticulous *alpujarreño* fashion. Good, medium-priced food, using locally grown ingredients, is available, and there's a library and fascinating art and artefacts everywhere. To reach it, follow the short signposted path (at times muddy and/or rather overgrown) from the GR7, cross the Guadalfeo (more a stream than a river) and head about 80m upstream to a path heading up to the right with an 'Alquería de Morayma 400m' sign: in fact, it's more like 600m.

The more budget-conscious should continue on the GR7, past the turn-off to Alquería de Morayma, and head to Cádiar, a metropolis for these parts with around 2000 people. **Pensión Montoro** (☎ 958 76 89 00; Calle San Isidro 20; s/d with bathroom €10/20), 250m from the church, has plain, basic rooms.

ALTERNATIVE ROUTE: VIA BUSQUÍSTAR
1¼ hours, 4.4km

Walking from Ferreirola via the town of Busquístar gives you an opportunity to stock up on supplies (there are several grocery stores) if necessary, as well as avoid the particularly steep Escarihuela de los Baños de Panjuila. This route adds about 30 minutes to the day's hike. Twenty minutes out of Ferreirola, where the trail forks, follow the GR142 and the 'Ruta Medieval' (PR-A299), cutting across the hillside rather than descending. After 30 minutes, you arrive on the lower west edge of Busquístar. Hike up to the main road, then descend again by Bar Vargas, following the paved street down a couple of turns and continuing down, past a plaza and heading left. A cobblestone path – a centuries-old mule track, used by silk traders during Moorish times – zigzags down to the ravine and back up the other side, joining up with the main route at the paved road (the A4132), one hour after leaving Busquístar.

OPTIONAL DAY 3: ALQUERÍA DE MORAYMA TO MAIRENA

The GR142 connects Cádiar and Mairena, which means that it's perfectly possible to link the two-day Alpujarras I: The Low Route that you've just completed with the two-day Alpujarras II: The High Route (below) thus making it a five-day binge of hiking glory. But we don't exactly recommend it as a pleasant outing: this optional day is a bracing 29km, and it passes through an exceptionally difficult and unscenic stretch, along an overgrown river valley that is either dry and sweltering or ankle-deep in mud, and, at 29km, the full day's hike can't be recommended as a pleasant one. If you'd like to continue from Cádiar to Mairena, it's best to take the bus from Cádiar at 11.25am (confirm the schedule at Alquería de Morayma), arriving in the scruffy lowland town of Ugíjar in one hour. From here, you can take a taxi to Mairena (€20), or walk the remaining 5km, a steady uphill climb of about two hours. If you follow this strategy, request detailed trail notes from Las Chimeneas in Mairena (p300), as the last half-hour of the route follows a complex series of landmarks. A taxi all the way from Cádiar to Mairena costs about €40; call **Auto-Taxi Barbero** (☎ 696 50 62 70) in Cádiar.

Day 1: Mairena to Bérchules
7 hours, 20.5km

This is a somewhat long walk, setting the stage for a more leisurely following day, but if you prefer to split the load differently, you can overnight in Yegen instead (and perhaps also take the loop trail into the dramatic valley below). From Las Chimeneas in Mairena, walk northwest along the main road, soon crossing a bridge. Shortly after, on a right-hand bend opposite the village exercise park, take a track running sharp right uphill. Turn left at the top of the short hill, where you'll see a red-and-white paint marker, indicating the GR7, on a rock wall. This dirt track dips and rises several times over the next 15 minutes or so, passing orchards and farm plots. At the top of a rise, a GR7 post marks the trail leading off to the left. It joins another track, skirting the back of a small structure, and continues on straight – the only option without winding up in a private yard.

You come down into a gully 10 minutes later: turn left down a path marked by a cairn and red-and-white paint stripes on the rock behind it (the paint stripes may be obscured by vegetation). In 25 minutes this path descends to and crosses the **Río Nechite**, in its pretty valley. About six minutes beyond the river, at a fork, take the lower, left-hand option. Entering the small village of **Nechite** eight minutes later, follow the street to the left, then go left, downhill, at the first fork, then right at a T-junction. Turn right at the bottom of this street, passing the Santa Lucía fountain, and follow the street toward Nechite's church. Turn right on the street before the church, where a paved *acequia* channel comes down to the main road. At the top of the street, bear right and head around the curve, where you'll see a GR7 sign to Válor, pointing up to a trail. After 10 minutes, the trail turns to rocks only, then runs along an *acequia*, becoming very overgrown. Stay on level ground and follow the greenest growth; a GR7 post appears in a couple of minutes, after the dense brush you emerge on a dirt track. Follow this briefly to continue on the trail leading to the top of **Válor**, one of the larger Alpujarras villages. Turn left down the road. You emerge on the main road through Válor, beside **Restaurante El Puente** (*bocadillos* €3-4, mains around €8), a fine spot for a bite of lunch. **Hostal Las Perdices** (☎ 958 85 18 21; www .balcondevalor.com, in Spanish; Calle Torrecilla; s or d with bathroom €30), a few hundred metres to the left (east) along the main road, has clean, straightforward rooms.

Take the street downhill opposite Restaurante El Puente, then turn right along the back of the large church to a plaza. Off the southwest corner, follow the 'Sendero de Launa' sign; at the T-intersection, turn left, then right at the next junction, heading uphill. You pass the small Ermita de Nuestra Señora de Lourdes on your left, then the street leads out of the village by a medieval bridge, the **Puente de la Tableta**. There are picnic tables down by the stream.

Follow the road uphill from the bridge, marked by a 'Yegen 4.5km' sign. After a few minutes, don't miss a GR7 post directing you left, away from the main highway that's visible in the distance. Go right at forks

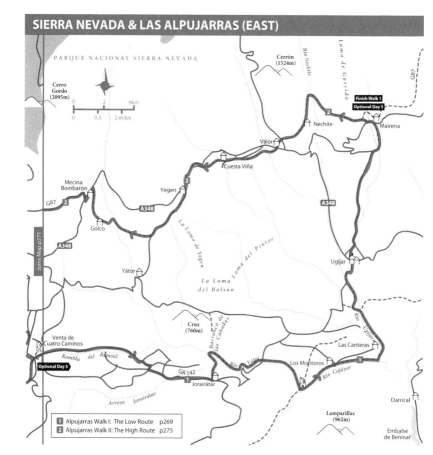

SIERRA NEVADA & LAS ALPUJARRAS (EAST)

10 and 15 minutes later, and left down a tarmac road after a further five minutes. In five minutes this brings you into the hamlet of **Cuesta Viña**, at the far end of which is a green-tiled enclosure with a concrete arch, containing half a dozen *ferruginous* (iron-bearing) springs – all worth a sip as each has a different strength.

Walk up past the right side of the springs building. Just past the top of a shabby picnic area, a GR7 post indicates your path bending up and leftward. Ten minutes up, at the top of the hill after an abandoned two-storey *cortijo*, the trailheads right, likely obscured by tall grasses, then rises steeply. In 10 minutes, cross the Válor-Yegen road. A few minutes later, turn left along a vehicle track to rejoin the road

after 60m. Turn right and you reach **Yegen** within 15 minutes.

This is the village made famous by writer Gerald Brenan, whose house, just off Yegen's fountain plaza, is marked by a plaque. To reach the fountain plaza, turn left off the main road at your first opportunity, bearing left at the T-junction; Brenan's house is straight across and just downhill. Local walks include a 1.9km Sendero Gerald Brenan: you can pick up a leaflet on them at the **Café-Bar Nuevo La Fuente** (☎ 958 85 10 67; www.pensionlafuente.com, in Spanish; Calle Real 38; s/d €22/30), on the fountain plaza, a friendly place with eight very clean rooms.

El Rincón de Yegen (☎ 958 85 12 70; s/d with bathroom €30/42), the first building you reach as you enter Yegen, has the village's most comfortable rooms and a good, medium-priced restaurant.

To leave town, head past the Brenan house, then fork right. Pass a supermarket down a street to the left, then, down on level ground, the town hall (*ayuntamiento*) on the right as you enter a long plaza. Leave by the street at its far end, continuing straight on until you approach the village edge. Follow the concrete road bending left past a GR7 marker post on the right. The track passes the village cemetrey, then winds downhill in an overall southwesterly direction. After 20 minutes turn right at a GR7 signpost to Golco. The track becomes a footpath. After two or so minutes take the lower, left option at a fork; the path grows narrow and muddy. When you reach the stream bed (likely dry, or barely muddy), turn right and walk up the bed itself. After a minute, the trail turns left and heads up a short rise. The path then climbs indistinctly in a northwesterly direction through an area of boulders: watch for a GR7 paint mark on rocks off to the left.

The path becomes clear and leads down to a river crossing beside a poplar grove 20 minutes later. Veer left on the far bank and the path soon bends right, uphill. Five minutes later the trail goes to the right (indicated by a GR7 post). After another three minutes turn left along a semi-cobbled path that leads up to a concrete road. In 10 more minutes you reach **Golco**: turn right at a GR7 signpost to Mecina Bombarón, then straight on along a path marked by a GR7 post where the road bends sharp left. Your path climbs up across the terraces (follow the street lights) and in 20 minutes brings you up onto the main street of **Mecina Bombarón**. There are a couple of cafés in town, but no reliable lodging.

Walk left along the main road for around five minutes, then, just before the edge of town, turn right up a concrete road with a 'Ruta Pintoresca' sign. You soon reach Mecina's upper plaza, Plaza Vieja. Turn left up the street signed 'Sendero Acequeros, Bérchules 5km' and follow this round to the left at an almost immediate fork. After 10 minutes, soon after a radio mast, follow the trailheading left (downhill). Follow the *acequia*, cross a wooden footbridge, then bear right and up through an overgrown gully. Cross a dirt track, then ascend through a second gully. At the top, bear left on a dirt track, heading steadily upward. In 10 minutes, the track turns to cement, and you pass the edge of a pine wood. After another 10 minutes, go left (downhill) at a fork, following a 'Cortijo Cortes' sign. Bérchules comes into view ahead, but after five minutes, the track turns right (north) up the Bérchules valley. Two minutes later, look for a GR7 signpost pointing to the left, indicating a trail downhill. Within 30 minutes, you cross the Río Guadalfeo by a little bridge beside a ruined mill, and in 20 minutes more (fairly steeply uphill) you enter **Bérchules**. For accommodation in Bérchules see p297.

Day 2: Bérchules to Trevélez
5 hours, 14.5km

This is a rare stretch of Alpujarras trail that passes through no villages – carry all the water you'll need, and pack a picnic lunch. It's not an easy trail to start – finding your way out of Bérchules is the hardest part – but once on the main route, it's easy to follow. From the **Hotel Bérchules**, turn right, then, within 100m, follow a trail uphill to the right, near a 'Parque Natural' sign. At the top of the rise, bear right toward a large chestnut tree, then straight on, with a fence on your left and passing a water tank on your right. Follow this trail gently uphill, into the top part of Bérchules and a small plaza (Plaza Portón) with a fenced-in tree in the centre. In the square, turn left and head up the street past a *lavadero* (wash-house) and a fountain. It turns into a trail, passing between two stone walls and emerging onto a wider path, marked Calle Castillejo. Turn left, heading past a fountain and another 'Parque Natural' sign on a dirt path. Follow this gradually uphill, out of the shaded terraces and up to an open field; take the right-hand fork, heading toward a long single-storey building on the rise above. The trail zigzags up, crossing an *acequia* then heading left along the channel to meet a dirt track running just below the building. Look for a fainter vehicle track leading steeply off to your right, toward the left end of the building. This takes you up to a wide dirt road, where you turn left (nearly one hour from Hotel Bérchules).

> ## MOUNTAIN MEAL
> The *plato alpujarreño*, found on almost every Alpujarras menu, consists of sausage, ham, fried eggs, fried potatoes and maybe a black pudding, usually for around €7.

The road curves gently right, opening onto a view of Cádiar and Narila in the valley below, then bends left into a gully; 150m after the gully, take a narrow path right. When this soon meets the road again, take another track heading west (right) up the slope. Within 10 minutes you reach a path and a firebreak along the edge of a pine plantation. Follow the firebreak up, crossing straight over a good dirt road after 10 minutes; 600m beyond, go left along another wide dirt road through the trees. One hundred metres along this, fork left along a lesser track, marked with a 'Sendero Sulayr' sign, passing through a clear area then a second patch of trees. At the wood's far edge, follow a road up for 200m, then veer left through a gate, marked with a 'Parque Nacional' sign.

From here until close to Trevélez, you're on the GR240, called the Sendero Sulayr, a circular long-distance route around the Sierra Nevadas. It's well-marked with posts stamped with a flower insignia and bearing both green and red-and-white paint stripes. The dirt road you're on soon starts to climb steadily along the edge of the national park, across a rather bleak moor with superb eastward views. After 40 minutes, you reach a firebreak, and the road passes into a forest. Ten minutes later, you meet a dirt track, where signposts point left. A post at the top of the rise marks the **Loma de Juviles** ridge at 2000m, the highest point on this trek.

Follow the GR240 markers straight on along the track about 200m, then right as the trailheads downhill, zigzagging through the trees. At a five-way intersection with a firebreak, marked by another 'Parque Nacional' sign, the trail jogs left along the road, then descends into the trees again. After about 15 minutes (35 minutes from Loma de Juviles), you meet another track: a marker post at the junction indicates that you've rejoined the GR7. From here, it's about 1¼ hours' descent to the base

of Trevélez, all along a well-marked path (though you will have to pass through a closed wire gate about halfway along – be sure to shut it behind you). If you're staying at La Fragua, allow at least another 20 minutes to hike up to the top of Trevélez.

SIERRA NEVADA TRAVERSE

Duration 3 days
Distance 45km
Difficulty moderate–demanding
Start Trevélez (p302)
Finish Lanjarón (p299)
Transport bus
Summary A strenuous but rewarding route across the higher reaches of the Sierra Nevada – a spectacular wilderness with surprising animal and plant life – includes mainland Spain's highest and third-highest peaks.

The upper Sierra Nevada provides, in many ways, Andalucía's ultimate walking experience, for its altitude and climatic conditions and also for its forbidding, wild aspect – large tracts are a rugged wilderness of black mica schist rock and stones, with plenty of sheer faces and jagged crags.

The Sierra Nevada's *tresmiles* (peaks higher than 3000m) – the only ones in peninsula Spain outside the Pyrenees – are strung along a serpentine stretch of its main ridge between Cerro Pelao (3179m), 11km north of Trevélez (the nearest village to the high summits), and Caballo (3010m), 15km west of Trevélez. Our route heads straight up from Trevélez to the heart of the *tresmil* zone, takes in Mulhacén and Veleta, the two highest peaks in the range (with Alcazaba, the third-highest, as an optional side trip), then traverses southwest before descending to the spa town of Lanjarón. For some shorter options in the Sierra Nevada, see the boxed text Short Walks in the Sierra Nevada (p283).

ENVIRONMENT
During the Ice Ages Europe's most southerly glaciers formed in the Sierra Nevada, the last of them surviving into the early 20th century. Many of the tarns (alpine lakes) here lie in glacially deepened basins, or

cirques. For a visual guide to some of the most recognisable glacial landforms, see the boxed text Signs of a Glacial Past, (p28).

The Sierra Nevada's combination of high altitude and southern latitude gives it unique botanical variety. Among its 2100 plant species are 66 endemics – including its own species of narcissus, poppy, crocus, monkshood and gentian. Receding snows in the summer uncover much of this variety; most endemic species are found on rocky crags and cliffs above 2800m. Damp, grassy areas around the tarns, called *borreguiles*, also harbour many tiny flowering plants.

Pre-eminent among animals is the ibex, which numbers about 5000 in the Sierra Nevada. In summer you stand an excellent chance of seeing ibex anywhere above 2800m.

PLANNING
When to Walk
July, August and early September are best times to walk but even at these times the weather can change quickly. Try to pick a spell of settled, clear weather and keep a careful eye on any clouds that begin to settle on the mountains. Even under clear summer skies, the heights of the range can be blasted by strong, cold winds, and temperatures can fall close to freezing. By late September, expect it to get very cold at night above 2500m, perhaps with snow and storms. Year-round, the temperature on the summits averages 14°C less than in the highest Alpujarras villages. The first major snowfall is usually around mid-October. The high ground begins to thaw in May. In June there's often plenty of snow still on the ground.

What to Bring
You'll need warm gear up here even if the skies are a cloudless blue and you've been sweltering down in the valleys. This means plenty of clothing layers – including head covering and gloves – and a warm sleeping bag. You need food for three days, and a tent.

There's plenty of water from springs, streams and tarns, but there are also quite a lot of animals in the Sierra Nevada, so purification tablets are advisable. Start Day 1 with enough water to reach the Cañada de Siete Lagunas.

THE SIERRA NEVADA ROAD

Construction of the road over the Sierra Nevada from Granada to Capileira began in the 1920s for tourist purposes. A paved section to the top of Veleta (3395m) from the Granada side, touted as the highest road in Europe, was completed in 1935. In the 1960s this road was joined below the Veleta summit, at about 3250m, by a dirt road constructed from Capileira, thus creating a road right over the *sierra* – albeit one whose upper reaches would be blocked by snow for all but two or three months each year. A 7km dirt spur reaching to within 800m of the top of Mulhacén was added in 1974. This brought the two highest summits in the Sierra Nevada within reach of anyone with a car.

Growing concern for the alpine environment tolled the road's death knell as a public highway. In the mid-1990s, a permit system was introduced. Today, there are barriers on both sides of the range to stop drivers altogether, unless they have permits (very difficult to obtain). The southern barrier is at Hoya del Portillo (2150m), 12.5km above Capileira, and the northern one is at Hoya de la Mora (2475m), 3km up from the ski resort at Pradollano. From about late June to the end of October the Sierra Nevada national park operates two small **information offices** (open approximately 8.30am-2.30pm & 3.30-7.30pm daily) at Hoya de la Mora and Capileira while the main information office is the **Centro de Visitantes El Dornajo** (☎ 958 34 06 25; 10am-2pm & 6-8pm Apr-Sep, 10am-2pm & 4-6pm Oct-Mar).

The national park also runs a bus service providing access to the upper reaches of the range during the same summer periods. Details of these services are subject to change but at the time of writing a shuttle bus ran 21km up the Sierra Nevada Road from Capileira to the Mirador de Trevélez at 2680m and about 6km up from Hoya de la Mora (to the Posiciones del Veleta, at 3020m). Tickets (€4/6 one-way/return on either route) were sold at the Hoya de la Mora information post and at the Capileira information office.

Maps

Because of its larger scale, Editorial Alpina's 1:40,000 *Sierra Nevada, La Alpujarra* map just about gets the nod over Editorial Penibética's 1:50,000 *Sierra Nevada* map and the IGN 1:50,000 *Sierra Nevada* map.

Permits & Regulations

Overnight camping in the Sierra Nevada is permitted only above 1600m, at least 50m from high-mountain lakes and at least 500m from staffed *refugios* and vehicle tracks. It's advisable to check the latest regulations through a park information office. At the time of writing you were required to give prior notification of all camping by email, fax or letter to the park authorities: check the latest regulations at a park information office.

GETTING TO/FROM THE WALK

For more on getting to and from the walk see Trevélez p302.

THE WALK (see map p271)
Day 1: Trevélez to Cañada de Siete Lagunas
3½ hours, 7km, 1300m ascent

Around 4m up the street from Trevélez's Hotel La Fragua, turn right under an arch to a junction where you take the uphill option. Fifty metres up, turn left into a path indicated by a yellow arrow, various paint dashes and a wooden marker post with an arrow. This leads you up through cultivated areas to an outlying farmlet, **Cortijo Piedra Redonda**, with one stone building on each side of the path, 2km (40 minutes) from Trevélez. At a fork 100m beyond, a 'Campiñuela, Siete Lagunas' sign points you up to the left. In a couple of minutes you pass through a fence with your route confirmed by a green paint blob. In another two minutes go left at a fork of paths. Continue upwards, keeping to the right of a fence and helped by the occasional national-park path marker post. Around 30 minutes from Cortijo Piedra Redonda the path swings northward to parallel the Acequia Gorda irrigation channel. The path crosses the channel after 10 minutes and angles up through a pine plantation. You pass through another fence 40 minutes from the Acequia Gorda, cross another irrigation channel and continue upward to **Cortijo**

de la Campiñuela (2400m), composed of a ruined stone building, a threshing floor (a flat area paved with stones) and a tumbledown corral.

A clear path now climbs more gently northwest towards the Chorreras Negras, two waterfalls tumbling over black stones. After 30 minutes, cross the Río Culo Perro and climb a path which soon heads for the **Chorreras Negras**. The path crosses the foot of the right-hand waterfall, 30 minutes from the river crossing, then makes a steep 20-minute climb up beside the left-hand waterfall. At the top (2850m) you emerge suddenly in the Cañada de Siete Lagunas glacial basin. A shallow tarn, **Laguna Hondera**, stretches before you. The rock mass of Mulhacén looms ahead, with the crags of Alcazaba to its right. Laguna Hondera and several of the six other tarns in the basin are surrounded by grassy areas – good **campsites** (if you can get permission from the park authorities), but as alpine tarns are fragile environments, your camping habits should be impeccable – don't forget the national park rule banning camping within 50m of mountain lakes. On a rise just southeast of Laguna Hondera is the so-called **Refugio Natural de Siete Lagunas**, a trio of shelters formed by rock walls around a boulder, with room for about 10 people to stretch out. There are also a number of low **rock enclosures** providing some wind shelter.

SIDE TRIP: ALCAZABA
3–3½ hours, 6km

If you have reached the Cañada de Siete Lagunas by lunchtime and have reserves of energy, it's a fine idea to devote the afternoon to Alcazaba (Fortress). The name is entirely apt for this 3366m rock massif protected by awesome crags and precipices on every side but the southeast. Compared with neighbouring Mulhacén, barely a trickle of walkers tackle this giant.

Begin by walking up the ridge forming the northeast flank of the Cañada de Siete Lagunas. As you pick your way carefully over its first lot of crags, about 1¼ hours from Laguna Hondera, Alcazaba's pyramid-shaped summit cairn appears just west of north. You can walk to the right of and below the remaining crags of the ridge before veering right (north) up the

> ## WARNING
>
> Several parts of the route, including the summits of Mulhacén and Veleta and the ridge to the summit of Alcazaba, are bordered by precipices. Consider very carefully whether to proceed if clouds or mist form.

Alcazaba summit ridge (with a precipice on its west side). From the peak itself, two hours from Laguna Hondera, steep walls drop away to the north and west. There are great panoramas just about every way you look.

To return, you can – after retracing your steps most of the way southward down Alcazaba's summit ridge – descend the stony valley on the north side of the ridge that you ascended from the Cañada de Siete Lagunas. Make for a discernible pass in this ridge, southeast from Alcazaba's summit. Once there (30 minutes from the summit), you find that you're on a more northerly spur of the ridge than the one you ascended. Head south for 20 minutes, losing little height, to return to your original spur, from where it's a simple 30-minute descent to Laguna Hondera.

Day 2: Cañada de Siete Lagunas to Refugio Carigüela
6 hours, 13km

This day takes you to the Sierra Nevada's two highest summits, Mulhacén (3479m) and Veleta (3395m).

From the southeast end of Laguna Hondera, a path climbs to the east end of the Cuesta del Resuello (Cuerda del Resuello on some maps), the rocky ridge forming the southwest flank of the Cañada de Siete Lagunas, then follows the ridge upwards. As you climb, you'll understand how the Río Culo Perro (Dog's Arse River), flowing out of Laguna Hondera, got its name. Mulhacén's summit is around 630m higher than Laguna Hondera, and the altitude may slow you down. Where the path up the Cuesta del Resuello fades, spots of yellow paint and small cairns show the way, keeping towards the north side of the ridge.

Two hours from Laguna Hondera, you emerge on a path 400m south of the summit. Turn right, and in 10 minutes you're standing on the highest rock in peninsular Spain. The **summit** supports a small shrine, a roofless stone chapel and a couple of small stone shelters. Immediately behind the summit is a near-perpendicular 500m drop to the Hoya de Mulhacén basin. In clear weather the views take in such distant ranges as the Sierra de las Nieves, Sierra de Cazorla and even the Rif Mountains of Morocco.

Head back down the summit path but after 150m turn right at two small cairns to descend Mulhacén's steep west slope. About 20 minutes down, fork right to the **Collado de Mulhacén** (or Collado del Ciervo), where there are great views of Mulhacén's perpendicular north face, Alcazaba and the Hoya de Mulhacén. It's then a straightforward 15 minutes down to the **Refugio La Caldera**, 40m or 50m above Laguna de la Caldera, identical to Refugio Carigüela at the end of this day's walk. Another similar shelter, Refugio Pillavientos, is 20 minutes southwest along the Sierra Nevada road from Refugio La Caldera. A further accommodation option, 1¼ hours from Refugio La Caldera, is **Refugio Poqueira** (☎ 958 34 33 49; dm beds €9), a modern staffed *refugio* in the upper Poqueira valley. Breakfast (€3.50) and dinner (€10) are available. To reach it, follow the Río Mulhacén downhill for 2.3km to the 2500m level, then follow a path veering 750m southeast to the *refugio*.

To continue our route from Refugio La Caldera, take the path crossing the slope above the north side of Laguna de la Caldera, to reach the Loma Pelá (or Loma Pelada) ridge after 20 minutes. Fine views unfold ahead. Descend 10 minutes to the Sierra Nevada road and continue westward along this between the **Crestones de Río Seco** crags and the Lagunas de Río Seco tarns. The road passes through a nick in the rocks where the Crestones and the equally jagged **Raspones de Río Seco** meet. A few minutes later a gap in the Crestones gives dramatic views down into the Valdeinfiernos valley.

Passing under the almost sheer southeast side of Veleta, the road zigzags up to the 3200m **Collado del Veleta** (or Collado de la Carigüela del Veleta) pass. A tremendous westward panorama opens out, with the jagged Tajos de la Virgen ridge snaking west-southwest and Granada 25km northwest. A few metres above the pass, two hours from Refugio La Caldera, is **Refugio Carigüela**. This simple shelter, maintained in good condition, is free, always open, and has boards for 12 people to spread out sleeping bags, plus a table and benches.

From the *refugio* it's 30 minutes to the top of **Veleta**. A footpath up from the Collado del Veleta soon joins the paved Veleta summit road, which passes the top lifts of the Sierra Nevada ski station. The summit area is disfigured by a line of aerials and a small concrete building.

Day 3: Refugio Carigüela to Lanjarón
7½–8½ hours, 25km

From the Collado del Veleta, a path heads west-northwest 25 minutes down to the **Lagunillas de la Virgen**, a group of tarns about 250m lower. This northern side of the *sierra* can retain substantial snow cover well into the summer, in which case the tarns may appear as patches of snow or even be invisible.

From the southernmost of the *lagunillas* (small tarns), which is visible (snow permitting) as you descend, an excellent path climbs southwest across the boulder-strewn slopes of Tajos de la Virgen. About 50 minutes up you reach **Refugio Elorrieta,** on the ridge southwest of the Tajos de la Virgen crags. This multi-chambered *refugio* has great views but is a mess inside.

Refugio Elorrieta stands above the **Laguna de Lanjarón** (or Laguna de las Tres Puertas) at the head of the Lanjarón valley, a typical stony, high Sierra Nevada wilderness. Crossing into this valley you have crossed the watershed between waters flowing to the Atlantic and waters destined for the Mediterranean.

From Refugio Elorrieta follow the southwest path along the western side of Loma de Cañar. After 10 to 15 minutes this heads down right. Fork left about five minutes down, then right after a further five minutes. Your path leads down across the Río Lanjarón. Across the river the **Vereda Cortá** (Cut Path) rises along the craggy northwest flank of the valley. Around 30 minutes along is the feature that earns this path its name – a steep (but not very wide) gully slicing down across the path.

This requires an all-four-limbs scramble to the path's continuation, a metre or two higher on the far side of the gully, with the aid of a length of cable fixed in place as a handhold. Another half-hour or so brings you to the little **Refugio del Caballo**, even more of a last resort than Refugio Elorrieta. This *refugio* stands just above Laguna del Caballo and below the most westerly *tresmil* in mainland Spain, Caballo (3010m).

If you're not happy about the gully manoeuvre on the Vereda Cortá you have two alternatives, both involving an extra descent of about 200m and ascent of 150m. One is to go left at the second fork as you descend the Loma de Cañar, and cross the Río Lanjarón at any convenient spot about 1km down. The other is to backtrack a couple of minutes from the gully and descend the stony slope to the valley floor. In either case you then walk southwest along the valley, picking up a path which after about 15 minutes starts to climb towards Caballo. You'll reach the Refugio del Caballo around 30 minutes later.

A clear path across the left side of Caballo leads into a steady southwest descent. A stream 1¼ hours down, just after a pine plantation, is probably the last drinkable water before Lanjarón. Fifteen minutes later, fork left down to a concrete irrigation channel and, beyond, the **Refugio Ventura** (of similar standard to the Refugio del Caballo) among some grey rocks.

From Refugio Ventura continue down on a path heading south-southwest in and out of pines. At the foot of a brief straight-downhill section, the path steers to the right and becomes a dirt road. This winds downhill through pines, passing a small meteorological station 25 minutes from Refugio Ventura. From a southbound leg of the zigzag 40 minutes later, zip left down a steep firebreak. At the bottom of the firebreak, go 350m left (northward) along a dirt road, then turn right down a path which in 10 minutes emerges on a broader track, where you again turn right. In 15 minutes this winds down to a group of semi-derelict forestry buildings, **Casa Tello**. From the west end of Casa Tello take a path diverging westward from the track you came in on. Go left at a fork after 60m and follow this trail 15 minutes down (with the aid of red paint dashes) to a footbridge over

SHORT WALKS IN THE SIERRA NEVADA

The following are a few of the many possible ways to experience the Sierra Nevada in one or two days. Routes using the national park shuttle bus are of course dependent on bus schedules and departure points. Times and distances given for these walks assume the shuttle bus goes to Mirador de Trevélez. For more information on the shuttle bus see the boxed text The Sierra Nevada Road, p279. The Editorial Alpina 1:40,000 *Sierra Nevada, La Alpujarra* map is recommended.

TREVÉLEZ–MULHACÉN–TREVÉLEZ

10–11 hours, 18km

Follow the Sierra Nevada Traverse from Trevélez to the Cañada de Siete Lagunas and on to the summit of Mulhacén, then go back down again!

TREVÉLEZ–MULHACÉN–CAPILEIRA

7½ hours, 14km

Follow the Sierra Nevada Traverse from Trevélez to the summit of Mulhacén, descend southward to the Sierra Nevada Road and the Mirador de Trevélez. Catch the shuttle bus to Capileira.

TREVÉLEZ–MULHACÉN–CAPILEIRA

2 days, 22km

Follow the Sierra Nevada Traverse to the summit of Mulhacén, then descend to Refugio La Caldera and Refugio Poqueira (see Day 2 of the Sierra Nevada Traverse, p278). Sleep at Refugio Poqueira and descend to Capileira in four hours the next day via Cortijo de las Tomas and Barranco de Poqueira trail No 3, with yellow marker posts (shown on the recommended map).

TREVÉLEZ–MULHACÉNVELETA–CAPILEIRA

2 days, 36km

Follow the Sierra Nevada Traverse to Mulhacén and continue the same day to Refugio Carigüela, a strenuous 8½ hours' walking. The next day ascend Veleta and return to Refugio Carigüela and Refugio La Caldera (three hours), then either head southeast along the Sierra Nevada Road to pick up the shuttle bus to Capileira (this saves 5km), or descend to Refugio Poqueira (1¼ hours) and from there to Capileira (four hours) as per the preceding walk.

CAPILEIRA–MULHACÉN–CAPILEIRA

4 hours, 10km

After taking the shuttle bus to Mirador de Trevélez, walk to the top of Mulhacén and return the same way.

CAPILEIRA–MULHACÉN–CAPILEIRA

2 days, 18km

After taking the shuttle bus to Mirador de Trevélez, walk to the top of Mulhacén, descend to Refugio Poqueira and sleep there. The next day descend to Capileira as per the two-day Trevélez–Mulhacén–Capileira route.

CAPILEIRA–MULHACÉN–ALCAZABA–TREVÉLEZ

2 days, 24km

Take the shuttle bus, walk to the top of Mulhacén, descend by the Cuesta del Resuello (see Day 2 of the Sierra Nevada Traverse, p278) to the Cañada de Siete Lagunas and camp there. The next day ascend Alcazaba (see Side Trip: Alcazaba, p280), return to the Cañada de Siete Lagunas and descend to Trevélez.

the Río Lanjarón. Just upstream, opposite two inviting waterfalls, is a **picnic spot** too good to pass.

Follow the path up the east side of this valley, forking right beside a small irrigation channel after five minutes, and choosing right (downhill) at a junction after another 10 minutes, with a stone *cortijo* to your left. The track you are following is the **Camino de la Sierra**, an old *camino real*. You pass a long *cortijo* on the right about 45 minutes from the last-mentioned junction. Shortly after turn right down a side-track, then immediately left into a path marked by a red paint dash. After another 40 minutes, 40m past a small stone hut on the right and almost within spitting distance of the Lanjarón rooftops, diverge to the right down a path marked by another red paint dash. You emerge on the A348 road at the east end of Lanjarón 10 minutes later. The town centre is 1km to your right.

CABO DE GATA

Andalucía's 700km coast isn't all packed throngs of pink bodies à la Costa del Sol. Far from it. The most spectacular coastal scenery of all is around the arid Cabo de Gata promontory east of Almería, protected within the borders of the Parque Natural de Cabo de Gata-Níjar, which covers Cabo de Gata's 60km coast plus a thick strip of hinterland.

The combination of a dry, desert climate with the cliffs of the volcanic Sierra del Cabo de Gata plunging towards the azure and turquoise Mediterranean waters produces a landscape of stark grandeur. Between the cliffs and headlands are strung some of Spain's best and least crowded beaches – and no large towns.

ENVIRONMENT
Cabo de Gata, especially the *salinas* (salt-extraction lagoons) south of El Cabo de Gata village, is renowned for its birds. In spring many migratory birds call at the salinas while in transit from Africa or Doñana in western Andalucía to breeding grounds further north. A few flamingos (and many other birds) stay to breed, then others arrive in summer; by late August there can be 1000 flamingos here. Autumn brings the biggest numbers of migratory birds as they pause on their return south. In winter the *salinas* are drained after the autumn salt harvest.

Cabo de Gata's dry climate and poor soil yield unusual vegetation such as the dwarf

fan palm – Europe's only native palm – a bush usually less than 1m high with fans of lance-shaped blades. You'll also come across areas of prickly pear cactus and of sisal, a cactus-like plant with thick spiky leaves, both of which are grown commercially here – sisal for rope-making, prickly pear for food.

CLIMATE
With just 100mm of rain in an average year, Cabo de Gata is the driest place in Europe, and one of the hottest.

PLANNING
Information Sources
The main information office of the Parque Natural de Cabo de Gata-Níjar is the **Centro de Visitantes Las Amoladeras** (☎ 950 16 04 35; 10am-2pm & 6-9pm Jun-Sep, 10am-3pm Oct-May), 8km north of El Cabo de Gata village, on the road from Almería.

ACCESS TOWN
See Almería (p296).

CABO DE GATA COAST
Duration 3 days
Distance 52km
Difficulty easy–moderate
Start El Cabo de Gata (p298)
Finish Agua Amarga (p295)
Transport bus, taxi
Summary A coastal walk along southern Spain's most spectacular seaboard.

This walk follows the coast through a beautiful natural park, combining paths, dirt roads and occasional sections of paved road.

Given the locations of accommodation options, it's impossible to divide the walk into three approximately equal days. We've opted for a short third day, giving a chance to linger at some of the more secluded beaches late in the walk or to head off from the final destination, Agua Amarga, in good time. The walk could be done in two long days, but that leaves little time to enjoy Cabo de Gata's inviting beaches and coves. In fact, we recommend allowing at least one extra day for just that purpose!

PLANNING
When to Walk
You can walk here almost any time of year, though it is very warm right through from June to September. July and August in particular can be dangerously hot (there's absolutely no shade); in these months you would need to take it very slowly, cool off at beaches along the way and carry more water than usual. Spring can be beautiful and surprisingly green, if the winter has been a wet one, but September and October have the advantage that the sea is warm.

What to Bring
There's never more than 3½ hours between villages, so you only need to carry picnic food – but take plenty of water on each stage, particularly for the tough stretch from San Pedro to Agua Amarga on Day 3.

Maps
Editorial Alpina's 1:50,000 *Cabo de Gata-Níjar* map is best. The information offices at Las Amoladeras and San José normally have copies.

Permits & Regulations
Camping in the *parque natural*, and therefore along the walk route, is allowed only in the few designated camping grounds. It is tolerated at Playa San Pedro, but you should not count on it.

GETTING TO/FROM THE WALK
See El Cabo de Gata p298.

THE WALK
Day 1: El Cabo de Gata to San José
5½–6 hours, 21km

South of the village, you can choose between walking along the beach or the main road, or, more scenically, along a dirt track just inland, which edges the **Salinas del Cabo de Gata**, salt-extraction lagoons that are famous for their water birds (see Environment, p284). There are several **bird-watching hides** along the dirt track, starting about 2km south of the village.

About two-thirds of the way along the salt flats, the village of **La Almadraba de Monteleva** has a curious towered church at its north end. The salt from the *salinas* is piled up in great heaps here. South of La Almadraba, past the lagoons, pass through the hamlet of **La Fabriquilla**. After this, you must resort to the road for the 45-minute section of steep coast round to the **Faro del Cabo de Gata** lighthouse at the peninsula's southern tip.

A path from the lighthouse joins the road for the 15-minute climb to the **Torre Vigía**

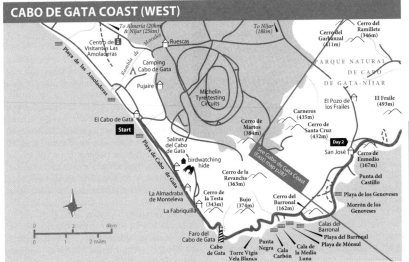

Vela Blanca, an 18th-century watchtower, 213m above sea level. You can avoid the road's long last hairpin by short-cutting up a gully. From the top, the eastward views along the next stretch of coast are magnificent. The road becomes dirt here and is barred to vehicles by a gate. It winds 25 minutes down to a similar barrier stopping traffic from the San José direction, then passes behind the enticing sandy beaches **Cala Carbón, Cala de la Media Luna** and **Playa de Mónsul**, all reachable by short tracks. The first two are generally less crowded in peak seasons, though Mónsul has some striking rock formations. To reach the next beaches after these, you can either walk back to the main road or walk up and across the dune at the east end of Mónsul.

Five minutes past Mónsul via the main road, opposite a parking pullout, take a path to the right towards, then past, an abandoned guardhouse. This leads to the **Calas de Barronal**, a string of gorgeous, isolated sandy beaches. The first you reach is a nudist beach, Playa del Barronal. Just before the water, bear left at a fork of sandy paths and spend 10 minutes working your way up to the little pass just left (north) of the highest of the hillocks rising to the east. From the pass head on down to the water. Tides permitting, you can walk round the foot of the cliffs to the next three beaches. Otherwise, you'll have to make your way over the intervening hills from beach to beach. Leave the last cove by the path climbing to the right across the hillside to the east. This curves left and, 10 minutes from the beach, crests a ridge where a marvellous view of the broad, 1km-long Playa de los Genoveses opens before you. Head down to and along the beach and, 100m before its northern end, go 100m inland to the start of an avenue between pines. At a crossing of tracks 170m along the pine avenue, turn right. The path leads 1km northeast to an old windmill, where you rejoin the dirt road towards San José (p301).

Day 2: San José to Las Negras
6 hours, 19km

Head north past Camping Tau (to get there from the centre, walk north along the beach, then turn left; make a left at the T, then a right and follow this as it curves). The road curves left into a T-junction; turn

right onto a gravel road. At a three-way junction after a few hundred metres, take the middle option. Continue 550m to the back of a house called La Atalaya. Just above the house, turn right and work your way up a footpath to the wider dirt road visible across the hillside above. Follow the road to the right, rounding the corner of the hillside, and continue for 1¾ hours to Los Escullos. There's a good cliff-top section at the start, after which it's a winding route, mostly away from the coast. You pass beneath **El Fraile** (493m), the highest peak on Cabo de Gata. The road becomes paved a few minutes before **Los Escullos**, where, close to the beach, you'll find the simple **Hotel Los Escullos** (☎ 950 38 97 33; www .hotelescullos.es, in Spanish; s/d €85/100) with an average-priced restaurant and the large **Camping Los Escullos** (☎ 950 38 98 11; www.losescullossanjose.com; site per person €7, four-person bungalow €80), some 900m back from the beach.

Head north along Playa del Arco. For the 1.5km (about 45 minutes) to the tiny village of **La Isleta del Moro**, you can continue by the water's edge except for a couple of brief sections, where trails run up and over the rocks. **Casa Café La Loma** (☎ 950 38 98 31; www.degata.com/laloma, in Spanish; s/d €35/57) on a small hill just above the village, is a friendly place with a part-vegetarian restaurant.

From the north end of La Isleta's Playa del Peñón Blanco, a path heads inland, initially following white posts. Unless you want to visit **Cala de los Toros**, a small black-sand beach backed by a splash of green trees, you should continue northeast cross-country to meet the road. Go uphill with the road to the **Mirador Las Amatistas** lookout, 30 minutes from La Isleta del Moro. You need to stay with the road as it heads inland towards the spooky former gold-mining settlement of Rodalquilar, a ghost town turned holiday village. **PanPePato** (☎ 950 38 97 03; mains €10-14;

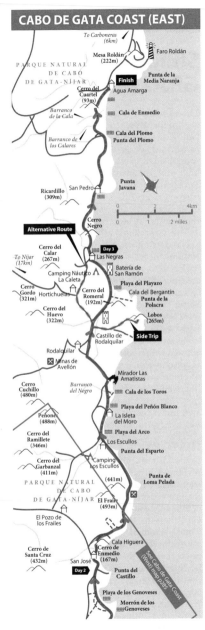

CABO DE GATA COAST (EAST)

right after crossing the dry river bed). **El Jardín de los Sueños** (☎ 950 38 98 43, 669 184118; www.eljardindelossuenos.es; d incl breakfast €90), just across the main road on the far side of town, is a lovely place to sleep, with a pool, gardens and great views of the valley.

Following the main road, northeast of Rodalquilar you pass the Hotel de Naturaleza, then a turning marked 'La Polacra' (see Side Trip: Lobos). About 300m along the road past the La Polacra turning, head right along a cement track. This passes the **Castillo de Rodalquilar**, which served as a refuge from 16th-century pirates, and 2km from the main road reaches **Playa del Playazo**, a good, sandy beach between two headlands (1¾ hours from the Mirador Las Amatistas).

At the north end of Playa del Playazo pick up the track heading north and follow the sign 'Sendero La Molata', which steers clear of the 18th-century Batería de San Ramón fort (now a private home) for an enjoyable 30-minute walk over the rocks to **Camping Náutico La Caleta** (☎ 950 52 52 37; www .vayacamping.net/lacaleta, in Spanish; site per person €6, four-person bungalows €100), in its own cove, where there's usually nude sunbathing (go on, we dare you!). This camping ground has little shade but a nice pool, restaurant and shop.

A paved road heads 750m north to Las Negras – see p299) for the low down on where to kip and eat.

SIDE TRIP: LOBOS
1¾ hours, 6.5km

It's worth the detour up 265m Lobos for magnificent views (adding about 1¼ hours to your day's walk). From the 'La Polacra' turning a paved road runs right to the top (3km, 50 minutes), with a gate barring vehicles about halfway. Lobos is topped by an 18th-century watchtower converted into a lighthouse.

From Lobos you can head northward down to the bay Cala del Bergantín, then on to Playa del Playazo by the pass between Cerro del Romeral and Cerrico Romero. The path fades in and out as far as Cala del Bergantín: just steer away from the cliffs, which have quite an overhang in places, and in one spot curve unexpectedly far inland.

closed Tue) is a good Italian restaurant on the main plaza (where the main road curves right, head straight into town, then turn

ANDALUCÍA

Day 3: Las Negras to Agua Amarga
4¼ hours, 12km

If you're more interested in optimal beach time rather than a thorough hike, consider making this day an out-and-back to San Pedro, packing a lunch and returning to Las Negras for the night. At the north end of Las Negras beach, a path heads inland and joins a dirt road from the back of the village (you can also find your way to this junction by following an orange 'Cala San Pedro' sign from the main street, then further hand-painted signs). This dirt road cuts up the hillside, levelling out as it gets closer to the water, then runs on the level back inland, around the back of Cerro Negro for 25 minutes. It then becomes a path high above the sea for another 25 minutes to **San Pedro**.

This isolated hamlet, with one of the finest beaches along the Cabo de Gata coast, was abandoned by its Spanish inhabitants some years ago; today a small floating population of travellers hang out here in tents, abandoned buildings and the odd cave. There are no formal services (though someone might sell you a warm beer or a loaf of bread), but there is a spring at the top of the hill before you descend to the beach.

There's no way out of San Pedro by land except up. Head up the beach and inland toward the round tower on the east side of the valley. From there, a path marked with cairns climbs steeply for 25 minutes, then gently for another 15, during which you suddenly find you're walking along the top of a cliff – take care! You come down the other side of the hill, about 1½ hours after leaving San Pedro, to **Cala del Plomo**, a beach of grey sand and pebbles with a couple of houses nearby. Three minutes along the road back from the beach, just before it bends, take a path to the right, opposite a stone wall and house; it's marked by a small post. In a few minutes this meets the Barranco de los Calares and follows it down to its meeting with the Barranco de la Cala, about 20 minutes all told from the road. If you wish to visit the nice little **Cala de Enmedio** beach, head right down the dry gulch about five minutes; for Agua Amarga, carry straight on (northward) and slightly uphill on a trail marked by a small post. This winds up and behind a small hill and will have you removing your boots on the beach at **Agua Amarga** in less than 40 minutes.

SIERRA DE GRAZALEMA

The Cordillera Bética gives a final flourish west of the white town of Grazalema before fading away to the coastal plains of Cádiz province. The Sierra de Grazalema (actually several small *sierras*) is neither particularly high nor extensive but it encompasses a variety of beautiful landscapes, from pastoral river valleys to precipitous gorges, from dense Mediterranean woodlands to rocky summits atop perpendicular cliffs.

The Grazalema hills and surrounding lowlands comprise the 517-sq-km Parque Natural Sierra de Grazalema. Within the park is a 30-sq-km *área de reserva* (reserve area) occupying most of the triangle between Grazalema, Benamahoma and Zahara de la Sierra. This contains much of the park's most spectacular territory and some of its finest walks. We certainly recommend these walks, but as entry to the reserve area is only allowed with a permit from the park office in El Bosque, which can be a little complicated to obtain, we focus instead on two equally fine walks outside the reserve area. You'll find information on walks in the reserve area under Sierra de Grazalema – Área de Reserva (p295) under Other Walks.

HISTORY
In the 13th to 15th centuries, this area was a Muslim–Christian frontier zone, hence the way villages huddle into the rocky hillsides for protection. Zahara de la Sierra's 13th-century Muslim-built castle fell to the Christians in 1407 and its brief recapture by Abu al-Hasan of Granada in 1481 provoked the Catholic Monarchs to launch the last phase of the Reconquista of Andalucía, leading to the fall of Granada in 1492. In the 19th century, with land ownership concentrated in the hands of a few, the area was renowned for banditry and poaching. In the mid-20th century swathes of forest were levelled for fuel and a big slice of the population departed in search of a more prosperous life elsewhere: you'll see many abandoned *cortijos* on your walks.

WARNING

Grazalema cattle always seem to have long, sharp horns pointing in your direction. It makes sense to walk near some cover (walls, fences, trees, rocks, thick undergrowth) that you could resort to if necessary.

ENVIRONMENT

Climbing El Torreón provides the best chance of spotting some of the park's 500 ibex. However, you'll see plenty of domesticated animals, including Iberian pigs, the black or dark brown breed that is turned into Spain's best ham, especially when (as it has ample opportunity to do here) it has eaten lots of acorns. The star of the bird population is the griffon vulture. Around 100 pairs live in the Garganta Verde and Garganta Seca gorges south of Zahara de La Sierra.

Much of the area is covered in beautiful Mediterranean woodland of holm- gall- and cork-oak, olive, *acebuche* (wild olive) and *algarrobo* (carob). The north flank of the Sierra del Pinar between Grazalema and Benamahoma supports a famous 3-sq-km *pinsapar*, the country's best preserved woodland of the rare Spanish fir (*pinsapo*). This handsome, dark-green tree survives in significant numbers only in pockets of southwest Andalucía and northern Morocco. Growing up to 30m high and able to live 500 years, it's one of 10 species around the Mediterranean that are relics of the extensive fir forests of the Tertiary period (which ended about 2.5 million years ago).

CLIMATE

The Sierra de Grazalema is the first major elevation encountered by prevailing warm, damp winds from the Atlantic. Consequently, this is one of the wettest parts of Spain (Grazalema town has the highest measured rainfall in the country at an average of 2153mm a year), and one of the greenest parts of Andalucía. Snow is fairly common in late January and February.

PLANNING
When to Walk
May, June, September and October are best. July and August can be unpleasantly hot.

Maps
We prefer the Junta de Andalucía/IGN 1:50,000 *Parque Natural Sierra de Grazalema* map, though it omits some good and obvious trails. More widely available locally is the Libros Penthalon 1:50,000 *Plano Topográfico del Macizo de Grazalema*, a revamp of some ancient SGE maps.

Information Sources
The nature park's main information office, the **Centro de Visitantes El Bosque** (☎ 956 72 70 29; Calle Federico García Lorca 1, El Bosque; 10am-2pm & 5-7pm Mon-Sat, 9am-2pm Sun) is in El Bosque. There are further information offices in Grazalema and Zahara de la Sierra.

ACCESS TOWN
See Grazalema (p299).

GRAZALEMA LOOP

Duration 6 hours
Distance 20km
Difficulty easy–moderate
Start/Finish Grazalema (p299)
Transport bus
Summary A walk through surprisingly remote valleys and passes, green woodlands and impressive limestone scenery.

There are several routes across the higher country between Grazalema and Benaocaz, 8km southwest as the crow flies. This walk follows one outward and another returning to Grazalema, with a total ascent of 1000m. Carry enough water for the whole of the walk.

GETTING TO/FROM THE WALK
For more on getting to and from the walk see Grazalema p299.

THE WALK
From Camping Tajo Rodillo walk five minutes up the A372, then turn left along a path with a 'Camino Peatonal' (pedestrian path) sign. This climbs gradually westward below the road. After 30 minutes it reaches a picnic shelter, the **Merendero del Boyar**. Go through a gate 50m to the right of this, with a sign 'Paso a Pie Salto del Cabrero'.

ANDALUCÍA

SIERRA DE GRAZALEMA

| 1 | Grazalema Loop | p289 |
| 2 | Benamahoma to Zahara de la Sierra | p291 |

To Algodonales (19km)

Finish Walk 2

Zahara de la Sierra

Embalse de Zahara-El Gastor

Portalejo

Puerto de la Breña

Garganta Seca

Garganta Verde

Alternative Route

Arroyo de Bocaleones

Gruta de la Ermita

To Ronda (29km)

Arroyo del

Sierra Margarita (1172m)

Laguna del Perezoso

Cerro de Cornicabra (1265m)

Puerto de los Acebuches

Alternative Route

El Portezuelo

Puerto de Albarranes

Cerro del Pilar (1301m)

Puerto de los Palomas

Brazo del Agua

Valdihuelo (1109m)

Sierra del Labradillo

Puerto del Pinar

El Torreón (1654m)

Pico San Cristóbal (1525m)

CA531

Rio de El Bosque

A372

Camping Los Linares

Benamahoma

Start Walk 2

To El Bosque (4km);
Villamartín (19km);
Seville (104km)

(975m)

Sierra de Albarracín

Sierra del Pinar

Puerto del Boyar

Merendero del Boyar

del Boyar

cortijo

Start / Finish Walk 1

Rio Guadalete

To Ronda (27km)

Grazalema

A372

Peñón Grande

Camping Tajo Rodillo

Llano del Endrinal

Sierra del Endrinal

Simancón (1561m)

Reloj (1535m)

A374

Arroyo Corredor

Salto del Cabrero

Casa del Dornajo

To Arcos de la Frontera

Tavizna

Silla (920m)

A373

Arroyo del Pajaruco

Benaocaz

Sierra del Caillo

Navazo Alto (1395m)

A374

Zona de Acampada Cintillo y Aguas Nuevas

0   2   2km

0   1   1 mile

Ubrique
To Gaucín (15km)

ANDALUCÍA

A dirt track leads 25 minutes southwest down to a white *cortijo*. Just before the *cortijo*, assorted signs direct you down to the left, through a gate and onto a path marked by a couple of green paint arrows. This descends through a gall-oak wood.

Thirty minutes from the *cortijo* the path starts to climb in a southwesterly direction. Just before the top of a rise, the path veers right between rocks, indicated by the odd green paint splodge or arrow, then bends left through a gate. It goes straight ahead after the gate, then veers right through terrain studded with limestone rocks. You descend to a flat, grassy area and curve westward through a gap between rocky ridges to the edge of the **Salto del Cabrero** (Goatherds' Leap) – a sloping fissure perhaps 500m long and 100m across, where the earth simply seems to have slipped 80m or 100m downwards – one hour from the white *cortijo*.

Return to the flat, grassy area and veer right to leave it by its south corner. Cross a small rise and head south towards **Benaocaz**, which soon becomes visible. You'll reach it in roughly an hour from the Salto del Cabrero, passing the Hostal San Antón as you walk up into the village. For food, continue about half a kilometre along the street to **Las Vegas** (Plaza de las Libertades; *media-raciones* €5.75).

The footsore have the option of returning to Grazalema by a Los Amarillos bus from Ubrique which passes through Benaocaz at 3.10pm (3.40pm Saturday, Sunday and holidays, although check times at the Grazalema tourist office before setting out). Otherwise head back to Hostal San Antón and follow the street along its right-hand (east) side. At the top of the street take the path passing the left-hand (west) side of Restaurante-Bar El Parral. This soon bends right (northeast) to pass through a gate five minutes from El Parral. As you follow the climbing path after the gate, keep looking for the indispensable yellow paint arrows. Twenty minutes beyond the gate the route turns left through a gate between two brick pillars. A further 20 minutes later look for a yellow arrow on the ground, pointing north, when you arrive in a small clearing with paths going every which way. Twenty minutes after that, you go through another gate: initially head north-northeast up the valley ahead but after 300m the path veers up the right (northeast). Ten minutes later you reach a bath serving as an animal drinking trough: look for a yellow arrow 25m uphill, pointing left (northeast). Follow this and soon you reach the **Casa del Dornajo**, an abandoned farmstead high in a holm-oak-strewn valley – the Casa is less impressive than your exertion in reaching it deserves, but still worth a breather beneath its trees!

From Dornajo start out northeast and almost immediately you're following blue paint arrows against the direction they point. The path bends northward across the lower slopes of **Simancón** (1561m), and 30 minutes from Dornajo you crest a rise where the Grazalema-Benamahoma road comes into view. The path descends to a gate about 15 minutes away. From the gate head 150m north, still against the blue arrows, then turn right at a path junction. This takes you over a rise past two cairns. Head northeast down to the bottom of the valley in front of you, which takes 30 minutes. At first there's a maze of sheep tracks, but a decent path materialises just right of centre after a few minutes. This switches to the left side of the valley about halfway down. Just after a water trough by the corner of a small pine plantation at the bottom of the valley, take the lesser path up to the left. This passes beneath the rock-climbers' crag **Peñón Grande** to emerge at the car park outside Camping Tajo Rodillo, 30 minutes from the trough.

BENAMAHOMA TO ZAHARA DE LA SIERRA

Duration 5 hours

Distance 14.5km

Difficulty easy

Start Benamahoma (p297)

Finish Zahara de la Sierra (p302)

Transport bus

Summary A beautiful walk through limestone hills, native oak woods and olive groves to the region's most spectacularly located village.

This walk takes you across some surprisingly remote country of thick woodlands and high pastures just outside the *área de reserva*. If you're doing some of the walks in the reserve area (see Sierra de Grazalema – Área de Reserva under More Walks, p295), this is one way of getting from the end of the Pinsapar walk to the jumping-off point for the Garganta Verde. Carry enough water for the whole walk.

ANDALUCÍA

GETTING TO/FROM THE WALK

For more on getting to and from the walk see Benamahoma p297 and Zahara de la Sierra p302.

THE WALK

At the bottom (west) end of Benamahoma, turn north by the Venta El Bujío bar. The side road crosses the Río de El Bosque and immediately divides. Take the left option, then turn right after 70m. Ignore a right fork opposite a pillared gate after a few minutes, but almost immediately turn 90 degrees to the right. Go through a gate, ignore a left turn soon afterwards, and the dirt road you are now on leads all the way to Zahara de la Sierra. However, a few worthwhile variations from the basic route are detailed in what follows.

The track soon starts climbing fairly steeply, with a few zigzags. Around 35 minutes from the last gate mentioned, with the track now more level, you pass through another gate as you head up the west side of the Breña del Agua valley. In a further 30 minutes there's a fenced enclosure on the left. Just 100m beyond this, a path branches left (north) shortly before the main track makes a sharpish right bend. Here you have a choice: if you stay with the main track (passing a *cortijo* after 10 minutes or so, going left at a junction at the Puerto de Albarranes 15 minutes later, and passing the *cortijo* El Portezuelo after another 10 minutes), you'll enjoy views of the **Cerro del Pilar** (1301m), **Sierra del Pinar** and **Cerro de Cornicabra** (1265m).

An alternative route is offered by the path, which saves you a few minutes and passes through some lovely woodlands. The path is not very clear at the start, but soon becomes so as it climbs 15 minutes to a little pass (925m). Descending, it bends a little to the right before emerging in a grassy upland valley with **Sierra Margarita** (1172m) rising from its west side. Head for the gate in the fence across the middle of the valley, where you rejoin the main track descending from El Portezuelo.

Just through the gate is the so-called **Laguna del Perezoso**, a shallow, stone-walled depression that collects rainwater but is often dry. The track continues ahead for five minutes, then begins a winding, 50-minute descent to the Arroyo del Parralejo (often

dry). From the *arroyo* there's a 20-minute ascent through perhaps the loveliest woods of the whole walk (mainly holm oaks and olives) to the Puerto de la Breña (600m).

Then it's downhill for 50 minutes to the Arroyo de Bocaleones issuing from the Garganta Verde. As you descend, you can see, to your right, some of the cliffs of the gorge, which is home to a large vulture colony. After passing Puerto do la Breña you could choose to pick up the Alternative Route (see Alternative Route: Colada de la Breña). From the Arroyo de Bocaleones you have around 40 minutes of up-and-down through olive groves to **Zahara**.

ALTERNATIVE ROUTE: COLADA DE LA BREÑA

35 minutes, 1.2km

It's possible to follow the old Colada de la Breña livestock route and avoid some of the main track's curves. Take the driveway down towards a *cortijo* on the right, a few minutes after the Puerto de la Breña. Turn left off the drive and follow a broad path northeast downhill for 10 minutes. Pass just to the right of another *cortijo*, then immediately veer to the left downhill. Pick up a clear trail running along for 20 minutes above the Garganta Seca stream, to rejoin the main track a few minutes before the Arroyo de Bocaleones.

SIERRA DE ARACENA (SIERRA MORENA)

Travel north from sultry Seville, over the burning southern plains, for a couple of hours and you'll reach a largely forgotten, mountain region known as the Sierra de Aracena (which forms a part of the Sierra Morena). Blissfully quiet, this is an area of rolling hills covered with a thick pelt of cork-oaks and pines and punctuated by winding river valleys, enchanting villages of stone and tile, and bustling market towns such as the area's 'capital', Aracena. Much of this little-discovered rural world – threaded with beautiful walking trails and blessed with a rich hill-country cuisine – lies within the 1840-sq-km Parque Natural Sierra de

Aracena y Picos de Aroche, Andalucía's second-largest protected area.

HISTORY

The pleasant climate and relatively fertile countryside of the Sierra de Aracena has meant that the region has been inhabited for around 5000 years. The hills around these parts have long been known to house large deposits of precious metals including gold and local legends say that it was from this area that Biblical King Solomon of Jerusalem obtained the gold for his magnificent temple. True or not, we do know that the Romans undertook a lot of mining around here – a tradition that continued until 2001 at the nearby Río Tinto mines.

Like the Sierra de Grazalema this area was a Muslim–Christian frontier, and Islamic reminders remain – just wait until you get a load of Almonaster la Real's *mezquita.*

At the start of the 20th century tourism started to grow and the regional 'capital' Aracena grew rapidly.

ENVIRONMENT

Keep your ears and eyes open and you'll find that the Sierra Morena as a whole is bustling with wildlife. Of the mammals the real five-star attraction is the beautiful Iberian lynx; the world's most endangered big cat. Doñana, with its 50 lynx has long been considered the best place to see them (and even there you have almost zero chance of spotting one), but evidence has recently emerged that the Sierra Morena now contains a slowly expanding population of 150 cats (concentrated around Andújar and Cardeña-Montoro in Jaen province). Other glamour-puss animals that inhabit the remote corners of the Sierra include wolves, black storks, imperial and booted eagles and black vultures. More commonly seen creatures include masses of summer butterflies, various lizards and snakes, as well as rabbits and foxes. The one creature you certainly won't be able to avoid are free-ranging pigs who scour the forest floors in search of acorns. It's these pigs that eventually become the best *jamón serrano* in all of Spain. Do remember to thank any pigs you see for this!

The typical trees of the area include cork-oaks, chestnuts and pines, as well as masses of spring flowers lighting up the sunny meadows.

CLIMATE

Subject to damp westerly winds coming off the Atlantic and with an altitude of up to 960m, the Sierra de Aracena is one of the wetter, and cooler, parts of Andalucía. Spring and autumn is mild to warm while summers have hot days and surprisingly cool nights. Winter can be downright cold.

PLANNING
When to Walk

Late April to June and September and October are best. July and August can be unpleasantly hot. In May, probably the best overall month, the hills are ablaze in colourful wildflowers.

Maps & Guides

Discovery Walking Guides *Sierra de Aracena* and the accompanying *Sierra de Aracena Tour & Trail Map* are superb and cover dozens of routes through these hills.

Other good sources are the *Parque Natural Sierra de Aracena y Picos de Aroche* (1:75,000), published by the Junta de Andalucía, and the IGN 1:25,000 sheets 917-1 *Galaroza*, 917-II *Cortelazor*, 917-III *Cortegana* and 917-IV *Aracena*. Also worth getting your mitts on is the Spanish language *Mapa Guía Siera de Aracena y Picos de Aroche.*

ACCESS TOWN

See Aracena p296.

ALÁJAR FIGURE OF EIGHT

Duration 6 hours

Distance 15km

Difficulty easy–moderate

Start/Finish Alájar

Transport bus

Summary A beautiful stroll through varied woodlands with the chance to enjoy expansive views, meadows of wild flowers, the spectacular Peña de Arias Montano as well as lunch in a gorgeous village.

GETTING TO/FROM THE WALK

Several buses a day run between Aracena and Alájar.

THE WALK

This sublime walk is a superb introduction to walking in the Sierra de Aracena and connects three of the area's most attractive villages in a figure of eight, allowing you to vary the route by starting from any of the three, or walking only part of the route. The whole walk takes about six hours at an average walking pace, not counting stops. The steeper bits are done downhill and there's nothing any modestly fit walker couldn't cope with.

Leave the main square at Alájar by the road heading west out of the village, pass an olive grove on your left and cross straight over the main road and take the track to **El Calabacino**, an international artist/hippy colony and a few creative signs from its inhabitants help you along your way. Your route crosses a stream on a wooden bridge, and a small, square, stone-and-brick church on your right, then ascends through a cork-oak forest. Ten minutes past the small church, fork directly right at an 'El Castaño' sign. Another 10 minutes of drifting through cork-oak forests with lots of trees and plants overhanging the path and you will cross a small stream bed (normally dry) to follow a path marked by a yellow paint dot. Within a further 10 minutes the path becomes a vehicle track through lovely flower bedecked meadows (perfect picnic territory). Fifteen minutes along this, carry straight on at a crossroads, and in three minutes more you crest a rise and the terracotta roofs of Castaño del Robledo come into view. Some 200m past the crest, take the shadier path diverging to the left, indicated by arrows pointing back the way you've just come from. This shady path runs parallel to the vehicle track so it's no great shakes if you stay on the wider road. After 10 to 15 minutes this track starts to veer down to the left, passing between tall cork oaks and gradually wending into **Castaño del Robledo**.

After lunch at one of Castaño's basic bar-restaurants, leave by the path through the **Área Recreativa Capilla del Cristo**, a shady picnic area with a little white-washed shrine on the north side of the HV5211 road passing the north side of the village, and pass by a field that's often full of pigs. To the left you'll soon be able to see Jabugo,

before you fork right at a tree with yellow-and-white paint stripes, 15 minutes from the *área recreativa* (recreational area). Your path starts winding downhill. Go straight on at a crossing of tracks after 10 minutes, and right at a fork one minute after that (a ruined stone building is up the left-hand path here). In 10 minutes Galaroza comes into view as you pass between its outlying *fincas* (rural properties). Cross a small river on a footbridge and emerge on the N433 road three minutes later. Walk left to **Galaroza** along the unpleasant N433 for around 800m then leave by the track on the left marked by a 'Sendero Ribera del Jabugo' route sign.

Fork right one minute out from the mentioned sign, then turn left four or five minutes later down to a footbridge that stretches over a stream. The path soon starts winding up the valley of the Río Jabugo, a particularly lovely stretch. Half an hour from the footbridge you will reach a vehicle track and cross roads marked with 'Camino de Jabugo a Fuenteheridos' and 'Camino de Galaroza a Castaño Bajo' signs. Take the right-hand fork towards Castaño Bajo, passing a couple of *cortijos* to cross the river on a low cement bridge. Turn left 50m past the bridge, then left at a fork 30m further on. You recross the river, then gradually wind up and away from it. Ten minutes from the river, turn left at a red-tile-roofed house (Monte Blanco) and for 15 minutes (mostly upward) you follow

ALÁJAR FIGURE OF EIGHT

a lightly cobbled road back to Castaño del Robledo, this time entering from the west.

To leave again, start retracing the route by which you arrived from Alájar earlier – up Calle Arias Montano from Plaza del Álamo, right along the first cobbled lane, up through the cork oaks to the crest then down to the crossing of tracks (30 minutes out of Castaño del Robledo). From here turn left, across the southwestern flank of **Castaño** (960m, the highest hill in the Sierra de Aracena) where you are rewarded with wonderful views over the *sierra*. The track curves sharply to the left after 12 to 15 minutes.

Some 300m further, turn right along a path beside a stone wall, which is marked by yellow paint. At a fork 10 minutes walk down from here, take the lesser path down to the right, and within another 20 minutes you will reach the **Peña de Arias Montano.** Leaving here, start along the paved road down the hill, but after 50m diverge right down on to a cobbled track. Within 10 minutes this track re-emerges on the road: follow the road down for 25m then turn right down a track through a gap in the wall. Cross the A470 a minute or two later to carry on down into the middle of Alájar. Find a chair in a bar, slump down, drink.

ALTERNATIVE ROUTE
3 hrs; 10km
If you want to make this walk shorter follow the first part of the walk from Alájar to Castaño del Robledo and, after some lunch there, return to Alájar following the route description in the last section of the main walk.

MORE WALKS

SIERRA DE GRAZALEMA
Área de Reserva
These walks are among the best in the Grazalema park, but access is controlled. The rules change from time to time, so it's well worth seeking advance information from the **Centro de Visitantes El Bosque** (☎ 956 72 70 29; Calle Federico García Lorca 1, El Bosque; 10am-2pm & 5-7pm Mon-Sat, 9am-2pm Sun) in El Bosque. At the time of writing you need a free permit

from the El Bosque park office for any of these walks. You can call or visit El Bosque up to 15 days in advance for this; do this as early as possible as the number of people allowed on each route is limited; you can arrange to collect permits at the Zahara visitors centre or Grazalema tourist office. For map advice see Planning (p289).

In July, August and September, when fire risk is high, some routes are wholly or partly closed, or you may be required to go with a guide from an authorised local company.

GRAZALEMA TO BENAMAHOMA VIA THE PINSAPAR
After a couple of steepish ascents in the initial third of this 14km walk, it's downhill most of the way. You walk up from Grazalema for 40 minutes to a parking area by the Zahara de la Sierra road (the CA531), just under 1km up from the A372. Here starts the footpath that leads across the northern slopes of the Sierra del Pinar. The thickest part of the *pinsapar* fir forest comes in the middle third of the walk, below the Sierra del Pinar's precipitous upper slopes.

EL TORREÓN
The highest peak of the Grazalema region, El Torreón (1654m) tops the Sierra del Pinar between Grazalema and Benamahoma. The ascent starts 100m east of the 'Km 40' marker on the Grazalema–Benamahoma road, about 8km from Grazalema. It's about 2½ hours up and 1½ hours down.

TOWNS & FACILITIES

Accommodation in Andalucía is generally much better value than in northern Spain – the exception to this rule being the beach resorts in high summer, and Seville and Granada at almost anytime.

AGUA AMARGA
☎ 950 / pop 1300
This is a pleasant fishing-cum-tourist settlement stretched along a straight, sandy beach. There is no ATM.

Hostal Restaurante La Palmera (☎ 950 13 82 08; Calle Aguada; d €60-90), at the eastern end of the beach, has 10 pleasant rooms. The attached restaurant is the most popular in town.

Hotel Family (☎ 13 80 14; www.hotelfamily.es; Calle La Lomilla; d with breakfast €85-120; mid-Dec-Nov) has nine frugally decorated rooms. They dish up excellent meals (mains €17-26). You pass Calle La Lomilla at the end of the walk.

Autocares Frahermar (☎ 29 02 12) in Almería runs to/from Agua Amarga once on Monday, Wednesdays, Friday, Saturday and Sunday; service increases to daily in July and August. An alternative is to take a taxi (€20, 20 minutes) to Carboneras, the next town north, where buses to Almería run four times on weekdays and once on weekends. There is no bus service connecting towns within the park. A taxi from Agua Amarga costs between €65 and €70 to Almería, El Cabo de Gata or anywhere else in the park, and it's a good idea to reserve at least a few hours ahead. **Taxi de Gata** (☎ 669 071442; www.taxidegata.com) is based in Níjar; **Taxi Ramón Ruíz López** (☎ 13 00 08, 606 414724) is in Carboneras.

ALMERÍA
☎ 950 / pop 177,000

The provincial capital is dominated by a fine 10th- to 15th-century fortress, the Alcazaba, which, along with the 16th-century cathedral, shouldn't be missed if you're passing through. You can stock up on food supplies at the **covered market** (Rambla del Obispo Orbera).

Information
For information on places around Almería province, visit the regional **tourist office** (☎ 27 43 55; Parque de Nicolás Salmerón; 9am-7pm Mon-Fri, 10am–2pm Sat & Sun).

Supplies & Equipment
El Libro Picasso (Calle Reyes Católicos 9) stocks a vast range of books and maps.

Sleeping & Eating
Clean and well kept, the **Albergue Juvenil Almería** (☎ 26 97 88; Calle Isla de Fuerteventura; under 26 yrs/others €18/24) is 1.5km east of the centre; take bus No 1 ('Universidad') from Rambla del Obispo Orbera in the centre.

Hostal Estación (☎ 26 72 39; hostalestacion@hotmail.com; Calle Calzada de Castro 37; d €48), near the train and bus station, is clean and basic. Nearer the centre, **Hotel Costasol** (☎ 23 40 11; www.hotelcostasol.com; Paseo de Almería 58; d €54) has some modern style, and spotless rooms with air-con.

Café Barea (Calle Granada 2; *tostadas* €3-5) is a bustling, old-fashioned *cafetería* with good breakfasts and snacks. Of the many excellent tapas bars in town, **Casa Puga** (Calle Jovellanos 7; drink & tapas €1.90, *raciones* €6-9) is one of the finest, serving free tapas with each drink and affordable *raciones* at tables in the back.

Getting There & Away
Almería's airport receives some international charter flights, and scheduled services from Barcelona and Madrid.

The combined bus and train station is on **Plaza de la Estación**, about 1km southeast of the city centre. Note that there is no luggage storage here. Buses come from Málaga (€16; 3½ to five hours; at least eight daily) and Granada (€12-13.50; two to four hours; at least 11 daily). Trains run to/from Granada (€15; 2¼ hours; four daily). There are also direct trains to and from Madrid and buses to and from Valencia and Barcelona.

ARACENA
☎ 959 / pop 7500

Sparkling white in its mountain bowl the thriving, old market town of Aracena is an appealingly lively place that's wrapped like a ribbon around a medieval church and ruined castle. With a stash of good places to stay and eat, it makes an ideal base from which to explore the Sierra de Aracena.

Information
Aracena Tourist Office (☎ 12 82 06; Calle Pozo de la Nieve; 10am-2pm & 4-6pm) It has some leaflets with basic walk descriptions and sells maps.

Sleeping & Eating
Molino del Bombo (☎ 12 84 78; www.molinodelbombo.com; Calle Ancha 4; s/d €30/60) is a wonderfully welcoming hotel with a tastefully rustic yet very comfortable style. It's hidden away at the top of town near the bull ring.

In the village of Castaño del Robledo, through which our walk passes, the **Posada del Castaño** (☎ 46 55 02; www .posadadelcastano.com; Calle José Sánchez Calvo 33; s/d with breakfast €40/50) has walkers foremost in mind and the young British owners (experienced walkers) are full of information and tips. They offer self-guided walking holidays (see website).

Eating is a highlight of Aracena. Of the many options don't miss chowing down the tapas of **Rincón de Juan** (Calle Jose Nogales; tapas €1.60-1.80, *raciones* €7-10) or for something more formal the **Meson Rural las Tinjas** (Calle Juan del Cíd Lōpez; mains €8-10) cannot fail to impress.

Getting There & Away

Casal (in Seville ☎ 954 99 92 62) operates buses between Aracena and Seville several times a day. From Aracena buses fan out to most of the surrounding villages.

BENAMAHOMA

☎ 956 / pop 500

This small, attractive village is 13km west of Grazalema and 4km east of El Bosque, on the A372.

Camping Los Linares (☎ 71 62 75; www .campingloslinares.com; site per person/ tent/car €5/5/4.50, four-person cabins €85; daily Jun-Sep, Sat & Sun Oct-May) is 600m up Camino del Nacimiento at the back of the village. There are several places to eat in the village.

The Grazalema–El Bosque bus, departing Grazalema at 5.30am Monday to Saturday, stops in Benamahoma; confirm departure times at the Grazalema tourist office.

BÉRCHULES

☎ 958 / pop 900

Cascading down the mountainside, the town of Bérchules is a popular stop for hikers.

Head almost 1km down to the main road at the foot of the village, where **Hotel Los Bérchules** (☎ 85 25 30; www.hotelberchules.com; Carretera de Bérchules 20; s/d with bathroom €35/45) has a pool, Bérchules' best restaurant and English-speaking hosts. If you arrive after the dinner hour, try the nearby **Bar Cuatro Vientos** (*raciones* €5) for satisfying tapas like rabbit with mushrooms.

CAPILEIRA

☎ 958 / pop 560

The highest of the three villages in the Barranco de Poqueira, Capileira offers the easiest access to day walks in the gorge and to the high Sierra Nevada. There is a supermarket here for supplies. For transport information see Getting There & Around (p268).

Sleeping & Eating

Hostal Atalaya (☎ 76 30 25; www .hostalatalaya.com; Calle Perchel 3; s/d €18/30, exterior d €35), 100m down the main road, offers pleasant, modernised rooms with breakfast included.

Cortijo Catifalarga (☎ 34 33 57; www .catifalarga.com; d €73-95, apt from €95) is a charmingly renovated farmstead. Its 500m driveway begins 750m up the Sierra Nevada road from the top of the village.

Bar El Tilo (Plaza Calvario; *raciones* €6-8) serves good-value *raciones*.

CAZORLA

☎ 953 / pop 8200

The attractive warren of twisting alleys that makes up the old quarter of Cazorla is the main launching pad for forays into the Parque Natural de Carzola.

Information

The **Oficina de Turismo Municipal** (☎ 72 08 75; Calle Narra 8; 10am-1pm & 5-7.30pm) is 200m north of Plaza de la Constitución.

Supplies & Equipment

You can stock up on supplies at plenty of bakeries and shops around the centre.

Sleeping & Eating

Hotel Guadalquivir (☎ 72 02 68; www .hguadalquivir.com in Spanish; Calle Nueva 6; s/d €36/48), just off the short main street Calle Doctor Muñoz, is a cheerful place with pretty rooms boasting bathroom, TV, air-con and heating.

Hotel Tharsis (☎ 72 13 13; www.tharsis cazorla.com; Calle Hilario Marco 51-53; s/d €51/65) This mid-range, mid-town hotel is a boon for motorists with its ample parking, friendly management and pleasant modern rooms behind a rather dull façade.

298 · ANDALUCÍA · Towns & Facilities

Mesón Don Chema (Calle Escaleras del Mercado 2; mains €10-18), down a lane off Calle Doctor Muñoz, serves up excellent local fare including venison, pork and the sizzling *huevos a la cazorleña*, a mixed stew of sliced boiled eggs, sausage and vegetables.

La Rincon de Victor (Plaza María; *raciones* €7-15) Take a heavy dose of locally flavoured tapas and meals, and combine with a great atmosphere and you have a memorable place to get stuffed.

Getting There & Away

Buses run by **Alsina Graells** head to Cazorla from Granada (€14.15; 3½ hours; two daily) stopping in Jaén, Baeza and Úbeda. The main stop in Cazorla is Plaza de la Constitución.

EL CABO DE GATA

☎ 950 / pop 170

Largely a cluster of holiday chalets and apartments, this is an amiable, low-rise place, set on a long, windswept beach that's either desolate or packed with Almería day-trippers. A bank on Calle Iglesia has an ATM.

Sleeping & Eating

Camping Cabo de Gata (☎ 16 04 43; www .campingcabodegata.com; site per person €6) is 1km from the beach, 2.5km north of the village by dirt roads. It has a restaurant.

Hostal Las Dunas (☎ 37 00 72; www .lasdunas.net; Calle Barrio Nuevo 58; s/d with bathroom €40/55), at the northern end of the village, has well-kept, modern rooms.

Hotel Blanca Brisa (☎ 37 00 01; www .blancabrisa.com; Calle Las Joricas 49; d €70) is a modern hotel, with comfortable rooms and a decent restaurant, at the entrance to the village.

Pizzeria Pedro (Calle Islas de Tabarca 2; Easter-Nov), round the corner from the Blanca Brisa, serves fine pizzas and pasta at middling prices.

Getting There & Away

Alsina Graells/ALSA (☎ 23 51 68; www .alsa.es) runs buses from Almería bus station to El Cabo de Gata (€2.50; one hour; six daily).

FERREIROLA

☎ 958 / pop 430

Set amid lush vegetation, Ferreirola is perhaps the most beautiful Taha village. For sleeping try the **Sierra y Mar** (☎ 76 61 71; www.sierraymar.com; Calle Albaicín; s/d with bathroom €42/62), which has nine highly individual rooms set around multiple patios and gardens, and its multilingual Danish and Italian hosts are both welcoming and highly knowledgeable about walking in the area. For an evening meal, or other lodgings (see p272), you need to walk back to Mecina or Mecinilla – just over 1km by road.

GRANADA

☎ 958 / pop 300,000

Home to the divine Alhambra palace and with a snowy Sierra Nevada backdrop, Granada is, for many, Andalucía's most magical city.

Information

The **Oficina Provincial de Turismo** (☎ 24 71 28; www.turismodegranada.com; Plaza de Mariana Pineda 10; 9.30am-7pm Mon-Fri, 10am–2pm Sat) is very helpful.

Supplies & Equipment

Cartográfica del Sur (☎ 20 49 01; www .cartograficadelsur.com, in Spanish; Calle Valle Inclán 2), just off Camino de Ronda, is an excellent map shop. Nearby is mountain equipment supplier **Deportes Sólo Aventura** (☎ 12 53 01; Camino de Ronda 1). IGN maps are also sold by the **CNIG** (☎ 90 93 20; Avenida Divina Pastora 7 & 9).

Sleeping & Eating

Just a short walk from the bus station and 2.5km northwest of the centre is **Camping Sierra Nevada** (☎ 15 00 62; www.campingsierranevada.com; Avenida de Madrid 107; site per person/tent/car €5.70/5.70/5.75). It has big clean bathrooms and a laundrette.

Albergue Juvenil Granada (☎ 27 26 38; Calle Ramón y Cajal 2; under 26 yrs/others €18/24), the HI hostel, is 1.7km west of the centre, with 89 comfy double and triple rooms, all with bathrooms.

Three friendly, clean and central *hostales* are **Hostal Venecia** (☎ 22 39 87; Cuesta de Goméraz 2; d €34, with bathroom €42),

Hostal Landázuri (☎ 22 14 06; www .hostallandazuri.com; Cuesta de Gomérez 24; s/d €36/45, s/d with shared bathroom €24/34) and **Hostal Arteaga** (☎ 20 88 41; www.hostalarteaga.com; Calle Arteaga 3; s/d/tr €40/49/60).

The Plaza Nueva area is a rich food-hunting ground. The bar **Bodegas Castañeda** (Calle Almireceros; *raciones* from €7) does magnificent tapas and *raciones*: seafood, omelettes, cheese, ham, pâtés – you name it. The cool neighbourhood of Realejo is also packed with tapas bars; **Los Diamantes** (Calle Navas 26; *raciones* €9-14), for fried seafood, is just the start.

Getting There & Away
Daily flights from Madrid and Barcelona are provided by **Iberia** (www.iberia.com), **Vueling** (www.vueling.com) and **Spanair** (www.spanair.com).

The **bus station** (Carretera de Jaén), nearly 3km northwest of the centre, has an internet café and luggage lockers. Services run to and from Madrid and Barcelona via Valencia; there is also a night bus direct to Madrid's Barajas airport.

The **train station** (Avenida de Andaluces), 1.5km northwest of the centre, has two daily services to/from Madrid and one or two to/from Barcelona via Valencia.

GRAZALEMA
☎ 956 / pop 2300
This neat, pretty little town nestles into a corner of beautiful mountain country and makes a superb base for the surrounding Sierra de Grazalema.

Information
Grazalema's **tourist office** (☎ 13 22 25; Plaza de España; 10am-2pm & 5-8pm Tue-Sun approx Easter-Oct, 10am-2pm & 4-6pm Tue-Sun rest of year) is helpful and the smattering of shops will furnish food and drink supplies.

Sleeping & Eating
At the top of the village beside the A372 to El Bosque is **Camping Tajo Rodillo** (☎ 71 62 75; www.campingtajorodillo.com; site from €12, per additional person or tent €5). In winter they only open at weekends.

Casa de las Piedras (☎ 13 20 14; www .casadelaspiedras.net; Calle Las Piedras 32;

s/d with shared bathroom €13/25, with private bathroom €40/50) is a good-value hostal with a restaurant serving hearty medium-priced meals.

Hotel Peñón Grande (☎ /fax 13 24 35; www.hotelgrazalema.com; Plaza Pequeña 7; s/d €38/55) is an excellent small hotel, with large, rustic-style but very comfortable rooms.

Among several places to eat on Calle Agua, off the central Plaza de España, is the excellent-value **Bar La Posadilla** (Calle Agua 19; *platos combinados* €2-6).

Restaurante Cádiz El Chico (Plaza de España 8; mains €6-13) is good for a more expensive meal, with excellent meat, egg dishes and fish.

Getting There & Away
Buses run by **Los Amarillos** (☎ 902 25 70 25) travel between Málaga and Grazalema via Ronda.

LANJARÓN
☎ 958 / pop 3800
Numerous places to stay and eat are strung along Lanjarón's lengthy main street.

There are plenty of places to put your head down for the night in and around the town the best value is the **Hotel Nuevo Palas** (☎ 77 01 11; www.hotelnuevopalas .com; Avenida de la Alpujarra 24; s/d €54/65) which has stylish rooms for a price you can't knock.

LAS NEGRAS
☎ 950 / pop 290
Set on a pebbly beach stretching towards an imposing headland of volcanic rock, Cerro Negro, the village of Las Negras attracts a vaguely trendy holiday clientele. There is a supermarket on the main street, Calle Bahía.

Hostal Arrecife (☎ 38 81 40; Calle Bahía 6; s/d with bathroom €26/38), with 11 rooms, is the only budget hotel. Other accommodation is mostly holiday apartments and houses to let, but you may find a few signs offering rooms by the night; you can also ask at the supermarket.

Pizza y Pasta (Mar-Nov; mains €7-10), just down from the main street, is a bright, friendly place serving exactly what the name suggests.

ANDALUCÍA

Alsina Graells/ALSA (☎ 902 42 22 42; www.alsa.es) runs buses to Almería once daily except Sunday, early in the morning.

MAIRENA
☎ 958 / pop 200

At the far eastern end of the Granada Alpujarras, Mairena is a small village with easy access to day walks higher up in the Sierra Nevadas, as well as the starting point for the traverse to Trevélez. There is a small market and an internet café, but no ATM.

Las Chimeneas (☎ 76 00 89; www .alpujarra-tours.com; Calle Amargura 6; r €70) is the de-facto walkers' centre here, with exceedingly well-informed owners who can suggest additional area walks.

The **restaurant** (*menú* €20) serves largely organic set meals. The village is not served by regular buses – you must take a taxi from Ugíjar or Bérchules.

MÁLAGA
☎ 952 / pop 720,000

This exuberant port city set against the sparkling blue Mediterranean is the region's chief international arrival point and has good connections with Madrid and other Andalucían cities.

Information

There's a useful **regional tourist office** (☎ 30 89 11; Pasaje de Chinitas 4; 9am-7.30pm Mon-Fri, 10am-7pm Sat, 10am-2pm Sun) off the central Plaza de la Constitución.

Supplies & Equipment

A good central outdoor equipment shop is **Deportes La Trucha** (☎ 21 22 03; Calle Carretería 100). You can stock up on food supplies at the colourful **Mercado Central** (Calle Atarazanas; early-1pm Mon-Sat).

Sleeping & Eating

Hotel Carlos V (☎ 21 51 20; Calle Císter 10; s/d €36/59) is recently renovated and offers sparkling rooms and excellent value. It's close to the Cathedral.

Hostal Derby (☎ 22 13 01; Calle San Juan de Dios 1; s/d €36/49) The Derby has spacious rooms some of which have massive views over the harbour.

Hostal Larios (☎ 22 54 90; www .hostallarios.com; Calle Marqués de Larios 9; s/d without bathroom €39/49, with

bathroom €48/58) This place easily out-does everything else in this class.

El Riad Andaluz (☎ 21 36 40; www .elriadandaluz.com; Calle Hinestrosa 24; s/d €70/90) Colourful and exotic, this gorgeous restored monastery offers eight rooms with Moroccan décor. It's a wonderful place to pamper tired muscles.

The city centre is peppered with eateries. The warehouse-like **Cladestino** (Calle Niño de Guevara 3; mains €9-17) has a great *menú* fusing north European and Latin treats. Friendly **El Vegetariano de la Alcazabilla** (Calle Pozo del Rey 5; mains around €9.50-12.50; closed Sun) concocts spectacular vegetarian dishes.

Getting There & Away

Many international carriers, including no-frills airlines, fly direct to Málaga: see Air (p351). Flying daily nonstop to/from Madrid, Barcelona, Bilbao and Valencia is **Iberia** (www.iberia.com). **Spanair** (www .spanair.com) flies from Barcelona and Madrid. **Vueling** (www.vueling.com) that links Málaga with Bilbao, Barcelona and Santiago de Compostela and **Air Europa** (www.air-europa.com) flies from Madrid, Barcelona and the Balearic Islands.

The **bus station** (☎ 35 00 61; Paseo de los Tilos) is 1km southwest of the centre. Buses come from Madrid (€21.50; six hours; at least nine daily), Granada (€10; two hours; 17 or more daily), and Seville (frequent service, €16; 2½ hours).

The **train station** (Explanada de la Estación), around the corner from the bus station, has super fast services to/from Madrid (€71.20-79.20; 2½ hours; six daily), and to/from Valencia and Barcelona (€58.40-129.40; 6½-13 hours; two daily). For Granada there are no direct trains, but you can get there in 2¼ hours for €13.45 with a transfer at Bobadilla.

PAMPANEIRA
☎ 958 / pop 330

This attractive Barranco de Poqueira village has the area's most useful information centre and a supermarket. For transport information see Getting There & Around (p268).

Sleeping & Eating

Two good-value *hostales* face each other at the entrance to the village: **Hostal**

Pampaneira (☎ 76 30 02; www
.hostalpampaneira.com; Avenida Alpujarra
1; d €40), with one of the cheapest restaurants
in the village (*menú del día* €9), and **Hostal
Ruta del Mulhacén** (☎ 76 30 10; www
.rutadelmulhacen.com; Avenida Alpujarra
6; s/d €36/45).

Casa Diego (Plaza de la Libertad 15;
mains €6-9), with a pleasant upstairs
terrace, is a good choice from the three
restaurants just along the street.

SAN JOSÉ
☎ 950 / pop 140
San José becomes a chic little resort in
summer, but out of season it's almost
deserted. Entering the town from the
direction of the walk follow 'Centro
Urbano' signs, which bring you onto the
main street, Avenida de San José, opposite
the **tourist office & park information
office** (☎ 38 02 99; 10am-2pm & 5-8pm,
closed Sun afternoon in winter). Calle Cala
Higuera, straight on, leads in 10 minutes
to the youth hostel and Camping Tau. One
block to the right along the main street is
San José's central intersection, where you'll
find an ATM. There are three supermarkets
on Avenida de San José.

Camping Tau (☎ 38 01 66; www
.parquenatural.com/tau; site per person/
tent/car €6 each, s/d €20/45; Apr-Sep) has
a shady little site some 300m back from San
José beach, on the north side of town.

There are a dozen or more *hostales* and
hotels. **Hostal Aloha** (☎ 38 04 61; www
.hostalaloha.com; Calle Cala Higuera; d
€55) is an appealing budget hotel with an
enormous pool on the back terrace.

Restaurante El Emigrante (Avenida
de San José; mains €9-14), at the central
intersection, is an excellent-value eatery
with a wide-ranging menu.

Autocares Bernardo (☎ 25 04 22; www
.autocaresbernardo.com) runs buses from
Almería and San José (three Mon-Sat,
two on Sun) and back (four Mon-Sat, two
on Sun).

SEVILLE
☎ 954 / pop 700,000
Steamy and passionate, Seville is an addiction
that can never be shaken. This is the home
of the glory and gore of bullfighting, the
soul-ripping sound of flamenco, the sombre

and spectacular Semana Santa (Holy Week)
processions and the jolly relief of Feria de
Abril. Cloaked in orange blossom and
dressed in art and culture, Seville is quite
simply a city you will never forget.

Information
There are several regional tourist offices
throughout the city. The most important
two are those at the **airport** (☎ 44 91
28; 9am-8.30pm Mon-Fri, 10am-6pm Sat,
10am-2pm Sun, closed holidays) and the
main one on **Avenida de la Constitución**
(☎ 22 14 04; Avenida de la Constitución
21; 9am-7.30pm Mon-Fri, 9am-3pm & 3-
7pm Sat & Sun, closed holidays); The staff
at the Constitución office are well informed
but often very busy.

Sleeping & Eating
Pensión Doña Trinidad (☎ 54 19 06;
www.donatrinidad.com; Calle Archeros 7;
s/d from €30/55) is a recently renovated
pension run by an elderly, but young-
at-heart couple who love to chitter-chatter
with anyone within range. They've managed
to put together one of the best cheapies in
Seville. The shiny rooms surround a plant-
filled, and traditionally tiled courtyard.

Un Patio en Santa Cruz (☎ 53 94 13;
www.patiosantacruz.com; Calle Doncellas
15; s/d €58/68) More of an art gallery
than a hotel the starched white walls
are coated in loud works of art, strange
sculptures and preserved plants. The
rooms are immensely comfortable and
there's a cool roof-top terrace with mosaic
Moroccan tables.

Hotel Sacristía Santa Ana (☎ 91 57
22; www.hotelsacristia.com; Alameda
de Hércules 22; d from €79) This utterly
delightful hotel is the best deal in Seville.
The setting on the Alameda is great for the
neighbouring bars and restaurants and the
hotel itself is a heavenly place with old-
fashioned rooms with big arty bedheads,
circular baths and cascading showers.

Nowhere else in Andalucía does food like
Seville. The city centre is filled with superb
places to eat, but these are a favourite
couple. **Vinería San Telmo** (Paseo Catalina
de Ribera 4; tapas €3.50, *media-raciones*
€10) If the thought of foie-gras with quail's
eggs and lychees or *rascacielos de tomate,
berenjena, queso de cabra y salmón* (which

roughly translates into a pyramid of tomato, goat cheese, aubergine and salmon) doesn't make you dribble then you're probably dead. **Los Coloniales** (Cnr Calle Dmitorio & Plaza Cristo de Burgos; tapas €2.50, *raciones* €10) It might not look like much from the outside but this is something very special. It's hard to pick a favourite dish as everything is outstanding, but we'd never turn down a plate of *chorizo a la Asturiana*, a divine spicy sausage in an onion sauce served on a bed of lightly fried potato. To follow up try the aubergines in honey.

Getting There & Away
Many international carriers, including no-frills airlines, fly direct to Seville: see Air (p351). Flying daily nonstop to/from several Spanish cities is **Iberia** (www.iberia.com), **Spanair** (www.spanair.com) and **Vueling** (www.vueling.com).

Seville has two bus stations. Buses to/from the north of Sevilla province, Huelva province, Portugal, Madrid, Extremadura and northwest Spain use the Estación de Autobuses Plaza de Armas. Other buses use the Estación de Autobuses Prado de San Sebastián, just southeast of the Barrio de Santa Cruz. Buses run roughly hourly to Huelva, Cádiz, Cordoba, Granada, Malaga and Madrid.

Seville's train station, **Estacin Santa Justa** (Avenida Kansas City), is 1.5km northeast of the centre. There's also a city-centre **Renfe information & ticket office** (Calle Zaragoza 29). Fourteen or more superfast AVEs whizz daily to/from Madrid in just 2½ hrours. Every one to two hours trains rattle off to Cádiz and Cordoba while several a day chug down to Huelva, Granada and Malaga.

TREVÉLEZ
☎ 958 / pop 800
Trevélez, set in a deep gash in the Sierra Nevada's southern flank, is a frequent starting point for ascents of the high Sierra Nevada peaks.

Along the main road you're confronted by a welter of ham and souvenir shops, but an exploration of the upper parts reveals a lively, typically Alpujarran village. La General bank just above the main road has an ATM. There's a Coviran supermarket

on the street approaching Hotel La Fragua from the Plaza del Barrio Medio.

Sleeping & Eating
A kilometre south of Trevélez along the A4132 road towards Busquístar is **Camping Trevélez** (☎ 85 87 35; www.campingtrevelez.net; site per person/small tent/car €4.50/4/3.80). It's set on a terraced and tree-coated hillside and has a good-value restaurant.

Near the top of the village, **Hotel La Fragua** (☎ 85 86 26; www.hotellafragua.com; Calle San Antonio 4; s/d with bathroom €33.50/45) has pleasant rooms, some with balconies, and is popular with walkers – some of whom may rise earlier, and more noisily, than you'd like to!

Mesón La Fragua (mains €9-12), just along the street from Hotel La Fragua, does excellent meals ranging from good vegetarian dishes to great lamb stews. Also good is **Mesón Joaquín** (Calle Puente; mains €9-14), just west of the main junction.

Getting There & Away
Alsina Graells/ALSA (☎ 23 51 68; www.alsa.es) runs buses to/from Granada (€8.50; three hours; two daily).

ZAHARA DE LA SIERRA
☎ 956 / pop 1600
Topped by a crag with a ruined castle dating back to the 13th century, Zahara has a superb setting above the Zahara-El Gastor reservoir. The Grazalema park's **Centro de Visitantes Zahara de la Sierra** (Zahara Catur; ☎ 12 31 14; Plaza del Rey 3; 9am-2pm & 4-7pm daily) is in the village centre.

Hostal Marqués de Zahara (☎/fax 12 30 61; www.marquesdezahara.com; Calle San Juan 3; s/d with bathroom €30/50), a converted mansion in the village centre, has comfy rooms.

You won't go wrong at either of two neighbouring establishments on Calle San Juan: **Restaurante Los Naranjos** (meat & fish mains €6-12) or **Bar Nuevo** (*menú* €8).

Comes (☎ 952 87 19 92) operates buses between Zahara and Ronda. Ronda is on the Málaga–Grazalema bus route. There's no bus service between Zahara and Grazalema.

Camino de Santiago

HIGHLIGHTS

- Watching the setting sun from the gates of **Roncesvalles** (p334) and thinking about the long road ahead
- Appreciating warm, animated conversation, intriguing walking companions and welcome rest in simple *albergues* after long days of walking
- Revelling in the solitude of **Castilla's** flat plain (p305), with the wind combing endless fields of wheat that roll off into distant nothingness
- Admiring the sun filtering through the countless stained-glass windows in **León's** beautiful cathedral (p332), creating a divine kaleidoscope
- Giving thanks for a safe journey at the altar of **Santiago's** cathedral (p330) after walking 783km in one month

Number of pilgrims completing the Camino:	1985: 2491	1995: 19,821	2005: 93,921

'The door is open to all, to sick and healthy, not only to Catholics but also to pagans, Jews, heretics and vagabonds', so go the words of a 13th-century poem describing the Camino. Eight hundred years later these words still ring true. The Camino de Santiago (Way of St James) originated as a medieval pilgrimage and for more than 1000 years people have taken up the Camino's age-old symbols – the scallop shell and staff – and set off on the adventure of a lifetime. They have risked life and limb to reach the tomb of St James, the apostle, in the Iberian Peninsula's far northwest. Today, this magnificent long-distance walk – spanning 783km of Spain's north from Roncesvalles, on the border with France, to Santiago de Compostela in Galicia – attracts walkers of all backgrounds and ages, from countries around the world. No wonder. Its laundry list of assets (culture, history, nature, infrastructure) is impressive, as are its accolades; for not just is it Europe's Premier Cultural Itinerary and a Unesco World Heritage site, but for pilgrims who complete the mammoth undertaking it's a pilgrimage the equal of one to Jerusalem and by finishing it you're guaranteed a healthy chunk of time off purgatory.

To feel, absorb, smell and taste northern Spain's diversity, for a great physical challenge, for a unique perspective on rural and urban communities, to meet intriguing companions, as well as for the opportunity to immerse yourself in a continuous outdoor museum, this is an incomparable walk. *The door is open to all* – step on in.

CAMINO DE SANTIAGO

Camino de Santiago Maps

1. Roncesvalles to Logroño — p310
2. Logroño to Hontanas — p316
3. Hontanas to Terradillos de los Templarios — p320
4. Terradillos de los Templarios to Molinaseca — p322
5. Molinaseca to Palas do Rei — p326
6. Palas do Rei to Santiago de Compostela — p329

HISTORY

In the 9th century a remarkable event occurred in the poor Iberian hinterlands: following a shining star, Pelayo, a religious hermit, unearthed the tomb of the apostle James the Greater (or, in Spanish, Santiago). The news was confirmed by the local bishop, the Asturian king and later the Pope. Its impact is hard to truly imagine today, but it was instant and indelible: first a trickle, then a flood of Christian Europeans began to journey towards the setting sun in search of salvation. Europe and the incipient Spain would never be the same.

In that age, saintly relics were highly valued, traded as commodities and even invented with great vigour to further ecclesiastical and monarchical interests. Relics were believed to have their own will, legally justifying many cases of 'sacred thievery'. To see and, even better, touch a relic was a way to acquire some part of its holiness. The church cultivated the value of relics by offering pilgrims indulgences – a remittance of sins committed in this life. Pilgrimage was by parts devotion, thanks and penance as well as an investment for one's future permanent retirement.

Compostela became the most important destination for Christians after Rome and Jerusalem. Its popularity increased with an 11th-century papal decree granting it Holy

Year (*Año Santo* or *Año Jacobeo* in Spanish, and *Xacobeo* in Galician) status: pilgrims could receive a plenary indulgence – a full remission of one's lifetime's sins – during a Holy Year. These occur when Santiago's feast day (25 July) falls on a Sunday (which happens at intervals of six, five, six and then 11 years): if you want to complete the pilgrimage in one of these Holy years then you'd better get your boots on quick because the next one is the year this book is published – 2010 and the next one isn't until 2021!

An obvious question persists: What were the remains of Santiago – martyred in Jerusalem in 44 AD – doing in northwest Iberia? Here, medieval imagination and masterminding take over. The accepted story suggests that two of Santiago's disciples secreted away his remains in a stone boat; set sail in the Mediterranean, passed through the Straits of Gibraltar and moored at present-day Padrón (see the boxed text The Scallop Shell, p311). Continuing inland for 17km, they buried his body in a forest named Libredon (present-day Compostela). All was forgotten until Pelayo saw the star.

The story's veracity is irrelevant. The fact that it was believed led to the mass movement of millions of pilgrims; the Camino's birth; the subsequent taming of the Iberian wilderness, unseen since the Roman colonisation; the spread of Romanesque and Gothic art styles (see the boxed text Romanesque & Gothic Art & Architecture, p317); and a major influx of settlers and of religious orders that established pilgrims' *hospitales* (wayside guesthouses) and monasteries.

These factors helped to safeguard and repopulate the northern territories gained through the Christian *Reconquista* (reconquest) of Muslim Spain. Directly linked to the *Reconquista* as the Christians' holy hero, Santiago made several appearances at major battles as Matamoros (Moor-Slayer). With sword raised, he would descend from the clouds on a white charger to save the day. Santiago is thus apostle, pilgrim (both images are found throughout Europe) and the violent moor-slayer (limited to Spain and South America, where the conquistadors carried his image).

The 11th and 12th centuries marked the pilgrimage's heyday. The Reformation was devastating for Catholic pilgrimages and by the 19th century the Camino nearly died out. In its startling late 20th-century reanimation, which continues today, it's most popular as a personal-cum-spiritual journey of discovery rather than one primarily motivated by religion.

ENVIRONMENT

Starting in the low western Pyrenees (1057m) of Navarra amid thick, well-maintained deciduous forests (beech, hazel and linden), the Camino drops onto rolling plains. Wild roses, stinging nettles, broom and blackberries appear on the first and nearly every other day. Navarra's rich cultivated fields produce cereals, red wine grapes and white asparagus.

In La Rioja the chalky, clay and alluvial silt soils support vineyards that produce excellent red wines – Spain's best-known abroad. Common riverbank species include black poplar, which is used for paper production, common alder and willow. Wildflowers (best in May and June) include mallow, milfoil, rue, thistles, cornflower and bellflower. Cereal fields are often red with poppies.

The *meseta* (high tableland) dominates the landscapes of Castilla y León (Burgos lies at 860m and León at 829m). Cereal crops roll endlessly and evergreen oaks sparsely shade the plains. North–south river systems (Ríos Carrión, Pisuerga, Cea, Bernesga and Órbigo) cut across the Camino and once made the pilgrimage much more challenging than it is now. The Camino returns to the mountains in western León, where Mediterranean aromatic thyme, lavender, rockrose and sage grow by the wayside. In the El Bierzo region, nestled between two mountain systems, cherry trees, red pepper plants and red wine grape vines thrive.

Forests and endless hills return in Galicia: chestnuts, oaks, then pines and, finally, eucalyptuses. The land is perpetually green along the undulating descent to Compostela, the Camino's lowest point (260m). In this rich dairy and farming country, common crops include potato, corn, cabbage and grelos, the leafy green that makes the soup *caldo gallego* distinctive. Inheritance practices here led to the continual division of land and its demarcation by unending stone walls and innumerable hamlets, a marked contrast to the *meseta's* larger, widely scattered settlements.

Birds are the most visible wildlife. The most obvious is the white stork (see the boxed text Storks, p312), found from Navarra to El Bierzo.

CLIMATE

Navarra and La Rioja have wet and blustery springs, hot summers and fairly mild winters, with snow in the higher elevations of Navarra. Castilla y León has relentlessly hot summers and cold, snowy winters. Cold northern winds, off the Cordillera

---

WHAT'S IN A NAME?

All the derivations of 'Santiago' (Sant Iago) can be confusing. The original Latin *Iacobus* became Jakob in German, James in English, Jacques in French, Jaume in Catalan, Jacopo in Italian, Xacobe in Galician and even Diego (as in San Diego).

The origin of 'Compostela' is another etymological conundrum. Some theorists argue that it means 'starry field' in Latin, referring to the hermit's discovery, while others suggest the more sedate Latin *compostium*, or burial ground.

MEDICINAL PLANTS

The great variety and richness of flora growing beside the way proved crucial for pilgrims and the staff of the hospices. For example, herb Robert came in handy for blisters; its crumbled, fresh leaves were mixed with honey and the compound was applied over the wound three times a day.

Dull-sounding common ragwort has another, even less appealing name – stinking willy – which possibly says something about the state of the Medieval pilgrims' personal hygiene! Known in Spanish as *hierba de Santiago*, it was fried in oil and then applied between the toes to soothe broken, irritated skin.

Fennel boiled in milk was the equivalent of a modern-day power drink used to counteract low energy. To treat flatulence and indigestion it was boiled in water and drunk after meals. A remedy for sore, inflamed feet – as common among walkers centuries ago as they are today – is a footbath of cool water, vinegar and salt. Many *albergues* keep buckets on hand just for this purpose.

Cantábrica, often sweep the *meseta*. In Galicia, expect rain at any time of year and mild temperatures. People should expect cold conditions and snow from December to May in any of the mountainous areas of Navarra, León and Galicia.

PLANNING

Although in Spain there are many *caminos* (paths) to Santiago, by far the most popular is, and was, the Camino Francés, which originated in France, crossed the Pyrenees at Roncesvalles and then headed west for 750km across mountains, wheat and wine fields, and forests of the regions of Navarra, La Rioja, Castilla y León and Galicia.

Waymarked with cheerful yellow arrows on everything from telephone poles to rocks and trees, the 'trail' is a mishmash of rural lanes, paved secondary roads and footpaths all strung together. Scallop shells, stuck in cement markers or stylised on blue-and-yellow metal signs, also show the way.

There is no official starting point. Nowadays many people walk or cycle varying lengths based on different criteria: time, interest or challenge.

A very popular alternative is to walk only the last 100km (the minimum distance allowed) from Sarria in Galicia in order to earn a Compostela certificate of completion given out by the Catedral de Santiago de Compostela. Modern pilgrims carry a Credencial del Peregrino (Pilgrim's Credential), which they can get stamped daily in churches and bars, and at *albergues* and *refugios*.

For more information about the Credencial and the Compostela certificate, visit the cathedral's **Oficina de Acogida de Peregrinos** (Pilgrim's Office; ☎ 981 56 88 46; Rúa do Vilar 1; www.archicompostela .org/Peregrinos/; 9am-9pm).

Maps

The IGN's 1:600,000 *Mapa del Camino de Santiago* is available in the bookshops of the route's major cities.

PLACE NAMES

In Navarra the Spanish and Basque names for settlements appear together, whereas in Galicia local signs and village names are in Galego (Galician). We do the same.

Books

Countless reams of paper and parchment are dedicated to the Camino. A fascinating text is the 12th-century *Liber Sancti Jacobi* (Book of St James), a five-chapter manuscript detailing the pilgrimage. The fifth chapter is a fascinating guidebook to the way, describing the places, the rivers, the relics and the people encountered (the description of whom gets downright obscene!). It's available in English as *The Pilgrim's Guide to Santiago de Compostela*, translated by William Melczer.

For modern reading try the following:

Culture: David Gitlitz and Linda Davidson's *The Pilgrimage Road to Santiago*: *The Complete Cultural Handbook* is well worth its weight.

Analysis: Anthropologist Nancy Frey explores the pilgrimage's modern resurgence in *Pilgrim Stories: On and Off the Road to Santiago.*

Guidebook: Millán Bravo Lozano's *A Practical Guide for Pilgrims* provides great maps and route descriptions.

Religious/Spiritual Account: Joyce Rupp gives a compelling account of the inner journey in *Walk in a Relaxed Manner.*

Esoteric: Paulo Coelho's mystical journey described in *The Pilgrimage* is an international bestseller.

Information Sources

Tourist offices along the Camino usually provide free local, regional and Camino-specific brochures.

Thousands of Camino-related websites cover topics from history to practical advice and personal experiences. Useful sites with many links include the following:

www.caminolinks.co.uk A complete, annotated guide to many *camino* websites.

www.csj.org.uk Confraternity of St James online bookshop offering historical and practical information, and detailed guides to the alternative *caminos*.

www.mundicamino.com Excellent, thorough descriptions and maps of all of the *caminos*.

www.santiago-today.com A huge selection of news groups from where you can get all of your questions answered plus planning information.

www.pilgrimage-to-santiago.com Has everything in one place, from the basics to a useful FAQ forum.

Pilgrim's Credential

Most people who walk, even if not religious, carry the Credencial del Peregrino (Pilgrim's Credential/Passport). An accordion-fold document, it gives bearers access to the well-organised system of *albergues* or *refugios* along the route – see the boxed text Albergues Along the Camino Francés, p308. You can obtain the Credencial upon starting in Roncesvalles (see p334) and in major cities along the way.

The Compostela certificate, obtained from the Oficina del Peregrino in Santiago de Compostela, is proof of completing the journey. To receive the Compostela, the Credencial must be ink-stamped twice each day (eg at churches, hostels, *albergues*, bars, cafés and almost any business you will stop in along the way) of the walk. It's imperative to complete the last 100km to Santiago de Compostela (a cumulative 100km done piecemeal is not accepted). At the Oficina del Peregrino, you will be asked to affirm that the journey was made for spiritual or religious motives.

Tours

If you want a guided trip, there are numerous outfits that organise walking and cycling tours of varying duration. **On Foot in Spain** (www.onfootinspain.com) offers guided cultural walking tours along the Camino Francés and Camino Portugués. Flexible, self-guided options where you walk on your own but are provided with maps, route notes, reserved accommodation and luggage transfers are offered by **World Walks** (www.worldwalks.com).

Friends of the Camino associations around the world also provide invaluable information, especially the **Confraternity of St James** (☎ 020 7928 9988; www.csj.org.uk; 27 Blackfriars Rd, London, SE1 8NY, UK).

GATEWAY

See Pamplona (p333).

CAMINO DE SANTIAGO

Duration 30 days
Distance 783km
Difficulty moderate–demanding
Start Roncesvalles (p334)
Finish Santiago de Compostela (p213)
Transport bus, train
Summary A magnificent route that traverses the north of Spain along back roads, forest tracks and agricultural fields through more than 1000 years of Spanish history, art and culture. And, if that weren't enough, you'll spend less time burning in Hell!

There are actually many Caminos de Santiago. Medieval pilgrims simply left home and picked up the closest and safest route to Compostela. Many of these became established in and outside Spain (see More Pilgrim Walks, p330). We describe the

ALBERGUES ALONG THE CAMINO FRANCÉS

The Camino has an extensive system of pilgrim *albergues* and all stages end at one. Other day-end accommodation options are also listed.

Run by parishes, local governments, Camino associations and private owners, *albergues* or *refugios* generally have bunks without sheets in communal dorms, toilets, showers (sometimes sex-segregated) and kitchens. They maintain opening hours (usually 3pm to 10pm, closed after 8am) and the vast majority do not take reservations. Some rely on pilgrims' donations to operate while others charge a fee (from €5 to €10). Help with cleaning the facilities is appreciated. Some are staffed by a *hospitalero voluntario* (volunteer attendant) who may spend part of a vacation, or may even work full-time, looking after pilgrims. To stay, present the Credencial to the *hospitalero*.

In July and August, when the way is at its busiest, local and regional governments frequently make additional facilities (eg, *polideportivos* or gymnasiums) available to walkers. Inquire at the local *albergue*.

Since space is limited in summer, it's common, unfortunately, to encounter a '*refugio* race' mentality: getting up very early to reach the next *refugio* and queue up for hours in order to ensure a bed space, instead of enjoying the walk. Resist the rat race.

most popular, the Camino Francés, from the Pyrenees to Santiago de Compostela in 30 stages. Walking daily for a month is demanding; schedule at least five weeks to allow for rest days, cultural visits or to break up longer stages. Depending on your pace and goals, the walk is feasible in fewer or more stages.

To divide the route into shorter sections, in two weeks the stretch from León (from Day 14) can be safely entertained. With a week the beautiful Galician portion, beginning in Cebreiro (from Day 24), offers a scenic introduction. The initial week in Navarra, from Roncesvalles to Logroño, in the region of La Rioja, is a true highlight. If you crave solitude and desolation or have never walked in a seemingly horizonless landscape, then try walking from Burgos to Hontanas (Day 11) or Castrojeriz (Day 12).

The distances given here will vary from those in other guidebooks: ours are from *albergue* to *albergue* for consistency and to avoid the frustration of reaching the town gate and realising that the *albergue* is 1km further. All times given are actual walking time and do not include rest stops.

The route regularly passes through villages and cities. In the walk description, settlements are either referred to as having a bar and/or restaurant, or all services, signifying a bar, restaurant, pharmacy, bank, market, shops etc. Potable water is

readily available in bars or from treated village fountains. Many restaurants offer an inexpensive *menú del día*, which usually includes three courses, wine or water and bread. All prices given are for high season (usually Easter and Jul–mid-Sep).

Trail markers (from bright-yellow painted arrows on trees, rocks and houses, or blue metal signs with stylised yellow shells, to ceramic shells and cement blocks) are frequent and easy to follow, making detailed maps and a compass superfluous. The Camino Francés corresponds to the GR65 long-distance trail throughout Navarra; red-and-white slashes join the yellow arrows. The walk is essentially one-way (east to west) and the yellow arrows reflect that. Local economic interests can influence the yellow arrows' direction through or around villages (for example, unnecessarily passing a particular bar). Sometimes it's necessary to choose between two diverging paths. We describe the best (ie the most attractive, those with the highlights) and summarise the alternatives.

PLANNING
When to Walk

The walk is feasible year-round, but the best months are May, June, September and October. Spring offers long days and visual splendour – rivers are full, hillsides burst with wildflowers and the *meseta's* cereal crops sway green. Anticipate some showers and cool mornings. The unbearable heat and crowds of July and August diminish by September and October, and shades of brown dominate the landscapes. Be prepared to encounter snow at higher elevations and on the *meseta* any time from November to early May.

July is Santiago de Compostela's month of celebration. The 25th is the Feast of Santiago and Galicia's 'national' day. The night before, Praza do Obradoiro comes alight with Os Fogos do Apóstolo, a spectacular light, music and fireworks show that dates back to the 17th century and culminates in a mock burning of the Mudéjar (an Islamic-influenced style of the 12th and 13th centuries) facade to commemorate the city's razing by Muslims in 997. The town authorities organise processions, numerous concerts – notably in Praza da Quintana – and other cultural activities.

What to Bring

Many people, expecting hardship, carry too much. All supplies are readily available in towns and villages. A sleeping bag, though, is essential. Some *albergues* have coin-operated washing machines.

Walkers frequently suffer blisters (*ampollas* in Spanish) and various pains (knee, back or tendons). Pharmacies stock necessary supplies, but bring any favourite

WARNING

Dogs are usually leashed and more bark than bite. Nonetheless, some people complain about aggressive, wild dogs and carry a stick for protection.

remedy. Stiff, alpine walking boots are not recommended. The variety of surfaces and long stretches of gently rolling terrain require more flexible, all-round, sturdy walking shoes or boots. In the summer many people also walk in sandals, trekking sandals and Crocs.

In the summertime shorts or light trousers are ideal for most of the route. But remember that Galicia loves rain, so keep a waterproof jacket handy.

GETTING TO/FROM THE WALK

From Pamplona buses run to Roncesvalles (€5.40; 1½ hours, one daily Mon-Sat).

THE WALK
Day 1: Roncesvalles to Zubiri
6–7 hours, 22.6km

Lace up your boots, take a deep breath and put your best foot forward. The Camino begins! Walk 100m down the N135 (towards Pamplona), cross and enter a tree-lined path for 15 minutes. Where the forest opens, veer left, continuing to the N135 and **Burguete** (Auritz; all services), famous for its white *caseríos* (farmhouses) with red shutters and as Hemingway's trout-fishing getaway in *The Sun Also Rises* (the book that put Pamplona and its legendary Sanfermines festival well and truly on the international map). From the plaza, dominated by the San Nicolás de Bari church, continue 100m and turn right down a dirt road leaving Burguete. Cross the stream over a wooden bridge to a wide, paved then dirt lane through pastures to a gate and stream. Cross this and then another stream soon thereafter. The path rolls through woods (hawthorn is abundant) making a 10-minute ascent. Descend 1.5km to **Espinal** (Aurizberri; all services), a picturesque hamlet founded in 1269.

Turn left and, just past mid-village and a **curious fountain** (potable water), left again onto an ascending paved road which 400m later converts to dirt. Fork right onto

CAMINO DE SANTIAGO

RONCESVALLES TO LOGROÑO

a dirt trail, soon entering a spruce and then a beech wood. Climb the wooden stairs and turn right 90 degrees, enjoying great field

and valley views (left). Descend to the N135 at the **Alto de Mezquíriz** (925m), cross and continue straight ahead.

Viscarret (Biskarreta; with fountain) is 3km from here. The rocky trail descends steeply through a beech wood and parallel to the N135, opening to it after 1.5km. Continue 20m along the road and turn right up a boxwood-enveloped trail that leads to a paved road and Viscarret.

Walk through **Viscarret**, over the N135, and then turn left down an imitation-stone path that converts to dirt after 400m. At the N135, cross onto a dirt path that leads to Lintzoain. Note the *frontón*, a court on which *pelota vasca* (or *jai alai* in Basque) – a type of handball popular in Navarra and the Basque Country – is played. Past the fountain (a long trough), turn right up a street that becomes a 5km undulating path through pine, oak, box, and beech to the **Alto de Erro** (801m). Cross the highway and continue descending on the forest and dirt path (passing the crumbling Venta del Puerto, once an inn for pilgrims and now a cow stable) to Zubiri (526m). Enter across the **Puente de la Rabia**, so nicknamed because livestock were circled three times around the central pillar to cure rabies. The magnesite factory, clearly visible on descent, sustains the local economy. To reach the *albergue* continue to the main road (aka Avenida Roncesvalles), passing the church and a fountain. Cross the road, turn right and in 175m reach the non-descript building on the left.

Day 2: Zubiri to Pamplona
5½–6½ hours, 21.3km
Cross back over Zubiri's bridge and turn right up a cement lane. After 150m the trail converts to dirt and rolls for 1km to a sealed road. Veer left, ascending the road for 500m, and continue along this unpleasant section, above the factory, before descending to the right on a trail. The winding footpath passes two hamlets – Ilarraz and Esquirotz (fountain) – before reaching **Larrasoaña**, which has a bar-restaurant, fountain and *albergue*.

To continue, head left towards Akerreta. The path narrows through a pine and oak forest, slowly approaching the Río Arga. Cross it at **Zuriain** (with fountain). Turn left at the N135 and continue for 600m.

THE SCALLOP SHELL

An important symbol since at least the 11th century, the scallop shell appears on a backpack, hat or tunic in nearly all images of Santiago or his followers from the 12th century onwards. The symbol's origin remains a mystery. The most colourful legend explains that when the martyred James arrived on the Galician coast in his stone boat a pagan wedding almost turned to disaster when the bridegroom and his horse crashed into the sea (upon seeing the strange sight) and began to drown. James demonstrated his goodwill by saving them from the waves; when they arose, scallop shells covered their bodies.

The Roman *Finis terrae* (end of the earth), today Fisterra, lies 90km west of Santiago and was the site of an important sun cult; souls were believed to live on an island somewhere beyond. *Finis terrae* became a popular post-Santiago destination for pilgrims. Roman influence also left a Venus cult; its prime symbol was the scallop shell. The scallop served as a talisman against evil as well as a symbol of fertility, rebirth and rejuvenation. Most likely these pre-existing pagan beliefs became fused with the Santiago pilgrimage, and the shell, with its rich symbology and abundance on the coast, was quickly incorporated. Originally, it was only worn by pilgrims after reaching Santiago. Today, most people wear it from the start.

Turn left down a paved road towards Ilurdotz. Cross the bridge and turn right onto a dirt path that leads to an abandoned mine. The trail turns right, ascending to Irotz (with fountain) and then the hamlet of Zabaldika straddling the N135. Turn left onto the N135 and cross at a picnic spot (with fountain and toilet). The path ascends and skirts the hillside – passing a restored house – to the highway (Carretera de Irún). Cross via a tunnel and turn right up the road that winds down to the Río Ultzama, an Arga tributary. Cross the **Romanesque bridge** to Trinidad de Arre (currently a boys' seminary) **monastery** with *albergue*. Continue left.

The Camino makes a beeline through **Villava** (Atarrabia; home town of five-time Tour de France winner Miguel Induráin), first along the Calle Mayor and then the Avenida de Serapio Huici for 2km to Burlada's Calle Mayor. Near the end of Burlada, by Talleres Garysa, turn right onto a pedestrian crossing over the Francia-Irún highway. Continue along the acacia-lined footpath and then a narrow road to the 14th-century Magdalena bridge. A modern *cruceiro* (cross), dedicated to Santiago, marks the foot of the bridge. Cross and veer right through the park, circling briefly below the city's ramparts before ascending to Pamplona's impressive, stone-gated northern entrance, the **Portal de Francia**. The way through the old quarter is well marked with blue-and-yellow trail markers. Take Calle del Carmen, turning right onto

Calle de Mercaderes. Fork right onto the Antigua Rúa del Mentidero to the Plaza Consistorial (town hall). Just beyond is the **San Saturnino** (also San Cernín) church and *albergue* (see also Pamplona, p333).

Day 3: Pamplona to Puente la Reina

6–7½ hours, 27.9km

The described route goes via Eunate; to reduce the walk by 3.5km take the Alternative Route (see p312) once you reach Muruzábal.

With San Saturnino church on the left continue straight, then fork left onto Calle Mayor. Continue on Calle Bosquecillo to Avenida Navas de Tolosa. Cross the city park along a stone path skirting the 16th-century defensive Ciudadela. Turn hard right and cross Calle Vuelta del Castillo and Avenida Sancho el Fuerte to Calle Fuente de Hierro, descending past the Universidad de Navarra. Reaching a T-junction, turn right and cross the wooden footbridge.

Continue 4.8km to **Cizur Menor**, with a bar-restaurant. Up the hill to the right are the *albergue* and the **Romanesque Iglesia de San Miguel**. Continue straight through the village crossroads and then veer right (a medieval fountain is on the left) onto a footpath past a *frontón* and through a housing development. Reaching a sealed road, head right and after 700m, turn hard left onto a trail through wheat fields.

Aim for windmill-studded **Sierra del Perdón**, 8.5km ahead. The trail becomes

STORKS

In spring and summer you'll inevitably see and hear the elegant *cigüeña* or European white stork, which, after passing the winter in North Africa, flies to the Iberian Peninsula to reproduce. White storks almost always settle near human populations, in contrast to their shy black relatives, which hide in the woods. They construct or reinhabit huge, complex nests perched in high places, such as water pumps, telephone poles or chimneys. Church bell-towers are a preferred nesting site and a single tower is sometimes crowded with three or four heavy nests. The distinctive chatter of clapping beaks is frequently heard.

a lane and in 4.6km reaches **Zariquiegui** (with fountain) and a Romanesque church. En route, hilltop Galar village (left) and the ruins of Guendulain (right) are visible. The more pronounced ascent of the *sierra* begins. Near the summit the dry Fuente Reniega (Renouncement Fountain) is part of a pilgrim legend. The Devil tempted a dehydrated pilgrim to renounce his faith in exchange for water. He refused and in return Santiago appeared and led him to a spring. At the summit (780m), a wind-power company has mounted a sculpture depicting medieval pilgrims and saying: 'Where the Way of the Stars and the Way of the Wind meet'. The phrase refers to the ancient linking of the Milky Way (*vía láctea* in Spanish) with the Camino, as they roughly parallel. According to legend, Charlemagne was the first pilgrim to Compostela; he found his way by following the Milky Way.

The next 10km are laid out in a sweeping westward view. Cross the road and descend the initially steep, loose-stone path through an oak and boxwood forest. Continue through rolling fields to **Uterga** (with fountain). Exit the village heading left on a downhill dirt path. At the bottom, take a path to the right, passing cultivated fields, almond trees and vineyards to **Muruzábal**, with fountain and bar.

From the small plaza, turn left past a 16th-century palace. Descend out of town along a sealed then dirt road for 2.5km

to the highway and the octagonal, 12th-century, Romanesque Ermita Nuestra Señora de Eunate (with fountain). Possibly a Knights Templar construction (See the boxed text Knights Templar, p318), it was also a pilgrims' cemetery.

Cross the car park to the picnic area and take a dirt path for 800m to the highway. Or continue 1.4km along the road to reach Puente la Reina (347m) at the convent and Iglesia de Crucifijo (both on the left) and the *albergue* **Padres Reparadores** (right).

ALTERNATIVE ROUTE: VIA OBANOS
1–1½ hours, 4.3km

Leave Muruzábal along the main road and turn right on a descending path for 1km to Obanos (with fountain and all services). Obanos' fame resides in the legend of fratricide between two saints, Felicia and Guillermo. The Iglesia San Juan Bautista houses the ghoulish relic of Guillermo (his cranium covered in silver) in the sacristy. Pass under the arch to the left of the church and descend (right) to Puente la Reina. On the N111 a modern pilgrim statue marks the historic junction of the Camino Francés and Camino Aragonés.

Day 4: Puente la Reina to Estella
5–6 hours, 22.7km

Walk through Puente la Reina, cross the bridge and turn left for 100m. Cross the highway and turn right onto a dirt path that narrows to an ascending trail. Snake up the embankment to the summit where Mañeru's church steeple appears. Continue to **Mañeru** (with fountain), crossing through the village and exiting via Calle Forzosa. Soon you'll pass the cemetrey, hemmed in with white walls and planted with cypress. Cemetreies in this region (and, later, in Castilla y León) are on the outskirts of town, in contrast to Galicia, where they are in the churchyards.

Passing between vineyards, cereals and olive trees, the dirt trail winds pleasantly for 2.7km to the compact and labyrinthine **Cirauqui** (a Basque word meaning 'nest of vipers'). The village retains some medieval walls, the arched portal, a hub-shaped urban plan and the **Iglesia de San Román**—justifiably famous for its 13th-century lobed-arch Mudéjar portal. At the columned plaza, deviate from the arrows and turn right to ascend to the church. The fountain is by the church's main door. Descend steeply left from the church plaza, turning sharply right once out of the village.

Cypress trees flank the impressive stretch of nearly 2000-year-old **calzada romana** (stone-paved Roman road) that descends over a **Roman bridge** and up to the N111. Cross the highway. Turn left onto a dirt road that descends to a medieval bridge and continues nearly 2km along the Roman *calzada* to the N111 again. Turn right onto a smaller, sealed road passing under a modern aqueduct to the Río Salado. The 12th-century *Pilgrim's Guide* narrates a grim story: Several Frankish pilgrims, arriving at the river bank, asked two Navarrese men sharpening their knives on the other side if the water was safe for their horses. They assented. The Frankish horses drank deeply and collapsed, dead, and the knife-wielders had fresh horse skins. The Franks were not in a position to argue. Cross the bridge and ascend to **Lorca** (with fountain).

Villatuerta (with fountain) lies 4km away along paths through cereal fields and plastic-covered rows of white asparagus. Pass Villatuerta's church and take the main street to the road. Cross and keep straight along a dirt path running parallel to the N111 and passing the Ermita de San Miguel. Descend along stairs to a picnic area, cross the road and take a sinuous trail to the Río Ega, crossed via a wooden bridge. After 1km of lane, head right along a cement road that reaches **Estella** (Lizarra; 465m) and the *albergue* on Rúa Curtidores in 1km.

Day 5: Estella to Los Arcos
5½–6 hours, 22.4km
Carry plenty of water for the long stretch between Villamayor and Los Arcos. Leave Estella via Rúa Curtidores and Calle San Nicolás. After the second roundabout and petrol station, ascend right onto a dirt road. After 1.2km either fork left (recommended) to Azqueta via the 12th-century Monasterio de Irache, or veer right downhill directly to Azqueta (via Hotel Irache).

To pass the monastery, fork left downhill, cross the highway and ascend a lane to the ingenious red wine and water fountain installed by Bodegas Irache (the adjacent winery) in 1991. Continue past

the monastery, following the stone wall to a fork (a longer route continues straight along the base of 1045m-high Montejurra to Luquín). Turn right, cross the highway and head left passing behind **Hotel Irache**. As you walk past a housing development, castle-topped Monjardín (894m) fills the western sky. Continue 3.2km to **Azqueta**, first through oak forest and then turning sharply left uphill, bordering cereal fields. Azqueta's fountain is in the tiny plaza.

Leaving the village, veer right down a dirt lane and circle a cow stable. The route gently climbs to the base of Monjardín, passing the restored 13th-century Fuente de los Moros (questionably drinkable water) below the ruins of the Roman-based Castillo de Deyo. Continue to the quiet village of **Villamayor**, which has an *albergue*, fountain and bar-restaurant. Head off left downhill through red-soil vineyards to an agricultural track. Reach Los Arcos in 12km through wheat and asparagus fields and an odd series of rounded hills studded with conifers. **Los Arcos** (444m) suddenly appears. Enter the village and continue straight ahead, passing an *albergue*, then turn right to the main square, dominated by the **Iglesia de Santa María**. Pass under the only remaining arch and cross the road to the *albergue municipal* (on the right).

Day 6: Los Arcos to Logroño
7½–9 hours, 28.8km
From the *albergue municipal*, turn right onto a dirt road, passing the cemetrey on your right. A macabre statement etched in the archway reads: 'I was what you are. You will be what I am.' A mostly flat and straight 6.7km remain to **Sansol**. After 3.7km, near a hut, veer right onto a marked dirt road that continues left to a sealed road. Sansol is clearly visible. Turn left onto the road and in 1.3km reach Sansol. The yellow arrows zigzag through the streets without ascending to the church. Outstanding panoramic views of **Torres del Río** below make the effort to ascend worthwhile.

Descend out of town and cross the highway (at a dangerous blind curve!) to a descending footpath. The water from the fountain at the bottom is not drinkable. A steep ascent through Torres' streets leads to the **Iglesia de Santo Sepulcro**, another

12th-century octagonal masterwork linked to the Knights Templar.

Leave Torres, heading straight up from the church to its highest point, and exit past the cemetrey. The rural road runs parallel to the highway and then crosses it, ascending left along a path to the **Ermita Señora del Poyo**, where the Virgin of Le Puy appeared, leaving behind a statue which refused to be moved – thus the chapel.

Over the next kilometres pay careful attention to the arrows. Descend to the road and continue along it briefly before turning right onto a footpath. After 600m the footpath reaches a road. Turn left on the road and briefly continue before veering onto a clay road. Immediately fork right (it's unmarked). Viana's bell tower is visible on the horizon. Descend through the Barranco Mataburros (literally, 'donkey-killing ditch') following the graded lane to the highway. Cross and ascend on a dirt trail. Viana's church appears, still 3km away.

At the foot of this historic frontier town, the trail crosses the highway and ascends to the **Plaza de los Fueros**. Here you'll find a fountain, all services and an *albergue*. The adjacent **Iglesia de Santa María**, with its concave Renaissance portal and soaring Gothic interior, is especially interesting.

Logroño lies 9km from Viana, but is partially hidden behind a flan-shaped hill (Cerro de Cantabria, with pre-Roman, Roman and medieval remains). Leave Viana, skirting the ruins of **Iglesia de San Pedro**, and walk down past apartments. Follow several well-marked zigzags out of Viana through a housing development and veer left with the arrows onto a path through gardens. Cross a sealed road and then walk parallel to the N111 (towards Logroño). Cross and turn left onto a sealed road that reaches the **Ermita Santa María de las Cuevas**. Continue on a dirt road past the Embalse de las Cañas. Head right up to and cross the highway, continuing to a crossroads at the Navarra-La Rioja border. Take the red asphalt trail (passing under two tunnels) around the Cerro de Cantabria's north side, finally reaching Logroño's cemetery. Enter the city over the Río Ebro via the **Puente de Piedra**. The first street to the right, Rúa Vieja, leads to the *albergue* in 200m.

Day 7: Logroño to Nájera
7½–9 hours, 30km

Six kilometres of cement starts the day. Follow the paving-stone scallops through the cobbled old quarter along the Rúa Vieja past the pilgrim's fountain in the Plaza de Santiago to Calle Barriocepo. Where it ends turn right to exit via the remnant of the city's medieval walls. Cross the car park and continue round the Plaza Alférez Provisional to the long Calle Marqués de Murrieta. Reaching two petrol stations (on either side of the road), turn left onto Calle Entrena, passing an industrial zone, and continue through a tunnel below the highway. Continue 2.4km along a flat cement footpath to the agreeable surprise of the **Embalse de la Grajera** reservoir.

Circling to the right, the trail ascends through vineyards to a sawmill. The large billboard bull on the hill once advertised Osborne sherry. Turn left along the highway for 300m and then cross it, descending along a path that affords views of hilltop Navarrete. Make a beeline to the village via an overpass and past the 12th-century ruins of Hospital de San Juan de Acre. One of its portals now serves as Navarrete's cemetrey door on the other side of town.

Navarrete has all services and an *albergue*. Wrapped like a blanket round the hill, Navarrete retains its medieval character with its cobbled, narrow streets and labyrinthine layout. *Alfarerías*, pottery shops, where the area's red clay soil is worked, have been fundamental to the local economy since Roman times. The magnificent Baroque altarpiece of the **Iglesia de la Asunción** merits a stop.

There are no fountains or villages in the next 16km to Nájera, unless you take the alternative route (see below). Follow the trail markers out of Navarrete down to the N120 (towards Burgos). Follow the N120 for 500m to the cemetery. The dirt trail runs parallel to the N120 for 300m until the path veers left through vineyards, olives and fruit trees, reaching a sealed road at the Vitivinícola de Sotes building. Turn left, descending along the road to the N120. Take the dirt trail parallel to the highway for 1.5km to a fork. Either continue straight (recommended) or turn left and make a 500m detour through Ventosa (with *albergue* and fountain).

OF SAINTS & CHICKENS

As you enter Santo Domingo de la Calzada cathedral's south door, you'll see a pair of live white chickens (exchanged for a fresh pair every 15 days) that are kept in an elevated chicken coop on the western wall. This odd custom dates back to the famed miracle of Santo Domingo. A young pilgrim, travelling with his parents to Santiago, was accused of pilfering silver from a local tavern. In reality the barmaid, her amorous advances rejected, had angrily slipped the silver into his knapsack and notified the authorities. To his parents' horror, the pilgrim was strung up on the gallows. Praying, they continued to Santiago and then returned. Surprisingly, rather than encounter his decomposing body, they found him well – yet still hanging, with the saint supporting his feet. They ran to the judge who, having just sat down to eat roast chicken, refused to be bothered. When the pilgrims insisted, the judge exclaimed that if their son were innocent the chickens would rise from his plate and crow. And they did, giving the town its motto: *'Donde la gallina cantó después de asada'* (Where the hen crowed after being roasted).

In the cathedral it's considered good luck to find a chicken feather or to hear them crowing. Look also for the wooden fragment of the gallows hanging on the wall above the south transept and, in town, don't miss the 'hanged pilgrim' pastries found in many bakeries.

From the fork continue 2.5km to where cairns mark the initially rocky ascent to the Alto de San Antón (670m), offering great views of Nájera, still 7.5km away. The track descends, crosses the highway, and skirts round two telecommunications antennae and a gravel works. Cross a footbridge and continue to **Nájera** (485m). Cross the Río Najerilla and enter the old quarter, built directly into the huge, red walls rising behind the town. Parallel to both the river and the wall is the fascinating Benedictine **Monasterio de Santa María la Real**; adjacent to it, on the right, is the *albergue*.

Day 8: Nájera to Santo Domingo de la Calzada
4½–5½ hours, 21.6km

Follow the road that curves round the monastery (right) and continues uphill (10 minutes) on first a sealed road, then a red-dirt road flanked by pines and cliffs. Descending through a ravine, the way flattens past vineyards to a sealed road and continues 5km to **Azofra**, which has a fountain, two *albergues* and all services.

Leave Azofra down the main street to the road. Turn right and after 100m turn left onto a dirt lane passing a large *rollo* (a medieval juridical pillar used to hang villains) converted into a cross. Climbing a small hill, the lane descends close to the N120, turns left and then parallels the highway to a sealed road. Cross the sealed road to pick up the dirt lane again.

For 700m the path cuts across wheat fields rolling away on either side and then ascends. At the top, the trail flattens to **Cirueña** (with fountain). Entering the village, take the main road to the right; in 150m, with hops to the right, the path turns left and undulates for 6km to **Santo Domingo de la Calzada**. At the main highway, turn left along the footpath, entering the historical quarter along Calle Mayor, which houses an *albergue*. Fifty metres down the street from this *albergue municipal* is an excellent new *albergue* that takes the pilgrim into the 21st century with its computer room and chill-out lounge!

Day 9: Santo Domingo de la Calzada to Belorado
5½–6½ hours, 23.4km

Entering Burgos province within Castilla y León, the way rolls through valleys surrounded by high tablelands. Continue straight along Calle Mayor to the N120. Cross the Río Oja (giving La Rioja its name) using Domingo's refitted bridge. Take a path right and in 1.3km return to the N120 and cross to a dirt road parallel to the N120 on its left. Continue 2.5km to a fork. Either go left on a dirt lane (recommended), reaching Grañón's back door in 2.3km (a sign indicates 3.2km but that distance includes an unnecessary detour), or continue straight for 1.9km along the dangerous N120.

After 1.5km of gentle ascent along the lane, a sign suggests two ways to enter

LOGROÑO TO HONTANAS

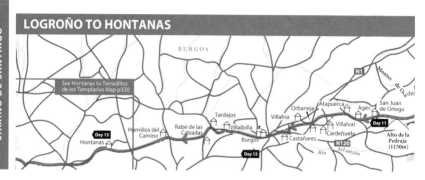

Grañón (with fountain and bar). Ignore the long right-hand option and continue straight on, passing the cemetrey before reaching Grañón's highest point. To enter the village, turn right down its main street. Once fully walled, it had two monasteries and a pilgrims' *hospital*. The restored main altar of the **Iglesia de San Juan Bautista** is a masterpiece of 16th-century Renaissance art. Find the curious *albergue*, built into the church's southern wall; pilgrims wash laundry on top of the vault!

From the high point continue straight, cross a sealed road and then pass between the *frontón* and the fountain, leaving the village on a dirt track for 350m (turn right at the T-junction, then immediately left). Reaching a farm, head right, cross the bridge and then turn left on the second dirt road. In 2.7km reach Redecilla. En route a sign marks the border between La Rioja and Castilla y León. **Redecilla del Camino**, straddling the highway, has a fountain, *albergue* and bar-restaurant. Cross the N120 and turn left through the village. The **Iglesia Virgen de la Calle** contains an exceptional Romanesque baptismal font resting on eight columns.

At Calle Mayor's far end, take a dirt road that parallels the N120's left side, detouring to **Castildelgado** (with fountain). Continue on the sealed road to **Viloria de Rioja** (the fountain's water is not potable) and then **Villamayor del Río** (with a fountain). At the entrance to **Belorado** (770m), cross the highway and enter along the dirt path which veers right, below the cliffs, past the parish *albergue* and nearby Iglesia Santa María. The other *albergue* is off the main plaza.

Day 10: Belorado to San Juan de Ortega
7–8 hours, 24.8km

Get supplies in Villafranca Montes de Oca as San Juan de Ortega has no shop. Descend across the Plaza Mayor and turn left onto Calle Hipólito Bernal and continue along Avenida Camino de Santiago. Leave Belorado, following the convent wall to the N120. Cross the road and the Río Tirón along a wooden footbridge. Follow a dirt trail parallel to the N120. After passing the petrol station, cross the highway and pick up the dirt trail which leads to **Tosantos** (with fountain) in 5km. Nuestra Señora de la Peña, the eye-catching church excavated into the hill on the right just before reaching Tosantos, contains another miraculous Romanesque image. In less than 2km the trail reaches deserted-looking **Villambistia** (with fountain). Typical of rural Castilla y León, these are adobe villages. Follow the trail markers to the highway and **Espinosa del Camino** (with fountain).

Leave the tranquil village along a dirt road. En route an overgrown pile of rocks on the right are the vestiges of **San Felices** – a great 9th-century Mozarabic monastery (Mozarabic design incorporated Arabic elements or techniques into Christian structures and was pre-Romanesque). Continue to the highway and turn right to **Villafranca Montes de Oca**, which has a fountain, bar-restaurant and *albergue*. This 'Village of Franks' is named after the traders, artisans and settlers who took advantage of the reduced taxes and privileges offered by monarchs to repopulate Muslim territories gained during the *Reconquista*.

Leave Villafranca (948m) by walking right (and steeply upwards) behind the **Iglesia de Santiago**, and for 12km wind through the desolate **Montes de Oca** among oaks and conifers to **San Juan** (1000m). The only fountain en route, **Fuente Mojapán**, is 1.5km from Villafranca at a lookout with picnic benches (near the top of the long initial ascent). The climb then gently ascends through oaks and flattens before reaching its highest point, **Alto de la Pedraja** (1150m), at a cross commemorating Spanish Civil War victims.

The wide trail descends and then ascends the steep gully initiating a fairly flat stretch of 7.5km – shadeless despite the trees – that eventually leads to the monastery. The *albergue* is in the monastery complex.

Day 11: San Juan de Ortega to Burgos
7–8 hours, 26km
Burgos merits a leisurely visit, thus we give city lodging options (see p331). The described walk avoids 7km of industrial

ROMANESQUE & GOTHIC ART & ARCHITECTURE

The medieval Romanesque and Gothic art and architectural styles arrived on the Iberian Peninsula via the Camino de Santiago. Christian Europe's first 'international' style Romanesque was developed at the beginning of the 11th century as an expression of feudal thought and as a post-millennium gesture of gratitude for the world's survival. It was spread via religious orders and pilgrimages across Europe. Solid and permanent, buildings constructed in this style used thick, squared walls, massive columns, semicircular arches and barrel vaults, and had few windows. Churches had three or five naves, a Latin cross floorplan, a cupola above the crossing, one or more semicircular apses and a pilgrims' ambulatory. Romanesque sculpture (incorporated into the building) and painting (which covered the interior walls completely!) accomplished a didactic, rather than decorative, function; the illiterate devout 'read the Bible' through the images, which sought to stimulate piety and fear of the Church. A common representation was Pantocrator (Christ) as powerful king and inflexible judge, seated on his throne and surrounded by the evangelists (Matthew, Mark, Luke and John) symbolically represented as an angel, lion, bull and eagle.

The Gothic style surfaced in the 12th century in conjunction with a general socioeconomic shift of power from the country to the city. Using the pointed arch and the ribbed vault, buildings – especially cathedrals – strove for height and luminosity (representing the light of God). The basilica (rectangular) floorplan, wider at the transept, also had an ambulatory and chapels behind the altar. The high walls incorporated stained-glass and rose windows inside and flying buttresses and needle-like pinnacles on the outside. The painting and sculpture sought realism and beauty rather than to present a message to be read. The Virgin Mary appears more frequently and Christ as judge is substituted for Christ as man who suffers on the cross. Sculptures are found on portals, chorus seats, gargoyles and altars, while painting (on wood) appears principally on altarpieces. Both reflect a greater preoccupation with light, movement, perspective and naturalism.

mess and busy streets by following the Río Arlanzón's peaceful, though paved, course.

Leave the monastery, walking along the road to a crossroads. From here, continue straight for almost 3km on a flat, dirt path enveloped in a thick forest of oak and conifers. Reaching a meadow, pass through the wire shepherds' gate and descend to **Agés** (with fountain). Cross the village and continue 2.5km along a paved road to **Atapuerca**, which has a fountain, *albergue* and bar.

Nearby, in Sierra de Atapuerca, archaeologists actively work on hugely important excavations of human remains dating from 800,000 years ago as well as a potential predecessor of Homo sapiens and a Neanderthal, dubbed H. antecessor. An information office in Atapuerca organises visits to the excavation sites.

Leaving the village, turn left, after the fountain on a dirt path, ascending 2km to the summit (1060m). Enjoy exceptional views to Burgos. The path descends to the valley, reaching a dirt road. Turn left onto the road and 300m later fork right (even if the arrows are painted out) to reach Orbaneja on a trail that winds pleasantly through wheat fields. (The left fork to Orbaneja is 1.5km longer, paved and passes through Villalval, with a bar, and Cardeñuela.)

From **Orbaneja** (with fountain and bar), follow the road heading west (right) for 700m to a bridge. Cross the *autovía* (highway). Immediately afterwards, by an abandoned military outpost, turn left onto a footpath skirting the outpost. After 1.3km the path circles an airfield following the cyclone fence until the trail veers left to **Castañares**. Turn right onto the trail paralleling the highway. Continue 1.5km to the Metal Ibérica factory (on the right), and turn left, crossing the highway. This turn is easy to miss! Take a dirt lane that soon converts to asphalt and passes through Villayuda (Ventilla; with fountain) and leaves under the train's pedestrian tunnel. It soon reaches Capiscol, a suburb of Burgos.

At the road either turn left (recommended) for the river route (3.3km to the cathedral) or follow the road (4.2km to the cathedral) right to the N1 (Calle Vitoria) by a petrol station, rejoining the conventional, waymarked city trail.

To follow the river, turn left. Head right, following the walkway to the **Puente El Cid**. Continue through the sycamore-shaded **Espolón** to the **Puerta de Santa María**, the dramatic stone gateway which leads to the cathedral plaza. The newly opened municipal *albergue* is located directly behind the Cathedral.

Day 12: Burgos to Hontanas
8–9½ hours, 31.8km
After the initial 10km of mostly sealed roads, the way enters a magnificent no-man's-land; the meaning of *meseta* becomes vividly clear. Get supplies in Burgos or Tardajos (much more limited) as neither Hornillos nor Hontanas has a market.

From the *albergue*, follow the river walkway for 2km to a stone bridge. Cross the bridge and then cross the road to El Parral City Park. Follow the trail back out of the park to the Hospital del Rey (today a university building). Continue straight along the footpath parallel to the main road for 700m to a roundabout and head right onto Calle Pérez Galdós. The street becomes dirt and winds between poplars and fields to **Villalbilla** (with fountain and *albergue*). Skirting the village, reach its

---

KNIGHTS TEMPLAR

Beginning in the 11th century as a consequence of the Crusades, religious military orders developed to combat the Muslims, and recuperate and defend holy places and the roadways connecting them. Spain and the Camino de Santiago, had its share of these orders. The most famous were the Knights of the Temple of Solomon (or Knights Templar) founded in Jerusalem in 1118. Despite poor beginnings, the order soon achieved great power, with numerous possessions; it became the most established bank of the period.

Not surprisingly, the order attracted various enemies, among them Phillip IV of France. In 1307 he ordered the detention of the Knights Templar, tortured many and confiscated their wealth , his actions were based on unfounded accusations including devil worship. The order was finally suppressed in 1312.

small train station and veer right through agricultural fields to the highway. Cross and take a dirt lane that parallels the highway to **Tardajos**, complete with all services, fountain and an *albergue*. Cross through the village, leaving via a paved road that veers left, reaching **Rabé de las Calzadas** (with fountain) in 2km.

Leave Rabé on a dirt road passing an *albergue* (right) and a chapel and cemetrey (on the left). The way climbs a small hill, flattens out and continues for a seemingly endless 8km to **Hornillos del Camino** (825m). There's a fountain to the right of the trail 2.4km from Rabé. For some, this stretch (and the next to Hontanas) is mentally fatiguing as the horizon stretches to infinity. Others feel liberated, far from the sights and sounds of 'civilisation'. Hornillos has a fountain, *albergue* and bar (which serves sandwiches).

Leave Hornillos, forking right to take a dirt road (past cellars tunnelled into the hillside) for 600m. Ascend to the crossroads marked with white limestone field stones and veer left. The path flattens and rolls off into nothing. Crossing two minor dirt roads, continue to an unanticipated dip marked with a red Santiago cross. Off to the left a small, solitary structure (painted with a red Knights Templar cross) is the small oasis of Sanbol, which has an *albergue* and a fountain with very cold water. The way continues without turns for 5km to Hontanas (930m). The church's bell tower suddenly pierces the sky, signalling your arrival. Past the church on the right you'll find the *albergue*.

Day 13: Hontanas to Boadilla del Camino

8–9½ hours, 29.6km

Buy supplies for day's end in Castrojeriz or continue for an additional 4.5km to Frómista (see Day 14). Leaving Hontanas, cross the highway (towards Castrojeriz) onto a path that rejoins the road 4km later. Another 5km remain to Castrojeriz. Countless poplar, linden and elm leaves rustle musically along the way. Outside Castrojeriz, the road reaches the lamentable ruins of the Gothic **Convento de San Antón**. When ergotism, or St Anthony's Fire (a gruesome disease causing reddened extremities, burning skin boils and

eventually gangrene), broke out across Europe in the 10th and 11th centuries, the saint's order blessed pilgrims with their symbol, the Greek letter tau, as insurance against the malady. The west rose window has the tau woven into the tracery. There is an *albergue* here.

The road continues to **Castrojeriz** (808m), a *sirga* wrapped round the hill's southern slope and topped with a castle, still impressive despite its ruined state. Entering town, pass the churches of the Virgen del Manzano, Santo Domingo (with a small museum) and San Juan. All services are available, including two *albergues*. Descend out of town, crossing the highway to a dirt road, and over the medieval stone then wooden bridge.

Steeply ascend the imposing hill for 1.2km to the summit of **Mostelares** (900m); an unexpected botanic garden greets you. The dirt path continues for 500m along the high *mesa* before abruptly descending to flat farmland and finally reaching a picnic area, Fuente del Piojo (Louse Fountain). Continue along the paved road for 1km and turn left onto a field road which descends past the **Ermita San Nicolás**, a small Romanesque church converted by an Italian Camino association into a simple *albergue*. Cross the 11-arch medieval bridge spanning the Río Pisuerga, the natural border between Burgos and Palencia provinces.

Head right on the wide dirt road to the village of **Itero de la Vega** (with fountain and an *albergue*). Leave Itero via a paved road and continue on a wide dirt-and-stone road for a long 8km to adobe **Boadilla del Camino** (795m). A shady, wheeled fountain on the left offers welcome respite. Follow the arrows to reach both *albergues*.

Day 14: Boadilla del Camino to Carrión de los Condes

7½–8½ hours, 27km

Leave Boadilla via the marked dirt road. Reaching a large barn and *palomar*, turn left and continue on the flats until gently rising to the Canal de Castilla. Designed for irrigation, transport and grain milling, the 240km of these waterways are primarily used today for irrigation. Continue for 4km along the canal's left shoulder until you get to the sluice gate (above the locks) and cross it via the footbridge.

HONTANAS TO TERRADILLOS DE LOS TEMPLARIOS

Continue straight along the road to **Frómista**, which has all services and an *albergue*. Frómista's highlight is the **Iglesia de San Martín**, a fine example of Romanesque architecture, famous for its 100 interior capitals and 315 exterior stone-sculpted figures (called corbels) gracing the eaves.

Leave Frómista along a sycamore-flanked walkway towards Carrión de los Condes. Once beyond the overpass, turn right onto the Senda de Peregrinos (Pilgrims' Path) running parallel to the highway. In 3km reach **Población de Campos**, with a fountain, bar and *albergue*.

From Población to Villalcázar there are two options: either roughly follow the Río Ucieza's course (recommended) or walk 9km along the Senda de Peregrinos. The former is more scenic, tranquil and 1.3km longer.

To reach the river, at the end of Población turn left before reaching the road leading to the Senda de Peregrinos. Veer right onto a dirt road that soon turns left then reaches Villovieco (with fountain) in 3.5km.

Continue past the village, cross over a bridge and immediately turn right onto a dirt trail which parallels the river. In 1.3km reach a dirt road and another bridge to the right (do not cross the bridge). A sign suggests turning left to Villarmentero and the Senda, but we recommend continuing straight along the river using the wide, flat trail. Follow the river for 3.7km to a sealed road and turn left. Passing the large Ermita Virgen del Río, continue for 1.8km to **Villalcázar de Sirga**. It has all services, a fountain and an *albergue*. This is one of the few villages with a documented Templar presence, and the central remnant of their powerful past is the

magnificent 13th-century **Iglesia de Santa María la Blanca** (see the boxed text Knights Templar, p318). The carved southern facade, the chapel of Santiago with the seated Virgen Blanca (south transept) and the altarpiece of Santiago (north transept) are especially noteworthy.

Continue on the Senda de Peregrinos, the only option now, for 6km to **Carrión** (830m). Walk up the main street past, first, the private *albergue* of the Clarisas (on the left) and then the parish *albergue* behind the Iglesia Cristo del Tiempo.

Day 15: Carrión de los Condes to Terradillos de los Templarios
7½–9 hours, 27km

On the flat, shadeless 16km stretch between Carrión and Calzadilla, studded with oaks and a few poplars, there's one fountain.

Descend to and cross the Río Carrión, passing the **Monasterio de San Zoilo**, now converted into a beautiful hotel. Continue straight through two consecutive crossroads (towards Villotilla). Three dreary kilometres of highway lead to and pass the Abadía Benevivere, founded in 1085 and now a farm. Cross the new bridge and after 700m reach and cross the highway heading straight onto a flat stone-and-dirt path – a Roman highway that connected Bordeaux to Astorga. In 2km, next to a tall poplar and a concrete marker which reads 'Hospital de Don García', is the fountain. In the next 10km you will reach **Calzadilla de la Cueza**, with a fountain, bar-restaurant and *albergue*.

Trail markers lead to the N120 where an information panel explains four alternative routes to San Nicolás del Real Camino. Initially we describe 'Ruta 4' to Ledigos and then from there 'Ruta 3: Al Palomar' because it's the most scenic and tranquil.

Turn right onto the N120 and after crossing the Río Cueza take the Senda, which parallels the highway's left shoulder. At a fork, 200m later, take 'Ruta 4' and continue 5.3km to **Ledigos**, which has a fountain, bar (which serves sandwiches but no meals) and *albergue*. Cross the highway to the sealed road (towards Población de Arroyo) and in 300m turn right onto an agricultural road. A large, circular *palomar* sits on the left. In 500m make a sharp left onto a path that leads to **Terradillos de los Templarios** (880m) in 2km. At the village entrance, veer right to find the *albergue* 100m further along on the left. Sit down and have a very cold drink. You're halfway there. How do you feel?

Day 16: Terradillos de los Templarios to Burgo Ranero
9–10½ hours, 32km

Castilla y León's wheat fields have been both Spain's breadbasket and a wool-industry centre. Large flocks of sheep are a common sight on the *meseta* walks.

Leave Terradillos on the first dirt road going left (west), to the right of an electricity tower, after entering the village. Ignore the uphill arrows; they return to the highway and the Senda. Continue 1.4km to the sealed road. Turn left and after 400m, veer right down a dirt lane passing a hand-pump fountain. Medieval Villaoreja once existed here. Continue to **Moratinos** (with fountain) and 2.5km later **San Nicolás del Real Camino** (with fountain) appears.

Cross the quiet village to a small poplar grove. The arrows diverge: turn right to the Senda, which runs parallel to the highway to reach Sahagún in 5.8km, or continue straight (west) along the unmarked dirt-and-gravel lane for 7.3km to Sahagún; the latter (recommended) is more tranquil and scenic. At the first junction, continue straight on the dirt track; at the second, make a right-angled turn right. Trail markers begin again. After a gentle ascent to a barren plateau, Sahagún appears ahead. Descend to an unmarked T-junction and turn right to the N120, then left onto the Senda. After 300m, cross a bridge and either continue straight on the Senda or cross the N120 (recommended) to the

agricultural road that leads to the Mudéjar-style **Ermita Virgen del Puente** – note the brick construction and horseshoe arches – surrounded by poplars. Continue under an overpass and enter **Sahagún de Campos**, which has all services and an *albergue* – in the restored Trinidad church. Sahagún's monuments are excellent examples of Mudéjar architecture. Celebrated examples include the San Tirso, San Lorenzo and La Peregrina churches.

Leave Sahagún via Calle Rey Don Antonio. With the neoclassical **Arco de San Benito** on the right, cross the 11th-century bridge over the Río Cea. To the right, the legendary Field of the Lances acquired its name when 40,000 of Charlemagne's Christian soldiers died here fighting to free the north of Muslim influence and make the pilgrimage road safe. It's now a municipal **camping ground**. Take the Senda parallel to the road and in 3.6km cross the N120 to rejoin the Senda straight ahead. After 250m reach another crossroads with two options. Straight ahead leads to Calzada del Coto (which has an *albergue*) on a rugged, desolate, poorly marked alternative that reaches Mansilla de las Mulas after 35.5km along the Via Traiana. Exceptionally hot in summer, during one 25km stretch the route lacks food, water or accommodation opportunities; only Calzadilla de los Hermanillos breaks the monotony.

Instead, at the crossroads, take the Senda de Peregrinos, marked with a cross, which heads west for 32km to Mansilla de las Mulas. Take the Senda reaching **Bercianos del Real Camino** in 5.5km, which has a fountain and *albergue*, and 8km later **Burgo Ranero** (878m). The *albergue* is across the street from the Hostal El Peregrino.

Day 17: Burgo Ranero to León
10–11½ hours, 37.7km

This long, often windy, stage is easily divided by stopping in Mansilla de las Mulas, a sizable town with *albergue* and all services, after 19.3km.

Next to a pond at the west end of Burgo Ranero, the Senda de Peregrinos begins again. After 12.5km of solitary, uninterrupted, barren plains (crossing the railway tracks once) the way reaches sleepy **Reliegos**, which has a fountain,

TERRADILLOS DE LOS TEMPLARIOS TO MOLINASECA

bar-restaurant and *albergue*. Leave Reliegos, passing the *frontón* to the Senda de Peregrinos, and 6km later enter **Mansilla de las Mulas** via the Puerta de Santiago gateway, passing a modern monument to the tired pilgrim. The *albergue* is along the pilgrim's road. Mansilla's odd coat of arms depicts a *mano* (hand) over a *silla* (saddle). The name Mansilla, though, probably derives from the town's beginnings as a Roman *mansionella* (way station).

Leave town, crossing the bridge over the **Río Esla**, and walk parallel to the N120 on a dirt trail for 4km to Villamoros de Mansilla. Continue through the village and take the Senda parallel to the N120, crossing a 20-arch bridge to the footpaths of **Villarente**, with fountain and all services. At the end of Villarente, after passing the petrol station, turn right onto a dirt trail that ascends to **Arcahueja** (with fountain). Descend to a junction: continue straight (recommended) to **Valdelafuente** (with fountain) or turn left to the highway route. In 1.5km from the fork, the dirt road ends at a sealed road. Turn left to reach the N120 and in 600m reach the Alto del Portillo (890m). Descend along the left side of the N120 for 2km and turn left to enter the León suburb of **Puente Castro**.

Continue straight, crossing a footbridge, and 1km further on, at the end of Avenida

de Madrid, the paths to the two *albergues* diverge. To reach the *albergue municipal*, on the city's outskirts, turn left onto Avenida Fernández Ladreda, and then left again on Calle Monseñor Turbado to the Colegio Huérfanos Ferroviarios (CHF) building. It's also a youth hostel. To reach the *albergue* Madres Carbalajas in 1.2km, and the historical quarter, continue straight on Avenida Alcalde Miguel Castaño, turning right onto Calle Barahona just after Plaza Santa Ana. Barahona converts to Puerta Moneda. Turn right onto Calle Escurial and 100m later you'll find the convent on the right, across from Plaza Santa María.

Day 18: León to Villar de Mazarife

5½–6½ hours, 21.5km

As Villar de Mazarife is very small, buy supplies in Virgen del Camino.

From Calle Puerta Moneda continue straight to Calle Herreros, which merges with Calle La Rúa. Turn right on Calle Ancha and continue uphill, turning left into the cathedral's Plaza Regla.

From the plaza take the first left down Sierra Pambley to Dámaso Merico to Recoletas and finally turn right onto Calle El Cid. Continue to Plaza San Isidoro and turn left down the stairs to Calle Ramón y Cajal. Turn right and then left onto Calle

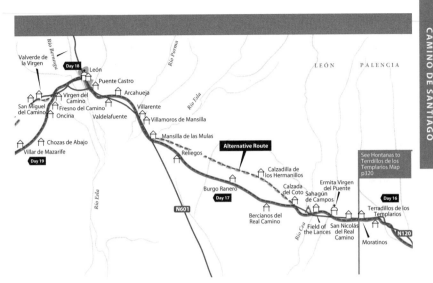

Renueva, which becomes Avenida Suero de Quiñones. Continue past the Hostal de San Marcos and over the medieval bridge to the N120.

Continue 1.5km through houses and high-rises to a small plaza where the trail crosses the train tracks via a pedestrian walkway before rejoining the N120. Veer left to avoid a dangerous curve before returning to, and crossing, the N120. Take Calle La Cruz, which ascends past the entrances to subterranean *bodegas* on the left. After the road flattens, continue straight for 1.2km to the N120. Take the parallel sealed trail past the petrol station to enter **Virgen del Camino**, which has a fountain and all services. The facade of the church, built in 1961, is the work of José María Subirachs (sculptor of stylistic and expressionist modern art) and contains 13 bronze statues (12 apostles – Santiago points to Compostela – and the Virgin Mary).

After the church, cross the N120 and descend along the sealed road. Two options rejoin in Hospital de Órbigo (see Day 19): the isolated, dirt roads via Villar de Mazarife (recommended) after 28.6km, or the Senda and highway via Villadangos after 24.3km. Along the latter, the route enters the villages of Valverde de la Virgen, San Miguel del Camino and, 14km beyond Virgen del Camino, **Villadangos**, which has all services and an *albergue*. The next 10km parallel the N120, passing San Martín del Camino (with *albergue*) and Puente Órbigo before reaching Hospital.

The clearly marked way to Villar de Mazarife undulates along dirt trails and minor roads past **Fresno del Camino** (with fountain), **Oncina** (with fountain), and **Chozas de Abajo**, and after 13.5km reaches Mazarife. Albergue Ramón is on the left 150m after the first houses Albergue. Loli is next to the church.

Day 19: Villar de Mazarife to Astorga
8–10 hours, 32km

To shorten this long stage you could stop in at the *albergue* of either **Hospital de Órbigo** (after 15km) or **Santibáñez** (after 20km). Santibáñez has no services.

Leave Mazarife, following the sealed road for 6km to a crossroads. Continue straight onto a dirt road and in 3.5km pass two canals and reach Villavante. Continue straight without entering Villavante (ignore arrows leading to the village). Cross the train tracks and the highway over a bridge to an industrial park that soon reaches the N120. Cross the highway and enter **Puente Órbigo**, aiming for its church adorned with massive stork's nests.

Turn left over the long stone bridge spanning the dammed Río Órbigo. Its 19 arches date from the 13th to the 19th centuries. Dubbed the Paso Honroso, the bridge gained fame in 1434 when Don Suero de Quiñones challenged all-comers to a jousting tournament to assuage the torments of an unrequited love. Dispatching some 300 knights over the course of one month, Suero triumphed and later made a pilgrimage to Santiago in thanks. **Hospital de Órbigo** has all services and two *albergues* (the parish one on the main street and the municipal one 500m through the poplar forest right, north, of the bridge).

Leave Hospital following its long main street (crossing a busy road once) to a fork. Either head straight for 1.5km to the road and an additional 9km parallel to the main road where the two options rejoin at the Crucero de Santo Toribio, or turn right (recommended) and for 11.5km enjoy tranquillity and rural life.

Turning right, walk a very flat 2km through cultivated fields to **Villares de Órbigo** (with fountain and bar). Turn left and then right past a *lavadero* (place to wash clothes) and fountain. Continue straight, crossing a sealed road and bridge, to a dirt footpath that turns left, ascending along the hillside (look for fragrant lavender and thyme) to a sealed road. Turn right, descending to **Santibáñez de Valdeiglesias** (with fountain and *albergue*). Reaching mid-village, before its subterranean fountain, turn right up the street and veer right out of the village for 7km to the Crucero de Santo Toribio (905m), ascending and descending through fields and forest.

Framed by mountains, Astorga spreads out majestically below. Descend to and pass through **San Justo de la Vega**, which has a fountain and all services. After crossing the bridge, turn right and then immediately left along a dirt track that in 1.8km leads to the main road. Turn right (crossing the train tracks) and turn left down the first road and then right. At the T-junction turn left and then make a hairpin right turn to ascend steeply into **Astorga** (873m). On the right, 50m further along, are the remains of a Roman villa complete with intact mosaic flooring.

The *albergue municipal* is on a parallel street off to the left.

Day 20: Astorga to Rabanal del Camino
5–6½ hours, 21.1km

Leave Astorga along Calle San Pedro and cross the NVI to the descending sealed road (towards Castrillo de los Polvazares). After 3.5km reach **Murias de Rechivaldo**, which has a fountain, *albergue* and bar-restaurants. Note the stone and wood construction, distinctive door jambs, balconies and slate roofs typical of the Maragatería – the area west of Astorga reaching to the summit beyond Foncebadón. Leave Murias along a dirt track. In 2.6km cross the road and continue along a Senda parallel to the road to reach **Santa Catalina de Somoza**, which has a fountain and *albergue*, in 1.8km. Cross the village and then continue along the Senda to **El Ganso** (with fountain and *albergue*).

The last 7km to Rabanal del Camino (1156m) is a continuous ascent along Senda and road. Be sure not to veer right to Rabanal el Viejo. At the base of Rabanal, either fork left to reach the *albergues* municipal and Pilar or fork right (immediately passing a tiny market and guesthouse on the left) to the *albergue*.

Day 21: Rabanal del Camino to Molinaseca
7–8 hours, 26.5km

Fountains en route are unreliable. Get water in Rabanal, El Acebo (17km) and Riego de Ambrós (20.5km).

Ascend Calle Real, taking a trail to the paved road, and ascend the road for 4.2km to **Foncebadón**, a small village with a few seasonal residents. Fork left and ascend through the village, past the church. The 12th-century hermit Gaucelmo ran a pilgrims' hospital here and there's now an *albergue*. Veer left onto a lane that soon ascends round the hill to the road. Cross and take the parallel trail that soon ends at the summit of **Monte Irago** (1504m) and the **Cruz de Ferro** (Iron Cross).

A highly emblematic monument of the Camino, the simple iron cross, rises out of a long, wooden trunk planted in a *milladoiro* (huge mound of stones). The Romans called these cairns 'mountains of Mercury' in honour of the walkers' deity. Continuing an age-old tradition, many pilgrims throw stones (some brought from home), which represent symbolic weights or sins, onto the pile.

The route runs parallel to the paved road for 2.2km to the largely abandoned, yet still inhabited, village of **Manjarín**. A bell may be rung in greeting as you approach a modern-day Knight Templar, Tomás, who runs a simple *albergue*.

Continue on the undulating highway before descending 12.5km to Molinaseca. The way alternates between stretches of highway and dirt paths, passing two villages. **El Acebo** has a fountain, bar-restaurant and some *albergues*. **Riego de Ambrós** has a fountain, bar-restaurant and an *albergue*. Note the slate roofs and overhanging wooden balconies with external staircases that are typical of the area.

Leaving El Acebo, an iron bicycle commemorates the death of a German pilgrim killed en route to Compostela. Continue along the road and veer left through broom to Riego de Ambrós. From Riego the path zigzags downhill through chestnut groves and open scrub to the road. Walk 100m along the road and turn right onto a dirt track. Descend to **Molinaseca** (620m), a beautiful village on the banks of the Río Meruelo, crossing the Romanesque bridge. To reach the municipal *albergue* continue walking 1km through Molinaseca on the main street and then the main road.

Day 22: Molinaseca to Villafranca del Bierzo
7–8 hours, 29.6km

Leave Molinaseca along the highway. After 2km of gentle ascent, Ponferrada comes into sight. Either continue along the highway (recommended) or take a trail to the left that makes a long (1.8km) unnecessary detour via Campo. Continuing on the highway, cross the Río Boeza and enter **Ponferrada** (meaning Iron Bridge) along Avenida de Molinaseca. At the first crossroads, turn left onto Avenida del Castillo and 400m later, next to the Iglesia del Carmen, you'll find the *albergue*. Continue straight to the famed **Castillo de los Templarios**, finished in 1282. The knights used it until their disbandment 30 years later. The mammoth complex overlooking the Río Sil has been extensively modified since then; now, fortunately, the town is renovating it.

Turn right uphill to reach the tourist office (in a stone building on the left) and the Plaza de la Encina with bars and the **Virgen de la Encina church**. From the plaza entrance, turn left and descend the stairs. Turn left, crossing the bridge, and then right on Calle Río Urdiales. Turn right onto Avenida Huerta del Sacramento and 1km later, turn right at Avenida de la Libertad. Passing mountains of coal, take the first left turn through **Compostilla**, passing the villages of **Columbrianos**, **Fuentes Nuevas** and **Camponaraya** (with all services) over the next 7km.

After Camponaraya, turn left along a dirt road next to the Cooperativa Viñas del Bierzo. After crossing the bridge, continue through vineyards along a dirt track for 2.5km to a sealed road. Descend along the road 1.5km to **Cacabelos**, which has all services including *albergues*. Depart across the Río Cúa and continue 4.5km along the highway, passing **Pieros** (with fountain). After the Km 406 highway sign, turn right onto a dirt trail that leads through vineyards and fruit trees in 2.8km to Villafranca del Bierzo (511m). Immediately on the right is the *albergue municipal* and on the left, past the Romanesque **Iglesia de Santiago**, is the stone *albergue* of Jesús Jato, built by and for pilgrims.

Day 23: Villafranca del Bierzo to Cebreiro
8–9 hours, 30.8km

This stage is the most physically challenging of the Camino with a total ascent of 1280m. The conventional route leaves Villafranca and follows a highway for 10.5km to Trabadelo (and to Portela after 14.4km). We describe a more difficult but far safer and more beautiful way to Trabadelo. There are various *albergues* en route to break up the stage if necessary.

Drop into Villafranca, head towards the river and exit via the medieval footbridge and then a car bridge over the Río Burbia to a fork. Fork left for the highway option (passing Pereje, with *albergue*) to Trabadelo in 9km, or fork right initiating a long ascent of 480m (towards Pradela), first on the paved street and then a dirt-and-stone track. Enjoy increasingly excellent views of Villafranca and the Valle del Valcárcel. Flattening out along the ridge, the way heads

CAMINO DE SANTIAGO

MOLINASECA TO PALAS DO REI

towards a hill topped with communication towers. Descend among chestnuts (Pradela comes into sight off to the right) and at the first fork, bear left. After 600m, fork left again through chestnuts and descend for 3km. Cross a sealed road several times until finally descending into **Trabadelo** (which has an *albergue* and bars) from behind along an ancient access trail. Turn right and join the NVI in 1km.

Continue along the highway for 2.2km to **Portela** (with bar). In 400m, turn left at the petrol station, and 400m further along veer left onto the road towards Vega de Valcarce. Continue 5.5km to the Herrerías fork, along the way passing **Ambasmestas** (with fountain and bar-restaurants); **Vega de Valcarce** (with all services and two *albergues*); and **Ruitelán** (with a bar and *albergue*).

One kilometre past Ruitelán, where the sealed road forks, turn left, and descend to **Herrerías** (with fountain). Pass through the village and ascend the sealed road for 1km. Watch for the fork and descend left along a Galician *corredoira* (stone-cobbled lane). Ascend steeply for 1.5km to **La Faba**, with fountain, *albergue* and a sporadically open bar. Continue through the village, returning to the *corredoira*, which ascends through pastures and rolling hills to **Laguna de Castilla** (with fountain), the last village of León, in 2km. Around 150m beyond the village fork left onto a lane that reaches **Cebreiro** (1300m) in 2km. Soon after, spot the entry into Galicia and the first cement trail marker indicating that 153km remain to Santiago de Compostela. The countdown begins: every 500m another marker appears. Cebreiro's *albergue* is at the far western end of the small burgh.

Day 24: Cebreiro to Triacastela
5–6 hours, 19km

In Galicia, green and grey predominate, rain is a constant possibility (some would say certainty!) and the Galician language, Galego (see p375), is commonly spoken. Rural Galicia with its countless hamlets connected by *corredoiras*, granite churches, stacked-tomb cemetreies and unending hills is bound to enchant.

Leave Cebreiro on the main road (towards Triacastela) and in 2.5km reach **Liñares** (with bar), founded as a linen plantation. Ascend to the **Alto de San Roque** (1270m) either via the highway or by turning right down a sealed road that after 100m converts to a footpath and ascends to the pass. A large, dramatic pilgrim statue braces against the elements at the top. Turn right onto a path that descends 1km to **Hospital da Condesa**, which has a fountain and an *albergue*. Traverse the hamlet and rejoin the highway for 600m. Turn right onto a sealed road (towards Sabugos) and in 200m take a dirt trail that ascends to **Padornelo** (with fountain). Climb steeply to **Alto do Poio** (1313m). Two bar-restaurants mark the summit – the Camino's last high point. Walk along the highway for 700m and then veer right onto a lane that reaches **Fonfría** in 2.5km.

In the next 9km to Triacastela follow rural lanes past Viduedo, up Monte Caldeirón, and then descend continuously to Filloval and through forests of chestnut and oak on a dirt lane to As Pasantes (reached via a tunnel below the road) and Ramil, before finally entering Triacastela (665m). Immediately on the left is the Albergue Xunta and straight ahead, in town, is the Albergue Aitzenea.

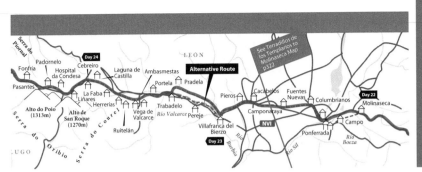

Day 25: Triacastela to Sarria
6½–7½ hours, 25.5km

To reach Sarria from Triacastela (where the trail splits at a T-junction) there are two options: left via Samos or right via San Xil. The former (highlight is Samos) is described here and the latter (its charm is rural) in the Alternative Route (see next column).

Turn left along the highway and continue parallel to the Río Oribio for 3.4km. Veer right down the marked, paved lane through **San Cristobo do Real**, over the Oribio and ascend past the hamlet's cemetry to a beautiful rural lane flanked with chestnuts and oaks. Keep straight on, crossing the Oribio again (near an in-use water mill) and then steeply ascend along a sealed road through **Renche** to the highway. Walk briefly along the road and descend (right) and reach Freituge in 1km. Mid-hamlet, fork right onto a rural lane that crosses the Oribio in 500m. Steeply ascend along the sealed road through a highway tunnel. Veer left onto a dirt lane that descends to **Samos** (510m).

Founded in the 6th century (the date is confirmed by a Visigothic tablet), the Samos **monastery** has a 9th- to 10th-century chapel and a wealth of Renaissance and Baroque art. The Benedictine monks run tours (€3; one hour). The highlight of the tours are the stunning **frescos** on the second floor. The village has all services and a monastic *albergue*.

From Samos, 15km remain to Sarria. Walk through and veer left out of the village, keeping the Oribio on your left. After the last houses, a footpath (left) parallels the road to the Teiguín river park (with fountain). After 150m, passing a bridge and water mill on the left, cross the main road and ascend a steep, sealed road. Continue 800m to **Pascais**. Just before its first houses, turn left onto a descending dirt lane. In 400m, after a farm, there's an unmarked fork. Fork left, skirting round the church and descending along a dirt lane to a sealed road. Continue 1.5km to a bridge (over the Río Frollais) guarded by an enshrined praying saint. The inscription reads: 'This bridge was made in the year 1840, those who cross entrust themselves to the souls of purgatory.' Soon thereafter, turn left onto a sealed road (towards Sivil) that is level and then climbs to **Aguiada** in 3.4km.

From Aguiada take the dirt Senda to the right of the road for 4km to **Sarria** (440m). In Sarria, cross the river, turn right on the street and then make a quick left, ascending a flight of penitential steps (Escalinata Maior) to Rúa Maior and the *albergue* at No 79.

ALTERNATIVE ROUTE: VIA SAN XIL
4½–5 hours, 18km

Fork right and follow the sealed road, turn left after crossing the highway, and in 1.7km reach **Balsa**. Cross its bridge and ascend right through woods to a sealed road. Turn right and soon reach **San Xil** (with fountain). In 2km ascend to the Alto de Riocabo (905m) and then descend to **Montán**. In 3km reach **Pintín** after passing through **Fontearcuda**. Continue, passing another hamlet, to **Calvor**, which has an *albergue*. The path runs parallel to the road for 350m until it turns right onto a sealed road (towards Aguiada). In 250m the two routes reunite in Aguiada.

Day 26: Sarria to Portomarín
6–7 hours, 23.7km

Today's walk passes through 23 hamlets (only the most important of which are marked on our map). Continue ascending along Rúa Maior past the Santa Marina (on the right) and Salvador (on the left) churches to a fountain. With the castle ruins ahead, turn right onto Avenida de la Feria, ascending to the Magdalena monastery (on the right).

Turn left, descending past the cemetery to a road. Turn right and in 150m turn left over a medieval bridge. The path runs parallel to the train tracks, crosses them and then after a wooden footbridge ascends through a dense chestnut forest. Ruins of a chestnut-drying hut are on the right. The path ascends to Vilei and then **Barbadelo**, which has an *albergue*. Barbadelo's church is a fine example of rural Galician Romanesque sculpture.

The Camino winds and bends along dirt, stone and sealed lanes through numerous signposted crossroads and hamlets, including Rente, **Peruscallo** (with bar), Lavandeira, Brea (from which you have a 'mere' 100km to go!), Morgade (with fountain and bar), **Ferreiros** (with *albergue* and bar), Mirallos, **Pena** (with fountain), Rozas, Pena dos Corvos (spectacular views and the first appearance of Galician pines), Moimentos, Mercadoiro, Montras, Parrocha and Vilachá. Finally, the route descends steeply to **Portomarín** (350m).

Cross the bridge over the Río Miño. Old Portomarín, submerged below, was sacrificed in 1956 to construct a dam. Turn right, ascending along the footpath below the city park. Turn left and in 150m you will reach the *albergue*.

Day 27: Portomarín to Palas do Rei
6½–7 hours, 26km

Cross the main plaza, descend along the columned main street to the main road and turn left. In 150m turn right and then cross the footbridge over the reservoir. Ascend Monte de San Antonio for 2km through forest to the highway at a brick factory. Cross to the Senda de Peregrinos, continuing for 1.6km to Toixibó and 3.8km further to Gonzar, which has an *albergue*.

Past the *albergue*, turn left to **Castromaior** where the first eucalyptus trees appear. Continue on the sealed road to the highway, walking parallel to it before descending left in 2.8km to **Alto do Hospital**, which has a

fountain, bar-restaurant and *albergue*. Leave Alto, crossing the highway over a bridge, and turn left, then 100m later turn right onto a sealed road (towards Ventas de Narón). Over the next 11km or so you'll pass through Ventas de Narón (with fountain), over the gentle Sierra de Ligonde (756m), then downhill through Previsa, Lameiros, **Ligonde** (with fountain and *albergue*), **Airexe** (with fountain and *albergue*), Portos (bar), Lestedo, Valos and, finally, **Brea**. The path runs parallel to the highway for 1.4km to Rosario and veers left past the camping ground and gym, entering **Palas do Rei** (605m) by the *albergue*, opposite the town hall.

Day 28: Palas do Rei to Ribadiso
6½–7½ hours, 27km

Ribadiso has no services other than an *albergue* but Arzúa, 2.5km further uphill, does. Along the way, shop in Melide for supplies.

Descend to the N547 and follow it to the Palas city limits. Before entering **Carballal**, cross the highway and climb through the village (with fountain) back to the N547. The route soon veers left on a descending trail to San Xulián do Camiño (with fountain). Cross a river and wind through an oak grove to Casanova, which has an *albergue*. In 2.5km the way reaches the border between Lugo and La Coruña. Turn left at the next crossroads along a dirt path to **Leboreiro** (with fountain); its Romanesque church has a simple image of the Virgin carved in the tympanum, and erotic corbels. Leave the village over its curious bridge to a path bordered by poplars and plains across Melide's industrial park (with fountain) for more than 2km. Descend to **Furelos** (with fountain). Cross the four-arch medieval bridge and continue for 1km to **Melide**, which has all services and an *albergue*.

Cross the town via Calle Principal to its main plaza. On fair days streetside *pulperías* (vendors of octopus boiled in copper pots and served *a la feria* on wooden plates with olive oil, red pepper and marine salt) provide a tempting excuse for a break. The **Iglesia de San Roque** and the 14th-century cross (to the left), considered Galicia's oldest, merit visits.

Follow the trail markers out of Melide past the cemetery and along a walled path to the highway. Cross the N547 and take the sealed road (towards San Martiño) for 200m before turning right (past the Romanesque **Iglesia de Santa María**). Over the next 5km pass Carballal, Parabispo and A Peroxa. In **Boente** (with fountain and bar), cross to the church and turn left through the village. Descend through eucalyptus groves and then ascend steeply to **Castañeda**, location of the 12th-century lime ovens used to make cement for Santiago de Compostela's cathedral. Pilgrims once carried stones from Triacastela to these ovens. Before reaching the N547 200m later, turn left towards Río, then veer right downhill. The way climbs a hill, descends, crosses the highway via an elevated bridge and then descends steeply to riverside **Ribadiso**. Two hundred metres above Ribadiso there's a bar. Cross the medieval bridge to the *albergue*, a restored 15th-century pilgrims' *hospital*. The closest alternative accommodation options are 2.5km and 3km further on, in Arzúa.

Day 29: Ribadiso to Arca
6–6½ hours, 23km
Alternative lodgings are available 1.5km before Arca, in Rúa. From Ribadiso, ascend towards the highway and turn left to pass through a tunnel under the N547. A footpath parallel to the highway reaches the centre of **Arzúa** (385m) in 2km.

Before reaching the main plaza, veer left down Calle Cima do Lugar (past the *albergue*) and go straight, leaving Arzúa via the stone-paved Rúa do Carme. Descend past the Fuente de los Franceses, and ascend through oaks past the Pazo As Barrosas (a country mansion). The dirt-and-stone lane reaches a stream, parallel to the path, and climbs to **Pregontoño**. The path forks right

out of the hamlet, through a tunnel and past three houses.

In A Peroxa (not to be confused with the one on Day 28) fork left onto the dirt road flanked by oak and fruit trees. Over the next 8km wind through the sleepy hamlets of Tabernavella, **Calzada** (with fountain), Boavista and, finally, **Salceda** (with fountain), where the path and highway run side by side. Just before Salceda, under a large chestnut tree, sits a rectangular stone mortar where apples were crushed for the fermented beverage, *sidra*.

Continue for 450m parallel to the N547, past a small shop-bar, and turn right onto a forest track. After a 200m climb, a pair of bronzed shoes unexpectedly commemorates the spot where a 63-year-old German pilgrim took his last steps in 1993. After Xen, Ras and Brea the path joins the highway at Rabiña and runs parallel to it to a pass and two roadside restaurants. Turn sharp right onto a dirt track flanked with eucalyptus that soon passes the **Albergue Xunta** in Santa Irene (the private *albergue* is across the N547). Continue downhill 850m through eucalyptus forest. Cross the highway to Rúa and continue downhill for 1.5km on a paved road to **Arca** (290m; also called Pedrouzo). Turn left onto the N547 and reach the *albergue* in 150m. Arca has three markets, and meals are available at a number of restaurants in town.

Day 30: Arca to Santiago de Compostela
5½–6 hours, 20.7km
Follow the N547 to Arca's tiny main plaza (1km) and turn right at the Casa do

PALAS DO REI TO SANTIAGO DE COMPOSTELA

Concello. Fifty metres past the school, turn left into the eucalypt forest. Continue for 3km to the N547 at **Amenal**. Cross and continue straight, entering a natural tunnel of rich vegetation and deep, dirt walls. Ascend for 2km, finally veering right to a roundabout on the main road. Turn left and look for two cement waymarks. You discover that up till now the distances given have been incorrect: there are 15km, not 12km, left to Santiago – somebody clearly has a sick sense of humour! Continue straight ahead, skirting the signal lights of the airport, and cross a sealed road. Descend to San Paio, known for the saint born in Pontevedra, martyred in Córdoba and popular throughout Galicia. Depart to the left and climb to a dirt road and eucalypt forest, reaching the first houses of **Lavacolla** (with bar-restaurant). The fame of Lavacolla is etymological – its name (literally, 'washing one's loins') describes medieval pilgrims' pre-arrival ablutions.

Pass Lavacolla's church, cross the N547 and in 150m reach the famed but nondescript Río Lavacolla. The last 10km to the cathedral square are sealed. Ascend for 5km through **Vilamaior**, past the large Galician and Spanish TV stations, and then turn left into San Marcos. From here medieval pilgrims sprinted to the nearby summit of **Monte do Gozo** (Mount Joy), dubbing the first to arrive 'king'. The cathedral's three spires are now in sight (barely!) for the first time. The summit's modest San Marcos chapel is overshadowed by the pilgrim sculpture in honour of the Pope and the 800-bed *albergue*, camp, bar-restaurant and amphitheatre.

Five kilometres of city streets remain. Descend straight, cross the highway bridge and round the left side of the roundabout. Continue straight to Rúa dos Concheiros. Turn left down the cobbled street to a roundabout. Cross to Rúa San Pedro, which leads to Porta do Camiño, one of the seven original entrances to the walled medieval city (the walls no longer exist). Granite flagstones lead up to the Praza de Cervantes and descend right through the Azabachería – the zone of the jet (petrified wood) artisans – then passes the Catedral de Santiago's north entrance and descends a flight of stairs to the grand Praza do Obradoiro.

Upon arrival, pilgrims usually mark the end with several rites: adding their hand imprint to the marble stone column at the cathedral's west end, hugging the large, Romanesque statue of Santiago and visiting the crypt containing his remains at the main altar. In Holy Years (see History, p304) the great *botafumeiro* (incense burner) is swung every day at the Pilgrims' Mass at noon, and is a sight to behold, especially from the north or south transept. To request the Compostela, head to the **Oficina del Peregrino** (☎ 981 56 24 29; www.archicompostela.org; Rúa do Vilar 1).

The only *albergue* in Santiago (and always threatened with closure) is the **Seminario Menor de Belvís**, 1km from the centre and accessed via Calle de las Trompas. Pilgrims are permitted to stay three nights. See also Santiago de Compostela (p213).

Now it's all done and dusted, and you're probably feeling a mixture of excitement and melancholy, you have two choices. The first is to remove your hiking boots and wonder what to do next with your life and the second is to leave those boots fused to your feet and carry on the journey to Fisterra and the end of the world…(see More Pilgrim Walks).

MORE PILGRIM WALKS

Though 91% of pilgrims walk the Camino Francés, some other historical pilgrimage routes are briefly described here. For guides to these routes see Books (p306).

Galicia's regional tourist offices have free *Roads to Santiago* brochures describing all except the Camino Aragonés.

Camino Aragonés

Using the higher Somport Pass in the Pyrenees, walk 146km through Aragón, joining the Camino Francés at Puente la Reina (see p312).

This quiet, more rugged route reveals the Pyrenees as peaks rather than lumps and descends gently through fertile valleys rich in monuments. The distance, intermittently waymarked, can be covered in five or six days.

Caminos del Norte

Pilgrims crossed the France–Spain border to Irún, reaching the Spanish Basque Country, and took the coastal route via San Sebastián, Bilbao and Santander to Ribadeo (Galicia) or headed inland via the Túnel de San Adrián (1443m) to La Rioja and the Camino Francés. Those sailing from the north landed (eg, in Santander or Gijón) and continued along the coast to Galicia or south to Fonsagrada and León via Oviedo. See www.gawthorpe40.freeserve.co.uk for information.

Vía de la Plata

From Seville, the Vía or Ruta de la Plata (Silver Way) runs 690km north to meet the Camino Francés at Astorga (see p324) via Zafra, Mérida, Cáceres, Salamanca and Zamora. Partly marked with yellow arrows, the route's infrastructure progressively improves. Passing through large cities and lengthy desolate stretches, water and people are scarce. Be prepared to carry supplies. Heat in Extremadura in July and August is unbearable, often more than 30°C.

Fisterra & Muxía

The 80km rural walk from Santiago de Compostela to the sea is feasible in three days passing through Negreira (with *albergue* and lodging), Olveiroa (with *albergue*), Cee and Corcubión (both with lodging), and Fisterra (with *albergue* and lodging). Continue another 30km north along the coast to Muxía, the legendary site of an encounter between Santiago and the Virgin Mary. Buses return daily from Fisterra and Muxía to Santiago.

Camino Portugués

From Lisbon a coastal route (via Porto and Tui) and two interior ones (via Braga and Verín or Ourense) reach Santiago. The coastal route is waymarked from Porto to Santiago and from the border at Tui. It's feasible in five days. The interior routes join a Vía de la Plata variant in Verín.

Camino Inglés

British pilgrims sailed to the ports of Ferrol or La Coruña and walked roughly 100km to Santiago. The two paths unite in Bruma (with *albergue*). The longer Ferrol section passes through the historic towns of Pontedeume and Betanzos.

TOWNS & FACILITIES

The following section includes information on Roncesvalles at the start of the Camino and all the major cities you will be passing through en route. Everywhere else you will presumably be staying in the pilgrim *albergues* that are found in most towns and villages along the way. For information on Santiago de Compostela see p213.

BURGOS

☎ 947 / pop 175,000

In the 15th century Burgos (860m), long associated with the pilgrimage, boasted 32 pilgrims' *hospitals*. Must-stops are the Gothic cathedral (which is a Unesco World Heritage site), considered one of Spain's masterworks for its interior and exterior opulence, the Gothic Iglesia de San Nicolás, and the *mirador* (lookout) below the castle ruins.

Information

The **regional tourist office** (☎ 20 31 25; www.turismocastillayleon.com; Plaza Alfonso Martínez 7; open daily) has excellent regional information. The **municipal tourist office** (☎ 28 88 74; www.aytoburgos.es, in Spanish; Plaza del Rey Fernando 2; open daily) has the lowdown on the city.

Sleeping & Eating

The decent **Albergue Municipal de Burgos** (☎ 460 922; Calle Fernán González 28; dm €3) is located directly behind the Cathedral. It consists of six floors with beds for 145 pilgrims. There are two private *albergues*. **Casa de Peregrinos Emaús** (Calle de San Pedro de Cardeña; donation) has just 16 beds. Similar is the **Albergue Divina Pastora** (☎ 20 79 52; Calle Lain Calvo 10; donation) which has 18 beds.

Pensión Peña (☎ 20 63 23; Calle Puebla 18, 2nd floor; s/d without bathroom from €20/26) This is an impeccable little place full of delightful individual touches, such as hand-painted wash basins.

CAMINO DE SANTIAGO

EL CID: THE HEROIC MERCENARY

Few names resonate through Spanish history quite like El Cid, the 11th-century soldier of fortune and adventurer whose story tells in microcosm of the tumultuous years when Spain was divided into Muslim and Christian zones. That El Cid became a romantic, idealised figure of history, known for his unswerving loyalty and superhuman strength, owes much to the 1961 film starring Charlton Heston and Sophia Loren. Reality, though, presents a different picture.

El Cid (from the Arabic *sidi* for 'chief' or 'lord') was born Rodrígo Diaz in Vivar, a hamlet about 10km north of Burgos, in 1043. After the death of Ferdinand I, he dabbled in the murky world of royal succession, which led to his banishment from Castilla in 1076. With few scruples as to whom he served, El Cid offered his services to a host of rulers, both Christian and Muslim. With each battle, he became ever more powerful and wealthy.

It's not known whether he suddenly developed a loyalty to the Christian kings or smelled the wind and saw that Spain's future would be Christian. Either way, when he heard that the Muslim armies had taken Valencia and expelled all the Christians, El Cid marched on the city, recaptured it and became its ruler in 1094 after a devastating siege. At the height of his powers and reputation, the man also known as El Campeador (Champion) retired to spend the remainder of his days in Valencia, where he died in 1099. His remains were returned to Burgos, where he lies buried along with his wife, Jimena, in the cathedral.

Hostal Acacia (☎ 20 51 34; www .hostalacacia.com; Calle de Bernabé Perez Ortiz 1; d with shower & washbasin from €30, s/d with bathroom from €25/37) This place, which is especially popular with pilgrims, hasn't raised its prices in years, during which time the rooms have, if anything, improved. The loquacious Trotsky-lookalike proprietor is a star attraction.

The king of Burgos tapas joints is the superb **Cervecería Morito** (Calle de la Sombrerería), a typical order is *alpargata* (lashings of cured ham with bread, tomato and olive oil; €2.70) and we challenge you to find better *calamares* (calamari) or *morcilla* elsewhere.

LEÓN

☎ 987 / pop 135,000

The most important inheritance of León (823m), originally a Roman garrison town, is its fine Romanesque and Gothic monuments. Highlights include the San Isidoro church; the Panteón Real, nicknamed the 'Sistine Chapel of Spanish Romanesque' for its exceptional Romanesque ceiling paintings; and the Santa María de la Regla cathedral, a French-influenced Gothic masterpiece with 2000 sq m of stained-glass windows.

Information

The **tourist office** (☎ 23 70 82; open daily) is on the cathedral plaza.

Sleeping & Eating

There are two *albergues* in León. The **Albergue del Monasterio de las Bene-dictinas** (☎ 25 28 66; Plaza Santa María del Camino; donation) has 125 beds and receives good feedback. The **municipal albergue** (☎ 08 18 32; Campos Góticos; dm €6) is smaller with just 64 beds and also receives good feedback.

Hostal Bayón (☎ 23 14 46; Calle del Alcázar de Toledo 6; s/d with washbasin €15/28, with shower €25/35) At this long-standing León favourite, the laid-back owner presides over cheerful, brightly painted rooms with pine floors.

Hostal San Martín (☎ 87 51 87; www .sanmartinhostales.com, in Spanish; Plaza de Torres de Omaña 1, 2nd fl; s without bathroom €20, s/d/tr with bathroom €28/40/52) In a splendid, recently overhauled 18th-century building, this engaging little place is an outstanding choice with light, airy and modern rooms (most with balcony).

Restaurante Luisón (Plaza Puerta Obispo 16; *menú del día* €8, meals €15-20) This place could only exist in Spain – basic surrounds, offhand waiters and terrific, hearty food that keeps the locals fortified during cold winters.

El Tizón (Plaza de San Martín 1; *menú del día* €13, meals €25-30) The tapas are good here, but the small sit-down restaurant, with an abundant set lunch, is even better.

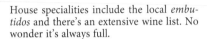

CAMINO DE SANTIAGO

House specialities include the local *embutidos* and there's an extensive wine list. No wonder it's always full.

LOGROÑO
☎ 941 / pop 147,000

The capital of the major wine-producing region of La Rioja, Logroño (384m) has long been a strategic and hotly contested city along the pilgrims' way. Just 18km south of town is Clavijo, the legendary site of Santiago's first appearance as Matamoros.

The facade of the Iglesia de Santiago has an excellent Matamoros image. Today the city is a stately place, with a heart of tree-studded squares, narrow streets and hidden corners, which you cannot help but feel contented in – and it's not just the wine.

Information
The **regional tourist office** (☎ 24 43 84; www.lariojaturismo.com; Paseo del Espolón; open daily) has excellent regional information including hiking and Camino details. The **Oficina de Información Logroño** (☎ 27 33 53; www.logroturismo.org; Calle de Portales 50; open daily) deals only with the city.

Sleeping & Eating
There are two *albergues* in Logroño. The **Albergue de Peregrinos de Logroño** (☎ 239 201; Rua Vieja 32; dm €3) has 90 beds and a kitchen. The **Albergue de Peregrinos Puerta del Revellín** (☎ 629 170447; Plaza Martíez Flamarique 4; dm €10) is smaller with just 40 beds.

Pensión La Bilbaina (☎ 25 42 26; Calle de Capitán Gallarza 10; s €25-30, d €36-40) A cute little place with clean and pleasing rooms.

Hostal La Numantina (☎ 25 14 11; Calle de Sagasta 4; s/d €35/55) This professional operation caters perfectly to the traveller's needs. The rooms are comfortable and homely and there's a communal TV room and ample tourist info.

For mouth-watering *pinchos*, head to Calle Laurel in the historical quarter. **Bar Soriano** (Calle Laurel 4) and **La Taberna de Baco** (Calle de San Agustín 10) are two places worth keeping your eyes peeled for.

PAMPLONA
☎ 948 / pop 196,000

Pamplona (Iruña), the capital of Navarra and location of the raucous San Fermín festivals in early July, is an ideal launching point for the Camino. Its highlights include the cathedral, museum, Calle Estafeta – where the running of the bulls (see p334) takes place – and the bars and cafés around Plaza del Castillo.

Information
The **tourist office** (☎ 42 04 20; www.navarra.es; Calle de Esclava 1; open 10am-2pm & 4-7pm Mon-Sat, 10am-2pm Sun) is extremely well-organised and has plenty of Camino and walking information.

Supplies & Equipment
On the town's outskirts, Decathlon, an excellent sports superstore, is best reached by taxi. In the city centre **elkar megadenda** (☎ 22 41 67; Calle Comedias 14) has a good range of hiking and Camino-related books and maps.

Sleeping & Eating
You'll find **Camping Ezcaba** (☎ 33 03 15; www.campingezcaba.com; Eusa-Oiricain; site per person/tent/car €4.90/5.35/4.90) 7km from Pamplona on the Pamplona-Irún (N121) highway.

There are two pilgrim *albergues* in Pamplona. The 24-bed **Albergue Casa Paderborn** (☎ 660 631656; Playa de Caparoso 6; dm €5) and **Albergue de Jesús y María** (☎ 662 570716; Calle Compañía; dm €5) bang in the centre and with 114 beds.

Habitaciones Mendi (☎ 22 52 97; Calle de las Navas de Tolosa 9; r €40) Full of the spirits of Pamplona past, this charming little guesthouse is a real find.

Hostal Don Lluis (☎ 679 385157; Calle de San Nicolás 24; r €40) Run by the chatty José, this *pensión* has a price that's hard to beat. The rooms are spacious and have character, and rather than a boring old shower you can make bubbles in the small baths.

For *pinchos* head to Calles San Nicolás (especially Bar-Restaurante Baserri, which also has an outstanding *menú* for €14) and the vegetarian **Sarasate** (menú €11-17). There's also a vibrant public market, open mornings, just off Plaza del Ayuntamiento.

Getting There & Away

AIR

Pamplona's **airport** (☎ 16 87 00), about 7km south of the city, has regular flights to Madrid and Barcelona. Bus 21 (€1) travels between the city (from the bus station) and the airport. A taxi costs about €13.

BUS

From the main **bus station** (☎ 22 38 54; Calle Conde Oliveto 8), buses leave for most towns throughout Navarra, although service is restricted on Sunday.

TRAIN

Pamplona's train station is linked to the city centre by Bus 9 from Paseo de Sarasate every 15 minutes. Tickets are also sold at the **Renfe agency** (☎ 902 24 02 02; Calle de Estella 8).

Trains run to/from Madrid (€51.80, three hours, three daily) and San Sebastián (from €14.70, two hours, three daily).

RONCESVALLES
☎ 948

Nestled quietly in the woods, there is an air of accomplishment to Roncesvalles

---

THE RUNNING OF THE BULLS

Liberated, obsessive or plain mad is how you might describe aficionados (and there are many) who regularly take part in Pamplona's Sanfermines (Fiesta de San Fermín), a nonstop cacophony of music, dance, fireworks and processions – and the small matter of running alongside a handful of agitated, horn-tossing *toros* (bulls) – that takes place from 6 to 14 July each year.

El encierro, the running of the bulls from their corrals to the bullring for the afternoon bullfight, takes place in Pamplona every morning during Sanfermines. Six bulls are let loose from the Coralillos de Santo Domingo to charge across the square of the same name (a good vantage point for observers). They continue up the street, veering onto Calle de los Mercaderes from Plaza Consistorial, and then sweep right onto Calle de la Estafeta for the final charge to the ring. Devotees, known as *mozos* (the brave or foolish, depending on your point of view), race madly with the bulls, aiming to keep close – but not too close. The total course is some 825m long and lasts little more than three minutes.

Since records began in 1924, 15 people have been killed during Pamplona's bull run. Many of those who run are full of bravado (and/or drink), and have little idea of what they're doing. Keeping ahead of the herd is the general rule. The greatest danger is getting trapped near a bull that has been separated from the herd – a lone, frightened, 500kg bull surrounded by charging humans can be lethal. Needless to say this is not an activity to be recommended.

Participants enter the course before 7.30am from Plaza de Santo Domingo. At 8am two rockets are fired: the first announces that the bulls have been released from the corrals; the second lets participants know they're all out and running. The first danger point is where Calle de los Mercaderes leads into Calle de la Estafeta. Here many of the bulls skid into the barriers because of their headlong speed on the turn. They can become isolated from the herd and are then always dangerous. A very treacherous stretch comes towards the end, where Calle de la Estafeta slopes down into the final turn to Plaza de Toros.

A third rocket goes off when all the bulls have made it to the ring, and a final one when they have been rounded up in the stalls.

Sanfermines winds up at midnight on 14 July with a candlelit procession, known as the Pobre de Mí (Poor Me), which starts from Plaza Consistorial. Another event, often no less pretty, is the Running of the Nudes, where members of People for the Ethical Treatment of Animals race naked along the same route as the bulls in protest against the event.

Concern has grown about the high numbers of people taking part in recent *encierros*. The 2004 fiesta was considered to be one of the most dangerous in recent years, with dozens of injuries, but no deaths. For the 2005 fiesta the authorities used a special antislip paint on the streets to cut down on bull skid, but there seemed to be just as many falls and there were several injuries, including four gorings. The 2008 event was also quite a bloody one with 45 serious injuries (four of them due to gorings) and in 2009 a young man from Madrid was gored and killed and several others injured. For dedicated *encierro* news check out www.sanfermin.com.

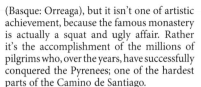

(Basque: Orreaga), but it isn't one of artistic achievement, because the famous monastery is actually a squat and ugly affair. Rather it's the accomplishment of the millions of pilgrims who, over the years, have successfully conquered the Pyrenees; one of the hardest parts of the Camino de Santiago.

Despite its ugliness the main event is the **monastery complex** (admission to cloister, chapter house & museum €2.30, guided tours adult/child €4.50/2.30; 10am-1.30pm & 3.30-7pm). It's open shorter hours from October to March. The 13th-century **Gothic Real Colegiata de Santa María** (10am-8.30pm) contains a much-revered, silver-covered statue of the Virgin beneath a modernist-looking canopy worthy of Frank Gehry. Also of interest is the cloister, which contains the tomb of King Sancho VII (El Fuerte) of Navarra, the apparently 2.25m-tall victor in the Battle of Las Navas de Tolosa, fought against the Muslims in 1212. Nearby is the 12th-century **Capilla de Sancti Spiritus**.

Information

People beginning in Roncesvalles often arrive a day ahead and get the Credencial at the Oficina del Peregrino below the arch at the entrance to the monastery. A few steps away, in an old mill house, is the **tourist office** (☎ 76 03 01; 10am-2pm & 4-7pm Mon-Sat, 10am-2pm Sun).

Sleeping & Eating

The **albergue** (€6) is a huge affair with around 100 beds. It's attached to the monastery complex.

If the *albergue* isn't for you then you have two other options. **Hostal Casa Sabina** (☎ 76 00 12; tw €50), which isn't great value and it's twin beds only – possibly to stop any hanky-panky so close to a monastery? **La Posada** (☎ 76 02 25; www.laposadaderoncesvalles.com; s/d €43/54) is a much more appealing option. The simple rooms have some gentle country charm and the staff is equally gentle.

Getting There & Away

A bus departs Roncesvalles at 9.20am every morning except Sunday for Pamplona (€5.40, 1 hour 40 minutes) via Burguete, and returns in the late afternoon.

Walkers Directory

CONTENTS

ACCOMMODATION

There's generally no need to book ahead for a room in the low or shoulder seasons. But when things get busier it's advisable (and in high periods it can be essential) to make a reservation if you want to avoid a wearisome search for a room. This is particularly true with mountain *refugios* (mountain huts) on busy routes in the summer. The last thing most people want to do at the end of a long day's hiking is to find no room at the inn and be forced to hike another three hours to the next *refugio*! At most places, a phone call earlier in the day is all that's needed.

Prices throughout this guidebook are high-season maximums. You may be pleasantly surprised if you travel at other times. What constitutes low or high season depends on where and when. Most of the year is high season in Barcelona, especially during trade fairs. August can be dead in the cities. Winter is high season around the ski resorts in the Pyrenees and low season in the Balearic Islands (indeed, the islands seem to shut down between November and Easter). July and August in the Balearics offer sun and fun, but finding a place to stay without booking ahead can be a pain. Weekends are high season for boutique hotels and *casas rurales* (country home, village or farmstead accommodation; see p338), but bad for business hotels in Madrid and Barcelona (which often offer generous specials then).

We divide accommodation categories into budget, midrange and top end. As prices vary greatly from one part of the country to another, the dividing line is somewhat arbitrary. In places such as Barcelona and Madrid, and other popular tourist locations, a budget place can mean anything up to €40/60 for an *individual/ doble* (single/double). At the higher end of this range you can generally expect to find good, comfortable rooms with private bathrooms. Shave a few euros off and you may find the place only has shared bathrooms in the corridor. In less-travelled regions, such as Extremadura, Murcia and Castilla-La Mancha, it can be relatively easy to find perfectly acceptable single/double rooms (usually with shared bathroom) for around €30/45. If you want to go for rock bottom then youth hostels, where a bed can cost anything up to €27 but more often around €12 to €21, are probably the best bet.

Midrange places in the big cities can cost up to about €200 for a fine double, and there are plenty of good and, on occasion, outright charming options for less. Anything above that price takes you into luxury level. Again, though, much depends on the location and period. Cities like Madrid and Barcelona, with busy trade fair calendars, can become more expensive still during such fairs. In many other parts of Spain you'd be hard-pressed to pay more than €150 for the best double in town.

A *habitación doble* (double room) is frequently just that: a room with two beds (which you can often shove together). If you want to be sure of a double bed (*cama matrimonial*), ask for it!

One website with online hotel booking facilities is **Hotelkey** (☎ 902 30 35 55; www.hotelkey.com). The national tourist office website (www.spain.info) is another option.

On the Trail
Day walks and some stages of longer walks begin and end within a bus ride of a population centre, where you'll normally find accommodation and sometimes a camping ground (see p338). Two other options on many longer walks are camping wild or staying in *refugios*.

CAMPING
A lightweight tent confers liberty and independence. If you have one, you can still opt for something cosier, should the mood take you. If you're without one, you're obliged to head for the nearest *refugio* or village – where you may arrive to find all options full. Those three or four extra kilos will more than justify themselves every time you pitch your tent.

However, you can't expect untrammelled freedom. *Parques nacionales* (national parks), many *parques naturales* (nature parks) and other protected areas prohibit or limit camping within their boundaries. There's also a regulation that says you're not allowed to camp wild within 1km of a camping ground.

Apart from such general restrictions, and others of more localised ambit, the opportunity for wild camping in Spain's open spaces is almost limitless. Within each walk, we indicate particularly attractive or convenient sites – but there are many more waiting to be discovered.

REFUGIOS
The larger *refugios* (mountain huts or refuges) are staffed and usually open from mid-June until mid-September though a minority of more accessible ones stay open year-round. During July and August in popular regions such as the Pyrenees, it's highly advisable to reserve in advance (you'll find contact details within the relevant walk descriptions). *Refugios* in the Sierra de Gredos and the Sierra de Guadarrama, both easy bus rides from Madrid, are usually packed solid every weekend.

Prices per person range from nothing to €12.50 a night and around €10 for dinner. There's rarely equipment for doing your own cooking though many bigger *refugios* set aside an area for this. Sleeping is normally in *literas*, long benches, sometimes double-decker, with mattresses running the length of the dormitory. Blankets are usually provided but not sheets.

Refugios are OK for a night or two. Many are fine, like a high-altitude youth hostel; others, where you're in a dormitory among

PRACTICALITIES

- Use the metric system for weights and measures.

- Bring an international adaptor because plugs have two round pins; the electric current is 220V, 50Hz.

- If your Spanish is up to it, try the following newspapers: *El País* (or the free, constantly updated, downloadable version, *24 Horas*, on www.elpais.es), the country's leading daily and left-of-centre oriented; *ABC*, for a right-wing view of life; Barcelona-based *La Vanguardia*, which on Friday has a great listings magazine for that city; and *Marca*, an all-sports (especially football) paper.

- Tune into Radio Nacional de España's (RNE)Radio 1 general interest and current affairs programmes; Radio 5 for sport and entertainment; and Radio 3 ('Radio d'Espop') for an admirable variety of pop and rock music. The most popular commercial pop and rock stations are 40 Principales, Cadena 100 and Onda Cero.

- Switch on the box to watch Spain's state-run Televisión Española (TVE1 and La 2) or the independent commercial stations (Antena 3, Tele 5, Cuatro, La Sexta and Canal Plus). Regional governments run local stations, such as Madrid's Telemadrid, Catalonia's TV-3 and Canal 33 (both in Catalan), Galicia's TVG, the Basque Country's ETB-1 and ETB-2, Valencia's Canal 9 and Andalucía's Canal Sur. Cable and satellite TV is becoming more widespread.

35 or more snoring people, are less fun. Their strong point is that the guardians are almost invariably friendly and well informed about walks in the area.

In some regions, there are unstaffed *refugios*, the best of which can be surprisingly cosy. However, at the end of the day, they're only as clean as the last group that passed through. Most unstaffed *refugios* remain open year-round and many others will allow access to one wing outside summer.

In Town
APARTMENTS, VILLAS & CASAS RURALES
Throughout Spain you can rent self-catering apartments and houses for varying amounts of time. Villas and houses are widely available on the main holiday coasts and in popular country areas.

A simple one-bedroom apartment in a coastal resort for two or three people might cost as little as €30 per night, although more often you'll be looking at nearly twice that much, and prices can jump even further in high season. More luxurious options with a swimming pool might come in at anything between €200 and €400 for four people.

Rural tourism has become immensely popular, with accommodation available in many new and often charming *casas rurales*. These are usually comfortably renovated village houses or farmhouses with a handful of rooms. They often go by other names, such as *cases de pagès* in Catalonia, *casas de aldea* in Asturias, *posadas* and *casonas* in Cantabria and so on. Some just provide rooms, while others offer meals or self-catering accommodation. Lower-end prices typically hover around €30/50 (single/double) per night, but classy boutique establishments can easily charge €100 or more for a double. Many are rented out by the week.

CAMPING & CARAVAN PARKS
Many hikers take advantage of Spain's numerous campsites (there are around 1000 officially graded *campings*). Some are well located in woodland or near beaches or rivers, but others are on the outskirts of towns or along highways.

Camping grounds usually charge per person, per tent and per vehicle – typically €4 to €8.50 for each. Children usually pay a bit less than adults. Many camping grounds close from around October to Easter.

HOSTELS
Spain's 250 or so youth hostels – *albergues juveniles,* not be confused with *hostales* (budget hotels) – are often the cheapest places for lone travellers, but two people can usually get a double room elsewhere for a similar price. Some hostels are only moderate value, lacking in privacy, often heavily booked by school groups, and with night-time curfews and no cooking facilities (although if there is nowhere to cook there is usually a cafeteria). Others, however, are conveniently located, open 24 hours and composed mainly of double rooms or small dorms, often with a private bathroom.

Prices at youth hostels often depend on the season, and vary between about €12 and €21 for under-26s and between €16 and €27 for those 26 and over. In some hostels the price includes breakfast.

You will sometimes find independent *albergues* offering basic dormitory accommodation for around €10 to €18, usually in villages in areas that attract plenty of Spanish walkers and climbers. These are not specifically youth hostels – although the clientele tends to be under 35. They're a kind of halfway house between a youth hostel and a *refugio.*

HOTELES, HOSTALES & PENSIONES
Officially, places to stay are classified into *hoteles* (hotels; one to five stars), *hostales* (one to three stars) and *pensiones* (basically small private hotels, often family businesses in rambling apartments; one or two stars).

In practice, places listing accommodation use all sorts of overlapping names to describe themselves, especially at the budget end of the market. In broad terms, the cheapest are usually places just advertising *camas* (beds). Most such places will be bare and basic; bathrooms are likely to be shared. Singles/doubles in these places generally cost from around €15/25 to €25/40.

A *pensión* is usually a small step up from the above types in standard and price. Some cheap establishments forget to provide soap, toilet paper or towels. *Hostales* are in much the same category. In both cases the better ones can be bright and spotless, with rooms boasting full en-suite bathroom. Prices can range up to €40/60 for singles/doubles in more popular/expensive locations.

The remainder of establishments call themselves *hoteles* and run the gamut of quality, from straightforward roadside places, bland but clean, through charming boutique premises and on to super luxury hotels.

BUSINESS HOURS

Generally, Spaniards work Monday to Friday from about 9am to 2pm and then again from 4pm or 5pm for another three hours. Shops are usually open similar hours on Saturday as well. The further south you go, the longer the afternoon break tends to be, with shops and the like staying closed until 6pm or so.

Big supermarkets and department stores are open from about 10am to 10pm Monday to Saturday. Shops in tourist resorts sometimes open on Sunday too.

Many government offices don't bother opening in the afternoon, any day of the year. In summer, offices tend to go on to *horario intensivo,* which means they can start as early as 7am and finish up for the day by 2pm.

Museums all have their own opening hours: major ones tend to open for something like normal Spanish business hours (with or without the afternoon break), but often have their weekly closing day on Monday.

As a general rule, restaurants open their kitchens for lunch from 1pm to 4pm and for dinner from 8pm to midnight. The further south you go, the later locals tend to go out to eat. While restaurants in Barcelona may already be busy by 9.30pm, their Madrid counterparts are still half-empty at this time. At lunch and dinner you can generally linger quite a while after the kitchen closes. Some, but by no means all, places close one or two days a week. Some also shut for a few weeks' annual holiday – the most common period for this is during August.

Bars have a wider range of hours. Those that serve as cafés and snack bars can open from about 8am to the early evening. Those that are more night-life bars may open in the early evening and close around 2am to 3am. Some places combine the two roles –

as the bars close the clubs open (generally from around midnight or 1am to around 5am or 6am).

CHILDREN

Walking with children in Spain is no more difficult than elsewhere in Europe. In some respects, it's easier. The Spanish in general are fond of children. There are no puritanical laws banishing them from places where alcohol is served and, since most cafés are open from breakfast until way after their bedtime, you can always pick up a soft drink or snack. Bear in mind, however, the late hour at which restaurants serve lunch and dinner, and ensure that you always have a cache of emergency provisions in your backpack.

Baby food, nappies (diapers), creams and potions and all the other paraphernalia of travelling with the very young are readily available in Spanish towns, though you may not find your favourite brand. If you're planning to walk in less populated areas, stock up in advance.

Before undertaking a route of several days, it might be wise to first establish a base camp and do a number of day or half-day walks to break your troops in.

Think also of combining walking with other activities such as beach fun. You could, for example, stay at Port de Sóller on Mallorca or on the Costa Blanca in Valencia.

Car-hire rates in Spain are much cheaper than in many parts of Europe and worth considering in preference to waiting with children for infrequent or nonexistent bus services.

There's a simple rule of thumb for calculating what kids can carry on a walk: most can comfortably walk their age and carry half of it. A 12-year-old, for example, should be able to walk about 12km per day in moderate terrain, carrying a backpack weighing around 6kg.

Lonely Planet's *Travel with Children* has lots of practical advice on the subject, along with first-hand travel stories from a host of Lonely Planet authors and others.

Walks suitable for families with children include the Sóller to Deià (see p244) and Barranc de Biniaraix & Embassament de Cúber (see p246) walks on Mallorca. Other possibilities are the Benamahoma to Zahara de la Sierra walk (see p291) in Andalucía's Sierra de Grazalema and a section of the Lake Walk (see p174) in the Cordillera Cantábrica. Throughout the text we have also mentioned where a walk can be easily shortened to make it family friendly.

The Pyrenees aren't particularly suitable for younger children. This said, Canillo in Andorra makes a great base for a few straightforward half-day walks such as the Basses de les Salamandres walk (see p105). Side trips listed at the end of a walk description and the More Walks section, which feature at the end of most chapters, can also be a source of ideas for family hikes.

CLIMATE

The *meseta* (high tableland of central Spain) and Ebro basin have a continental climate: scorching in summer, cold in winter, and dry. Madrid regularly freezes in December, January and February, and temperatures climb above 30°C in July and August. Valladolid on the northern *meseta* and Zaragoza in the Ebro basin are even drier, with only around 300mm of rain a year (little more than Alice Springs in Australia). The Guadalquivir basin in Andalucía is only a little wetter, and positively broils in high summer, with temperatures of 35+°C in Seville that kill people every year.

The Pyrenees and the Cordillera Cantábrica, backing the Bay of Biscay, bear the brunt of cold northern and northwestern airstreams, which bring moderate temperatures and heavy rainfall (three or four times as much as Madrid's) to the north coast. Even in high summer you never know when you might get a shower.

The Mediterranean coast and Balearic Islands get a little more rain than Madrid, and the south can be even hotter in summer. The Mediterranean, particularly around Alicante, also provides Spain's warmest waters (reaching 27°C or so in August). Barcelona's weather is typical of the coast – milder than in inland cities but more humid.

In general you can usually rely on pleasant or hot temperatures just about everywhere from April to early November. In Andalucía there are plenty of warm, sunny days right through winter. In July and August temperatures can get unpleasantly hot inland.

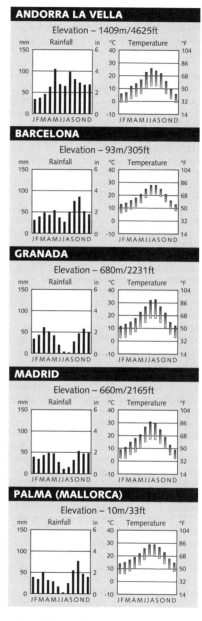

Snowfalls in the mountains have been known to start as early as October in some years and some snow cover can last all year on the highest peaks.

For more tips on the best times to travel, see p23.

Weather Information
Daily at around 9.30pm, both **TVE1** and **Antenna 3** (a private channel), show the weather forecast for the next 24 hours and beyond. Local papers usually have the weather prognosis in both visual and textual form.

Two excellent websites for all Spanish regions, including detailed forecasts for most mountain areas, is that of the **Instituto Nacional de Meteorología** (www.aemet.es) and **Canal Meteo** (www.canalmeteo.com; in Spanish).

If you speak Spanish well, you can also call Teletiempo (€0.41 per minute), the phone information service of the **Instituto Nacional de Meteorología**. The system is touch-tone interactive and speakers tend to gabble. To access it, dial ☎ 807 17 03 65. For mountain areas, dial ☎ 807 17 03 80 for the Pyrenees, substituting the final 80 for 81 for Picos de Europa, 82 for Sierra de Guadarrama, 83 for Sistema Iberico, 84 for Sierra Nevada and 85 for Sierra de Gredos.

CUSTOMS
Duty-free allowances for travellers entering Spain from outside the EU include 2L of wine (or 1L of wine and 1L of spirits), and 200 cigarettes or 50 cigars or 250g of tobacco.

There are no duty-free allowances for travel between EU countries but equally no restrictions on the import of duty-paid items into Spain from other EU countries for personal use. You *can* buy VAT-free articles at airport shops when travelling between EU countries.

DANGERS & ANNOYANCES
Spain is generally a pretty safe country. The main thing to be wary of is petty theft (which may of course not seem so petty if your passport, cash, credit card and camera go missing). Most visitors to Spain never feel remotely threatened, but, even on the remotest mountain trails, there's always the occasional experience.

DISCOUNT CARDS
If taking a break from the trail to indulge in some sightseeing never hesitate to ask if there are discounts for students, young people, children, families or seniors.

Senior Cards
There are reduced prices for people over 60, 63 or 65 (depending on the place) at various museums and attractions (sometimes restricted to EU citizens only) and occasionally on transport.

Student & Youth Cards
At some sites discounts (usually half the normal fee) are available to students and people under 18. An **ISIC** (International Student Identity Card; www.isic.org) may come in handy (there is also a teachers' version, **ITIC**) for travel discounts, but is not accepted at many tourist sites.

Student cards are issued by hostelling organisations, student unions and some youth travel agencies worldwide.

For nonstudent travellers under 25 there is also the **International Youth Travel Card** (IYTC; www.istc.org), which offers similar benefits.

You'll have more luck with a Euro<26 (www.euro26.org) card (known as Carnet Joven in Spain), which is useful for those under 26. For instance, Euro<26 cardholders enjoy 20% or 25% off most 2nd-class train fares, 10% or 20% off many ferries and some bus fares, good discounts at some museums, and discounts of up to 20% at some youth hostels.

EMBASSIES & CONSULATES
Spanish Embassies & Consulates
To find the details of any Spanish embassy or consulate, check out the **Ministry of Foreign Affairs** website (www.maec.es), click on Servicios Consulares and then choose the country you want. Among those with representation are:

Andorra (☎ 800 030; Carrer Prat de la Creu 34, Andorra la Vella)
Australia Canberra (☎ 02 6273 3555; emb .canberra@maec.es; 15 Arkana St, Yarralumla ACT 2600); Melbourne (☎ 03 9347 1966; 146 Elgin St, Carlton, Vic 3053); Sydney (☎ 02 9261 2433; Level 24, St Martin's Tower, 31 Market St, NSW 2000)
Canada Ottawa (☎ 613 747 2252; emb .ottawa@maec.es; 74 Stanley Ave, Ontario K1M 1P4); Montreal (☎ 514 935 5235; Ste

1456, 1 Westmount Sq, Québec H3Z 2P9); Toronto (☎ 416 977 1661; 2 Bloor St East, Ste 1201, Ontario M4W 1A8)

France (☎ 01 44 43 18 00; emb.paris @maec.es; 22 Ave Marceau, 75008 Paris)

Germany Berlin (☎ 030 254 00 70; www .info-spanischebotschaft.de; Lichtenstein- allee 1, 10787); Düsseldorf (☎ 0211 43 90 80; Hombergerstr 16, 40474); Frankfurt am Main (☎ 069 959 16 60; Niebelungenplatz 3, 60318); Munich (☎ 089 998 47 90; Ober- föhringerstr 45, 81925)

Ireland (☎ 01 269 1640; emb.dublin.info @mace.es; 17A Merlyn Park, Ballsbridge, Dublin 4)

Japan (☎ 03 3583 8531; emb.tokio@maec .es; 1-3-29 Roppongi Minato-ku, Tokyo 106-0032)

Morocco Rabat (☎ 07 63 39 00; emb.rabat @mae.es; rue Ain Khalouiya, Route des Zaërs, Km5.3, Souissi); Casablanca (☎ 02 22 07 52; 31 rue d'Alger); Tangier (☎ 09 93 70 00; 85 Ave Président Habib Bourghiba)

Netherlands (☎ 070 302 49 99; www .claboral.nl; Lange Voorhout 50, The Hague 2514 EG)

New Zealand (☎ 913 11 67; emb .wellington@mace.es; 56 Victoria St, Wellington 6142)

Portugal (☎ 01 347 2381; emb.lisboa @mae.es; Rua do Salitre 1, Lisbon 1269-052)

UK London (☎ 020 7235 5555; http://spain .embassyhomepage.com; 39 Chesham Pl, SW1X 8SB); Edinburgh (☎ 0131 220 1843; 63 North Castle St, EH2 3LJ); London consulate (☎ 020 7589 8989; 20 Draycott Pl, SW3 2RZ); Manchester (☎ 0161 236 1262; 1a Brook House, 70 Spring Gardens, M2 2BQ)

USA Washington DC (☎ 202 728 2340; embespus@mail.mae.es; 2375 Pennsyl- vania Ave NW, 20037); Boston (☎ 617 536 2506); Chicago (☎ 312 782 4588); Houston (☎ 713 783 6200); Los Angeles (☎ 213 938 0158); Miami (☎ 305 446 5511); New York (☎ 212 355 4080); San Francisco (☎ 415 922 2995)

Embassies & Consulates in Spain

The embassies are in Madrid. Some coun- tries also maintain consulates in major cities, particularly in Barcelona. Embassies and consulates include:

Australia Madrid (☎ 91 353 66 00; www .spain.embassy.gov.au; Plaza del Descu- bridor Diego de Ordás 3); Barcelona (☎ 93 490 90 13; Plaça de Galla Placidia 1)

Canada Madrid (☎ 91 423 32 50; www .canadainternational.gc.ca; Calle de Núñez de Balboa 35); Barcelona (☎ 93 204 27 00; Carrer d'Elisenda de Pinós 10; FGC Reina Elisenda)

France Madrid (☎ 91 423 89 00; www .ambafrance-es.org; Calle de Salustiano Olózaga 9); Barcelona (☎ 93 270 30 00; Ronda de l'Universitat 22B)

Germany Madrid (☎ 91 557 90 00; www .madrid.diplo.de; Calle de Fortuny 8); Barcelona (☎ 93 292 10 00; Passeig de Gràcia 111)

Ireland Madrid (☎ 91 436 40 93; Paseo de la Castellana 46); Barcelona (☎ 93 491 50 21; Gran Via de Carles III 94)

Japan (91 590 76 00; www.es.emb-japan .go.jp; Calle de Serrano 109, Madrid)

Morocco (91 563 10 90; www.embajada -marruecos.es; Calle de Serrano 179, Madrid)

Netherlands Madrid (☎ 91 353 75 00; www.embajadapaisesbajos.es; Avenida del Comandante Franco 32); Barcelona (☎ 93 363 54 20; Avinguda Diagonal 601); Palma de Mallorca (☎ 971 71 64 93; Calle de San Miquel 36)

New Zealand Madrid (☎ 91 523 02 26; www.nzembassy.com; Calle del Pinar 7); Barcelona (☎ 93 209 03 99; Travessera de Gràcia 64)

Portugal (91 782 49 60; www.embaja daportugal-madrid.org; Calle del Pinar 1, Madrid)

UK Madrid (☎ 91 700 82 00; www.ukin spain.com; Calle de Fernando el Santo 16); Consulate (☎ 91 524 97 00; Paseo de Recoletos 7/9); Barcelona (☎ 93 366 62 00; Avinguda Diagonal 477); Palma de Mallorca (☎ 971 71 24 45; Carrer del Convent dels Caputxins 4, Edifici B)

US Madrid (☎ 91 587 22 00; www.embusa .es; Calle de Serrano 75); Barcelona (☎ 93 280 22 27; Passeig de la Reina Elisenda de Montcada 23-25; FGC Reina Elisenda) Consular Agencies in A Coruña, Fuengirola, Palma de Mallorca, Sevilla and Valencia.

FOOD & DRINK

The food and drink in Spain can be so good that for many hikers the culinary highs can be as sublime as the mountain ones. Throughout Spain you'll find plenty of restaurants serving excellent regional food at very affordable prices. There are also a minority of fairly dire dumps, particularly in tourist haunts. A *mesón* is a simple eatery with home-style cooking, commonly attached to a bar. A *venta* was probably once an inn, and is usually off the beaten track, while a *marisquería* is a seafood restaurant.

Even the tiniest village will usually have a café or bar. Bars come in various guises, including *bodegas* (old-style wine bars), *cervecerías* (beer bars), *tascas* (bars that specialise in tapas, or bar snacks), *tabernas* (taverns) and even pubs. Many serve tapas and often have more substantial fare too.

Typical Spanish bar and restaurant food focuses largely upon typically Mediterranean ingredients such as olive oil (Spain produces one-third of the world's olive oil), garlic, onions, tomatoes and peppers (capsicum).

For variety, you can munch your way through a selection of *tapas* (bar snacks) or *raciones* (larger portions of the same), though this can work out to be expensive. The price, range and quality of à-la-carte items varies enormously from place to place. However, at lunch time especially, there's almost always a *menú del día* (menu of the day) or *menú de la casa* (house menu) available. Often simply called a *menú*, it has a set price and offers a choice of items. It typically consists of a starter, main course, a *postre* (dessert) and bread. A *bebida* (beverage), usually a choice of wine, beer or water, may also be included.

Just about every region in Spain has its specialities; the Basque Country and Catalonia have particularly rich local cuisines. Originating in Valencia, *paella* is a delicious saffron-coloured rice dish, simmered in richly flavoured stock that crops up on menus throughout Spain. There are two versions: one with chicken, rabbit, green beans, butter beans and sometimes a snail or two; and *paella de mariscos*, a fancier version scattered with seafood.

Fabada asturiana is an Asturian speciality, a rich stew guaranteed to dispel the chill of winter. It combines white beans, black pudding (blood sausage), hunks of chorizo (a spicy red sausage), cubes of pork fat and stewing beef, diced smoked ham and, optionally, a pig's ear – this heart-warming dish has been known to bring tears to the eyes of a hungry walker.

For the vocabulary to help you navigate a restaurant menu or a trip to the greengrocers, consult Lonely Planet's *Spain*, or its *Spanish Phrasebook*, which gives an even more comprehensive listing.

When to Eat

Spaniards normally eat late and this is reflected in restaurant hours. Lunch will typically be served from around 2pm and people won't look askance if you arrive as late as 4.30pm expecting to be served. Dinner is rarely offered before 9pm, so if you're ravenous after a long day of walking, make sure you have some snacks in your backpack to tide you over. However, outside normal opening hours many burger joints and places offer *platos combinados*, a largish serving of meat, seafood or omelette with trimmings.

The *refugios* that are staffed usually have different eating hours, serving dinner earlier, often in two sittings if it's a large place and is full to capacity.

On the Walk
REFUGIOS

Most staffed *refugios* serve breakfast and dinner. Some of the larger ones stay open all day and sell drinks, snacks and occasionally lunch. It's advisable to reserve dinner

---

WATER

Water is by far the best thirst-quencher when you're walking. It's also the most readily available way to rehydrate. Village *fuentes* (fountains or springs) are often reliable. Walk on if one is signed '*agua no potable*' (nondrinking water) but don't be too suspicious if it simply says '*agua no tratada*' (untreated water). In some mountain regions, above the cultivation line and away from areas where livestock graze, it's safe to drink straight from flowing streams. Take advice from locals and *refugio* wardens and carry water-purifying tablets. For information on how to treat water that seems suspect, see Water (p371).

at the same time as your bunk, though they'll never turn a hungry traveller away. You don't have to be staying at a *refugio* to order food so it's quite possible to enjoy an evening meal and then head away to camp somewhere more tranquil.

BUYING FOOD

There's usually at least one shop at the beginning and the end of each walk we describe. For walks longer than one day we indicate places en route where you can pick up supplies.

For wild camping, most of the major equipment shops sell dehydrated foods. You shouldn't have trouble picking up some form of high-energy food in even the smallest one-shop village.

Drinks

NON-ALCOHOLIC DRINKS

Agua mineral (bottled spring water) is widely available. You can buy it *sin gas* (still) and *con gas* (sparkling). Soft drinks, called *refrescos*, are also sold everywhere. Freshly squeezed fruit juices (*zumos*) are delicious and altogether healthier. If fresh fruit is out of season, you can buy juices cheaply in waxed cartons.

It's difficult to get a really bad coffee in Spain, where all but the humblest bar will have an espresso machine hissing away. You can order *café* (coffee) several ways: *solo*, small, black and pungently strong; *cortado*, a *solo* cut with a splash of milk; *café con leche*, coffee with milk; or *descafeinado* (decaffeinated). There's also *café americano*, black and weaker; ask for one in the villages and all you'll get in return is a quizzical stare. If you request tea, you'll probably be served a cup of hot water with a tea bag dangling in it.

ALCOHOLIC DRINKS

Just to take a look at the array of bottles behind even the most modest bar is enough to make your liver protest. Most drinkers in a bar will be sipping *vino* (wine), either *tinto* (red), *rosado* (rosé) or *blanco* (white). In Andalucía, and in fancier joints elsewhere, sherry – usually asked for as *un fino* – or its local equivalent is popular. In restaurants, the *vino de la casa* (house wine) is normally very palatable but you'll occasionally inhale some toxic paint stripper.

TRAVEL INSURANCE

Buy a policy that generously covers you for medical expenses, theft or loss of luggage and tickets, and for cancellation of and delays in your travel arrangements. It may be worth taking out cover for mountaineering activities and the cost of rescue. Check your policy doesn't exclude walking/hiking/trekking as a dangerous activity.

Buy travel insurance as early as possible to ensure you'll be compensated for any unforseen accidents or delays. If items are lost or stolen get a police report immediately – otherwise your insurer might not pay up.

For draught beer, ask for *cerveza de barril* or *cerveza de presión*.

HOLIDAYS

The two main periods when Spaniards go on holiday are Semana Santa (the week leading up to Easter Sunday) and August. At these times accommodation in resorts can be scarce and transport heavily booked, but other places are often half-empty.

There are at least 14 official holidays a year – some observed nationwide, some locally. When a holiday falls close to a weekend, Spaniards like to make a *puente* (bridge), meaning they take the intervening day off too. Occasionally when some holidays fall close, they make an *acueducto* (aqueduct)! National holidays are:

Año Nuevo (New Year's Day) 1 January
Viernes Santo (Good Friday) March/April
Fiesta del Trabajo (Labour Day) 1 May
La Asunción (Feast of the Assumption) 15 August
Fiesta Nacional de España (National Day) 12 October
La Inmaculada Concepción (Feast of the Immaculate Conception) 8 December
Navidad (Christmas) 25 December

Regional governments set five holidays and local councils two more. Common dates for widely observed holidays include:

Epifanía (Epiphany) or **Día de los Reyes Magos** (Three Kings' Day) 6 January

Día de San José (St Joseph's Day) 19 March
Jueves Santo (Good Thursday) March/ April. This is not observed in Catalonia and Valencia.
Corpus Christi June. This is the Thursday after the eighth Sunday after Easter Sunday.
Día de San Juan Bautista (Feast of St John the Baptist) 24 June
Día de Santiago Apóstol (Feast of St James the Apostle) 25 July
Día de Todos los Santos (All Saints Day) 1 November
Día de la Constitución (Constitution Day) 6 December

INTERNET ACCESS

Travelling with a laptop is a great way to stay in touch with life back home. Make sure you have a universal AC adaptor and a two-pin plug adaptor for Europe. Spanish telephone sockets are the US RJ-11 type. Most hotels and an increasing number of bars and cafés have wi-fi hotspots so you'll rarely struggle to get online. However, in some cases (such as in airports and some hotels) you must pay a fee to access the internet this way.

Mobile phones with internet access built into them work everywhere in Spain; you can often get a reception even in the remotest mountain areas, but remember, if you're using a foreign phone, downloading that junk email is going to cost you big-time!

If you intend to rely on internet cafés (commonly referred to as *cibers*), you'll need three pieces of information: your incoming (POP or IMAP) mail-server name, your account name and your password. Most travellers make constant use of internet cafés and free web-based email such as Yahoo (www.yahoo.com), Hotmail (www.hotmail.com) or Google's Gmail (www.gmail.com). You typically have to pay about €1.50 to €3 per hour to go online in most internet cafés.

Check out the websites on p26 before arriving in Spain.

MAPS

Make sure you get a hold of the latest versions of country maps, as a series of highway code changes in 2004 caused considerable confusion for a while.

City Maps

For finding your way around cities, the free maps handed out by tourist offices are often adequate, although more-detailed maps are sold widely in bookshops. The best Spanish series of maps are produced by Telstar, Alpina and Everest.

Small-scale Maps

Some of the best maps for travellers are by Michelin, which produces the 1:1,000,000 *Spain Portugal* map and six 1:400,000 regional maps covering the whole country. These are all pretty accurate, even down to the state of minor country roads, and are frequently updated; they are detailed yet easy to read. They're widely available in Spain. Also good are the GeoCentre maps published by Germany's RV Verlag.

Probably the best physical map of Spain is *Península Ibérica, Baleares y Canarias* published by the Centro Nacional de Información Geográfica (CNIG, www.cnig.es), the publishing arm of the Instituto Geográfico Nacional (IGN, www.ign.es). Ask for it in good bookshops.

Walking Maps

Two public sector bodies, the Instituto Geográfico Nacional (IGN) and the Servicio Geográfico del Ejército (SGE) of the Spanish army, produce maps at walker-friendly scales. Between them, they cover the whole country at 1:50,000 (with contours 20m apart) and 1:25,000 (with contours 10m apart). IGN produces new and updated maps at 1:25,000 while both bodies maintain their 1:50,000 series. IGN maps cost €3, and SGE sheets, €2.50.

Both series are produced strictly according to a grid, so depending how

---

PLACE NAMES

Where a regional language is spoken, we reflect predominant local usage; for example, in the Catalan Pyrenees we call a village, mountain or pass by its Catalan name, while in Galicia we use the Galician form. It's no big deal since the majority of names aren't significantly different from their equivalent in Spanish; for example, Mulleres for Molières, Urdiceta for Ordiceta and Astós for Estós.

WALKERS DIRECTORY

MAPS IN THIS BOOK

The maps in this book are based on the best available references, sometimes combined with GPS data collected in the field. They are intended to show the general routes of the walks we describe. They are primarily to help locate the route within the surrounding area. They are not detailed enough in themselves for route-finding or navigation. You will still need a properly surveyed map at an adequate scale – specific maps are recommended in the Planning section for each walk. Most chapters also have a regional map showing the gateway towns or cities, principal transport routes and other major features. Map symbols are interpreted in the legend on the inside front cover of this book.

On the maps in this book, natural features such as river confluences and mountain peaks are in their true position, but sometimes the location of villages and routes is not always so. This may be because a village is spread over a hillside, or the size of the map does not allow for detail of the path's twists and turns. However, by using several basic route-finding techniques (see p319), you will have few problems following our descriptions.

the grid boundaries fall your coastal map could be 75% sea, and a popular day walk might require two or more sheets. When buying maps, check carefully when a map was *actualizada* (updated) rather than when it was printed; the difference can be considerable.

Editorial Alpina (www.editorialalpina .com) produces more than 70 topographical maps in the *Guía Cartográfica* and *Guía Excursionista y Turística* series. The series combines information booklets in Spanish (and sometimes Catalan) with detailed maps at scales ranging from 1:25,000 (1cm to 250m) to 1:50,000 (1cm to 500m). They cover the Pyrenees and Catalonia fairly comprehensively and also cover parts of the Picos de Europa, Sierra de Cazorla and Sierra de Gredos. Most are at 1:25,000 with contours at 20m intervals. With their five to seven shades of colour, elevation shading stands out clearly. Newer editions, with green covers, are generally more accurate than their red-covered predecessors. Even so, while contours are accurate, some maps have the occasional blinding, disorienting error. The Institut Cartogràfic de Catalunya puts out some decent maps for hiking in the Catalan Pyrenees that are often better than their Editorial Alpina counterparts.

Two other private map companies that stand out for reliability and walker-friendliness are Prames, which produce excellent maps specifically for walkers in the Aragón region. Also regional and reliable are the maps produced by

Adrados Ediciones. You'll find them in major northern cities such as Oviedo and Santander in Cantabria, as well as in even the smallest villages around the Picos de Europa in the Cordillera Cantábrica.

UK-based **Discovery Walking Guides** (www.walking.demon.co.uk) publish excellent maps based on IGN 1:25,000 originals for the Balearic Islands and the Alpujarras region in Andalucía, among other Spanish destinations. Each comes in a handy pack with a detailed route description in English and new editions are being produced in an unrippable, unstainable, GPS-compatible format.

You can often pick up Editorial Alpina publications and CNIG maps at bookshops near trekking areas, and at specialist bookshops such as **Librería Desnivel** (☎ 902 24 88 48; www.libreriadesnivel.com; Plaza de Matute 6) or **Altaïr** (☎ 93 342 71 71; www.altair.es; Gran Via de les Corts Catalanes 616) or **Quera** (☎ 93 318 07 43; www .llibreriaquera.com; Carrer de Petritxol 2) in Barcelona. Some map specialists in other countries, such as **Stanfords** (☎ 020 7836 1321; www.stanfords.co.uk; 12-14 Long Acre, London WC2E 9LP) in the UK, also have a good range of Spain maps.

MONEY

As in 22 other EU nations, the euro is Spain's currency. The euro is divided into 100 cents. Coin denominations are one, two, five, 10, 20 and 50 cents, €1 and €2. The notes are €5, €10, €20, €50, €100, €200 and €500.

Exchange rates are given within the cover of this book and a guide to costs can be found on p24.

Spain's international airports have bank branches, ATMs and exchange offices. They're less frequent at road crossings into Spain now as Spain's neighbours – Andorra, Portugal and France – all use the euro.

Banks and building societies tend to offer the best exchange rates, and are plentiful: even small villages often have at least one. They mostly open from about 8.30am to 2pm Monday to Friday. Some also open Thursday evening (about 4-7pm) or Saturday morning (9am-2pm). Ask about commissions before changing (especially in exchange bureaux).

Prices in this guidebook are quoted in euros (€), unless otherwise stated.

ATMs

Many credit and debit cards (Visa and MasterCard are the most widely accepted) can be used for withdrawing money from *cajeros automáticos* (automatic telling machines – ATMs). This is handy because many banks do not offer an over-the-counter cash advance service on foreign cards (and where they do, the process can be wearisome).

The exchange rate used for credit and debit card transactions is usually more in your favour than that for cash exchanges. Bear in mind, however, the costs involved. There is usually a charge (hovering around 1.5% to 2%) on ATM cash withdrawals abroad. This charge may appear on your statements.

Cash

There is little advantage in bringing foreign cash into Spain. True, exchange commissions are often lower than for traveller's cheques, but the danger of losing the lot far outweighs such gains.

Credit & Debit Cards

You can use 'plastic' to pay for the vast majority of purchases. You'll often be asked to show your passport or some other form of identification when using

---

TAKING PHOTOS OUTDOORS

For walkers, photography can be a vexed issue – all that magnificent scenery but such weight and space restrictions on what photographic equipment you can carry. With a little care and planning it is possible to maximise your chance of taking great photos on the trail.

Light & Filters In fine weather, the best light is early and late in the day. In strong sunlight and in mountain and coastal areas where the light is intense, a polarising filter will improve colour saturation and reduce haze. On overcast days the soft light can be great for shooting wildflowers and running water and an 81A warming filter can be useful. If you use slide film, a graduated filter will help balance unevenly lit landscapes.

Equipment If you need to travel light carry a zoom in the 28–70mm range, and if your sole purpose is landscapes consider carrying just a single wide-angle lens (24mm). A tripod is essential for really good images and there are some excellent lightweight models available. Otherwise a trekking pole, pack or even a pile of rocks can be used to improvise.

Camera Care Keep your gear dry – a few zip-lock freezer bags can be used to double wrap camera gear and silica-gel sachets (a drying agent) can be used to suck moisture out of equipment. Sturdy cameras will normally work fine in freezing conditions. Take care when bringing a camera from one temperature extreme to another; if moisture condenses on the camera parts make sure it dries thoroughly before going back into the cold, or mechanisms can freeze up. Standard camera batteries fail very quickly in the cold. Remove them from the camera when it's not in use and keep them under your clothing.

For a thorough grounding on photography on the road, read Lonely Planet's *Travel Photography*, by Richard I'Anson, a full-colour guide for happy-snappers and professional photographers alike. Also highly recommended is the outdoor photography classic *Mountain Light*, by Galen Rowell.

Gareth McCormack

TAKING YOUR MOBILE PHONE

If you plan to take your own mobile phone to Spain, check in advance with your mobile network provider that your phone is enabled for international roaming, which allows you to make and receive calls and messages abroad.

- Consider buying an alternative SIM card for use on a local network in Spain. If your phone is not blocked (check before leaving home), you can buy any local pay-as-you-go SIM card.
- Take an international adaptor for the charger plug.
- Note your phone's number and serial number (IMEI number) and your operator's customer services number. This will help if your phone is stolen.
- For more advice on using mobile phones abroad go to www.ofcom.org.uk.

cards. Among the most widely accepted are Visa, MasterCard, American Express (Amex), Cirrus, Maestro, Plus, Diners Club and JCB. Many institutions add 2.5% or more to all transactions (cash advance or purchases) on cards used abroad – this charge does not generally appear on your bank statements.

If your card is lost, stolen or swallowed by an ATM, you can telephone toll-free to have an immediate stop put on its use. For **MasterCard** the number in Spain is ☎ 900 97 12 31, for **Visa** ☎ 900 99 11 24, for **Amex** ☎ 900 99 44 26 and for **Diners Club** ☎ 901 10 10 11.

Carrying your finances in the form of a credit or debit card is always the best way to go.

Moneychangers

As well as at banks, you can exchange both cash and travellers cheques at exchange offices – usually indicated by the word *cambio* (exchange). They abound in tourist resorts and other places that attract high numbers of foreigners. Generally they offer longer opening hours and quicker service than banks, but worse exchange rates. Their commissions are, on occasion, outrageous.

Tipping

The law requires menu prices to include a service charge; tipping is a matter of choice. Most people leave some small change if they're satisfied: 5% is normally fine and 10% generous. Taxi drivers don't have to be tipped but a little rounding up won't go amiss.

Travellers Cheques

Travellers cheques usually bring only a slightly better exchange rate than cash, usually offset by the charges for buying them in the first place and the commission you may have to pay to cash them in. Travellers cheques are also a pain to exchange, with many banks now refusing to accept them altogether. Plastic has by now largely supplanted travellers cheques for travel in Spain but the ultra-cautious may see them as a useful back-up measure in case of something going wrong with one's debit and/or credit cards.

TELEPHONE

The ubiquitous blue payphones are easy to use for international and domestic calls. They accept coins, phonecards *(tarjetas telefónicas)* issued by the national phone company Telefónica and, in some cases, various credit cards. Phonecards come in €6 and €12 denominations and, like postage stamps, are sold at post offices and tobacconists.

Mobile Phones

Spain uses GSM 900/1800, which is compatible with the rest of Europe and Australia but not with the North American GSM 1900 or the system used in Japan. From those countries, you will need to travel with a tri-band or quadric-band phone.

Phone Codes

Dial the international access code (☎ 00 in most countries), followed by the code for Spain (☎ 34) and the full number (including the code, 91, which is an integral part of the number). For example to call the number ☎ 91 455 67 83 from Madrid, you need to dial the international access code followed by ☎ 34 91 455 67 83.

The access code for international calls from Spain is ☎ 00. To make an international call, dial the access code, then dial the country code, area code and number you want.

International collect calls are simple. Dial 900 followed by the code for the country you're calling:

Australia ☎ 99 00 61
Canada ☎ 99 00 15
France ☎ 99 00 33
Germany ☎ 99 00 49
Ireland ☎ 99 03 53
Israel ☎ 99 09 72
New Zealand ☎ 99 00 64
UK for BT ☎ 99 00 44
US for AT&T ☎ 99 00 11, for Sprint and various others ☎ 99 00 13

For international directory inquiries dial ☎ 11825. Be warned: a call to this number costs €2!

Mobile phone numbers start with 6. Numbers starting with 900 are national toll-free numbers, while those starting 901 to 905 come with varying conditions. A common one is 902, which is a national standard rate number. In a similar category are numbers starting with 803, 806 and 807.

Phonecards

Cut-rate prepaid phonecards can be good value for international calls. They can be bought from *estancos* (tobacconists) and newsstands in the main cities and tourist resorts. If possible, try to compare rates because some are better than others. *Locutorios* (private call centres) that specialise in cut-rate overseas calls have popped up all over the place in the centre of bigger cities. Again, compare rates – as a rule the phonecards are better value and generally more convenient.

TIME

Mainland Spain and the Balearic Islands have the same time as most of the rest of western Europe: GMT/UTC plus one hour during winter and GMT/UTC plus two hours during the daylight-saving period, which runs from the last Sunday in March to the last Sunday in October.

The UK, Ireland, Portugal and the Canary Islands are one hour behind mainland Spain. Morocco is on GMT/UTC year-round. From the last Sunday in March to the last Sunday in October, subtract two hours from Spanish time to get Moroccan time; the rest of the year, subtract one hour.

Spanish time is US Eastern Time plus six hours and US Pacific Time plus nine hours.

During the Australian winter (Spanish summer), subtract eight hours from Australian Eastern Standard Time to get Spanish time; in the Australian summer subtract 10 hours.

Although the 24-hour clock is used in most official situations, you'll find people generally use the 12-hour clock for everyday use.

TOURIST INFORMATION
Local Tourist Offices

All cities and many smaller towns have an *oficina de turismo* or *oficina de información turística*. In the country's provincial capitals you'll sometimes find more than one

---

ON SPANISH TRAILS

In general, Spain is a very safe country for a woman alone, especially in rural walking areas. Before going to Spain for the first time, I was warned about the attention I might receive from the stereotyped macho ibérico (a man unashamed to express his virility and strength). Once there I discovered that the macho ibérico was, in fact, becoming an endangered species and that in the rare instance when unwanted advances were directed my way, a firm 'Dejame' (Deh-ha-may; meaning 'Leave me alone!') was sufficient to keep them at bay.

What did bother me at first were the long looks from both sexes. However, rather than an invasion of individual privacy, I found they are part of a Spanish cultural code in which people-watching is the norm. Stares don't necessarily have a secondary intent.

You don't see women walking alone in the mountains very often, and this does attract attention. Women on their own (mostly foreigners) provoke reactions among locals of surprise, admiration and concern. It's common to be warned not to go into the hills alone by both men and women repeating advice learned in childhood.

Nancy Frey

tourist office – one specialising in information on the city alone, the other carrying mostly provincial or regional information. National and natural parks also often have visitor centres offering useful information. Their opening hours and quality of information vary widely.

Turespaña (www.spain.info, www.tourspain.es), the country's national tourism body, presents a variety of general information and links on the entire country in its web pages.

VISAS

Spain is one of 25 member countries of the Schengen Convention, under which 22 EU countries (all but Bulgaria, Cyprus, Ireland, Romania and the UK) plus Iceland, Norway and Switzerland have abolished checks at common borders. Cyprus is preparing to join in 2010. For detailed information on the EU, including which countries are member states, visit http://europa.eu.

EU, Norwegian, Swiss and Icelandic nationals need no visa, regardless of the length or purpose of their visit to Spain. If they stay beyond 90 days, they are required to register with the police (although many do not). Legal residents of one Schengen country (regardless of their nationality) do not require a visa for another Schengen country.

Nationals of many other countries, including Australia, Canada, Israel, Japan, NZ and the US, do not need a visa for tourist visits of up to 90 days in Spain, although some of these nationalities may be subject to restrictions in other Schengen countries and should check with consulates of all Schengen countries they plan to visit. If you are a citizen of a country not mentioned in this section, check with a Spanish consulate whether you need a visa.

The standard tourist visa issued by Spanish consulates is the Schengen visa, valid for up to 90 days. A Schengen visa issued by one Schengen country is generally valid for travel in all other Schengen countries.

WOMEN WALKERS

You'll be very unlucky if you have any problems on the trails that are related specifically to your sex. Like walkers everywhere, Spanish hikers tend to be fairly socially enlightened. Younger ones are relaxed in their dealings with the opposite sex, and older walkers are usually free of the prurient interest in foreign women that some 'dinosaurs' still carry over from the repressive social climate of the Franco era.

In towns, you may get the occasional unwelcome stare, catcall or unnecessary comment, to which the best – and most galling – response is indifference. And don't get too paranoid about what's being called; the *piropo* – a harmless, mildly flirty compliment – is deeply ingrained in Spanish society and, if well delivered, is even considered gallant. Serious harassment is not frequent and Spain has one of the developed world's lowest incidences of reported rape.

Sleeping arrangements in many *refugios* often involve a single- or double-decker bench running from one side of the dormitory to the other where male and female, young and old, snore side by side. If this worries you, pack a tent and retain your independence.

In general, as anywhere, it might be risky for a woman to hitch alone.

For general advice consult *Handbook for Women Travellers*, by M & G Moss.

Transport

CONTENTS

GETTING THERE & AWAY

Spain is one of Europe's top holiday destinations and is well linked to other European countries by air, rail and road. Regular car ferries and hydrofoils run to and from Morocco, and there are ferry links to the UK, Italy, the Canary Islands and Algeria. The existence of budget airlines has revolutionised travel in Europe. Flying is generally the fastest and cheapest way of reaching Spain from elsewhere in Europe. On the other hand, the per-person carbon emissions are greater than travelling, say, by train, (although they're not as great as being the sole person in a large 4x4 driving the same distance).

Some good direct flights are available from North America. Those coming from Australasia will usually have to make at least one change of flight.

ENTERING THE COUNTRY
Passport

Citizens of the 27 European Union (EU) member states and Switzerland can travel to Spain with their national identity card alone. If such countries do not issue ID cards – as in the UK – travellers must carry a full valid passport. All other nationalities must have a full valid passport.

By law you are supposed to have your passport or ID card with you at all times. It doesn't happen often, but it could be embarrassing if you are asked by the police to produce a document and you don't have it with you. You will need one of these documents for police registration when you take a hotel room.

AIR

High season in Spain generally means Christmas/New Year, Easter and, roughly, June to September. This varies, depending on the specific destination. You may find reasonably priced flights available to Madrid in August because it is stinking hot and everyone else has fled to the mountains or the sea. As a general rule, November to March are when airfares to Spain are likely to be at their lowest, and the intervening months can be considered shoulder periods.

Airports & Airlines

The main gateway to Spain is Madrid's **Barajas airport** (Aeropuerto de Barajas; nationwide flight information ☎ 902 40 47 04; www.aena.es), although many European direct flights serve other centres, particularly Barcelona, Málaga, Palma de Mallorca, Bilbao and Valencia. Charter flights and low-cost airlines (mostly from the UK) fly direct to a growing number of regional airports, including A Coruña, Alicante, Almería, Asturias, Girona (for the Costa Brava and Barcelona), Ibiza, Jerez de la Frontera, Murcia, Reus and Seville.

THINGS CHANGE...

The information in this chapter is particularly vulnerable to change. Check directly with the airline or a travel agent to make sure you understand how a fare (and ticket you may buy) works and be aware of the security requirements for international travel. Shop carefully. The details given in this chapter should be regarded as pointers and are not a substitute for your own careful, up-to-date research.

Iberia, Spain's national carrier, flies to most Spanish cities (many via Madrid) from around the world but is generally the expensive way to go.

Among the airlines that fly to and from Spain are the following:

Aer Lingus (EI; in Ireland ☎ 0818 365000; www.aerlingus.com)
Air Berlin (AB; ☎ 902 32 07 37, in Germany 01805 737800; www.airberlin.com)
Air Europa (UX; ☎ 902 40 15 01; www.aireuropa.com)
Air Nostrum (IB; ☎ 902 40 05 00; www.airnostrum.es)
American Airlines (AA; in the US ☎ 800 433 7300; www.aa.com)
BMI (BD; ☎ 91 275 46 29, in the UK 0870 607 0555; www.flybmi.com)
British Airways (BA; ☎ 902 11 13 33, in the UK 0870 850 9850; www.britishairways.com)
Brussels Airlines (SN; ☎ 807 22 00 03, in Belgium 0902 516000; www.flysn.com)
Continental (CO; ☎ 900 96 12 66, in the USA 800 231 0856; www.continental.com)
Delta (DL; ☎ 901 11 69 46, in the USA 800 221 1212; www.delta.com)
EasyJet (U2; ☎ 807 26 00 26, in the UK 0905 821 0905; www.easyjet.com)
FlyGlobeSpan (Y2; in the UK ☎ 0871 271 0415; www.flyglobespan.com)
Germanwings (4U; ☎ 91 625 97 04, in Germany 0900 1919100; www.germanwings.com)
Iberia (IB; ☎ 902 40 05 00; www.iberia.es)
Jet2 (LS; ☎ 902 88 12 69, in the UK 0871 226 1737; www.jet2.com)
Lufthansa (LX; ☎ 902 22 01 01, in Germany 01805 838426; www.lufthansa.com)
Meridiana (IG; in Italy ☎ 39 78952682; www.meridiana.it)
Monarch (ZB; ☎ 800 09 92 60, in the UK 0870 040 5040; www.flymonarch.com)
Norwegian Air Shuttle (DY; in Norway ☎ 815 21815; www.norwegian.no)
Royal Air Maroc (AT; www.royalairmaroc.com)
Ryanair (FR; ☎ 807 22 00 32, in the UK 0871 246 0000, in Ireland 0818 303030; www.ryanair.com)
Singapore Airlines (SQ; ☎ 902 01 25 14; www.singaporeair.com)
Spanair (JK; ☎ 902 13 14 15; www.spanair.com)
Swiss (LX; ☎ 901 11 67 12, in Switzerland 0848 700700; www.swiss.com)
Thomson Fly (BY; in the UK ☎ 0871 231 4691; www.thomsonfly.com)
Transavia (HV; ☎ 807 07 50 22, in the Netherlands 0900 0737; www.transavia.com)
US Airways (US; ☎ 901 11 70 73, in the US 800 428 4322; www.usairways.com)
Vueling (VY; ☎ 902 33 39 33; www.vueling.com)
Windjet (IV; ☎ 900 99 69 33; w2.volawindjet.it)
Wizz (W6; ☎ 807 45 00 10, in Hungary 06 9018 1181; http://wizzair.com)

Tickets

The internet is increasingly the easiest way of locating and booking reasonably priced seats. This is especially so for flights from around Europe, regardless of whether you are flying with major carriers like Iberia or low-cost airlines.

There is no shortage of online agents:

www.cheaptickets.com
www.ebookers.com
www.expedia.com
www.flightline.co.uk
www.flynow.com
www.lastminute.com
www.openjet.com
www.opodo.com
www.planesimple.co.uk
www.skyscanner.net
www.travelocity.co.uk
www.tripadvisor.com

Australia

Cheap flights from Australia to Europe generally go via South-East Asian capitals.

BAGGAGE RESTRICTIONS

Airlines impose tight restrictions on carry-on baggage. No sharp implements of any kind are allowed onto the plane, so pack items such as pocket knives, camping cutlery and first-aid kits into your checked luggage.

If you're carrying a camping stove you should remember that airlines also ban liquid fuels and gas cartridges from all baggage, both check-through and carry-on. Empty all fuel bottles and buy what you need at your destination.

There are hardly any direct flights. Singapore Airlines, however, does fly direct to Barcelona via Singapore.

STA Travel (☎ 134 782; www.statravel.com.au) and **Flight Centre** (☎ 133 133; www.flightcentre.com.au) are major dealers in cheap airfares, although discounted fares can also be found at your local travel agent. For online bookings, try www.travel.com.au.

Continental Europe

Air travel between Spain and other places in continental Europe is worth considering if you are short on time. Short hops can be expensive, but for longer journeys you can often find airfares that beat overland alternatives.

In France, have a look at **Anyway** (☎ 0892 302 301; http://voyages.anyway .com), **Lastminute** (☎ 04 66 92 30 29; www .lastminute.fr) and **Nouvelles Frontières** (☎ 01 49 20 64 00; www.nouvelles -frontieres.fr).

In Germany, **STA Travel** (☎ 069 7430 3292; www.statravel.de) is one of the best student and discount travel agencies.

Amsterdam is a popular departure point and a good budget-flight centre. Try **Air Fair** (☎ 0900 7717717; www.airfair.nl). **Kilroy Travels** (☎ 0900 0400636; www .kilroytravels.nl) is also worth checking out.

The best place to look for cheap fares in Italy is **CTS** (Centro Turistico Studentesco e Giovanile; ☎ 06 4411166; www.cts.it), which has branches in cities throughout the country.

In Portugal, **Tagus** (☎ 707 220000; www .viagenstagus.pt) is a reputable travel agency with branches around the country.

South America

Iberia and a series of South American national airlines connect Spain with Latin America. Most flights converge on Madrid, although some continue to Barcelona.

Asatej (www.asatej.com) is a Hispanic youth travel organisation, with offices in Argentina and Mexico.

UK & Ireland

No-frills airlines are big business for travel between the UK and Spain. EasyJet and Ryanair are the main operators. Prices vary wildly according to season and also depend on how far in advance you book. Prices have recently risen and once you add on all the extras (baggage fees, booking fees, credit card fees, check-in fees – the list with some seems endless) then it can end up costing much the same as with the scheduled airlines.

Discount air travel is big business in London. Advertisements for many travel agencies appear in the travel pages of the weekend newspapers, such as the *Independent,* the *Guardian* on Saturday and the *Sunday Times*.

STA Travel (☎ 0871 230 0040; www .statravel.co.uk) and **Trailfinders** (☎ 0845 058 5858; www.trailfinders.com), both of which have offices throughout the UK, sell discounted and student tickets.

From Ireland, check out offers from Aer Lingus and Ryanair.

US

Several airlines fly 'direct' (many flights involve a stop elsewhere in Europe en route) to Spain, landing in Madrid and Barcelona.

Discount travel agencies in the US are known as consolidators. San Francisco is the ticket-consolidator capital of America, although some good deals can be found in other big cities. The *New York Times, Los Angeles Times, Chicago Tribune* and *San Francisco Examiner* all produce weekly travel sections. **STA Travel** (☎ 1800 781 4040; www.statravel.com) has offices around the country. **Travel Cuts** (☎ 1800 592 2887; www.travelcuts.com) is a similar operation.

Discount and rock-bottom options from the US include charter, stand-by and courier flights. Stand-by fares are often sold at 60% of the normal price for one-way tickets. **Courier Travel** (www.couriertravel .org) is a search engine for courier and stand-by flights.

LAND

You can enter Spain by train, bus and private vehicle along various points of its northern border with France (and Andorra) and the western frontier with Portugal. Bus is generally the cheapest option but the train is more comfortable, especially for long-haul trips.

Border Crossings

The main road crossing into Spain from France is the highway that links up with Spain's AP7 tollway, which runs down to Barcelona and follows the Spanish coast south (with a branch, the AP2, going to Madrid via Zaragoza). A series of links cut across the Pyrenees from France and Andorra into Spain, as does a coastal route that runs from Biarritz in France into the Spanish Basque Country.

The A5 freeway linking Madrid with Badajoz crosses the Portuguese frontier and continues on to Lisbon, and there are many other road connections up and down the length of the Hispano-Portuguese frontier. As Spain, France and Portugal are members of the EU and the Schengen area (see p350) there are usually no border controls between them. The tiny principality of Andorra is not in the EU, so border controls (and customs checks for contraband) remain in place.

Bus

Eurolines (www.eurolines.com) and its partner bus companies run an extensive network of international buses across most of western Europe and Morocco. In Spain they serve many destinations from the rest of Europe, although services often run only a few times a week.

See individual country sections for more information on bus transport.

Car & Motorcycle

When driving in Europe, always carry proof of ownership of a private vehicle. Third-party motor insurance is required throughout Europe.

Every vehicle should display a nationality plate of its country of registration. A warning triangle (to be used in case of breakdown) is compulsory. In Spain two reflective jackets are also compulsory and police do check that you have them.

Prebooking a rental car before leaving home will enable you to find the cheapest deals (for multinational agencies, see p357).

No matter where you hire your car, make sure you understand what is included in the price and your liabilities.

Your vehicle could be searched on arrival from Andorra. Spanish customs look out for contraband duty-free products destined for illegal resale in Spain. The same generally goes on arrival from Morocco or the Spanish North African enclaves of Ceuta and Melilla. In this case the search is for controlled substances.

See p357 for comprehensive information on road rules, petrol, insurance and other driving tips for Spain.

Train

The principal rail crossings into Spain pierce the Franco-Spanish frontier along the Mediterranean coast and via the Basque Country. Another minor rail route runs inland across the Pyrenees from Latour-de-Carol to Barcelona. From Portugal, the main line runs from Lisbon across Extremadura to Madrid.

Direct trains link Barcelona with Paris, Geneva, Zürich, Turin and Milan at least three times a week. Direct overnight trains also connect Paris with Madrid. Check details on the website of **Renfe** (www.renfe.es), the Spanish national railway company.

Andorra

Regular buses connect Andorra with Barcelona (including winter ski buses and direct services to the airport) and other destinations in Spain (including Madrid) and France.

France

BUS

Eurolines (www.eurolines.fr) heads to Spain from Paris and more than 20 other French cities and towns. It connects with Madrid (17¾ hours), Barcelona (14¾ hours) and many other destinations. There is at least one departure per day for main destinations.

TRAIN

About the only truly direct trains to Madrid and Barcelona are the *trenhoteles,* which are expensive sleeper trains. There are daily services from Madrid and Barcelona to Paris.

There are several other less luxurious possibilities to Spain. Two or three TGV (high-speed) trains leave from Paris Montparnasse for Irún, where you change to a normal train for the Basque Country and onwards. Up to three TGVs also put you on track to Barcelona (leaving from

Paris Gare de Lyon), with a change of train at Montpellier or Narbonne. One or two daily direct services connect Montpellier with Barcelona (and on to Murcia).

For more information on French rail services check out the **SNCF** (www.voyages-sncf.com) website.

Morocco

Buses from several Moroccan cities converge on Tangier to make the ferry crossing to Algeciras, and then fan out to the main Spanish centres. Several companies, including **A**LSA (www.alsa.es), run these routes.

Portugal

BUS

AutoRes (www.auto-res.net) runs one or two buses a day from Lisbon to Madrid via Badajoz. The trip takes 7½ to nine hours.

Other services from the Portuguese capital run to Seville via Aracena; to Málaga via Badajoz, Seville, Cádiz, Algeciras and the Costa del Sol; and to Granada via Albufeira, Huelva, Seville, Málaga and Almuñécar.

Another service runs north via Porto to Tui, Santiago de Compostela and A Coruña in Galicia. Local buses cross the border from towns such as Huelva in Andalucía, Badajoz in Extremadura and Ourense in Galicia.

TRAIN

An overnight sleeper train runs daily from Lisbon to Madrid, and another train connects the Portuguese capital with Irún. See **Renfe** (www.renfe.es) for details.

UK

BUS

Eurolines (www.nationalexpress.com/eurolines) runs buses to Barcelona, Madrid and other Spanish destinations several times a week. The London terminal is at **Victoria Coach Station** (Buckingham Palace Rd). Journey times (including a wait in Paris of up to two hours) can range from 24 to 26 hours to Barcelona and from 25 to 30 hours to Madrid.

CAR & MOTORCYCLE

You can take your car across to France by ferry or via the Channel Tunnel on **Eurotunnel** (www.eurotunnel.com). The latter runs four crossings (35 minutes) an hour between Folkestone and Calais in the high season.

TRAIN

The passenger-train service **Eurostar** (www.eurostar.com) travels between London and Paris, from where you can connect with trains to Spain. Alternatively, you can purchase a train ticket that includes crossing the English Channel by ferry, SeaCat or hovercraft.

SEA

Ferries run to mainland Spain regularly from the Canary Islands, Italy, North Africa (Algeria, Morocco and the Spanish enclaves of Ceuta and Melilla) and the UK. Most services are run by the Spanish national ferry company, **Acciona Trasmediterránea** (www.trasmediterranea.es).

Canary Islands

An Acciona Trasmediterránea car ferry leaves from Santa Cruz de Tenerife (2pm) every Thursday and from Las Palmas de Gran Canaria (8am) every Monday for Cádiz. It's a long and bumpy ride, taking about 44 hours from Santa Cruz (with a stop in Santa Cruz de Palma) and 34 from Las Palmas (with a stop in Arrecife).

Italy

Ferries run daily from Genoa to Barcelona, and up to six times a week from Civitavecchia (near Rome) and Livorno (for Florence and Pisa).

Morocco

You can sail from the Moroccan ports of Tangiers, Al Hoceima and Nador, as well as from Ceuta or Melilla (Spanish enclaves on the Moroccan coast), to Almería, Málaga, Algeciras, Gibraltar and Tarifa. The routes are Melilla–Almería, Al Hoceima–Almería, Nador–Almería, Melilla–Málaga, Tangier–Gibraltar, Tangier–Algeciras, Ceuta–Algeciras and Tangier–Tarifa. All routes usually take vehicles as well as passengers.

The most frequent sailings are from Algeciras to Tangier (taking 1¼ to 2½ hours) and Ceuta (35 to 45 minutes). Extra services are put on during the peak summer period (mid-Jun – mid-Sep) to cater for the stream of Moroccans resident in Europe heading home for the holidays, and the Tangier–Tarifa route may be restricted to people with EU passports or EU residence papers during this period.

Acciona Trasmediterránea (www .trasmediterranea.es) and various other companies compete for business.

UK
PLYMOUTH/PORTSMOUTH TO SANTANDER
From Plymouth and Portsmouth, **Brittany Ferries** (www.brittany-ferries.co.uk) runs a car ferry once a week to Santander from mid-March to mid-November.

PORTSMOUTH TO BILBAO
P&O Ferries (www.poferries.com) operates a service from Portsmouth to Bilbao. As a rule there are sailings every three days, year-round.

VIA FRANCE
You can transport your car by ferry to France from the UK. **Norfolkline** (www .norfolkline.com) fast boats take about 1¾ hours to cross from Dover to Dunkirk. **P&O Ferries** (www.poferries.com) has frequent car ferries from Dover to Calais (1¼ hours).

GETTING AROUND

You can reach almost any town or village in Spain by train or bus, and services are efficient and, generally, cheap. Getting to some of the trailheads though is a different matter and your own wheels give you the most freedom in this respect.

AIR
Airlines in Spain
Iberia and its subsidiary, Iberia Regional-Air Nostrum, have an extensive network covering all of Spain. Competing with Iberia are Spanair and Air Europa, as well as the Spanish low-cost company Vueling, and EasyJet and Ryanair. Between them they cover a host of Spanish destinations.

Generally, domestic flights are most easily booked on the airlines' websites. It is worth shopping around, and for return flights there is nothing to stop you booking each leg with a different airline.

BOAT
Ferries and hydrofoils link the mainland (La Península) with the Balearic Islands.

The main national ferry company is **Acciona Trasmediterránea** (www.trasmedi terranea.es). It runs a combination of slower car ferries and modern, high-speed, passenger-only fast ferries and hydrofoils. On overnight services between the mainland and the Balearic Islands you can opt for seating or sleeping accommodation in a cabin.

BUS
A plethora of companies provide bus links, from local routes between villages to fast intercity connections. It is often cheaper to travel by bus than by train, particularly on long-haul runs, but also less comfortable.

Local services can get you just about anywhere, but most buses connecting villages and provincial towns are not geared to tourist needs. Frequent weekday services drop off to a trickle on Saturday and Sunday. Often just one bus runs daily between smaller places during the week and none operate on Sunday. It's usually unnecessary to make reservations; just arrive early enough to get a seat. Unless a walk begins in a village or town then it's generally safe to say that you won't be able to access the trailhead by bus.

For longer trips (such as Madrid to Seville or to the coast), and certainly in peak holiday season, you can (and should) buy your ticket in advance. On some routes you have the choice between express and all-stops services.

In most larger towns and cities, buses leave from a single bus station (estación de autobuses). In smaller places, buses tend to operate from a set street or plaza, often unmarked. Locals will know where to go. Usually a specific bar sells tickets, although in some cases you may have to purchase tickets on the bus. Bus travel within Spain is not overly costly. The trip from Madrid to Barcelona costs around €27 one way.

CAR & MOTORCYCLE
Automobile Associations
The **Real Automóvil Club de España** (RACE; ☎ 902 40 45 45; www.race.es) is the national

automobile club. They may come to assist you in case of breakdown, but in any event you should obtain an emergency telephone number for Spain from your own insurer.

Bring Your Own Vehicle

If bringing your own car, remember to have your insurance and other papers in order (see p354).

Driving Licence

All EU member states' driving licences are fully recognised throughout Europe. Those with a non-EU licence are supposed to obtain a 12-month International Driver's Permit (IDP) to accompany their national licence, which your national automobile association can issue. If you want to hire a car or motorcycle you will need to produce your driving licence.

Fuel & Spare Parts

Petrol (*gasolina*) in Spain is pricey, but generally cheaper than in its major EU neighbours (including France, Germany, Italy and the UK).

Prices vary between service stations (*gasolineras*). Lead-free (*sin plomo*; 95 octane) costs around €1.09 per litre. Diesel (*gasóleo*) comes in at €0.94 per litre. Both of these prices are based on September 2009 averages.

Petrol is about 10% cheaper in Gibraltar than in Spain and 15% cheaper in Andorra. It's about 35% cheaper in Spain's tax-free enclaves of Ceuta and Melilla in North Africa.

Hire

A selection of multinational car rental agencies:

Autos Abroad (☎ in the UK 0845 029 1945; www.autosabroad.com)
Avis (www.avis.es)
Budget (☎ in the US 800 527 0700; www.budget.com)
Europcar (www.europcar.es)
Hertz (www.hertz.es)
National/Atesa (☎ 902 10 01 01; www.atesa.es)
Pepecar (☎ 807 41 42 43; www.pepecar.com) A local low-cost company.

To rent a car in Spain you have to have a licence and be aged 21 or over. Although

those with a non-EU licence should also have an IDP, you will find that national licences from countries like Australia, Canada, New Zealand and the US are often accepted.

Insurance

Third-party motor insurance is a minimum requirement in Spain and throughout Europe. Ask your insurer for a European Accident Statement form, which can simplify matters in the event of an accident. A European breakdown-assistance policy such as the AA Five Star Service or RAC Eurocover Motoring Assistance is a good investment.

Car-hire companies also provide this minimum insurance, but be careful to understand what your liabilities and excess are, and what waivers you are entitled to in case of accident or damage to the hire vehicle.

Road Rules

Drive on the right. In built-up areas the speed limit is 50km/h (and in some cases, such as inner-city Barcelona, 30km/h), which increases to 100km/h on major roads and up to 120km/h on *autovías* and *autopistas* (toll-free and tolled dual-lane highways, respectively). Cars towing caravans are restricted to a maximum speed of 80km/h. The minimum driving age is 18 years.

Motorcyclists must use headlights at all times and wear a helmet if riding a bike of 125cc or more. The minimum age for riding motorbikes and scooters of 80cc and over is 16; for those 50cc and under it's 14. A licence is required.

Spanish truck drivers often have the courtesy to turn on their right indicator to show that the way ahead of them is clear for overtaking (and the left one if it is not and you are attempting this manoeuvre).

At traffic circles (roundabouts), vehicles already in the circle have the right of way.

The blood-alcohol limit is 0.05%. Breath tests are common and if found to be over the limit you can be judged, condemned, fined and deprived of your licence within 24 hours. Fines range up to around €600 for serious offences. Non-resident foreigners will be required to pay up on the spot (at

30% off the full fine). Pleading linguistic ignorance will not help – your traffic cop will produce a list of infringements and fines in as many languages as you like. If you don't pay, or don't have a Spanish resident to act as guarantor for you, your vehicle could be impounded.

HITCHING

Hitching is never entirely safe in any country in the world and we don't recommend it. Travellers who decide to hitch should understand that they are taking a small but potentially dangerous risk. People who do choose to hitch will be safer if they travel in pairs and let someone know where they are planning to go.

Having said that, if you're cruising without a car then you're simply going to have no option but to hitch to many trailheads and in general you'll find that if you're in a quiet mountain area and look like a walker then you won't have to wait long for someone to pick you up.

Hitching is illegal on *autopistas* and *autovías*, and difficult on other major highways. Choose a spot where cars can safely stop before highway slipways, or use minor roads. The going can be slow on the latter, as the traffic is often light.

TRAIN

Renfe (☎ 902 24 02 02; www.renfe.es) is the national train system that runs most of the services in Spain. There are also a handful of small private rail lines.

Spain has several types of trains. For short hops, bigger cities such as Madrid, Barcelona, Bilbao, Málaga and Valencia have local networks known as *cercanías*. Long-distance (aka *largo recorrido* or Grandes Líneas) trains come in all sorts of different flavours. They range from all-stops *regionales* operating within one region, to the high-speed Tren de Alta Velocidad Española (AVE) trains that link Madrid with Barcelona, Burgos, Huesca (via Zaragoza), Málaga, Seville and Valladolid (and in coming years Madrid–Valencia via Cuenca, and Madrid–Bilbao). A whole host of modern intermediate-speed services (Alaris, Altaria, Alvia, Arco and Avant) offer an increasingly speedy and comfortable service around the country, and have improved services vastly

on such shorter-distance runs as Madrid–Toledo and Barcelona–Lleida. Slower long-distance trains include the Talgo and Intercity.

You'll find *consignas* (left-luggage facilities) at all main train stations. They are usually open from about 6am to midnight and charge from €3 to €4.50 per day per piece of luggage.

Classes & Costs

All long-distance trains have 2nd and 1st classes, known as *turista* and *preferente*, respectively. The latter is 20% to 40% more expensive. Some services have a third, superior category, called *club*. Fares vary enormously depending on the service (faster trains cost considerably more) and, in the case of some high-speed services such as the AVE, on the time and day of travel. If you get a return ticket, it is worth checking whether your return journey is by the same kind of train. If you return on a slower train than the outward-bound trip you may be entitled to a modest refund on the return leg. Alternatively, if you return by a faster train you will need to pay more to make your return ticket valid for that train.

Tickets for AVE trains are by far the most expensive. A one-way trip in 2nd class from Madrid to Barcelona (on which route only AVE trains run) could cost as much as €160 (less if booked ahead on the web). Flying is often cheaper (although more of a hassle) and the bus certainly is. By contrast, the trip on the slower but much longer run from Barcelona to Oviedo costs a very reasonable €56.

Children aged between four and 12 years are entitled to a 40% discount; those aged under four travel free (except on high-speed trains, for which they pay the same as those aged four to 12). Buying a return ticket often gives you a 10% to 20% discount on the return trip. Students and people up to 25 years of age with a Euro<26 Card (Carnet Joven in Spain) are entitled to 20% to 25% off most ticket prices.

Buying tickets in advance on the internet can also bring significant discounts (as much as 60% on some AVE services for tickets bought at least 15 days in advance).

On overnight trips within Spain on *tren-hoteles* it's worth paying extra for a *litera* (*couchette*; a sleeping berth in a six- or four-bed compartment) or, if available, single or double cabins in *preferente* or *gran clase* class. The cost depends on the class of accommodation, type of train and length of journey. The lines covered are Madrid–La Coruña, Barcelona–Córdoba–Seville, Barcelona–Madrid (and on to Lisbon) and Barcelona–Málaga.

Reservations

Reservations are recommended for long-distance trips and you can make them in train stations, Renfe offices and travel agencies, as well as online (this can be a little complicated though). In a growing number of stations you can pick up prebooked tickets from machines scattered about the station concourse.

TRANSPORT

Clothing & Equipment

You don't need to spend a fortune on gear to enjoy the outdoors, but you do need to think carefully about what you pack to make sure you're comfortable and prepared for an emergency. Taking the right clothing and equipment on a walk can make the difference between an enjoyable day out or a cold and miserable one; in extreme situations, it can even mean the difference between life and death.

The gear you need for your walking holiday will depend on the type of walking you plan to do. For simple day walks on a warm and sunny day you might get away with little more than sandals/light shoes, a hat, shorts, shirt and a warm pullover. For longer walks, or those in alpine regions, especially if you're camping, the list becomes longer.

We recommend spending as much as you can afford on quality walking boots, backpack, jacket and, if camping, a tent and sleeping bag. These are likely to be your most expensive items but are a sound investment, as they should last for years.

CLOTHING

There are a couple of items that are essential items for every walk (even if they sometimes spend all day in your backpack). These are a waterproof jacket, overtrousers, sun protection and, of course, a good pair of boots (and socks to go with them). You should also consider whether gaiters would be useful on your chosen walk. See the box text on p362.

Layering

A secret of comfortable walking is to wear several layers of light clothing, which you can easily take off or put on as you warm up or cool down. Most walkers use three main layers: a base layer next to the skin; an insulating layer; and an outer, shell layer for protection from wind, rain and snow.

For the upper body, the base layer is typically a shirt of synthetic material such as polypropylene, with its ability to wick moisture away from the body and reduce chilling. The insulating layer retains heat next to your body, and is often a windproof synthetic fleece or down jacket. The outer shell consists of a waterproof jacket that also protects against cold wind.

For the lower body, the layers generally consist of either shorts or loose-fitting trousers, polypropylene 'long-john' underwear and waterproof overtrousers.

Waterproof Shells

For some of the walks in this book, for example the Cabo de Gata Coast walk (p284) in Andalucía you're highly unlikely to need any form of jacket, but for the majority of walks included here you will need one. In addition to the buying hints in the box text on p362 also make sure the sleeves are long enough to cover warm clothes underneath and that the overall length of the garment allows you to sit down on it.

Footwear

Your footwear will be your friend or your enemy, so choose carefully. The first decision to make is boots or shoes. Runners (trainers) are fine over easy terrain but, for more difficult trails and across rocks and scree, most walkers agree that the ankle support offered by boots is invaluable. If you'll be using crampons or walking in snow you need the rigid sole of a walking boot. Leather boots are heavier and less water resistant than fabric boots lined with a breathable membrane such as Gore-Tex, but pierce a hole in Gore-Tex-lined fabric boots – a more likely occurrence than with a leather boot – and their water resistance will go from hero to zero in an instant.

EQUIPMENT
Backpack

Your backpack will be fighting with your boots for the honour of most important bit of kit, so invest as much as you can in a good bag.

It can be tough deciding whether to go for a smaller or bigger pack. This can depend on your destination and whether you plan to camp or stay in *refugios* (mountain huts or refuges). Your pack should be large enough so that you don't need to strap bits and pieces to the outside. However, if you buy a bigger pack, then you're certain to fill it with stuff you never use and all this extra weight will quickly send your enjoyment levels spiralling downwards.

CHECKLIST

This list is a general guide to the things you might take on a hike. Your list will vary depending on the kind of hiking you want to do, whether you're camping or planning on staying in hostels or B&Bs, and on the terrain, weather conditions and time of year.

CLOTHING

- boots and spare laces
- gaiters
- hat (warm), scarf and gloves
- jacket (waterproof)
- overtrousers (waterproof)
- runners (training shoes), sandals or thongs (flip flops)
- shorts and trousers or skirt
- socks and underwear
- sunhat
- sweater or fleece jacket
- thermal underwear
- T-shirt and long-sleeved shirt with collar

EQUIPMENT

- backpack with liner (waterproof)
- first-aid kit*
- food and snacks (high energy) and one day's emergency supplies
- insect repellent
- map, compass and guidebook
- map case or clip-seal plastic bags
- pocket knife
- sunglasses
- sunscreen and lip balm
- survival bag or blanket
- toilet paper and trowel
- torch (flashlight) or headlamp, spare batteries and globe (bulb)
- water container
- whistle

OVERNIGHT WALKS

- cooking, eating and drinking utensils
- dishwashing items
- matches and lighter
- sewing/repair kit
- sleeping bag and bag liner/inner sheet
- sleeping mat
- spare cord
- stove and fuel
- tent, pegs, poles and guy ropes
- toiletries
- towel
- water purification tablets, iodine or filter

OPTIONAL ITEMS

- altimetre
- backpack cover (waterproof, slip-on)
- binoculars
- camera, film and batteries
- candle
- emergency distress beacon
- GPS receiver
- groundsheet
- mobile phone**
- mosquito net
- notebook and pen
- swimming costume
- walking/hiking/trekking poles
- watch

* see the First-Aid Check List (p366)
** see Mobile Phones (p348)

BUYING TIPS

BACKPACK

For day walks, a day-pack (30–40L) will usually suffice, but for multiday hikes you will need a backpack of between 45L and 90L. A good backpack should be made of strong fabric such as canvas or Cordura, a lightweight internal or external frame and an adjustable, well-padded harness that evenly distributes weight. Even if the manufacturer claims your pack is waterproof, use heavy-duty liners.

FOOTWEAR

Runners or walking shoes are fine over easy terrain but, for more difficult trails and across rocks and scree, the ankle support offered by boots is invaluable. Nonslip soles (such as Vibram) provide the best grip. Buy boots in warm conditions or go for a walk before trying them on, so that your feet can expand slightly, as they would on a walk. Most hikers carry a pair of sandals or thongs (flip flops) to wear at night or rest stops. Sandals are also useful when fording waterways.

GAITERS

If you will be hiking through snow, deep mud or scratchy vegetation, gaiters will protect your legs and help keep your socks dry. The best are made of strong fabric, with a robust zip protected by a flap, and secure easily around the foot.

OVERTROUSERS

Choose a model with slits for pocket access and long leg zips so that you can pull them on and off over your boots.

SLEEPING BAG & MAT

Down fillings are warmer than synthetic for the same weight and bulk but, unlike synthetic fillings, do not retain warmth when wet. Mummy bags are the best shape for weight and warmth. The given figure (–5ºC, for instance) is the coldest temperature at which a person should feel comfortable in the bag (although the ratings are notoriously unreliable).

An inner sheet helps keep your sleeping bag clean, as well as adding an insulating layer. Silk 'inners' are lightest; however, liners also come in cotton or polypropylene.

Self-inflating sleeping mats work like a thin air cushion between you and the ground; they also insulate from the cold. Foam mats are a low-cost, but less comfortable, alternative.

SOCKS

Hiking socks should be free of ridged seams in the toes and heels.

STOVES

Fuel stoves fall roughly into three categories: multifuel, methylated spirits (ethyl alcohol) and butane gas. Multifuel stoves are small, efficient and ideal for places where a reliable fuel supply is difficult to find. However, they tend to be sooty and require frequent maintenance. Stoves running on methylated spirits are slower and less efficient, but are safe, clean and easy to use. Butane gas stoves are clean and reliable, but can be slow, and the gas canisters can be awkward to carry and a potential litter problem.

TENT

A three-season tent will fulfil the requirements of most hikers. The floor and the outer shell, or fly, should have taped or sealed seams and covered zips to stop leaks. Most hikers find tents of around 2kg to 3kg a comfortable carrying weight. Dome- and tunnel-shaped tents handle windy conditions better than flat-sided tents.

WATERPROOF JACKET

The ideal specifications are a breathable, waterproof fabric, a hood that is roomy enough to cover headwear but still allows peripheral vision, capacious map pocket, and a heavy-gauge zip protected by a storm flap.

CLOTHING & EQUIPMENT

Sun Protection

Even on cloudy days it's very easy to get sunburnt at altitude so make sure you have a sun hat (preferably wide-brimmed, with a chin strap), sunglasses and high-factor sun cream handy.

Walking Poles

They might not look like anything more than a silly gadget but lightweight, telescopic walking poles help you balance and, best of all, ease the jarring on your knees during steep descents.

Stove Fuel

In Spain, the most reliable option is to carry a butane/propane stove since their *cartuchos* (cartridges) are the only widely available fuel source. Some *droguerias* (shops selling household products) stock *alcohol de quemar* (methylated spirits).

BUYING GEAR

For the sake of convenience it's best to bring all the gear you'll need with you. This said, Spain is a good place to pick up new items at reasonable prices. If you need to top up en route, look for a *tienda de deportes* (sporting goods shop).

NAVIGATION EQUIPMENT

Maps & Compass

You should always carry a good map of the area in which you are walking (see p345), and know how to read it. Before setting off on your walk, ensure that you understand

---

HOW TO USE A COMPASS

This is a very basic introduction to using a compass and will only be of assistance if you are proficient in map reading. For simplicity, it doesn't take magnetic variation into account. Before using a compass we recommend you obtain further instruction.

1. Reading a Compass

Hold the compass flat in the palm of your hand. Rotate the bezel (4) so the red end (7) of the needle (6) points to the N (north point; 8) on the bezel. The bearing is read from the dash (3) under the bezel.

2. Orienting the Map

To orient the map so that it aligns with the ground, place the compass flat on the map. Rotate the map until the needle is parallel with the map's north/south grid lines and the red end is pointing to north on the map. You can now identify features around you by aligning them with labelled features on the map.

3. Taking a Bearing from the Map

Draw a line on the map between your starting point and your destination. Place the edge of the compass on this line with the direction of travel arrow (2) pointing towards your destination. Rotate the bezel until the meridian lines (5) are parallel with the north/south grid lines on the map and the N points to north on the map. Read the bearing from the dash.

4. Following a Bearing

Rotate the bezel so that the intended bearing is in line with the dash. Place the compass flat in the palm of your hand and rotate the base plate (1) until the red end points to N on the bezel. The direction of travel arrow will now point in the direction you need to walk.

5. Determining Your Bearing

Rotate the bezel so the red end points to the N. Place the compass flat in the palm of your hand and rotate the base plate until the direction of travel arrow points in the direction in which you have been walking/hiking/trekking. Read your bearing from the dash.

1	Base plate
2	Direction of travel arrow
3	Dash
4	Bezel
5	Meridian lines
6	Needle
7	Red end
8	N (north point)

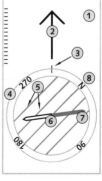

the contours and the map symbols, plus the main ridge and river systems in the area. Also familiarise yourself with the true north–south directions and the general direction in which you are heading. On the trail, try to identify major landforms such as mountain ranges and gorges, and locate them on your map. This will give you a better understanding of the region's geography.

Buy a compass and learn how to use it. The attraction of magnetic north varies in different parts of the world, so compasses need to be balanced accordingly. Compass manufacturers have divided the world into five zones. Make sure your compass is balanced for your destination zone. There are also 'universal' compasses on the market that can be used anywhere in the world.

GPS

Originally developed by the US Department of Defense, the Global Positioning System (GPS) is a network of more than 20 earth-orbiting satellites that continually beam encoded signals back to earth. Small, computer-driven devices (GPS receivers) can decode these signals to give users an extremely accurate reading of their location – to within a few metres, anywhere on the planet, at any time of day, in almost any weather. The cheapest hand-held GPS receivers now cost around $250 (although these may not have a built-in averaging system that minimises signal errors). Other important factors to consider when buying a GPS receiver are its weight and battery life.

Remember that a GPS receiver is of little use to walkers unless used with an accurate topographical map. The receiver simply gives your position, which you must then locate on the local map. GPS receivers will only work properly in the open. The signals from a crucial satellite may be blocked (or bounce off rock or water) directly below high cliffs, near large bodies of water or in dense tree cover and give inaccurate readings. GPS receivers are more vulnerable to breakdowns (including dead batteries) than the humble magnetic compass – a low-tech device that has served navigators faithfully for centuries – so don't rely on them entirely.

For a complete rundown on GPS use, consider picking up a copy of a book such as *GPS Made Easy* by Lawrence Letham.

Health & Safety

Spain is a pain-free travel destination as far as health and safety goes, and you're unlikely to suffer from any nasty illness while on the trail. Having said that, things can and do go wrong every now and then. Keeping healthy on the trail depends on your predeparture preparations, your daily health care while travelling and how you handle any medical problems that develop. While the potential problems can seem quite daunting, in reality most hikers in Spain suffer from nothing worse than the occasional blister or twisted ankle and an over-filled belly from too much restaurant indulgence.

BEFORE YOU GO

Bring medications in their original, clearly labelled, containers. A signed and dated letter from your physician describing your medical conditions and medications, including generic names, is also a good idea. If carrying syringes or needles, be sure to have a physician's letter documenting their medical necessity.

Some of the walks in this book are physically demanding and most require a reasonable level of fitness. Even if you're tackling the easy or easy–moderate walks, it pays to be relatively fit, rather than launch straight into them after months of fairly sedentary living. If you're aiming for the demanding walks, fitness is essential.

Unless you're a regular walker, start your get-fit campaign at least a month before your visit. Take a vigorous walk of about an hour, two or three times per week and gradually extend the duration of your outings as the departure date nears. If you plan to carry a full backpack on any walk, carry a loaded pack on some of your training jaunts.

If you have any known medical problems or are concerned about your health in any way, it's a good idea to have a full check up before you start walking. It's far better to have any problems recognised and treated at home than to find out about them halfway up a mountain. It's also sensible to have had a recent dental check up since toothache on the trail with solace a couple of days or more away can be a miserable experience, and dental fillings are more likely to come loose at high altitude.

INSURANCE

If you're an EU citizen, a European Health Insurance Card, available from health centres or, in the UK, post offices, covers you for most medical care in public hospitals. It will not cover you for non-emergencies or emergency repatriation home. So even with the card, you will still have to pay for medicine bought from pharmacies, even if prescribed, and perhaps for a few tests and procedures. The card is no good for private medical consultations and treatment in Spain; this includes virtually all dentists, and some of the better clinics and surgeries. Citizens from other countries should find out if there is a reciprocal arrangement for free medical care between their country and Spain. If you do need health insurance, strongly consider a policy that covers you for ambulances and the worst possible scenario, such as an accident requiring an emergency flight home.

HEALTH & SAFETY

Find out in advance if your insurance plan will make payments directly to providers or reimburse you later for overseas health expenditures; if you have to claim later make sure you keep all documentation. The former option is generally preferable, as it doesn't require you to pay out of your own pocket in a foreign country.

Spanish residents should check their health insurance covers them for remote-area ambulance rescue services.

Worldwide travel insurance is available at www.lonelyplanet.com/travel_services. You can buy, extend and claim online anywhere – even if you're already on the road.

RECOMMENDED VACCINATIONS

No jabs are necessary for Spain. However, the World Health Organization (WHO) recommends that all travellers should be covered for diphtheria, tetanus, measles, mumps, rubella and polio, regardless of their destination. Since most vaccines don't produce immunity until at least two weeks after they're given, visit a physician at least six weeks before departure.

INTERNET RESOURCES

There is a wealth of travel health advice to be found on the internet. For further information, **Lonely Planet** (www.lonely planet.com) is a good place to start. The **WHO** (World Health Organization; www .who.int/ith) publishes a superb book called *International Travel and Health,* which is revised annually and is available online at no cost. Another website of general interest is **MD Travel Health** (www.mdtravelhealth .com), which provides complete travel health recommendations for every country and is updated daily.

It's usually a good idea to consult your government's travel health website before departure, if one is available:

Australia (www.dfat.gov.au/travel)
Canada (www.travelhealth.gc.ca)
UK (www.dh.gov.uk/en/healthcare/health advicefortravellers)
USA (wwwn.cdc.gov/travel)

Other decent health-related websites include:

Age Concern (www.ageconcern.org.uk) Advice on travel for the elderly.
Fit for Travel (www.fitfortravel.scot.nhs.uk) General travel advice for the layperson.
Marie Stopes International (www.mariest opes.org.uk) Information on women's health and contraception.
MD Travel Health (www.mdtravelhealth.com)

FIRST-AID CHECKLIST

- Acetaminophen (paracetamol) or aspirin
- Adhesive or paper tape
- Antibacterial ointment for cuts and abrasions
- Antibiotics
- Antidiarrhoeal drugs (eg loperamide)
- Anti-inflammatory drugs (eg ibuprofen)
- Antihistamines (for hayfever and allergic reactions)
- Bandages, gauze swabs, gauze rolls
- DEET-containing insect repellent for the skin
- Elasticised support bandage
- Iodine tablets or water filter (for water purification)
- Nonadhesive dressing

- Oral rehydration salts
- Paper stitches
- Permethrin-containing insect spray for clothing, tents and bed nets
- Pocket knife
- Scissors, safety pins, tweezers
- Sterile alcohol wipes
- Steroid cream or cortisone (for allergic rashes)
- Sticking plasters (Band-Aids, blister plasters)
- Sun block
- Sutures
- Syringes & needles – ask your doctor for a note explaining why you have them
- Thermomete

Travel health recommendations for every country; updated daily.

FURTHER READING

Travel with Children, from Lonely Planet, includes advice on travel health for younger children. Other recommended references include *Travellers' Health* by Dr Richard Dawood (Oxford University Press) and *International Travel Health Guide* by Stuart R Rose, MD (Travel Medicine Inc).

Other useful health guides for walkers include:

o *Medicine for Mountaineering & Other Wilderness Activities,* by James A Wilkerson, is an outstanding reference book for the layperson. It describes many of the medical problems typically encountered while trekking.

o *The Mountain Traveller's Handbook,* by Paul Deegan, includes chapters giving medical and safety advice as well as valuable information on all aspects of travelling in mountainous regions.

IN SPAIN

AVAILABILITY & COST OF HEALTH CARE

If you need an ambulance, call ☎ 061. For emergency treatment go straight to the *urgencias* (casualty) section of the nearest hospital.

Good health care is readily available, and *farmacias* (pharmacies) offer valuable advice and sell over-the-counter medication. In Spain, a system of *farmacias de guardia* (duty pharmacies) operates so that each district has one open all the time. When a pharmacy is closed, it posts the name of the nearest open one on the door.

Medical costs are lower in Spain than many other European countries, but can still mount quickly if you are uninsured.

INFECTIOUS DISEASES

Fungal Infections

Sweating liberally, probably washing less than usual and going longer without a change of clothes mean that long-distance walkers risk picking up a fungal infection, which, while an unpleasant irritant, presents no danger.

Fungal infections are encouraged by moisture. So wear loose, comfortable clothes, wash when you can, and dry yourself thoroughly. Try to expose the infected area to air or sunlight as much as possible and apply an antifungal cream or powder like tolnaftate.

Giardiasis

Symptoms include stomach cramps, nausea, a bloated stomach, watery, foul-smelling diarrhoea and frequent gas. Giardiasis can appear several weeks after you have been exposed to the parasite. The symptoms may disappear for a few days and then return; this can go on for several weeks.

Seek medical advice if you think you have giardiasis, but where this is not possible, tinidazole or metronidazole are the recommended drugs. Treatment is a 2g single dose of tinidazole or 250mg of metronidazole three times daily for five to 10 days.

TRAVELLERS DIARRHOEA

If you develop diarrhoea, be sure to drink plenty of fluids, preferably an oral rehydration solution, such as Dioralyte. If diarrhoea is bloody, persists for more than 72 hours or is accompanied by a fever, shaking, chills or severe abdominal pain, you should seek medical attention.

ENVIRONMENTAL HAZARDS

Altitude

Lack of oxygen at high altitudes (over 2500m) affects most people to some extent. The effect may be mild or severe and occurs because the air pressure is reduced, and the heart and lungs must work harder to oxygenate the body. Symptoms of acute mountain sickness (AMS) usually develop during the first 24 hours at altitude but may be delayed up to three weeks. Mild symptoms include headache, lethargy, dizziness, difficulty sleeping and loss of appetite. AMS may become more severe without warning and can be fatal. Severe symptoms include breathlessness, a dry, irritative cough (which may progress to the production of pink, frothy sputum), severe headache, lack of coordination and balance, confusion, irrational behaviour, vomiting, drowsiness and unconsciousness. There is no hard-and-fast rule as to what is too high: AMS has been fatal at 3000m,

COMMON AILMENTS

BLISTERS

To avoid blisters make sure your walking boots or shoes are well worn in before you hit the trail. Your boots should fit comfortably with enough room to move your toes; boots that are too big or too small will cause blisters. Similarly for socks – be sure they fit properly and are specifically made for walkers; even then, check to make sure that there are no seams across the widest part of your foot. Wet and muddy socks can also cause blisters, so even on a day walk, pack a spare pair of socks. Keep your toenails clipped but not too short. If you do feel a blister coming on, treat it sooner rather then later. Apply a simple sticking plaster, or preferably one of the special blister plasters that act as a second skin.

FATIGUE

A simple statistic is that more injuries happen towards the end of the day than earlier, when you're fresher. Although tiredness can simply be a nuisance on an easy walk, it can be life-threatening on narrow exposed ridges or in bad weather. You should never set out on a walk that is beyond your capabilities on the day. If you feel below par, have a day off or take a bus. To reduce the risk, don't push yourself too hard – take rests every hour or two and build in a good half-hour lunch break. Towards the end of the day, take down the pace and increase your concentration. You should also eat properly throughout the day; nuts, dried fruit and chocolate are all good energy-giving snack foods.

KNEE STRAIN

Many walkers feel the judder on long steep descents. Although you can't eliminate strain on the knee joints when dropping steeply, you can reduce it by taking shorter steps which leave your legs slightly bent and ensure that your heel hits the ground before the rest of your foot. Some walkers find that tubular bandages help, while others use hi-tech, strap-on supports. Walking poles are very effective in taking some of the weight off the knees.

although 3500 to 4500m is the usual range for altitude sickness.

Fortunately, altitude sickness is only going to be a potential problem on a handful of the higher altitude walks featured in this book and, unless you are extraordinarily unlucky, on none are you likely to ascend high enough to suffer from a severe attack.

Treat mild symptoms by resting at the same altitude until recovery, usually a day or two. Paracetamol or aspirin can be taken for headaches. If symptoms persist or become worse, however, *immediate descent is necessary*; even 500m can help. Drug treatments should never be used to avoid descent or to enable further ascent.

The drugs acetazolamide and dexamethasone are recommended by some doctors for the prevention of AMS; however, their use is controversial. They can reduce the symptoms, but they may also mask warning signs; severe and fatal AMS has occurred in people taking these drugs. In general we do not recommend them for travellers.

To prevent acute mountain sickness:

○ Ascend slowly – have frequent rest days, spending two to three nights at each rise of 1000m. If you reach a high altitude by trekking, acclimatisation takes place gradually and you are less likely to be affected than if you fly directly to high altitude.

○ It is always wise to sleep at a lower altitude than the greatest height reached during the day if possible. Also, once above 3000m, care should be taken not to increase the sleeping altitude by more than 300m per day.

○ Drink extra fluids. The mountain air is dry and cold and moisture is lost as you breathe.

○ Evaporation of sweat may occur unnoticed and result in dehydration.

○ Eat light, high-carbohydrate meals for more energy.

○ Avoid alcohol as it may increase the risk of dehydration.

○ Avoid sedatives.

Bites & Stings

BEES & WASPS

Bees and wasps only cause real problems to those with a severe allergy (anaphylaxis). If you have a severe allergy to bee or wasp stings, carry an 'EpiPen' or similar adrenaline injection.

MOSQUITOES

Mosquitoes are found in most parts of Europe. They may not carry malaria, but can cause irritation and infected bites.

SNAKES

It's highly unlikely that you will even see a snake let alone hang out with one long enough to get bitten. The only venomous snake that is even relatively common in Spain is Lataste's viper. It has a triangular-shaped head, grows up to 75cm long, and is grey with a zigzag pattern. It lives in dry, rocky areas, away from humans. Its bite can be fatal and needs to be treated with a serum, which state clinics in major towns keep in stock. Also to be avoided is the Montpellier snake, which is blue with a white underside and prominent ridges over the eyes. It lives mainly in scrub and sandy areas, but keeps a low profile and is unlikely to be a threat unless trodden on.

Despite the odds of seeing a snake being low, you should still do what you can to minimise your chances of being bitten by always wearing boots, socks and long trousers when walking through undergrowth where snakes may be present. Don't put your hands into holes and crevices.

If bitten, immediately wrap the bitten limb tightly, as you would for a sprained ankle, and then attach a splint to immobilise it. Keep the victim still and seek medical help; it will help if you can describe the offending reptile. Tourniquets and sucking out the poison are now comprehensively discredited.

TICKS

Always check all over your body if you have been walking through a potentially tick-infested area as ticks can cause skin infections and other more serious diseases. Ticks are most active from spring to autumn, especially where there are plenty of sheep or deer. They usually lurk in overhanging vegetation, so avoid pushing through tall bushes if possible.

If a tick is found attached to the skin, press down around the tick's head with tweezers, grab the head and gently pull upwards. Avoid pulling the rear of the body as this may squeeze the tick's gut contents through its mouth into your skin, increasing the risk of infection and disease.

Smearing chemicals on the tick will not make it let go and is not recommended as a solution.

OTHER INSECTS

In forested areas watch out for the hairy reddish-brown caterpillars of the pine processionary moth. They live in silvery nests up in the pine trees and, come spring, leave the nest to march in long lines (hence the name). Touching the caterpillars' hairs sets off a severely irritating allergic skin reaction.

Some Spanish centipedes have a very nasty but nonfatal sting. The ones to watch out for are those with clearly defined segments, which may be patterned with, for instance, black and yellow stripes.

Scorpions are found in Spain and their sting can be distressingly painful, but they are not considered fatal.

HOW TO PREVENT MOSQUITO & MIDGE BITES

- Wear light-coloured clothing.
- Wear long trousers and long-sleeved shirts.
- Use mosquito repellents containing the compound DEET on exposed areas (prolonged overuse of DEET may be harmful, especially to children, but its use is considered preferable to being bitten by disease-transmitting mosquitoes).
- Avoid perfumes or aftershave.
- Use a mosquito net impregnated with mosquito repellent (permethrin) – it may be worth taking your own.
- Impregnating clothes with permethrin effectively deters mosquitoes and other insects.

Cold

HYPOTHERMIA

This occurs when the body loses heat faster than it can produce it and the core temperature of the body falls.

It is frighteningly easy to progress from very cold to dangerously cold due to a combination of wind, wet clothing, fatigue and hunger, even if the air temperature is above freezing. If the weather deteriorates, put on extra layers of warm clothing: a wind and/or waterproof jacket, plus wool or fleece hat and gloves are all essential. Have something energy-giving to eat and ensure that everyone in your group is fit, feeling well and alert.

Symptoms of hypothermia are exhaustion, numb skin (particularly toes and fingers), shivering, slurred speech, irrational or violent behaviour, lethargy, stumbling, dizzy spells, muscle cramps and violent bursts of energy. Irrationality may take the form of sufferers claiming they are warm and trying to take off their clothes.

To treat mild hypothermia, first get the person out of the wind and/or rain, remove their clothing if it's wet, and replace it with dry, warm clothing. Give them hot liquids – not alcohol – and some high-energy, easily digestible food. Do not rub victims: instead, allow them to slowly warm themselves. This should be enough to treat the early stages of hypothermia. The early recognition and treatment of mild hypothermia is the only way to prevent severe hypothermia, which is a critical condition.

FROSTBITE

This refers to the freezing of extremities, including fingers, toes and nose. Signs and symptoms of frostbite include a whitish or waxy cast to the skin, or even crystals on the surface, plus itching, numbness and pain. Warm the affected areas by immersion in warm (not hot) water or with blankets or clothes, only until the skin becomes flushed. Frostbitten parts should not be rubbed. Pain and swelling are inevitable. Blisters should not be broken. Get medical attention right away.

Heat

DEHYDRATION & HEAT EXHAUSTION

Dehydration is a potentially dangerous and generally preventable condition caused by excessive fluid loss. Sweating combined with inadequate fluid intake is one of the commonest causes in trekkers, but other important causes are diarrhoea, vomiting, and high fever – see Diarrhoea (p367) for more details about appropriate treatment in these circumstances.

The first symptoms are weakness, thirst and passing small amounts of very concentrated urine. This may progress to drowsiness, dizziness or fainting on standing up, and finally, coma.

It's easy to forget how much fluid you are losing via perspiration while you are trekking, particularly if a strong breeze is drying your skin quickly. You should always maintain a good fluid intake – a minimum of 3L a day is recommended.

Dehydration and salt deficiency can cause heat exhaustion. Salt deficiency is characterised by fatigue, lethargy, headaches, giddiness and muscle cramps; salt tablets are overkill, just adding extra salt to your food is probably sufficient.

HEATSTROKE

This is a serious, occasionally fatal, condition that occurs if the body's heat-regulating mechanism breaks down and the body temperature rises to dangerous levels. Long, continuous periods of exposure to high temperatures and insufficient fluids can leave you vulnerable to heatstroke.

The symptoms are feeling unwell, not sweating very much (or at all) and a high body temperature (39°-41°C or 102°-106°F). Where sweating has ceased, the skin becomes flushed and red. Severe, throbbing headaches and lack of coordination will also occur, and the sufferer may be confused or aggressive. Eventually the victim will become delirious or convulse. Hospitalisation is essential, but in the interim get victims out of the sun, remove their clothing, cover them with a wet sheet or towel and then fan continually. Give fluids if they are conscious.

Snow Blindness

This is a temporary painful condition resulting from sunburn of the surface of the eye (cornea). It usually occurs when someone walks on snow or in bright sunshine without sunglasses. Treatment is to relieve the pain – cold cloths on closed eyelids may help. Antibiotic and anaesthetic eye drops are not necessary. The condition usually resolves itself within a few days and there are no long-term consequences.

Sun

Protection against the sun should always be taken seriously. Particularly in the rarified air and deceptive coolness of the mountains, sunburn occurs rapidly. Slap on the sunscreen and a barrier cream for your nose and lips, wear a broad-brimmed hat and protect your eyes with good quality sunglasses with UV lenses, particularly when walking near water, sand or snow. If, despite these precautions, you get yourself burnt, calamine lotion, aloe vera or other commercial sunburn relief preparations will soothe.

Food

If your food is poor you can soon start to lose weight and place your health at risk.

Make sure your diet is well balanced. Cooked eggs, meat, tofu, beans, lentils and nuts are all reliable ways to get protein. Fruit is a good source of vitamins. Eat plenty of grains, such as rice, and bread.

For longer treks, consider taking vitamin and iron pills.

TRAUMATIC INJURIES

Detailed first-aid instruction is outside the scope of this book, but here are some tips and advice. Walkers should consider taking a first-aid course before hitting the trail to ensure they know what to do in the event of an injury.

Cuts & Scratches

Wash and treat with antiseptic even small cuts and grazes. Dry wounds heal more quickly so avoid bandages and plasters that keep wounds wet. A sign of infection is the skin margins of the wound becoming red, painful and swollen. More serious infection can cause swelling of the whole limb and of the lymph glands. The patient may develop a fever, and will need medical attention.

Sprains

Ankle and knee sprains are common injuries among hikers, particularly when crossing rugged terrain. To help prevent ankle sprains, wear boots that have adequate ankle support. If you do suffer a sprain,

---

WATER

Many diseases are carried in water in the form of bacteria, protozoa, viruses, worms and insect eggs etc. In Spain tap water is always fine to drink, but some village fountains might be spewing forth untreated tap water (in which case it will normally be signed '*agua no potable*'). Quenching your thirst from mountain streams is a more dicey prospect. If you're at, or very close to, the source then it's probably OK to drink it, but if the source is some distance away and if the water might have been polluted in any way by animals then you must treat it before drinking.

WATER PURIFICATION

The simplest way of purifying water is to boil it thoroughly. Vigorous boiling should be satisfactory; however, at high altitude water boils at a lower temperature, so germs are less likely to be killed. Boil it for longer (10 minutes) in this environment.

You can also use a chemical agent to purify water. Chlorine and iodine are usually used, available from outdoor equipment suppliers and pharmacies. Chlorine tablets will kill many pathogens, but not some parasites like giardia and amoebic cysts. Iodine is more effective in purifying water. Follow the directions carefully and remember that too much iodine can be harmful.

Consider purchasing a water filter. There are two main kinds of filter. Total filters take out all parasites, bacteria and viruses and make water safe to drink. They are relatively expensive, but they can be more cost effective (and environmentally friendly) than buying bottled water. Simple filters (which can be a nylon mesh bag) take out dirt and larger foreign bodies from the water so that chemical solutions work much more effectively; if the water is dirty, chemical solutions may not work at all. It's very important when buying a filter to read the specifications, so that you know exactly what it removes from the water.

immobilise the joint with a firm bandage, and, if feasible, immerse the foot in cold water. Distribute the contents of your pack among your companions. Once you reach shelter, relieve pain and swelling by keeping the joint elevated for the first 24 hours and, where possible, by putting ice on the swollen joint. Take simple painkillers to ease the discomfort. If the sprain is mild, you may be able to continue your walk after a couple of days. For more severe sprains, seek medical attention as an X-ray may be needed to find out whether a bone has been broken.

Fractures

Indications of a fracture (broken bone) are pain (tenderness of the affected area), swelling and discoloration, loss of function or deformity of a limb. Unless you know what you are doing, you shouldn't try to straighten an obviously displaced broken bone. To protect from further injury, immobilise a nondisplaced fracture by splinting it, usually in the position found, which will probably be the most comfortable position.

Fractures of the thigh bone require urgent treatment as they involve massive blood loss and pain. Seek help and treat the patient for shock. Fractures associated with open wounds (compound fractures) also require more urgent treatment than simple fractures as there is a risk of infection. Dislocations, where the bone has come out of the joint, are very painful, and should be set as soon as possible.

Broken ribs are painful but usually heal by themselves and do not need splinting. If breathing difficulties occur, or the person coughs up blood, medical attention should be sought urgently, as it may indicate a punctured lung.

Internal Injuries

These are more difficult to detect, and cannot usually be treated in the field. Watch for shock, which is a specific medical condition associated with a failure to maintain circulating blood volume. Signs include a rapid pulse and cold, clammy extremities. A person in shock requires urgent medical attention.

Major Accidents

Falling or having something fall on you, resulting in head injuries or fractures is always possible when walking, especially if you are crossing steep slopes or unstable terrain. Following is some basic advice on what to do in the event of a major accident.

If a person suffers a major fall:

- Make sure you and other people with you are not in danger.
- Assess the injured person's condition.
- Stabilise any injuries, such as bleeding wounds or broken bones.
- Seek medical attention (see p374).

If the person is unconscious, immediately check whether they are breathing – clear their airway if it is blocked – and check whether they have a pulse – feel the side of the neck rather than the wrist. If they are not breathing but have a pulse, you should start mouth-to-mouth resuscitation immediately. In these circumstances it is best to move the person as little as possible in case their neck or back is broken.

Check for wounds and broken bones – ask the person where they have pain if they are conscious, otherwise gently inspect them all over (including their back and the back of the head), moving them as little as possible. Control any bleeding by applying firm pressure to the wound. Bleeding from the nose or ear may indicate a fractured skull. Don't give the person anything by mouth, especially if they are unconscious.

You'll have to manage the person for shock. Raise their legs above heart level (unless their legs are fractured), dress any wounds and immobilise any fractures, loosen tight clothing, keep the person warm by covering them with a blanket or other dry clothing, insulate them from the ground if possible, but don't heat them.

General points to bear in mind are:

- Simple fractures take several weeks to heal, so they don't need fixing straight away, but they should be immobilised to protect them from further injury. Compound fractures need urgent treatment.
- If you do have to splint a broken bone, remember to check regularly that the splint is not cutting off the circulation to the hand or foot.
- Most cases of brief unconsciousness are not associated with any serious internal injury to the brain but, as a general rule of

thumb in these circumstances, any person who has been knocked unconscious should be watched for deterioration. If they do deteriorate, seek medical attention straight away.

WOMEN'S HEALTH

Walking is not particularly hazardous to your health. However, women's health issues can be a bit trickier to cope with when you are on the trail.

Menstruation

A change in diet, routine and environment, as well as intensive exercise, may lead to irregularities in your menstrual cycle. It's particularly important during the menstrual cycle to maintain good personal hygiene. Antibacterial hand gel or pre-moistened wipes can be useful if you don't have access to soap and water. Because of hygiene concerns and for ease while on an extended trip, some women prefer to temporarily stop menstruation; discuss your options with a doctor before you go.

Thrush (Vaginal Candidiasis)

Antibiotic use, synthetic underwear, tight trousers, sweating, contraceptive pills and unprotected sex can lead to fungal vaginal infections. The most common is thrush (vaginal candidiasis). Symptoms include itching and discomfort in the genital area, often in association with a thick white discharge. The best prevention is to keep the vaginal area cool and dry and to wear cotton, rather than synthetic, underwear and loose clothes. Treat thrush with clotrimazole pessaries, a vaginal cream or, if these are not available, a vinegar or lemon-juice douche or yoghurt. To prevent thrush, eat fresh yoghurt regularly or consider taking acidophilus tablets.

Urinary Tract Infection

Dehydration and 'hanging on' can result in urinary tract infection and cystitis. Symptoms include burning when urinating and having to go frequently and urgently. Sometimes there's blood in the urine. Drink plenty of fluids and urinate regularly. If symptoms persist, seek medical attention because a simple infection can spread to the kidneys, causing a more severe illness.

SAFETY ON THE WALK

You can significantly reduce the chance of getting into difficulties by taking a few simple precautions. These are listed in the boxed text Hike Safety – Basic Rules, below. For suggestions on recommended clothing and equipment see p360.

CROSSING RIVERS

Sudden downpours are common in the mountains and can speedily turn a gentle stream into a raging torrent. If you're in any doubt about the safety of a crossing, look for a safer passage upstream or wait. If the rain is short-lived, it should subside quickly.

If you decide it's essential to cross (late in the day, for example), look for a wide, relatively shallow stretch of the stream rather than a bend. Take off your trousers and socks, but keep your boots on to prevent injury. Put dry, warm clothes and a towel in a plastic bag near the top of your pack. Before stepping out from the bank, unclip your chest strap and belt buckle. This makes it easier to slip out of your backpack and

---

HIKE SAFETY – BASIC RULES

○ Allow plenty of time to accomplish a walk before dark, particularly when daylight hours are shorter.

○ Study the route carefully before setting out, noting the possible escape routes and the point of no return (where it's quicker to continue than to turn back). Monitor your progress during the day against the time estimated for the walk, and keep an eye on the weather.

○ It's wise not to walk alone. Always leave details of your intended route, number of people in your group, and expected return time with someone responsible before you set off; let that person know when you return.

○ Before setting off, make sure you have a relevant map, compass, whistle, and that you know the weather forecast for the area for the next 24 hours.

swim to safety if you lose your balance and are swept downstream. Use a walking pole, grasped in both hands, on the upstream side as a third leg, or go arm in arm with a companion, clasping at the wrist, and cross side-on to the flow, taking short steps.

DOGS

During walks in settled and farming areas, you're likely to encounter barking dogs – tethered or running free. Regard any dog as a potential attacker and be prepared to take evasive action: even just crossing the road can take you out of its territory and into safety. A walking pole may be useful, though use it as a last resort.

LIGHTNING

If a storm brews, avoid exposed areas. Lightning has a penchant for crests, lone trees, small depressions, gullies, caves and cabin entrances, as well as wet ground. If you are caught out in the open, try to curl up as tightly as possible with your feet together and keep a layer of insulation between you and the ground. Place metal objects such as metal-frame backpacks and walking poles away from you. The Pyrenees is renowned for huge and incredibly violent thunderstorms. These are most common at the end hot August days and can appear out of nowhere. If you see large thunder clouds starting to form, look for somewhere safe to shelter as soon as possible.

RESCUE & EVACUATION

If someone in your group is injured or falls ill and can't move, leave somebody with them while another one or more goes for help. They should take clear written details of the location and condition of the victim, and of helicopter landing conditions. If there are only two of you, leave the injured person with as much warm clothing, food and water as it's sensible to spare, plus the whistle and torch. Mark the position with something conspicuous – an orange bivvy bag, or perhaps a large stone cross on the ground. Remember, the rescue effort might be slow, perhaps taking days to remove the injured person.

Emergency Communications

Emergency communications are well developed in Spain but in remote mountain areas our general reliance on satellite and digital technology somewhat falls to pieces when you find yourself stranded in a valley with surrounding mountain peaks blocking all satellite signals!

When communicating with the emergency services be ready to give information on where an accident occurred, how many people are injured and the injuries sustained. If a helicopter needs to come in, what are the terrain and weather conditions like at the place of the accident?

TELEPHONE

Whatever the crisis, a call to ☎ 112 will alert the emergency services.

However, don't expect your mobile phone to elicit action up high in the mountains; often as not, there's no coverage.

Some walkers carry an emergency distress beacon, which transmits an internationally recognised distress signal when activated.

DISTRESS SIGNALS

If you need to call for help, use these internationally recognised emergency signals. Give six short signals, such as a whistle, a yell or the flash of a light, at 10-second intervals, followed by a minute of rest. Repeat the sequence until you get a response. If the responder knows the signals, this will be three signals at 20-second intervals, followed by a minute's pause and a repetition of the sequence.

Helicopter Rescue & Evacuation

If a helicopter arrives on the scene, there are a couple of conventions you should be familiar with. Standing face on to the chopper:

o Arms up in the shape of a letter 'V' means 'I/We need help'.
o Arms in a straight diagonal line (like one line of a letter X) means `All OK'.

For the helicopter to land, there must be a cleared space of 25m x 25m, with a flat landing pad area of 6m x 6m. The helicopter will fly into the wind when landing.

In cases of extreme emergency, where no landing area is available, a person or harness might be lowered.

Language

Spain has one official national language, Spanish, and four co-official languages: Basque, Catalan, Galician and Aranese.

As the country's national language, Spanish (often referred to as *castellano*, or Castilian) is understood by everyone and spoken fluently by nearly all. In global terms it's the most widely spoken of the Romance languages – the group of languages derived from Latin, which includes French, Italian and Portuguese.

Like Castilian, Catalan *(català)* is a Romance language; including the dialects spoken in the Balearic Islands (Islas Baleares), Andorra and much of the Valencia region (where it's usually referred to as *valenciano*), Catalan is the most widely spoken of Spain's four regional languages. It has a rich literary history and culture; you'll even find a substantial volume of Catalan writing about trekking and mountaineering, many titles unavailable in any other language. Signs in Catalunya are frequently only in Catalan – fortunately, the written forms of Catalan and Spanish are very similar.

Galician *(Galego)* is also a Romance language. It is very similar to Portuguese – in fact, up until the 13th century they were pretty much identical. The debate over the status of Galician as a dialect of Portuguese or a separate language still rages today.

Basque *(euskara)* has long been a conundrum for linguists. As it bears no relation to any any other language, its origins remain obscure. It's spoken by a minority in the País Vasco (Basque Country – called Euskadi in Basque) and in Navarra.

Aranese *(aranés)* is a form of Gascon, a dialect of the Occitan language, and is spoken mainly in the Aran Valley. A minority language, it has a few thousand speakers and is taught in schools in the region.

People will generally be happy to converse with you in Spanish. Away from the main tourist areas and big cities, English isn't as widely spoken as many visitors expect, so it's a good idea to gain some knowledge of simple conversational Spanish before you travel. It isn't difficult to pick up, particularly if you have even the most basic grounding in French, Italian or Portuguese. Communicating at any level with the people you meet will prove both useful and rewarding.

If you need to ask for something in English in an out-of-the-way place, your best bet is often to approach someone under 30 – anyone who's been through the education system since about 1985 will have studied four to five years of English.

For more information and practical phrases, get a copy of Lonely Planet's *Spanish Phrasebook*. It also has a two-way dictionary and includes special sections covering Basque, Catalan and Galician.

GENDER IN SPANISH

As in all Latin-based languages, Spanish nouns and adjectives are marked for gender. Where two optional endings (for example soy *diabético/a*) are given in the following words and phrases, the first variant is for a male speaker, the second for female.

PRONUNCIATION

Spanish pronunciation isn't too difficult; apart from a few throat-rasping exceptions, many Spanish sounds resemble their English counterparts. There's also a very clear and consistent relationship between pronunciation and spelling; if you can read it, you can say it. Stick to the following rules and you'll have few problems making yourself understood.

LANGUAGE

Vowels

Unlike English, each of the vowels in Spanish has a uniform pronunciation, which doesn't vary. For example, the letter 'a' has one pronunciation rather than the numerous variations we find in English, such as in 'cake', 'care', 'cat', 'cart' and 'call'. Many words have a written acute accent. This accent (as in *días*) usually indicates a stressed syllable – it does not change the sound of the vowel. Vowels are pronounced clearly even if they are in unstressed positions or at the end of a word.

a	somewhere between the 'a' in 'cat' and the 'a' in 'cart'
e	as in 'met'
i	somewhere between the 'i' in 'marine' and the 'i' in 'flip'
o	similar to the 'o' in 'hot'
u	between the 'u' in 'put' and the 'oo' in 'loose'

Consonants

Some Spanish consonants are the same as their English counterparts. The pronunciation of others varies according to which vowel follows. The Spanish alphabet also contains the letter **ñ**, which isn't found in the English alphabet. Until recently, the clusters **ch** and **ll** were also officially separate consonants, and you're likely to encounter many situations – for example in lists and dictionaries – in which they're still treated that way.

b	soft, as the 'v' in 'van'; also (less commonly) as in 'book' when word-initial or preceded by a nasal such as **m** or **n**
c	as in 'cat' when followed by **a**, **o**, **u** or a consonant; before **e** or **i** as the 'th' in 'thin'
ch	as in 'choose'
d	as in 'dog' when word-initial; elsewhere as the 'th' in 'thin' – or not pronounced at all
g	as in 'go' when followed by **a**, **o**, **u** or a consonant; before **e** or **i**, a harsh, breathy sound, like Spanish **j**
h	always silent, as in 'honest'
j	a harsh, guttural sound similar to the 'ch' in Scottish *loch* or a discreet clearing of the throat
ll	similar to the 'y' in 'yellow'
ñ	a nasal sound like the 'ni' in 'onion' or the 'ny' in 'canyon'
qu	(they always occur together) as the 'k' in 'kick'
r	a rolled or trilled sound; longer and stronger when initial or doubled
s	as in 'send', never as in 'fusion', 'mission' or 'miser'; often not pronounced at the end of a word
v	pronounced the same as **b**
x	as the 'x' in 'taxi' when between two vowels; as the 's' in 'so' when it precedes a consonant
z	as the 'th' in 'thin'
y	on its own (when it means 'and') it's pronounced as 'i'; elsewhere it sounds somewhere between the 'y' in 'yonder' and the 'g' in 'beige', depending on the region – pronounce it as 'y' and you'll be understood everywhere

GREETINGS & CIVILITIES

Good morning.	*Buenos días.*
Good afternoon.	*Buenas tardes.*
Hello./Goodbye.	*Hola./Adios.*
See you later.	*Hasta luego.*
Yes./No.	*Sí./No.*
Please./Thank you.	*Por favor./Gracias.*
That's OK./You're welcome.	*De nada.*
Excuse me.	*Perdón./Perdona.*
Sorry./Excuse me.	*Lo siento./Discúlpeme.*

USEFUL PHRASES

What's your name?
¿Cómo te llamas/Cómo se llama usted? (inf/pol)
My name is ...
Me llamo ...
What's the time?
¿Qué hora es?
Please wait for me here.
Espérame aquí, por favor.
Do you speak English?
¿Habla inglés?
I (don't) understand.
(No) Entiendo.
Please speak more slowly.
Por favor, habla más despacio.
Just a minute.
Un momento.
Could you write it down, please?
¿Puede escribirlo, por favor?
How do you say ...?
¿Cómo se dice ...?
What does ... mean?
¿Qué significa ...?

SIGNS

Entrada	Entrance
Salida	Exit
Información	Information
Abierto	Open
Cerrado	Closed
Prohibido	Prohibited
Comisaría	Police Station
Servicios/Aseos	Toilets
Hombres/Caballeros	Men
Mujeres/Damas	Women

GETTING AROUND

When does the ...	*¿Cuándo sale/llega*
leave/arrive?	*el ...?*
boat	*barco*
bus/intercity bus	*autobus/autocar*
train	*tren*
first	*primer*
last	*último*
next	*próximo*
timetable	*horario*
I'd like to hire a ...	*Quisiera alquilar un ...*
car	*coche*
taxi	*taxi*
I'd like a ... ticket.	*Quisiera un billete ...*
one-way	*sencillo*
return	*de ida y vuelta*

Where's the bus stop?
¿Dónde está la parada de autobús?
Can you take me to ...?
¿Puede llevarme a ...?
I want to go to ...
Quiero ir a ...

DIRECTIONS

ahead/behind	*mas adelante/detrás*
below/above	*debajo/encima de*
before/after	*antes/después (de)*
up/down	*arriba/abajo*
flat/steep	*llano/empinado*
ascent/descent	*subida/bajada*
near/far	*cerca/lejos*
on the other side of	*al otro lado de*
towards/away from	*hacia/desde*
north/south	*norte/sur*
east/west	*este/oueste*
Go straight ahead.	*Siga todo recto/derecho.*
Turn left.	*Gire a la izquierda.*
Turn right.	*Gire a la derecha*

AROUND TOWN

I'm looking for ...	*Estoy buscando ...*
a bank	*un banco*
a chemist/pharmacy	*una farmacia*
the market	*el mercado*
the police	*la policía*
the post office	*los correos*
a telephone	*un teléfono*
the tourist office	*la oficina de turismo*

What time does it open/close?
¿A qué hora abren/cierran?

ACCOMMODATION

I'm looking for ...	*Estoy buscando ...*
a hotel	*un hotel*
a guesthouse	*una pensión*
the youth hostel	*el albergue juvenil*

What's the address?
¿Cuál es la dirección?
Do you have any rooms available?
¿Tiene habitaciones libres?
Where is the bathroom?
¿Dónde está el baño?

I'd like a ...	*Quisiera una ...*
bed	*cama*
single room	*habitación individual*
double room	*habitación doble*
room with a	*habitación con*
bathroom	*baño*
How much is it ...?	*¿Cuánto cuesta ...?*
per night/person	*por noche/persona*
per tent	*por tienda*

SHOPPING

Where can I buy ...?	*¿Dónde puedo comprar ...?*
I'd like to buy ...	*Quisiera comprar ...*
How much is it?	*¿Cuánto cuesta?*

TIME, DAYS & NUMBERS

What time is it?	*¿Qué hora es?*
today/tomorrow	*hoy/mañana*
in the morning	*de la mañana*
in the afternoon	*de la tarde*
Monday	*lunes*
Tuesday	*martes*
Wednesday	*miércoles*
Thursday	*jueves*
Friday	*viernes*
Saturday	*sábado*
Sunday	*domingo*

LANGUAGE

0	*cero*
1	*uno*
2	*dos*
3	*tres*
4	*cuatro*
5	*cinco*
6	*seis*
7	*siete*
8	*ocho*
9	*nueve*
10	*diez*
11	*once*
12	*doce*
13	*trece*
14	*catorce*
15	*quince*
16	*dieciséis*
17	*diecisiete*
18	*dieciocho*
19	*diecinueve*
20	*veinte*
21	*veintiuno*
22	*veintidós*
30	*treinta*
31	*treinta y uno*
40	*cuarenta*
50	*cincuenta*
60	*sesenta*
70	*setenta*
80	*ochenta*
90	*noventa*
100	*cien/ciento*
200	*doscientos*
1000	*mil*
one million	*un millón*

HEALTH

I'm ill.	*Estoy enfermo/a.*
I need a doctor.	*Necesito un doctor.*

I'm ...	*Soy ...*
asthmatic	*asmático/a*
diabetic	*diabético/a*
epileptic	*epiléptico/a*

I'm allergic to ...	*Soy alérgico/a a ...*
antibiotics	*los antibióticos*
penicillin	*la penicilina*

antiseptic	*antiséptico*
aspirin	*aspirina*
condoms	*preservativos/condones*

EMERGENCIES

Help!	*¡Socorro!/¡Auxilio!*
Call a doctor!	*¡Llame a un doctor!*
Call the police!	*¡Llame a la policía!*
There's been an accident.	*Ha habido un accidente.*
Go away!	*¡Váyase!*
Where is the toilet?	*¿Dónde están los servicios?*

contraceptive	*anticonceptivo*
diarrhoea	*diarrea*
medicine	*medicamento*
nausea	*náusea*
tampons	*tampones*

WALKING
Preparations

Where can we buy food supplies?
¿Dónde podemos comprar comida?
Can I leave some things here?
¿Puedo dejar algunas cosas aquí ?
I'd like to talk to someone who knows this area.
Quisiera hablar con álguien que conozca esta zona.
Where can we hire a guide?
¿Dónde podemos alquilar un/una guía?
We are thinking of taking this route.
Pensamos tomar esta ruta.
Is the walk very difficult?
¿Es muy difícil el recorrido?
Is the track (well) marked?
¿Está (bien) señalizado el sendero?
Which is the shortest/easiest route?
¿Cuál es la ruta más corta/más fácil?
Is there much snow on the pass?
¿Hay mucha nieve en el collado?
We'll return in one week.
Volverémos en una semana.

Clothing & Equipment

altimetre	*altímetro*
backpack	*mochila*
batteries	*pilas*
bootlace	*cordón de bota*
boots	*botas*
camp stove	*hornillo*
candle	*vela*
canteen/water bottle	*cantimplora*
compass	*brújula*
cooking pot	*cazo*
crampons	*crampones*
gaiters	*polainas*
gas cartridge	*cartucho de gas*
ice axe	*piolet*
kerosene	*keroseno*

methylated spirits	*alcohol de quemar*
pocketknife	*navaja*
provisions (food)	*comida*
rainjacket	*anorak/chubasquero*
rope	*cuerda*
runners/trainers	*zapatillas*
sleeping bag	*saco de dormir*
sleeping mat	*colchoneta aislante*
sunblock	*protector solar*
sunglasses	*gafas de sol*
tent	*tienda*
torch/flashlight	*linterna*
walking poles	*palos telescópicos*

On the Walk

How many kilometres to ...?
¿Cuántos kilómetros hay hasta ...?
How many hours' walking?
Hace cuántas horas de marcha?
Does this track go to ...?
¿Este sendero va a ...?
How do you reach the summit?
¿Cómo se llega a la cumbre?
Where are you going to?
¿A dónde va?
Can you show me on the map where we are?
¿Puede señalarme en el mapa dónde estamos?
What is this place called?
¿Cómo se llama este lugar?
We're doing a walk from ... to ...
Estamos haciendo una excursión desde ... a ...

bridge/footbridge	*puente/pasarela*
to carry	*llevar*
circuit	*circuito*
climb (to climb)	*escalada (escalar)*
fence	*cerco/alambrado*
firebreak	*cortefuego*
to fish	*pescar*
to follow	*seguir*
mountain guide	*guía de montaña*
mountaineer	*montañero*
park ranger/ refugio warden	*guarda*
path/trail	*sendero/senda*
refuge/mountain shelter	*refugio*
route	*ruta*
short cut	*atajo*
signpost	*señal/marca*
ski field	*pista de esquí*
traverse	*travesía*
village	*pueblo/aldea*
a walk	*una excursión*

WALKING SIGNS

Camino Particular	Private Road
Camping	Camping Ground
Campo de Trio	Shooting Range
Coto Privado de Casa	Private Hunting Area
Cuidado/Ojo con el Perro	Beware of the Dog
Finca Particular	Private Farm
Prohibido el Paso	No Entry
Propriedad Privada	Private Property
Toro Suelto	Loose Bull

Map Reading

altitude difference	*desnivel*
contour lines	*curvas de nivel*
map	*mapa*
metres above sea level	*metros sobre el nivel del mar*
spot height	*cota*

Weather

What will the weather be like?
¿Qué tiempo hará?
Tomorrow it'll be cold.
Mañana hará frío.
It's going to rain.
Va a llover.
It's windy/sunny.
Hace viento/sol.
It's raining/snowing.
Está lloviendo/nevando.
It's clouded over.
Se ha nublado.

clear/fine	*despejado*
cloud/cloudy	*nube/nublado*
fog/mist	*neblina/niebla*
ice	*hielo*
rain (to rain)	*lluvia (llover)*
snow (to snow)	*nieve (nevar)*
wind	*viento*
high/low tide	*altamar/bajamar*
spring melt/thaw	*deshielo*
storm	*tormenta*
summer/autumn	*verano/otoño*
winter/spring	*invierno/primavera*

Camping

Where's the best place to camp?
¿Dónde está el mejor lugar para acampar?
Can we put up a tent here?
¿Podemos montar una tienda aquí?
Is it permitted to make a fire?
¿Está permitido hacer fuego?

LANGUAGE

I have a gas/petrol stove.
Tengo un hornillo a gas/gasolina.
I'm going to stay here (two) days.
Voy a quedarme (dos) días aquí.

bivouac — *vivac*
to camp — *acampar*
campfire/fireplace — *hoguera*
campsite — *sitio de acampar*

Difficulties
Careful! — *¡Cuidado!*
Is it dangerous? — *¿Es peligroso?*
Can you help me? — *¿Puede ayudarme?*
I'm thirsty/hungry. — *Tengo sed/hambre.*
I'm lost. — *Estoy perdido/a.*
Can you repair this? — *¿Puede arreglarme ésto?*

Features
avalanche — *alud*
branch or tributary of lake — *afluente*
cairn — *hito*
canyon/gorge — *cañón/barranco*
cave — *cueva*
cliff — *acantilado*
coast/shoreline — *costa*
confluence — *confluencia*
creek/small river — *arroyo*
crevasse — *grieta*
fjord/sound — *ría*

frontier/border — *frontera/límite*
glacier — *glaciar*
hill — *colina*
island — *isla*
lake — *lago*
landslide — *desprendimiento*
lookout — *mirador*
moraine — *morena*
mountain — *montaña*
mountain chain — *cordillera/sierra*
névé/permanent snowfield — *nevero*
pass — *collado*
plain/flat terrain — *llanura/planicie*
plateau/tableland — *meseta*
range/massif — *sierra/macizo*
rapids — *catarata*
river — *río*
riverbank/shoreline — *orilla*
ridge/spur — *espolón/cresta*
slope/rise — *cuesta/pendiente*
spring — *fuente/manantial*
stream/brook — *riachuelo*
summit/peak — *cumbre/cima/pico*
thermal springs — *aguas termales*
tide — *marea*
torrent — *torrente*
valley — *valle*
waterfall — *cascada*
wood/forest — *bosque*

Also available from Lonely Planet:
Spanish Phrasebook

Glossary

Unless otherwise indicated, glossary terms are in Castilian Spanish (*castellano*). Other languages are listed in brackets and are abbreviated as follows: Aran = Aranese, Arag = Aragonese, Bas = Basque (*euskara*), Cat = Catalan, Eng = English, Gal = Galician. Words that appear in italics within definitions have their own entries.

A

abrigo – shelter
acequia – irrigation channel
agua potable – drinking water
aiz – (Bas) rock, spur
albergue – shelter or refuge
albergue juvenil – youth hostel
alde – (Bas) neighbourhood
aldea – hamlet
alpujarreño – from Las Alpujarras
área de acampada – free camping ground, usually with no facilities
área de reserva – reserve to which access is restricted
arroyo – stream, brook or creek
autonomía – autonomous region: Spain's 50 provincias are grouped into 17 such units
autopista – tollway
autovía – toll-free, dual-carriage highway
ayuntamiento – district or town council; town hall

B

bable – Asturian language
bahía – bay
balneario – spa or health resort
barranc – (Cat) *barranco*
barranco – gully or ravine
barrio – district or area
bide – (Bas) path
bocadillo – long sandwich
bodega – old-style wine bar; wine cellar
borda – (Cat) mountain hut used in summer by shepherds and cowherds
bosque – forest
braña – stone hut or cabin found in the Cordillera Cantábrica

C

cabaña – cabin, hut

cabo – cape, promontory
cala – cove, small bay
calle – street
calzada – roadway
calzada romana – stone-paved Roman road
camí – (Cat) *camino*
camino – footpath, track, path, trail or road
camino real – state-maintained *camino*
campa – (Gal) treeless land or meadow
cañada – drovers' road
capilla – chapel
carrer – (Cat) *calle*
carretera – public road or highway
carta – menu
casa – house or building
casa de labranza – *casa rural* in Cantabria and Asturias
casa de pagès – *casa rural* in Catalunya
casa rural – rural house or farmstead with rooms to let
cascada – waterfall or cascade
castellano – Castilian; a term often used in preference to 'español' to describe the national language
castillo – castle
castro – fortified circular village, usually pre-Roman
català – (Cat) Catalan language; a native of Catalunya
caza – hunting
cervecería – beer bar
charca – pond or pool
charco – pool or puddle
circo – *cirque*
cirque – (Eng) corrie or bowl at the head of a valley, typically formed by glaciation
CNIG – Centro Nacional de Información Geográfica: it distributes IGN maps
col – (Eng) mountain pass
coll – (Cat) *col*
collada – (Arag) *col*
collado – *col*
coma – (Cat) *cirque*
comú – local authority (Andorra)
comunidad autónoma – *autonomía*
concha – shell
cordillera – mountain range
corniche – (Eng) coastal road or path

corredoira – (Gal) stone-cobbled rural lane connecting hamlets in Galicia
corrie – (Eng) *cirque*
cortijo – farm or farmhouse, especially in Andalucía
costa – coast
coto – area where hunting rights are reserved to a specific group of people; also cairn, boundary or boundary marker
couloir – (Eng) gully
cromlech – Megalithic stone structure
cruceiro – (Gal) stone cross marking crossroads
cuesta – slope or hillside

D

dehesa – woodland pasture
devesa – in Galicia, woodland combining Atlantic and Mediterranean species
desfiladero – gorge, defile or narrow pass between mountains
DNI – Documento Nacional de Identidad; Spanish identification card
dolmen – megalithic stone table

E

embalse – reservoir or dam
ermita – wayside chapel or hermitage
erratic – (Eng) a solitary rock different from those around it
erreka – (Bas) stream
estación de autobuses – bus station
estación de tren/ferrocarril – train station
estanh – (Aran) *estanque*
estanque – pool, small lake or tarn
estany – (Cat) *estanque*
etxe – (Bas) house
Euskadi – (Bas) Basque Country

F

faro – lighthouse
finca – building or piece of land, usually rural
font – (Cat) *fuente*
fonte – (Gal) *fuente*
forau – (Arag) cave or pothole
fuente – spring, fountain or water source

G

gallego – Galician language; a native of Galicia
garganta – throat; also gorge or ravine
golada – (Gal) *col* or pass
GR – Gran Recorrido (long distance), a

classification of some walking routes; also the prefix of some road numbers in Granada province
guía – guide

H

harri – (Bas) spur
hito – cairn; also landmark
hondartza – (Bas) beach
hórreo – granary in Galicia and Asturias
hospice – pilgrims' hospital
hospital – literally, hospital; also wayside guesthouse
hospitalero – *albergue* or *refugio* attendant on pilgrim route
hostal – inexpensive hotel
hoyo – hole, pit; bable word for *jou*

I

ibaia – (Bas) river
ibón – (Arag) small lake or tarn
iglesia – church
IGN – Instituto Geográfico Nacional, producing countrywide maps
illa – (Cat & Gal) *isla*
isla – island
iturria – (Bas) fountain
IVA – Impuesto sobre el Valor Añadido, or Value-Added Tax (VAT)

J

jou – hollow or pothole in Asturias

K

karst – (Eng) characteristic spiky landforms of a limestone region
kasko – (Bas) summit, peak
koba – (Bas) cave

L

lago – lake
laguna – pool or lagoon
lagunillo – small lake; tarn
lepoa – (Bas) pass
librería – bookshop
llano – plain
loma – low ridge

M

macizo – massif
madrileño/a – native of Madrid
mapa – map
marisquería – seafood restaurant
mendatea – (Bas) mountain pass
mendia – (Bas) mountain

mendikatea – (Bas) range
menhir – Megalithic upright, standing stone
menú del degustación – fixed-price sampler of local dishes
menú del día – fixed-price, usually three-course, meal which often includes a drink
mercado – market
merendero – picnic spot
meseta – high tableland of central Spain
mesón – simple eatery with home-style cooking
mirador – lookout
mojón – boundary marker or large cairn
monasterio – monastery
montebajo – scrub or undergrowth
moraine – (Eng) rock debris swept down by glaciers and dumped as the ice melts
morisco – Muslim converted to Christianity in medieval Spain
mudéjar – Muslims living under Christian rule in medieval Spain; their characteristic style of architecture
muga – border marker or boundary

N

nava – high plain in Andalucía
nevera – pit or building used for making ice from snow
nevero – permanent, high-level snowfield

O

oficina de turismo – tourist office

P

palloza – thatch-roofed stone dwelling in the eastern *sierras* of Galicia
parador – luxury state hotel; many occupy historic buildings
parque nacional – national park
parque natural – nature park
pensión – boarding house or guesthouse
peregrino – pilgrim
pic – (Cat) *pico*
pico – peak or summit
piedra – stone or rock
pinsapar – woodland of Spanish firs
pista – trail or track
pla – (Cat) *llano*
plan – (Arag) *llano*
plato combinado – fixed-price dish with three or four items served on the same plate
playa – beach
port – (Cat) *puerto*
potable – (Eng) safe to drink

pozo de nieve – snow-storage pit
prado – meadow
praia – (Gal) *playa*
prat – (Cat) *prado*
presa – dam
pueblo – village or small town
puente – bridge
puerta – gate or door
puerto – port; also pass

R

ración – serving of food larger than tapas
rambla – seasonal watercourse; also avenue
refugi – (Cat) *refugio*
refugio – mountain hut or refuge
Renfe – Red Nacional de los Ferrocarriles Españoles, the national railway network
reserva nacional de caza – national reserve, where hunting is permitted but controlled
ría – estuary in Galicia and Asturias
río – river
riu – (Cat) *río*
rúa – (Gal) street
ruta – route

S

senda – path or track
sendero – footpath
serra – (Cat & Gal) *sierra*
SGE – Servício Geográfico del Ejército, producing countrywide maps
sierra – mountain range
sima – pothole, sink hole or fissure

T

taberna – bar or tavern
tapas – bar snacks
tarn – (Eng) small mountain lake or pond
tasca – bar, particularly specialising in *tapas*
teito – thatch-roofed stone cabin
tienda – shop; also tent
torrente – beck, mountain stream or narrow valley
tree line – (Eng) altitude above which trees can no longer survive
tresmil – peak higher than 3000m
true left/right bank – (Eng) side of the riverbank as you look downstream
tuc – (Cat) peak, summit

U

ugalde – (Bas) river
urbegia – (Bas) spring

V

vado – ford
vall – (Cat) *valle*
valla – fence or barrier
valle – valley
vega – pasture or meadow
vía pecuaria – drovers' road

vivac – bivouac
volcán – volcano

Z

zona de acampada – *área de acampada*
zubi – (Bas) bridge

Behind the Scenes

THIS BOOK

This guidebook was commissioned in Lonely Planet's Melbourne office, and produced by the following:

Publisher Chris Rennie
Associate Publisher Ben Handicott
Commissioning Editors Bridget Blair, Janine Eberle
Cover Designer Brendan Demsey
Cover Image Research Naomi Parker
Internal Image Research Jane Hart
Project Manager Jane Atkin
Thanks to Graham Imeson, Andy Lewis, Mik Ruff, Yuki Kamimura
Production [recapture]

CONTRIBUTING AUTHORS

The following authors contributed to the research and writing of sections of this book.

JON BOWEN – THE PYRENEES

Jon Bowen has travelled all over the world, but can normally be found near his home in North Devon, tramping along coast paths in search of undiscovered surf spots, taking photographs, and writing. Author of two surfing books, *Surfing Moods* and *Perfect Surf*, he also contributed to a walking book of North Devon, *A Boot Up North Devon*.

LUDOVIC BUDILLON – SISTEMA CENTRAL

Born in the heart of the French Alps, Ludovic started mountain walking with his dad at the foot of the highest peak in Europe, Mont Blanc. After wearing out his first walking shoes in the French and Swiss Alps and Austria, Ludovic moved further afield to New Zealand where he explored the beautiful coastline of Tasman Bay and the glacier area of the southwest. Back in France, Ludovic spends his winters in Tignes mountaineering and skiing. He had an eventful time updating the Alta Ruta de Gredos hike for this book: he lost his sleeping bag on the first day and spent a night in a mountain hut with 12 women prisoners (don't ask!).

NANCY FREY & JOSE PLACER – GALICIA

Nancy and Jose met on the Camino de Santiago in 1994. Jose, a Santiago de Compostela native, was taking a break from his law career and Nancy, a cultural anthropologist, was researching the boom of the contemporary pilgrimage. Subsequently, she published *Pilgrim Stories: On & Off the Road to Santiago*. They combined their love of writing and hiking by contributing to different editions of Lonely Planet's *Walking in Spain* and *Walking in Scotland*. In 1999 Jose and Nancy founded On Foot

BEHIND THE SCENES

THE LONELY PLANET STORY

Fresh from an epic journey across Europe, Asia and Australia in 1972, Tony and Maureen Wheeler sat at their kitchen table stapling together notes. The first Lonely Planet guidebook, *Across Asia on the Cheap*, was born.

Travellers snapped up the guides. Inspired by their success, the Wheelers began publishing books to Southeast Asia, India and beyond. Demand was prodigious, and the Wheelers expanded the business rapidly to keep up. Over the years, Lonely Planet extended its coverage to every country and into the virtual world via lonelyplanet.com and the Thorn Tree message board.

As Lonely Planet became a globally loved brand, Tony and Maureen received several offers for the company. But it wasn't until 2007 that they found a partner whom they trusted to remain true to the company's principles of travelling widely, treading lightly and giving sustainably. In October of that year, BBC Worldwide acquired a 75% share in the company, pledging to uphold Lonely Planet's commitment to independent travel, trustworthy advice and editorial independence.

Today, Lonely Planet has offices in Melbourne, London and Oakland, with over 500 staff members and 300 authors. Tony and Maureen are still actively involved with Lonely Planet. They're travelling more often than ever, and they're devoting their spare time to charitable projects. And the company is still driven by the philosophy of *Across Asia on the Cheap*: 'All you've got to do is decide to go and the hardest part is over. So go!'

in Spain Walking & Hiking Educational Adventures, and since then have led hundreds of groups along the magnificent trails of northern Spain. They live in a small village on the Galician coast and have three kids.

ANTHONY HAM – ANDALUCÍA

A Madrid-based writer and photographer, Anthony divides most of his year between Africa, the Spanish capital and the charms of Cádiz Province in Andalucía. Whenever he can, he leaves the modern world behind and treks out into the wilderness, whether it be the Dogon Country in Mali in West Africa, or the Sierra de Grazalema in Cádiz's hinterland, one of his favourite corners of the country.

ZORA O'NEILL – ANDALUCÍA

Having cruised Granada and Almeria by car for Lonely Planet's newest *Andalucia* edition, Zora was delighted to return for a trip on foot, with time to dawdle in villages and opportunity to work up a real appetite for eggs and sausage. She went native when her trusty 15-year-old Vasques bit the dust in the Alpujarras, and Spanish boots from a general store proved a worthy replacement. Zora lives in New York City, but often travels to the American Southwest to hike.

MARION POIZEAU – ANDALUCÍA

As a child, Marion grew up near the Alps and enjoyed hiking, snowboarding and making movies about the area. Later she started travelling to other places where she could pursue these activities, like Réunion, Patagonia and New Zealand. Between travels, she also lived and worked in Valencia in Spain where she learned to speak Spanish.

MILES RODDIS – VALENCIA & SISTEMA CENTRAL

Miles was the coordinating author for the last two editions of *Walking in Spain*. This time, he has enjoyed exploring Valencia, the region where he and his wife have lived for 20 years. It's the 50th Lonely Planet guide that he's written or contributed to – his very first outing was a single chapter of Lonely Planet's *Walking in Britain*. These days, he writes mainly about Mediterranean lands: Spain, Italy and France, including a couple of editions of *Walking in France*.

PATRICK SALMON & RHONDA STURGES – THE PYRENEES

An Australian currently living in England and working in sports development, Patrick has had a vast amount of trekking experience, particularly in the Nepal and the Tibet Himalaya, as well as the South American Andes. The Spanish Pyrenees provided Rhonda's first overnight experience of walking. She has previously undertaken day walks throughout England and has travelled extensively throughout Africa, Australia and Asia.

ELSA TARANTINO – PYRENEES, CORDILLERA CANTÁBRICA & SISTEMA CENTRAL

Brought up in the UK from an Italian background, Elsa spent lots of time as a young girl on the winding mountain passes between the UK and Italy. Later on these travels inspired her to become a tour guide taking clients over and around various European mountain passes. She now lives in the Southwest of France at the foot of the Pyrenees which gives her lots of chances to give her hiking boots a work out.

HAMAL VILLAR LÁZARO – MALLORCA

Born in Mallorca because his mother thought it was an ideal place to grow up, Hamal has known the island mountains since childhood. Nowadays he is mountain guide in Mallorca and the other mountain ranges in Spain, and also works as an outdoor activities instructor. When he's not travelling and adventuring around Europe or hiking with clients you'll find him running up the mountains on his free days in Mallorca.

OUR READERS

Many thanks to the travellers who used the last edition and wrote to us with helpful hints, useful advice and interesting anecdotes:

Judith Barrett, Rick Bignell, Helen De Mamiel, Lauren Edwards, Alex Hamilton, Ann Hooke, Edouard Imbeau, Frances & Andrea Lench, Josie Lodder, Nicolas Pesenti, Paul Shewry, Keith Tapp, Matthew Titler, J W Van Der Graaf, Murray Woodburn

ACKNOWLEDGMENTS

Internal photographs Stuart Butler p2 (#2), p5 (#2, #3); Jon Bowen p3 (#6); p7 (#3) blickwinkel/ Alamy; p9 (#2) Juanvi Carrasco/Alamy; p9 (#1) Loetscher Chlaus/Alamy; p6 (#3) David R Frazier Photolibrary,Inc/Alamy; p9 (#3) Chris Howes/Wild Places Photography/Alamy; p8 (#2) Life File Photo Library Ltd/Alamy; p7 (#3) Cro Magnon/Alamy; p11 (#3) Alberto Paredes/Alamy; p6 (#2) Pixtal Images. All other photographs by Lonely Planet Images,

and by Karl Blackwell p10 (#2); Bethune Carmichael p8 (#3); Alby De Tweede p2 (#5); Krzysztof Dydynski p4 (#3); Christopher Herwig p7 (#1); Philip Game p12; Roberto Gerometta p5 (#1); Matt Fletcher p4 (#1, #2); Karl Lehmann p10 (#1); Nacho Moro p10 (#3); Juan Jose Pascual p6 (#1); Oliver Strewe p11 (#2); David Tomlinson p3 (#1).

All images are the copyright of the photographers unless otherwise indicated. Many of the images in this guide are available for licensing from Lonely Planet Images: www.lonelyplanetimages .com.

THANKS
Stuart Butler

To produce a book of this scale, covering hundreds of kilometres of the best trails in Spain, is a mammoth undertaking and I'm therefore incredibly indebted to my fellow walkers: Elsa Tarantino, Miles Roddis, Zora O'Neill, Ludo Budillon, Anthony Ham, Marion Poizeau, Hamal Lázaro, Nancy Frey and Jose Placer, Jon Bowen and Rosanna Rothery, Patrick Salmon and Rhonda Sturges.

Thank you also to all the hikers, tourist office staff and others who helped on the way.

Finally, a huge thank you once again to Heather who, despite being from two-to-six months pregnant, walked most of these trails with me and in the process amazed every other hiker we passed!

Index

INDEX

LONELY PLANET OFFICES

Australia
Head Office
Locked Bag 1, Footscray, Victoria 3011
☎ 03 8379 8000, fax 03 8379 8111
talk2us@lonelyplanet.com.au

USA
150 Linden St, Oakland, CA 94607
☎ 510 893 8556, toll free 800 275 8555
fax 510 893 8572
info@lonelyplanet.com

UK
2nd fl, 186 City Rd,
London EC1V 2NT
☎ 020 7106 2100, fax 020 7106 2101
go@lonelyplanet.co.uk

Mixed Sources
Product group from well-managed
forests and other controlled sources
www.fsc.org Cert no. SGS-COC-005002
© 1996 Forest Stewardship Council

PUBLISHED BY LONELY PLANET PUBLICATIONS PTY LTD

ABN 36 005 607 983

Printed by Fabulous Printers Pte Ltd
Printed in Singapore